T0341260

The Routledge Companion to the Professions and Professionalism

The Routledge Companion to the Professions and Professionalism is a state-of-the-art reference work which maps out the current developments and debates around the sociology of the professions, and how they relate to management and organizations.

Supported by an international contributor team specializing in the disciplines of organizational studies and sociology, the collection provides extensive coverage of this field of research. It brings together the core concepts and issues, and has chapters on all the key aspects of professions in both the public and private sectors, including issues of governance and regulation. The volume closes with a set of international case studies which provide valuable practical insights into the subject.

This Companion will be an indispensable reference source for students, scholars and educators within the social sciences, especially within management, organizational studies and sociology. It will also be highly relevant for those working and studying in the area of professional education.

Mike Dent is Emeritus Professor, Staffordshire University and Visiting Professor at the University of Leicester, UK.

Ivy Lynn Bourgeault is Professor in the Telfer School of Management at the University of Ottawa, Canada.

Jean-Louis Denis is Full Professor at the École Nationale d'Administration Publique (ÉNAP), Canada.

Ellen Kuhlmann is a Senior Researcher at the Medical Management Centre, Karolinska Institutet, Sweden.

Routledge Companions in Business, Management and Accounting

Routledge Companions in Business, Management and Accounting are prestige reference works providing an overview of a whole subject area or sub-discipline. These books survey the state of the discipline including emerging and cutting-edge areas. Providing a comprehensive, up-to-date, definitive work of reference, Routledge Companions can be cited as an authoritative source on the subject.

A key aspect of these Routledge Companions is their international scope and relevance. Edited by an array of highly regarded scholars, these volumes also benefit from teams of contributors which reflect an international range of perspectives.

Individually, Routledge Companions in Business, Management and Accounting provide an impactful one-stop-shop resource for each theme covered. Collectively, they represent a comprehensive learning and research resource for researchers, postgraduate students and practitioners. Published titles in this series include:

The Routledge Companion to the Professions and Professionalism

Edited by Mike Dent, Ivy Lynn Bourgeault,
Jean-Louis Denis and Ellen Kuhlmann

LONDON AND NEW YORK

First published 2016
by Routledge
4 Park Square, Milton Park, Abingdon, Oxon OX14 4RN

and by Routledge
605 Third Avenue, New York, NY 10017

First issued in paperback 2022

Routledge is an imprint of the Taylor & Francis Group, an informa business

Publisher's Note
The publisher has gone to great lengths to ensure the quality of this reprint but points
out that some imperfections in the original copies may be apparent.

British Library Cataloguing in Publication Data
A catalogue record for this book is available from the British Library

Library of Congress Cataloguing in Publication Data
Names: Dent, Mike, 1944– editor.
Title: The Routledge companion to the professions and professionalism /
edited by Mike Dent, Ivy Bourgeault, Jean-Louis Denis and Ellen Kuhlmann.
Description: Abingdon, Oxon; New York, NY : Routledge, 2016. |
Series: Routledge companions in business, management and accounting |
Includes bibliographical references and index.
Identifiers: LCCN 2015049544| ISBN 9781138018891 (hardback) |
ISBN 9781315779447 (ebook)
Subjects: LCSH: Professions. | Professional employees. | Professional ethics. |
Personnel management. | Knowledge management.
Classification: LCC HD8038.A1 R68 2016 | DDC 331.702–dc23
LC record available at http://lccn.loc.gov/2015049544

ISBN 13: 978-1-03-247726-8 (pbk)
ISBN 13: 978-1-138-01889-1 (hbk)
ISBN 13: 978-1-315-77944-7 (ebk)

DOI: 10.4324/9781315779447

Typeset in Bembo
by Out of House Publishing

Contents

Contents

Contents

Figures and charts

Tables

Contributors

Roman Abramov is an Associate Professor of Sociology at the National Research University, Higher School of Economics, Moscow, Russia. He specializes in the sociology of professions, educational policy, urban studies, the history of social sciences and memory studies.

Stephen Ackroyd is Professor Emeritus at Lancaster University Management School, UK, Honorary Professor at Leicester Management Centre, UK, and Visiting Professor at Ostfold University, Norway. He has written or edited ten books, and, in addition to his work on the professions, he is also known for his research and writing on organizational misbehaviour, the organization of large companies in Britain and change in the public sector. His published works include standard works in the field of organizational behaviour, such as his *The Organisation of Business* (2002) and, written and edited with others, *The Handbook of Work and Organisation* (2005).

Tuba Agartan is an Associate Professor of Health Policy and Management at Providence College, Rhode Island, USA. Her research interests are at the interface of social policy and sociology, with a focus on comparative health policy, professions and health-care reform, global health and governance. She has published in several journals, including *Journal of Health Politics, Policy and Law*, *Journal of Comparative Policy Analysis*, *Social Science & Medicine* and *Current Sociology*.

Swethaa Ballakrishnen is a Postdoctoral Associate at the Division of Social Sciences, New York University, Abu Dhabi. Her research broadly investigates globalization, organisational innovation and labour market stratification in emerging markets. In particular, she is interested in the ways in which global professional markets and their perceptions (both actual and assumed) orient and organize individual outcomes, interactions and institutions. In her NSF-funded doctoral dissertation, Ballakrishnen explored the case of elite law firms in India, which have been at the forefront of creating gender-friendly outcomes, oftentimes without intention or specific agency.

Cecilia Benoit received her PhD from the University of Toronto, Ontario, Canada. She is currently a scientist at the Centre for Addictions Research of British Columbia and Professor in the Department of Sociology at the University of Victoria. Apart from ongoing research focused on the occupation of midwifery and the organization of maternity care in Canada and internationally, Benoit is involved in a variety of projects that employ mixed methodologies to investigate the health of different vulnerable populations. Her work has appeared in several journals, including *Health Psychology*, *Archives of Sexual Behavior*, *Social Science & Medicine*, *Sociology of Health & Illness* and *Journal of Health Psychology*.

Ingrid Biese is a postdoctoral researcher and lecturer in the Department of Management and Organisation at the Hanken School of Economics in Helsinki, Finland. For her PhD she studied women who opt out of successful careers to adopt new lifestyles, and she has recently started her postdoctoral research project on men who do the same. Ingrid regularly engages in public debates on issues pertaining to sustainable career models and new solutions for work, for example through her blog: theoptingoutblog.com.

Debby Bonnin is Associate Professor of Sociology and the Head of Department of Sociology at the University of Pretoria, South Africa. She has a PhD in Sociology from the University of Witwatersrand. Her research is in the field of industrial and economic sociology, where current projects include interests in the sociology of professions, textile designers and the home furnishings sector of the textile industry as well as supply chains in the textile industry. She teaches in the area of the sociology of South Africa, globalization, and gender and work.

Alan Borthwick is an Associate Professor in the Faculty of Health Sciences, University of Southampton, UK. His research has largely focused on the contemporary and historical sociology of the allied health professions in the UK and Australia, and in particular on the profession of podiatry. He is the UK editor-in-chief of the *Journal of Foot and Ankle Research*, and holds several roles in the UK College of Podiatry.

Ivy Lynn Bourgeault, PhD, is a Professor in the Telfer School of Management at the University of Ottawa and the Canadian Institutes of Health Research (CIHR) Chair in Gender, Work and Health Human Resources. She leads the pan-Canadian Health Human Resources Network with funding from Health Canada and the CIHR. She has been a consultant to various provincial ministries of health in Canada, to Health Canada and to the World Health Organization. Her recent research focuses on the migration of health professionals and their integration into the Canadian health-care system. Dr Bourgeault is the co-founder of the bilingual Canadian Society for the Sociology of Health.

Patrick Brown is an Assistant Professor in the Department of Sociology at the University of Amsterdam, the Netherlands. His research explores how organizations, groups and individuals handle uncertainty within health-care contexts. He is currently writing up a study on trust in the value-for-money regulation of medicines in England, with Mike Calnan. He has published widely on processes of trust, risk and hope in journals such as *Social Science & Medicine*, *Social Studies of Science* and *Sociology of Health & Illness*. Recent books include *Making Health Policy* (2011) and *Trusting on the Edge* (2012).

Viola Burau is Associate Professor of Public Policy at Aarhus University in Denmark and Senior Researcher at CFK – Public Health and Quality Improvement, a research centre in the central Denmark region. Her research interests lie in the changing organization of welfare services, especially issues of governance and the multiple roles played by professions. She has published widely in *Sociology of Health & Illness*, *Social Policy & Administration* and *BMC Health Services Research*, among others, and recent publications focus on the complexities of care coordination and the contribution of health-care professionals to processes of organizational change.

Michael Calnan is a medical sociologist who is interested in the sociology of health, medicine and health policy, and has researched and published extensively on a wide range of health-related topics. His books include: *Health, Medicine and Society: Key Theories, Future Agendas* (2000), *Work*

Stress: The Making of a Modern Epidemic (2002), *Trust Matters in Health Care* (2008), *The New Sociology of the Health Service* (2009) and *Trusting on the Edge* (2012). His current research interests include the study of trust relations in health systems, including comparative work in Australia and India, and the study of ageing and dignity in health care.

Teresa Carvalho is a senior researcher at the Centre for Research in Higher Education Policies (CIPES) and an Assistant Professor at the University of Aveiro, Portugal. She develops research in public reforms and has a special interest in issues related to the role of professionals in formulating and implementing public policies. She has been coordinator of the ESA network of the Sociology of Professions (RN19) since 2013. She has published research in new public management, the sociology of professions and academic careers, both in book chapters and in journals such as *Higher Education Policy, International Journal of Public Administration* and *Journal of Professions and Organization*. She is also co-editor of *The Changing Dynamics of Higher Education Middle Management* (2010) and *Professionalism, Managerialism and Reform in Higher Education and the Health Services* (2015).

Marta Choroszewicz is a university lecturer and a postdoctoral researcher at the University of Eastern Finland, Joensuu Campus. She has taught courses on qualitative and quantitative methods, sociology of gender and the relationships between gender, work and migration. Her research interests include gender in the legal profession, gendering processes in organizations, gender and age in the professions, gender inequality and comparative research.

Jean-Louis Denis, PhD, is Full Professor at the École Nationale d'Administration Publique (ÉNAP) and holds the Canada research chair on governance and transformation of health-care organisations and systems at ÉNAP. He is a visiting professor at the Department of Management, King's College London. He pursues research on governance and change process in health-care organizations and systems. He is a member of the Royal Society of Canada, fellow of the Canadian Academy of Health Sciences and, since December 2014, has been director of the Research Centre of Charles Lemoyne Hospital.

Mike Dent is Emeritus Professor, Staffordshire University and Visiting Professor at Leicester University in the UK. He continues to research and publish widely on the comparative study of the professions and management within health-care organizations, new public management, and health-care computing as well as user and citizen involvement in its various forms. His articles have appeared in a range of leading academic journals, including *Public Administration, Organization, Organizational Studies* and *Sociology of Health & Illness*. The recent research has been funded and enabled principally by the NIHR SDO and European COST.

Colin Haslam is Professor of Accounting and Finance at Queen Mary University of London. His research consolidates work undertaken on financialization into a unique 'business model' conceptual framework. This framework of analysis explores how contradictions embedded in stakeholder networks and interactions impact upon a reporting entity's financial performance and viability. A recent text, *Redefining Business Models: Strategies for a Financialized World* (2013), consolidates this analytical approach.

Jeff Hearn is Guest Faculty Research Professor in the humanities and social sciences, based in Gender Studies, Örebro University, Sweden, and Professor of Sociology, University of Huddersfield, UK. He has also been Reader at the University of Bradford, Faculty Research

Professor in the Social Sciences, Manchester University, UK, and Professor of Management and Organisation, Hanken School of Economics, Finland. His most recent books include *Rethinking Transnational Men*, co-edited with Marina Blagojević and Katherine Harrison (2013), and *Men of the World: Genders, Globalizations, Transnational Times* (2015).

C.R. (Bob) Hinings is Professor Emeritus in the Alberta School of Business, University of Alberta. He has received the Distinguished Scholar Award from the Organization and Management Theory Division of the US Academy of Management. He is a Fellow of the Royal Society of Canada and of the US Academy of Management, as well as an Honorary Member of the European Group for Organizational Studies.

Liisa Husu is a Finnish sociologist and gender expert, Professor of Gender Studies and Head of the Centre for Feminist Social Studies at Örebro University, Sweden, and Co-Director of the three-university GEXcel International Collegium for Advanced Transdisciplinary Gender Studies. Her research interests focus on gender dynamics in science, academia and research policy, and women's research careers. She has been actively engaged in several national and European research projects and actions related to gender processes and gender equality in science and research activities, facilitated eight European conferences on gender equality in higher education and is currently a partner in the EU FP7 project GenPORT.

Elena Iarskaia-Smirnova is a Professor of Sociology at National Research University, Higher School of Economics, Moscow, Russia. She also works as an editor-in-chief of the peer-reviewed *Journal of Social Policy Studies*. Her research interests include the sociology of profession, gender, welfare policy, social work, disability studies, and qualitative and visual methodology.

Ian Kirkpatrick is Professor in Work and Organisation. His research focuses on the changing management of professional organizations across both public and private sectors. He has published widely in a range of leading academic journals, including *Public Administration, Organization, British Journal of Management, Work, Employment & Society* and *Sociology of Health & Illness*. Ian is also co-author of two recent books: *The New Managerialism and Public Service Professions* (2004) and *Managing Residential Childcare* (2005). He has been involved in a number of large research projects, including studies funded by the Department of Health, the Economic and Social Research Council and the European Science Foundation.

Mia von Knorring is senior researcher in medical management at the Medical Management Centre, Department of Learning, Informatics, Management and Ethics (LIME), Karolinska Institutet, Sweden. Her research focuses on how work in health-care organizations is organized and managed – formally and informally – and how this impacts on the role-taking of and interaction between managers and professionals, the work conditions of employees, quality of care and patient outcome. In 2014, she was awarded the Leadership Promotor of the Year prize by the Swedish Leadership Academy in Healthcare.

Anne Kovalainen is Professor of Entrepreneurship at the University of Turku, Finland. Anne is an economic sociologist by education; she has worked as Minna Canth Academy Professor at the Academy of Finland and as vice-chair of the Research Council for Culture and Society at the Academy of Finland. She has held visiting professorships at Stanford University, London School of Economics, Roskilde University and University of Technology, Sydney. Her research interests include gender, economic sociology, entrepreneurship, critical studies, knowledge society, societal change and research methods.

Ellen Kuhlmann is currently a Senior Researcher at Goethe-University, Germany and associated to the Medical Management Centre, Karolinska Institutet Stockholm, Sweden. She has previously held positions as interim professor in Germany and guest professor at Aarhus University, Denmark. She is the President of Research Committee 52 'Professional Groups' of the International Sociological Association. Recent publications include *The Palgrave International Handbook of Healthcare Policy and Governance* (2015) and a Special Issue of *Health Policy* on 'Health workforce governance in Europe'.

Kevin T. Leicht is Professor and Head of the Department of Sociology at the University of Illinois Urbana-Champaign. He has written extensively on changes in the professions and white-collar occupations and the role that economic and political ideologies play in altering the content and evaluation of professional work. His research has been funded by the US National Science Foundation, National Institutes of Health, Ford and Spencer Foundations. His most recent books focus on the economic decline of the US middle class.

Annick Lepage is a PhD candidate at École National d'Administration Publique (ÉNAP) in Montreal. Her research interests include professional dynamics, interprofessional collaboration and professionalism. Her doctoral research explores more specifically the relationship between the evolution of professionalism, new organizational imperatives and the related impact on the system of profession.

Maria Athina (Tina) Martimianakis is Assistant Professor in the Department of Paediatrics and Scientist at the Wilson Centre for Research in Education at the University of Toronto. She is also affiliated with the Higher Education Group at the Ontario Institute for Studies in Education, where she teaches graduate courses in the health professions education stream. Drawing on critical social science theories, she studies the interface of discourse, governance and identity. Her research explores the effects of neoliberal politics and globalization discourses on higher education and professional education.

Sølvi Mausethagen is an Associate Professor at the Centre for the Study of Professions at Oslo and Akershus University College of Applied Sciences, Norway. Her research interests involve teacher work and professionalism, educational governance and accountability. She is currently leading a research project on practices of data use in Norwegian municipalities and schools.

Ruth McDonald is Professor of Health Science Research and Policy at the University of Manchester, UK. Her research concerns organizational change and professional behaviours in health settings. Much of this in recent years has focused on financial incentives to change professional behaviour in the UK and beyond, and she has published widely on the subject. Prior to entering academia, Ruth was a finance director in the UK National Health Service.

Linda Muzzin is Associate Professor and Coordinator of the Higher Education Group at the Ontario Institute for Studies in Education of the University of Toronto, where she teaches graduate courses on faculty in colleges and universities, professions and education, social theory and research methods. Her recent research and writing focuses on equity for contingent faculty, the effects of neoliberalism on professional faculty and faculty in Aboriginal-oriented northern colleges.

Susan Nancarrow is Professor of Health Sciences and health services researcher at Southern Cross University in Australia. Her primary research interests explore the ways that health workforce dynamics can be used to enhance health-care efficiency. She has a background in allied health service delivery and management and has worked in Australia and England.

Elena Neiterman is a lecturer at the School of Public Health and Health Systems. She received her PhD from the Department of Sociology of McMaster University, Ontario, Canada. Her research interests include health policy analysis, health human resources, work retention, and migration and integration of internationally educated health-care professionals.

Seppo Poutanen is Senior Researcher and Docent of Sociology at the School of Economics in the University of Turku, Finland. Seppo is trained both in philosophy and sociology, and his areas of expertise include social epistemology, social theory, sociology of science, methodology of social sciences and economic sociology. Seppo has acted as Visiting Fellow in several universities internationally (e.g. Stanford University, London School of Economics, University of Essex, and the University of Technology Sydney, Business School), and one of his current research projects, with Professor Anne Kovalainen, focuses on the rise of the entrepreneurial university.

Shaun Ruggunan is a senior lecturer in Human Resources Management at the University of KwaZulu-Natal, South Africa. His PhD in industrial organizational and labour studies examined the transformation of global labour markets for seafarers. Shaun has published on seafaring labour markets and professional milieus of medical specialist doctors. He teaches in research methodology, critical management studies and human resources management.

Michael I. Reed is Emeritus Professor of Organizational Analysis, Cardiff Business School, Cardiff University, UK. He has published widely in major international journals, such as *Organization Studies, Journal of Management Studies* and *Research in the Sociology of Organizations*, on his major research interests encompassing the study of organizational elites, new organizational control regimes and changing forms of expert/professional labour. He is a founding editor of the journal *Organization*.

Mike Saks is Research Professor in Health Policy at University Campus Suffolk, UK, and Visiting Professor at the University of Lincoln, UK, and the University of Toronto, Canada. He has published over a dozen books with top publishers on professions, health care and research methods.

Rui Santiago is Associated Professor at the University of Aveiro, Portugal, senior researcher at the Centre for Research in Higher Education Policies (CIPES) and Vice-President of the Portuguese Society of Education Sciences. His main research interests are public reforms, higher education governance and management and the academic profession. He has published diverse book chapters and articles in journals such as *Higher Education, Minerva, Higher Education Quarterly, Higher Education Policy* and *Análise Social*. He is also co-editor of *The Changing Dynamics of Higher Education Middle Management* (2010), *Non-University Higher Education in Europe* (2008) and *Professionalism, Managerialism and Reform in Higher Education and the Health Services* (2015).

Christiane Schnell is a researcher at the Institute of Social Research at the Goethe-University of Frankfurt in Germany. Her research is situated in the field of sociology of work and professions. She has worked in particular on the empirical analysis and theoretical interpretation of the field of cultural work, the financial sector and the pharmaceutical industries. Since 2013, Dr Schnell has been chair of the section of Sociology of Professions in the German Sociology Association and Co-coordinator of the Research Network Sociology of Professions in the European Sociology Association.

Jens-Christian Smeby is a Professor and Deputy Director of the Centre for the Study of Professions at Oslo and Akershus University College of Applied Sciences, Norway. His research interests include professional learning in education and work and the nature of professional knowledge and expertise. He is the editor of *Professions and Professionalism* and co-editor of *From Vocational to Professional Education* (Routledge 2015). He has published in *Journal of Education and Work*, *Studies in Higher Education*, *Higher Education* and *Research Policy*, among others.

Crawford Spence seeks to understand the work of financial professionals – accountants, analysts, fund managers – from a sociological perspective. His most recent work is centred on the globalization of professional service firms, with a particular focus on their expansion in Asia. Other research interests include corporate social responsibility, business history and the sociology of calculation.

Evelien Tonkens, sociologist, is Full Professor of Citizenship and Humanization of the Public Sector at the University of Humanistic Studies in Utrecht, the Netherlands. Before that, she was professor of Active Citizenship at the University of Amsterdam and Member of the Dutch Parliament for the Green Left. Her research interests include changing ideals and practices of citizenship, professionalism and publicness.

Nicolette van Gestel is Professor of New Modes of Governance at TIAS School for Business & Society, Tilburg University, the Netherlands. Her research interests include public management reform in social security, employment services and health care. She has published books and chapters as well as articles in journals, including *Public Administration*, *Public Money & Management*, *Organization Studies*, *Human Resource Management*, *Personnel Review*, *European Journal of Industrial Relations* and *European Journal of Social Work*. Since 2007 she has co-chaired the EGOS Standing Working Group 'Organizing the Public Sector: Public Governance and Management'.

Stephen A. Webb is Professor of Social Work at Glasgow Caledonian University in Scotland. Previous to this, he was Director of the Institute for Social Inclusion and Well-being, University of Newcastle, New South Wales, Australia, and Professorial Research Fellow at University of Sussex, UK. Webb's critical analysis 'Some considerations on the validity of evidence-based practice in social work' (2001) is the world's most cited article in the field and is the most influential recent publication in social work.

Sirpa Wrede is Professor of Ethnic Relations and the Director of CEREN, the Centre for Research on Ethnic Relations and Nationalism at the Swedish School of Social Science at the University of Helsinki, Finland. Her research focuses on the impact of globalization on professional work as well as on ethnic relations in working life. Her research areas include welfare-state restructuring, especially from the point of view of the rapid increase of immigration to Finland. She is an internationally recognized expert on professional occupations and has led several Academy of Finland projects on care-work occupations and on the incorporation of migrant workers in care work and in Finnish working life in general. Currently, she serves as the President of the Nordic Sociological Association.

General introduction

The changing world of professions and professionalism

Mike Dent, Ivy Lynn Bourgeault, Jean-Louis Denis
and Ellen Kuhlmann

Introduction

This book brings together perspectives and analyses from sociological and organisational studies on the professions and professionalism. These are of particular relevance to our understanding of the contemporary globalised world of professional work and its organisation. The professions have long held a fascination for many of us and they are seen by many as not simply 'jobs' but as 'vocations'. This assumption has meant, particularly in the past, that the study of professions has often had a normative emphasis. Yet, as Johnson (1972) famously pointed out, professions developed more as a means of controlling an occupation than necessarily as an altruistic service to others (although these may not be mutually exclusive). It is one of the challenges of researching the 'professions' that the term shares an everyday usage with the complex realities of those occupations variously identified as professions. One may wonder why this obfuscation continues. We could, for example, refer instead to 'knowledge work' or 'expert occupations' (Brint 1993; Reed 1996; Muzio *et al.* 2008) – extending the term to include the traditional as well as the newer professions. Yet the evidence and debates currently point to the newer expert occupations being identified as professions alongside the older ones, but not as professions as we have previously known them. To explain, Reed (1996, p. 586), for example, has identified financial and business consultants, project/R&D engineers and computer/IT analysts as examples of this expert group, which he refers to as *entrepreneurial professions*. This is, in part, because their control strategy is a market-based one. Others, including Muzio and colleagues (2008, p. 5, 2011), prefer the term *expert occupations* to apply to this group of occupations characterised as having 'no mandatory [professional] membership or official credentials' (Muzio *et al.* 2008, p. 5). Meanwhile, the older professions, particularly law and accountancy, have not remained unchanged, for they too have adapted to the conditions of late modernity (Giddens 1990; Reed 1996), increasingly becoming international, global, businesses. The world of the professions and professionalism is undergoing constant transformation as it responds to the market and economic ideologies that are promoting a different role for governments within many sectors (including, for example, higher education, health and social services) alongside the increasing task and technological complexities that also impact on the status and role of professionals.

The resilience of the professions as an influential form of occupational organisation is an intriguing one for it is in spite of the economic and policy challenges, including the financial crises that the public and private sectors everywhere have had to confront in recent decades. These realities, however, have transformed – in highly contested ways – the delivery of welfare-state services and with it the work of the health, educational and social care professionals. They have also contributed to the pressures to rationalise and marketise the delivery of professional services in the private sector and the concomitant growth of the *managerial professional business* (MPB) (Greenwood and Hinings 1993). This is a change in emphasis from collegiality to managerialism that at least 'implies a contamination if not displacement of professionalism' (Muzio and Kirkpatrick 2011, p. 394). There have also been serious questions raised around the question of trust and risk within professional organisations more generally (Brown and Calnan 2016, Chapter 9 of this volume), including law and finance. The latter concerns have led to the imposition of external, state-controlled, governance arrangements. All of these trends have major implications for the discourse around the professions and professionalism and have played a significant part in shaping the structure of this Routledge Companion. By way of introduction, we will set out, and thereby emphasise, the global context of professional work, preceded by a discussion on the growing diversity within those expert occupations known as professions.

The diversity of professions

While it is the case that there are various occupations and activities that are commonly referred to as professions or professional, when one 'drills down', one finds that these 'professions' do not always share common institutional arrangements or cognate histories. They are different 'species' of occupations whose professional status is as much a public appellation – or labelling – as it is one sought by the practitioners themselves. IT and computer specialists, for example, are commonly referred to as 'professionals' although many of them will not be members of a professional organisation (Muzio *et al.* 2008, p. 5). Moreover, in the UK at least, there is no legal compulsion for these specialists to have completed accredited programmes of training, nor any requirement for them to be registered (Dent 1996, pp. 59–60). It would appear that the maintenance of professional jurisdiction is not viewed as a major issue for the occupation in that it is organised more in line with the logic of *entrepreneurial professionalism* (Reed 1996) referred to earlier. On the other hand, nursing, which is widely organised as a profession, with legal recognition and registration, continues to pursue and consolidate its professionalisation through such strategies as advanced practice recognition (i.e. nurse practitioners) (Dent 2003, pp. 21–23). These two examples (computing and nursing) also illustrate a general point about the different contexts of professional work. Where the work is largely within the public sector, the autonomy and status of these professions have been influenced by their relations with the state to a greater extent than those in the private sector. By contrast, the professions working substantially in the private sector are far more directly shaped by the markets in which they operate. Much, although certainly not all, of the English-language literature on the professions has been distinctively Anglo-American. Burrage and Torstendahl (1990), Macdonald (1995) and, perhaps most significantly of all, Abbott (1988) have all emphasised the differences in organisation, traditions and institutional arrangements between continental Europe and Scandinavia compared to the UK, North America and Australasia. What has received less attention has been developments in the post-colonial world. Yet, given the globalisation of knowledge work and professional organisation (Faulconbridge and Muzio 2012), this is an oversight that is surprising. Here too was a world of another kind of 'semi-professionalisation' that ensured the white colonial doctor, lawyer and accountant maintained an ascendancy within the field. With the coming of independence in the mid twentieth century, the fate of the professionals took different trajectories in Asia than in Africa (see Part IV in this volume).

The changing world of professions and professionalism

Before the arrival of the neo-liberal politics and policies of Reaganism and Thatcherism ushered in during the 1980s, the professions were a disparate group of well-organised occupations with varying degrees of elite status and career security. Then the study of the professions would have been understood either in neo-Weberian terms of social closure or from a neo-Marxian labour process approach (Davies 1996, pp. 661–662; Ackroyd 2016, Chapter 1 in this volume). Although even then there was a growing fascination among scholars with Foucauldian analyses of professional activities, particularly in relation to the concepts of governmentality and surveillance (Johnson 1995; Fournier 1999). As has been described in detail in a number of treatises, the neo-Weberian approach emphasises the strategies of professions to restrict access and monopolise critical work activities as a means of establishing and maintaining high status and rewards. The neo-Marxian approach emphasises the issue of control over the work processes and the looming threat of 'proletarianisation', where occupational control is eroded (Dent 2003, pp. 27–30). The Foucauldian approaches initially pointed to the role of the professions in disciplining citizens in order that they become self-regulating (law-abiding, hard-working) members of society (Johnson 1995, p. 12). There is also important work being done on the influence of gender, exemplified by the work of Hearn *et al.* (2016, Chapter 4 in this volume), Witz (1992) and Davies (1996) reflecting a growing appreciation of the nuanced and context-sensitive way in which patriarchal inequalities play out within and between professions. A more contemporary intersectionality perspective which includes other key concerns with ethnicity or race, class and age has complicated and enriched our understanding of trends amongst the professions (Kuhlmann and Bourgeault 2008).

Whereas much of the literature on gender and the professions came from sociologists, other new developments were the product of organisational analysts. Probably the most significant example here has been the sociologically based version of new institutionalism that came to prominence in the 1990s (Powell and DiMaggio 1991), and the cognate archetype theory particularly associated with the works of Hinings, Greenwood and Cooper (e.g. 1999). Both of these related approaches have been extensively applied to the analysis of the professions within organisations, as in the case of Brock, Powell and Hinings' (1999) very useful collection of studies on accounting, health care and law. Recent works have also explored further the notion of concomitant changes within professions and organisations to accommodate various institutional and technological changes (Noordegraaf 2011). Organisational researchers, including anglo-governmentalists like Rose (2000) and critical realists, including Reed (2016, Chapter 14 in this volume), also pay attention to how professions become mobilised by broader political and ideological forces that shape their roles and work. These works suggest that the day-to-day life of professionals is increasingly conditioned by what is happening within organisations – organisations being conceived here as a mediating space between broader social forces and the reality of work.

Generally, the neo-liberal policies of deregulation within the economy and labour markets have proven to be a real test for many professions in both the private and public sectors. For those working within the private sector, these policies created apparently wondrous – but in some cases disastrous – opportunities for those working within banking and finance – as witnessed in the 2008 banking crisis (e.g. Posner 2011; Haslam 2016, Chapter 16 in this volume), while within the public sector what became known as new public management (NPM) has been the primary neo-liberal instrument that has changed the scripts for those professionals working within the organisations of the welfare state and radically reoriented their autonomy (Dent and Barry 2004).

This autonomy became subject, for the first time, to explicit controls and governance – and their work has become subject to an increasing standardisation delineated by national guidelines and protocols, whether they are social workers, school teachers, nurses or hospital physicians. All these managerial innovations have changed the work situations of the professionals in the public and private sectors, but they have not eradicated them; nor do they look likely to do so.

Much of this discussion can be interpreted as addressing the question: to what extent, in this neo-liberal era, have the professionals been subjugated to managerial, performative, controls? Power (1997) argued, for example, that the medical profession had been colonised by medical audit. Conversely, it is possible that some professionals themselves have colonised the managerial roles (Thomas and Hewitt 2011), and this links directly with the debate around the role of the 'hybrid' within the professions (Muzio and Kirkpatrick 2011, p. 392; Noordegraaf 2015; Kirkpatrick 2016, Chapter 12 in this volume).

There are a range of possibilities here. Hybrids may be professionals with managerial responsibilities who exercise their responsibilities in the interests of their professional colleagues. Alternatively, they may fulfil their managerial role more corporately and in line with the broader management agenda. A third possibility is the hybrid professional/manager, fulfilling a syncretic role within the professional organisation as, for example, within a law or accountancy firm organised as a managed professional business (MPB) (Hinings *et al.* 1999) or an acute hospital (Dent *et al.* 2012). In general terms, the variations in professionals' approach to managerial roles are shaped by whether they are – broadly speaking – 'middle', or 'senior' management roles, for the latter may offer an alternative career path away from professional work while the former is firmly embedded within it. Examples here might be doctors as heads of clinical directorates (middle-management role) vs a doctor as the CEO or director of a large hospital.

This debate around 'hybridisation' reflects elements of earlier, sociological, ones around the putative dilution of professional autonomy encapsulated in the deprofessionalisation (Haug 1975) and proletarianisation (McKinlay and Arches 1985) theses (which have been briefly summarised by Freidson 1994, pp. 133–136 and Macdonald 1995, pp. 61–63), in the sense that the involvement in management might be assumed to weaken professional autonomy. Alternatively, hybridisation may reflect a wholly new negotiated professional order, one characterised by new forms of internal stratification and segmentation. These are developments presaged in Freidson's argument (Freidson 1994, p. 142) and they reflect an extension of Bucher and Strauss' (1961) concept of professional segmentation (later extended by Carpenter (1977) and Melia (1987)). Certainly, the classic dichotomy of profession vs bureaucracy has long since broken down, with multiple consequences on the status, roles and legitimacy of professionals as new hybridised forms have emerged reflecting this new context.

Another noticeable development in the wake of neo-liberalism – and the global economic crises – has been the increased interest and concern over the issue of trust. Giddens (1990, p. 88) asked the question:

> [W]hy *do* most people, most of the time, trust in practices and social mechanisms about which their own technical knowledge is slight or non-existent?
>
> *(emphasis in the original)*

He suggests that a 'hidden curriculum' within formal education is the likely cause. This issue of trust has become increasingly important within the public sector, largely because of the impact of NPM, and with it the pressure for greater performativity, as well as the subsequent movement towards the new governance (Newman 2001, pp. 86–95; Osbourne 2006). We make no assumption here that professionalism exhibited high levels of integrity in earlier times, only that with the new governance arrangements, the issue of trust receives even greater attention. As Brown and Calnan point out in this volume (2016, Chapter 9), we have seen a paradigm shift towards a new regulatory regime in relation to many professions. No longer is the issue of trust implicit; instead, the professionals increasingly have to make it clear why trust in them is justified, for example in the publication of performance data. This is something that has been developing widely within the area of medicine and health care. All of this change is suggestive of a realignment of the institutional and organisational logics of professionalism and managerialism. This has led to a range of responses, including synergetic collaboration evidenced, for example, in the oft-cited exemplary health professional model of Kaiser-Permanente in the United States (e.g. Dent, Kirkpatrick and Neogy 2012). This is an example that caught the attention of health policy people, particularly in the UK, for it seemed to offer an innovative model useful for the UK's National Health Service (NHS) to emulate (Light and Dixon 2004). The attraction was its cost effectiveness and its integrated system of proactive health care which emphasises keeping people healthy. This approach thus saves money as fewer people then become sick (Light and Dixon 2004, p. 763). What perhaps has been less widely recognised is that the doctors within this health maintenance organisation (HMO) work much more closely with management than is the case elsewhere in the USA, or indeed in other health-care systems. For the Kaiser-Permanente HMO, this working relationship proved to be particularly helpful when its survival was seriously challenged in the 1980s. Subsequently, the doctors took on even greater involvement in management with the establishment of 'physician-managers' selected by central management and responsible to them (Dent et al. 2012, p. 115). This 'hybridisation' has proven an attractive model for other organisations (Noordegraaf 2015; Kirkpatrick 2016, Chapter 12 in this volume), although it needs to be distinguished from the contested co-existence of historically established collegial practices alongside the newer managerialist ones, in a situation identified as 'sedimentation' by Cooper et al. (1996). Metaphorically, the older collegial practices equate to a stratum of rock laid down in a previous geological age which may break through the more recent managerial 'strata' in disruptive ways. Unlike rocks, however, this version of 'sedimentation' operates on a much shorter timescale and is readily observable in hospitals and universities, where collegial and managerial practices may co-exist uneasily together (Kitchener 1999, p. 198; Dent et al. 2012, p. 117).

Recent sociological research has responded to these developments, among others, by placing changes in the professions in the context of governance and highlighting the bonding of professionalism and other forms of governing. Several authors discuss the role of professional groups as active players in the NPM and leadership models (Burau and Bro 2015; Kuhlmann and Von Knorring 2014). These developments in the sociology of professions show many overlaps with '(neo-)institutionalist' concepts, as described previously, and they open the door for closer connections of professions with organisation science and management studies, thus mirroring changes in governance (Bourgeault and Merritt 2015; Currie et al. 2012; Denis and van Gestel 2015; Kirkpatrick et al. 2015; Leicht 2015; McGivern et al. 2015; Muzio and Kirkpatrick 2011; Numerato et al. 2011; Suddaby and Viale 2011).

The linkage of the professions with governance creates a new appeal to organisation and management studies, as described previously. Hence, the focus on macro- and meso-level dimensions of governance is not as novel as it might seem at first glance. Moreover, contemporary debates draw on a classic strand of scholarship that placed the professions in the contexts of state regulation (including complex forms of 'governmentality') and citizenship (Bertilsson 1990; Johnson 1995; Torstendahl and Burrage 1990). Viewed through this lens, the embeddedness of the professions in wider 'modernisation agendas', like public sector reforms and new modes of citizenship (Kuhlmann et al. 2016, Chapter 2 in this volume), and the regulatory power of professions and professionalism as a host for knowledge production, ethics and trust comes into view (Burau and Bro 2015; De Vries *et al.* 2009; Kuhlmann 2006; Tonkens and Newman 2011; see also Brown and Calnan 2016, Chapter 9 in this volume, and Carvalho and Santiago 2016, Chapter 10 in this volume).

This most recent strand of research into the professions also embodies professions–state connections but expands the scholarly debate in different ways. This includes transformations of the concept of 'state', geographical expansion and cross-country comparison. For instance, globalisation and new emergent forms of transnational governance can be researched through the lens of professionalism and professions (Faulconbridge and Muzio 2012; Seabrooke 2014; Wrede 2012). The concepts of profession and professionalism developed in mature welfare states and Anglo-American countries are now applied to emergent service economies in other countries and areas of the world (Bonnin and Ruggunan 2013). Furthermore, international research and cross-country comparative approaches into the professions and professionalism are gaining significance (Allsop *et al.* 2009; Kuhlmann *et al.* 2015).

If anything, the professions and professionalism and their analysis have experienced something of a renaissance but in ways more compatible with the prevailing managerial ideology. Freidson, in his book on professionalism as the 'third logic', made a cogent argument for the continued '[o]ccupational control of the division of labor' (2001, p. 59) for that group of specialists we typically call professionals. But this is now even more subject to ongoing negotiations around jurisdiction (p. 60). Thus we find changing boundaries in specialisation, for example, as between nursing and medicine, academic research and teaching, law and legal-advice work. But we also see a shift in management–professions relations over the issue of leadership (see Reed Chapter 14 in this volume) and, as Fournier (1999) pointed out a few years ago, the notion of professionalism is now being employed extensively as a managerial motivational tool and linked to new forms of leadership (Denis and van Gestel 2015). The professions have had to adapt to the radical changes of the new millennium; there have been changes, quite radical ones too, but they are still with us. The question is as much about the 'why' as it is about the 'how' this is possible.

Conclusion and outline of contents

We have made a case here as to how professions and professionalism are not fixed concepts but reflect a fluid set of institutional arrangements. They are, as Burrage, Jarausch and Siegrist (1990, p. 207) very usefully pointed out, subject to changes depending on the specific *jurisdictional* relations within and between occupations and professions and the state as well as employers and clients – and the country within which they are situated.

This Companion to the Professions and Professionalism has been designed and written in order to address the question of 'what are and whither go' the professions and professionalism in this new, rapidly globalising age. It is organised into five parts covering the elements we have identified. Each part is preceded by an introduction by one of the editors to provide an overview of its authors and contents.

Part I provides an assessment of contemporary theory and institutional practices internationally. Ackroyd provides a detailed account of the sociological and organisational theories, while Kuhlmann, Agartan and Von Knorring, Tonkens, and Hearn *et al.* each provide research-based analyses of current developments in the crucial areas of governance, and involvement of service users and citizens, as well as, crucially, gender and diversity. This section closes with Saks' review of the theories of power in the analysis of the profession.

Part II provides in-depth approaches into governance as an umbrella concept under which we can explore developments in the professions and changing modes of professionalism. Burau begins with introducing the concept of governance through professions as experts, while

McDonald and Spence discuss new forms of managing the performance of professions and Poutanen and Kovalainen illustrate the new connections between the professions and entrepreneurialism. Meanwhile, Brown and Calnan remind us about the building of trust through professionalism, and Carvalho and Santiago illustrate the persistence and change in the role of knowledge as the core of professionalism.

Part III deals with the relationship between organisations, management and the professions. Hinings looks at works in the last thirty years on the restructuring of professional organisations. Kirkpatrick analyses the emergence of hybrid roles that combine professional and managerial roles in organisations. Leicht analyses the professionalisation of management and its implications for other professions. Reed assesses the implications for professionals of a call for more leadership in public sector reforms. Finally, Denis and Van Gestel explore the theme of professionals in organisational change.

Part IV addresses the interface of global and local professionalism particularly within emerging economies. The section begins with Haslam's analysis of the role and global reach of accounting, finance and banking professionals. Next, there are three case studies of the unique context of local professionalism in South Africa, India and Russia. Bonnin and Ruggunan describe how the key changes in South Africa are part of the post-apartheid project of racial and, to a lesser extent, gendered transformation. In India, Ballakrishnen details how professionalism is being reorganised in the face of the globally focused nature of professional work. We then travel to the Russian Federation with Iarskaia-Smirnova and Abramov, who argue that one must understand the historical changes that occurred before, during and after state socialism in order to understand Russian professions today. The final chapter in this section by Bourgeault, Wrede, Benoit and Neiterman provides an overview and conceptual model for the analysis of the migration and integration of expert labour.

Part V concludes the volume with a series of case studies across a range of professions. Each of these discusses current issues that challenge their jurisdictions and autonomy in the different ways identified in the earlier parts of the Companion. The chapters variously integrate the themes of governance, management and international comparison and the implications for our current understanding of the sociology of professions and professionalism.

References

Abbott, A. (1988) *The System of Professions: An Essay on the Division of Labour*, Chicago and London: The University of Chicago Press.

Ackroyd, S. (2016) 'Sociological and Organisational Theories of Professions and Professionalism', in M. Dent, I. Bourgeault, J.-L. Denis and E. Kuhlmann (eds) *The Routledge Companion to the Professions and Professionalism*, London: Routledge, pp. 15–30.

Allsop, J., Bourgeault, I. L., Evetts, J., Le Bianic, T., Jones, K. and Wrede, S. (2009) 'Encountering Globalization: Professional Groups in International Context', *Current Sociology*, 57(4), pp. 487–510.

Bertilsson, M. (1990) 'The Welfare State, the Professions and Citizens', in R. Torstendahl and M. Burrage (eds) *The Formation of Professions: Knowledge, State and Strategy*, London: Sage, pp. 144–133.

Bonnin, D. and Ruggunan, S. (2013) 'Towards a Sociology of Professions', *South African Review of Sociology*, Special Issue 44(2), pp. 1–6.

Bourgeault, I. and Merritt, K. (2015) 'Deploying and Managing Health Human Resources', in E. Kuhlmann, R. B. Blank, I. L. Bourgeault and C. Wendt (eds) *The Palgrave International Handbook of Healthcare Policy and Governance*, Basingstoke: Palgrave, pp. 306–324.

Brint, S. (1993) *In an Age of Experts: The Changing Role of Professionals in Politics and Public Life*, Princeton, NJ: Princeton University Press.

Brock, D., Powell, M. and Hinings, C. R. (1999) *Restructuring the Professional Organization: Accounting, Health Care and Law*, London: Routledge.

Brown, P. and Calnan, M. (2016) 'Professionalism, Trust and Cooperation', in M. Dent, I. Bourgeault, J.-L. Denis and E. Kuhlmann (eds) *The Routledge Companion to the Professions and Professionalism*, London: Routledge, pp. 129–143.

Bucher, R. and Strauss, A. (1961) 'Professions in Process', *American Journal of Sociology*, 66, pp. 325–334.

Burau, V. and Bro, F. (2015) 'The Making of Local Hospital Discharge Arrangements: Specifying the Role of Professional Groups', *BMC Health Services Research*, 15, p. 305.

Burrage, M. and Torstendahl, R. (eds) (1990) *The Professions in Theory and History: Rethinking the Study of the Professions*, London: Sage.

Burrage, M., Jarausch, K. and Siegrist, H. (1990) 'An Actor-Based Framework for the Study of the Professions', in M. Burrage and R. Torstendahl (eds) *The Professions in Theory and History: Rethinking the Study of the Professions*, London: Sage, pp. 203–225.

Carpenter, M. (1977) 'The New Managerialism and Professionalism in Nursing', in M. Stacey, M. Reid and R. Dingwall (eds) *Health and the Division of Labour*, London: Croom Helm, pp. 165–195.

Carvalho, T. and Santiago, R. (2016) 'Professionalism and Knowledge', in M. Dent, I. Bourgeault, J.-L. Denis and E. Kuhlmann (eds) *The Routledge Companion to the Professions and Professionalism*, London: Routledge, pp. 144–150.

Cooper, D. J., Hinings, C. R., Greenwood, R. and Brown, J. L. (1996) 'Sedimentation and Transformation in Organizational Change: The Case of Canadian Law Firms', *Organizational Studies*, 17(4), pp. 623–647.

Currie, G., Lockett, A., Finn, R., Martin, G. and Waring, J. (2012) 'Institutional Work to Maintain Professional Power: Recreating the Model of Medical Professionalism', *Organization Studies*, 33(7), pp. 937–962.

Davies, C. (1996) 'The Sociology of Professions and the Professions of Gender', *Sociology*, 30(4), pp. 661–678.

Denis, J.-L. and van Gestel, N. (2015) 'Leadership and Innovation in Healthcare Governance', in E. Kuhlmann, R. B. Blank, I. L. Bourgeault and C. Wendt (eds) *The Palgrave International Handbook of Healthcare Policy and Governance*, Basingstoke: Palgrave, pp. 425–440.

Dent, M. (1996) *Professions, Information Technology and Management in Hospitals*, Aldershot: Avebury.

Dent, M. (2003) *Remodelling Hospitals and Health Professions in Europe: Medicine, Nursing and the State*, Basingstoke: Palgrave Macmillan.

Dent, M. and Barry, J. (2004) 'New Public Management and the Professions in the UK: Reconfiguring Control?', in M. Dent, J. Chandler and J. Barry (eds.) *Questioning the New Public Management*, Aldershot: Ashgate, pp. 7–20.

Dent, M., Kirkpatrick, I. and Neogy, I. (2012) 'Medical Leadership and Management Reforms in Hospitals: A Comparative Study', in C. Teelken, E. Ferlie and M. Dent (eds) *Leadership in the Public Sector: Promises and Pitfalls*, London: Routledge, pp. 105–125.

Faulconbridge, J. R. and Muzio, D. (2012) 'Professions in a Globalizing World: Towards a Transnational Sociology of the Professions', *International Sociology*, 27(1), pp. 136–152.

Fournier, V. (1999) 'The Appeal of "Professionalism" as a Disciplinary Mechanism', *The Sociological Review*, 47(2), pp. 280–307.

Freidson, E. (1994) *Professionalism Reborn: Theory, Prophecy and Policy*, Cambridge: Polity Press.

Freidson, E. (2001) *Professionalism: The Third Logic*, Cambridge: Polity Press.

Giddens, A. (1990) *The Consequences of Modernity*, Cambridge: Polity Press.

Greenwood, R. and Hinings, C. R. (1993) 'Understanding Strategic Change: The Contribution of Archetypes', *Academy of Management Journal*, 36(5), pp. 1053–1081.

Haslam, C. (2016) 'Accountancy, Finance and Banking: The Global Reach of the Professions: Accounting for Professionalism in a Financialized Banking Business Model', in M. Dent, I. Bourgeault, J.-L. Denis and E. Kuhlmann (eds) *The Routledge Companion to the Professions and Professionalism*, London: Routledge, pp. 235–250.

Haug, M. R. (1975) 'The Deprofessionalization of Everybody', *Sociological Focus*, 8, pp. 197–213.

Hearn, J., Biese, I., Choroszewicz, M. and Husu, L. (2016) 'Gender, Diversity and Intersectionality in Professions and Potential Professions: Analytical, Historical and Contemporary Perspectives', in M. Dent, I. Bourgeault, J.-L. Denis and E. Kuhlmann (eds) *The Routledge Companion to the Professions and Professionalism*, London: Routledge, pp. 57–70.

Hinings, C. R., Greenwood, R. and Cooper, D. (1999) 'The Dynamics of Change in Large Accounting Firms', in D. Brock, M. Powell and C. R. Hinings (eds) *Restructuring the Professional Organization: Accounting, Health Care and Law*, London: Routledge, pp. 130–153.

Johnson, T. J. (1972) *Professions and Power*. London: Macmillan.

Johnson, T. (1995) 'Governmentality and the Institutionalization of Expertise', in T. Johnson, G. Larkin and M. Saks (eds) *Health Professions and the State in Europe*, London: Routledge, pp. 2–14.

Kirkpatrick, I. (2016) 'Hybrid Managers and Professional Leadership', in M. Dent, I. Bourgeault, J.-L. Denis and E. Kuhlmann (eds) *The Routledge Companion to the Professions and Professionalism*, London: Routledge, pp. 175–187.

Kirkpatrick, I., Hartley, K., Kuhlmann, E. and Veronesi, G. (2015) 'Clinical Management and Professionalism', in E. Kuhlmann, R.B. Blank, I.L. Bourgeault and C. Wendt (eds) *The Palgrave International Handbook of Healthcare Policy and Governance*, Basingstoke: Palgrave, pp. 325–340.

Kitchener, M. (1999) '"All Fur Coat and No Knickers": Contemporary Organizational Change in United Kingdom Hospitals', in D. Brock, M. Powell and C. R. Hinings (eds) *Restructuring the Professional Organization: Accounting, Health Care and Law*, London: Routledge, pp. 183–199.

Kuhlmann, E. (2006) *Modernising Health Care: Reinventing Professions, the State and the Public*, Bristol, UK: Policy Press.

Kuhlmann, E. and Bourgeault, I. L. (eds) (2008) 'Reinventing Gender and Professions: New Governance, Equality and Diversity', *Equal Opportunities International*, Special Issue, 27(1), pp. 5–121.

Kuhlmann, E. and Von Knorring, M. (2014) 'Management and Medicine: Why We Need a New Approach to the Relationship', *Journal of Health Services Research & Policy*, 19(3), pp. 189–191.

Kuhlmann, E., Agartan, T., Bonnin, D., Hermo, J. P., Iarskaia-Smirnova, E., Lengauer, M., Ruggunan, S. and Singh, V.P. (2015) 'The Professions in an International Perspective: Opening the Box', *Globale Dialogue, ISA online Magazine*, 5(3), http://isa-global-dialogue.net/professions-in-an-international-perspective-opening-the-box/ (last accessed 22 January 2016).

Leicht, K. T. (2015) 'Market Fundamentalism, Cultural Fragmentation, Post-Modern Skepticism, and the Future of Professional Work', *Journal of Professions and Organization*, 2, pp. 1–15.

Light, D. W. and Dixon, M. (2004) 'Making the NHS More Like Kaiser Permanente', *British Medical Journal*, 326(7442), pp. 763–765.

Macdonald, K. M. (1995) *The Sociology of the Professions*, London: Sage.

McGivern, G., Currie, G., Ferlie, E., Fitzgerald, L. and Waring, J. (2015) 'Hybrid Manager-Professionals' Identity Work: The Maintenance and Hybridization of Professionalism in Managerial Contexts', *Public Administration*, 93(2), pp. 412–432.

McKinlay, J. and Arches, J. (1985) 'Towards the Proletarianization of Physicians', *International Journal of Health Services*, 15, pp. 161–195.

Melia, K. (1987) *Learning and Working: The Occupational Socialization of Nurses*, London: Tavistock.

Muzio, D. and Kirkpatrick, D. (2011) 'Introduction: Professions and Organizations: a Conceptual Framework', *Current Sociology*, 59 (4), pp. 389–405.

Muzio, D., Ackroyd, S. and Chanlat, J.-F. (2008) 'Introduction: Lawyers, Doctors and Business Consultants', in D. Muzio, S. Ackroyd and J.-F. Chanlat (eds) *Redirections in the Study of Expert Labour: Established Professions And New Expert Occupations*, Basingstoke: Palgrave Macmillan, pp. 1–28.

Muzio, D., Hodgson, D., Faulconbridge, J., Beaverstock, J. and Hall, S. (2011) 'Towards Corporate Professionalization: The Case of Project Management Consultancy and Executive Search', *Current Sociology*, 59(4), pp. 443–464.

Newman, J. (2001) *Modernising Governance*, London: Sage.

Noordegraaf, M. (2011) 'Risky Business: How Professionals and Professional Fields (Must) Deal with Organizational Issues', *Organizational Studies*, 32(10), pp. 1349–1371.

Noordegraaf, M. (2015) 'Hybrid Professionalism and Beyond: (New) Forms of Public Professionalism in Changing Organizational and Societal Contexts', *Journal of Professions and Organization*, 2(2), pp. 187–206 (doi: 10.1093/jpo/jov002).

Numerato, D., Salvatore, D. and Fattore, G. (2011) 'The Impact of Management on Medical Professionalism: A Review', *Sociology of Health and Illness*, 34, pp. 626–644.

Osbourne, S. (2006) 'The New Public Governance', *Public Management Review*, 8(3), pp. 377–387.

Posner, R. A. (2011) *A Failure of Capitalism: The Crisis of '08 and the Descent into Depression*, Cambridge, MA: Harvard University Press.

Powell, W. W. and DiMaggio, P. J. (eds) (1991) *The New Institutionalism in Organizational Analysis*, Chicago, IL: The University of Chicago Press.

Power, M. (1997) *The Audit Society: The Rituals of Verification*, Oxford: Oxford University Press.

Reed, M. I. (1996) 'Expert Power and Control in Late Modernity: An Empirical Review and Theoretical Synthesis', *Organization Studies*, 17(4), pp. 573–597.

Reed, M. I. (2016) 'Leadership and "Leaderism": The Discourse of Professional Leadership and the Practice of Management Control in Public Services', in M. Dent, I. Bourgeault, J.-L. Denis and E. Kuhlmann (eds) *The Routledge Companion to the Professions and Professionalism*, London: Routledge, pp. 200–214.

Rose, N. (2000) 'Government and Control', *British Journal of Criminology*, 40(2), pp. 321–339.

Seabrooke, L. (2014) 'Epistemic Arbitrage: Transnational Professional Knowledge in Action', *Journal of Professions and Organization*, 1(1), pp. 49–64.

Suddaby, R. and Viale, T. (2011) 'Professionals and Field-Level Change: Institutional Work and the Professional Project', *Current Sociology*, 59(4), pp. 423–442.

Thomas, P. and Hewitt, J. (2011) 'Managerial Organization and Professional Autonomy: A Discourse-Based Conceptualization', *Organization Studies*, 32(10), pp. 1373–1393.

Tonkens, E. and Newman, J. (2011) 'Active Citizens, Active Professionals', in J. Newman and E. Tonkens (eds) *Participation, Responsibility and Choice: Summoning the Active Citizen in Western European Welfare States*, Amsterdam: Amsterdam University Press, pp. 201–215.

Torstendahl, R. and Burrage, M. (eds) (1990) *The Formation of Professions: Knowledge, State and Strategy*, London: Sage.

De Vries, R., Dingwall, R. and Orfali, K. (2009) 'The Moral Organization of the Professions: Bioethics in the United States and France', *Current Sociology*, 57, p. 555.

Witz, A. (1992) *Professions and Patriarchy*, London: Routledge.

Wrede, S. (2012) 'Nursing: Globalization of a Female-Gendered Profession', in E. Kuhlmann and E. Annandale (eds) *The Palgrave Handbook of Gender and Healthcare* (2nd edn), Basingstoke: Palgrave, pp. 471–487.

Part I

Theories and contemporary context of professions and professionalism

Introduction

Mike Dent

Earlier in 2015, during the time we were putting together this Companion, I was watching on TV the French TV drama series that was broadcast in the UK as *The Spiral*. The original French title is *Engrenages*, which I understand has the figurative meaning of being 'caught up in the system' (Larousse-Bordas, 1997). This is in itself a good way of introducing the professions and professionalism, for the professions and professionalism have intriguing, various and changing relations with 'the system', by which I mean the economy, society and state. But to return to the TV series, it is the French legal profession as well as the police who play a significant role in the drama. Whatever licence has been taken in the service of dramatic storytelling, it is clear that the French legal system – and the profession that works within it – operates differently from that in the UK and North America. These latter countries' legal systems have been shaped by common-law principles, whereas in France – and much of continental Europe – the system of law is based on the Napoleonic code (Krause, 1996, p. 139). Yet, even while the two legal systems are very different, we can still recognise that the work of advocates and magistrates in France corresponds, however loosely, to that of barristers and judges in Britain and similarly to the attorneys and judges in the USA. By extension, we recognise other professions as they exist within different countries across the globe even though their organisation may be somewhat different. In this current section, the chapters are focused primarily on Europe, the UK and the USA; the issues of professional organisation and practice elsewhere are treated in greater depth within Part IV (Global Professionalism and the Emerging Economies).

In this first group of chapters, our contributors set out key concepts and theories for the understanding and analysis of professions and professionalism. These are specifically discussed in the first chapter, which reviews the sociological and organisational theories underpinning research and provides an assessment of recent developments (Ackroyd). Similarly, too, the closing chapter deals with professions and power (Saks), including issues of policy. Between these two broadly foundational chapters there are three chapters that set out, in some detail, key themes that are crucially shaping the professions and professionalism today: governance, including how this relates to globalisation (Kuhlmann *et al.*), service users as citizens and consumers (Tonkens), and gender and diversity (see Hearn *et al.*). Together, these provide the bedrock for the following thematic sections and case studies.

References

Krause, E. A. (1996) *Death of the Guilds: Professions, States and the Advance of Capitalism, 1930 to the Present.* New Haven, CT: Yale University Press.
Larousse-Bordas (1997) *BBC French Dictionary.* London: BBC Books.

1

Sociological and organisational theories of professions and professionalism

Stephen Ackroyd

Introduction

In everyday speech to be professional requires only that a person is paid for their work and/or adopts a business-like approach to it. Professionalism is an attitude to work which anyone may adopt. Researchers understand professions and professionalism differently, however. For them, professionals are members of a limited group of high-status service occupations such as medicine, engineering and law. In addition to being repositories of authoritative knowledge, these occupations have some common features: restricted entry, high-level qualifications and stringent tests of competence, together with distinctive types of formal organisation. It is because of the high status and supposed effectiveness of established professions that aspects of their outlook and behaviour are claimed for work of every type.

The delivery of expert services by discrete, independent and high-status occupations, each with a monopoly of a specialised type of knowledge, is not the only way of organising the supply of expertise. Thus, the question of how professions have come into being, and what sustains their continuing importance in the modern world (around a thousand years after their first creation) is important and an issue on which the theories to be considered in this chapter have a bearing.

Outline of the chapter

This chapter considers, first, the historically important and theoretically distinct approaches to the professions which provide insights into their origins and character. Second, it is then proposed that the resulting accumulated research has so broadened our understanding that there is now a widely shared knowledge of the kinds of professions that have emerged and of the processes of change typically affecting them. Third, whilst there is agreement on many fronts, there remain some important theoretical differences concerning the causes of change and how to explain them. The chapter concludes with a brief discussion of the likely future of professions and predicts further decline in their importance.

1 Historical schools of thought

Analysts of professions usually distinguish different schools of thought (Suddaby and Muzio, 2015). There are benefits in approaching history in this way. It is economical in presenting the range of opinions about the professions and indicates something of the differences of emphasis in the writings of leading researchers. But the idea of distinctive theories is misleading if it is assumed that contributions only make sense within a particular perspective and there is no common ground between them. The proposition that different perspectives are fundamentally incommensurable because they are conceptually distinct is not as widely accepted as it was. Today it is thought there are findings in common between different approaches to the professions, including ideas about processes of change.

1.1 Traits of professions

Early writers on the professions, amongst other things, made some attempt to describe the characteristics of professions which made them distinct from other occupations. From this the suggestion has been made that the first approach to the professions was something called 'trait theory'. One problem with this is that there was (and still is) only limited agreement as to what the traits of professions are or why they are important. Also, a list of traits alone is insufficient for a theory, which requires proposals about causality to be made.

Whether there was an agreed list of traits in early works is highly doubtful. One of the key texts usually cited as the start of trait theory is by Carr-Saunders and Wilson (1933). This was certainly written before the literature on professions proliferated in the 1950s. But it is difficult to find a list of attributes of professions there. Analysing professions is not considered until Part III of the book and the discussion is inconclusive. The evidence considered is drawn from documents produced by a sample of British professional associations, and discussion is tied to views recorded. This writing has conceptual elements, but they stem from the authors' concern with improving the quality of the population (eugenics). Other texts also supposedly foundational for trait theory by Cogan (1953) and Greenwood (1957) were written for members of particular occupations – educationists and social workers respectively. It is difficult to see these as serious contributions to theory.

The traits envisaged by writers increased with time, however. Most lists referred to expertise, a consistent body of knowledge, and certification of competency. Willensky (1964) discussed a sequence in which traits might be acquired, whilst others also tried to measure them (Millerson, 1964; Hickson and Thomas, 1967), but there were many exceptions and anomalies. There was a teleological cast to this listing. Professions were successful because of their attributes: prolonged education, specialised knowledge, regulatory associations, developed rules and codes of ethics etc. Too often it was simply assumed that these traits must be the cause of professional effectiveness, but how and why was unanalysed.

1.2 Functionalist accounts

The first recognisably theoretical account of the professions was functionalism. Functionalism proposes that groups and institutions exist because they are functional for society. The theory is described as 'holistic' because the reasons for the parts taking their form is sought in the character of the whole. This approach developed strongly in North America after 1950, but originated in Europe in the nineteenth century. A key source of ideas here was Emile Durkheim (d 1917), who thought civic and professional organisations (with their origins in antiquity) would continue to be valuable elements of economically advanced societies (translated, 1957). Durkheim thought modernisation of society could lead to continuing political instability, but that professions and civil organisations would act as counter-balancing sources of power and authority to the state and military (Turner, 1992). Such institutions would provide a differentiated condition of culture (the 'conscience collective') appropriate to economically developed societies, and supporting social responsibility and altruism. Thus, professions contribute to order and avoidance of (a) authoritarianism (by the state or political power) and (b) rootlessness and anarchy (anomie). The functionality attributed to institutions in this theory was thus highly qualified. It was not suggested institutions necessarily contribute to social order, but that appropriate institutions will improve functionality and avert incipient crisis.

Durkheim's approach was taken up by another key figure, Talcott Parsons, whose new variant of functionalism was popularised in America after World War II. In his mature work, Parsons (1953) proposed a theory featuring the self-adjusting tendencies of groups and organisations within society. Durkheim's idea that functionality was not automatic and needs to be fostered was lost. In its place was the idea that society would automatically tend towards equilibrium. In Parsons' thought, integration occurred through four processes – adaptation (necessary to meet changed economic and political conditions), new goal attainment (innovation necessary to effective competition and in response to changed conditions), reintegration (necessary for institutions to accommodate change) and pattern maintenance or latency (homeostasis to provide continuity).

It might be thought that Parsons would conclude that professions contribute more to integration and homeostasis than to innovation, but this is incorrect. Brante suggests (2011) that Parsons discussed professions as part of a range of elite occupations, including business executives and administrators, which he regarded as functionally similar. All these occupations alike were seen as bearers of progressive, rational values, all feeding off and indebted to developments within pure science. These ideas give a limiting idea of the professions, and do not allow key questions such as why some professions are developed to an exceptional degree but others are not. Parsons also had little to say about the different types of formal organisation of professions, except to imply that the more functional for society they are, the more developed occupations would be.

Functionalists assume that professions serve the public good and are altruistic (Goode, 1957). However, such claims were generally not tested. Despite attempts to put the study of professionalism on an objective basis, for example by the use of measurement by Millerson (1964), such methods were difficult to develop and apply. Indeed, many noticed practices that were obviously self-serving rather than altruistic, such as suspending the operation of market processes and relying on professional judgement as the basis of provision. Many also noted the tendency of professional groups to limit supply of qualified practitioners, so increasing rewards as well as sustaining quality. Problems arising from the contentions of functionalism thus grew in the 1970/80s.

Functionalist thinking was also widely applied to organisations. The influential 'Aston Group', for example, assumed organisations adapted their structures to remain functional and efficient. These researchers set out to study large samples of firms, and their approach was called contingency theory because they thought organisations must adapt to market, technical and other environmental 'contingencies'. In their research they found two types of organisation approximating bureaucracy: what they called 'work-flow bureaucracies' and 'personnel bureaucracies' (Pugh and Hickson, 1976, p. 161). The latter are large, service organisations typically employing many professionals. Thus the Aston researchers suggested that bureaucratic organisations and professionals within them would adapt to externally imposed demands for change. As contemporary research showed, however, adaptation was not automatic and there were sometimes groups within existing structures who would resist change (Burns and Stalker, 1961). Subsequent research into the professions has amply shown this tendency amongst professionals (Ackroyd, 1996).

1.3 Conflict theory

Marx (d 1883) and Weber (d 1920) saw conflict as basic to understanding social change. Neither presented extended work on modern professions, but later researchers developed a distinctive approach to professions from their initial insights.

For Marx, the main source of professional revenue would be from services provided to capitalists or other members of the middle class. The existence of such groups as lawyers and managers was to be understood in terms of their relationship with the capital-owning class. This was a different explanation from that of functionalists, being cast in terms of self-interested motives of professionals, and related to their relative social position. Weber was more aware of the range of historical variation in the beliefs and practices of groups and their connections with society, but, like Marx, he assumed self-interest was endemic. In the first chapter of *Economy and Society*, Weber compares the operation of social groups, and he proposes, amongst other things, that groups can be artificially closed in various ways. This is a possibility he illustrated briefly with the case of lawyers in early modern England (1968, pp. 43–47). The idea of closure by social groups, as developed by Weber's followers, has made an important contribution to the explanation of social processes (Parkin, 1979). It has also been applied with good effect to the analysis of professions (MacDonald, 1995; Murphy, 1988).

The conflict approach to professions, then, focuses on the (often latent) practices of professions designed to restrict supply of services. In this approach, educational requirements, registration and licensing are now recast as devices to restrict the supply of skilled labour and so to enhance status and earnings. Using these ideas, Johnson (1972) pinpointed a key feature of established professions. They had, he suggested, a high level of control over membership and used this to sustain the quality of services and enhance the social standing and earnings of existing members. Johnson called these professions 'collegiate professions' because they are controlled by the college of the qualified membership. Control was actually secured by a strong professional association empowered to license competent practice, membership of which was obligatory. He concluded that professions are not a type of occupation so much as 'a peculiar means of occupational control' (1972, p. 27).

M. S. Larson (1977) extended this view, pointing out that the labour market is potentially weakening for occupations competing to translate their particular skills into social and economic rewards. She analysed what the professions did as 'occupational development projects'. Larson shows that professions undertake their projects by attaining control of the market for skilled work. Freidson (1986, 2001) also suggested the professional project aimed to control the terms of trade and conditions of work (the professional labour process). These ideas became widely perceived as appropriate from the end of the 1970s, when social and economic change intensified in the West, sharpening social and economic differences. At that time, right-wing governments in the UK and USA attempted to extend the operation of the market and to weaken the power of professions. At this time, too, income became increasingly important as an indicator of status. Occupational prestige was connected with standards of living more so than any putative status deriving from a supposed contribution to greater social good.

The conflict approach does not suggest the only motive behind professional organisation is pursuit of status or wealth to the exclusion of other objectives, nor is it conceivable that professions pursue their aims without regard to other groups. Such suggestions oversimplify the proposed causality here. Professions seek to suspend the operation of open markets for labour by controlling the right to designate who is allowed to claim and sell expertise. Thus professionals certainly seek high earnings and status, but they also must attend to the quality and value of their services, which also leads them to control entry. Understanding this motivational pattern means analysts must consider the institutional circumstances in which professions initially achieved their privileged position and the strategies they have used in this context to advance. The idea of a professional project allows the analyst to trace the processes by which occupations have developed themselves and to explain their relative success. Thus the conflict approach gives rise to a systematic research agenda into the development of forms of professionalism and professional organisation.

1.4   Professions as exponents of discourses

A development in the study of professions in the 1990s entailed a new focus on the ideas professionals espouse and how these are organised into professional narratives or discourses. Discourses deploy ideas and arguments that sustain practices. Attention to discourses addresses questions of how professionals conduct themselves to establish the legitimacy of their activities. At the time, attention to such matters was often seen as part of an intellectual movement away from the concerns of traditional ideas, and especially theories like functionalism and conflict theory, which purport to explain general movements of society and history.

The approach has serious intellectual provenance. A key text for its development was Berger and Luckmann's path-finding work (1966). This has various sources of intellectual inspiration, one of which is the sociology of knowledge, which suggests that what is known by people and accepted as true is shaped by the form of society and set of institutions in which those convictions were created. Berger and Luckmann also draw on two other types of literature: first, American social psychology with its roots in pragmatist philosophy. This contributes ideas about the way subjective ideas produce a perception that there is a world outside of us, which seems to be external and fixed, though it is actually produced and reproduced by everyday actions. Amongst the key contributors here was G. H. Mead (1934), who argues that it is through the use of language and symbolism that people differentiate themselves from others and create their identity. Analytically viewed, our sense of reality is sustained by our shared participation. A third ingredient is the philosophy of writers such as Sartre (existentialism) and Heidegger (phenomenology), who share the conviction that people need not regard their lives as being externally determined. Berger and Luckmann did not fully draw out the political implications of their writing, but they did help produce a new emphasis in social study which made 'the social construction of reality', and the role of key groups in doing this, fundamental.

Researchers using this perspective applied to the professions (Fournier, 1999; Dent and Whitehead, 2002; Anderson-Gough et al., 1999) have been sensitive to the ways in which professions have sought to negotiate their way of looking at things and to persuade others of its validity. The discourses of groups are so formative they shape the individual's sense of self and identity.

1.5   Holism resurgent: institutions and archetypes

Some claim today that institutional theory is a new and distinctive approach to the study of organisations (Suddaby and Muzio, 2015). However, this approach shares many assumptions of functionalism, including the basic idea that organisations are largely shaped by entities outside them. In this case it is not, as it was with functionalism, society that has the formative role, it is the 'organisational field' of similar organisations (Powell and DiMaggio, 1991). Thus, formative effects shape organisations within a field, constraining them to adopt a similar structure and to act in similar ways. A particular institutional field is identified, and its constitution is then considered to explain the entities within. However, if formative effects are primarily from field to organisations, how does change in fields occur? More seriously, if this is the main formative effect, it is hard to say how fields arise in the first place. Actually, change is seen to require intervention by leading groups, and professions are often seen as key agents of change in this way.

Institutional theorists suggest that modern organisations are little different from other institutions, and the appropriate way to analyse them is as social phenomena with special qualities which artificially restrict and channel the action of individuals. Thus, existing institutions are constitutive models, establishing the available range of viable organisational types and types of acceptable actions (Muzio et al., 2013). Within institutions, the perceptions and activities of participants are shaped by specific, identifiable cognitive schemas, scripts, and ways of thinking. The need for continuity and stability is achieved within the organisation by established norms of conduct and ritual actions and outside by the tendency for institutions to adopt similar forms. The main thrust is to explain the similarity or 'isomorphism' of institutions by seeing them as conforming to the expectations of established practice in their fields. However, the approach seemingly ignores the well-established accounts of organisations and the differences between them and institutions. Modern organisations are usually thought of as deliberately designed to meet limited objectives, in contrast to institutions with customary forms serving multiple purposes. For Weber and Tonnies, modern organisations, as distinct from traditional institutions, are marked by their rationality and specialisation. Thus, arguably, whether they fully realise it or not, professions are important to institutionalists because they fall between these two types of entities, having properties of both. Professions have existed for hundreds of years and yet they are repositories of advanced knowledge. This makes them both traditional and modern.

Archetype theory is the leading institutional theory applied to organisational change, particularly change in professions (Hinings and Greenwood, 1988). It offers accounts of how professional organisations are capable of change, despite their tendencies to continuity and persistence. To advance their argument, these researchers introduce the concept of a 'design archetype' (Hinings and Greenwood, 1988). This proposes that an organisation as a whole consists of, first, 'a set of structures and systems...' that, second, '... consistently embodies a single interpretative scheme' (Greenwood and Hinings, 1993, p. 1055). Thus the organisational structure is shaped by deeper values shared by organisational members. These values relate to how organisations define their domain, the relevant principles of governance and criteria for evaluation. These authors emphasise the formative importance of culture by claiming that interpretive schemes embody 'prevailing conceptions of what an organization should be doing, of how it should be doing it and how it should be judged' (Hinings and Greenwood, 1988, p. 295).

Dominant interpretive schemes of organisations are shared by members and other organisations and are thus held to originate outside the individual organisation. They are 'ideational templates ... originating outside the organization and ... relevant to a population of organizations within an organizational field' (Greenwood and Hinings, 1996, p. 1026). It is assumed that within a given 'institutional sphere', strong pressures for archetypal conformity will operate upon individual organisations. These pressures are forceful in professional fields. Nevertheless, change in organisations does occur, and professional organisations can innovate. The argument developed is that the changing environment, as interpreted by organisational members, is the inner mechanism of change. It is this interpretation that produces ideas about the need for change and the form it might take. Hinings and Greenwood formulate their view that a new design archetype must be developed as a workable model before successful change can take place (1988).

2   Professions in process

As has been shown, in recent decades there has been a great deal of work completed by researchers considering the professions and especially in studying the changing character of professional organisations. Not long ago it was held that different theoretical approaches in social science are fundamentally different perspectives, producing results that cannot be connected or used in conjunction. This view itself was derived from the idea of scientific paradigms, a concept from the sociology of science (Kuhn, 1962) which was applied to the study of organisations (Burrell and Morgan, 1979). Today it is possible to see these ideas as in some ways seriously misleading, among other things, possibly impeding the accumulation of knowledge. Hence, in this chapter it will be suggested that knowledge of the professions and professionalism has actually developed a great deal and there are now large areas of common ground shared by researchers, which can be initially summarised as follows.

First, professions and their organisations are now seen to be dynamic. Looked at through the quotidian details of professional practice, as discourse analysts suggest, it is hard to avoid such a conclusion. As a result of this work, it is recognised that professions undertake substantial tasks of persuasion as a part of their practical activity. Today, it is not really credible to study the professions without investigating the substance of professional motivations and outlooks. The key question now is not whether the views of professionals and the discourses they develop are interesting, but what role they play in processes of change.

Second, although there is recognition of complexity in the process of continuity and change of professions, there are now some well-known patterns. Whilst there are short-term changes in the forms and subjects of professional discourses, there is enormous continuity in professional relationships and the structures of professional organisations. It seems clear that some professions have developed into distinctive forms which have been slow to change. However, there are identifiable pathways to the production of distinctive professional forms and these are well known in Britain and North America, but perhaps less so elsewhere. Thus, although there is recognition that professions are dynamic, change has limits. Professionals as active agents have to work through existing sets of relationships within specific organisational forms and organisational fields. There is thus, in many aspects of professional practice, a bias towards conservatism, a tendency to stick with what is known. The fascination of professions resides in how they combine the creation of new knowledge but do so within deeply traditional structures and relationships. Today, as will be discussed below, it is possible to distinguish a great deal about the pathways taken in the process of creation, development and change of professions and to be clear about their patterns of organisation.

2.1   Contemporary forms of professional organisation

In the following account, consideration of the processes of continuity and change is undertaken in the context of known types of professions. Four distinctive types of professions are presented and the pressures for change to which each have been and are now subject are also discussed. The following classification of the professions relates to the ideal types of profession seen in Britain and North America and has many similarities with other typologies (Reed, 1996).

2.1.1   Collegiate professions

Collegiate professions are descendants of the original form of the profession (Johnson, 1972). Both the professional association and the constituent professional organisations until recently lacked a single executive head, indicated at the organisational level by use of the partnership form. The professional body is, however, strongly regulatory of conduct, being governed by the qualified membership. Licensing of practitioners by professional bodies is a key feature, allowing effective occupational closure. Another key feature is that the organisation delivering services is typically owned and controlled by the principal providers of services. Thus collegiate professions are of interest because of the long-term survival of features of the traditional organisational form. But this does not mean there is no change. Until towards the end of the last century, both law and medicine were good examples of collegiate professions, but whether medicine can claim this in the UK today is doubtful. Though not initially collegiate professions, architecture and leading sections of accountants have joined this group.

2.1.2 Are collegiate professions viable?

Collegiate professions bear the imprint of history. In such matters as their self-regulation and partnership membership they are unlike other organisations. In the UK and USA there is thus some vitality in the traditional professions, as is indicated by the use of the partnership form which combines ownership and control of firms in the hands of professionals (Empson, 2007). However, some of the collegiate firms are very large indeed. The largest legal firms – sometimes called 'megalaw' (Flood, 1996) – are firms with thousands of partners and tens of thousands of employees. These are commercial law firms specialising in global legal services. Their large scale and the fact that, these days, not all of the lawyers are partners, may be thought to compromise the model. With the large commercial law firm there has been a trend towards increasing hierarchy and permanent employee status for lower-level professionals (Muzio and Ackroyd, 2005). However, smaller legal practices, lacking access to global markets for legal services, have also tended to grow in size and geographic coverage, so that the single or very small legal practice is increasingly rare. Changes in the institutional arrangements for the training of lawyers have led to the reworking of closure, from reliance on the external labour market to control of promotion and access to partnerships within firms (Muzio, 2004).

As has been mentioned, archetype theorists argue that a new organisational 'design archetype' has emerged to supersede the traditional profession involving the use of professional managers to coordinate activities within firms and improve efficiency. Instead of the higher levels of professional organisations being exclusively made up of senior professionals, as in the traditional collegiate firm, archetype theorists think a managed professional business (MPB) has emerged. Drawing on their research including small samples in law and accountancy (Cooper et al., 1996; Brock et al., 1999), it is suggested that the MPB is becoming dominant. This form is said to be a 'clear departure' (Powell and DiMaggio, 1991, p. 8) from the earlier form. At the heart of the MPB is an interpretive scheme stressing different values, such as efficiency, client centredness and managed modes of governance (Cooper et al., 1996). A limited amount of quantitative research has tested these propositions, but there are reasons for thinking the trend towards collegiate professional firms controlled by managers is not supported by data relating to the population of English legal firms. First, because there is huge demand for professional services and profits are high, such firms have grown prodigiously and become global providers without any commensurate growth in numbers of managers (Ackroyd and Muzio, 2007). Second, as has been argued by Freidson (2001) and Perkin (1989), professional priorities and logic are different from managerial and entrepreneurial ideas. For this reason, they are uneasy collaborators (Raelin, 1985). If the institutionalists are right and management practices and logic have become dominant over professional logic, there has been really substantial change in these firms. Whether they are truly professional firms or just another managed business is in question.

Architects and leading sections of accountancy share the attributes of law firms. Here, too, leading organisations are global firms and still partnerships (Pinnington and Morris, 2002). Although the number of global accountancy firms reduced to four in 2002 with the collapse of Arthur Andersen in the wake of the Enron scandal, the numbers of accountants employed in large accountancy firms has not fallen.

By contrast with these developments, there have been movements in the other direction – from collegiate professionalism to organisational professionalism. The medical profession in Britain has been less successful than lawyers in reorganising and preserving independence from external control. Their position was weakened once their main employers became the state (1948). However, it was not until more recently that, among other things, reforms of medical education have wrested control of the supply of trainee doctors away from the main professional body (the British Medical Association). At the same time, externally imposed changes to medical education have weakened the content of medical training (Bolton *et al.*, 2011). There have been many studies of changes in the medical profession in response to policy changes in the UK in recent decades. In particular, the introduction of new managerial procedures and quasi-markets has weakened professional autonomy and the ability of professionals to control their work. Dent (2008) argued that external controls of medical practice have intensified hospital doctors' work, and this has had an impact on the division of labour between doctors and other health professionals. Dent and colleagues (Dent and Barry, 2004) enumerate the new agencies involved in the emerging managerialised health care and the new procedures they have introduced. In addition to these increased controls, there has been growing intrusion of private capital into the provision of medical services (Pollock, 2005) in all areas – both in hospital provision and primary care.

Reviewing the evidence regarding the legal and medical professions, it is clear there are important differences in the success with which the collegiate form has been preserved and developed.

2.2   Organisational professions

Many contemporary professions have never approximated the collegiate pattern. Mostly, they have secured effective licensing of practitioners and so a significant degree of occupational closure, but typically their members do not own or control their own organisations and are thus largely dependent on employment in large organisations and subordinated to executive power. Thus we call them organisational professions.

There are two sub-variants, professions dependent on modern industrial and commercial organisations and those dependent on employment by the state. The first group, e.g. engineers, usually originated as specialised employees in industry and commerce. The status of engineers as professionals turned on the relative success with which (a) the profession closed itself to unqualified entrants and (b) raised the perceived quality of work of qualified persons. Even today, this profession does not have exclusive rights to the use of the designation 'engineer', though some branches have achieved high status and rewards. Although there are examples of professional firms owned and run by these professionals, and which therefore qualify to some extent as collegiate professions, the majority of these professionals are employed in large organisations. Some professions – accountants and pharmacists, for example – advanced themselves by making regulatory bargains with the state. Contemporary joiners of this group are human resource managers and project managers.

2.2.1   The experience of private sector organisational professions

In Britain and North America, many occupations consolidated their position as professions in the late nineteenth century but a few have moved beyond the status of organisational professions.

Accountancy has partly developed into a collegiate profession, whilst other parts remain in the organisational professional form. With origins in book-keeping, accountancy became indispensable to business in the nineteenth century by developing crucial expertise, forming professional associations and licensing practitioners. The state also developed an interest in the regulatory potential of accountants in the control of businesses. By the end of the first half of the twentieth century, members of the Chartered Accountants Association in the UK, which assiduously constructed its identity as the elite group, were increasingly able to set themselves up as private partnerships, and here has been the emergence of large accountancy firms. Executives with accountancy qualifications were also recruited in increasing numbers to the boards of companies. In the UK in 2010, there were around 100,000 doctors with practice licences, but nearly three times that number of licensed accountants. The number of students registered with the professional accountancy bodies in the UK at the time (170,000) was more than half the number of qualified professionals in practice, suggesting buoyant growth. The numbers in training in accountancy now dwarfs the numbers in engineering, mathematics and the sciences.

The development of organisations needing specialised expertise was the key condition for growth of professions in the late nineteenth century. Professional bodies made extra-contractual bargains with their employers concerning the supply of expert employees and their working conditions, but they remained employees. Whereas many accountants have made a successful move into private practice, only a small fraction of engineers, surveyors and pharmacists are partners of organisations supplying these services. Given the importance of engineering in British industrial history, the failure of the engineers to become a powerful and independent profession in the nineteenth century is striking. Today the downward trend in this profession is the compelling point of interest. In 2010, the British Engineering Council argued that there will be a large shortfall in the numbers of engineers in training, estimating that 100,000 trainee engineers would shortly be required simply to replace the engineers likely to retire in the next five years. However, employment opportunities for qualified engineers are in decline and the lack of recruits to training places and degree courses realistically reflects this.

There are some examples of occupations developing towards organisational professions. These include project managers and human resource managers. Hodgson's studies (2002) of project managers suggest that neither recent formation nor proximity to private capitalism are necessarily inimical to the achievement of professional organisation. The expertise of project management is in demand in the age of 'fast-capitalism', as corporations restructure themselves through the use of subsidiaries and supply chains and adopt business processes that involve the extensive use of projects. Hodgson's analysis captures the efforts of this occupation to apply the early techniques of project management outside of their context of discovery, which was heavy mechanical engineering. The occupational development of project managers has entailed the partial redefinition of project management as a crucial business competence which secures timely, efficient and effective accomplishment of defined goals in challenging environments. This process of 'projectification' (evocative of the imperialistic tendencies of established professions) is an example of how a professional project inevitably begins with the need to create a stable market for a service (Larson, 1977; Macdonald, 1995) then continues by establishing a strong link between an occupation's cognitive base and areas of practice which it seeks to institutionalise. Hodgson documents the efforts made by the members of this occupation through its professional associations to achieve closure on its chosen occupational domain.

THE EXPERIENCE OF PUBLIC SECTOR ORGANISATIONAL PROFESSIONS

The second group of organisational professions is dependent on public sector organisations. Professionals in teaching, social work, nursing and (in the UK) medicine, typically find employment in state organisations. Most of these professions can trace their beginnings in the nineteenth century. However, the rise of the modern welfare state in the twentieth century, which these professionals helped to design, is where they began to organise themselves most effectively. By the use of professional associations, qualifications and informal closure in the workplace, these groups have systematically enhanced their status and earnings. However, these professions are highly dependent on the state for employment and careers, and so, with the recent reduction of state support for welfare, they are suffering accordingly.

Macdonald has referred to the 'regulative bargain' between professional occupations and the state (1995). In accord with this, Johnson defined professionals employed by the state as in a situation where 'the state intervenes in the relationship between practitioner and client to define needs and/or the manner in which such needs are catered for' (1972, p. 77). Historically, professionals in public services provided selective support to citizens on behalf of the state. Thus it is perhaps more accurate to say these professions intruded themselves between the state and the potential recipients of state benefits, defining both their needs and allowable types of provision. Here organisational professions exchange skilled work with career prospects in return for a degree of autonomy in service delivery. As well as a high degree of freedom to organise services, these occupations were granted 'structurally determined privileges' (Cousins, 1987, p. 106), such as employment security and the right to regulate their own education and conduct in a manner something like the collegiate professions (Flynn, 1999).

Many note that welfare-state organisations were extensively colonised by professionals over much of the last century (Laffin, 1998), but such accounts are apt to understate the extent of the symbiosis between public sector professions and emergent public sector services. Public sector organisations evolved alongside the development of occupations providing skilled labour and there was mutual adaptation. Indeed, until the late 1970s, there was a substantial degree of consensus about the inevitability of professional self-regulation in the public sector, and professionals exclusively controlled these organisations (Clarke and Newman, 1997). Certainly, control of welfare organisations by professionals did not involve much directive management. Managers were mostly drawn from the ranks of the professionals themselves and their main task was ensuring service standards whilst defending practitioner autonomy (Ackroyd et al., 1989, p. 613).

Thus, in these circumstances, it seems unlikely that much radical change would originate from service providers or be automatically produced by the organisational field, as institutional theory suggests is likely. After 1980, rather abruptly in historical terms, through legislation and administrative directives, government began to impose what is called new public management (NPM) on public sector services, and this had a direct impact on the work of professionals. Given the existing regulatory bargain, NPM involved the revocation of existing arrangements and provoked resistance. One policy aimed directly at eroding professional power involves the use of unqualified personnel – nursing and teaching assistants, for example – for the provision of services. The response of professional groups to NPM has been variable. One study showed that the stronger a professional organisation was, the more concerted its opposition to NPM was also (Kirkpatrick et al., 2005). However, almost everywhere, professions have been weakened by NPM.

2.1.3 The rise of new or corporate professions

Around the turn of the twentieth century, there was a period of innovation in business-related occupations, especially in the UK and USA. These ranged from advertising and marketing, to public relations and information and systems analysts. Amongst these occupations, management consultants are the most prestigious and most analysed. Today, the status and income of many of these occupations is high. Leading management consultancy firms challenge the status and rewards of the heights of the traditional professions. It is the occupation of choice for graduates from the best universities. And yet key features of traditional professionalism are largely absent from these new occupations. There were the beginnings of attempts to form professional associations when the first management consultancies were formed, but they are still not highly developed. There is little interest shown by consultants or the owners of consultancy firms in affirming qualifications as a guarantee of service quality, or in acquiring other features of professional organisation. The profit-making effectiveness of these occupations is the main plank of their rhetoric and preferred discourses.

The question of why new expert occupations did not adopt traditional professional strategies more fully or press for their advantages is open. The literature has emphasised such factors as the difficulty of the routinisation and commodification of consultants' expertise, the challenge of establishing reliability and legitimacy of consultants' knowledge, the uniqueness of business services and the evolving nature of clients' needs. These features supposedly make it difficult to represent this knowledge as similar to that of established professions (Clark and Fincham, 2002). Alternatively, the extent of the differences between the consultants' knowledge base and that of traditional professions may be exaggerated. The suggestion that there is something intrinsic to the knowledge used in consultancy that makes it unlike other types of knowledge is not defensible. We should recall that many professions were regarded at earlier points in history as having fragmented and elusive knowledge (Kipping *et al.*, 2006). A formalised body of knowledge is as much a result of a successful professionalisation project as it is a prerequisite for one.

Almost no new business-services occupations have made serious moves to adopt the procedures and policies of the professions, so they pose an interesting puzzle. These occupations probably should not be considered professions, so widely do they depart from the traditional practices and forms of organisation.

3 Remaining issues and controversies

Five approaches to the professions have been distinguished here. Of these, the trait approach does not have enough substance to be considered a separate theory. Discourse analysis has serious intellectual provenance and can be construed as a new perspective. On the other hand, findings from this approach can be considered as giving emphasis to aspects of professional practice substantially overlooked hitherto. Insights here bring new depth to the understanding of professional practices, which are not incompatible with other major approaches such as institutionalism and conflict theory. Moreover, institutionalism is a redirection of the holistic and functionalist mode of theorising. Given these points, it can be argued there are actually only two main types of theorising about the professions. These are functionalism/institutionalism and conflict theory. Even these are less different than might be imagined.

Both the major approaches to the professions envisaged here involve similar conceptions of their subject matter, recognising different empirical levels. Both recognise the motivations and outlook of professionals and professional occupations. Both see outlooks and orientations as emerging and operating within broader relationships and structures comprising the organisational field (similar organisations), the system of the professions (the set professional occupations (Abbott, 1988)), the institutional field (the variety of organisations with which professions have to deal). What differs is mostly the way in which accounts of particular professions and the changes affecting them are conceived and assembled to propose explanations of what is happening. Institutionalism relies heavily on the putative characteristics of organisational fields and other collective levels as the basis for accounting for similarity of attitudes of professionals, continuity in the form of professional organisations and the functionality of professions. Conflict theorists see the motivations of professions as self-interested, and, although their conceptions are shaped by their understanding of organisational and other fields, the actual properties of fields are emergent from the activities of groups and are strongly shaped by powerful actors. They see the big battalions in the economy and polity as key, being capable of influencing and even directing what happens at the level of the organisational field. Thus fields usually reflect historic compromises between groups and are as likely to be dysfunctional as functional.

Differences between contemporary theorists are clearly seen in accounts of change. For institutionalists, the need for change arises from the environment and is met by innovation amongst the professionals and professional firms that are more insightful and enterprising. Some groups initiate change, but it is largely consensual. Innovation is creative, functional and oriented towards the interests and values of the wider community as well as of the instigators. The alternative conflict view conceives of groups defensively or opportunistically in pursuit of their own interests, and generally beneficial outcomes when they occur are accidental. There is much inertia in the system. However, change occurs in response to external opportunities and threats, usually resulting from the activities of politically and economically powerful groups operating in the general institutional field. Change is not so much 'required by the environment' but is the result of actions by businesses and/or the state which threaten or give opportunities to the professions. Reactions of professional organisations and changed interactions between them and other groups do not turn out precisely as any one group plans, and potentially dysfunctional outcomes at the levels of professional and institutional fields are possible. Thus the system of professions is the outcome of diverse, defensive and self-serving motivations of particular occupations pursued over time. What has emerged is an imbricated system of professions with much duplication and overlapping. What makes it valuable is precisely what Durkheim averred a century ago: it is a diffuse locus of power providing a counterweight to the big battalions in the economy and polity.

Contemporary understanding of the professions often lacks sufficient appreciation of the historical depth of the processes of development in the manner brought out by Durkheim and Weber. It is difficult to explain the development of the professions without reference to the institutional context at the time of formation, as well as in the present. The collegiate structure, with decentred power and lack of single executive heads, comes down to us from the original professions, which developed in a period of autocratic kingly power. The organisational professions could not have emerged to the extent they have without the complicity of business and the deals struck between them. Public sector organisational professions can only have grown given the formation of the welfare state, and they are now under severe pressure because this arrangement is being renegotiated or withdrawn (Kirkpatrick *et al.*, 2005).

This analysis has the professions in Britain and North America as its primary points of reference. Application to other contexts will require reference to the organisational forms and properties of the new context. How professionals have conceived their professional development projects and negotiated their way between the interests of business organisations, community interests and the state will explain much about any system of the professions under scrutiny. A key difference from those found in continental Europe, for example, is the extent of state sponsorship and protection of professions, which is in contrast to the limited concern in Britain and America (Burrage and Torstendahl, 1990).

4 Conclusion: limits to professionalisation and the demise of professional society

Whatever theoretical view is taken, it is difficult to conclude that professions are as important as they were even a few decades ago. Only a few traditional professions are thriving, and then arguably only because of buoyant markets for the services they offer. Indeed, the leading organisations of these types are a very few huge firms very unlike the relatively small partnerships of the past. Amongst organisational professions there are many signs of weakness. Some of those operating mainly in the private sector are in rapid numerical decline, whilst those in the public sector are having their autonomy reduced and freedom of action encroached upon by the new policies of the state. There is also the rise of new forms of expert occupations, corporate professions that have few of the attributes of traditional professions. If they are professions, and there must be doubt about the matter, their organisation and contractual position are far removed from traditional professions. Despite high status, good earnings and social importance, the most recently formed expert occupations seem to be largely free of the impulse to professionalise. They are new forms of private corporation as much as they are occupations. In sum, there is much to support the view that the professions are in decline.

Not so long ago some commentators (Freidson, 2001; Perkin, 1989, 1996) argued that professions were becoming more influential in modern society. The idea was that their practices embody a distinct mode of organising and logic, which were supposedly becoming increasingly important. Perkin (1989) took the idea furthest, referring to the rise of 'professional society' in England after 1880 and developing extensively in the twentieth century. Later he argued that, in several leading powers in the world, professional elites were taking a leading role in decision-making and social development (1996). That professions and systems of professions embody an alternative logic to entrepreneurship and administration, for example, is undoubtedly correct. But with the benefit of only a short period of hindsight, it seems clear that these authors over-emphasised the extent of the growth of professions and their influence. In the recent past, there is more evidence for the development of market ideas and their domination of decision-making and organising, and, with this, acute challenges have been offered to professionalism as a mode of organisation.

References

Abbott, A. (1988) *The System of Professions: An Essay on the Division of Expert Labor.* Chicago: University of Chicago Press.

Ackroyd, S. (1996) 'Organisation Contra Organisations: Professions and organisational Change in the United Kingdom'. *Organization Studies* 17(4), pp. 599–621.

Ackroyd, S. and Muzio, D. (2007) 'The Reconstructed Professional Firm: Explaining Change in English legal practices'. *Organization Studies* 48(5), pp. 1–19.

Ackroyd, S., Hughes, J. A. and Soothill, K. L. (1989) 'Public Sector Services and Their Management'. *Journal of Management Studies* 26(6), pp. 603–619.

Anderson-Gough, F., Grey, C. and Robson, K. (1999) 'The Service Ethic in Two Professional Service Firms'. *Human Relations* 53(9), pp. 1151–1174.

Berger, P. and Luckmann, T. (1966) *The Social Construction of Reality*. Harmondsworth: Penguin.

Bolton, S., Muzio, D. and Boyd-Quinn, C. (2011) 'Making Sense of Modern Medical Careers: The Case of the UK's National Health Service'. *Sociology* 45(4), pp. 682–699.

Brante, T. (2011) 'Professions as Science-Based Occupations'. *Professions and Professionalism* 1(1), pp. 4–20.

Brock, D., Powell, M. and Hinings, C.R. (eds) (1999) *Restructuring the Professional Organisation: Accounting, Healthcare, and Law*. London: Routledge.

Burns, T. and Stalker, G. (1961) *The Management of Innovation*. London: Tavistock.

Burrage, M. and Torstendahl, R. (eds) (1990) *Professions in Theory and History: Rethinking the Study of the Professions*. London: Sage.

Burrell, G. and Morgan, G. (1979) *Sociological Paradigms and Organisational Analysis*. London: Heinemann.

Carr-Saunders, A. and Wilson P. (1933) *The Professions*. Oxford: Oxford University Press.

Clark, T. and Fincham, R. (2002) *Critical Consulting*. Oxford: Blackwell.

Clarke, J. and Newman, J. (1997) *The Managerial State*. London: Sage.

Cogan, M. (1953) 'Towards a Definition of Professions'. *Harvard Educational Review* 23, pp. 33–50.

Cooper, D., Hinings, C. R., Greenwood, R. and Brown, J. (1996) 'Sedimentation and Transformation: The Case of Canadian Law Firms'. *Organization Studies* 17(4), pp. 623–647.

Cousins, C. (1987) *Controlling Social Welfare*. Brighton: Wheatsheaf.

Dent, M. (2008) 'Medicine, Nursing and Changing Professional Jurisdictions'. In D. Muzio, S. Ackroyd and J.-F. Chanlat (eds) *Redirections in the Study of Expert Labour*. Basingstoke: Palgrave Macmillan, pp. 101–117.

Dent, M. and Whitehead, S. (eds) (2002) *Managing Professional Identities*. London: Routledge

Dent, M. and Barry, J. (2004) 'New Public Management and the Professions in the UK: Reconfiguring Control'. In M. Dent, J. Chandler and J. Barry (eds) *Questioning the New Public Management*. Aldershot: Ashgate, pp. 7–20.

Durkheim, E. (1957) *Professional Ethics and Civic Morals*. London: Routledge.

Empson, L. (2007) *Managing the Modern Law Firm*. Oxford: Oxford University Press.

Flood, J. (1996) Megalaw in the Global Order: The Cultural, Social, Economic Transformation of Global Legal Practice'. *International Journal of the Legal Professions* 3, pp. 169–214.

Flynn, R. (1999) 'Managerialism, Professionalism and Quasi-Markets'. In M. Exworthy and S. Halford (eds) *Professionals and the New Managerialism in the Public Sector*. Buckingham: Open University Press, pp. 18–36.

Fournier, V. (1999) 'The Appeal to "Professionalism" as a Disciplinary Mechanism'. *The Sociological Review* 47(2), pp. 280–307.

Freidson, E. (1986) *Professional Powers: A Study of the Institutionalization of Formal Knowledge*. Chicago, IL: University of Chicago Press.

Freidson, E. (2001) *Professionalism: The Third Logic*. Chicago, IL: University of Chicago Press.

Goode, W. (1957) 'The Community within a Community: The Professions'. *American Sociological Review* 22, pp. 194–200.

Greenwood, E. (1957) 'The Attributes of a Profession'. *Social Work* 2(3), pp. 44–55.

Greenwood, R. and Hinings, C. R. (1993) 'Understanding Strategic Change: The Contribution of Archetypes'. *Academy of Management Journal* 36(5), pp. 1053–1081.

Greenwood, R., and Hinings, C. R. (1996) Understanding Radical Organizational Change: Bringing Together the Old and New Institutionalism'. *Academy of Management Review* 21(4), pp. 1022–1054.

Hickson, D. and Thomas, M. (1967) 'Professionalisation in Britain: A Preliminary Measurement'. *Sociology* 3(1), pp. 37–53.

Hinings, C. R. and Greenwood, R. (1988) *The Dynamics of Strategic Change*. Oxford: Blackwell.

Hodgson, D. (2002) 'Disciplining the Professional: The Case of Project Management'. *Journal of Management Studies* 39(7), pp. 803–821.

Johnson, T. J. (1972) *Professions and Power*. London: Macmillan.

Kipping, M., Kirkpatrick, I. and Muzio, D. (2006) 'Overly Controlled or Out of Control? Management Consultants and the New Corporate Professionalism'. In J. Craig (ed.) *Production Values: Futures for Professionalism*. London: Demos, pp. 153–165.

Kirkpatrick, I., Ackroyd, S., and Walker, R. (2005) *The New Managerialism and the Public Service Professions*. Basingstoke: Palgrave Macmillan.

Kuhn, T. (1962) *The Structure of Scientific Revolutions*. Chicago, IL: University of Chicago Press.

Laffin, M. (1998) *Beyond Bureaucracy: Professions in the Contemporary Public Sector*. Aldershot: Ashgate.

Larson, M. S. (1977) *The Rise of Professionalism: A Sociological Analysis*. Berkeley, CA: University of California Press.

Macdonald, K. M. (1995) *The Sociology of the Professions*. London: Sage.

Mead, G. H. (1934) *Mind, Self and Society*. Chicago, IL: University of Chicago Press.

Millerson, G. (1964) *The Qualifying Professions*. London: Routledge & Kegan Paul.

Murphy, R. (1988) *Social Closure: The Theory of Monopolization and Exclusion*. Oxford: Clarendon Press.

Muzio, D. (2004) 'The Professional Project and the Contemporary Re-organisation of the Legal Profession in England and Wales'. *International Journal of the Legal Profession* 11(1/2), pp. 33–50.

Muzio, D. and Ackroyd, S. (2005) 'On the Consequences of Defensive Professionalism: The Transformation of the Legal Labour Process'. *Journal of Law and Society* 32(4), pp. 615–642.

Muzio, D., Brock, D. and Suddaby, R. (2013) 'Professions and Institutional Change'. *Journal of Management Studies* 50(5), pp. 699–721.

Parkin, F. (1979) *Class, Inequality and Political Order*. London: Tavistock.

Parsons, T. (1953) *The Social System*. Glencoe, IL: The Free Press.

Perkin, H. (1989) *The Rise of Professional Society: England Since 1880*. London: Routledge.

Perkin, H. (1996) *The Third Revolution: Professional Elites in the Modern World*. London: Routledge.

Pinnington, A. H. and Morris, T. (2002) 'Transforming the Architect: Ownership Form and Archetype Change'. *Organisation Studies* 23(2), pp. 189–211.

Pollock, A. (2005) *NHS Plc: The Privatisation of Our Health Care*. London: Verso.

Powell, W. W. and DiMaggio, P. (eds) (1991) *The New Institutionalism in Organizational Analysis*. Chicago, IL: Chicago University Press.

Pugh, D. and Hickson, D. (1976) *Organizational Structure in Its Context*. Farnborough: Saxon House.

Raelin, J. (1985) *The Clash of Cultures: Managers and Professionals*. Boston, MA: Harvard University Press.

Reed, M. (1996) 'Expert Power and Control in Late Modernity: An Empirical Review and Theoretical Synthesis'. *Organization Studies* 17(4), pp. 573–597.

Suddaby, R. and Muzio, D. (2015) 'Theoretical Perspectives on the Professions'. In L. Empson, D. Muzio, J. Broschak and R. Hinings (eds) *The Oxford Handbook of Professional Service Firms*. Oxford: Oxford University Press, pp. 25–47.

Turner, B. (1992) 'Preface to the Second Edition'. *E. Durkheim's Professional Ethics and Civic Morals*. London: Routledge.

Weber, M. (1968) *Economy and Society: An Outline of Interpretive Sociology*. G. Roth and C. Wittich (eds). Los Angeles, CA: University of California Press.

Willensky, H. (1964) 'The Professionalisation of Everyone?'. *American Journal of Sociology* 70(1), pp. 137–158.

2

Governance and professions

Ellen Kuhlmann, Tuba Agartan and Mia von Knorring

Introduction

Governance and professions are bound in complex ways. As policy experts, organizational managers, lawyers and providers of a wide range of services from teachers, doctors and carers to social workers, the professions serve as mediators between the state and its citizens, while professionalism is oiling the machinery of organizations and service provision (Kuhlmann, 2006; Suddaby & Viale, 2011). Over recent years, new public management (NPM) and marketization, as well as transnationalism and globalization, have challenged these relationships, but the transformations have not weakened the bonding of professions and governance.

Professions have been the target groups of NPM reforms aiming towards greater control and, at the same time, the value of professionalism and the self-governing capacities of professions have been reinvented in the current debates over governance and leadership (Dent, 2005; Teelken *et al.*, 2012; Denis & van Gestel, 2015; HCPC, 2015). Furnished with self-governing capacities, public trust and state support, the professions are perfectly equipped for leadership in public sector organizations. Professionals enjoy overall high levels of trust of the citizens, while doctors and some other health professions are leading the tables in most, if not all, countries (see Chapter 9 by Brown & Calnan). As policy experts, the professions produce the evidence on which public sector services and policy interventions are built (see Chapter 6 by Burau), being able to legitimate unpopular decisions through the power of scientific knowledge (see Chapter 10 by Carvalho & Santiago). Professionals also often act as 'champions of the people', thereby protecting the most vulnerable groups in society (Tonkens & Newman, 2011).

This seemingly paradoxical situation of professions being both the 'officers' and the 'servants' (Bertilsson, 1990) of the public and their dominant role in institutional change (Suddaby & Viale, 2011) calls for a systematic revision of the traditional theoretical concepts in the field of professions. Furthermore, new professional groups and market segments are emerging that lie across traditional national, sectoral, occupational and organizational boundaries, such as, for instance, clinical managers or textile designers (Von Knorring *et al.*, 2010; Bonin & Ruggunan, 2013; Kirkpatrick *et al.*, 2015). Consequently, there is need to shift the focus from 'boundaries', 'contradicting logics' and 'social exclusion' (Larson, 1977; Freidson, 2001) towards the bonds and bridges between professions and governance and the demand for more inclusive forms of professionalism (Kuhlmann & Von Knorring, 2014).

The chapter begins with an overview of the contingencies in the relationships between professions and governance. This includes major challenges like transnationalism and the bonding of professions–organizations–management. This is followed by case studies from the healthcare sector in Germany, Sweden and Turkey that provide in-depth illustrations of how professions and governance are connected in changing societies. Finally, some conclusions are drawn as to whether and how professions and governance are bonded as 'partners in crises' rather than counterforces in contemporary public sectors.

The concept of governance and the professions: historical bonds revisited

Governance is described as 'governing without government' (Rhodes, 1996), and consequently, closely linked to NPM and leadership. A common denominator of the new governance models is the shift of regulatory power from the macro-level of government towards the meso-level of the organizations and a variety of stakeholders and professional actors (Muzio & Kirkpatrick, 2011; Dent et al., 2012). Governance includes qualitatively new dimensions of regulation and policy that connect different levels of policymaking and may also serve as a tool of policy implementation.

Newman (2005), for instance, described new governance as different sets of governing that include social and cultural, as well as institutional practices. She argues that changing governance is not simply the result of pressure, whether from above or below. Instead, it embodies a remaking of people, politics and public spheres, and complex dynamics rather than a uniform tendency and direction of change (Newman, 2005). From this perspective, professionalism is one specific governance practice that intersects in a dynamic way with other forms of governing (Kuhlmann, 2006). Some authors have discussed these new intersections as 'hybridization' of different modes of governing (Tuohy, 2012).

It is important to understand that professions are connected to the state and its governing bodies through a number of ties, as various authors have explained from different theoretical angles (Bertilsson, 1990; Johnson, 1995; Burau et al., 2009). Weakening one tie, therefore, does not necessarily provoke substantive changes. Moreover, professional power needs the support of the state, and the state needs the professions to develop policy and politics and guarantee service provision. However, new governance has transformed national arrangements and also has global effects. New spheres of transnational governance have been created that act above and beyond the nation state; the European Union is a specific example of an emerging mode of transnational governance (Suddaby & Viale, 2011; Faulconbridge & Muzio, 2012; Seabrooke, 2014). How, then, can professions flourish if the key role of the state is transformed by complex governance arrangements, and how do new arrangements affect the role of professions and the concept of professionalism?

The professionals as citizens and mediators

From an historical point of view, the rise of professionalism and the emergence of professional projects are characteristic of civic societies (Bertilsson, 1990). As the new emerging group of experts and knowledge workers, the professions gained full significance in the developing welfare states of the early twentieth century and experienced a 'golden age' after World War II (Bertilsson, 1990). Professional power is closely linked to knowledge (Freidson, 1986), but the state has been an important player when it comes to legitimizing the power–knowledge nexus of professionalism (Johnson, 1995). And in turn, professions are highly effective buffers of social conflict, acting as mediators between states and citizens, while professionalism furnishes hegemonic claims of nations, governments, organizations and social groups with the legitimacy and authority of scientific knowledge (for an overview, see Kuhlmann, 2006).

The welfare states had a vital interest in the expansion of professions and professionalism. The concept of the welfare state (regardless of its specific type) promised access to social services for the citizens and this, in turn, has fuelled the provision and expansion of markets for professionalized work. From the public's perspective, these services offered by the professions became a yardstick for the success of welfare states to translate the concept of social citizenship into the practice of social services. Added to this, professionalism also serves as an ideological model for 'justifying inequality of status and closure of access in the occupational order' (Larson, 1977, p. xviii).

The gender order of societies is a prime example to highlight the normative power and important role of professions in modern societies. Historically, professionalization processes were inevitably linked with the social exclusion of women and non-White men. The 'dominance' of a few elitist professions, like law and medicine, has been backed up by the 'deference' of numerous women (and men), who were either completely denied the status of an expert and professional worker or were clustered in low-status professions, often termed 'semi-professions'. Professionalization was – and still is to some extent – deeply structured by the gender order of society (Barry et al., 2003; Kuhlmann & Bourgeault, 2008). This order creates ongoing 'glass ceiling' effects and status inequality for women in traditionally male-dominated areas, like medicine, despite an increasingly balanced sex ratio in the medical profession at large in most western countries. Also, the gender order serves female-gendered professions like nursing to back up their claims for professionalization and create professional identities, as Wrede (2012) has shown for the nursing profession in Finland.

Hence, changing gender arrangements and increasing professional migration, as well as emergent new economies, have changed the social composition of the professions, thereby challenging professionalism as a White male project of resource-rich countries (Bonnin & Ruggunan, 2013). The traditional forms of boundary work and elitist professionalism in healthcare, backed up by nation-state support are no longer sustainable in times of equal opportunity policies, increasing numbers of women doctors and new demand for skill-mix and task-shifting (Bourgeault & Merritt, 2015). The changes underway in different countries raise more general questions on the logics of professionalism as a mode of organizing the public sector.

The logics of professionalism

US sociologist Freidson (2001) has argued that professionalism is based on knowledge and serves as a 'third logic' next to the rational–legal bureaucracy developed by Max Weber, which represents managerialism, and Adam Smith's model of the free market, which represents consumerism (2001, p. 179). From different theoretical approaches, a major body of the literature has dealt with the formalized knowledge system as a resource for professional power to gain occupational closure and dominance over other groups (Freidson, 1986; and Chapter 10 by Carvalho & Santiago). Viewed through the lens of contradicting logics (Light, 2010), the new modes of governing through performance management appear as external forces imposed on professions that challenge professional power and self-regulatory competencies.

There has for a long time been scholarly debate into the problematic limitations of professionalism as necessarily opposed to other forms of regulation. Johnson (1995), arguing from the perspective of an English sociologist, proposed to overcome the static and contradictory conception of external regulation and professionalism by taking up the Foucauldian concept of governmentality. More recently, integrated governance approaches and a growing body of empirical research into changing boundaries between management and professionalism have added further evidence and expanded the theoretical concepts towards neo-institutionalism and organization studies (Dent et al., 2012; Reay & Hinings, 2009; Suddaby & Viale, 2011; Kuhlmann et al., 2013).

The role of professions in contemporary public sectors can only be fully understood if we bear in mind the double role of professions as 'officers' and 'servants', as Bertilsson (1990) has argued from the perspective of the Nordic welfare states. Governments across the world need the power of professional knowledge to legitimize political decisions and new policies, in particular in the light of austerity politics and more critical and knowledgeable citizens as service users (Kuhlmann, 2006).

The transformations underway in the public sectors of different countries and the emergent public sector services across the world (see Chapters 16–20, in Part IV) cannot be explained in dualist and dichotomous frameworks, such as 'from welfare states to neoliberal marketization'. Moreover, professions and organizations are 'collective agents', as Muzio and Kirkpatrick (2011, p. 390) argue, with distributed responsibility for public sector services. The 'collective' momentum and embeddedness of the professions in publics and public sector services may be best explained by the figure of the 'citizen professional' (Kuhlmann, 2006, pp. 15–33; see also Chapter 3 by Tonkens). This approach highlights the bonding of professions and governance and, consequently, calls for a critical review of theoretical explanations into the role of professions in contemporary public sector transformations.

Relocating professions in new emergent spheres of governance

Changes in the relationship between governance and professions and demand for more integrated forms of professionalism are relevant on all levels of governance. Within this context, a more integrated professionalism has many different facets, including more equal social (gender) relationships as well as the softening of occupational boundaries, the new connections between professions and organizations through NPM regimes, and the critical approaches to hegemonic claims for autonomy, to name only some. The qualitatively new dimensions of the bonds between professions and governance are most obvious when looking at new emergent spheres of governance. Here, the politics of globalization, internationalization and Europeanization have created new modes of both transnational governance and agency of professions; this will be illustrated in more detail later in this chapter using gender-sensitive medicine as an example.

As a common denominator of these developments, the different sets of governing (Newman, 2005) are becoming more complex, mixed and permeable. This may lead to processes of 're-stratification' in the professions (Freidson, 2001; McDonald, 2012; Kirkpatrick et al., 2015) that separate the emergent administrative and knowledge elites from a growing body of rank-and-file workers, thereby reinforcing divisions of work and inequality in the professional workforce. However, as Muzio and Kirkpatrick (2011, p. 390) highlight, organizations and professions are 'collective agents' and the developments may also 'represent a way in which professions, as "corporate entities", are able to reinforce or even extend their dominance over organizations or field of practice' (2011, p. 396). Similarly, Suddaby and Viale argue that professionals are furnished with:

> critical social skills that are essential for effecting field-level change. These skills make professionals uniquely qualified to engage in 'institutional work', i.e. creating, maintaining or

altering institutions… they shift sides of professional control to new contexts, new vehicles and new organizational fields.

(Suddaby & Viale, 2011, p. 436)

These approaches suggest that professions are not only able to survive in new emergent volatile spheres of governance but are well equipped to actively reconfigure contemporary governance and public sectors. The professions may be relocated in changing public sectors in various ways and new stratifications may emerge, but the bonds between professions and governance are being reinforced, as the examples below highlight in more detail.

Transnationalism: professional agency in volatile spheres of governance

Globalization has created new spaces beyond the regulatory architecture of national states, and this in turn raises a number of new questions about the established bonds between the state, its citizens and the professions and the transformations of these relationships. Despite the centrality of the state in the study of professions (Johnson, 1995), research and theorizing have largely failed to reflect adequately on the geopolitical and cultural contexts of a specific concept of 'state' (especially the model of the welfare state and its European roots) that for many years served as a blueprint for the concepts of 'profession' and 'professionalism'.

Only recently have globalization and transnationalism gained more attention in the study of professions, and there is still a lack of comparative approaches. Existing research has highlighted persisting 'path dependency' in the country-specific responses of professions 'to neoliberal institutional pressures' (Leicht *et al.*, 2009, p. 581). This suggests that the state is still a key actor that determines the scope of professional action, agency and self-regulatory powers (Leicht *et al.*, 2009). At the same time, new supranational and transnational regulatory bodies are increasingly relevant and 'international organizations are a force encouraging global standards' (Allsop *et al.*, 2009, p. 487). New bodies and forms of governing beyond nation states may develop their own rules of how to govern the professions (Faulconbridge & Muzio, 2012).

Here, the emergent new field of gender medicine provides an interesting example of how the bonds between governance and professions are tightened up transnationally in the absence of a strong state-government and (conservative) national elites of the medical profession and how this may even transform core concepts of professional knowledge. It is well known that medicine has emerged as a science that is strongly biased towards male actors and based on a masculinist concept of science and the human body that claims 'neutrality' of formalized knowledge and supremacy of men's perspectives over women's experience. However, the legitimizing power of this approach is on the wane, and a new medical speciality of gender medicine, gender-sensitive policies in major institutions of the healthcare state, evidence-based gender-specific data and gender-specific curricula are emerging in some countries and areas – although slowly and not uncontested.

Changes towards more gender-sensitive healthcare and medicine are fostered by many different players: an international women's health and gender equality movement, gender mainstreaming policies and equal opportunity approaches of international organizations (like the World Health Organization, the United Nations and the European Union), more gender-sensitive and women-friendly standards and target setting of international research and funding organizations and high-level journals, and regulatory bodies with high international scientific and market power, such as the Food and Drug Administration (FDA) in the USA (for details, see Kuhlmann and Annandale, 2012).

The example of gender-sensitive medicine reveals that a highly conservative medical profession that is firmly rooted in, and tied to nation-state governance arrangements may be re-located in transnational spheres of governance in ways that foster innovation and change in the entire 'institutional field', to borrow the term from Suddaby and Viale (2011, p. 436). The developments might in future even lead to restratification processes (like new emergent fields of gender medicine) and more generally, to changes in the knowledge basis of the profession.

Medicine is not the only example of the transformative powers of transnational governance within professional fields. Seabrooke, for instance, has recently introduced the concept of 'epistemic arbitrage' (defined as exploitation of opportunities between bodies of professional knowledge) and argued that transnational environments 'are especially permissive of epistemic arbitrage and professional mobilization' (2014, p. 49). Furthermore, Quack, drawing on law-making in large international law firms and international legal associations, has revealed that:

> in the absence of strong government, transnational law develops, to a significant degree, from decentralized rule-setting led by legal practitioners in large law firms and international professional associations … recurrent efforts of multiple professional actors to make sense of their legal transactions generate a working level of relationships while all of the actors maintain their distinct cultural and institutional reference frames.
>
> *(2007, pp. 658, 660)*

Taken together, the research suggests that professionalism is embedded in new emergent spheres of transnational governance in public sectors – which increasingly also include private players like large multinational pharmaceutical firms or private NGOs – and that these processes may foster professional agency in new ways.

Hybridization: professions as organizational agents

The hybridization metaphor (Tuohy, 2012) highlights further important changes in contemporary governance. Here, the focus is mainly on the governance shifts towards operational and actor-centred governance and the meso–micro levels of organizations and professions. Developments in the field of healthcare and the new connections between management and professionalism, including new groups of clinical managers, are the most prominent example of these transformations (Saltman *et al.*, 2011; Kirkpatrick *et al.*, 2015).

Changes may impact in the structure and processes of healthcare organizations like hospitals, in the health professions (e.g. restratification processes and new interdisciplinary educational programmes), and in the concept of professionalism (e.g. more inclusive and participatory approaches). Transformations happen in the 'minds of doctors' and those of managers (Von Knorring *et al.*, 2010; Kuhlmann *et al.*, 2013) as well as in the organizations and institutions of the healthcare systems (Burau *et al.*, 2009; Saltman *et al.*, 2011). These processes are not always systematically connected and may be uneven and even contradictory, but scholarly debate increasingly highlights their connectedness and this, in turn, calls for critical revisions of the traditional focus on boundaries in the study of professions.

Organizational research and management studies, in particular, have contributed innovative approaches to the professions and management relationships (Muzio & Kirkpatrick, 2011). Several authors have highlighted the blurring of boundaries between professionalism, conceptualized as 'internal' mode of governing, and managerialism as an 'external' governance approach attempting to improve control and transparency of elitist professional knowledge. For instance, Waring and Currie (2009) have studied the management of knowledge around clinical risks in the National Health Service (NHS) in the United Kingdom and revealed 'that doctors respond to change through a number of situated responses that limit managerial control over knowledge and reinforce claims to medical autonomy' (2009, p. 755). Waring and Currie have introduced three categories for an in-depth description of the strategies applied by doctors: 'co-optation', 'adaptation' and 'circumvention'. This research brings into view that management approaches and tools are 'co-opted into professional work as a form of resistance, with professionals being competent in management practice, rather than being co-opted into management roles' (Waring & Currie, 2009, p. 774). At the same time, doctors may incorporate managerialist logics and work styles, thus transforming professionalism from 'within' the profession (Kuhlmann, 2006).

Cross-country comparative research has added further evidence of the bonding of professions to organizational settings and revealed varieties of relocations. For example, Dent and colleagues (2012) have compared medical leadership in England, Denmark, the Netherlands and the USA and highlighted the ways in which national institutions have shaped professional development. Thus, path dependency still matters in restratification processes.

A comparison of changing modes of control in clinical practice in seven European countries has recently shown that healthcare systems make use of both managerial controls and professional self-governing capacities as well as of markets and public controls. But they vary in the ways the different sets of governing and managing professional performance are coordinated (Kuhlmann et al., 2013). Consequently, coordination may serve as a taxonomy for comparing clinical governance. The findings also call for a closer look at the bonds between professionalism and managerialism to better understand the implementation of governance changes and the agency of professions in organizations and healthcare systems.

Furthermore, the example of gender medicine described previously confirms the capacity of medicine to transform its boundaries and innovate its knowledge base in order to respond to new demand and international pressure. Similarly, Plochg and colleagues (2009) have highlighted important transformations underway in medical professionalism to better respond to healthcare needs. Taken together, the findings illustrate what Suddaby and Viale (2011, p. 436) describe from the perspective of institutional/organizational theorists as 'critical social skills' of professionals and Quack (2007, p. 636) as 'decentralized rule-setting' of professions that make change happen in organizations and the wider public sector, be it law or healthcare services.

In summary, a discourse of hybridization has challenged classic approaches to professionalism as boundary work and exclusionary strategy. At the same time, the hybridization discourse lacks institutional embeddedness and sensitivity to power relations, and it is, therefore, time to bring flesh to the bones of the hybrid professionals. Here, more critical theoretical approaches and empirical research locate the figure of a hybrid professional in the institutional contexts of healthcare systems, thereby identifying organizational settings that foster integrated modes of professionalism, leadership and innovation (Kuhlmann et al., 2013; Denis & van Gestel, 2015; HCPC, 2015; Kirkpatrick et al., 2015; see also Chapters 11–15 in Part III). How the professions are located in these new emergent spheres of governing depends on contexts; and overall, the path-dependencies of the nation states and systems remain strong factors.

Case studies: health professions and governance in Germany, Sweden and Turkey

We have chosen healthcare in Germany, Sweden and Turkey as case studies to illuminate the importance of contexts to professional governance. Healthcare is interesting for various reasons. First, in medicine we find a highly standardized knowledge system and strong international forces that create similar concepts of professionalism and an umbrella for supranational and transnational governance. Second, health policy, organizations and service provision follow similar goals of universal coverage and 'good' care for patients. Our case studies below take four major dimensions into account, namely the position of doctors in the institutional governance arrangements, the introduction of NPM reforms, the leadership of doctors, and new forms of clinical management in relation to the state–professions bonds.

While the modes of professionalism and the goals are similar, the institutional conditions and healthcare systems are different. Germany is a classic Bismarckian-style health system with corporatist governance in a high-income country. Sweden is a prime example of a high-income country with universal healthcare and decentralized governance, and Turkey is a middle-income country with a mixed system that combines centralized governance with market reforms (Tatar *et al.*, 2011; Agartan, 2012; Anell *et al.*, 2012; Busse & Blümel, 2014). Thus, the selected cases provide opportunities to explore the bonds between professions and governance in different governance settings and social contexts.

Germany: Professionalism in a corporatist governance system

The Bismarckian healthcare system in Germany is the oldest welfare model in the world. It is based on corporatism, network-based governance and institutional integration of doctors in the major bodies and regulatory settings. This system is characterized by federalism, fragmentation of outpatient and inpatient care and statutory health insurance (SHI), with healthcare jointly funded by compulsory contributions from employers and employees, although mixed forms, including co-payments of patients, are on the increase. The statutory contribution system ensures free healthcare for all citizens that are members of the health insurance funds. Approximately 50 per cent of doctors are self-employed office-based generalists and specialists, while most others are salaried employees in hospitals. All doctors who treat patients that are members of the statutory health insurance funds must, by law, be registered with the regional Association of Statutory Health Insurance (SHI) Physicians.

The state has established the legal framework for collecting and distributing funds for healthcare, while delegating responsibility for administration and decision-making to a network of public law institutions with the 'Federal Joint Committee' (*Gemeinsamer Bundesausschuss*) as its major steering body. The associations of SHI physicians and the SHI funds form the two pillars of the joint self-administration charged with cooperating to make decisions in the public interest. Within this framework, the Association of SHI physicians represents the provider side (including all healthcare professions), while the SHI funds represent the user side. As a regulatory model, the joint-self-administration of SHI care is based on the principle of balancing, and curbing different interests – including those of the state (Blank & Burau, 2014; Busse & Blümel, 2014).

The 2000 Health Reform Act introduced, for the first time, structural change and pilot projects that impacted on the corporatist partnership-based SHI system by strengthening both market and state powers. Within this context, the introduction of disease management programmes (DMPs) for chronic illnesses in ambulatory (outpatient) care are the clearest sign of intervention in the SHI system. First introduced in 2002, DMPs are shaped by the politics of cost-containment and financial incentives for both the SHI funds and the doctors. Although the programmes attempted to improve the quality of care through the standardization of treatment and a number of new models of quality and safety management, they did not establish a coherent system of target setting, monitoring and evaluation with benchmarks. There are also few sanctions against doctors who provide poor quality of care (Kuhlmann, 2006).

In this situation, office-based doctors have taken the tools of management on board, but primarily in those areas where they are able to design the instruments and outcomes, as, for instance, in quality management and the development and implementation of evidence-based clinical guidelines. In contrast, improved rights of patients and better involvement in decision-making were less popular among office-based doctors (generalists and specialists), as shown by a representative survey conducted with office-based doctors in two large associations of SHI physicians (Kuhlmann, 2006).

Another important area of changing governance is hospitals. Besides a diagnosis-related group-based reimbursement system (DRGs), a number of steering tools have been introduced in recent years, mainly attempting to improve control of budgets and providers (especially doctors) coupled with new modes of quality and safety management (Saltman et al., 2011). Here, a recent European comparative study reveals a paradox of corporatist governance: as policy player, the medical profession is integrated in hospital governance (connected through key regulatory bodies, for instance), but in ways that ensure medical power on macro- and micro-levels of governance, even if the balance of power is shifting towards the sickness funds and a more interventionist state (Kuhlmann et al., 2013). The key question, therefore, is no longer *whether* management and professions are connected, but *how* the two modes of governing are coordinated.

In the German case, the new forms of governing medical performance have increased the connections between management and professionalism on all levels and areas, but the regulatory bodies and tools are often not adequately coordinated. This leads to some fragmentation in the coordination between the top level of hospital management and the level of the department/unit as well as between budget management and quality/safety management. In this situation, professional powers are strongest at the level of the department and in the area of quality management (Kuhlmann et al., 2013).

In summary, the governance of medical performance has been transformed but remains firmly located in the SHI system. Consequently, the implementation of governance changes depends, first and foremost, on negotiations between doctors and sickness funds. Within this context, the medical profession holds a strong leadership position, also in relation to other health professions. Here, network-based configurations of SHI governance (based on the two pillars of sickness funds and physicians' associations) and system-based fragmentation of governing powers provide opportunity for doctors to actively transform the bonds between governance, the state and the citizens.

Sweden: professionalism in a universalist governance system

Similar to the other Scandinavian countries, Sweden has a long tradition of a universalist social welfare system, where healthcare is a public responsibility, mainly financed through taxes and hospital care delivered by public providers. In relation to the provider groups, almost all healthcare professionals in Sweden are salaried employees in inpatient and outpatient care, comprising physicians, nurses and a wide range of other healthcare vocational groups.

The Swedish healthcare system is also, by tradition, characterized by decentralization. While the state provides the overall framework for healthcare policy, the twenty-one County Councils/regions are responsible for funding and provision of healthcare services to the population in their respective geographical regions. Consequently, most healthcare reforms are developed and implemented at county-council level and this has created significant variation in the organization and delivery of healthcare services. More recently, reforms are aiming to shift regulatory power towards the state in order to reduce existing regional differences and ensure equal access to services for all citizens (Anell et al., 2012; Blank & Burau, 2014).

Interestingly, the attempt to overcome the problems of decentralized healthcare policy through stronger state-level reforms is marching in step with an increasing significance of new governance instruments on meso- and micro-levels of healthcare governance. More specifically,

NPM and market-oriented policies have been part and parcel of health reform in Sweden since the 1990s. These policies were introduced to weaken the regulatory power of the healthcare state and its monopoly on the provision of welfare services (on national and county levels), but also to improve provider control and strengthen the voice and choice of the citizens and service users in healthcare policy.

Clearly, cost efficiency and quality improvement have also been important driving forces of reforms. This includes the introduction of market mechanisms such as a purchaser–provider split and more expanded opportunities for patients to choose their healthcare provider, as well as new forms of privatization of services hitherto not very common in the Swedish system, including the availability of health services fully paid for by the users. This is still the exception and mainly limited to large cities and elective services, however (Anell *et al.*, 2012; Blank & Burau, 2014).

Within the context of NPM and market-based elements of governance, management is enjoying overall higher currency in all areas of healthcare and all provider groups, while quality management is a particularly interesting case to illustrate the multifaceted connections of governance changes. Here, ideas from total quality management (TQM, in Swedish: *kvalitetsstyrning*) were imported into the new healthcare policy and had a growing influence on both the concepts of management and the day-to-day practice of physicians. The idea of 'control' of doctors seems, at a first glance, to be in contrast to the integrated governance structure of the Swedish welfare system and traditionally high levels of trust in the medical professions' commitment to quality care. However, the focus on control turned out to reinforce the bonds between the state and the medical profession. This was possible due to the importance of high-quality service provision in Swedish healthcare institutions and the general culture that caused a mutual dependency between doctors (as citizen-professionals) and policymakers/ government.

Furthermore, NPM reforms and strong commitment to quality management strengthen managerial influence. This has led to an increasingly stronger manager position in relation to the medical profession. Here, the Department Manager Reform of 1997 marked a final step in separating the healthcare manager role and the doctor's role. It opens the position of clinical department manager (a direct manager over physicians) to professionals or vocational groups other than doctors. Consequently, governance reforms not only transform the medicine–management connections but may also impact more generally on the role of doctors in clinical settings and the position of other health professionals (Von Knorring *et al.*, 2016).

At the same time, empirical research has revealed that the new managers do not develop their own professional identity to respond to new demand for leadership but refer to the medical professions' behaviour; this may weaken the manager role in relation to the medical profession (Von Knorring *et al.*, 2010, 2016). This result brings tensions and paradoxes into view. According to the logics of NPM reforms and new medical management concepts, the managers are charged with control of doctors and therefore expected to change the legacy of strong state–professions in universalist welfare systems. Obviously, this does not necessarily happen as expected in theory.

In summary, the universalist system in Sweden has a long tradition of close connections between the state and the professions, specifically doctors. This case study illustrates how the bonding may be 'institutionalized' and professional expertise integrated into 'governmentality', as Johnson (1995, p. 2) put it. As we have seen from the examples, the 'institutionalization of expertise' (Johnson, 1995, p. 2) does not easily leave its trajectories into governance just because of a 'diversification' in some areas, but it may search out new avenues, for instance through increasingly involving doctors and nurses in management.

Turkey: professionalism in a mixed governance context

It has proven difficult to categorize Turkey's healthcare system due to its fragmented nature. In terms of financing, it could be considered closer to a social health insurance (SHI) model (Wendt *et al.*, 2013): the three insurance funds – for formally employed workers, retired state employees, and the self-employed – were non-profit financing institutions which collected social insurance contributions. These social insurance contributions were the largest source of funding (43.9%) in 2008 (Tatar *et al.*, 2011). Alongside this SHI system, there was a tax-financed primary care system that provided care through publicly owned and operated healthcare centres. Moreover, unlike in other SHI systems, corporate actors in Turkey, such as the social insurance funds, trade unions and doctors' associations were not accorded a central role in the governance of the healthcare system. Rather, along the lines of a command-and-control system, many decisions involving the contents of the comprehensive benefits package or methods of remuneration were decided in a top-down manner, and, partly due to its large role in service provision, the central government held day-to-day operating authority.

The 2003 Health Transformation Programme brought about major changes in the financing, provision and regulation dimensions of the Turkish health system. One of the most important changes was the creation of a single-payer system by uniting the public insurance funds under the Social Security Institution (SSI). The Health Transformation Programme adopted new payment mechanisms that emphasized performance, granted public hospitals some degree of autonomy, established the directorate of Public Hospitals Institution, and redefined the Ministry of Health (MoH) as a planning and supervising authority. Improving efficiency and effectiveness of healthcare delivery was assigned a high priority, and new quality standards tied to performance payments were implemented in all hospitals. Thus, market elements were combined with managerialism and expanded the audit and inspection culture.

At first glance, this trend seems to be largely similar to high-income welfare states. However, reforms in middle-income countries such as Turkey combined elements of marketization and managerialism with universalism largely because reforms had to address problems of access to healthcare services and lack of insurance coverage (Agartan, 2012). Second, in the Turkish case, the reforms were devised and implemented in a top-down manner with very limited participation of stakeholders. Third, and most importantly, at least in this initial stage (2003–10), this particular combination of managerialism, marketization and universalism has strengthened state power.

Although Turkey has experimented with NPM reforms within the framework of the Health Transformation Programme, we have not yet observed the parallel changes in governance where the regulatory power shifts from the macro-level of government towards the meso-level of organizations and to a variety of actors. Additionally, major decisions on financing, such as setting the contribution rates and co-payments, are made by the government within the boundaries set by the Health Reform Act (5510), with no influence of corporate actors. The benefits package is also defined by law, and the SSI (the single payer) issues Health Implementation Guides that list the services, prices and service delivery rules for public and private providers (Tatar *et al.*, 2011).

Currently, corporate actors, such as doctors' associations, do not have a formal role in governing the financing of healthcare services. Rather, professional self-governance is limited to licensing, certification and monitoring of professional conduct. Some of the important corporate actors such as the Turkish Medical Association remain staunch critics of the Health Transformation Programme and believe that the particular combination of managerial and market-based reforms has undermined their professional autonomy. However, the recent wave of reforms that focus on governance and quality improvement create new areas of governance at the meso-level where doctors may play an important role.

First, doctors have always been the backbone of leadership in the Turkish healthcare system, occupying managerial positions in the MoH's central organization and provincial health directorates as well as in public hospitals. It would be interesting to observe what kinds of opportunities (and challenges) the shifts in the governance of public hospitals towards financial and managerial autonomy would create for doctors. Second, the next phase of reforms (focusing on quality and regulatory issues) may open up new areas for health professions. Recent criticisms of the Health Transformation Programme highlighted the need for building professional interest in quality as well as a culture of quality improvement (OECD, 2014).

Furthermore, there is growing need for new groups of clinical managers in Turkey who may adopt new tools of management, such as evidence-based clinical guidelines, and use them in ways that reflect professional values and priorities. The MoH has played a leading role in developing clinical guidelines in primary care; working groups for frequently diagnosed diseases were established with participation of some of the stakeholders (Tatar *et al.*, 2011). But the MoH needs professions to reach its targets of improved quality and efficiency. In sum, a mixed model of governance is emerging in Turkey, where centralist public governance is combined with new market elements. In this process, new bonds are forming among the state, the professions and the market.

Conclusion

This chapter set out to explore the relationships between governance, professions and professionalism and the changes created by new modes of governing. We have illuminated the bonds between governance and professions and argued the need to overcome static concepts of professions and professionalism as opposed to other forms of governing. Moreover, as citizens and organizational actors, the professions are embedded in the governance of public sectors. Our examples reveal that the bonds between professions and governance are flexible and malleable and, at the same time, shaped by national architectures of governance.

One important conclusion drawn from our case studies is that the goals and the toolbox of governance may be similar across healthcare systems while the impact in the relationship between the state and the professions, as well as between the professions and organizations, may take different forms. Furthermore, processes of relocation of the professions are underway on macro-, meso- and micro-levels of governance that may create new bonds or strengthen existing ones. Consequently, this calls for multi-level governance approaches to explore the intersecting dynamics in the transformations underway in contemporary societies.

The results bring the complexity of transformations and new emergent forms of professionalism into view in ways that we cannot explain in traditional categories of conflict, exclusion and jurisdiction. These effects of changing governance, management and leadership models are perhaps best understood in terms of intersectionality – to borrow a concept from diversity and gender studies. An intersectionality approach suggests that the connection of different sets of governance may create different results depending on how these sets are connected (for examples, see Kuhlmann & Annandale, 2012). Change in one dimension may trigger dynamics in the governance architecture and the organizational settings that open new spaces for the professions as policy actors and organizational agents (Muzio and Kirkpatrick, 2011). Path dependency is important but does not fully determine this space, because different interests may overlap and new alliances may be volatile and less predictable.

Bringing the bonds between professions and governance into perspective may help us to understand the importance of professions as 'mediators' between state and citizens' interests and as 'change agents' in public sector policy and services. Viewed through this lens, professions and governing bodies/policymakers – in mature welfare states as well as in emergent capitalist service societies – are bonded by the demand for sustainable public sectors and services for the citizens, although the various players involved in public sector governance may have different ideas on how these goals may best be achieved.

References

Agartan, T. I. (2012) Marketization and universalism: Crafting the right balance in the Turkish health care system. *Current Sociology*, 60(4), 456–471.

Allsop, J., Bourgeault, I. L., Evetts, J., Le Bianic, T., Jones, K. & Wrede, S. (2009) Encountering globalization: Professional groups in international context. *Current Sociology*, 57(4), 487–510.

Anell, A., Glenngård, A. H. & Merkur, S. (2012) Sweden: Health system review. *Health Systems in Transition*, 14(5), 1–187.

Barry, J., Dent, M. & O'Neill, M. (eds) (2003) *Gender and the Public Sector*. London: Routledge.

Bertilsson, M. (1990) The welfare state, the professions and citizens, in R. Torstendahl & M. Burrage (eds), *The Formation of Professions. Knowledge, State and Strategy*. London: Sage, pp. 144–133.

Blank, R. B. & Burau, V. (2014) *Comparative Health Policy* (4th edn). Basingstoke: Palgrave.

Bonnin, D. & Ruggunan, S. (2013) Towards a South African sociology of professions. *South African Review of Sociology*, 44(2), 1–6.

Bourgeault, I. & Merritt, K. (2015) Deploying and managing health human resources, in E. Kuhlmann, R. B. Blank, I.L. Bourgeault & C. Wendt (eds), *The Palgrave International Handbook of Healthcare Policy and Governance*. Basingstoke: Palgrave, pp. 306–324.

Burau, V., Wilsford, D. & France, G. (2009) What is it about institutions? Reforming medical governance in Europe. *Health Economics, Policy and Law*, 4, 265–282.

Busse, R. & Blümel, M. (2014) Germany: Health system review. *Health Systems in Transition*, 16(2), 1–61.

Denis, J.-L. & van Gestel, N. (2015) Leadership and innovation in healthcare governance, in E. Kuhlmann, R. B. Blank, I. L. Bourgeault & C. Wendt (eds), *The Palgrave International Handbook of Healthcare Policy and Governance*. Basingstoke: Palgrave, pp. 425–440.

Dent, M. (2005) Post-new public management in public sector hospitals? The UK, Germany and Italy. *Policy & Politics*, 33, 623–636.

Dent, M., Kirkpatrick, I. & Neogy, I. (2012) Medical leadership and management reforms in hospital: a comparative study, in C. Teelken, E. Ferlie & M. Dent (eds), *Leadership in the Public Sector: Promises and Pitfalls*. London: Routledge, pp. 105–125.

Faulconbridge, J. R. & Muzio, D. (2012) Professions in a globalizing world: Towards a transnational sociology of the professions. *International Sociology*, 27(1), 136–152.

Freidson, E. (1986) *Professional Powers: A Study of Formal Knowledge*. Chicago, IL: University of Chicago Press.

Freidson, E. (2001) *Professionalism: The Third Logic*. Oxford: Polity Press.

HCPC – Health & Care Professions Council (2015) *Preventing Small Problems from Becoming Big Problems in Health and Care*. Research Report, London: HCPC.

Johnson, T. (1995) Governmentality and the institutionalization of expertise, in T. Johnson, G. Larkin & M. Saks (eds), *Health Professions and the State in Europe*. London: Routledge, pp. 2–14.

Kirkpatrick, I., Ackroyd, S. & Walker, R. (2005) *New Managerialism and Public Sector Professionalism*. London: Palgrave.

Kirkpatrick, I., Hartley, K., Kuhlmann, E. & Veronesi, G. (2015) Clinical management and professionalism', in E. Kuhlmann, R. B. Blank, I. L. Bourgeault & C. Wendt (eds), *The Palgrave International Handbook of Healthcare Policy and Governance*. Basingstoke: Palgrave, pp. 325–340.

Kuhlmann, E. (2006) *Modernising Health Care: Reinventing Professions, the State and the Public*, Bristol, UK: Policy Press.

Kuhlmann, E. & Bourgeault, I.L. (2008) Gender, professions and public policy: New directions. *Equal Opportunities International*, 27(1), 5–18.

Kuhlmann, E. & Annandale, E. (eds) (2012) *The Palgrave Handbook of Gender and Healthcare* (2nd edn). Basingstoke: Palgrave.

Kuhlmann, E. & Von Knorring, M. (2014) Management and medicine: Why we need a new approach to the relationship. *Journal of Health Services Research & Policy*, 19(3), 189–191.

Kuhlmann, E., Burau, V., Correia, T., Lewandowski, R., Lionis, C., Noordegraaf, M. & Repullo, J. (2013) 'A manager in the minds of doctors': A comparison of new modes of control in European hospitals. *BMC Health Services Research*, 13: 246.

Larson, S. M. (1977) *The Rise of Professionalism*. Berkeley, CA: University of California Press.

Light, D. W. (2010) Health-care professions, markets and countervailing powers, in C. E. Bird, P. Conrad, A. M. Fremont & S. Timmermans (eds), *Handbook of Medical Sociology* (6th edn). Nashville, TN: Vanderbilt University Press, pp. 270–289.

Leicht, K. T., Walter, T., Sainsaulieu, I. & Davies, S. (2009) New public management and new professionalism across nations and contexts. *Current Sociology*, 57(4), 581–605.

McDonald, R. (2012) Restratification revisited: The changing landscape of primary medical care in England and California. *Current Sociology*, 60(4), 441–455.

Muzio, D. & Kirkpatrick, I. (2011) Introduction: Professions and organizations – a conceptual framework. *Current Sociology*, 59(4), 389–405.

Newman, J. (2005) Introduction, in J. Newman (ed.), *Remaking Governance: People, Politics and the Public Sphere*. Bristol, UK: Policy Press, pp. 1–15.

OECD (2014) *OECD Reviews of Health Care Quality. Turkey 2014: Raising Standards*. Paris: OECD.

Plochg, T., Klazinga, N. & Starfield, B. (2009) Transforming medical professionalism to fit changing health needs. *BMC Medicine*, 7, 64.

Quack, S. (2007) Legal professionals and transnational law-making: A case of distributed agency. *Organization*, 14(5), 643–666.

Reay, T. & Hinings, C. R. (2009) Managing the rivalry of competing institutional logics. *Organization Studies*, 30(6), 629–652.

Rhodes, R. A. W. (1996) The New Governance: Governing without government. *Political Studies*, XLIV, 652–667.

Saltman, R. B., Durán, A. & Dubois, H. F. W. (2011) Introduction: Innovative governance strategies in European public hospitals, in R. B. Saltman, A. Durán & H. F. W. Dubois (eds), *Governing Public Hospitals*. Copenhagen: WHO, pp. 1–33.

Seabrooke, L. (2014) Epistemic arbitrage: Transnational professional knowledge in action. *Journal of Professions and Organization*, 1(1), 49–64.

Suddaby, R. & Viale, T. (2011) Professionals and field-level change: Institutional work and the professional project. *Current Sociology*, 59(4), 423–442.

Tatar, M., Mollahaliloğlu, S., Sahin, B., Aydın, S., Maresso, A. & Hernández-Quevedo, C. (2011) Turkey: Health System Review. *Health Systems in Transition*, 13(6), 1–186.

Teelken, C., Ferlie, E. & Dent, M. (eds) (2012) *Leadership in the Public Sector: Promises and Pitfalls*. London: Routledge.

Tonkens, E. & Newman, J. (2011) Active citizens, active professionals, in J. Newman & E. Tonkens (eds), *Participation, Responsibility and Choice: Summoning the Active Citizen in Western European Welfare States*. Amsterdam: Amsterdam University Press, pp. 201–215.

Tuohy, C. H. (2012) Reform and the politics of hybridization in mature health care states. *Journal of Health Politics, Policy and Law*, 37(4), 611–632.

Von Knorring, M., de Rijk, A. & Alexanderson, K. (2010) Managers' perceptions of the manager role in relation to physicians: A qualitative interview study of the top managers in Swedish healthcare. *BMC Health Services Research*, 10: 271.

Von Knorring, M., Alexanderson, K. & Eliasson, M. A. (2016) Healthcare managers' construction of the manager role in relation to the medical profession. *Journal of Health Organization & Management*, forthcoming.

Waring, J. & Currie, G. (2009) Managing expert knowledge: Organizational challenges and managerial futures for the UK medical profession. *Organization Studies*, 30(7), 755–778.

Wendt, C., Agartan, T. I. & Kaminska, M. (2013) Social health insurance without corporate actors: Patterns of self-regulation in Germany, Poland and Turkey. *Social Science & Medicine*, 86, 88–95.

Wrede, S. (2012) Nursing: Globalization of a female-gendered profession, in E. Kuhlmann & E. Annandale (eds), *The Palgrave Handbook of Gender and Healthcare* (2nd edn). Basingstoke: Palgrave, pp. 471–487.

3

Professions, service users and citizenship

Deliberation, choice and responsibility

Evelien Tonkens

Introduction

Changing ideals of citizenship over the past decades have influenced the theory and practice of professionalism in numerous ways. Demands for citizen involvement and empowerment emerged against a background of critiques of professional power and challenges to the traditional relationship between professionals and service users (Freidson, 1970). Citizens were to be empowered through the extension of choice and voice, while the recognition of citizen expertise would transform the hierarchy of professional expertise and authority. Citizens were to be respected as persons in their own right, not defined or pigeon-holed in accordance with professional diagnoses of needs and conditions. The power position of allegedly self-interested professionals in the bureau-professional regime of the welfare state gave rise to new public management (NPM) – a supposedly more client-centred alternative (Clarke & Newman, 1997; Pollitt, 2003).

How have changing ideas about citizenship impacted upon the relationship between professionals and citizens/patients? An extensive literature discusses how professionalism has changed under the influence of system changes such as NPM, public choice and/or marketization (Evetts, 2011; see Chapter 2 by Kuhlmann *et al.*). Much less attention has been paid to how changing conceptions of citizenship have influenced professional theory and practice. In this chapter I pursue this theme. I first briefly introduce the concept of citizenship and then discuss three emergent ideals of citizenship that have affected professional practice in the public sector more generally and in healthcare in particular: deliberation, choice and responsibility.

The concept of citizenship

The concept of citizenship entered healthcare in the 1990s (Newman & Tonkens, 2011). Liberal interpretations of citizenship that stressed individual rights (Heater, 2004) provided a lens for patient activism, bridging the potentially conflicting goals of equal treatment (by virtue of being human) and special treatment (for suffering from an illness) (Ootes *et al.*, 2010). Echoing T. H.

Marshall (1950), to claim citizenship is to claim that one is a bearer of rights to services that compensate for one's illness or handicap, so that one may participate in society as an equal citizen.

Citizenship can also be seen through a more communal lens, in line with republican and/or communitarian tenets (Heater, 2004) that emphasize the obligations of citizens towards the community and/or the public good. In this interpretation, professionals as well as patients, customers, consumers and service users have civic obligations. 'Citizen professionals' can exercise control and influence not only in defence of their professional interests but also to promote public goals such as social justice (cf. Kuhlmann, 2006). Professionals must decide how to act in situations of ambiguity, guided by both their professional ethos and their political values. They sometimes silently subvert policy prescriptions, using their discretion to 'translate' policies to suit local contexts or to privilege particular goals. They may also use spaces of agency to assert the values of care or the public ethos against managerial logic.

Professionals can bring their own citizenship into the service relationship, using it as a resource to resolve the dilemmas of everyday work as well as to exercise a more expansive 'subversive citizenship' (Barnes & Prior, 2009). Sometimes this happens silently, behind closed doors, for instance when professionals manipulate registers to serve patients rather than insurance companies (Tonkens et al., 2013a). Prior (2009) uses the concept of counter-agency to describe processes of revision, resistance and refusal on the part of frontline staff, who must implement policies whose effects they see as harmful or iniquitous. While the citizenship of professionals deserves attention in its own right, this chapter focuses on the citizenship of (potential) patients as it bears on professional practice.

Deliberation

There is by now an impressive body of practice as well as research on citizen/patient deliberation in the provision of healthcare (Baggott, 2005; Milewa et al., 2002), including forums such as citizens' panels, boards, trusts, juries, service user consultations, governance boards and evaluation projects. The internet and other new technologies have expanded opportunities for such participation. Many opportunities for deliberation cater to organized patient groups such as, in the United Kingdom, National Voices and Diabetes UK. In response to more emancipated citizenries, professionals are increasingly accepting 'public accountability' and entering into 'real dialogue with their publics', 'inviting public response and involvement in the profession's effort to clarify its mission and responsibilities' (Sullivan, 2004, p. 19).

Although the push to involve citizens in deliberation emerged from the criticism of authoritarian and paternalistic professionals (Tonkens, 2010, 2011; Tonkens et al., 2013b), concrete practices more often target managers, witnessed in forums where citizens/patients can discuss issues such as planning and organizational targets. Although some authors argue that citizens are empowered by such deliberation, many others have grown disillusioned with the extent of real citizen influence. Critics argue that power holders do not really intend to empower citizens, that citizen involvement is mere window dressing, theatre (Milewa, 2004), or the pursuit of the 'holy grail of community control' (Baggott, 2005, p. 548). Power holders only play 'the user card' if it is in their interests to appear democratic (Harrison & Mort, 1998, p. 66). While there are exceptions, such as the self-help groups of patients living with diabetes and HIV/AIDS in Sweden, the drive to involve citizens often hides new forms of manipulation, control and hedging in (Baggott, 2005; Hodge, 2005). In general, citizens are only empowered through effective training and participation (Carr, 2007; Cowden & Singh, 2007).

Representation

An important factor undermining the influence of service users in decision-making bodies is their lack of representativeness. Citizens active on boards and in councils – in healthcare as well as in other fields – are generally far from representative of the whole group of users: they tend to be older, more highly educated, more often white and male (Fung, 2003). They have more radical ideas than the groups they are supposed to represent. In particular, highly educated men are not only more often present but exert greater influence than the others who are also present. They talk more easily and loudly, and are more skilled in rhetoric. This results in the privileging of their voices.

The argument of weak representation, however, is often used selectively and strategically. If citizens express opinions considered unwelcome by policy-makers or professionals, these are often dismissed as non-representative (Harrison & Mort, 1998). Institutions tend to control who can participate and who cannot, and therefore which voices will be listened to. They also often dismiss issues of more democratic representation as irrelevant or unworthy of serious pursuit (Cowden & Singh, 2007).

What makes (more representative forms of) citizen involvement so difficult? I first examine what citizens as patients or carers bring to the table. As mentioned above, citizens often participate in bodies that deliberate on managerial issues. In such settings, citizens are positioned as quasi-experts, invited to discuss issues such as planning, budgeting, or abstract, long-term policy goals – issues where their personal experiences cannot easily be integrated. In such situations, bringing in one's personal experiences as a patient almost inevitably detracts from the broader institutional agenda.

In a study of patient and public councils in the UK, Brooks (2006) found that professionals with weaker status tend to more readily assert their expertise. Nurses were more annoyed than medical doctors by patients bringing in their own experiences, and more often dismissed patient experiences as trivial, too personal, and an attack on their own expertise. Patients in turn did not feel heard by nurses and grew frustrated. Brooks explains this by the weak status of the nurses, whose own expertise is undervalued in the hospital.

Experience or expertise?

Carr finds that patient experiences are often dismissed as 'too distressing and disturbing' (2007, p. 271). Patients then feel that unrealistic demands are being placed on them, for example having to express themselves in managerial terms. Most patients, Milewa (1997) argues, are neither well equipped nor interested in deliberating policy issues such as budgeting. The issues that they want to discuss – and which officials need to create room for – are closer to their personal experiences (Milewa, 1997).

But making room for patient experiences and allowing them to play a meaningful role in patient–doctor dialogue is apparently no easy task. At best, patient experiences are often relegated to legitimizing decisions that have already been made. Citizen experiences that do not do so are neglected and placed outside the order of things (Hodge, 2005).

Furthermore, the power imbalance between citizens and professionals/managers rarely improves when patient experiences are brought in. Professionals and managers retain the power to neglect them. This could be different, Carr (2007) argues, if officials would also talk about their experiences and if, more generally, passions and conflict were an accepted part of deliberation. Following Mouffe, Carr argues that attaining an equitable power balance entails all involved parties bringing in their emotions and experience. In Brooks' (2006) above-mentioned research on patient and public councils, placing this issue explicitly on the agenda proved to be the turning point. When patients were invited to talk about why they felt frustrated and what they thought they could bring to the table – their personal involvement – nurses began to listen.

Scott's (1998) notion of *metis* may be helpful here. Scott contrasts *metis* – 'a wide array of practical skills and acquired intelligence in responding to a constantly changing natural and human environment' (1998, p. 213) – with *techne*, by which he means supposedly universal, abstract knowledge, logically deducted from general principles regardless of time, place, tradition, or local circumstance. While Scott formulated this contrast for the field of planning, it can easily be applied to other fields.

Scott analysed the failures of planning in, among other places, the 1920s Soviet Union and 1960s Tanzania, where large-scale projects were hatched on drawing boards and in architectural and planning offices, far removed from daily practice. Often with the best intentions, planners took pride in this remoteness as well as in an aesthetics that saw their work as the complete reinvention of the world as it was. Projects then failed, Scott (1998) argues, because they did not recognize the value of citizens' local, non-standardized knowledge – for example that one should, in a particular valley, seed a particular plant after another has blossomed or after a particular migrating bird has arrived, rather than on a fixed date of the calendar. Experiential expertise in deliberative democracy can also be understood as *metis*: as particular, local knowledge that cannot be directly transferred to different situations.

Being open to a broader range of expertise implies not only inviting citizens in the early stages of planning, but also – and perhaps more importantly – in the process of implementation, where *metis* can be crucial. Whereas citizens today are most often involved in the early stages of a process – where a 'go or no go' decision is at stake – Fung (2003) argues that the implementation stage is when everyday experiences are most informative and bringing them in most corrective. Nor should citizen experiences be restricted to those of current service users; past and potential users have much to contribute as well.

Nevertheless, experience and expertise are not equally valued. Expertise is generally considered more important, and is also usually held by people (e.g. experts and managers) who are deemed more important. More often than not, Fung (2003) argues, participation has a 'laissez-faire' character, based on the naive belief that citizens can exert influence and power if only they are given the occasion to speak. While the structure of the discussion and participation process has serious ramifications, it is often neglected. Citizens' power and influence can only be exerted when participation is well organized (Fung, 2003; Cawston & Barbour, 2003; Dzur, 2004) and led by an objective and fair chair (Fung, 2003).

Also, citizens do not spontaneously possess the capacity to participate (Milewa, 1997) and are often easily intimidated. They therefore need to be trained in the art of exerting influence. Fung (2003) reveals how training and the structure of discussion directly influence the power and influence citizens can exert. Training and structure are particularly empowering for less-educated citizens. Promoting structured rather than laissez-faire participation may help balance the inequality of expertise and experience and thus augment mutual respect. I will return to this theme in discussing informal participation further below.

Consensus versus battle

How the dialogue between citizens/patients and professionals is structured clearly matters. Here we can distinguish between the consensus model of deliberation and the agonistic model (Elstub,

2006). The consensus model, inspired by the work of German sociologist Habermas, posits that the strength of deliberative democracy lies in the need for all participants to formulate their arguments in terms that can convince others. Personal interests do not convince others and are thus not accepted as valid.

The consensus model requires participants to abandon their personal interests and adopt impartial stances. In this way, deliberative democracy is the best guarantee that they will focus on the public interest. In the consensus model, participants are citizens, not consumers; they can and should consider both their own interests and those of others and/or the 'general' interest. Research shows that citizens on average are capable of making these distinctions (Wolsink, 2006). Consumers have meagre roles in civic democracy, as they are not meant to deliberate on the public good (Walsh, 1994). The consensus model encourages citizens and professionals to sit together in decision-making bodies, focusing on shared interests and the public good rather than group interests.

In contrast, the agonistic model posits that what is proclaimed to be the public interest is simply partial, personal interest in disguise. The agonistic model does not require participants to put aside their personal and partial interests but to express them. There is no point in only considering arguments that are acceptable to all, as the consensus model demands. Note that the agonistic model does not deny the importance of public reason. It posits that public reason arises, not out of consensus but from the confrontation of differences. From this confrontation and its related power struggle, wise decisions are born.

> It is only through allowing citizens to express their private interests in a deliberatively democratic arena where they will hear of the experiences and information of others that they might come to appreciate their private interests conflict with what they perceive [to be] the common good.
>
> *(Elstub, 2006, p. 27)*

Deliberative democracy should not strive for impartiality but for 'enlarged thinking' (Elstub, 2006, p. 27). Most older forms of deliberative democracy, including client boards and platforms, are based on the agonistic model; many newer forms, such as interactive policy-making and joined-up governance, are based on the consensus model. Fung and Wright (2003) find that most citizen groups begin with an agonistic (in their terms, 'adversarial') model and then move towards the consensus ('collaborative') model over time when they experience success. But taking this step demands a different skill set. New people who do not have a history of conflict with the former adversary are often better suited for the new role.

In sum, citizen influence through participation in boards and panels is generally limited. Although criticism of professional dominance was the impetus to form these boards in the first place, many of these forums focus more on managerial issues than professional ones. While there is often little room for patients' emotions and experiences in these settings, citizen participation can be improved when all participants express emotions and experiences and participation is structured rather than laissez-faire.

Negotiation

If formal participation in boards and forums often fails to empower citizens, what do we observe in the realm of informal participation – in the everyday interactions between citizens (as patients or carers) and professionals? As citizens become more emancipated, better educated, and have greater access to medical information, they often diagnose themselves before turning to medical experts. Professional authority is no longer self-evident: it has to be won! Increasingly, relationships between doctors and patients are based on negotiation.

However, not all patients are sufficiently competent or clear-headed; they may be too vulnerable (sick, old, exhausted, or confused) or lack the necessary literacy and bureaucratic or negotiating skills to interact with professionals on a more equal footing. Comparative research in eleven European countries has shown that many vulnerable people do not wish to negotiate with professionals but to enter into caring relationships with them (Bastiaens et al., 2007).

Other studies have shown that citizens value access to proper services more than participation (Contandriopoulos, 2004). This requires flexibility and responsiveness on the part of professionals, who must then judge when to support, when to intervene, and when to negotiate. They must decide when to return to their traditional forms of expertise and authority and when to attempt to share power with newly independent and assertive service users. This implies some loosening of the knowledge–power knot of traditional professional authority, and the weaving in of new skills and forms of power.

What is at stake is neither the resilience of professional power nor its demise, but a reordering of power and authority. Power is not simply a ball that can be handed from professionals to citizens; authority and expertise today have multiplied, become more diffuse and conditional. Citizens and professionals today enter into relationships of negotiation, attuning, and calibration (Mol, 2008), where 'traditional boundaries between expert and lay become blurred' (Cawston & Barbour, 2003, p. 721). This creates new challenges for professionals, who face the daunting task of combining proper dialogue with their publics and taking 'public leadership in solving perceived public problems' (Dzur, 2004, p. 18). They must 'both exercise authority and share it' (Dzur, 2004, p. 12). This dual task – of exercising and sharing authority – is what makes being a professional so challenging today (Kremer & Tonkens, 2006).

What is the role of patients' personal experiences in informal participation? Sennett (2003) argues that both professionals and patients have different kinds of expertise that should be mutually acknowledged. Professionals are experts in diagnosis and treatment; citizens are experts in how it feels to live with diabetes or cancer, a demented partner or a handicapped child, what it is like to lie in the operating room without knowing what is going to happen, and when. Professionals should try to understand by way of empathy; except for those rare cases when they have suffered the same illness, professionals should acknowledge that patients know better. Conversely, patients should recognize that, as far as diagnosis and treatment are concerned, professionals in the end generally know better.

Thanks to the internet and patient organizations, many citizens today have significant expertise on their own illness. Chronic patients especially often spend many years gathering information and may know more about their illness than many doctors. Such 'expert patients' thus often possess both medical expertise and expertise born of experience: they know about different types of treatment and how it feels to use them. Nevertheless, treatment options still need to be negotiated with doctors and nurses, who will have broader experience with, for example, a range of patients rather than with this one particular patient.

We also need to examine how patient experiences are understood. If experiences are viewed as something deep, personal, fixed, and therefore inaccessible to others, bringing in experiences tends to close down rather than open up discussion. To effectively discuss experiences within doctor–patient exchanges, a non-essentialist understanding of experience is helpful – one that recognizes that experiences change, for example under the influence of ideas about what is considered appropriate to experience and feel (Hochschild, 2003). When knowledge based on these experiences is treated as fluid and open to discussion, there is more room for the effective exchange of views.

In short, informal participation is more directly focused on patients' relationships with professionals; it provides more room for discussing patients' experiences and tends to be experienced as more empowering. Experience should be recognized as a different type of expertise, while a non-essentialist understanding of experience supports this empowerment.

Choice

Freedom of choice has long been a demand of citizens locked into dependent relationships with government bureaucracies and public service providers. The introduction of consumerist models of participation in a marketplace of public and private goods can be viewed, in part, as a response to longstanding struggles by service users for more flexible and accessible models of delivery. As the focus shifts to the individual, choice-making citizen-consumer, these struggles have become de-collectivized and depoliticized. Enhancing the power of customers or consumers – placing their needs and demands at the centre of the service relationship – has underpinned numerous reforms in healthcare and beyond. Professionals are there to serve, not patronize – with a smile rather than a sermon. Clients will set the rules through 'demand steering' (Pollitt, 2003), and professionals who bully their clients will lose their contracts.

Osborne and Gaebler (1992) blamed governments for keeping their 'clients' passive and for denying them choice. Bureaucratic state institutions are sluggish due to their hierarchical chains of command and their preoccupation with rules and regulations; the government is as out of date as a dinosaur and slow as a snail, unable to respond to the needs of clients. Professionals would be 'exercising power over would-be customers, denying choice, through the dubious claim that "professionals know best"' (Clarke & Newman, 1997, p. 15). Sehested (2002, p. 1516) describes how, in Denmark, professionals in public organizations were seen as motivated by self-interest, only fighting for more resources to increase their own status and prestige. Citizens were invited to view themselves as market actors, expressing choice in a new marketplace of public and private goods. The result was what Evetts (2011) terms commodification:

> Professional service work organizations are converting into enterprises in terms of identity, hierarchy and rationality.... The commodification of professional service work entails changes in professional work relations.... Relationships between professionals and clients are ... being converted into customer relations.... The service itself is increasingly focused, modelled on equivalents provided by other producers, shaped by the interests of consumers and increasingly standardized.
>
> *(Evetts, 2011, pp. 415–416)*

The commodification of care can entail marketization, greater consumer-orientation, or a combination of the two. Much of the debate on the market reform of healthcare focuses on curative care (Pollitt *et al.*, 2010), with little attention to the long-term or 'incurable' sector. Even where there is no market for healthcare products, such as in emergency services, professionals have been recast as service providers and patients as consumers (Newman & Tonkens, 2011). Although there is no competition between emergency services to 'maximize' production, there is a growing expectation that emergency nurses 'serve the customer' well.

The degree of commodification varies between countries and sectors. For example, both the Dutch healthcare reforms of 2006 and the German reforms of 2007 to 2009 installed regulated competition between private insurance companies, between service providers, and ultimately between healthcare professionals. In the Netherlands, insurance companies gradually gained more freedom to (not) sign contracts with organizations and individual professionals and to set the terms. Compared to their Dutch counterparts, German medical professionals were more successful in softening competition and preserving their autonomy (Kuhlmann, 2011). In the UK, the National Health Service tempers the reach of marketization (though not that of 'demand steering') (Fotaki, 2011).

Transparency – by way of performance measurement – is deemed necessary to facilitate patient choice. Performance measurement, it is claimed, provides citizens with the necessary information to see for themselves that a service is failing and to vote with their feet; it thus empowers citizens by enabling them to make informed choices between providers (Power, 1997). Professionals and organizations must prove their performance and submit detailed reports on both the processes and outcomes of their services. As a consequence, Dutch medical specialists spend 26 per cent of their time on paperwork and fulfilling procedural demands, up from only 6 per cent 25 years earlier (Kanters *et al.*, 2004). The advent of publicly available performance rankings further contributes to performance pressure.

Some authors argue that commodification and choice are necessary in order to correct paternalistic doctors who presume they know what is best for their patients without inquiring about their preferences, and who fail to admit failures and blame colleagues for their own mistakes (Noordegraaf, 2007; Evetts, 2011).

Criticisms of commodification

Numerous authors have criticized the commodification of healthcare – for 'squeezing out' democratization through its 'supermarketized' vision (Cowden & Singh, 2007, p. 7) and for choice coming at the expense of voice (Baggott, 2005). The centrality of the user in a marketplace of public and private goods has been censured as the further commodification of basic human needs and welfare. The idea of the user as a consumer of public services has been criticized for undermining trust relationships between professionals and service users (Vabø, 2006).

It is often argued that commodification threatens the professions. Elliott Freidson (2001), in his seminal book *Professionalism: The Third Logic*, argues that the logic of professionalism is radically different from the logic of both the market and the state. Professionals share a professional ideology. They are dedicated to a higher, transcendent goal, to be distinguished from the making of profit, applying bureaucracy's rules and regulations, or reaching political targets. In healthcare, professionals are assumed to be dedicated to their patients' health, not to their own bank accounts or their patients' preferences (Freidson, 2001, p. 122).

According to Freidson, the logic of professionalism needs active support from citizens and the state. Citizens have to submit to a moderate amount of paternalism, or at least medical expertise; they have to accept that their preferences cannot rule supreme because 'the doctor knows best' – be it to a certain extent and under certain conditions. The state has to ensure that doctors do not fall prey to the all-encompassing power of the market by guaranteeing them an income. The commodification of healthcare is perceived as a two-pronged attack on what Freidson (2001, p. 217) has dubbed 'the soul of professionalism' – by both elevating the status of consumer preferences and letting market forces loose on professional practices.

A more recent but similar argument comes from the political philosopher Michael Sandel (2012), who argues that marketization can breed corruption, by which he means loosening morals among newly created service providers and consumers. Similarly, Krizova traces the decline of professional autonomy to marketization. Professional autonomy used to be in the patient's best interest; its erosion might therefore cause 'a decrease in altruistic or service-oriented attitudes toward patients' (Krizova, 2008, p. 111). Diefenbach (2009, p. 897) argues that commodification can lead to concentrating on 'cash cows' and the 'deletion of activities that are not profit-making'.

In a survey of doctors, dentists and physiotherapists in the Netherlands, Groenewegen and Hansen (2007) found that their respondents feared obligatory competition with peers would diminish cooperation and come at the cost of patient well-being. Over 90 per cent feared pressure to treat patients according to their insurance status rather than their medical condition; over 80 per cent disapproved of such a situation.

Similarly, a review of competition, freedom of choice, and personalized care in health and social services in England and Sweden showed no evidence of marketization empowering users (Fotaki, 2011). Patients generally make scant use of available choices. To the extent that they do so, their choices concern time and place of treatment in the UK and the choice of doctors in parts of Sweden (Fotaki, 2011, p. 941). While patients still value choice, they mostly rely on doctors, probably due to the vulnerability that comes with ill health and the inequality of information.

In sum, the promise of freedom of choice in the commodification of healthcare has recast professionals as service providers and patients as consumers entitled to services and choice. But in practice, patients are less enthusiastic about choice than is often assumed, and make scant use of available options to choose between healthcare providers. As the exercise of choice by patients is limited, so, too, is its likely impact on professionalism. Nevertheless, the conditions created to make choice possible – such as transparency about performance and performance indicators – do impact upon professionalism, not least by creating more red tape.

Responsibility

A third way in which changing ideals of citizenship have influenced professional practice concerns the 'responsibilization' of citizens. Responsibilization – a consequence of individualization – is the tendency to make citizens increasingly responsible for their own health and healthcare (Ilcan & Basok, 2004; Fotaki, 2011). It entails managing one's own healthcare, living a healthy lifestyle, behaving in a sexually responsible manner, and establishing a network of people for mutual support. As responsibilization is the most recent of the three changes in citizenship ideals discussed here, there is, as yet, little empirical evidence on how it affects professional practice.

Here it makes sense to distinguish between bottom-up and top-down responsibilization. In the bottom-up scenario, citizens themselves demand more responsibility, such as when diabetes patients demand more control over their own use and management of medicines. In the top-down scenario, politicians, health experts and/or public debate demand that citizens live more responsibly, for example that they quit smoking and start exercising.

Top-down responsibilization returns professionals to the paternalistic roles that were attacked in the 1970s in Western Europe and the USA (Freidson, 1970). Today, failure to live responsibly is deemed sufficient reason for health and social workers – armed with both carrots and sticks – to intervene through outreach programmes, to try to 'get behind the front door' to identify social problems and offer care and advice. In contrast, bottom-up responsibilization places professionals in negotiating roles, as discussed in the section on participation.

The top-down responsibilization of citizens runs counter to critical citizenship – a way to discipline and dominate by delegating responsibility to citizens (Ilcan & Basok, 2004) while the welfare state withdraws from its previous obligations, leading to the depoliticization of healthcare policy (Eriksson, 2012).

As the expectations placed on citizens to live responsibly grow, so too does the tendency towards professional paternalism. The more parents are exhorted to take responsibility for their children's health, diet and weight, the more reasons professionals have to intervene and, ultimately, to take custody of children and responsibility away from parents.

Conclusion

Changing ideals of citizenship over the past decades have influenced the theory and practice of professionalism in numerous ways. While the ideal of citizen participation grew out of the criticism of authoritarian and paternalistic professionals, the dominant form of citizen participation to date – formal deliberation in boards and councils – has affected managers more than professionals. Citizen participation in such formal venues, where there is little room for voicing personal experiences, has failed to empower citizens and has, for many, been an exercise in disillusionment.

A vast number of studies have thus pointed to ways in which citizen participation can be improved. First, participation should be structured rather than laissez-faire. Second, it should privilege experience over expertise – provided that experience is not treated as the ultimate truth but open to discussion and change. Third, representation should be conceived as more than just descriptive representation, or the presence of citizens on panels and boards. Fourth, the tension between public and personal/group interests should be treated as something that professionals as well as citizens struggle with.

Informal participation within direct citizen–professional relationships provides more room for the discussion and recognition of patient experiences and tends to be experienced as more empowering. A non-essentialist understanding of experience supports dialogue.

In many countries, the second ideal – greater choice – is directly related to the commodification of healthcare. Professionals here are recast as service providers, patients as consumers entitled to services and choice. However, the reality is that patients commonly are not eager to take on the consumer role and therefore the implications for professionalism have been minimal. On the other hand, the managerial mechanism of performance indicators, as well as pressures for transparency, have had a real impact upon professionalism simply by introducing more regulations within the clinics.

Empirical studies on the impact of the third ideal – the responsibilization of citizens – remain limited in number. This ideal may well have the contradictory effect of encouraging more equal relationships between citizens and professionals based on negotiation, and the abandonment of citizens in the name of personal responsibility as well as a return to paternalism when personal responsibility is found wanting.

In conclusion, changing modes of citizenship have contradictory effects on professionalism and the professions. The proliferation of choice encourages patients to be consumers, possibly increasing their power but also threatening to undermine trust in healthcare providers. Greater patient choice also impacts professionals indirectly by encouraging policies on transparency that create more competition between professionals and more red tape. While the responsibilization of citizens may push professionals towards more controlling and disciplining practices, it is too early to draw any firm conclusions. As for citizen participation, formal deliberation in boards and councils may be meaningful for patient collectives, but affects managers more than professionals. Informal citizen participation thus seems to most stimulate the development of a more democratic, civic professionalism, as it opens new ways for democratic and instructive dialogue.

Acknowledgement

The author wishes to thank Takeo David Hymans for his excellent editing of this chapter.

References

Baggott, R. (2005) A funny thing happened on the way to the forum? Reforming patient and public involvement in the NHS in England. *Public Administration,* 83(3), pp. 533–551.

Barnes, M. & D. Prior (eds) (2009) *Subversive Citizens: Power, Agency and Resistance in Public Services*. Bristol, UK: Policy Press.

Bastiaens, H., P. Van Royen, D. Rotal Pavlic, V. Raposo & R. Baker (2007) Older people's preferences for involvement in their own care: A qualitative study primary health care in 11 European countries. *Patient Education and Counseling*, 68, pp. 33–42.

Brooks, F. (2006) Nursing and public participation in health: An ethnographic study of a patient council. *International Journal of Nursing Studies*, 45, pp. 3–12.

Carr, S. (2007) Participation, power, conflict and change: Dynamics of service user participation in the social care system of England and Wales. *Critical Social Policy*, 27, pp. 266–276.

Cawston, P. G. & R. S. Barbour (2003) Clients or citizens? Some consideration for primary care organisations. *British Journal of General Practice*, 53, pp. 716–722.

Clarke, J. & J. Newman (1997) *The Managerial State: Power, Politics and Ideology in the Remaking of Social Welfare*. London: Sage.

Contandriopoulos, D. (2004) A sociological perspective on public participation in health care. *Social Science & Medicine*, 58, pp. 312–330.

Cowden, S. & G. Singh (2007) The 'user': Friend, foe or fetish? A critical exploration of user involvement in health and social care. *Critical Social Policy*, 27, pp. 5–23.

Diefenbach, T. (2009) New public management in public sector organizations: The dark sides of managerialistic 'enlightenment'. *Public Administration*, 87(4), pp. 892–909.

Dzur, A. W. (2004) Democratic professionalism: Sharing authority in civic life. *The Good Society*, 13(1), pp. 6–14.

Elstub, S. (2006) Towards an inclusive social policy for the UK: The need for democratic deliberation in voluntary and community associations. *Voluntas: International Journal of Voluntary and Non-Profit Organisations*, 17, pp. 17–39.

Eriksson, K. (2012) Self-service society: Participative politics and new forms of governance. *Public Administration*, 90(3), pp. 685–698.

Evetts, J. (2011) A new professionalism? Challenges and opportunities. *Current Sociology*, 59(4), pp. 406–422.

Fotaki, M. (2011) Towards developing new partnerships in public services: Users as consumers, citizens and/or co-producers in health and social care in England and Sweden. *Public Administration*, 89(3), pp. 933–955.

Freidson, E. (1970) *Professional Dominance: The Social Structure of Medical Care*. New Brunswick: Transaction.

Freidson, E. (2001) *Professionalism: The Third Logic*. Cambridge: Polity.

Fung, A. (2003) *Empowered Participation: Reinventing Urban Democracy*. Princeton, NJ: Princeton University Press.

Fung, A. & E. O. Wright (eds) (2003) *Deepening Democracy: Institutional Innovations in Empowered Participatory Governance*. London: Verso.

Groenewegen, P. P. & J. Hansen. (2007) *De Toekomst van de Witte Jas. Professies en de Toekomst: Veranderende Verhoudingen in de Gezondheidszorg*. Leusden: Springer.

Harrison, S. & M. Mort (1998) Which champions, which people? Public and user involvement in health care as a technology of legitimation. *Social Policy & Administration*, 32, pp. 60–70.

Heater, D. (2004) *Citizenship: The Civic Ideal in World History, Politics and Education*. Essex, UK: Longman.

Hochschild, A. R. (2003) *The Commercialization of Intimate Life*. Berkeley, CA: University of California Press.

Hodge, S. (2005) Participation, discourse and power: A case study in service user involvement. *Critical Social Policy*, 25, pp. 164–179.

Ilcan, S. & T. Basok (2004) Community government: Voluntary agencies, social justice and the responsibilisation of citizens. *Citizenship Studies*, 8(2), pp. 129–144.

Kanters, H. W., Van der Windt, W. and Ott, M. (2004) Geen wildgroei managers in de zorg. *Prismant*, 6 January 2004.

Kremer, M. & E. Tonkens (2006) Authority, trust, knowledge and the public good in disarray. In J. W. Duyvendak, T. Knijn & M. Kremer (eds), *Professionals between People and Policy*. Amsterdam: Amsterdam University Press, pp. 122–136.

Krizova, E. (2008) Marketization of health care and changes in the professional status of the medical profession. In N. E. Zeegers & H. E. Bröring (eds), *Professions under Pressure: Lawyers and Doctors between Profit and Public Interest*. The Hague: Boom, pp. 99–111.

Kuhlmann, E. (2006) Traces of doubt and sources of trust: Health professions in an uncertain society. *Current Sociology*, 54(4), 607–620.

Kuhlmann, E. (2011) Citizenship and healthcare in Germany: Patchy activation and constraint choices. In J. Newman & E. Tonkens (eds), *Participation, Responsibility and Choice: Summoning the Active Citizen in Western European Welfare States.* Amsterdam: Amsterdam University Press, pp. 29–45.

Marshall, T. H. (1950) *Citizenship and Social Class and Other Essays.* Cambridge: Cambridge University Press.

Milewa, T. (1997) Community participation and health care priorities: Reflections on policy, theatre and reality in Britain. *Health Promotion International,* 12, pp. 161–167.

Milewa, T. (2004) Local participatory democracy in Britain's health service: Innovation or fragmentation of a universal citizenship? *Social Policy &Administration,* 38, pp. 240–252.

Milewa, T., G. Dowswell & S. Harrison (2002) Partnerships, power and the 'new' politics of community participation in British health care. *Social Policy and Administration,* 36, pp. 796–809.

Mol, A. (2008) *The Logic of Care: Health and the Problem of Patient Choice.* London: Routledge.

Newman, J. & E. Tonkens (eds) (2011) *Participation, Responsibility and Choice: Summoning the Active Citizen in Western European Welfare States.* Amsterdam: Amsterdam University Press.

Noordegraaf, M. (2007) From 'pure' to 'hybrid' professionalism: Present-day professionalism in ambiguous public domains. *Administration & Society,* 39(6), pp. 761–85.

Ootes, S., A. J. Pols, E. Tonkens & D. Willems (2010) Bridging boundaries: The concept of 'citizenship' as a boundary object in mental healthcare. *Medische Antropologie,* 22(2), pp. 375–388.

Osborne, D.E. & T. Gaebler (1992) *Reinventing Government: How the Entrepreneurial Spirit Is Transforming the Public Sector.* Reading, UK: Addison-Wesley.

Pollitt, C. (2003) *The Essential Public Manager.* Berkshire, UK: Open University Press.

Pollitt, C., S. Harrison, S. Dowswell, S. Jerak-Zuiderent & R. Bal (2010), Performance regimes in health care: Institutions, critical junctures and the logic of escalation in England and the Netherlands. *Evaluation,* 16(1), pp. 13–29.

Power, M. (1997) *The Audit Society: Rituals of Verification.* Oxford: Oxford University Press.

Prior, D. (2009) Policy, power and the potential for counter-agency. In M. Barnes & D. Prior (eds), *Subversive Citizens: Power, Agency and Resistance in Public Services.* Bristol, UK: Policy Press, pp. 17–31.

Sandel, M. (2012) *What Money Can't Buy: The Moral Limits of Markets.* New York: Farrar, Straus and Giroux.

Scott, J.C. (1998) *Seeing Like a State: How Certain Schemes to Improve the Human Condition Have Failed.* New Haven, CT: Yale University Press.

Sehested, K. (2002) How new public management reforms challenge the roles of professionals. *International Journal of Public Administration,* 25(12), pp. 1513–1537.

Sennett, R. (2003) *Respect in an Age of Inequality.* New York: Norton.

Sullivan, W. (2004) Can professionalism still be a viable ethic? *The Good Society,* 13(1), pp. 15–20.

Tonkens, E. (2010) Civicness and citizen participation in social services: Conditions for promoting respect and public concern. In T. Brandsen, P. Dekker & A. Evers (eds), *Civicness in the Governance and Delivery of Social Services.* Baden-Baden: Nomos, pp. 83–98.

Tonkens, E. (2011) The embrace of responsibility: Citizenship and the governance of social care in the Netherlands. In J. Newman & E. Tonkens, *Participation, Responsibility and Choice: Summoning the Active Citizen in Western Welfare States.* Amsterdam: Amsterdam University Press, pp. 45–66.

Tonkens, E., C. Broer, M. Heerings & N. Van Sambeek (2013a) Pretenders and performers: Professional responses to the commodification of health care. *Social Theory & Health,* 11(4), pp. 368–387.

Tonkens, E., M. Hoijtink and H. Gulikers (2013b) Democratizing social work. In M. Noordegraaf & B. Steijn (eds), *Professionals under Pressure: The Reconfiguration of Professional Work in Changing Public Services.* Amsterdam: Amsterdam University Press, pp. 161–178.

Vabø, M. (2006) Caring for people or caring for proxy consumers? *European Societies,* 8(3), pp. 403–422.

Walsh, K. (1994) Citizens, charters and contracts. In N. Abercrombie, R. Keat & N. Whiteley (eds), *The Authority of the Consumer.* London: Routledge, pp. 189–206.

Wolsink, M. (2006) Invalid theory impedes our understanding: A critique of the persistence of the language of Nimby. *Transactions of the Institute of British Geographers,* 31(1), pp. 85–91.

4

Gender, diversity and intersectionality in professions and potential professions

Analytical, historical and contemporary perspectives

Jeff Hearn, Ingrid Biese, Marta Choroszewicz and Liisa Husu

Few women even now have been graded at the universities; the great trials of the professions, army and navy, trade, politics and diplomacy have hardly tested them. They remain even at this moment almost unclassified.

(Woolf, 1929, p. 82)

Introduction

The fields of gender studies, gender and organizations, diversity and diversity management, and intersectionality studies have all grown extensively in recent years as ways of analysing social divisions. Each and all of these have major implications for the analysis of professions, even if the issues they raise have often not been at the forefront of mainstream studies. In this chapter, we consider the relevance of gendered intersectional analysis for the understanding of professions, potential professions and professionalization. Indeed, put this way, we may ask: is it really possible to analyse professions and professionalization without considering gender and gender relations? To read some of the classics in the vast literature on professions, you would think so.

The first part of the chapter considers some issues of gender, diversity and intersectionality that are relevant in the analysis in and around professions. This section continues by turning to the examination of the intersectional gendered structures, processes and other issues within professions. The next main section examines the historical gendering of professions. The chapter continues with two contemporary case studies that set out some of the complexities of gendered intersectional analysis of professions. The first is on an established profession, namely law. The increasing entry of women into such traditionally male-dominated professions raises new questions regarding the still limited inclusion of women across the profession. The second concerns a less clear-cut case of a profession, namely business management, with a focus on women managers opting out of successful careers. The chapter concludes with a short consideration of future changes for gender, diversity, intersectionality and professions.

Professions, 'neutrality' and power

Professions and analysts of the professions alike have characteristically valued the neutralized lists of traits of professions or professional traits: universalistic standards; specificity of professional expertise; affective neutrality; status achieved through individual performance; decision-making based on the client's interest not the practitioner's self-interest (the service ethic); and control by voluntary association (extended expert training, internalized codes of practice, and control by peers) (Blau and Scott, 1963, pp. 60–63). As Blau and Scott put it so clearly, in contrasting professional and bureaucratic orientations: '(p)rofesssionals in a given field constitute a colleague group of equals' (p. 63). Seen thus, professions appear to embrace voluntaristic and communal reason and reasonableness, even progressive reasonable critique; they are open-minded and powerful – and gendered throughout. Indeed, what is more honourable than the (gender-)neutrality of the 'true (male) professional', with identifiably separate occupational status. All this has in sum provided firm ground for neutral(ized), 'gender-neutral', analyses of the occupational separation and 'specialness' of professions.

Interestingly, the study of professions is itself long and historically dominated by high-ranking professional white men commenting on other high-ranking professional white men, such as Carr-Saunders and Wilson (1933) and Hughes (1963). The operation of the 'established professions' intermingled with their analysis by men not so dissimilar to themselves. Analysts have taken the Schutzian imperative – that analytical concepts should be such that they would be understandable to the (in this case, professional male) actors themselves and those (other professionals) involved around them – at its word. Classic texts, such as *Professional Men* (Reader, 1966) and *Boys in White* (Becker *et al.*, 1976) say it all. In this context, it is no wonder that these presumed 'neutral' occupational democracies became, from the 1970s, subject to critique as forms of ideological, privileged power blocs (Elliot, 1972; Johnson, 1972), primarily in terms of class and occupation,[1] rather than gender or other social divisions.

Gendering, diversifying and intersectionalizing professions

In contrast to class-based approaches to professions and power, professions are often characterized by a variety of social divisions and social differences, including, but not limited to, occupational class. These include social divisions: internally within professions; externally in relation to those outside, including other professions; and between those within professions and those served, or not, by the professions. For example, in medicine, there are characteristic gender and status divisions between physicians in internal medical specialisms; between physicians, medical management, and nurses; and between physicians and patients. Such social divisions and social differences in and around professions have at times been clear and categorical, as in the historical construction of some professions as the sole territory of men, the gendering of professional men and masculinities, and what it means to be professional.

In considering social divisions and social differences in professions, we begin with the question of gender (Hearn, 1982; Davies, 1996; Witz, 1992; Riska, 2014). Despite some clear historical, and indeed contemporary, social divisions in the professions and professional work, much mainstream analysis of the professions has been and still often remains distinctly non-gendered. These issues have not been at the centre of mainstream analysis of professions and professionalization. In this sense, professions could be said to be not so different from other work, organizational and institutional phenomena. Gendering occurs in gendered distributions and gendered practices, even when professions and professional organizations comprise only men or only women. Typical patterns include:

- *Gendered valuing of public-domain professional work over work in the private domain.* Men's professional work has frequently been valued over women's. Women typically carry the double burden of childcare and unpaid domestic work, even a triple burden of care for dependents, old people, and people with disabilities. In addition, the professions are often involved in work across the public–private boundary, with gendered expertise to advise and seek to resolve problems and issues in the private domain and/or close to the body (Stacey and Price, 1981).
- *Gendered divisions, inclusions and exclusions of professions and professional labour and authority,* including between professions and other occupations, and between professionals and those professions may seek to assist. Women and men tend to specialize in particular types of professional labour or sectors, creating vertical and horizontal divisions. Gendered valuations of formal authority and informal status and standing also vary within and between professions. Moreover, women are more likely to face contradictory messages about gender-appropriate professional behaviour, which, on one hand, sustain gendered divisions, but, on the other, may provide women with some flexibility in how to respond to the gendered professional norms (Pierce, 2010).
- *Gendered processes between the centre and margins of professions.* These may be literally or metaphorically spatial in distributions of power and activity between the centre and margins of professional organizations. 'Front-line' professional activities are often staffed by women; 'central' and managerial activities more often by men. The 'main aim' of professions tends to be dominantly defined by men (cf. Cockburn, 1991).
- *Gendered processes in sexuality.* Most professions have reproduced dominant heterosexual norms, ideology and practices. Indeed (hetero)sexual arrangements in private generally provide the base infrastructure for professional organizations, principally through women's unpaid reproductive labour (Hearn and Parkin, 1987/1995). These contexts may impact and influence professional activities, such as the sexual dynamics in counselling, therapeutic or mentoring relations, including with those of dissident sexualities (Morgan and Davidson, 2008).
- *Gendered processes in harassment, bullying and physical violence in and around professions* have been a relatively neglected aspect, but one that impacts on all the other features in profound and constraining ways (Hearn and Parkin, 2001). This includes such activities by, to and between professionals, for example violence and abuse experienced within the health system.
- *Gendered processes in professional interactions, and individuals' internal mental work,* that maintain, or disrupt, other gendered patterns, and concern how professionals and those people served, or not, by them make sense of gendering (Acker, 1992), such as the emotion work of both professionals and their clients (Hearn, 1982).
- *Gendered professional symbols, images and forms of consciousness,* for example, in media, decor, and material, technical, scientific and professional objects (Acker, 1992), for instance, the props of professional expertise, such as legal attire or the white coat.

All of these basic issues of organizational and organizing are highly relevant to the professions, professional organizations, their internal dynamics, and their relations with other professions and occupations, including those that formally or informally aspire to become labelled as professions. In summarizing these issues, some of the examples above refer to 'women' and 'men', and thus it should be made clear that gendering applies as much to men and masculinities as to women and femininities: gender is not a synonym for women. Moreover, these are not the only gender categories; gender and sexual categories have expanded, as, for example, with LGBTIQ+ (lesbian, bisexual, gay, transgender, intersex, queer, and further non-normative gender and sexual orientations). Gender is thus much more than cisgender,[2] and indeed debates on the very meaning of gender have become more complex and contingent as studies of gender, work, organizations and professions have become more established (Hearn and Husu, 2012).

Similarly, and more generally, professions are characterized by comparable processes in relation to other social divisions and social differences, such as ethnicity and racialization, in terms of, for example, inclusions and exclusions. This becomes clear when locating professions in international, comparative and transnational contexts. Indeed, much of the historical development of professions has been influenced by processes of imperialism and colonialism, for example, in the Anglophone world, professions and professionals have historically been more often white, and educated in the metropole(s). In the latter half of the twentieth century, professions became much more diversified in terms of ethnicity and skin colour, whether educated in the metropole(s) or locally, and sometimes also continuing to serve metropolitan populations.

Moreover, social divisions and social differences do not operate separately, but in diversity and in intersectional ways. Having said this, diversity and intersectionality can mean many things. The concept of diversity tends to be applied more descriptively to the diverse range of social categories in a given situation, occupation, organization or, in this context, profession. The term intersectionality generally refers to intersections between categories, social divisions or social differences. Beyond that, it has, however, been used in many different ways – between relatively fixed social categories, in the making of such categories, in their mutual constitution, in transcending categories. McCall's (2005) clarification of different interpretations of intersectionality is especially useful, distinguishing approaches that are:

- inter-categorical: adopting existing analytical, relatively fixed categories, with the focus on relations between them, as in gendered, ethnicized/raced labour markets amongst health professionals;
- intra-categorical: using more provisional categories; acknowledging stable, even durable, relationships that social categories represent at a given point in time; maintaining a critical stance toward categories; and focusing on particular social groups at neglected points of intersection: 'people whose identity crosses the boundaries of traditionally constructed groups', such as the Afro-Caribbean upper-middle-class barrister;
- anti-categorical: not seeing categories as basic, and instead deconstructing categories, such as the white heterosexual able-bodied bishop.

This framework moves, in broad terms, from more modernist inter-categorical conceptions of intersectionality to more ambiguous intra-categorical conceptions, to poststructuralist anti-categorical conceptions. These distinctions also mirror, to some extent, discussions of more essentialist and more constructionist approaches to difference. More essentialist approaches to difference tend to highlight differences between groupings and treat groupings as relatively internally homogeneous, whether members of a profession or marked (for example, black or minority ethnic) or unmarked (for example, white or majority ethnic) category of professionals; more constructionist approaches tend to focus more on variations within groups: for example, not all women physicians are alike; not all minority ethnic lawyers are alike.[3]

Gender, diversity and intersectionality are also extremely relevant for the analysis of inter-professional relations, where, for example, one professional group is granted higher status than another, in part by virtue of its association with a higher-status social category or combination of social categories. On the other hand, it is quite likely that the combination or intersection of status categories may conflict or be ambiguous in relation to professional status, for example when a black working-class-background doctor treats a white upper-class patient.

Historical perspectives

The various gendered and intersectional processes and approaches noted in the previous section take specific historical and dynamic forms. The historical gendering of professions has moved from the incipient pre- or proto-professions, sometimes with a strong presence of women, to what were often originally virtually men-only, or sometimes strictly men-only, established professions (for example, law, medicine, clergy), and their own growing gendered complexity, onto the development of the welfare professions and what were sometimes, disparagingly, called the 'semi-professions' (Etzioni, 1969) with many women in their so-called rank and file, to the emergence of a whole host of newer modern or even postmodern professions, with more flexible gendered definitions and gendered occupational practices. Here we use the terms 'potential professions' and 'aspiring professions' in preference to such critiqued terms as 'semi-professions', or even 'the other professions' (Abbott, 1988).

In broadly non-industrial society, women were engaged in tasks, activities and spheres of responsibility that were later to be taken over by the men of the professions. This may be clearest in the area of medicine and the care of the body (for example, Ehrenreich and English, 1973, 1974), but it also applies to some extent in the arenas of divinity and law, through various forms of 'wise women', 'healers', operating across of the boundaries of life and death. Indeed, in the Christian world 'for eight … centuries. From the fifth to the thirteenth, the other-worldly, anti-medical stance of the Church … stood in the way of the development of medicine as a respectable profession' (Ehrenreich and English, 1974, p. 13). According to early Christian missionary and Norman practices, 'Male physicians were rare, since time and desire for study were almost confined to monks, Jews and others debarred from the supreme masculine occupation of fighting' (Manton, 1965, p. 57). This pattern was disrupted through a combination of the church, state, universities, science and capitalism, and the men who dominated there: in 'the medical occupations the seventeenth and eighteenth centuries witnessed an increasing division of labour and a concomitant exclusion of women from the higher and more lucrative branches which were emerging' (Parry and Parry, 1976, p. 164).

In eighteenth-century England, the high-status professions, such as barristers, became an occupational route for sons, especially the younger sons, of the gentry, while men or the subordinated 'lower branches' (Reader, 1966), and aspiring groups, such as attorneys and solicitors, were recruited from the families of tradesmen and artisans. This points to the ways in which gendered divisions, between classed men, have been (re)produced in and by the professions. Most importantly, until the end of the nineteenth century, and often later, higher education, one of the prerequisites for entry into the 'established professions', was denied to women in most countries. With women's entry into higher education, albeit in an uneven way internationally, higher education, universities and science in its broad sense themselves became arenas for professional contestation.

In addressing such historical complexities, it is very important to distinguish professional activity and professional institutionalization. For example, women were involved in professional activities and tasks throughout the history of education and science but became excluded with its institutionalization (Schiebinger, 1999). In the late eighteenth century, women were hired as 'professional' astronomical 'computer' women, yet with low pay and no opportunities to advance in their career; observatories, such as Harvard College Observatory, hired numerous women as 'computers', to perform star observation and arithmetic work (Rossiter, 1982).

The international historical literature on the women pioneers in the professions in their modern form is extensive. The position of women entering, or re-entering, medicine in the nineteenth-century United States has been recorded by the sisters Elisabeth and Emily Blackwell

61

(1860) in *Medicine as a Profession for Women*. A major early overview of women's entry into the professional associations in the USA was that by Breckenridge in her 1933 report, *Women in the Twentieth Century*, sometimes initially through the formation of parallel women's professional associations, such as the Medical Women's National Association. There are many other accounts of women entering law, higher education, veterinary surgery, and so on.

A classic account is that by Agnes Sjöberg (1964/2000), the first woman to become a veterinary surgeon in Europe and the first woman in Europe to obtain a doctorate in veterinary medicine. The Rector who admitted her to study at the University of Dresden in 1911, did so first on a probationary basis, assuming that 'a woman would be especially suited to treat small animals' (p. 32), even if her specialism was horses. In her autobiography, Sjöberg goes on to describe in vivid detail the responses from the other, all male, students, in the lecture theatre ('a terrible noise was created in the hall. The students stamped their feet and shouted "hinaus" [out]' (p. 34), and more generally ('They said: "… if we could get this first devil woman away, so there would not be more of them, but if she is able to continue, next year there can be many more hags on these benches"' (p. 35).

There are well-developed arguments, both for and against women being in the professions, often tending to emphasize either sexual/gender difference or gender/sexual sameness. Difference arguments against women's inclusion have sometimes relied on forms of essentialist biologism, such as that intellectual work may damage the ovaries, as reported in the *Norwegian Journal of Medicine* in 1892 (see Husu, 2001, p. 33). Such thinking is not dead, as when Harvard President Lawrence Summers explained the under-representation of women in some natural science fields:

> It does appear that on many, many different human attributes – height, weight, propensity for criminality, overall IQ, mathematical ability, scientific ability – there is relatively clear evidence that whatever the difference in means – which can be debated – there is a difference in the standard deviation, and variability of a male and a female population.
>
> *(Summers, 2005)*

This highlights the question of men's responses, discriminations and resistances to women's entry, and how women themselves, and some men, articulated arguments in favour of women coming into the professions. Arguments for women's inclusion have included women's special contribution, for example in midwifery that might thus benefit from women's contribution, and the more fundamental argument of justice for women in broadening their own occupational choices. These twin arguments of gender complementarity (difference) and gender comparability (sameness) are also paralleled by arguments for diversity in various occupational fields, and in relation to gendered, sometimes intersectional, labour markets. For example, increasing women's representation in natural science, technology, engineering and mathematics can be justified (and opposed) in relation to women's choices, women's contribution and potential, industrial and labour market demands, and justice and equality. Likewise, gender or intersectional equality can be framed, alternatively: as a matter of individual choice, potential and contribution; as matters of organizational, occupational and labour market dynamics; or as a matter of the structuring of (professional) knowledge itself and what counts as (professional) knowledge (Hearn and Husu, 2011; Schiebinger, 1999). This last approach might be rather easily understood in professions such as law and medicine, but may be less obvious in, say, physics.

The very project of professionalization can be understood in some instances as patriarchal in form and content. Innovative feminist action can be incorporated into male domination through serving a man or an existing profession, as with nurses and care assistants, mainly women, often of lower class or ethnic status, who are subordinated to medical doctors, often men, often of higher class or ethnic status – in gendered, ethnicized professional hierarchies. Other mechanisms include reinforcement of the 'patriarchal feminine', advantageous positioning of men in sectors and hierarchies, and managerialist takeover (Hearn, 1982). Patriarchal relations can also be reproduced through professions being embedded within and mediated by patriarchal contexts (Witz, 1992). Collective action, between professions, aspiring or potential professions, and other occupations, involves the intersection of various (internal, intra-professional) exclusionary strategies and (external, inter-professional) demarcatory strategies of closure by the dominant group, and by various inclusionary strategies by subordinated groups in response. These strategies, for example, around and through legal and credential controls and tactics are enacted by gendered (and indeed intersectional) collective actors, not socially 'neutral' actors. This may be clear in using, say, other external, inter-professional collective actors, such as the state and the courts, with their own gendered intersectional structures and processes. In this way, framing some women, individually and collectively, can pursue the project of professional recognition, more or less successfully in the intersections of occupation, class, gender and further social divisions.

Such accounts have been much complicated in more recent times in several ways. First, the established contrasts between professions, on the one hand, and bureaucracy, organizations, management and the state, on the other, have become less and less tenable. The well-established contrast of professions and bureaucracy no longer holds so true. In some instances, gendered changes in these various forms of professions and professionalizations are bound up with shifting relations of state and capitalism. This prompted greater consideration of the variable relation of professions and the state (for example, as financier and regulator; through state education; and in state welfare professions) with hybrid forms of professionalized bureaucracies and bureaucratic professions (Noordegraaf and Stein, 2013). Professional independence, often male gendered, and allegiance to a professional association, can be overridden by state or other employer power.

Second is the greater attention to comparative approaches to the professions from the 1970s (Larson, 1977), but now accelerating, not least through greater international research cooperation. For example, the continental European model has often involved more direct state direction of professions than in the historical anglophone supposedly 'gentlemanly' model, noted above. The status of certain professions is also highly variable when seen in comparative terms. In the Soviet Union, the medical professional tended to be coded as women's work rather than as a male bastion into which women sought entry. Veterinary surgery has been a men's arena into which women are entering in greater numbers in some countries (Lofstedt, 2003), while in Finland it has long been dominated by women. Dentistry in Finland has traditionally been a female-coded profession, in clear contrast with other Nordic countries (Haavio-Mannila, 1975). In some post-socialist countries, there is a significantly higher proportion of women in the university professoriate and in scientific, technology, engineering and medical research than in some Western Europe countries (EU Directorate-General for Research and Innovation, 2013). Similarly, while there are some broadly consistent patterns in professional specialisms, there are also great variations across countries. For example, child psychiatry has been much more of a woman's specialism in Finland than the Scandinavian countries; medicine has generally been more male-dominated in Denmark than in other Nordic countries, but not so radiology (Riska, 1998).

Third, there have been more recent trends in many countries towards the entry of greater numbers of women, including women from less privileged status groups, into established professions (Walby, 1997), alongside more men entering and rising up professions formerly seen as women's arenas (Simpson, 2005). We continue with this theme in more detail below.

Thus there are multiple and various possible historical, local, national, comparative, international and transnational forms of gendering, diversifying and intersectionalizing of the professions. To illustrate this complexity, the next main section addresses two contemporary international case examples: first, women working in an established profession, law, in two European countries, one post-communist, the other not; and then women leaving, or considering doing so, what might be seen as the incipient profession of business management, across Finland and the USA. These both, albeit in different ways, examine intersections of gender, occupation and national context.

Contemporary international cases

Women lawyers in Finland and Poland: managing competitive pressures, expectations and identities

The increasing entry of women in the male-dominated professions, such as the legal profession, raises many questions regarding the still limited inclusion of women lawyers across all segments of the profession. Changes in legal education and the market for legal services have contributed to the greater number of women entering the legal profession. The opening of law to women has resulted in what may appear to be equality of career opportunities between women and men, which in turn normalizes women lawyers' less favourable professional status and fewer career opportunities. While women are increasingly entering legal education and the legal profession, they are under-represented in the upper levels of law firms across countries (Bolton and Muzio, 2007; Pinnington and Sandberg, 2013; Choroszewicz, 2014). Due to the increasing role of law firms as sites in the social reproduction of the professional elite, scrutiny of women lawyers' professional status has shifted towards women practising law within the corporate segment of the legal profession (Kay and Hagan, 1998; Walsh, 2012).

Gendering processes within the legal profession also involve women's active participation in the reproduction of career choices perceived as appropriate for them due to their certain skills, competence and life experience (for example, Bolton and Muzio, 2007; Pierce, 2010). Further insights into such gendering processes arise through cross-national research, as, for example, of Finnish and Polish women lawyers.[4] Specifically, some of women's professional choices are informed not only by their sense of what is occupationally advantageous but also by their gendered identity about the professional expectations and career opportunities marked as appropriate for them as women lawyers. In both Finland and Poland, women's professional labour market position is being enhanced by their competitive potential, particularly with regard to quality of client service. The basis of competition in the market for legal services, in the globalizing economy, is shifting from traditionally formulated competences based predominantly on legal knowledge and legal reasoning towards other qualities which facilitate good rapport with clients. Lawyers and law firms experience increased pressure to differentiate themselves in terms of market niche and quality of legal services. This has facilitated recognition of attributes associated with the hegemonic ideals of femininity as a set of powerful resources which have been undervalued in traditionally male-dominated professions, in order to be more attentive to clients' needs and satisfaction. Thus, women lawyers' competitiveness is enhanced by their interpersonal and cooperative abilities as nowadays sought after in law firms.

The emerging asymmetry in the relations between lawyers and their clients exposes lawyers to pressures to conform to their clients' expectations in order to retain enduring relations with them. Lawyers, like other service providers, are increasingly expected to engage in intensive interactions with valued clients. This pressure is particularly salient in law firms in which lawyers are subject to the influence of prestigious and influential clients who consider it legitimate to demand legal assistance specifically tailored to their needs. Some Finnish and Polish women lawyers feel particularly predisposed to display care and concern for their clients along with the legal assistance. In legal specializations that provide legal advice for weaker and disadvantaged clients, they are expected to perform emotional labour not necessarily expected from male colleagues (Pierce, 2010, p. 181). This applies in such legal specializations as family and inheritance law, and compensation lawsuits, which provide women lawyers with flexibility to draw on skills that they, as women, are expected to possess. However, such specializations are usually characterized by slower career advancement, lower wages, and less power and authority.

In these ways, challenges linked to gender equality in the legal profession in Finland and Poland appear somewhat similar in both countries. In order to retain their competitiveness and move towards legal specializations and positions of greater salary, influence and authority in the legal profession, women lawyers are expected to be able to live up to the traditional understanding of success. Women lawyers clearly have more agency with regard to career choices and greater opportunities to devise their own ways of combining career and personal life, which are not necessarily available to women of other occupational groups. They are also subject to more competitive professional pressures and expectations to fit traditional models of success, particularly strong in the most prestigious positions within the legal profession. This gendered notion of success is built upon stereotypically masculine working patterns and career advancement, which are only increasing nowadays in terms of working time and availability to clients – due to the asymmetry in the relations between lawyers and clients. It is not enough that women lawyers are formally granted equal career opportunities if their access to the most professionally favoured positions is still conditioned by their ability to fit into men-tailored professional expectations, working patterns and career commitment.

At the same time, the pattern of Finnish and Polish women attorneys' careers demonstrates that national contexts, Nordic and post-communist respectively, shape in different ways the competitive potential of women attorneys. Women's access to the most prestigious positions is dependent on women's support systems, including formal work–life reconciliation policies, flexible working arrangements, professional autonomy, equal career opportunities, workplace mentoring, and spousal and family support. Women lawyers in Finland benefit from the Finnish welfare state that provides women with greater opportunities to realize their career aspirations and orientation towards a balanced life. Finnish women lawyers have more flexibility to use and benefit from gender-appropriate attributes and competencies across legal specializations, work positions and law firms compared to their Polish counterparts. By contrast, the career opportunities of Polish women attorneys are undercut by their greater family responsibilities compared to male spouses, less flexible working arrangements, and lesser gender equality and poorer work–life reconciliation policies. Thus, Polish women attorneys tend to opt for more independent or joint law practices in order to avoid the acute trade-offs between a rewarding career and a fulfilling personal life posed by many law firms in Poland. In this respect, the operation of gender as an axis of social inequality continues to persist, underpinned by gendered professional expectations and conditions which encourage women and men to enact different qualities, competences and orientations. Gender, as a source of embodied cultural capital, still shapes women's professional experience and career choices in both Finland and Poland, if in rather different ways. These gendered expectations and conditions hamper equality in the legal profession in both Finland and Poland.

Business management in Finland and the USA: opting out of a new profession?

This second case study shows some similarities and differences. This concerns a less clear-cut case of professions or a possible potential profession, namely business management, with a focus not on working within the profession but on women opting out of successful careers. Traditionally, business management has not been considered a profession, and there has been disagreement regarding whether or not it should be, and whether or not business managers have a professional orientation. However, there are several aspects of management, many of which are also gendered, that are comparable to professions. Management assumes many of the appearances of professions, although it may play down or evade certain ethical responsibilities and obligations (Khurana *et al.*, 2005), which can be seen as intersectionally gendered. Similarly to certain professions where male power and prestige have historically dominated and often persist, corporate environments tend to follow masculinist norms and ideals. Business management, with its particular forms of professional commitment – corporate, vocational, expert – which relate in turn to gender and other axes of power and inequality, is therefore an interesting case to consider when examining gender, diversity and intersectionality in professions.

These masculinist (professional) corporate environments in turn provide the backdrop for various forms of career development, coping, sense-making, and indeed resistance. One such, and sometimes rather dramatic, form of response is opting out from the professional corporate life, examined here through the study of interview narratives of fifteen women aged between 30 and 50 from Finland and the USA who opted out of successful business careers to adopt new ways of living and working that accommodate different interests and areas of life.[5] This perspective – of exit – raises a further set of gendered professional processes that may intersect with age, generation, family situation, national location and other social divisions and differences. And what is the significance of opting out in terms of gender and diversity? Could opting out be seen as gendered professional, or indeed unprofessional, behaviour?

The case of women opting out of successful careers in business management helps create an understanding of the gendered experiences of women professionals in masculinist professional cultures: what it is that pushes them out and what they are looking for in the new lifestyles they opt in to instead. For example, some successful women managers reported difficulties creating coherent narratives of their lives and work in the masculinist working environment, as they combined having a career with motherhood. Women with children are typically drawn between the individualistic world of work and the self-sacrificing motherhood schema, and while work often spills over into the private sphere, care responsibilities have to be kept invisible in the office (Blair-Loy, 2003). Women who opt out often leave their high-powered careers to adopt new lifestyles where they can live and work on their own terms, and where they can combine different interests and areas of life (McKie *et al.*, 2013; Mainiero and Sullivan, 2006). After opting out of the corporate environment, women generally experience a sense of authenticity and control, of finally being able to be themselves.

Finland and the USA are both Western countries; however, the culture, political, and social systems differ. Finland is a welfare state and is rated one of the most gender-equal in the EU. After having children, Finnish women face a reality quite different from that of US women. In Finland, there is a tradition of both partners working, and mothers and fathers have a right to subsidized maternity, paternity and parental leave until the child is three years of age, after which they are guaranteed employment by their employers upon their return to work. In addition, there is high-quality subsidized day care in Finland, while in the USA there is a nanny and stay-at-home 'mom' tradition, mainly as a result of expensive and poor availability of high-quality day care.

Despite these differences, the narratives of the US and Finnish women were remarkably similar. The women and their narratives were bound together, to some extent, by their expertise, agentic and other resources, educational and work experiences, and occupational potential and possibilities; although national differences seemed less significant, or at least less apparent, intersections of gender, work and family were important.

Interestingly, none of the women interviewed originally planned to opt out. They were all ambitious with plans to pursue a career and reportedly liked their jobs. Although having children was not the main cause of their desire to opt out, the situation became especially poignant for these women after they became mothers – it became increasingly challenging to combine a career with their care responsibilities, and it also became more difficult for these women to create coherent narratives about their lives and work. Previous research has argued that due to the hectic nature of living in contemporary society, it is, in fact, difficult for individuals to create coherent life narratives (see, for example, Elliott and Lemert, 2006), and for women combining careers with children, it becomes even more so. With current technology, employees – especially those pursuing careers – are expected to be available 24/7, and thus work often spills over into the private sphere (Blair-Loy, 2003). Working mothers thus find themselves answering emails and phone calls while caring for their children. Ironically, however, this does not go both ways; issues pertaining to the home and to their children are generally expected to be kept invisible at work, making these women feel that it was not appropriate to reveal their maternal selves in the workplace. And correspondingly, many women in the study felt that they could not be themselves before they opted out. At the same time, career women with children are typically drawn between two very contradicting schemas: the individualistic world of work, on the one hand, and self-sacrificing, intensive motherhood on the other (Blair-Loy, 2003). Both schemas demand complete availability and devotion and are fundamentally ideological opposites. As a result, many successful female managers, especially with children, tend to find it challenging to consolidate the two detrimentally different ideologies, adding to the difficulty of creating coherent narratives about their lives and their work. There is an intimate link between coherence and a sense of well-being (Linde, 1993) and, correspondingly, these women reported feeling exhausted and overwhelmed by the time they made the decision to opt out.

However, it was not until the situation became untenable and the women experienced some sort of a crisis that they finally decided to take the step. Although children are factored in, this was often not the main reason for opting out. Previous research has shown that women often use children as a reason to explain why they leave, as they are generally applauded for being good mothers, and this is easier than confronting an employer with the real reasons for leaving, such as gender discrimination, an unsupportive corporate culture or simply difficulties combining career and motherhood (Stone, 2007; McKie et al., 2013). However, contrary to much other research on opting out, only two of the women in this study became stay-at-home mothers, and all fifteen women were all highly ambitious and had a desire to continue working, either immediately or eventually. They left to create new lifestyles where they could combine meaningful work with other areas of life, where they had control over their time and their lives, and where they themselves could decide when and how they worked and when they spent time with their children, instead of having it decided for them by an employer or the demands of the corporate culture.

All the women expressed how, in their new lifestyles, they finally felt like they could 'be themselves'. They felt a sense of authenticity, which they had not felt in their previous careers, and this sense of authenticity, in turn, added to a sense of coherence and contentment. What was notable in all the narratives was that whatever it was these women ended up doing instead, they did so with a new mindset. No longer did they conform to the expectations and demands of the masculinist corporate culture and career model, they no longer worried so much about how others perceived them, and they were determined to live and work according to their own values and standards. So while opting out could be seen as unprofessional behaviour, these women had a will to continue being professional, but simply to do it on their own terms, in a sustainable way.

Some concluding remarks on the future...

The field of gender, diversity and intersectionality in and around the professions is very far from stable. There are numerous changes and challenges in and for both the professions and their analysis. First, there are shifts in the international gendered intersectional divisions of labour, partly through huge migrations, bringing greater inter-ethnic and inter-racialized professional processes and encounters. Second, transnational formations, such as virtual collaboration, are increasingly powerful constructors of professional knowledge. Information and communication technologies themselves bring new forms of gendered intersectional professional work at the interface and mutual construction of humans and technologies. Transnational professionals may learn and need to learn what has been called (gendered, intersectional) epistemic arbitrage (Seabrooke, 2014), within transnational inter-organizational contexts. Third, there is the impact of neoliberalism, especially pressures towards privatization and individualism. In this situation, the professionalization project may become more individualized, more separated from professional associations and specific employers. This may lead to concerns about the 'professionalization of everyone' (cf. Wilensky, 1964) but now in neoliberal form: portfolio careers, organizations as temporary employing 'hotels', and the professionalized, self-monitoring, entrepreneurial body as an individual project. Finally, we note the emergence of new professions and powerful professional expertise, for example linked to biotechnologies or climate change, highlighting new intersectionalities with non-humans and the environment more broadly (Kaijser and Kronsell, 2014). The combination of such various trends and moves may even make professions in their current forms redundant.

Thus the gendered and intersectional structuring of and in professions and professionalization projects, at macro, meso and micro levels, are both historically well established and taking new forms. To approach the study and analysis of professions and professionalization as neutral phenomena and without attending to gender and intersectional structures, processes and change is unscientific and careless indeed.

Notes

1 Interestingly, Marx and Weber had rather little to say on professions, preferring to focus on class and bureaucracy as key concepts. This can be understood to some extent in terms of how the professions were formed and established at their time of writing. Rather, one might argue that both Gramsci (1971), on hegemony, organic intellectuals and those professionally engaged in cultural work, and Althusser (1971), in terms of repressive and ideological state apparatuses, have more to say here.

2 Cisgender refers to an equivalence, assumed equivalence or match between gender assigned at birth, people's bodies, and their personal identity or self-perception (Schilt and Westbrook, 2009).

3 The concept of intersectionality has a rich feminist and anti-racist history (see, for example, Crenshaw, 1989; Brah and Phoenix, 2004), and is sometimes seen as one of the major contributions of feminist thought. Intersectional perspectives, and the complex social phenomena to which they refer, go under many different names, including inter-relations of oppressions, multiple oppressions, multiple social divisions, mutual constitution, multiple differences, hybridities, simultaneity, multiculturalisms, multiplicities, post-colonialities, as well as diversity.

4 The remainder of this section draws extensively on recent research on Finnish and Polish women lawyers (Choroszewicz, 2014).

5 The remainder of this section draws extensively on recent research on women who have opted out of business management (Biese, 2013).

Acknowledgement

This chapter arises partly from the Swedish Research Council project, 'Feminist theorisings of intersectionality, transversal dialogues and new synergies', and the Academy of Finland project, 'Social and economic sustainability of future working life: policies, (in)equalities and intersectionalities in Finland'.

References

Abbott, A. (1988) *The System of Professions: An Essay on the Division of Expert Labour*. Chicago, IL: Chicago University Press.

Acker, J. (1992) 'Gendering Organizational Theory'. In A. J. Mills and P. Tancred (eds), *Gendering Organizational Analysis*. Newbury Park, CA: Sage, pp. 248–260.

Althusser, L. (1971) *Lenin and Philosophy and Other Essays*. New York: Monthly Review Press.

Becker, H., Geer, B., Hughes, E.C. and Strauss, A.L. (1976) *Boys in White*. Chicago, IL: University of Chicago Press.

Biese, I. (2013) *Opting Out: A Critical Study of Women Leaving Their Careers to Adopt New Lifestyles*. Adelaide: University of South Australia.

Blackwell, E. and Blackwell, E. (1860) *Medicine as a Profession for Women*. New York: New York Infirmary for Women.

Blair-Loy, M. (2003) *Competing Devotions: Career and Family among Women Executives*. Cambridge, MA: Harvard University Press.

Blau, P. M. and Scott, W. R. (1963) *Formal Organizations: A Comparative Approach*. London: Routledge & Kegan Paul.

Bolton, S. and Muzio, D. (2007) 'Can't Live With 'em; Can't Live Without 'em: Gendered Segmentation in the Legal Profession'. *Sociology*, 41(1): 47–61.

Brah, A. and Phoenix, A. (2004) 'Ain't I a Woman? Revisiting Intersectionality'. *Journal of International Women's Studies*, 5(3): 75–86.

Breckinridge, S. (1933) *Women in the Twentieth Century*. New York. McGraw-Hill.

Carr-Saunders, A. M. and Wilson, P. A. (1933) *The Professions*. Oxford: Clarendon.

Choroszewicz, M. (2014) *Managing Competitiveness in Pursuit of a Legal Career: Women Attorneys in Finland and Poland*. Joensuu: University of Eastern Finland.

Cockburn, C. K. (1991). *In the Way of Women: Men's Resistance to Sex Equality in Organizations*. London: Macmillan.

Crenshaw, K. (1989) 'Demarginalizing the Intersection of Race and Sex: A Black Feminist Critique of Antidiscrimination Doctrine, Feminist Theory and Antiracist Politics'. *University of Chicago Legal Forum*, 140: 139–167.

Davies, C. (1996) 'The Sociology of Professions and the Profession of Gender'. *Sociology*, 30(4): 661–678.

Ehrenreich, B. and English, D. (1973) *Witches, Midwives and Nurses: A History of Women Healers*. New York: Feminist Press.

Ehrenreich, B. and English, D. (1974) *Complaints and Disorders: The Sexual Politics of Sickness*. New York: Feminist Press.

Elliot, P. (1972) *The Sociology of Professions*. London: Macmillan.

Elliott, A. and Lemert, C. (2006) *The New Individualism: The Emotional Costs of Globalization*. London: Routledge.

Etzioni, A. (ed.) (1969) *The Semi-Professions and Their Organization*. New York: Free Press.

EU Directorate-General for Research and Innovation (2013) *She Figures: Gender in Research and Innovation*. Brussels: European Commission.

Gramsci, A. (1971) *Selections from the Prison Notebooks*. London: Lawrence & Wishart.

Haavio-Mannila, E. (1975) *Sex Roles among Physicians and Dentists in Scandinavia*. Helsinki: University of Helsinki Institute of Sociology, Research Report 206.

Hearn, J. (1982) 'Notes on Patriarchy, Professionalization and the Semi-Professions'. *Sociology*, 16(2): 184–202.

Hearn, J. and Husu, L. (2011) 'Understanding Gender: Some Implications for Science and Technology'. *Interdisciplinary Science Reviews*, 36: 103–113.

Hearn, J. and Parkin, W. (1987/1995) *'Sex' at 'Work'*. New York: St Martin's.

Hearn, J. and Parkin, W. (2001) *Gender, Sexuality and Violence in Organizations*. London: Sage.

Hughes, E. C. (1963) 'Professions'. *Daedalus*, 92: 655–668.

Husu, L. (2001) *Sexism, Support and Survival in Academia*. Helsinki: University of Helsinki Press.

Johnson, T. (1972) *Professions and Power*. London: Macmillan.

Kaijser, A. and Kronsell, A. (2014) 'Climate Change through the Lens of Intersectionality'. *Environmental Politics*, 23(3): 417–433.

Kay, F. M. and Hagan, J. (1998) 'Raising the Bar: The Gender Stratification of Law-Firm Capital'. *American Sociological Review*, 63(5): 728–743.

Khurana, R., Nuhria, N. and Penrice, D. (2005) *Is Business Management a Profession?* HBS Working Knowledge, Harvard Business School. http://hbswk.hbs.edu/item/4650.html.

Larson, M. S. (1977) *The Rise of Professionalism*. Berkeley, CA: University of California Press.

Linde, C. (1993) *Life Stories: The Creation of Coherence*. Oxford: Oxford University Press.

Lofstedt, J. (2003) 'Gender and Veterinary Medicine'. *Canadian Veterinary Journal*, 44(7): 533–535.

McCall, L. (2005) 'The Complexity of Intersectionality'. *Signs*, 30: 1771–1800.

McKie, L., Biese, I. and Jyrkinen, M. (2013) '"The Best Time Is Now!" The Temporal and Spatial Dynamics of Women Opting in to Self-Employment'. *Gender, Work and Organization*, 20(2): 184–196.

Mainiero, L. A. and Sullivan, S. E. (2006) *The Opt-Out Revolt: Why People Are Leaving Companies to Create Kaleidoscope Careers*. Mountain View, CA: Davies Black.

Manton, J. (1965) *Elizabeth Garrett Anderson*. New York: Dutton.

Morgan, L. M. and Davidson, M. J. (2008) 'Sexual Dynamics in Mentoring Relationships: A Critical Review'. *British Journal of Management*, 19: S120–S129.

Noordegraaf, M. and Steijn, B. (2013) *Professionals under Pressure: The Reconfiguration of Professional Work in Changing Public Services*. Amsterdam: Amsterdam University Press.

Parry, N. and Parry, J. (1976) *The Rise of the Medical Profession*. London: Croom Helm.

Pierce, J. (2010) 'Women and Men as Litigators: Gender Differences on the Job'. In J. Goodman (ed.), *Global Perspectives on Gender and Work*. Plymouth, UK: Rowman & Littlefield.

Pinnington, A. H. and Sandberg, J. (2013) 'Lawyers' Professional Careers: Increasing Women's Inclusion in the Partnership of Law Firms'. *Gender, Work and Organization*, 20(6): 616–631.

Reader, W. J. (1966) *Professional Men: The Rise of the Professional Classes in Nineteenth-Century England*. New York: Basic.

Riska, E. (1998) 'Further Rationalization of Medicine: The Reconfiguration of the Medical Profession'. *Research in the Sociology of Health Care*, 15: 111–127.

Riska, E. (2014) 'Gender and the Professions'. In W. C. Cockerham, R. Dingwall and S. R. Quah (eds) *The Wiley Blackwell Encyclopedia of Health, Illness, Behavior, and Society*. London: John Wiley & Sons, pp. 633–637.

Rossiter, M. W. (1982) *Women Scientists in America*. Baltimore, MD: Johns Hopkins University Press.

Schiebinger, L. (1999) *Has Feminism Changed Science?* Cambridge, MA: Harvard University Press.

Schilt, K. and Westbrook, L. (2009). 'Doing Gender, Doing Heteronormativity: "Gender Normals," Transgender People, and the Social Maintenance of Heterosexuality'. *Gender & Society*, 23(4): 440–464.

Seabrooke, L. (2014) 'Epistemic Arbitrage: Transnational Professional Knowledge in Action'., *Journal of Professions and Organization*, 1(1):, pp. 49–64.

Simpson, R. (2005) 'Men in Non-Traditional Occupations: Career Entry, Career Orientation and Experience of Role Strain'. *Gender, Work and Organization*, 12(4): 363–380.

Sjöberg, A. (1964) *Euroopan ensimmäinen naiseläinlääkäri [Europe's first woman veterinary doctor]*. Helsinki: Lasipalatsi.

Stacey, M. and Price, M. (1981) *Women, Power and Politics*. London: Tavistock.

Stone, P. (2007) *Opting Out? Why Women Really Quit Their Careers and Head Home*. Berkeley, CA: University of California Press.

Summers, L. (2005) 'Remarks at NBER Conference on Diversifying the Science & Engineering Workforce', Cambridge, MA, January 14, 2005. Harvard: The Office of the President. www.harvard.edu/president/speeches/summers_2005/nber.php.

Walby, S. (1997) *Gender Transformations*. London: Routledge.

Walsh, J. (2012) 'Not Worth the Sacrifice? Women's Aspirations and Career Progression in Law Firms'. *Gender, Work and Organisation*, 19(5): 508–531.

Wilensky, H. (1964) 'The Professionalization of Everyone'. *American Journal of Sociology*, 70: 137–158.

Witz, A. (1992) *Professions and Patriarchy*. London: Routledge.

Woolf, V. (1929) *A Room of One's Own*. Oxford: Oxford University Press.

5

Professions and power

A review of theories of professions and power

Mike Saks

Introduction

The concept of power is at the heart of the consideration of the nature and role of professional groups in society, from the classic professions of law and medicine to other professional occupations, including accountancy, architecture, nursing and social work. The centrality of this concept has been highlighted by its significance in the work of sociologists of professions in the range of theoretical analyses of professions that have been produced to aid the interpretation of both the historical and contemporary activities of professional groups. These analyses underline that not only is the definition of a profession fundamentally contested, but – most importantly in this context – so is the concept of power itself in terms of the origins of professions and their relationship to other bodies in and beyond the division of occupational labour.

This chapter is illustrated through examples from different countries in the modern world inside and outside organizations and in the public and private sectors, as well as across a number of professional groups at the macro and micro level. Here particular, but not exclusive, reference to the Anglo-American context is made to exemplify key points. The analysis starts by outlining chronologically the mainstream theoretical perspectives in sociology on professions. It focuses specifically on the various ways in which the concept of power is employed in each, against the backcloth of a rapidly changing world and debates about the shifting power of professional groups.

In this exploration, it is argued that a neo-Weberian approach to professional power linked to the self-interests of professional groups, with relevant counterfactuals, might be seen to have a number of advantages compared to other theoretical analyses. Having examined some of the benefits of a neo-Weberian approach, the chapter considers in more detail through a neo-Weberian lens the meaning of the concept of power. This is seen to be multidimensional and to operate at varying levels. The chapter then examines from the standpoint of power the shifting relationship both within and between professional groups in the context of the state and the market – against the backcloth of the growing voice of citizens.

In this regard, the chapter will ask, amongst other things, whether the power of professions can be seen to be waning – particularly in the context of contemporary neo-Weberian debates about deprofessionalization. In a related manner, it considers the new forms that professions may now be taking in organizational and other contexts and the extent to which the rise of the new public management (NPM) and other developments have affected their power in a fast-changing international socio-economic climate. In so doing, it recognizes that professions and power can also be analysed at a micro level in terms of professional–client relationships in a manner related to wider structures of professional power.

Sociological theories of professions and power

Key theories of professions in the Anglo-American context span historically from the relatively benevolent taxonomic approach to more critical perspectives – including symbolic interactionism, Marxism, Foucauldianism and discourse analysis. In examining chronologically how these approaches conceive of the relationship between professions and power at a macro and micro level, the chapter reviews such contributions and assesses the theoretical and methodological issues they have posed in the development of the sociology of professions. As such, the purview of the chapter is broad, ranging from the analysis of more supportive to more challenging theories of the professions.

The benevolent taxonomic approach to professions

The taxonomic approach to professions, which was particularly influential in the 1950s and 1960s, focused on the positive differences of professions from other occupations – which were defined in terms of characteristics like high-level expertise and a public-interest orientation. There were two variants, the first of which was the trait approach, which largely consisted of atheoretical listings of various attributes of a profession, from altruistic codes of ethics to the educational qualifications required for entry – as illustrated by Greenwood (1957) in relation to social work. This approach need not detain us here as power did not figure explicitly except in so far as the features of professions bolstered the authority of professionals over clients.

Nonetheless, power was more central to the second variant of taxonomy, that of structural functionalism. Functionalists like Goode (1960) gave a more theoretically cogent account of professions like psychology and medicine in industrial societies – in which it was argued that there was a functional relationship between professional groups and the wider society. In this sense, the elevated position of professions in the social system – underwritten by the state – was typically seen as related to their esoteric knowledge of great importance to society. This high standing was given in return for ensuring the protection of the public, not least through the establishment and implementation of professional codes of ethics.

In this functionalist account, power was very important as its exercise was seen as a system property designed to realize collective ends. This was highlighted by Parsons (1967: 308), who saw power as the 'generalized capacity to secure the performance of binding obligations by units in a system of collective organization when the obligations are legitimized with reference to their bearing on collective goals and where in case of recalcitrance there is a presumption of enforcement by negative situational sanctions'. A profession was therefore seen as facilitating the performance of functions in, and on behalf of, the social system – exercising power in collective goal fulfilment, based on value consensus.

However, the taxonomic approach has been heavily criticized – not least in terms of its uncritical view of professions, which seemed to be rather more oriented towards legitimating professional ideologies as opposed to depicting how professions operate in practice (Roth 1974). This is generally fair comment on the functionalist variant of this approach on which this section focuses, albeit with the exception of sophisticated contributors like Parsons (1967), who adopted a model of professions based on 'ideal types' against which judgements about their operation might be made, rather than endeavouring to depict some kind of immutable professional reality.

For critics of functionalist analyses of professions, though, this deferential view of such occupational groups gave an all too starry-eyed interpretation of the operation of power. This is because the starting point for functionalist conceptualizations was centred on a presumption about the existence of professional communities as part of a societal consensus, rather than as elements of a conflicting landscape characterized by zero-sum games. As such, the exercise of professional power at a structural level was seen as a platform for meeting system needs, rather than as a resource underpinning struggles with other groups in society – in a manner comparatively blind to internal divisions within professions.

Having said this, a more critical view of professions and power was precipitated by wider socio-political changes in Britain and the United States associated with the rise of the 1960s and 1970s counterculture. This was driven by attacks on scientific progress, in which a subculture emerged that was sceptical about technocratic solutions to problems and sought alternative lifestyles – embracing everything from mysticism to hallucinogenic drugs (Roszak 1995). As a result, established professions in areas from architecture and education to law and medicine were variously assailed, amongst other things, for not only their lack of effectiveness but also the dehumanization and disempowerment they evoked.

Critical perspectives on professions

(a)   Symbolic interactionism

Paradoxically, the initial main group of critics of the taxonomic view of professions and power came not from a macro, but a micro, perspective – in the form of symbolic interactionism, which particularly reacted to the reification of professions by functionalist writers. Instead of stressing the differences of professions from other occupations, interactionists like Hughes (1963) emphasized the similarities of professional groups like doctors and lawyers to more stigmatized workers such as exotic dancers and janitors. These groups, it was argued, faced parallel dilemmas in managing their occupational roles and identities – with the concept of a profession being seen simply as an honorific label won in the politics of work.

This micro-orientation, though, did not mean that the concept of power disappeared from the landscape. On the contrary, as Dennis (2005) has argued, in the front-of-stage analysis of interactionists it was acknowledged that political and economic power was important in shaping the way that rules were set and labels established. Here he notes that power was manifested in the relationships established at a micro level – not least between professionals and their clients. Thus, for example, within interactionist studies in Britain and the United States, teachers and other educational professionals were seen as having the power to define situations for their students and to impose identities on them.

As such, interactionism as an approach to the professions has primarily focused on the local use of power in the negotiation over the ascription of labels of professionalism – with all the implications that these carry for their occupational incumbents in practice. Revealing as this is in stripping away reflexive assumptions about professionals and their ideologies, and providing insights into the symbolic politics of work, it came with a price. This was that too little attention was given to detailing the historical background and wider structures of power that influence success or failure in gaining and sustaining professional standing (Saks 2012). Such a gap, though, was addressed in other more critical emerging perspectives.

(b)   The neo-Marxist approach

In terms of the operation of professions and power, the neo-Marxist approach can scarcely be accused of shirking from undertaking historical and macro-structural analyses in Western capitalist societies. The approach itself, though, masks differentiation and diversity – centrally including on which side of the divide between capital and labour specific professions should be placed theoretically. In this respect, leading professions have variously been viewed as either a 'professional-managerial class' acting as agents of capitalism in surveillance and control functions for the bourgeoisie (Ehrenreich and Ehrenreich 1979) or a part of the capitalist class itself, without themselves necessarily owning the means of production in the classic Marxist idiom (Navarro 1986).

What is clear, though, is that the typically privileged position of professional groups, from accountants and architects to doctors and social welfare occupations, is seen as derived in a different way from structural functional contributors. For neo-Marxists, as has been seen, the power underpinning professions is linked to their role in the class relations between the bourgeoisie and the proletariat rather than as a system resource directed towards societal goal attainment. Thus, for example, Poulantzas (1973: 104), in his structural neo-Marxist account, defined power as 'the capacity of a social class to realize its specific objective interests' in the class struggle, in which professional privileges stem from serving the dominant class.

The neo-Marxist approach to professions and power, however, has itself been open to criticism. Although this approach takes several forms, one issue is that it usually adopts a tautological view of state power under capitalism as inevitably functioning in the long-term interests of the capitalist class. As a result, the neo-Marxist approach often shields from empirical assessment conflicting claims about both the operation of the state and the nature and role of professional groups that it sanctions (Saunders 2007). The pre-eminence of this approach to the sociology of professions in the 1970s and 1980s also came under challenge with the collapse of socialist regimes in Eastern Europe, including most prominently the Soviet Union in the early 1990s (Saks 2015).

(c)   The Foucauldian approach

A further approach in Anglo-American sociology in considering professions and power as an antidote to more benevolent views of professionalism was provided by Foucauldianism, initiated by the French philosopher Michel Foucault. Like structural functionalism, this approach sees power as a ubiquitous feature of human activities in terms of its effects, but differs by being rather more cynical about its operation at a macro level. Employing the concept of governmentality – in which Johnson (1995) sees the state as a cluster of institutions, procedures, tactics, calculations, knowledge and technologies related to the outcome of governing – followers of Foucault (1978) have challenged the ideology of the rationality of scientific progress associated with professions in relation to institutional fields such as hospitals, prisons and schools.

Donzelot (1979) provides a good example of the way in which the Foucauldian perspective has been employed to dissect the use of power and knowledge by the professions involved in policing the family, from social workers to psychiatrists. He shows how power has been employed to render populations governable in the previously predominantly private domain of the family. Nettleton (1992), meanwhile, has considered the historical relationship between dental power and knowledge – underlining the role of dentists and dental knowledge in the surveillance, monitoring and normalization activities carried out in the task of governing. In this way, both studies highlight that power is not simply exercised by a particular class, as is so often portrayed in neo-Marxist accounts, but pervasively permeates everything from actions and attitudes to discourse, learning and everyday lives.

Nonetheless, Foucauldianism too has its frailties in its intriguing archaeological excavation of power and knowledge in the process of governance. In studying professions from this perspective, for example, the approach is difficult to operationalize as it is based on a model in which the state and the professions are seen as inextricably intertwined following the political incorporation of expertise (Saks 2012). Foucauldians have also been held to treat data in cavalier fashion and to pitch their analyses at too high a level of abstraction (Macdonald 1995) – again opening up claims about pursuing self-fulfilling arguments. In sum, its critical analysis of professions and power, while presenting a refreshing if chilling view of a complex modern world, has sometimes been conducted without sufficient attention to methodological rigour.

(d) Discourse analysis

But if questions remain about the operationalization of Foucauldian studies of professions and power, more recently a number of sociologists of the professions have retreated from 'big picture' theories to micro-oriented discourse analysis in countering the positive macro theorising of the functionalists. Although the study of discourse is a central part of the Foucauldian idiom, this form of analysis has more in common with the earlier symbolic interactionist perspective (Gubrium and Holstein 2003). Fournier (1999) pioneered this approach in her consideration of recruitment and advertising – examining the way in which groups like managers and supervisors use the notions of professions and professionalism to defend or extend their power in the workplace.

As with interactionism, discourse analysis is based on a less rigid categorization of professional groups than in some other theoretical approaches. It has since been employed in a wide span of areas, from architecture (Cohen *et al.* 2005) to executive coaching, medicine and psychotherapy (Graf, Sator and Spranz-Fogasy 2014). In the former case, the authors examined the accounts given by architects of the workings of their profession in different organizational contexts, including the enhancement of power through emphasizing creativity and expertise. The latter case meanwhile brings more clearly into vision the micro focus of the approach in understanding power relations in practitioner–client interaction.

In this sense, discourse analysis illuminates the culture of professionalism in terms of power and extends the range of occupations that are open to examination as part of the study of professions. Its focus on narratives in ground-level relationships in private and public sector settings is both a strength and weakness – as, like interactionism, it risks losing sight of wider structures of power. Against this, though, it is possible to weave discourse analysis into a broader framework by linking the ideologies that it studies to wider professional interests in the politics of work (Saks 2012). A key way in which this can be achieved is through the neo-Weberian approach that is now outlined.

The neo-Weberian approach to professions and power

Main aspects of the neo-Weberian approach

It is claimed here that the now widely adopted neo-Weberian approach can be highly fruitful in analysing professions and power in the Anglo-American context on which this chapter primarily focuses. The reason for this is that it addresses the main vulnerabilities of the theoretical perspectives so far considered. In the first place, it allows the exercise of power in the professions to be empirically examined, avoiding the benevolent presumptions about professional groups typically embedded in the trait and functionalist variants of the taxonomic approach. Neo-Weberianism also transcends the micro focus of interactionism and discourse analysis by enabling a macro structural analysis based on an understanding of the historical processes involved in generating front-of-stage activities.

Moreover, in developing a neo-Weberian approach to professions and power, the analysis is helpfully based on the interests of professional groups and other stakeholders within a sophisticated theoretical, conceptual and methodological framework – with a more open view of the state as an institution that has power in its own right and does not necessarily represent in ongoing fashion particular groups or classes (Smith 2009). As such, the strait jacket provided by limiting neo-Marxist assumptions surrounding the operation of the state under capitalism can be circumvented, as can the tendency of Foucauldians to base their analyses on less than systematic analyses of historical and other evidence. Without denying the insights offered by other perspectives, this provides a persuasive basis for adopting a neo-Weberian assessment of power in relation to professions.

The neo-Weberian approach is derived from the work of Max Weber and is centred on the concept of exclusionary social closure in the market (Parkin 1979). This is pivoted on occupational groups winning and sustaining formal legal boundaries, sanctioned by the state, defining a profession – with a single register based on credentialism creating a limited group of eligibles and ranks of insiders and outsiders. The process of gaining a professional monopoly is driven by the exercise of macro political power in a competitive marketplace where successful occupations typically enhance their position in terms of income, status and power, privileging themselves as against other occupational groups in the division of labour.

This should not mask differences in approach within a neo-Weberian perspective as, amongst other things, not all such contributors directly link their analyses to the concept of social closure. However, in such cases, their frame of reference is at least derivable from market closure. Thus, for example, Johnson (1972) sees professional groups as defined by collegiate producer control over the consumer, in contrast to patronage and mediative relationships. Similarly, Freidson (1994) sees professionalism as centred on legitimate, organized autonomy over technical issues and work organization. Nonetheless, all neo-Weberian analyses are rooted in the exercise of power, even if this is less explicitly articulated in the work of Freidson as compared to other contributors (Macdonald 1995).

In medicine, the neo-Weberian approach to professions and power is well exemplified by Berlant (1975), who argues that the *de facto* and *de jure* monopolies that emerged in Britain and the United States respectively came into being as a result of the tactics of competition employed by doctors and the different socio-political conditions that they faced in a liberal era. In the no less classic case of law, the approach is illustrated by the use of professional power to form the bar associations in early nineteenth-century America that acted as a platform to winning market control (Halliday 1987) and the political in-fighting that led to legal monopolies of solicitors and barristers in Britain under the authority of the Law Society and the Bar Council (Burrage 2006).

Criticisms of the neo-Weberian approach

Despite the comparative strengths of neo-Weberianism in understanding the dynamics of professions and power in the Anglo-American setting, as Saks (2010) has documented, it does not itself stand above criticism. One issue is the need for greater empirical rigour in applying the approach. This is highlighted by the much-cited work of Johnson (1972), who does not evidence his claim that doctors – having established a professional monopoly – used their power to irrationally constrain the roles of professions auxiliary to medicine in their own interests. Perucci (1973) also gives little basis for his view that professions use their power to protect their own interest when this conflicts with the public welfare. Paradoxically, this is the mirror image of the benevolent and unsubstantiated assumptions of taxonomy that have been so heavily attacked in the sociology of professions.

A second related weakness of the neo-Weberian approach is that its proponents are unduly disparaging about the self-interested use of power by professional groups. In the case of law, for example, Johnson (1972) reflexively claims that the politically inspired work of the legal profession lacks relevance to black and feminist groups, while similarly denigratory and unsubstantiated remarks are made by Beattie (1995) about the adverse effects of professional tribalism in health care. This flies in face of evidence about professional power being used for the public good through the *pro bono* activities of American lawyers (Granfield and Mather 2009) and the activities of British midwives and nurses – despite tensions between them – as 'knowledgeable doers' in serving clients (Borsay and Hunter 2012).

If this argues for greater balance in understanding the relationship between professions and power, a third area of criticism of neo-Weberian accounts is that they often fail to consider professions in the wider occupational division of labour. Thus, for instance, practitioners of complementary and alternative medicine (CAM) and health support workers have been little studied by neo-Weberians compared to doctors, in part because of their marginal standing (Saks 2008). Yet, having largely failed to professionalize, these groups shed valuable light on explaining the outcome of attempts to gain professional social closure in terms of power and interests. However, this does not undermine the neo-Weberian approach any more than the foregoing criticisms, as they relate to its application rather than the utility of the analytical tools provided.

A brief comment here is finally needed on the view of Sciulli (2005) that the neo-Weberian concept of exclusionary social closure is limited mainly to Britain and the United States in the modern world in addressing the relationship between professions and power. Formal professional independence from the state is certainly less common in continental Europe, where professionals in areas such as health and education are largely employed by, and have managerial accountability to, public sector bureaucracies (Evetts 2006). But even here there is great variability – in Germany, for example, professional social closure has been achieved in law in a similar fashion to medicine (Rogowski 1995), paralleling the position of doctors in societies such as Australia, Canada and New Zealand (Allsop and Jones 2008).

Conceptualizing the extent of such closure on a sliding scale, therefore, the neo-Weberian approach remains one of the more potent theoretical frameworks for examining professions and power internationally – from understanding the political forces that lead to the establishment of professional monopolies to charting the privileges that derive from the power generated in the market through professionalization. Having said this, more discussion is needed about the meaning of the concept of power within this frame of reference, including its link to professional interests – not least regarding how such interests are theorized and, even more significantly, how they can be effectively operationalized.

The concepts of power and interests in analysing professionalism

Considerations about power – whether in a neo-Weberian or some other theoretical sense – can essentially be defined in terms of the ability to achieve a desired outcome, which typically includes the capacity to influence others. However, as the analysis of theoretical perspectives in the sociology of professions demonstrates, when the inquirer moves beyond the neo-Weberian notion of power as the realization of the interests of the powerful and the capacity to produce favourable effects in terms of such interests, the universe becomes fuzzier and more contestable – not only as regards studying power conceptually, but also in understanding it empirically (Smith 2009).

The dimensions of power

This is well highlighted by Lukes (2005), who argues that there are three competing dimensions of power. The one-dimensional view of power is based on the well-known analysis by Dahl (1961) of issue areas in a city in the United States in which professions were involved – urban redevelopment, public education and political nominations. In order to assess empirically the exercise of power, Dahl used subjectively expressed views to represent interests and compared these to outcomes to gauge which party or parties prevailed in political decision making. His conclusion from studying observable conflicts of policy preferences was that American society had a pluralistic power structure rather than a system run by one or more dominant elites in professional, corporate or other areas.

However, the positivist approach taken by Dahl was famously considered biased, superficial and restrictive by his critics Bachrach and Baratz (1970). They outlined a two-dimensional conception of power which takes into account that some issues may never be explicitly aired in the first place because of the exercise of power. Their framework therefore does not simply emphasize initiating, deciding and vetoing proposals, on which Dahl focused, but also recognizes that power may be exercised by confining the scope of decision making to relatively safe issues. As such, by adopting a wider concept of interests than Dahl, Bachrach and Baratz encompassed both decision making and non-decision making.

Nonetheless, as Lukes (2005) notes, this approach is also flawed. Its difficulties arise from the fact that, first, it adopts a methodologically individualistic view of power based on the probability of specific participants realizing their wills and, second, it again relies on identifying the exercise of power in observable, overt or covert, conflict. As such, it excludes the possibility of false or manipulated consensuses by definitional fiat – in which potential as well as actual issues are kept out of political debate. The issue here then becomes how interests are to be ascribed on the three-dimensional view of power. Lukes acknowledges that this is not straightforward, but believes that insights can be drawn from considering how people behave in abnormal times when hegemony is removed.

Lukes (2005) is right to highlight the possibility of actors generally and professional groups in particular mistaking their interests and to draw attention to issues of false consciousness in analysing the operation of power. He is also wise to avoid the dangers of simply imputing interests to such actors without empirical reference, as is common in relation to class interests among Marxist writers (see, for instance, Poulantzas 1973). However, his own position in seeking relevant counterfactuals for gauging interests by observing how professional and other groups act when the wider apparatus of power is removed or relaxed is fraught with problems. Even if the influence of other sources of power is ruled out, any inferences will absurdly be drawn philosophically from a barren asocial arena.

Operationalizing the concepts of power and interests

But if Lukes (2005) does not provide a meaningful solution to the dilemmas posed in terms of empirically operationalizing the concepts of power and interests in considering the relationship between professions and power, there is a more incisive way forward. This has been signposted by Saunders (2007), who argues that professional and other interests should be seen as the objective achievement of benefits and the avoidance of costs in given situations, based on such indicators as income, status and power. Significantly, these are central to assessing life chances in a neo-Weberian approach and have become key touchstones within this perspective of the privileges obtained in professional projects.

Saks (1995) has both developed and applied this approach in his detailed neo-Weberian analysis of the response of the medical profession to acupuncture in nineteenth- and twentieth-century Britain. He argues that the interests of doctors were generally advanced in terms of income, status and power by distancing themselves from, and repelling challenges by, non-medically qualified acupuncturists in the professionalization process. However, this situation changed after the 1960s and 1970s counterculture where a developing client voice and rapidly increasing public demand for CAM made its selective medical incorporation a preferable strategy, in a manner avoiding the legitimation of outsiders and sustaining the dominance of the biomedical paradigm of doctors.

The study by Saks (1995) also significantly involved a more systematic approach to evaluating the role of professional self-interests in decision making, in light of the lack of rigour in previous research. To establish this relationship based on the exercise of power, it was also held to be necessary, amongst other things, to show that the decision reached was consistent with the professional interests concerned; that the profession involved possessed sufficient political resources to have influenced the decision under consideration; and that other plausible explanations could be ruled out – in this case, a range of factors from competing medical priorities and the diffusion of knowledge of acupuncture to the power of the drug companies and its safety and effectiveness.

Current issues about professions and power

However, lest the analysis of professions and power moves too far into the realm of methodology within a neo-Weberian approach, it is time to broaden the chapter to highlight a number of mainstream contemporary areas of focus in this field. The issues briefly covered here from a neo-Weberian perspective include the impact of NPM on professions; organizational professionalism and professionals in organizations; the deprofessionalization and restratification of professions; professional dominance and inter-professional working; and the dynamics of professional practitioner–client interaction. Having given an overview of the territory pervaded by the exercise of power, each of these areas will now be considered in turn – with a final commentary on feminist theory about professions and power.

The impact of the new public management on professions

The NPM which has developed at a time of restricted resources and financial stringency in neo-liberal societies with the explicit aim of increasing the efficiency of public services and providing a greater user focus has challenged the power of public service professions in areas such as health, social services and education. Although it has been a less integrated and uniform force than often presented, its introduction has been seen to increase the accountability and control of professional groups in the market, following practices in the private sector (Dent, Chandler and Barry 2004). As such, it has been held to have significantly impacted on these groups, from imparting new cultural values to increasing flexibility.

However, the extent of the impact of NPM on the power of professions has been much debated. Some have argued that professions have largely been able successfully to resist managerial control (Carvalho 2014). Others have claimed that it has led to hybrid professionalism in which the pattern of occupational control contains both managerial and professional strands (Noordegraaf 2007). It has also been asserted that NPM is well advanced in reining in the autonomy of professions in the neo-Weberian sense – causing new types of control over occupations previously seen as obstacles to change (Evetts 2006). Clearly, this remains a matter for empirical examination in particular countries and professional settings, but the ramifications of this debate have spilt over into the discussion of the power of professions in organizations.

Organizational professionalism and professionals in organizations

In this respect, Evetts (2013) has argued that the shifting balance of power has led to a move from occupational professionalism to organizational professionalism. Here occupational professionalism is taken to involve collegial authority based on trust relationships with employers and clients and discretionary judgements. Organizational professionalism, on the other hand, is seen as a discourse of control centred on rational-legal authority used by managers in work organizations, involving standardization and performance management. Whatever their respective virtues, both of these ideal types of professionalism derive from Weber – where organizational professionalism is associated more with the increasing bureaucratization of modern societies than the concept of exclusionary social closure.

Nonetheless, the direction of change claimed by Evetts (2013) can be contested. Faulconbridge and Muzio (2008), for example, argue that the effects of globalization, technology and competition on professionalism in multinational law firms in Britain are moderated by professional values and interests. Similarly, Jonnergård and Erlingsdóttir (2012) discovered that professional strategies are more significant than organizational affiliations in shaping the adoption of quality reforms in medicine in Sweden – in a situation where Svensson and Evetts (2010) note there has been ever greater convergence between models of professionalism in continental Europe and the Anglo-American setting, through more integrated professional work organizations, as well as increasing marketization.

This context may help to account for the increasing political conflicts identified within a neo-Weberian approach at a meso level between professionals and the organizations in which they are employed – with the former expecting to be self-directing and the latter seeking obedience from subordinates (Thompson and McHugh 2009). The degree of organizational conflict in the exercise of power, however, may be reduced where there are legal restrictions on the provision of professional services – as in the case of areas like medicine, law and accountancy in the United States – which Freidson (1994) has noted can offer some protection to the independence of professionals from direct employer control.

The deprofessionalization and restratification of professions

Another related facet of current debates about professions and power is the wider question of whether in neo-Weberian terms professional groups in modern societies have become increasingly deprofessionalized. This viewpoint was classically presented by Braverman (1974) within the neo-Marxist framework of proletarianization. He claimed that skilled professional and other tasks were being fragmented as a result of managerial endeavours to control the labour process and cheapen the cost of wage labour as capitalism developed. Such issues have resurfaced in a neo-Weberian framework in relation to a number of specific professions – not least law and medicine (Epstein 2013).

The question of the deprofessionalization of medicine has been particularly intensively debated in the Anglo-American context. Saks (2015) argues that physicians in the United States – notwithstanding internal stratification within the profession – have suffered a decline in income, status and particularly power in face of the growing corporatization of medicine and the rise of managed care, which has reduced their control of medical decision making. In contrast, in Britain the medical profession has typically been successful in maintaining its privileges through the strong state shelter of the National Health Service – even if government concern about patient protection has recently led to a more regulated rather than autonomous pattern of self-regulation.

However, in Britain in a differentiated profession, the distribution of power has not remained static. More specifically, over the past two or three decades there has been a restratification of the English medical profession, in which the standing of general practitioners has risen compared to the burgeoning number of hospital-based medical specialists – first through an elevated position in Primary Care Groups and Primary Care Trusts and now through their lead roles in Clinical Commissioning Groups (Saks 2015). Agreeing criteria against which deprofessionalization and/or restratification is to be benchmarked for further research into the power and interests of the medical and other professions, though, remains contentious.

Professional dominance and inter-professional working

This spills on to the next main area of focus in the neo-Weberian analysis of power and professionalism – the question of professional dominance, which has been taken to refer not only to the cultural authority of professions in society and their power over users of services but also to the relational aspects of the power base of professional groups (Elston 2004). In the latter respect, in each professionalized field, there is typically one or more top professions in the pecking order, with professional groups further down the line based on 'dual closure'. This term is employed by neo-Weberian writers to define semi-professional groups like teachers and social workers, which contain some elements of exclusionary closure mixed with aspects of usurpationary closure centred on union-style collective action (Parkin 1979).

This is traditionally reflected in the stratified hierarchy in health care in Britain and the United States defined by Turner (1995), with the dominant medical profession at the summit. Closely behind in terms of power come limited health professions such as dentists and optometrists, whose operation is restricted to specific parts of the body. Then follow subordinated health professions such as nurses and the professions allied to medicine, and finally excluded health practitioners like many CAM groups which lie outside orthodox medicine. In sketching out this tiered health-care hierarchy, it is again vital to note – as underlined by the rising power of general practitioners in England outlined above – that the comparative position of each profession is fluid and very far from fixed in the politics of work.

In terms of power and its exercise in the marketplace, the notion of shifting territorial relationships is reinforced in Britain, the United States and continental Europe by Abbott (1988) across a much broader system of professions, from accountancy to law. He sees them as vying with each other for the right to control the provision of services and activities in their interrelated occupational jurisdictions. The concept of such turf wars also brings into focus the obstacles related to silo-based power that impedes inter-professional working. These have increased the importance of examining how to facilitate collaboration between health and social care at all levels in providing effective individualized care for clients (Pollard *et al.* 2010).

The dynamics of professional practitioner–client interaction

This highlights that structures of power at the macro and meso level have implications for the interaction between professional practitioners and clients at the micro level. This is illustrated further by Strong (2001), whose study of over a thousand child health consultations in the Anglo-American context showed that the most prevalent mode of interaction was bureaucratic. Here the interaction was framed by the idealized competence and expertise of doctors, while the concerns of parents – who were assumed to lack knowledge – were subordinated to medical interests, notwithstanding the gentility of the consultation. More recent research has shown this pattern of medical power and authority to prevail generally in such interactions and to be supported by legal rules, despite extensions to patient rights (Le Roux-Kemp 2011).

Moreover, in terms of the growing client voice, it is important to note that professionals can still be prey to using their power in patient management in a less than supportive manner on a one-to-one basis. In law, for instance, Bogoch (1997), writing from a feminist perspective, found patterns of dominance in interactions between lawyers and their clients based on language – including such aspects as the control of discourse, interruptions, topic control, and challenges – which were amplified by a greater pattern of deference among female clients towards male lawyers. In a similar vein in terms of minority groups, medical practitioners have been found to discriminate against 'difficult' patients such as alcoholics and the mentally ill who fall into the category of 'dirty work' (Shaw 2004).

The dynamics of professional practitioner–client interaction underline another key focus in terms of power from a neo-Weberian standpoint – that of inequalities in service delivery and access to services which may be manifested anywhere from the micro to the macro level. Inequalities between social groups have been shown frequently to mirror inequalities of power and position within the professions themselves, not least in health care in Britain and the United States (Saks 2014). This is also exemplified by studies of professional projects in law, teaching and management in Britain by Bolton and Muzio (2008), who discovered patterns of gendered exclusion, segmentation and stratification in these areas.

The latter account is a clear exception to the claim that neo-Weberian studies of the professions are too often gender blind and permeated by masculine visions of such occupations (Davies 1995). In this respect, Witz (1992) classically argued from a feminist perspective that professionalization in medicine and nursing has been a gendered historical process based on the exercise of power by men in a patriarchal society. The need to more explicitly open up the study of professions and power to a feminist lens has more recently been underlined by Kuhlmann and Annandale (2012), who call for greater gender mainstreaming in health care, in which the implications for women of any planned action – whether it be legislation, policies or programmes – are scrutinized such that gender inequality is not perpetuated.

Conclusion

This chapter has now covered much of the central literature on professions and power as they figure in theory and indeed history – encompassing a range of professional groups, countries and issues. As the various sociological contributions considered highlight, both the definition of professions and the concept of power are contested. However, the value of a neo-Weberian approach has been advocated here because – despite some weaknesses in its operationalization – it arguably provides a strong general theoretical framework for the analysis of the relationship between the two. It has therefore been within this perspective that a number of current key issues related to professions and power have been profiled.

Another aspect of professions and power in a political rather than a purely academic sense is the variety of questions that this chapter raises about future policy directions in relation to professional groups in modern societies. These are accentuated within a neo-Weberian perspective by the centrality to professionalism of the achievement of exclusionary social closure, based on successful interest-based lobbying of the state by selected occupational groups. How far, therefore, at a macro level is ongoing state support justified for the privileged position of professions in the market? Or, put another way, to what extent does the power that has made such groups professionalized warrant special underwriting from the state, which is itself subject to many political influences?

Such pragmatic political questions concerning professions and power pertain to each of the different levels of analysis of this area. For instance, in what ways might professionals in interactional contexts be regulated or developed to ensure more sensitive and less disempowering dealings with clients? How far is it defensible for professional expertise to be protected in terms of power within organizational decision making? And how might knowledge of power and interests in the professions be strategically harnessed through informed leadership to advance the public interest in the increasing web of organizational and managerial interests in which they are embroiled in the wider society?

The 'public interest' is, of course, a politicized concept which is even more contested than the notions of professions and power. Indeed, it is easy to come to the view that – given the multiplicity of competing interpretations – rather than trying to define the public interest, it may be simpler to consider it purely as an ideology used to advance the cause of the powerful in debate. Despite the difficulties, though, this argument not only entails relinquishing political responsibility but also testifies to the centrality of the concept of power in understanding privileged groups like professions, who regularly deploy altruistic ideologies in support of their interests and actions in ever-changing modern societies.

References

Abbott, A. (1988) *The System of Professions: An Essay on the Division of Expert Labour*, Chicago, IL: Chicago University Press.

Allsop, J. and Jones, K. (2008) 'Protecting patients: International trends in medical governance', in Kuhlmann, E. and Saks, M. (eds) *Rethinking Professional Governance: International Directions in Health Care*, Bristol, UK: Policy Press.

Bachrach, P. and Baratz, M. (1970) *Power and Poverty: Theory and Practice*, New York: Oxford University Press.

Beattie, A. (1995) 'War and peace among the health tribes', in Soothill, K., Mackay, L. and Webb, C. (eds) *Interprofessional Relations in Health Care*, London: Edward Arnold.

Berlant, J. L. (1975) *Profession and Monopoly: A Study of Medicine in the United States and Great Britain*, Berkeley, CA: University of California Press.

Bogoch, B. (1997) 'Gendered lawyering: Difference and dominance in lawyer-client interaction', *Law and Society Review* 31(4): 677–712.

Bolton, S. and Muzio, D. (2008) 'The paradoxical processes of feminization in the professions: The case of established, aspiring and semi-professions', *Work, Employment and Society* 22(2): 281–299.

Borsay, A. and Hunter, B. (eds) (2012) *Nursing and Midwifery in Britain Since 1700*, Basingstoke, UK: Palgrave Macmillan.

Braverman, H. (1974) *Labour and Monopoly Capital: The Degradation of Work in the Twentieth Century*, New York: Monthly Review Press.

Burrage, M. (2006) *Revolution and the Making of the Contemporary Legal Profession: England, France and the United States*, New York: Oxford University Press.

Carvalho, T. (2014) 'Changing connections between professionalism and managerialism: A case study of nursing in Portugal', *Journal of Professions and Organization* 1(2): 176–190.

Cohen, L., Wilkinson, A., Arnold, J. and Finn, R. (2005) '"Remember I'm the bloody architect!" Architects, organizations and discourses of profession', *Work, Employment and Society* 19(4): 775–796.

Dahl, R. (1961) *Who Governs? Democracy and Power in an American City*, New Haven, CT: Yale University Press.

Davies, C. (1995) 'Competence versus care? Gender and caring work revisited', *Acta Sociologica* 38: 17–31.

Dennis, A. (2005) 'Symbolic interactionism and the concept of power', *British Journal of Sociology* 56(2): 191–213.

Dent, M., Chandler, J. and Barry, J. (eds) (2004) *Questioning the New Public Management*, Aldershot, UK: Ashgate.

Donzelot, J. (1979) *The Policing of Families*, New York: Pantheon.

Ehrenreich, B. and Ehrenreich, J. (1979) 'The professional-managerial class', in Walker, P. (ed.) *Between Capital and Labour*, Brighton: Harvester Press.

Elston, M. A. (2004) 'Medical autonomy and medical dominance', in Gabe, J., Bury, M. and Elston, M. A. (eds) *Key Concepts in Medical Sociology*, London: Sage.

Epstein, R. (2013) 'Big Law and Big Med: The deprofessionalization of legal and medical services', *International Review of Law and Economics* 38: 64–76.

Evetts, J. (2006) 'Short note: The sociology of professional groups', *Current Sociology* 54(1): 133–143.

Evetts, J. (2013) 'Professionalism: Value and ideology', *Current Sociology Review* 61(5–6): 778–796.

Faulconbridge, J. and Muzio, D. (2008) 'Organizational professionalism in globalizing law firms', *Work, Employment and Society* 22(1): 7–25.

Foucault, M. (1978) *Discipline and Punish: The Birth of the Prison*, New York: Random House.

Fournier, V. (1999) 'The appeal to "professionalism" as a disciplinary mechanism', *Social Review* 47(2): 656–673.

Freidson, E. (1994) *Professionalism Reborn: Theory, Prophecy and Policy*, Chicago, IL: University of Chicago Press.

Goode, W. J. (1960) 'Encroachment, charlatanism and the emerging profession: Psychology, sociology and medicine', *American Sociological Review* 25: 902–14.

Graf, E., Sator, M. and Spranz-Fogasy, T. (2014) *Discourses of Helping Professions*, Amsterdam: John Benjamins.

Granfield, R. and Mather, L. (eds) (2009) *Private Lawyers and the Public Interest: The Evolving Role of Pro Bono in the Legal Profession*, New York: Oxford University Press.

Greenwood, E. (1957) 'The attributes of a profession', *Social Work* 2(3): 45–55.

Gubrium, J. and Holstein, J. (2003) 'Analyzing interpretive practice', in Denzin, N. and Lincoln, Y. (eds) *Strategies of Qualitative Inquiry*, Thousand Oaks, CA: Sage.

Halliday, T. C. (1987) *Beyond Monopoly: Lawyers, State Crises, and Professional Empowerment*, Chicago, IL: University of Chicago Press.

Hughes, E. (1963) 'Professions', *Daedalus* 92: 655–668.

Johnson, T. (1972) *Professions and Power*, London: Macmillan.

Johnson, T. (1995) 'Governmentality and the institutionalization of expertise', in Johnson, T., Larkin, G. and Saks, M. (eds) *Health Professions and the State in Europe*, London: Routledge.

Jonnergård, K. and Erlingsdóttir, G. (2012) 'Variations in professions' adoption of quality reforms: The cases of doctors and auditors in Sweden', *Current Sociology* 60(5): 672–689.

Kuhlmann, E. and Annandale, E. (2012) 'Bringing gender to the heart of health policy, practice and research', in Kuhlmann, E. and Annandale, E. (eds) *The Palgrave Handbook of Gender and Healthcare*, Basingstoke, UK: Palgrave Macmillan, 2nd edn.

Le Roux-Kemp, A. (2011) *Law, Power and the Doctor-Patient Relationship*, Saarbrücken: VDM Publishing.

Lukes, S. (2005) *Power: A Radical View*, Basingstoke, UK: Palgrave Macmillan, 2nd edn.

Macdonald, K. (1995) *The Sociology of the Professions*, London: Sage.

Navarro, V. (1986) *Crisis, Health and Medicine: A Social Critique*, London: Tavistock.

Nettleton, S. (1992) *Power, Pain and Dentistry*, Buckingham, UK: Open University Press.

Noordegraaf, M. (2007) 'From "pure" to "hybrid" professionalism: Present-day professionalism in ambiguous public domains', *Administration and Society* 39(6): 761–785.

Parkin, F. (1979) *Marxism and Class Theory: A Bourgeois Critique*, London: Tavistock.

Parsons, T. (1967) *Sociological Theory and Modern Society*, New York: Free Press.

Perucci, R. (1973) 'In the service of man: Radical movements in the professions', in Halmos, P. (ed.) *Professionalization and Social Change*, Sociological Review Monograph No. 20, Keele, UK: University of Keele.

Pollard, K., Thomas, J. and Miers, M. (eds) (2010) *Understanding Interprofessional Working in Health and Social Care: Theory and Practice*, Basingstoke, UK: Palgrave Macmillan.

Poulantzas, N. (1973) *Political Power and Social Classes*, London: New Left Books.

Rogowski, R. (1995) 'German corporate lawyers: Social closure in autopoietic perspective', in Dezalay, Y. and Sugarman, D. (eds) *Professional Competition and Professional Power: Lawyers, Accountants and the Social Construction of Markets*, London: Routledge.

Roszak, T. (1995) *The Making of a Counter Culture*, Berkeley, CA: University of California Press.

Roth, J. (1974) 'Professionalism: The sociologists' decoy', *Work and Occupations* 1: 6–23.

Saks, M. (1995) *Professions and the Public Interest: Medical Power, Altruism and Alternative Medicine*, London: Routledge.

Saks, M. (2008) 'Policy dynamics: Marginal groups in the healthcare division of labour in the UK', in Kuhlmann, E. and Saks, M. (eds) *Rethinking Professional Governance: International Directions in Healthcare*, Bristol, UK: Policy Press.

Saks, M. (2010) 'Analyzing the professions: The case for a neo-Weberian approach', *Comparative Sociology* 9: 887–915.

Saks, M. (2012) 'Defining a profession: The role of knowledge and expertise', *Professions and Professionalism* 2: 1–10.

Saks, M. (2014) 'Professions, marginality and inequalities', *Sociopedia*. Available at: http://www.isa-sociology. org/publ/sociopedia-isa/, last accessed 16 September 2015.

Saks, M. (2015) *The Professions, State and the Market: Medicine in Britain, the United States and Russia*, Abingdon, UK: Routledge.

Saunders, P. (2007) *Urban Politics: A Sociological Interpretation*, Abingdon: Routledge.

Sciulli, D. (2005) 'Continental sociology of professions today: Conceptual contributions', *Current Sociology* 53(6): 915–942.

Shaw, I. (2004) 'Doctors, "dirty work" patients, and "revolving doors"', *Qualitative Health Research* 14(8): 1032–1045.

Smith, M. (2009) *Power and the State*, Basingstoke, UK: Palgrave Macmillan.

Strong, P. (2001) *The Ceremonial Order of the Clinic: Parents, Doctors and Medical Bureaucrats*, Aldershot, UK: Ashgate.

Svensson, L. and Evetts, J. (2010) 'Introduction', in Svensson, L. and Evetts, J. (eds) *Sociology of Professions: Continental and Anglo-Saxon Traditions*, Göteborg: Daidalos.

Thompson, P. and McHugh, D. (2009) *Work Organisations: A Critical Approach*, Basingstoke, UK: Palgrave Macmillan, 4th edn.

Turner, B. (1995) *Medical Power and Social Knowledge*, London: Sage, 2nd edn.

Witz, A. (1992) *Professions and Patriarchy*, London: Routledge.

Part II

Governing the professions and professionalism

Introduction

Ellen Kuhlmann

The relationship between professions and the state and the importance of professionalism as a facilitator of public sector services and societal development have been key issues in the study of professions for many years. More recently, the traditional focus on 'professions and the state' has expanded towards the concept of 'governance'. Governance marks a policy shift from 'government to governance' (Rhodes, 1996) and comprises different sets and operational levels, including the provider organizations of public sector and other services and the actors involved (Newman, 2001). While the professions have always been connected to hierarchical forms of governance like state regulation, the era of new public management (NPM) and new governance has expanded these connections towards new actors and novel forms of professionalism, as, for instance, the emergent connections with management and entrepreneurialism illustrate.

Following from Chapter 2 on 'governance and professions' in Part I of this Companion, this collection of articles now provides in-depth analyses of the various ways the professions and professionalism are connected to governance and how these connections are currently created, re-created and newly defined. Opening the box of the 'professions-and-governance', the first chapter (Viola Burau) in this series of governance research takes a closer look at the embeddedness of the professions in society and their role as policy experts and direct involvement in policymaking processes. The following chapters focus on the different sets of governance, taking into account the operational dimensions of governance and the 'hybridization' processes (Tuohy, 2012) as well as 'governmentality' (Johnson, 1995) and discourse approaches to professionalism.

New emergent forms of governing often use financial incentives to influence the behaviour of professionals (Ruth McDonald & Crawford Spence). Similarly, elements of entrepreneurialism and market-based logics are increasingly gaining currency in public sector services, including the service, delivery and organization of professional groups (Seppo Poutanen and & Anne Kovalainen). These developments illustrate important changes in the professions and the concept of professionalism. New forms of governing may further the importance of the organization as well as the creation of emergent forms of more integrated professionalism. This seems to be a general trend as observed in different countries and professional groups, while the impact may vary between professional groups and organizational contexts. Consequently, the assumption of fundamentally different 'logics' of professionalism (Freidson, 2001) as opposed to other forms of regulation, as well as the view of professions as inevitably driven by self-interest and social closure, are oversimplified and no longer sustainable.

In contrast to the new developments, which show mixed forms of governance and 'hybridization' between the professional self-governing tools and managerial and organizational modes, the remaining two chapters in this part address traditional dimensions of professionalism, namely the importance of trust and formalized knowledge. Trust (Patrick Brown & Michael Calnan) is connected to professionalism in complex ways and 'embodied' by a certain type of professional, such as doctors or nurses. Citizens' trust in the professions and their services comes on the back of more general trust in public policy and functioning in society and, consequently, blatant bureaucratic control does not work as it provokes mistrust in the professional services. Finally, knowledge as the 'currency of competition' (Abbott, 1988) of the professions is the fundament of 'modernity' and the establishment of 'knowledge societies' which enables decision-making procedures based on formalized knowledge, standardization and scientific evidence (see Chapter 10, by Theresa Carvalho & Rui Santiago). The 'making' of knowledge and its bonding to the professions is therefore embedded in new governance models, including, for instance, performance management, evaluations and target-setting based on scientific evidence.

Taken together, the chapters in Part II provide a snapshot of contemporary developments in the professions and reveal how these developments intersect with governance changes. The chapters and the related case studies tell their own stories and use different methodological and empirical approaches and tools, but they all reveal a common trend. The authors illustrate an overall growing relevance of more integrative forms of professionalism and new professional roles and areas of expertise in public sector services and society. This, in turn, calls for theoretical approaches and empirical research that are sensitive to contexts and capable of understanding professions and governance as dynamic, intersecting and malleable relationships.

References

Abbott, A. (1988) *The System of Professions*. Chicago, IL: Chicago University Press.

Freidson, E. (2001) *Professionalism: The Third Logic*. Oxford: Polity Press.

Johnson, T. (1995) Governmentality and the institutionalization of expertise, in T. Johnson, G. Larkin & M. Saks (eds), *Health Professions and the State in Europe*. London: Routledge, pp. 2–14.

Newman, J. (2001) *Modernising Governance*. Bristol, UK: Policy Press.

Rhodes, R. A. W. (1996) The New Governance: Governing without government. *Political Studies*, XLIV, 652–667.

Tuohy, C. H. (2012) Reform and the politics of hybridization in mature health care states. *Journal of Health Politics, Policy and Law*, 37(4), 611–632.

6

Governing through professional experts

Viola Burau

Introduction

Following the neo-Weberian perspective, professions have long been understood as a form of social closure (Freidson, 1970, 2001). At the micro level, professions use highly specialized knowledge as stepping stones for practising with relative autonomy and for dominating the division of labour in their respective fields of work. At the macro level, professions seek to create shelters from both state interventions and market forces. In contrast, this chapter focuses on the societal embeddedness of professions and analyses how professional expertise can be used as a source for governing in contemporary societies. The perspective on embeddedness opens up for study the multiple ways in which professions are connected to society, and vice versa. This includes questions about governing and about the specific processes structuring professional fields, policies and organizations.

As the next section argues, embeddedness is on the rise for a number of reasons. Changes in society, government politics, as well as in science and the professions themselves, highlight the governing potential of professional experts. The remainder of the chapter discusses how to conceptualize this development in theoretical terms and introduces four perspectives: governmentality, welfare governance, organization studies and gender. The governmentality perspective highlights governing through the institutionalization of expertise, how this is predicated on both autonomy and control as well as historically contingent. The welfare-governance perspective draws attention to sector-specific strategies of governing through institutional adaptations that are part of a complex knowledge–power knot, where professions are both agents and under pressure as well as subject to policy and country contingencies. The organization-studies perspective is concerned with governing through the agency of professions in processes of organizational change, where professions pursue their interests in specific organizational contexts. Finally, the gender perspective stresses the salience and ambivalences of governing through professions, where highly gendered contingencies limit the potential for governing.

Why embeddedness?

The underlying argument is that the nature of *both* professions and government has been changing. In relation to the first point, Brint (1994), for example, suggests that professions have moved from being social trustees to being professional experts. As social trustees, the legitimacy of professions is built on a combination of possessing expert knowledge and practising to the greater good of society. As professional experts, professions still draw legitimacy from their knowledge, but only to the extent that knowledge and its underpinning credentials prove their value in relation to organizational functions and market forces (Brint, 1994). The nature of knowledge is more formally than socially important (see Chapter 10 by Carvalho and Santiago).

There are a number of reasons for the greater embeddedness of professions in societies (Brint, 1994). Among others, professions have grown in size and the ensuing internal competition has made professions more fragmented. For example, following the expansion of higher education since the 1960s, stratification among universities has increased. Within the profession of university academics, there are growing divides, for example between elite and rank-and-file academics or between predominantly research and predominantly teaching active academics. This, together with different ways of critiquing professionalism, has weakened the institutions supporting social trustee professionalism, especially its underlying moral fabric.

A prominent example of the weakening moral fabric of professionalism is a number of severe cases of medical malpractice in the UK in the late 1990s, which led to a radical overhaul of the system of professional self-regulation more generally (Fenton & Salter, 2009). Medical performance came to be regulated externally to a greater extent in the form of the government's clinical governance policy and the General Medical Council's revalidation policy. By extension, the perspective of professional expertise raises questions about the political influence of professions and, more specifically, what influence professions enjoy under what circumstances (Brint, 1990). Professional experts thus become an integral part of the question 'who governs?'.

This is also the focus of recent contributions to the science studies literature. Maasen and Weingart (2005), for example, are concerned with the interdependence of the relations between science and politics. They see this as the consequence of a twofold development, whereby science has become more democratic and politics has become more scientific. On the one hand, through the greater availability of information, for example through the internet, scientific knowledge is demystified and also is subject to greater critical scrutiny. Institutionally, one consequence is that user representatives are increasingly included in expert committees, sitting side by side with professional experts. On the other hand, the policy process increasingly draws on expert knowledge to legitimize interests and decisions. One indication of this is the notion of evidence-based policy-making and the use of expert panels.

The interdependent relations between science and the political system give rise to different types of mutual references. Examples of such coupling are: the proliferation of expertise to legitimate political/business decisions; the ubiquity of experts reflecting an increasing specialization of knowledge; the diversity of institutional bases for individual experts well beyond universities; the explicit use of partisan rather than 'objective' knowledge to support specific sets of political/business interests; and the commodification of knowledge whereby expert advice is supplied without demand. Based on the case of interdisciplinary research, Maasen and Lieven (2006) highlight the double-edged nature of the interdependence between science and politics: it strengthens the public accountability of science, but this comes at the price of greater control of science. The concrete measures employed are continuous monitoring and reporting as well as the accomplishment of visible results, which also fit well the overall move towards an audit society (Maasen & Lieven, 2006).

In parallel with the move of seeing professions as embedded in society, the view of the nature of government has also changed. Policy analysis and public administration have traditionally focused on government as an organizationally distinct entity. With reforms of the public sector since the 1980s, the nature of government has been in a state of flux. The reforms have drawn on softer, less openly hierarchical forms of governing and have also to a greater extent included sub-central/supranational levels of governing together with actors from beyond the public sector (Kooiman, 2000; Kazepov, 2010). More recent contributions to the literature thus focus on governance instead of government, which they see as a complex process. Governance spans different levels and, in addition to hierarchy, also draws on other forms of coordination, especially networks but also markets (Bell & Hindmoor, 2007; Dingeldey & Rothgang, 2010; Osborne, 2010).

In relation to the second point, the shift in perspective from government to governance has opened the view for professions and their potential contribution to governing (see Chapter 2 by Kuhlmann *et al.*), especially as mediators between welfare states and citizens (Noordegraaf, 2011). For example, in her study of the modernization of healthcare in Germany, Kuhlmann (2006) critically examines the remaking of professionalism (and especially medical professionals) in the context of the new modes of governing. Similarly, Duyvendak and colleagues (2006) assess how new welfare policies in the Netherlands concerned with contractualization/accountability, managerialism and privatization/marketization offer a springboard for both questioning and redefining the influence of professionals in welfare services. Indeed, from a broader comparative perspective, Kuhlmann and Burau (2008) argue that, in relation to healthcare, the new regulatory tools at the same time increase the control of clinical practice and offer a lever for reasserting medical power.

Professions and governmentality

One way to conceptualize governance through professional experts is the notion of governmentality (Johnson, 1995; Fournier, 1999). This goes back to Foucault's (1979) view of governing as a highly complex activity, or rather set of activities, which encompasses different institutions, procedures, tactics, calculations, forms of knowledge and technologies. Professions are part and parcel of governmentality: they represent the institutionalization of expertise, which in turn is a condition for the exercise of political power. For example, states create professions to respond to specific problems of governing and, as such, professions become part of the formation of states.

For Sweden, Evertsson (2000) shows how the creation of a centrally planned welfare state opened new professional fields for female welfare professions and how the state was quick to establish relationships with occupational groups whose skills appeared to be particularly suitable in the welfare political context. In this process of governing, states depend on professions and their autonomy as much as professions depend on the intervention of the state (Johnson, 1995). In this way, the notion of governmentality offers a deeper understanding of the nature of the independence between states and professions in processes of governing.

While Johnson's perspective is primarily historical, Fournier (1999) more clearly positions professions in the context of contemporary governments. As she explains, liberal government is about both autonomy and control and more specifically about the government of autonomous conduct. Governing concerns the structuring of domains of possibility for action and subjectivity, and in this process governing also constitutes free-willed subjects (Fournier, 1999). The overall legitimacy of this form of governing rests on an argument about working in the name of truth. At the same time, truth claims need to be legitimate and meaningful vis-à-vis those whose lives are governed by such truths.

Expertise offers a specific form of legitimization of such truth claims, and contemporary societies are characterized by the proliferation of expert knowledge. For example, in relation to patient safety reforms in England, Waring (2007, p. 164) argues that the emergence of 'safety science' offers a knowledge base that allows managers to legitimately evaluate clinical performance.

Such forms of knowledge are embedded in professional competences and this helps to further legitimize truth claims (Fournier, 1999). Importantly, competence relates not only to knowledge but also to practice or conduct, and professions have to inscribe themselves in a network of accountability. For example, Pickard (2010) shows that the development of geriatric medicine in the United Kingdom after the Second World War was predicated not only on the availability of new knowledge about the possibilities for treating older people but also on the use of this knowledge for discharging older people from long-stay beds.

In summary, the governmentality perspective sets the focus on governing through the institutionalization of expertise, and on how this is predicated on both autonomy and control. The perspective also stresses the historical contingency of governing arrangements.

Professions and welfare governance

Another way to conceptualize governance through professional expertise is the concept of governance. In comparison to governmentality, the governance perspective has emerged from public administration and accounts for specific strategies of governing. As welfare states are a major area of governance, and as professions play a key role in the definition and delivery of welfare services, the main focus of the literature is on welfare governance. Clarke and Newman (1997) present professions as one of the three building blocks of the governance of the post-war welfare state; the other two are bureaucracy and democratic accountability. This building block is based on a double logic of representation, whereby bureaucracy serves the 'public interest', whereas professions have a focus on the 'public good'. Professionalism is not only an occupational strategy that defines the entry into a profession and negotiates its power but also an organizational strategy (Clarke & Newman, 1997). As such, it shapes how relationships and power in organizations are coordinated. For example, hospitals have traditionally been organized based on medical specialties and this reflects the dominant position of doctors in the health division of labour.

New public management reforms

Clarke and Newman (1997, pp. 63–64) contrast the post-war settlement with new public management (NPM) reforms since the 1980s, whose rhetoric built on a frontal attack on 'professional (welfare) bureaucracies'. The main focus was on the 'fundamental' problems of the existing governing regime, and this offered a stepping stone for presenting the qualities of management. Indeed, this became a recurring discursive figure and, for example, as part of its modernization of the public sector, the New Labour government labelled public sector professions as part of an old-fashioned 'producer monopoly' (Newman, 2001, p. 83).

What are the implications for the role of professions in welfare governance? A linear perspective predicts displacement, or rather subordination, whereby welfare governance comes to be dominated by managers and professionals are marginalized. However, in practice, the picture is more mixed, and Clarke and colleagues (2007) see public sector change as a process of institutional adaptation. This goes hand in hand with strategies of co-option, whereby NPM redefines professional concerns in managerial terms (Clarke & Newman, 1997). For example, over the last decades, reforms of elderly care in the Nordic countries have redefined quality, from quality as care delivered by highly trained professionals to quality as user choice and measurable standards (Dahl & Rasmussen, 2012).

Contemporary welfare governance is more hybrid in nature and professions continue to play an important role, although under different terms. Professions are part of relevant networks, but together with public and other non-public agencies; there is also space for new occupational groups at the same time that the boundaries of established professions are becoming softer (Newman, 2013). For example, Newman (2001) suggests that for welfare professions in the United Kingdom, the management of performance under New Labour included elements of both managerial control and professional self-control. Measuring outputs through performance indicators and specifying process through standards were examples of the former, whereas the growing focus on quality was associated with the latter.

In their comparative study of the management of medical performance in four European countries, Burau and colleagues (2009) also find that professional self-regulation is combined with other forms of governance, especially based on the logic of hierarchy. The assertion of public controls was the main challenge underlying pre-reform arrangements, but the extent to which hierarchy gains in strength and how this affected the overall balance with professional self-regulation varies among countries. In the United Kingdom, the reforms have generated more hierarchy, challenging the parallel regime of professional self-regulation. In Italy, instead, the strengthening of hierarchy is less extensive and, above all, incomplete. The situation is similar in Denmark, except that there hierarchy is complete. The strengthening of hierarchy is also moderate in Germany but coincides with a weakening of professional self-regulation.

The specific constellations of governing arrangements reflect differences in macro-institutional contexts, especially related to the healthcare state and its relative centralization as well as the nature of medical authority. For example, in the United Kingdom, the combination of the entrenched command-and-control healthcare state and highly centralized governing arrangements has given the government extensive governing capacities, and all the new regulatory agencies operate at arm's length from each other as quasi-government bodies.

Also, with a similar healthcare state, Denmark sees the introduction of a national systematic standards-based programme. Yet, following the focus on consensus-finding in the context of highly decentralized governing arrangements, this is a public body, which functions as a coordination hub for public authorities at sub-central and central levels. Similarly, in Germany, subjecting the component parts of the system of joint self-administration to tighter substantive and procedural regulation reflects a healthcare state that has traditionally been more decentralized corporatist. Here, the governing capacities of the state are mainly related to defining (and redefining) the overall framework in which joint self-administration operates; this includes both procedural and substantive issues and is achieved by initiating legislation.

Welfare governance and institutional adaptation

Contemporary welfare governance puts professional knowledge into new contexts, where professions are both agents and under pressure. Conceptually, Clarke and colleagues (2007; also Newman, 2013) present the idea of the knowledge–power knot to capture more fully the complex position of professions in welfare governance. Welfare governance is a process of institutional adaptation, interpretation and translation; this is shaped by a set of interdependent dynamics, which can be thought of as the four corners of a diamond. The two axes represent the main forces in public services, which originate from the relations between government and the public and from the relations between professions and organizations respectively.

The specific accommodations between the four corners are highly context dependent (Newman, 2013), but are variations arising from the following interplay: 'the public places new expectations, government makes new demands, organizations tighten managerial logics, occupations become more uncertain' (Newman, 2013, p. 45). For example, Harrison (2002, p. 465) argues that changes in health policy in England since the late 1990s have led to the emergence of 'scientific-bureaucratic medicine'. This was a response to a variety of pressures: the inherent element of control corresponded very well to the heightened managerial ambitions of the government developed as part of NPM reforms since the 1980s, as well as to the quasi-market structures of the healthcare service; and control further addressed the concerns of the public following high-profile cases of medical malpractice, which also left the medical profession with considerable uncertainty about the system of professional self-regulation.

The welfare governance perspective draws attention to sector-specific strategies of governing through institutional adaptation that are part of a complex knowledge–power knot, where professions are both agents and under pressure as well as subject to policy and country contingencies.

Professions and organizational studies

The previous two perspectives have in common that they focus on the macro level of governing and examine the role of professions in this process. In contrast, the literature on organization studies of professions has the meso level of organizations as its starting point and analyses how professions contribute to maintaining and changing organizations (Muzio & Kirkpatrick, 2011; see also Chapters 11 to 15 in Part III of this Companion). This perspective is particularly relevant as NPM reforms draw on softer, non-hierarchical as well as decentralized forms of governing (Kazepov, 2010; Kuhlmann & Burau, 2015). Organizations have thus become important arenas for governing; indeed, they are increasingly conceived as policy instruments to bring about change and improvements in the public sector.

Professions and change

Like the literatures on governmentality and welfare governance, interdependence is also a central concern of the organizational-studies perspective. This builds on a view of organizations as interrelated systems of professions (Kirkpatrick & Ackroyd, 2003). For example, Kirkpatrick and colleagues (2011) suggest that the formal health division of labour is shaped by both the projects of professions and the rational design of managers. In this respect, management itself has become an increasingly contested issue and the central question is who controls management and in what ways; as discussed in more detail below, professions have become more management-minded (Noordegraaf, 2011). At the level of actors, professions emerge as agents of organizational change as much as organizations offer a platform for professional development (Muzio & Kirkpatrick, 2011). Numerato and colleagues (2012) illustrate this in their discussion of co-optation of healthcare management by doctors: management first and foremost involves doctors who employ a complex set of tactics. This process does both: it secures centrally and managerially defined goals, and it allows sufficient leeway to reinforce medical professionalism.

Within this body of literature, there are different types of research. One set of studies analyses the changing role and nature of professions in the dynamics of organizations. For example, Muzio and colleagues (2013; similarly Suddaby & Viale, 2011) take processes of institutionalization as their starting point and thereby highlight the broader role of professions in constructing, organizing and ordering social life. Following on from this, changes in professional projects naturally have repercussions in the organizational fields where professions work and indeed can lead to endogenous organizational change (Suddaby & Viale, 2011, p. 425).

Institutionalization thus offers a switchboard for the development of both organizations and professions, and from this switchboard professions emerge as key agents of institutional change. This encompasses a range of roles (Scott, 2008): cultural-cognitive agents, who offer conceptual tools to define issues; normative agents, who provide norms, standards and principles to guide human action; and regulative agents, who take part in the formulation, implementation and interpretation of rules and regulations. Further, Suddaby and Viale (2011) identify the different strategies professions employ when acting as institutional agents. This may include: opening up new spaces for the expertise of professions; populating existing organizational spaces with new actors; and redrawing boundaries and rules governing a specific organizational field.

In contrast, Noordegraaf (2007) examines the relations between organizations and professions through the notion of hybridity. This describes a situation where professions are not merely embedded in organizational contexts but deeply connected to organizations. More specifically, contemporary professionalism encompasses different approaches to governing, drawing on managerial, market as well as professional logics. This allows for diverse roles in the maintenance and change of organizations. A powerful example is the ambivalent role of epidemiological knowledge, which at the same time is rooted in and can strengthen the logic of professionalism, and can be connected to the logic of management and be used as a means of external control (Numerato et al., 2012). At the level of actors, this may be reflected in the emergence of manager professionals and professional managers, who in their practice navigate between those different logics of governance, and who thereby connect professional practice and organizational actions in new ways.

Noordegraaf (2011) further specifies the role of professions in organizations by introducing the notion of organized professionalism. Here management-minded professionals become engaged in managing multiplicity by making connections to broader organizational, economic or political demands. The task of organizing professional work is increasingly managerial in nature as it has to address external changes relating to working conditions, multi-professionalism and new risks. This is underlined by Waring and Currie (2009) in their case study of knowledge management of medical doctors in the United Kingdom. The authors find that managerial expertise can in fact become detached from managers as persons/roles and instead can become part of professional practice. At one level, this helps to maintain professional autonomy, while at another level, it makes professional practice and identities increasingly managerial.

Postma and colleagues (2014) further expand on the concept of organized professionalism. Based on a case study of neighbourhood nurses in the Netherlands, the authors argue that organizing work does not necessarily always come from above. Instead, organizing work can be an intrinsic part of professional practice, but which has received a new meaning in the face of changes in organizational conditions and policies. This is what the authors call 'articulation work' (Postma et al., 2014, p. 61).

Interplay between professions and organizations

Another set of studies takes one step back and explores what determines the specific interplay between professions and organizations. Comparisons across different professions or countries typically highlight variations and at the same time offer a lever for analysing the contexts which help account for the very same variations. For example, Kirkpatrick and colleagues (2009) compare relations between doctors and managers in Denmark and England. The authors suggest that the specific stratifications emerging in hospitals reflect different legacies of state–professions relations, which in turn shape the collective strategies of doctors and their willingness to engage with management at the level of organizations.

Similarly, in a study of hospital governance in six European countries, Kuhlmann and colleagues (2013) identify three patterns of control which exhibit different degrees of integration. The differences relate not only to organizational but also to macro-level contexts, namely the governance structures of hospitals and the institutional characteristics of healthcare states respectively.

In summary, the organization-studies perspective is concerned with governing through the agency of professions in processes of organizational change, where professions pursue their interests in specific organizational contexts.

Professions and gender

Governing through experts builds on embeddedness, but it does not stop with governmentality, welfare governance and organizations. Instead, embeddedness also includes society at large and the gendered structures of society. In fact, as the literature on welfare service professions suggests, governing through gender is highly salient and, as such, also highlights the ambivalences of governing through professional experts.

The traditionally gendered nature of many occupational fields has meant that women-dominated welfare professions like social workers, nurses and midwives have been a prime leverage point for governing, for example in connection with the building of the welfare state. This particularly applies to the universalistic (welfare) states in Nordic countries, where states have been proactive in creating extensive educational opportunities, public sector jobs and work-related social rights (Evertsson, 2000). As a result, welfare service professions enjoy a strong position in these countries. Nevertheless, in other countries, the state also plays an important role as potential ally, enabling and actively supporting professional projects of welfare service professions (Henriksson *et al.*, 2006). For example, Sandall *et al.* (2001) examine the changing occupational role and status in the social structure of healthcare in four countries and conclude that states are central to supporting and protecting the jurisdictional claims of midwives. The specific stance the state adopts vis-à-vis welfare service professions reflects broader political and cultural systems that affect women's caring work (Benoit & Heitlinger, 1998).

However, the (historically) tight relationship with the state and its governing activities also means that welfare service professions became more closely tied to government agendas. For example, in relation to Finland, Henriksson *et al.* (2006) suggest that the marketization of welfare services from the 1990s onwards has resulted in a substantial weakening of the welfare service arenas and the scope of professional projects. Similarly, in their comparison of the impact of neoliberalism on maternity services in Australia and Canada, Benoit and colleagues (2010, p. 480) find that 'state concepts of market relations contribute to commodifying labour and birth through initiatives that maintain an obstetrical monopoly over childbearing, enhancing rather than presenting alternatives to medical dominance'.

These examples are potentially problematic as governing through professional experts more or less explicitly builds on some degree of congruence of interests and corresponding projects. A sustained disconnect between the two parties is likely to lead to conflict and undermine the sustainability of governing arrangements in the long term. Hence, the crucial question is to what extent welfare service professions and professions more broadly can take advantage of policy reforms. This ability is likely to be contingent and therefore vary considerably.

Conclusion

The notion of professional experts as introduced by Brint (1994) sets focus on the deep-seated embeddedness of professions in society, and professions move centre stage concerning questions about the 'who' and the 'how' of governance. As the science-studies literature emphasizes, knowledge emerges as an important switchboard in such processes, whereby science is becoming more politicized in as much as politics is becoming more scientific. Changes in governments and politics help to further sustain this development, as they involve a greater openness to new ways of governing and the multiple roles professions can play in this.

However, the four theoretical perspectives introduced in this chapter define the embeddedness of professions in different ways. The literature on governmentality focuses on the macro level and conceptualizes embeddedness as the institutionalization of expertise, whereby professions become a condition for governing. The literature on welfare governance also remains at the macro level, but has a more sector-specific focus; it conceives embeddedness through processes of institutional adaptation, interpretation and translation, which places professions in a complex knowledge–power knot. In contrast to the first two, the literature on organizational studies is concerned with the meso level and sees embeddedness in the agency of professions in processes of organizational change. The literature on gender in relation to welfare service professions spans across macro and meso levels and stresses the salience of embeddedness and its ambivalences.

Embeddedness represents the basic infrastructure for governing through professional experts, but this raises questions about the relative potential of this form of governing. Here all four theoretical perspectives stress that the ability to govern is closely related to the existence of professional opportunities. The literature on governmentality argues that governing is predicated on both professional control and autonomy. In a similar way, governing within the frame of the knowledge–power knot introduced by the literature on welfare governance puts professions under pressure and also involves them as agents. As the literature on organizational studies emphasizes, organizational change occurs through professions pursuing professional development. The literature on gender in relation to welfare service professions confirms this but also highlights the limits of this potential.

In summary, the literature suggests there is considerable potential for governance through professional experts. At the same time, the four bodies of literature agree that this governing potential is highly contingent. The literature on governmentality highlights historical contingencies and in particular the specific characteristics of liberal government. The literature on welfare governance points to policy-related contingencies as well as contingencies related to the system-level differences across countries. The main focus of the literature on organization studies is on contingencies related to different organizational contexts, while the literature on welfare service professions stresses the highly gendered nature of such contingencies. Importantly, contingencies make it more difficult to predict the specific governing potential, but they do not necessarily undermine the potential to govern through professional experts.

In terms of future research, it is therefore important to set more explicit focus on the potential of governing through professional experts and to use the full range of available conceptual perspectives.

References

Bell, S. and A. Hindmoor (2007) *Rethinking governance: The centrality of the state in modern society*. Cambridge: Cambridge University Press.

Benoit, C. and A. Heitlinger (1998) 'Women's health care work in comparative perspective: Canada, Sweden and Czechoslovakia/Czech Republic as case examples'. *Social Science & Medicine*, 47 (8), pp. 1101–1011.

Benoit, C., M. Zadoroznyi, H. Hallgrimsdottir, A. Treloar and K. Taylor (2010) 'Medical dominance and neoliberalisation in maternal care provision: The evidence from Canada and Australia'. *Social Science & Medicine*, 71(3), pp. 475–481.

Brint, S. (1990) 'Rethinking the policy influence of experts: from general characterizations to analysis of variation'. *Sociological Forum*, 5(3), pp. 361–385.

Brint, S. (1994) *In an age of experts: The changing role of professionals in politics and public life*. Princeton, NJ: Princeton University Press.

Burau, V., D. Wilsford and G. France (2009) 'Reforming medical governance in Europe: What is it about institutions?'. *Health Economics, Policy and Law*, 4(3), pp. 265–282.

Clarke, J. and J. Newman (1997) *The managerial state: Power, politics and ideology in the remaking of social welfare*. London: Sage.

Clarke, J., J. Newman and N. Smith (2007) *Changing publics and changing public services*. London: Sage.

Dahl, H. M. and B. Rasmussen (2012) 'Paradoxes in elderly care: The Nordic model'. In A. Kamp and H. Hvid (eds), *Elderly care in transition: Management, meaning and identity work*, pp. 29–49. Copenhagen: Copenhagen Business School Press.

Dingeldey, I. and H. Rothgang (eds) (2010) *Governance of welfare state reform: A cross national and cross sectoral comparison of policy and politics*. Cheltenham: Edward Elgar.

Duyvendak, J. W., T. Knijn and M. Kremer (eds) (2006) *Policy, people, and the new professional: De-professionalisation and re-professionalisation in care and welfare*. Amsterdam: Amsterdam University Press.

Evertsson, L. (2000) 'The Swedish welfare state and the emergence of female welfare state occupations'. *Gender, Work and Organization*, 7(4), pp. 230–241.

Fenton, L. and B. Salter (2009) 'Competition and compromise in negotiating the new governance of medical performance: The clinical governance and revalidation policies in the UK'. *Health Economics, Policy and Law*, 4(3), pp. 283–303.

Foucault, M. (1979) 'On governmentality'. *Ideology and Consciousness*, 6, pp. 5–22.

Fournier, V. (1999) 'The appeal to "professionalism" as a disciplinary logic'. *Sociological Review*, 47(2), pp. 281–307.

Freidson, E. (1970) *Profession of medicine: A study of the sociology of applied knowledge*. New York: Dodd, Mead.

Freidson, E. (2001) *Professionalism: The third logic*. Chicago, IL: University of Chicago Press.

Harrison, S. (2002) 'New Labour, modernisation and the medical labour process'. *Journal of Social Policy*, 31, pp. 465–485.

Henriksson, L. S. Wrede and V. Burau (2006) 'Understanding professional projects in welfare service work: Revival of old professionalism?'. *Gender, Work and Organization*, 13(2), pp. 174–192.

Johnson, T. (1995) 'Governmentality and the institutionalization of expertise'. In T. Johnson, G. Larkin and M. Saks (eds), *Health professions and the state in Europe*, pp. 7–24. London: Routledge.

Kazepov, Y. (2010) 'Rescaling social policies towards multi-level governance in Europe: some reflections on processes at stake and actors involved'. In Y. Kazepov (ed.), *Rescaling social policies: Towards multilevel governance in Europe*, pp. 35–72. Aldershot: Ashgate.

Kirkpatrick, I. and S. Ackroyd (2003) 'Archetype theory and the changing professional organization: A critique and alternative'. *Organization*, 10(4), pp. 731–750.

Kirkpatrick, I., P. K. Jespersen, M. Dent and I. Neogy (2009) 'Medicine and management in a comparative perspective: The case of Denmark and England'. *Sociology of Health and Illness*, 31(5), pp. 642–658.

Kirkpatrick, I., M. Dent and P. K. Jespersen (2011) 'The contested terrain of hospital management: Professional projects and healthcare reforms in Denmark'. *Current Sociology*, 59(4), pp. 489–506.

Kooiman, J. (2000) 'Societal governance: levels, models and order of social-political interaction'. In. J. Pierre (ed.), *Debating governance: Authority, steering, and democracy*, pp. 138–164. Oxford: Oxford University Press.

Kuhlmann, E. (2006) *Modernising health care: Reinventing professions, the state and the public*. Bristol: Policy Press.

Kuhlmann, E. and V. Burau (2008) 'The "healthcare state" in transition: national and international contexts of changing professional governance'. *European Societies*, 10(4), pp. 619–634.

Kuhlmann, E. and V. Burau (2015) '"Soft governance" and the knowledge-bonds in professionalism: Case studies from the healthcare sector in Germany'. In E. Pavolini and T. Klenk (eds), *Restructuring welfare governance: Marketization, managerialism, and welfare state professionalism*. Cheltenham: Edward Elgar.

Kuhlmann, E., V. Burau, T. Correia, R. Lewandowski, C. Lionis, M. Noordegraaf and J. Repullo (2013) 'A manager in the minds of doctors: A comparison of new modes of control in European hospitals'. *BMC Health Services Research*, 13, p. 246.

Maasen, S. and O. Lieven (2006) 'Transdisciplinarity: A new mode of governing science'. *Science and Public Policy*, 33(6), pp. 399–410.

Maasen, S. and P. Weingart (2005) 'What's new in scientific advice to politics?'. In S. Maasen and P. Weingart (eds), *Democratization of expertise? Exploring novel forms of scientific advice in political decision-making*, pp. 1–19. Dordrecht/London: Springer.

Muzio, D. and I. Kirkpatrick (2011) 'Introduction: professions and organizations – a conceptual framework'. *Current Sociology*, 59(4), pp. 389–405.

Muzio, D., D. Brock and R. Suddaby (2013) 'Professions and institutional change: Towards an institutionalist sociology of the professions'. *Journal of Management Studies*, 50(5), pp. 699–721.

Newman, J. (2001) *Modernising governance: New Labour, policy and society*. London: Sage.

Newman, J. (2013) 'Professionals, power and the reform of public services'. In M. Noordegraaf and B. Steijn (eds), *Professions under pressure: The reconfiguration of professional work in changing public services*, pp. 41–54. Amsterdam: Amsterdam University Press.

Noordegraaf, M. (2007) 'From "pure" to "hybrid" professionalism: Present-day professionalism in ambiguous public domains'. *Administration and Society*, 39(6), pp. 761–785.

Noordegraaf, M. (2011) 'Risky business: how professionals and professional fields (must) deal with organizational fields'. *Organization Studies*, 32, pp. 1349–1371.

Numerato, D., D. Salvatore and G. Fattore (2012) 'The impact of management on medical professionalism: A review'. *Sociology of Health & Illness*, 34(4), pp. 626–644.

Osborne, S. P. (2010) 'The (new) public governance: a suitable case for treatment?'. In S. P. Osborne (ed.), *The new public governance: Emerging perspectives on theory and practice of public governance*, pp. 1–16. London: Routledge.

Pickard, S. (2010) 'The role of governmentality in the establishment, maintenance and demise of professional jurisdictions: The case of geriatric medicine'. *Sociology of Health & Illness*, 32(7), pp. 1072–1086.

Postma, J., L. Oldenhof and K. Putters (2014) 'Organized professionalism in healthcare: Articulation work by neighbourhood nurses'. *Journal of Professions and Organization*, 1(2), pp. 61–77.

Sandall, J., I. L. Bourgeault, W. J. Meijer and B. A. Schüecking (2001) 'Deciding who cares: winners and losers in the late twentieth century'. In R. De Vries, C. Benoit, E. R. van Tejlingen and S. Wrede (eds), *Birth by design: Pregnancy, maternity care, and midwifery in North America and Europe*, pp. 117–138. New York: Routledge.

Scott, W. R. (2008) 'Lords of the dance: Professions as institutional agents'. *Organization Studies*, 29, pp. 219–238.

Suddaby, R. and T. Viale (2011) 'Professions and field-level change: Institutional work and the professional project'. *Current Sociology*, 59(4), pp. 423–442.

Waring, J. (2007) 'Adaptive regulation and governmentality: Patient safety and the changing regulation of medicine'. *Sociology of Health & Illness*, 29(2), pp. 163–179.

Waring, J. and G. Currie (2009) 'Managing expert knowledge: Organizational challenges and managerial futures for the UK medical profession'. *Organization Studies*, 30(7), pp. 755–778.

7

Professions and financial incentives

Ruth McDonald and Crawford Spence

Introduction

Early social scientific accounts of occupations described characteristics or traits which defined them as professions (Macdonald, 1995). These included the existence of a code of professional conduct and a professional organization, as well as service for the public good (Millerson, 1964). More critical sociologists working within Marxian and Weberian traditions have for many years argued that professional groups put their own interests before those of the wider society (Saks, 1995).

However, such accounts tend to view interests in rather simple terms (Swedberg, 2005). For example, Alford's (1975) conceptualization of the medical profession as a dominant structural interest in healthcare systems tends to assume that these 'interests' are determined according to the structure of social, economic and political institutions that exist at any given time. It also places a heavy emphasis on the importance of financial 'interests'. This might imply that changing behaviour is best achieved by manipulating the financial incentives professionals face. In a range of settings, financial incentives are increasingly being used as part of an attempt to influence professional behaviour.

In this chapter we examine how the financial incentives faced by professionals in the fields of medicine and accountancy impact on their behaviour. These professions are very different. Medicine has traditionally been seen as a vocation and doctors are expected to exercise altruism when discharging their duties. In contrast, accountancy has been described as abandoning its social or public good orientation and replacing it with a narrow 'keep the client happy' commercial one (Hanlon, 1994). As we discuss below, however, both groups of professionals face financial incentives which attempt to influence their behaviour. We suggest that these are powerful influences in helping to reconfigure professional fields.

The changing context of professionalism

Professionalism has traditionally been seen as a means of organizing and controlling group members that contrasts with other hierarchical and bureaucratic forms of control (Macdonald, 1995). This means that professionals are self-regulating and enjoy a degree of autonomy which is not available to members of other occupational groups. Professional ethics are overseen by the professionals' own institutions and associations, in the context of collegial, rather than hierarchical, relationships between practitioners. Linked to this, professionals are trusted to exercise judgement in the best interests of the client.

The context in which professionals work has, however, seen much change in recent years. We have witnessed a shift away from trusting professionals towards holding them to account against measurable criteria. Giddens views trust in professional experts as an essential component of modernity, yet '[w]idespread lay knowledge of the modern risk environment leads to the awareness of the limits of expertise' (Giddens, 1990, p. 130; see also Chapter 9 by Brown and Calnan). In the context of a 'risk society', various commentators identify trust in professionals as declining. Beck (1992) asserts that an increasing public awareness of risk and uncertainty has been accompanied by a loss of faith in experts. Despite this trend, the medical profession has largely escaped the sort of critical public scrutiny experienced by other professions. For Beck, the '*internal definition-making power of medical practice*' (Beck, 1992, p. 208, emphasis in the original) means that it can counter criticism from external sources by the creation of new social facts.

In addition to the shifting views of society, the organizational context in which professionals work is changing. The emphasis on collegiality amongst peers embodied by the traditional model of professionalism suggests equality amongst professional group members in terms of probity and competence. Yet, writing about the medical profession, Freidson (1985) identified a process of 'stratification' which involved an administrative elite guiding and evaluating the performance of professionals against standards developed by a knowledge elite (Freidson, 1985, p. 22). According to Freidson, this process enabled elites to exert control over members of the profession whilst helping maintain medicine's position of pre-eminence. This ensured the continued dominance of the medical model and the profession's ability to determine its own fate (Freidson, 1985).

The developments Freidson outlined were seen as enabling the profession to resist attempts at control from outside. More recently, however, the autonomy of professionals has come under increasing challenge from a range of sources such as clients and/or third-party payers, as well as managers within their organizations. Evetts (2005) identifies: 'an ideal-type organizational professionalism' which

> is a discourse of control used increasingly by managers in work organizations. It incorporates rational-legal forms of authority and hierarchical structures of responsibility and decision-making. It involves the increased standardization of work procedures and practices and managerialist controls. It relies on externalized forms of regulation and accountability measures such as target-setting and performance review.
>
> *(Evetts, 2005, p. 9)*

Such processes are likely to have a significant impact on professional behaviour. Grey (1994), writing in the context of the accountancy profession in the UK, suggests that the pursuit of career, which involves, amongst other things, conformity to organizational expectations and assessment via performance review, has implications for the way professionals behave. He describes how work, for some people, is important:

> not just for those reasons of collegiate identification highlighted by the sociology of the professions ... Instead, work is a part of the entrepreneurial project of the self ... a process of the achievement of self through work which is offered within organisations as career and which is expressed by individuals through career.
>
> *(Grey, 1994, p. 482)*

Career is both controlling and benevolent, since conformity to organizational expectations will help individuals achieve their potential. The process Grey describes resonates with writings from the sociology of professions, however, since notions of the appropriate self are formulated as part of socialization processes which inculcate norms and clarify expectations about appropriate forms of selfhood.

Financial incentives

Grey does not use the phrase financial incentives, but they are implied, since the financial rewards that career progression brings are likely to be an important part of the process he describes. For the purposes of this chapter, we define an incentive as something that is intended to encourage people to do something. Increasingly, in recent years, there has been a tendency to treat incentives more explicitly. These attempts to influence professional behaviour reflect a general trend away from placing implicit trust in individuals and organizations to carry out their duties towards actively influencing their performance (Harrison and Smith, 2003). Whilst individuals may respond to financial incentives in the short run, they may be negative reinforcers in the long run, since they may conflict with intrinsic motivation – the individual's desire to perform a task for its own sake. This is because they signal to the individual that they are not trusted to perform in the absence of inducements (Frey, 1997).

Much of the literature on financial incentives is informed by economics and cognitive psychology. However, these approaches tend to downplay or ignore the concept of a shared professional identity, with associated norms and behaviours. Moving to a more social (as opposed to atomistic individual) perspective provides some insights into the contextual issues which influence behaviour (McDonald, 2015). Furthermore, features of the wider system in which professionals work may have an impact as well. Reforms in the wider context (as opposed to immediate organizational factors) may threaten worker motivation and behaviour if they embody values that are antithetical to those on the receiving end.

Literature from the sociology of the professions draws our attention to the fact that professional groupings exhibit shared norms and behaviours. The introduction of measures to increase professional accountability and enforce formal standards, even if they are linked to financial rewards, may clash with the desire for professional autonomy (McDonald et al., 2010). In the following sections, we explore the impact of financial incentives in the context of medicine and accountancy.

Asking 'what impact do incentives have on professionals?' is likely to result in the answer 'it depends on the context'. We choose two contexts – English primary medical care and accountants, and the empirical material reported on here is drawn from two large studies. The research examining medical professionals involved interviews with general practitioners working in England. The accountancy material is from a study into the 'Big 4' accounting firms and involved interviews with accountants in England and Canada.

Whilst primary medical care and accountancy are very different, the context is similar in some respects. Traditionally, accountants and English primary care doctors have worked in partnership arrangements. However, as we illustrate in what follows, this context is changing. Accountants and doctors face increasingly challenging and turbulent environments. This includes greater emphasis on competition and choice, clients who are becoming increasingly challenging and the professionalization of management (Brock et al., 1999). The neat distinction between traditional bureaucracy and professional modes of organizing no longer reflects the changing context in which professionals work. The incentive structures faced by professionals contribute to this process of change as we explain in what follows.

Medical professionals and financial incentives: the case of English primary care

As various commentators have noted, the autonomy of medical professionals has been increasingly challenged in recent decades (Kirkpatrick *et al.*, 2005; McKinlay and Marceau, 2008). As part of this process, third-party payers in health systems internationally have placed emphasis on standardized treatment protocols that codify knowledge and reduce discretion. More recently, a proliferation of policy initiatives has sought to link financial rewards to performance (McDonald *et al.*, 2010; McDonald, 2015).

In England, primary care doctors are general practitioners (GPs), who have traditionally been independent contractors to the National Health Service (NHS). The national GP contract is the result of a negotiated process involving representatives of both the GP profession and the state. However, in 1990, a new contract, which contained a handful of performance targets, was imposed on the profession despite its opposition. This opposition has been interpreted as a rejection of the 'contract state' and related market reforms pursued by the then Conservative Thatcher government (Lewis, 1998).

The election of a Labour Government in 1997 signalled the start of a new era in health policy. In 2000, the NHS Plan (Department of Health, 2000) outlined various policy objectives aimed at modernizing primary care. These included increased emphasis on performance-based rewards. The view that the existing general medical services (GMS) contract was outdated and inflexible was shared by the medical profession as well as the state in a context of poor morale in general practice, long hours and low pay relative to hospital doctors, difficulties in recruiting GPs and poor work–life balance (National Audit Office, 2008).

A new contract came into effect in April 2004. A prominent element of this, the Quality and Outcomes Framework (QOF), comprised 146 indicators of quality of care. Since then, a large percentage of practice income has been dependent on achieving these targets. The QOF includes the concept of exception reporting. This allows practices to exclude patients from performance calculations where, for example, patients do not attend for review, or where a medication cannot be prescribed due to a contraindication or side effect. The contract reforms also offered GPs the ability to opt out of the responsibility for providing care 'out of hours' (OOH) and resulted in significant increases in income for GP partnerships (Batty, 2003). These factors may explain why, unlike in 1990, most GPs in 2003 voted in favour of the new GMS contract in a national ballot. As part of the process of reform, substantial investment in primary care was planned (National Audit Office, 2008).

In line with its intention to increase competition amongst healthcare providers, the government introduced policies to promote patient choice and to allow money to follow patients to providers of their choice. Practice-based commissioning (PBC), was intended to be a key enabler of patient choice (Department of Health, 2004). Under PBC, practices or (more commonly) groups of practices were provided with an 'indicative budget' for commissioning secondary care (hospital) services. The intention was that GP commissioners would identify a variety of different providers for their patients and increase the choices on offer by directly providing or commissioning new services themselves. In addition, PBC was intended to control, and ultimately reduce, the overall rate of GP referrals to hospitals. As part of the process aimed at opening up the market in healthcare for NHS patients, the reforms gave GPs a new role as commissioners of care. In this role they could choose to commission care from private-sector providers of secondary care services, although this might compromise their commitment to 'the NHS ethos'.

The reforms also allowed private-sector providers of primary care to enter the market and enabled existing GP partnerships to compete with these providers. The reforms also created a strong financial incentive to remain within budget. In the context of rising demand and costs, the implications were that GPs should reduce the volume of referrals to hospital and/or prescription medication.

In 2006, Primary Care Trusts (PCTs) in England, who commission primary care services from local general medical practices, were given new powers to negotiate contracts with commercial companies (APMS or Alternative Providers of Medical Services contracts) and employ GPs directly (PCT Medical Services contracts) (Heins *et al.*, 2009). These reforms were also expected to help PCTs shift from being passive payers to active commissioners of primary care and to encourage more competition in primary care provision.

The medical case study is based on a large study undertaken between 2007 and 2010, which involved interviewing English primary care doctors to explore their experiences of financial incentives (McDonald *et al.*, 2010). Quotes are from doctors, unless otherwise indicated.

Quality targets and changes in practice

Doctors interviewed for the study were very aware of the QOF targets against which their performance was measured and were generally supportive of the target regime. Practice team members were very conscious of targets and reported processes for monitoring performance levels on an ongoing basis, taking remedial action where necessary. In common with McDonald *et al.* (2007), we found evidence of new strata emerging within practices, with groups of staff 'chasing' other members of the practice team. Clinicians, for the most part, did not object to this scrutiny and monitoring. Often non-doctors, such as practice managers and nurses, were involved in this process of 'chasing' too. Over time, many clinicians adapted, with the result that they no longer needed 'chasing'. One practice manager described approaching individuals on an ongoing basis, but this process was no longer necessary 'because everybody knows what they're doing' (ID141 Practice Manager). Doctors were very aware of the surveillance process, feeling 'quite managed and watched… don't feel like you do have a completely free rein'. (ID216), as one doctor described it.

All of the doctors described positive benefits flowing from QOF, but often the suggestion was made that the potential benefits lay in improving standards in other, deficient, practices.

> Where I was working before I was with this single-handed guy, when QOF first came in. His QOF scores were quite good, but it was just a load of rubbish because he was making them up. He was making up blood pressures.
>
> *(ID19)*

Although, as the above quote implies, they also suggested that high scores in some deficient practices were the result of dubious activities. This willingness and enthusiasm for challenging poor performance in other practices is something to which we return below.

As part of the process of reorganizing care delivery in response to the reforms, there was an increasing trend towards devolving work to nurses who were practice employees. The partners received a large pay rise during the first three years of the QOF (National Audit Office, 2008). The influx of new money created incentives to limit the number of partners in the organisation since profits are shared between partners. This resulted in a trend towards recruiting salaried doctors. In some cases, these were additional staff, but in others, when partners left, they were replaced by salaried GPs. This created a hierarchy within the practice and led to resentment from some salaried GPs. They complained of being paid less and given more of the additional work, such as home visits, compared with partners.

Whilst some salaried GPs felt that they were treated as second class compared to partners, some partners also suggested that salaried doctors were not committed to their work. There was a suggestion that partners worked harder and gave additional effort in ways that salaried doctors would not.

In a context where partnerships were in limited supply, some salaried GPs felt they had no exit options, despite their frustrations. For others, working hard, despite feeling unfairly treated, was seen as a requirement to be offered a partnership in one's existing practice. There were also frustrations expressed by salaried GPs about the QOF targets. Salaried employees had little influence or choice with regard to hitting targets, although some did report refusing to pursue targets where they disagreed with their content.

For some doctors, however, there was an acceptance that partnership status was something that should be earned rather than an automatic entitlement. This suggests that norms relating to expectations may be changing amongst newer entrants to the GP profession.

> I don't think you should assume that you should just have a partnership. That would be like joining a legal firm and expecting that you're going to be a partner. In most businesses, you earn your partnership by delivering.
>
> *(ID231)*

Cost containment and clinical freedom

Although PBC involved scrutiny of referrals, the process was not seen in emotive terms. Targets for reductions in referrals were agreed by elite PBC GPs, and proposals for reinvesting savings were dependent on approval from PBC elites, but, by and large, rank-and-file GPs did not express undue concern about the process. Participation in PBC was voluntary and even amongst GPs who were not PBC zealots, there was an acceptance that participation was beneficial since savings could be reinvested in other services. GPs described scrutinising referrals as a peer-review process carried out in a non-threatening manner 'so we can bore down to great detail without us feeling huffy that we're being criticised' (ID297). Some who were initially 'horrified by it' described getting used to the process and ultimately viewing it as useful (ID101).

Accountability and performance monitoring

QOF performance data for each practice are available on the internet, although English GPs have not traditionally been involved in competing for patients. However, policies to expand the market for primary care by encouraging new entrants have been introduced to address perceived deficiencies in existing primary medical care provision (McDonald, 2009). Coupled with the moves by commissioners to actively monitor performance and commission services – as opposed to merely acting as paymasters – this appeared to have contributed to a willingness amongst English GPs for poor performance in other practices to be addressed. The fact that private providers might be found wanting when scrutinized on a common set of indicators may have been part of the appeal of this approach for some GPs.

New strata

New strata of 'chasers' included GPs and others who acted to monitor practice staff, including GP partners within their own practice. Additionally, in the context of PBC, what might be conceptualized as an administrative elite comprises members of PBC boards who volunteered to serve in this capacity. Since not all practices were represented at board level, new hierarchies were developing which involved scrutiny of practice activities by GPs from other practices. However, although not all English GPs were happy with new ways of working, most were relatively accepting of these changes and many welcomed them, despite the constraints on individual autonomy which accompanied them.

There are a number of reasons which might help explain this state of affairs. These include the voluntary nature of participation in the new working arrangements. Furthermore, the rank-and-file GPs who undertake elite roles are very different from Freidson's elites, who 'do not, and perhaps cannot do the daily work of the profession, and therefore may not be able to understand, let alone sympathize with, the problems of daily work' (1983, p. 289).

Standardization and regulation from outside and from within

The relatively positive reactions to the reforms are perhaps understandable, given that guidelines and evidence-based practice have been part of the landscape of British general practice for many years (Checkland, 2004). This is reflected in the comments of study GPs that QOF was consistent with existing practice. Amongst 'chased' GPs, there was little complaint about being on the receiving end of prompts and reminders from other members of the practice team. In some cases, reservations were expressed about particular targets and guidelines but, for the most part, not about the principle of 'peer' review and targets. Most rank-and-file GPs were content to respond when chased and let 'elite' members do the work of organizing the process, and they welcomed the development of new services made possible from PBC savings.

Furthermore, there was support amongst elites and rank-and-file GPs for a more proactive approach to tackling poor performance, leading in extreme cases to decommissioning services from existing providers. The provision of evidence-based targets and guidelines appears to be viewed by many GPs as assisting them in delivering a quality service, with little evidence that it is perceived as constraining their autonomy.

The GPs appeared to have few reservations about greater standardization. Rather than leading to deepening divisions, actions to address poor performance were welcomed by many rank-and-file GPs. A refusal to judge others has traditionally been a key element of the medical identity (Bosk, 1979), yet the GPs in our study highlighted poor performance in neighbouring practices, suggesting that stricter sanctions should be applied. In a context where individual GPs and practices are being compared against each other, where practice activities contribute to consortium performance and market reforms are enabling primary care commissioning and provision to be contracted out to private limited companies, one interpretation is that rank-and-file GPs and elites have a common interest in ensuring that their fellow GPs and practices are behaving in a way that does not undermine the standing of the profession. These changes do not necessarily threaten the ability of the profession to socialize members into an attitude of loyalty towards colleagues. However, in a context where performance measurement is viewed by GPs as legitimate, this loyalty is unlikely to be unconditional.

Restratification and the empirical findings

In an environment where medicine is increasingly governed, rank-and-file English GPs saw the actions of elites as legitimate and, for the most part, did not appear to regard them as unduly interfering with their ability to exercise 'autonomy'. The standards by which English medical professionals are judged relate to resource use (PBC) and adherence to guidelines (QOF and PBC), which are generally relatively uncontroversial. Scrutiny involves assessment of compliance against clear standards rather than an investigation into the ethics of individual practice assessed against a vague notion of what constitutes professional conduct. The creation of clear and largely uncontentious standards depersonalizes the process of scrutiny. The questions asked by elites do not concern detailed examination of the particular ethics and actions of individual practitioners, but are merely a judgement of whether a particular standard was achieved.

At the same time, the fact that scrutiny is conducted by fellow professionals as opposed to NHS managers may also account for the acceptability of these processes to English GPs (Sheaff *et al.*, 2004). Confining review by colleagues to specific areas of clinical practice means that new forms of collegial practice enable professionals to continue to exercise considerable autonomy in other areas. At the same time, the voluntary nature of arrangements can be interpreted as allowing GPs to reconcile their need for autonomy and their 'choice' to respond to prompts and 'chasing' from elites.

Despite this, PBC was beginning to change the context of medical work, with groups of doctors taking responsibility for fixed budgets, requiring them to modify their practice. This may be interpreted as a mechanism by which the state (via medical elites) is shifting responsibility on to medical professionals and reducing their ability to exercise discretion.

In the English context, medical professionals might be interpreted as responding to state policies aimed at 'enforced self-regulation' (Dent, 2005). Hood and colleagues describe this as involving 'the deployment of heavier regulatory tackle against the incompetent or recalcitrant, while lightening the regulatory yoke over good performers' (2000, p. 296).

The findings suggest that English GPs have adapted to state pressures by developing new forms of self-regulation. Waring identified a process of 'adaptive regulation', suggesting that this might be viewed as part of an ongoing process enabling the medical profession to 'respond, even resist, and "move with the times" whilst maintaining or not excessively fracturing the enduring norms of professionalism' (Waring, 2007, p. 175). There are parallels in the data with other studies which describe doctors as reordering their ways of working in a way which combines self-surveillance and self-control with a defence of professional norms of self-regulation (Dent, 2005).

Big 4 accountants

Just as English medical partnerships have undergone institutional change leading to/driven by the introduction of financial incentives and accountability structures, so too have UK and Canadian accounting partnerships in the last 20 years undergone something of a commercial revolution which has changed the way in which accounting professionals conceive of and execute their work. The case study referred to below was undertaken between 2010 and 2014 in the two countries, involving 36 interviews with partners in accounting firms.

Modern accountants are much more concerned to translate their knowledge and skills into social and (particularly) economic rewards (Larson, 1977) than their counterparts in the past. The focus of this section is specifically on the 'Big 4' accounting partnerships. We focus on these organizations specifically for a number of reasons. Firstly, their sheer size makes them worthy of analysis in their own right. Their market share dwarfs that of their counterparts. For example, 99 out of 100 audits of FTSE 100 companies are undertaken by Big 4 firms (FRC, 2013). Secondly, the Big 4 have become so influential in shaping both national and international accounting regulation in recent years (Suddaby *et al.*, 2007) that they effectively set the professional agenda (in their own form) for others to follow. As such, that which is observable in Big 4 firms might be thought of as portentous of future trends in the profession more generally.

Although accounting has always been interested in money, the profession's relationship to profit seeking has historically been tempered by a wider compact with society (Spence and Carter, 2014). Whilst it is perhaps too crude to suggest that accountants have historically been honoured servants of the public interest (Freidson, 1994), one could at least reasonably conclude that their own status and economic position has followed as a by-product of rendering a service conceived of by the state as socially necessary. In some ways, accounting has operated as something of a semi-autonomous field (Bourdieu, 1996). What will be argued below is that this autonomy in recent years has been heavily circumscribed as the accounting field (read profession) has been rapidly colonized by market logics, which bring with them a whole concomitant raft of financial incentives.

For the Big 4, as with other professional services firms, their globalization has led to a much greater focus on revenue generation, new areas of business and profitability. As a result of this increasing colonization by the economic field, the types of behaviour exhibited by partners has changed quite dramatically in recent years. One phenomenon that encapsulates this change is the slow death of the 'technical partner'. Technical partners can be described as accountants who embody a very high level of technical expertise. This might manifest itself in significant hands-on experience in audits, up-to-date knowledge of the latest accounting standards or the ability to conceptualize and execute an especially complicated tax vehicle for clients. Such partners still exist, but they are, we were told, a 'dying breed' (Canada Audit Partner).

Rather, contemporary partners in Big 4 firms spend the vast majority of their time on 'business development'. What this essentially entails is proactively selling and cross-selling services to clients, managing relationships with clients and representing the firm in the business community. As one partner put it, within Big 4 firms today you need to have 'hunters, killers and skinners' (UK Retired Managing Partner) which denotes a process of finding work, winning work and delivering work. Partners are much more concerned with 'hunting' and 'killing', while 'skinning' is left to the technical people who, these days, are unlikely to be partners and more likely to be directors or senior managers.

This is a far cry from the scenario in (then) Big 6 firms 20 years ago, when partners were much more focused on actually delivering work and far less concerned about aggressively winning work:

> Back in [previous firm – circa 25 years ago] they would sit around for someone to knock on the door and say 'would you be kind enough to do my accounts?' 'We'll have a look at it, consider it and get back to you'. Now you do anything that you can to get that business.
>
> *(UK Managing Partner)*

This managing partner described how his firm was a 'gentleman's club' when he first joined in the 1980s, where the partners did very little actual work and where the barriers to ascension were defined much more in terms of who your father was and what school you went to. That technical expertise was associated with feet up on the desk or golf on a Friday afternoon says something about the power dynamics within firms at the time. Since then, partners now argued that things have become more 'meritocratic' (UK Corporate Finance Partner). Meritocracy in this sense essentially means that Big 4 partners are expected to perform and meet financial targets whereas, in the past, accounting was done, to some extent, for accounting's sake.

Essentially, during the 1990s, with neoliberalism in full swing, the accounting field lost its last vestiges of autonomy and started to become colonized full force by the laws of the market. In other words, financial incentives became the primary criteria by which partner and firm performance were measured. The emergence of financial incentives is evident from the story of a clear-out in the UK office of a Big 4 firm from the mid 1990s. This clear-out was described evocatively by the following interviewee as the 'year of the knives':

> At one point, here three of us made partner the same day, that was 49, 50 and 51 partners just for the Scottish practice. Only £26 million in income, so it was not very profitable. Then, we took that partner number down to about 26 in a 12–13 month period. So it was a quite brutal … The younger partners coming through were saying 'wait a minute, I could be earning more money somewhere else, so why don't we go and sort it!' So we did and we became very profitable up here.
>
> *(UK Corporate Finance Partner)*

When asked why this sudden change came about and where the new focus on performance came from, interviewees gave general responses referring to the changing economic climate, denoting those changes as natural or inevitable. Research looking at changing partner requirements in the legal field tells a similar story of increased commercialism and financial incentives creeping into law firms almost as an inevitable consequence of globalization (Galanter and Henderson, 2008).

This new emphasis on financial accountability to one's fellow partners had significant implications, not only for who made partner, but for other salaried positions as well. In the early 1990s, career structures in the then Big 6 saw managers move to senior manager. The next grade above senior manager was partner. Further, there was an explicit 'up or out' policy whereby, after a certain amount of time as senior manager, one needed to either make the step up to partner or find a job elsewhere. Employee turnover was therefore high but the number of partners within a firm was also relatively high compared to the present situation.

Around the mid 1990s, at the same time as the commercial revolution within these firms was in full swing, a new category was introduced in between senior manager and partner. This was variously called director, principal, or associate partner, depending on the firm in question and the geographical context. This new category offered existing non-performing partners the opportunity of a safe haven to which they might retreat. One Canadian audit partner explained how, in the mid 1990s, there were lots of people who were 'being carried' by other partners who 'were performing' and, rather than ask them to leave, they could be demoted to a position that was more prestigious than senior manager and which still had a 'market-facing title'. The current managing partner of the office which instigated the 'year of the knives' described how things had changed over the course of the last 20 years:

> If you look at the structure, in 1992 we would have 52 partners in Scotland turning over a third of what we turn over now. We have now got probably 17/18 partners. How did we do that? Because a lot of the guys that would have been partner are now directors.
>
> *(UK Managing Partner)*

Essentially, the introduction of these new salaried positions had two effects within accounting partnerships. First, they offered a career option for people who had spent perhaps ten years previously working within the firm, preventing talent loss for the organization and reducing notoriously high attrition rates. Second, they increased 'leverage' – the ratio of staff to equity partners. This latter phenomenon had the effect of greatly increasing profit-per-partner figures. Again, the same phenomenon has been observed in law firms over the period (Galanter and Henderson, 2008).

Directors essentially fulfil the function that the technical partners of the past would. In other words, they are the skinners of the firms rather than the hunters or the killers. These specialists, we were told by more than one partner, were 'second-class citizens' (Canada Retired Managing Partner), 'boffins' (UK Audit Partner) or 'geeks' (UK Tax Partner).

We have described in this section the death of the technical partners and his (invariably 'his' rather than 'her') replacement by a more commercially oriented partner whose main interests revolve around responding to financial incentives. This is not to say that financial incentives have replaced an archetypal commitment to the provision of robust accounting services. Rather, it is to point out that the delivery of those services is undertaken by subordinates rather than the leaders of Big 4 firms.

Functionalist interpretations of this change in work delegation might suggest that this is merely a result of the growth of firms and the need to develop a cadre of leaders who spend more time on oversight rather than delivery. However, a whole host of concomitant changes have been engendered by the birth of the new commercial partner. Essentially, the language of public interest and professional ethics has been replaced by the more solipsistic and financially focused terminology of 'risk management'. Technical experts are there within firms not so much to ensure the successful delivery of a professional service as to ensure that the entrepreneurial partners' backs are covered as they gravitate around their local business communities trying to increase profit-per-partner figures.

In other words, the meaning of professionalism has changed within these firms or, rather, there are now multiple meanings of professionalism depending on what pay grade one observes. This multiplicity notwithstanding, it is clear from the present research that a more commercial, entrepreneurial conception of professionalism dominates the traditional, archetypal conception. Financial incentives have been very successful in reconfiguring the professional field in this respect.

Conclusion

As we have outlined, there has been a tendency in recent years for professionals to be subject to more explicit financial incentive regimes than was previously the case. This means that rather than trusting autonomous professionals to 'do the right thing', greater emphasis is placed on linking actions to rewards. The complex contexts in which professionals work are often characterized by multiple and competing goals. This can create tensions for professionals who may be incentivized to prioritize certain goals over others. Choosing to pursue financial incentives might be seen as at odds with professional behaviour (e.g. choosing cheap treatments when these are not in the interest of the patient). However, it might also be seen as indicative of a new form of professionalism which reflects the aims of the broader organization in which professionals are working.

The cases illustrate the importance of the organizational dimension in the process of governing professionals and changing notions of professionalism. The findings we describe, with an emphasis on targets and performance monitoring and related financial incentives, resonate with the concept of organizational professionalism (Evetts, 2004). Linked to this, our findings also highlight the social nature of responses to incentives. Norms are changing within organizations. New ways of working in response to revised incentive structures are becoming embedded in organizational routines and practices in a way which gives them some legitimacy amongst professionals.

As illustrated in our case studies, a growing emphasis on financial incentives has contributed to changes in the two professions we describe. In many respects, the context of accountants working in the private sector is very different from that of doctors. However, an environment in which partners scrutinize the behaviour and performance of salaried accountants has some similarities with medical practice. The potential to achieve promotion and partnership status, combined with internal surveillance mechanisms, acts as an incentive to prioritize certain behaviours over others. In both cases, incentives have contributed to the creation of new strata, with career progression taking on a new dimension in the context of diminishing access to partnership status.

For salaried GPs, there is some evidence of acceptance that partnership status is becoming seen as something to be worked for over time rather than an entitlement. This appears to involve developing an appropriate form of selfhood (Grey, 1994) which is in accordance with organizational norms and expectations. At the same time, salaried GPs are seen as second-class doctors by some members of their profession.

There are some similarities with the creation of new salaried positions (directors) in the big accounting firms (second-class citizens, as one interviewee described them). Yet, whereas directors are unlikely to achieve partnership status, salaried doctors often aspire to this. Indeed, it is this ambition which incentivizes certain activities, even though it may also reduce morale to some extent.

As outlined earlier, responses to incentives depend on the context. Reactions of doctors in Turkey (Yuzden and Yildirim, 2014), France (Saint Lary et al., 2013) and California (McDonald and Roland, 2009), for example, to financial incentive reforms differed from those in England. It is too early to say at this stage whether changes initiated in those countries will ultimately lead to similar trends to those observed in England. It is certainly true that financial incentives can lead professionals to engage in illegal activity (Cunningham and Harris, 2006; NHSBA, 2014), and such extreme cases hit the headlines in the popular press. There is a danger in focusing on these dramatic incidents since, as we have shown, there are other effects of incentives which are more widespread and are likely to have enduring impacts on notions of professionalism and professional governance.

References

Alford, R. (1975) *Health Care Politics*. Chicago, IL: University of Chicago Press.

Batty, D. (2003) 'Q&A: GP Contract'. *The Guardian*, Friday 20 June, at: www.guardian.co.uk/society/2003/jun/20/politics.theissuesexplained (last accessed 25 January 2016).

Beck, U. (1992) *Risk Society: Towards a New Modernity*. London: Sage.

Bosk, C. L. (1979) *Forgive and Remember: Managing Medical Failure*. Chicago, IL: University of Chicago Press.

Bourdieu, P. (1996) *The Rules of Art*. Cambridge, UK: Polity Press.

Brock, D., Powell, M. and Hinings, C.R. (1999), *Restructuring the Professional Organization*. London: Routledge.

Checkland, K. (2004) 'National Service Frameworks and UK General Practitioners: Street-level Bureaucrats at Work?'. *Sociology of Health & Illness*, 26, pp. 951–975.

Cunningham, G. and Harris, J. (2006) 'Enron and Arthur Andersen: The Case of the Crooked E and the Fallen A'. *Global Perspectives on Accounting Education*, 3, pp. 27–48.

Dent, M. (2005) 'Post-New Public Management in Public Sector Hospitals? The UK, Germany and Italy'. *Policy & Politics*, 33(4), pp. 623–636.

Department of Health (2000) *The NHS Plan. A Plan for Investment. A Plan for Reform*. London: The Stationery Office.

Department of Health (2004) *Practice-Based Commissioning: Engaging Practices in Commissioning*. London: Department of Health.

Evetts, J. (2004) *Organizational or Occupational Professionalism: Centralized Regulation or Occupational Trust*. Paper presented at ISA RC52 Interim Conference, Versailles, France, 22–24 September.

Evetts, J. (2005) *The Management of Professionalism: A Contemporary Paradox*, Paper presented at Changing Teacher Roles, Identities and Professionalism Conference, Kings College, London, 19 October 2005.

Financial Reporting Council (FRC) (2013) *Key Facts and Trends in the Accountancy Profession*, at: www.frc.org.uk/News-and-Events/FRC-Press/Press/2013/June/FRC-issues-Key-Facts-and-Trends-in-the-Accountancy.aspx (last accessed 25 January 2016).

Freidson, E. (1983) 'The reorganization of the professions by regulation'. *Law and Human Behavior*, 7, pp. 279–290.

Freidson, E. (1985) 'The Reorganisation of the Medical Profession'. *Medical Care Review*, 42(1), pp. 11–35.

Freidson, E. (1994) *Professionalism Reborn: Theory, Prophecy and Policy*. Cambridge, UK: Polity Press.

Frey, B. (1997) *Not Just for Money: An Economic Theory of Personal Motivation*. Cheltenham, UK: Edward Elgar.

Galanter, M. and Henderson, W. (2008) 'The Elastic Tournament: A Second Transformation of the Big Law Firm'. *Stanford Law Review*, 60(6), pp. 1867–1930.

Giddens, A. (1990) *The Consequences of Modernity*. Stanford, CA: Stanford University Press.

Grey, C. (1994) 'Career as a Project of the Self and Labour Process Discipline'. *Sociology*, 28, pp. 479–497.

Hanlon, G. (1994) *The Commercialisation of Accountancy: Flexible Accumulation and the Transformation of the Service Class*. London: Macmillan.

Harrison, S. and Smith, C. (2003) 'Medical Autonomy and Managerial Authority in the National Health Service'. *Competition and Change*, 7(4), pp. 243–254.

Heins, E., Pollock, A. and Price, D. (2009) 'The Commercialisation of GP Services: A Survey of APMS Contracts and New GP Ownership'. *British Journal of General Practice*, 59, pp. e339–e343.

Hood, C., James, O. and Scott, C. (2000) 'Regulation of Government: Has It Increased, Is It Increasing, Should It Be Diminished?'. *Public Administration*, 78(2), pp. 283–304.

Kirkpatrick, I., Ackroyd, S. and Walker, R. (2005) *The New Managerialism and Public Service Professions: Change in Health, Social Services and Housing*. New York: Palgrave.

Larson, M.S. (1977) *The Rise of Professionalism: A Sociological Analysis*. California: University of California Press.

Lewis, J. (1998) 'The Medical Profession and the State: GPs and the GP Contract in the 1960s and the 1990s'. *Social Policy & Administration*, 32(2), pp. 132–150.

Macdonald, K. M. (1995) *The Sociology of the Professions*. London: Sage.

McDonald, R. (2009) 'Market Reforms in English Primary Medical Care: Medicine, Habitus and the Public Sphere'. *Sociology of Health and Illness*, 31, pp. 659–672.

McDonald, R. (2015) 'Financial incentives and the governance of performance'. In E. Kuhlmann, R. H. Blank, I. L. Bourgeault and C. Wendt (eds), *The Palgrave International Handbook of Healthcare Policy and Governance*, pp. 393–408. Basingstoke, UK: Palgrave.

McDonald, R. and Roland, M. (2009) 'Pay for Performance in Primary Care in England and California: Comparison of Unintended Consequences'. *Annals of Family Medicine*, 7, pp. 121–127.

McDonald, R., Harrison, S., Checkland, K., Campbell, S. and Roland, M. (2007) 'Impact of Financial Incentives on Clinical Autonomy and Internal Motivation in Primary Care: An Ethnographic Study'. *British Medical Journal*, 334, pp. 1357–1359.

McDonald, R., Cheraghi-Sohi, S., Tickle, M., Roland, M., Doran, T., Campbell, S., Ashcroft, D. and Sanders, C. (2010) *The Impact of Incentives on the Behaviour and Performance of Primary Care Professionals*, Report for the National Institute for Health Research Service Delivery and Organisation Programme, at: www.nets.nihr.ac.uk/__data/assets/pdf_file/0008/64295/FR-08-1618-158.pdf (last accessed 25 January 2016).

McKinlay, J. and Marceau, L. (2008) 'When There Is No Doctor: Reasons for the Disappearance of Primary Care Physicians in the U.S. during the Early 21st Century'. *Social Science & Medicine*, 67, pp. 1481–1491.

Millerson, G. (1964) *The Qualifying Associations: A Study in Professionalism*. London: Routledge & Kegan Paul.

National Audit Office (2008) *NHS Pay Modernisation: New Contracts for General Practice Services in England*. London: The Stationery Office.

NHSBA (2014) 'GP Who Falsified 1700 Patient Records Sentenced for £62K NHS Fraud'. www.nhsbsa.nhs.uk/4472.aspx (last accessed 25 January 2016).

Saint Lary, O., Bernard, E, Sicsic, J., Plu, I., Francois-Pursell, I. and Franc, C. (2013) 'Why Did Most French GPs Choose not to Join the Voluntary National Pay-For-Performance Program'. *PLOS One*, 14, pp. 117–131.

Saks, M. (1995) *Professions and the Public Interest*. London: Routledge.

Sheaff, R., Marshall, M., Rogers, A., Roland, M., Sibbald, B. and Pickard, S. (2004) 'Governmentality by Network in English Primary Healthcare'. *Social Policy & Administration*, 38(1), pp. 89–103.

Spence, C. and Carter, C. (2014) 'Exploring the Professional Habitus in Big 4 Accounting Firms'. *Work, Employment & Society*, 6(28), pp. 946–962.

Suddaby, R., Cooper, D. J. and Greenwood, R. (2007) 'Transnational Regulation of Professional Services: Governance Dynamics or Field Level Organizational Change'. *Accounting, Organizations and Society,* 32, pp. 333–362.

Swedberg, R. (2005) *Interest*. Buckinghamshire, UK: Open University Press.

Waring, J. (2007) 'Adaptive Regulation or Governmentality: Patient Safety and the Changing Regulation of Medicine'. *Sociology of Health & Illness*, 29, pp. 163–179.

Yuzden, G. and Yildirim, J. (2014) 'A Qualitative Evaluation of Performance-Based Supplementary Payment System in Turkey: Physicians' Perspectives'. *Journal of Health Management*, 16(2), pp. 259–270.

8

Professionalism and entrepreneurialism

Seppo Poutanen and Anne Kovalainen

Introduction

Several major changes, including how globalization and digitalization are transforming the way we work, and how the current turmoil in the global and national economies is transforming the economic basis of societies, have raised a new set of questions concerning the role of professions in societies. Entrepreneurship and entrepreneurial activities have risen to the forefront as solutions for how professions may be organized in present and future societies, with individual professions, careers and even industrial sectors such as healthcare and welfare services changing to embrace these entrepreneurial roles, for example.

Recent research concerning professions has revolved round the new forms of governance associated with the principles of new public management (NPM) and related policies, such as auditing and monitoring, which have brought management principles into the everyday practices of professions. Existing literature covering professions focuses on several aspects of the effects resulting from the rise of NPM among professions (e.g. Evetts, 2011). Curiously enough, though, current literature provides little insight into how and in what ways market-based entrepreneurialism is in fact transforming current and future professions and their hierarchical relationships. This same dilemma also extends to existing literature on entrepreneurs and entrepreneurialism: research within entrepreneurship has paid little or no attention to questions such as professional qualifications and their maintenance, and mechanisms such as market closure, both highly relevant when explaining the development of professions.

NPM has been introduced in the literature as the vehicle that connects and embeds both professions and professionalism into the economy, with entrepreneurship being one form for the actualization of this process (Kovalainen and Sundin, 2012). It is therefore appropriate to question whether the newly established connections and linkages between professionalism and entrepreneurialism exist outside of the influences of current economic impacts.

This chapter investigates the connections, linkages and differences between professionalism and entrepreneurialism, two fields that demonstrate alignment in some theories, but less so in empirical research. Perhaps not surprisingly, these two academic disciplinary fields have developed separately with very different research agendas. There are several aspects through which professionalism and entrepreneurialism relate to each other, ranging from the classics such as

Weber and Schumpeter to NPM and marketization. It is thus of interest to analyse both disciplinary fields, and this is especially true when the business models of entrepreneurial activities cut across professional activities.

In the following text, the origins of the two academic disciplinary fields will be evaluated first, then the relationships between them and their current and future research areas will be briefly discussed. This discussion is illustrated with examples of recent empirical work. The chapter concludes with a reflection on the research agenda and the notion of blurring boundaries, possible interconnections and the future shaping of the research field in common for professional and entrepreneurial studies.

Classics uniting professionalism and entrepreneurialism research

Professions have long been part of the sociological classics and canon, not only through Marx and Weber but also through Durkheim's and Parsons' seminal works (Parsons, 1939; Durkheim, 1992; Kuhlmann, 2006; Evetts, 2013). Weber's influential work on professions and bureaucracy and on economy and society, Marx's writings on the formation of social classes and stratification, Durkheim's analysis of moral communities, and, later, Parsons' recognition of the relationship between professions and social order have formed the corpus of the theoretical foundation for the research on professions in many ways. These classics have also formed the intellectual core and a significant proportion of the theoretical basis for research conducted in relation to entrepreneurship and self-employment, and their positions in societal formation and economic development over an extended period of time (Swedberg, 1991; Kovalainen, 1995).

For Weber, professions were not the aim but the means by which the rationalization of society was progressing – essentially, the professions were part of the rationalization and bureaucratization processes within society (Weber, [1905]1960). These societal change processes were not initiated by or attached to specific occupational groups or professions; rather society exhibited change through the development of the occupations and professions on a more general basis. Professions were seen as promoting societies wherein knowledge and skills-based learning acted as the organizing mechanisms, and, as such, these professions became the key building blocks for societies no longer based on agricultural or manual labour alone. For Marx, professions had a more dynamic role as they were part of the overall class-formation process and were vehicles for emerging societal inequalities (Kalleberg, 2011).

For both Marx and Weber – albeit in differing ways – entrepreneurship was a crucial aspect of societal change, promoting capital accumulation that subsequently lead to inequality, therefore triggering dynamism in society. For the classics, entrepreneurship was first and foremost a societal force. Thus, it was not so much about individuality and individual aspirations as it was about societal change, in contrast to current mainstream entrepreneurship research, which often examines the relationships individuals have with firms and businesses as opposed to society as a whole.

Classics differentiating professionalism and entrepreneurialism research

Even if social science classics such as Marx and Weber can be extended and shared by both the entrepreneurship and professions research fields, the ways in which the concepts of professions and entrepreneurs have been discussed and dealt with in said works are very different. For Marx, and especially for Weber, the professions were inherently part of developing society and the formation of the normative social order, but the two discussed entrepreneurship in different manners. For Weber, an entrepreneur was a capitalist, and entrepreneurs were realized in Weber's texts as small business owners who belonged to the preceding phase of industrial development, superseded by larger and more complex organizational forms with more developed bureaucracy (and professional structures). For Marx, entrepreneurs were rent- and profit-seeking capitalists, or owners of some form of assets, petite bourgeoisie, and inherently part of the class structure.

The development of the social class structure, through the diminishing petite bourgeoisie, was related by the classics to the renewal of the economies through the commonly observed trend at that time of new profession formation. In the renewal period that took place at the beginning of the twentieth century, the perception of individual actions being the engines of societal development began to gain prevalence. The interest shown towards individuals and the capabilities of individual actions to act as engines for economic development, as opposed to state–profession relations or social classes and capital, became the distinguishing factor between the classics of entrepreneurship and those of the professions. According to Schumpeter, the foremost classical scholar in entrepreneurship research, the renewal of society and economy takes place through individual actions, irrespective of occupation or profession, and through continuous development and creative destruction (Schumpeter, [1912]1961).

In the works of Weber ([1905]1960), the seventeenth-century Protestant religious duties of individuals became the primary force for the economic activities that took place a century later. The Calvinist ethics and aspects of wealth accumulation and, following that, the rise of capitalism through the general 'entrepreneurial spirit' (Weber, [1905]1960; Schumpeter, ([1912]1961) created the origins of entrepreneurship as a research field. Schumpeter's ideas were highly influential for the Austrian school of economics (Hayek, 1945; von Mises, [1963] 1996), where entrepreneurs are placed at the centre of all progress (and failures) in societies and in economies, and where state governance in general and bureaucracy in particular are not beneficial for entrepreneurial activities.

With the advent of the developing theories of societal progress and industrial societies, individuals became subservient to complex societal structures and networks, with social orders based on skills, competencies and capital-based hierarchies, the same structures that were the common denominators for the classics when dealing both with professions and entrepreneurs. Since the classical works, developments within both entrepreneurship research and professions research have brought widely differing elements, theories and ways to describe and analyse the empirical subjects.

Inevitably, the growth of the state's role in the planning, regulation and education of professional groups meant that professions were not to be seen solely as a means to maintain the stability and civility of societies (as in Durkheim), but were instead increasingly seen as varied groups with differing and often conflicting interests. Views on the ways in which the relationship between professions and the state became an object of study thus vary.

At that time, the growth of the functions of the state did not relate to the development of the economy. To a large extent, the economy was pre-/early industrial: rent-seekers as well as small business owners were all seen as entrepreneurs. The qualification for an entrepreneur was the creation of economic dynamism, capital or rent-seeking activity, and no profession or knowledge-based capability were needed for the creation of economic disequilibrium. Austrian economics – influenced by Weber, but with Schumpeter, von Mises and Kirzner as key figureheads – focused on the economic development of societal and economic disequilibrium. As a result, entrepreneurs were seen as the engines of economic and societal development, and the state had a diminished or even no role to play in their development. This was contrary to the development of the professions and their role in societal development (Kovalainen, 1995).

Divergent and parallel approaches in professionalism and entrepreneurialism research

Professionalism research

Traditionally, professions have been analysed as entities that were regulated either by the state and its normative foundations or by the professional bodies that governed their entry and boundaries (e.g. Abbott, 1993). The state has usually played a regulatory role or has been in an active position in relation to the formation and functioning of professions. What is interesting is that the state has been largely missing from the analyses of entrepreneurship. If it is present at all, it is usually in the context of a distant and passive institution that mainly acts in a restrictive manner through legal and regulatory tasks such as taxation (Kuratko, 2007). The analyses of occupations, professions, professional work and professionalism were for quite a long time differentiated from each other through normative categorizations, or, more pragmatically, through the focus of analysis.

Further differentiation of research into work, occupations and professions has even resulted in some researchers announcing 'the death of the sociology of professions' (e.g. Gorman and Sandefur, 2011, p. 276), while other researchers see an ever-growing need to redefine and differentiate, as exemplified by the distinction between expert occupations (such as design) and semi-professions from true professions (such as medicine or law) (Noordegraaf, 2007). As a result of these re-differentiations, the need to refocus the analysis of professions arises anew.

The relationship between professions and the state is constantly changing and is full of tensions. This is not only due to the NPM structures that have entered into the workings of the state, but is even more a result of the changes in the professions themselves. Over time, the assumed and real sovereignty of professions has changed and partly evaporated, and, instead of state or professional bodies, governance is thought to reside in the practices and praxis of the field; governance may also lie in the praxis of organizations and organizational actors related to professions (see e.g. Greenwood and Suddaby, 2006; see also Chapter 2 by Kuhlmann *et al.*).

Some researchers have added ethical commitment to these definitions. Even when considering this altruistic notion, the professions cannot be seen as mere objects of new modes of governance. Instead, they have also become, as professional groups and as professionals, directly involved in governance (Kuhlmann, 2013) and as such, part of the governance structure. Thus, professionalism defined as a distinctive way of controlling and organizing work and workers extends the idea of work into said governance and self-governance. The definition also differentiates professionalism from professions as embodiments of knowledge and competence. The analysis of professionalism thus involves occupational change and the control of work in organizations and workplaces. The shift in the embodiment of expertise from an individual with a profession to an organization that defines professionalism has also meant a change in the unit of analysis (see also Chapters 11–15 in Part III of this Companion).

Entrepreneurship research

In entrepreneurship research, the development took another route. The classical, Austrian-economics-influenced (Kirtzner, 1973; von Mises, 1996; Hayek, 1945) view on entrepreneurs and entrepreneurship was strongly felt in research presented in the 1980s' and 1990s' entrepreneur-based literature. This research focused on individuals who were following their own strong visionary path and were subsequently creating economic development. Even today, the emphasis on individuals and individuality is rooted in the ways in which entrepreneurship is analysed as a societal and economic force and phenomenon. The 'individual-laden' mainstream orientation has much to do with the phenomenon of entrepreneurship being at the crossroads of economics, business studies and sociology (Kovalainen, 1995, p. 43), but said orientation can be considered as being rather functionalist in its philosophical origins and current research underpinnings.

Much entrepreneurial research has tried to take the positivistic approach, especially when trying to search for the ideal entrepreneur or the most suitable business start-up. Within entrepreneurship research, the questions of market invasion or NPM are rarely related to entrepreneurship when compared to the ways in which they are related to professions. It seems that neoliberalism, as defined and related to the general accounts of global transformations (e.g. Harvey, 2007), is seldom discussed in current entrepreneurial theory constructions.

In entrepreneurship research, the normatively laden redefinitions of the concept of the entrepreneur have aimed for further and more precise distinctions within the concept itself. The definitions have aimed to differentiate the small and medium-sized business owner from the 'true' entrepreneur who aims for new business and its growth. Further distinctions exist between 'intrapreneurs' (referring to initiatives by employees in organizations for new business activities), the serial entrepreneur (who have several time-sequenced business activities) and the 'corporate' entrepreneur (who aims for the renewal of existing organizations only) (Kuratko, 2007; Blackburn and Kovalainen, 2009, p. 129). The concepts or research surrounding these approaches have not dealt with the professions or their qualifications.

Increasing bifurcation of research since the 1990s has led to theoretical and methodological discussions about what are the most fruitful and relevant ways to empirically analyse professions and professionalism in contemporary society, ranging from traditional institutional theories to the Foucauldian 'knowing subject' and governance analyses, whereby profession becomes defined through professional practices and through professional knowledge in practice (e.g. Young and Miller, 2014). The self-reflections of the research fields of entrepreneurship, as in professions research, have only recently surfaced, and influences have begun to arrive from other disciplinary fields than entrepreneurship studies itself (Kovalainen and Sundin, 2012).

The concept of profession most often represents the generic category of occupational work and, even more, it seems to be contextually bound: no clear demarcation line exists among the occupations defined as professions and those that are not. This naturally raises the question of how the professions emerge and change. The process of 'becoming' a profession, 'professionalization', is a process whereby an occupation becomes defined as profession. The process of becoming classified as a 'profession' refers to fluidity and change and the malleability of the professions (e.g. Kuhlmann, 2013). The processual view underlines new types of insecurities within professions that were not present in the earlier analyses or theorizations of professions.

Insecurities such as declining status levels or unemployment bring new elements into the ways in which professions are seen and analysed in relation to the economy. They also bring several aspects of entrepreneurship into alignment with professionalism in new ways. The questions of NPM, managerialism, independence and power become aligned in new ways and require new analyses.

One example of such new analyses is the development of new professions and the changes in the higher education patterns for professions. Both represent a challenge for established professions and call for further analysis of the new professions from a new perspective. The new de-professionalization trends and processes additionally challenge current research on professions (Kuhlmann, 2013; Adams, 2015). Parallels between the two research fields are also to be found in the ways in which both traditions have developed new units of analysis and have subsequently widened their perspective over time. The current intersectionality of professionalism research and entrepreneurialism research is closely related to the emergence of new occupations, and to changes in the economies that push occupational development away from traditional spheres.

Professionalism, entrepreneurialism and new questions for research

How does entrepreneurship research recognize the distinction highlighted in recent new professionalism research between the two concepts of professions and entrepreneurs? It is noteworthy that the view regarding the entrepreneurial activities that take place within professionalism has developed along a different path than that found in professions research – as briefly described above – even if the classics of the subjects are shared. In the following section, some main threads are discussed and the relationships with professionalism studies are explored in order to validate joint research agendas.

With analysis of economies as social systems and as sources of global crises increasing, interest in entrepreneurship as part of capitalism and its consequences throughout economies has done likewise. Despite this programmatic idea, entrepreneurship as a research field has been argued to be fragmented as a scientific field, even if numerous attempts to create an integrated framework have been instigated in order to define the domain and broaden the individual orientation of the theories (e.g. Shane and Venkataram, 2000). Again, the question needs to be asked as to whether one unified theory of entrepreneurship can exist, let alone work in research when no unified ontological or epistemological certainty reigns within the discipline (Blackburn and Kovalainen, 2009). Given the vastly varied appearance and forms of entrepreneurship – ranging from sole entrepreneurship and self-employment to franchising and large companies – it is interesting that the research theories of entrepreneurship seldom analysed professionalism as an economic activity.

Both professionalism and entrepreneurialism research currently relate to the changing economic structures, and especially to the emergence of the immaterial knowledge economy and the new modes of production that have redesigned new professions as well as reorganizing the roles found within old professions and old types of entrepreneurship and the places in which they occur. For some professions, such as architects, accountants and lawyers, self-employment and entrepreneurship have in most countries been the most relevant way of organizing work around the core competence. Contract work as a form of self-employment, sub-contracting and companies based on expertise are ways of organizing the income from actual competence. The ways in which entrepreneurship has been part of this work organization are not extensively discussed, yet the very organization of work closely relates to business activities.

Old connections revisited

Historically, the professions emerged in the period of prospering welfare states that occurred in the twentieth century, as Kuhlmann (2013, e8) and several researchers of professions note. One of the new challenges for the analysis of professions and professionalism is that it should take into account the emergence of new types of professionalism that operate alongside the traditional model. Thus, the relevant questions no longer relate solely to the codification of professional knowledge, nor to institutions producing professionals or entry requirements. Instead, they now also relate to more indirect forms of exclusion and inclusion, and the entries and exits at the boundaries of professions.

Professions may enhance occupational change and regulate development (e.g. through higher education), and they also have the power to influence the policies of the state and governance, both by being part of the governance system and through exerting power within and outside of said governance. Professions are known to regulate their own fields through controlled content, as is postulated in classical professionalism (Noordegraaf, 2007), wherein occupations either establish a professional control or create occupational closure.

The state–professions relationship has been under analysis for quite some time (e.g. Saks, 2010), and in recent years, the notion of citizenship has been added. The configurations between state and professions, on the one hand, and professions and citizens, on the other, are relevant to one of the biggest profession research fields, namely medicine and healthcare (e.g. Kovalainen and Sundin, 2012; Dahl *et al.*, 2011). These configurations also relate to the broader societal context of professions, including transformations both within states and to states on the whole, globalization, and trends in the cultural, societal and material organization of services.

Within professions studies, the majority of research focuses on healthcare professions, with special attention being paid to medicine and nursing, and to some extent to legal professions, teaching, accounting, engineering, journalism and architecture. When 501 articles on the sociology of the professions field (US and UK-based) were analysed, the most usual questions in relation to professions concerned intersectionalities (such as gender, race, ethnicity, migration), regulations and public policies, work satisfaction and work organization (Adams, 2015, p. 157). The most common approach observed among the 501 articles Adams analysed was the use of a case study, although there were empirical divergences across regions and nations.

Single case studies have, according to Adams (2015), dominated the sociology of professions for at least a decade. In general, case studies focusing on single professions do not hinder or stop theorization on professions, but they may narrow the empirical base for arguing the changes, for example. In contrast, we would argue that addressing the societal – including markets – changes and theoretical variation in the ways of explaining these changes may have been different, and may also be addressed differently, in the USA in comparison to European studies on professions.

One nexus for entrepreneurship research and professions research can be found in the construction of professional identity in the new economic situation. In fact, the body of literature on professional identities is expanding rapidly. This is partly a result of gatekeeping within professions with the education system as the prevailing model, and, for most professions, the higher education system maintains a standardized ideology of professional identity. Education in relation to a profession such as accountancy or medicine entails not only the technical skills and knowledge required for standard accounting or medical practices but, more importantly, the formation of an appropriate professional identity.

The tensions between the 'formal' requirements of a professional identity often created within the education system and the existence of differing professional discourses both within and outside of professions have created growing ruptures. This has become prominent especially in those professions where norms strongly regulate professional ethics and work, such as in the legal profession, and especially in the medical professions, where concerns about students' unwillingness to conduct primary care, 'lifestyle priorities', 'lack of professionalism' and 'declining humanism', to mention a few, have been voiced by faculties and medical educators alike. Even recent literature on professional education within medicine gives normative definitions and instructions for professional identity, yet in a very positive and general manner, such as 'medical practitioners of the future will possess and demonstrate the qualities of the "good physician"' (Cruess *et al.*, 2014, p. 1446).

Partially connected to diverse opinions and tensions found within the process of identity construction of professions are larger societal changes that blur the clear-cut space that professions need to function. Even if professions developed in different ways on a national basis, global trends and transnationalism evens out the differences. One notable example of such a development is the transformation of welfare states into quasi-markets with neoliberal modes of governance. In this global trend, the professions – if they can be addressed as a unified occupational group – rarely remain unaffected and unchanged. The national differences become partly highlighted anew, partly evened out as global trends become 'domesticated' through national policies (Poutanen and Kovalainen, 2014).

The analysis of organizations as sites for professional control and domination has shifted the research emphasis to focus on inter-occupational competition (Muzio and Kirkpatrick, 2011). Competition becomes prevalent: how has the incorporation of management training as a way of increasing occupational/professional status and standing changed the ways in which professions enter the markets? Competition has also required the solid basis usual for professions, such as the standardization and formalization of entry into said profession, and the work tasks, qualifications and content of the work, all of which have become more transparent. This transparency relates to the management of the professions and, at the same time, it is built in to the very profession itself (e.g. Kuhlmann and Saks, 2008).

With the growth of global labour markets for some professionals, and global organizations 'domesticating' not only professionals but work patterns and practices, there is a significant amount of research relating to neo-Weberian theories of the professions and professionalism in a globalizing world (Faulconbridge and Muzio, 2011; Saks, 2010, 2011), as well as research on managerialism (Dent, 2005), and NPM and professions (Boyce, 2008; Thomas and Hewitt, 2011), again, keeping in mind the occupations which are most common in profession research (Vallas, 2011).

Future alignments/renewal of research agenda

There is notably less literature that covers the ways in which entrepreneurialism and entrepreneurship relate to professionalism, and how entrepreneurship and entrepreneurialism become integrated into the everyday work practices of professionals. The new modes of work shift the location in which entrepreneurial activities are carried out to reside inside professional work: the buzzword of the day is now that everybody is expected to be entrepreneurial in their personal mindset and entrepreneurially orientated in general, or, put another way, is expected to be an intrapreneur in their day-to-day activities. What types of challenges do these developments set for future research on professions and professionalism, on the one hand, and entrepreneurs and entrepreneurialism, on the other?

With the NPM managerial practices conducted in the public sector, interest in health and social care work and entrepreneurship has lately risen. Neither entrepreneurialism nor strong professionalism has been self-evident in healthcare occupations, but rather, with the current shifts in employment patterns, the market types of solutions become everyday solutions and entrepreneurship increases in relevance. In the global North, entrepreneurship within social and healthcare spheres has been growing during the 2010s, largely as a result of the change in the roles and responsibilities of states, municipalities and markets. We have analysed entrepreneurship in health and social care, and revealed that the ideology of care and gendered roles in care are intertwined (Kovalainen and Österberg-Högstedt, 2011).

Entrepreneurial activities among health professionals, for example, have most often been analysed as not having any effect on the professional skills and capabilities. Even if entrepreneurialism is increasingly related to the capturing of opportunities, and thus seen as a separate skill (McDaniel, 2006; Boyce, 2008) rather than closely aligned with the ways and the skills of the profession, this assumption is highly problematic, as it sets entrepreneurial skills apart from professional skills, an assumption which is based on the idea that there is a core professional skill set that remains intact, no matter what takes place contextually. The claim of profession and professionalism being a bundled set of skills that remains intact from training to the profession is in contrast with the current theoretical understanding of a contemporary individual with flexibilities, several skills and even multiple identities.

In order to find out whether that claim holds in an empirical context, we explored the ways in which those health and social care professionals that became entrepreneurs and started their own businesses constructed their professional identities. Using wide-ranging interview and survey data sets, we analysed the large group of healthcare professionals who had been working in the public healthcare sector in paid employment contracts, with collective benefits, such as solid salary levels, holidays and work-related benefits such as in-work training, and with some managerial tasks. The data is from Finland, where nationwide, high-quality public sector health and social care is the main healthcare employer, and where a sizeable level of professional qualifications are obtained via vocational and professional training.

All surveyed and interviewed healthcare professionals had previous working experience and contracts in the public sector and had started their own businesses based on their professional skills and experience (Kovalainen and Österberg-Högstedt, 2013). We controlled for the motivation for founding the business, that is, we took into account whether the motivation to start one's own business was a push or a pull, meaning either unemployment or disappointment with the public sector (push) or an interest in trying something new based on one's own skills and knowledge (pull).

Our analysis shows that while professional identity provided a sense of belonging and being an entrepreneur provided a sense of distinctiveness, these two work-related identities were not separate or necessarily different, but fluid and overlapping. Talk about the business was related to one's own capabilities within care, new solutions in care, and their costs and benefits, thus highlighting the aspect of building professional knowledge where the two elements – care profession and business profession – were entangled. (Kovalainen and Österberg-Högstedt, 2013, p. 19).

The results from our study of the healthcare professionals who moved from paid employment positions to entrepreneurial positions contradict the argument of an 'outer' layer of entrepreneurship that relates to the profession and leaves the core of the profession untouched. For most respondents in the survey, the differences between what counts as 'profession-based' work and what counts as 'entrepreneurial' work were not clear-cut or self-evident. Over time, these different professionalisms and work tasks merged with each other, bringing a new dimension to the professional knowledge of care and highlighting new assemblages in relation to professionalism, yet preserving the basic ideas of care work, such as its ethical dimensions. Whether features such as the ethics of care can be considered to be at the core of the profession or not is debatable (Kovalainen and Österberg-Högstedt, 2013).

Both historical and Foucauldian analyses have grown in importance regarding the increase in research on the processes of professions, the changes and conflicts found within professionalism, and the malleability of professional boundaries, work and organizations. Even Foucault's somewhat diluted influence has been vast in relation to the studies of economic phenomena, and, as a result, historians of professions, especially medical professions, have started to study and write about professionalization and have begun to emphasize the process view regarding profession building and construction. This led to criticism of the 'attribute studies of professionalization' and also of cross-cultural empirical data studies with functionalist aims. Instead, a growth in research using both contemporary and historical narratives took place. For example, during the 1980s, medical historians produced 'compelling narratives of change' that utilized a 'multidimensional model of professionalization [that] … included the ideas of both market and monopoly along with older attributes of professionalization' (Burnham, 1998, pp. 143–44; see also Ball, 2012).

A very different view of professionalism and entrepreneurialism is built through Foucauldian analysis which expands the view into the ways that ideologies work through professions. Entrepreneurship and professionalism become understood not as foci of research but as vehicles through which governance works in sectors and occupational groups such as education or healthcare (Kuhlmann, 2006; Thomas and Hewitt, 2011). An example of this is 'management as moral technology' among professions such as teachers. Through schemes of self-appraisal, school improvement and the development of professional skills in programmatic ways, teachers are urged to believe that their commitment to such processes will make the school and themselves more professional (Ball, 2012). The discourse analyses of professions and processes are suggested to better describe the socio-cultural aspects and ambiguities of professionalism in relation to present times (e.g. Thomas and Hewitt, 2011).

Conclusion

Research on professions and research on entrepreneurship have parallel developments and commonalities in terms of sharing some of the main classics in social sciences. Currently, the two fields are quite separate from each other, yet the interesting commonalities of the two have growing significance in the transformation of societies, such as markets and professions, globalization and new demands, to mention a few.

The intersections between new types of transnational professionals, migrating workers, gender and new types of global dependencies and interdependencies have been analysed and discussed widely in relation to changing care work, global care chains and professionals moving with the jobs (Dahl *et al.*, 2011; McDowell, 2014; Poutanen and Kovalainen, 2014), but also, to a lesser extent, in relation to other professions and their change, or indeed, in relation to the new economy. The new economy often refers to changes in the ways in which professional work is conducted, due to advances in information technology, globalization, and the commodification of knowledge. Studies of the new economy have shown how new technologies and production logic have rearranged work tasks and professions (Vallas, 2011) and, for example, care work on a global scale, irrespective of the profession in question.

The complexities of new skills demanded in the new economy, the hybrid forms of new professions and the widening of 'old' professions all call for changes to both professions and entrepreneurship research. Markets invade the logics of closure, and the new economy in its global form increases the variance within professions. Globalization strengthens the emphasis of spatial location, but also leads to detachment of the locational or spatial. At the same time, as professions change and renew, there are other types of challenge, which contradict the logic of the new economy.

Even with the growth of healthcare-related telephone call centres, which function irrespective of location, care as a profession typically requires the embodied presence of the carer and the cared-for. Care as a profession carries power in itself, as well as dependency and vulnerability. As work, care has become an example of global labour through global care chains, being partly market-based and partly fragmented through contracts. Hence these facts are challenged by professions, and as such, they are not enough to change the nature of the required *embodied presence* in care work and the *embodied location* of the care. Even as a profession, care as work still takes place in personal contact between carer and cared-for, but this embodied relationship carries in itself also a larger set of social relations within which the caring is done, perceived and assessed by others (Poutanen and Kovalainen, 2014).

The new trends within the occupations set differentiating tracks for research on professions. Coupled with those changes, new aspects of entrepreneurship as a new mode of organizing professional work in future societies (see Chapter 15 by Denis *et al.*) will also set new challenges for entrepreneurship research.

The theoretical frames through which entrepreneurialism is scrutinized within professionalism research are based on very different approaches and rather stable ontological positions, in which professions have 'core' identities – as outlined above – and markets and capitalism are distanced from this core. Thus, markets are thought to lie outside of professions and professionalism, and professions are often thought to be strangers to capitalism, even in cases where the profession mainly works 'at the markets', in the private sector. While professions have become empowered and, to some extent, are able to resist changes, this is not necessarily the case: in the case of most contemporary service occupations, professionalism is being imposed 'from above', such as through and by employers and managers. Here, the question of autonomy within professions and professionalism vis-à-vis entrepreneurialism becomes explicated and questioned anew.

Entrepreneurship and entrepreneurialism have entered the professions and professionalism vocabulary through globalization, new or emergent markets for services and new public management pervading the public sector and arenas of professions. Healthcare professionals are only one example, but, as such, the professional sector as a whole exemplifies many aspects of professions in the current global economy.

The late capitalism of the early twenty-first century is marked by new types of insecurities and tensions, opportunities and changes that are intensified by globalization. Marketization of the public sector, introduction of the quasi-markets and mechanisms such as NPM have served to transform both public and private sector organizations and their modes of operation, professions included. The adoption of business logic has led them to become more entrepreneurial in their modes of organizing activities and in their orientations. These managerial and market-orientated, entrepreneurial changes have become the current modus operandi, habits of working. All these transformations pose new types of challenges for research in professions but also in entrepreneurialism. The old and new professions amidst the globally functioning economy, with entrepreneurship and marketization mechanisms being infused as part of states, require bold new types of research questions and theoretically laden fresh analyses where these two phenomena are not separate but interconnected and interrelated.

References

Abbott, A. (1993) 'The sociology of work and occupations'. *Annual Review of Sociology*, 19: 187–209.

Adams, T. L. (2015) 'Sociology of professions: International divergences and research directions'. *Work, Employment and Society*, 29: 154–165.

Ball, S. J. (2012) 'Management as moral technology: A Luddite analysis'. In S. J. Ball (ed.), *Foucault and Education: Disciplines and Knowledge*, 2nd edn. Routledge: London, pp. 153–166.

Blackburn, R. and Kovalainen, A. (2009) 'Researching small firms: Past, present, future trends'. *International Journal of Management Reviews,* 11: 127–148.

Boyce, R. A. (2008) 'Professionalism meets entrepreneurialism and managerialism'. In E. Kuhlmann and M. Saks (eds), *Rethinking Professional Governance: International Directions in Healthcare*. London: Policy Press, pp. 77–92.

Burnham, J. C. (1998) 'How the idea of profession changed the writing of medical history'. *Medical History*, Suppl. 18. London: Wellcome Institute for the History of Medicine.

Cruess, R. L., Cruess, S. R., Boudreau, D., Snell, L. and Steinert Y. (2014) 'Reframing medical education to support professional identity formation'. *Academic Medicine*, 89: 1446–1451.

Dahl, H. M., Keränen, M. and Kovalainen, A. (2011) 'Introduction'. In H. M. Dahl, M. Keränen and A. Kovalainen (eds), *Europeanization, Care and Gender: Global Challenges*. Basingstoke, UK: Palgrave, pp. 1–17.

Dent, M. (2005) 'Post-new public management in public sector hospitals? The UK, Germany and Italy'. *Policy Polity*, 33: 623–636.

Durkheim, E. (1992) *Professional Ethics and Civic Morals*. London: Routledge.

Evetts, J. (2011) 'A new professionalism? Challenges and opportunities'. *Current Sociology*, 59: 406–422.

Evetts, J. (2013) 'Professionalism: Value and ideology'. *Current Sociology*, 61: 778–796.

Faulconbridge, J. R. and Muzio, D. (2011) 'Professions in a globalizing world: Towards a transnational sociology of professions'. *International Sociology*, 27: 136–152.

Gorman, E. and Sandefur, R. (2011) '"Golden Age", quiescence, and revival: How the sociology of professions became the study of knowledge-based work'. *Work and Occupations*, 38: 275–302.

Greenwood, R. and Suddaby, R. (2006) 'Institutional entrepreneurships in mature fields: The big five accounting firms'. *Academy of Management Journal*, 49: 27–48.

Harvey, D. (2007) *A Brief History of Neoliberalism*. Oxford: Oxford University Press.

Hayek, F. (1945) 'The use of knowledge in society'. *American Economic Review*, 35: 519–530.

Kalleberg, A. (2011) *Good Jobs, Bad Jobs: The Rise of Polarized and Precarious Employment Systems in the United States, 1970s to 2000s*. New York: Russell Sage Foundation.

Kirtzner, I. (1973) *Competition and Entrepreneurship*. Chicago, IL: University of Chicago Press.

Kovalainen, A. (1995) *At the Margins of the Economy: Women's Self-Employment in Finland 1960–1990*. Avebury: Ashgate.

Kovalainen, A. and Österberg-Högstedt, J. (2011) 'Finland's changing public sector: Business, trust and gender in municipalities'. *Nordiske Organisasjonsstudier,* 13: 57–73.

Kovalainen, A. and Österberg-Högstedt, J. (2013) 'Entrepreneurship within social and health care: A question of identity, gender and professionalism'. *International Journal of Gender and Entrepreneurship*, 5: 17–35.

Kovalainen, A. and Simonen, L. (1998) 'Neo-entrepreneurship in Finland in welfare services'. *Transfer*, 4: 462–490.

Kovalainen, A. and Sundin, E. (2012) 'Entrepreneurship in public organizations'. In D. Hjorth (ed.), *Handbook on Organisational Entrepreneurship*. Cheltenham, UK: Edward Elgar, pp. 257–280.

Kuhlmann, E. (2006) *Modernising Health Care: Reinventing Professions, the State and the Public*. Bristol, UK: Policy Press.

Kuhlmann, E. (2013) '"Riders in the Storm": The professions and healthcare governance'. *Saúde & Tecnologia,* 10: e6–e10.

Kuhlmann, E. and Saks, M. (2008) 'Introduction'. In E. Kuhlmann and M. Saks (eds), *Rethinking Professional Governance: International Directions in Healthcare*. London: Policy Press, pp. 1–14.

Kuratko, D. F. (2007) 'Corporate entrepreneurship'. *Foundations and Trends in Entrepreneurship*, 3: 151–203.

McDaniel, S. A. (2006) 'Self-employment: How individual choices interact with market economies'. *International Sociology*, 21: 796–805.

McDowell, L. (2014) 'Gender, work, employment and society: Feminist reflections on continuity and change'. *Work, Employment & Society*, 28: 825–837.

Muzio, D. and Kirkpatrick, I. (2011) 'Professions and organizations: a conceptual framework'. *Current Sociology*, 59: 389–405.

Noordegraaf, M. (2007) 'From "pure" to "hybrid" professionalism: Present-day professionalism in ambiguous public domains'. *Administration & Society*, 39: 761–785.

Parsons, T. (1939) 'The professions and social structure'. *Social Forces*, 17: 457–467.

Poutanen, S. and Kovalainen, A. (2014) 'What is new in the "New Economy"?'. In J. Gruhlich and B. Riegraf (eds), *Care as Critical Nexus Challenging Rigid Conceptualizations/Geschlecht und transnationale Räume*. Münster: Verlag Westphälisches Dampfboot, pp. 174–191.

Saks, M. (2010) 'Analyzing the professions: The case for the Neo-Weberian approach'. *Comparative Sociology*, 9: 887–915.

Saks, M. (2011) *Professions and the Public Interest: Medical Power, Altruism and Alternative Medicine*. London: Routledge.

Schumpeter, J. ([1912]1961) *The Theory of Economic Development*. Cambridge, MA: Harvard University Press.

Shane, S. and Venkataraman, S. (2000) 'The promise of entrepreneurship as a field of research'. *Academy of Management Review*, 25: 217–226.

Swedberg, R. (1991) *Schumpeter: A Biography*. Princeton, NJ: Princeton University Press.

Thomas, P. and Hewitt, J. (2011) 'Managerial organization and professional autonomy: A discourse-based conceptualization'. *Organization Studies*, 32: 1373–1993.

Vallas, S. (2011) *Work: A Critique*. Boston: Polity Books.

Von Mises, L. ([1963]1996) *Human Action: A Treatise on Economics.* New Haven, CT: Yale University Press.

Weber, M. (1905/1960) *The Protestant Ethic and the Spirit of Capitalism.* New York: Scribner's Sons.

Young, M. and Müller, J. (2014) 'From sociology of professions to sociology of professional knowledge'. In M. Young and J. Müller (eds), *Knowledge, Expertise and the Professions.* Oxford: Routledge, pp. 3–16.

9

Professionalism, trust and cooperation

Patrick Brown and Michael Calnan

Introduction

Professions and professional work require trust and in various senses are sustained by it (Elston, 2009). A close inspection of trust processes involving professions is thus important not only as a topic of interest in its own right, but moreover because considering what it means to trust can also shed significant light on the very nature of professions, the social contexts which they shape and within which they function. If, as we will argue, trust relations around various professions are shifting and increasingly being called into question, then this implies that the form and function of professions are also in a state of flux – and vice versa. The chapter below interrogates some of these changes, alongside some more enduring features, in exploring various ways of conceptually relating trust to a study of professions and professionals.

An awareness of the salience of trust is clearly apparent within many classic studies of professions. Some of the more critical perspectives depicted clients of professionals as relatively powerless and obligated, whereby 'on entering the domain of the profession ... the citizen is expected to give up all but the most humble rights, to put himself into the hands of the expert and trust his judgement and good intentions' (Freidson, 1970, p. 355). Trust in such analyses could be characterized by dependency and knowledge asymmetry in the face of hegemonic powers, where trust develops either as unwitting obeisance or as a 'forced option' (Greener, 2003; Barbalet, 2009). Meanwhile, more positive accounts emphasized the refinement and specialization of expert knowledge applied by professionals who were bound by fiduciary obligation. The enduring legacy and significance of a profession's symbolic value thus obliged the professional as much as the client (Parsons, 1975). Professionals were valued, therefore, through their proven ability to manage uncertainty and complexity on our behalf – with trust emerging from quality past experiences, while also underpinning interactions in the present and orientations to the future through binding mutual obligation.

As much as more classical approaches provide many useful starting points for analysing trust, the sociology of the professions has developed greatly since these earlier studies (as described elsewhere in this Companion), and moreover, the nature of trust around professions would appear to have been decidedly altered amidst the intensifying pressures of late-modern societies. This chapter will therefore focus upon more recent theoretical work on trust and professions, delineating five main themes around which the chapter will be structured: (a) the regulatory and organizational apparatus around professional work can usefully be illuminated through notions of abstract systems (Giddens, 1990) and related system-trust (Luhmann, 1979); (b) accordingly, challenges to self-regulation will be explored through the construction of a trust *crisis* and the contrasting narratives of professionals as self-interested knaves or more benevolent knights (Le Grand, 2010; Dixon-Woods *et al.*, 2011); (c) ostensible changes in levels of system-trust in professionals have led to shifts in the balance between trust and checking within the governance frameworks by which professionals are monitored and held accountable for their work (Davies and Mannion, 1999); (d) at a more micro-level, the nature of professional work relies on the ability of individual professionals to successfully embody the expertise and appropriate motivations which are intrinsic to winning trust (Calnan and Rowe, 2008), whereby interactions with clients may be influenced by changing regulation; and (e) dysfunctional aspects of the regulation and (external) governance of existing mainstream professions can help us understand challenges in effective facework, status and trust building for existing professions, as well as the investment of trust and hope in (re-)emerging professions. We will conclude the chapter by reflecting upon some new formats of professional trust dynamics emerging within late modernity (Kuhlmann, 2006; Brown and Calnan, 2011).

Within the chapter we refer to various cases and country contexts but focus mainly upon the British, and especially the English, medical profession. This choice is partly pragmatic (as the context we know best), but medicine is moreover seen as the archetypal profession in terms of uniquely high levels of trust, power and social influence (Elston, 2009, p. 18), yet it is where high levels of uncertainty and unpredictability make trust more explicit. England also represents an extreme case in the way that new formats of (external) regulation of professionals – not least medical professionals – and the related imposition of new public management (NPM) have been implemented in a particularly swift and stringent manner (Alaszewski, 2002; Moran, 2003; Dixon-Woods *et al.*, 2011). As we will explore in the first main section, trust, power and societal influence are vitally bound up with the nature of regulation and pressures towards change.

Regulation as a basis for system-trust

Systems of regulation: building trust through inclusion and exclusion

One of the key defining attributes of a profession, structures of (self-)regulation have changed dramatically over many centuries and are significant for understanding the power, status and general esteem of particular professions across wider society (Freidson, 1970). Moran (2003, p. 42) describes how in Britain the 'ancient professions' of clerics, lawyers and doctors came to be regulated via more formal and legal mechanisms following a series of reforms across the middle part of the nineteenth century. Yet while the British Apothecaries Act (1815), as with the Dutch Regulation of Medical Practice Act (1865 – *Wet regelende de uitoefening der geneeskunst*) and other laws across Europe, created much more formal legal delineations between professionals and outsiders, *within* the profession itself self-regulation remained relatively informal, 'cooperative' and 'light touch' (Moran, 2003, p. 42).

These nineteenth-century reforms of the ancient professions and creation of many new professions involved the instituting of a great many organizations that would go on to hold important symbolic value for how various professions have come to be viewed across wider societies. Perhaps most visible of all professions (Elston, 2009), the clear legal parameters regarding doctors' training and registration – especially the placing of these under peer scrutiny – helped to generate a sense of appropriate checks and balances which has laid the taken-for-granted basis of patients' interactions with medical professionals (Giddens, 1990).

The institution of the General Medical Council (GMC) (as it is now known) through the 1858 Medical Act can thus be seen as pivotal to the development of the 'modern' profession of medicine in Britain. The wider legislation and the GMC itself were partly the product of reformist political pressures, epitomized by the campaigning of Thomas Wakeley and *The Lancet* which he founded and edited. Railing against both the elitism of the medical establishment and the prevalence of 'quackery' in common approaches to disease, the reformists campaigned for a more meritocratic and scientifically trained medical profession (Burney, 2007). For Wakeley, the need for a more (meritocratic, non-elitist) inclusive yet (anti-quackery) exclusive profession went hand-in-hand:

> By excluding the medical rank and file from full membership, the [elitist] royal colleges demeaned the majority of medical practitioners before their public, implying that their qualifications were not sufficient to distinguish them from those practicing without a licence.
>
> *(Burney, 2007, p. 56)*

This quotation, written regarding a historical moment which was crucial to the forging of the modern medical profession, points to a number of important social dynamics around professions which are salient for our concerns regarding trust. First, the societal view of how a profession functions at an organizational level has important implications for how individual practitioners or groups of practitioners are perceived. Second, such a colouring of views of professionals often remains more implicit than explicit. Yet nevertheless, and third, changes to the central legal-organizational structures and functioning of a profession have important implications for members and non-members and how they are viewed by 'their public'.

Interpersonal trust interacting with system-trust

In further analysing the first of these three concerns, it is useful to consider interpersonal trust, placed in individual professionals, alongside broader views of a profession as an abstract system of expert knowledge (Luhmann, 1988; Giddens, 1990). Interpersonal trust has been defined as 'the optimistic acceptance of a vulnerable situation in which the truster believes the trustee will care for the truster's interests' (Hall *et al.*, 2001, p. 615). In accounting for such acceptance, Luhmann (1988, pp. 95–96) encourages us to think about the ways in which we make assumptions based upon what is familiar or, moreover, how we start to make sense of contexts which are unfamiliar. In both types of setting, we might navigate uncertainty by implicit reference to the symbolic meanings we associate with social actors and their actions, in relation to wider social systems (Luhmann, 1988; Möllering, 2005). Alternatively, in some other settings, we abstractly consider or assume the functioning of systems as a proxy for the actions of many individual professionals – in the absence of direct encounters with these professionals (Luhmann, 1988).

Whether we are trusting in a (familiar) family doctor with the drug she is asking us to ingest (but which could harm us), or whether we are 'trusting' in the system of aircraft maintenance which seeks to render our pending flight a safe one (but which could fall out of the sky), we adopt an 'attitude' which overlooks risk through a 'previous structural reduction in complexity' (Luhmann, 1988, p. 103). Our more or less precise understandings and/or assumptions regarding social systems of professional expertise, training in this expertise and the ongoing regulation of practice – in line with the state of the art – help us rule out large swathes of complexity such as those regarding the family doctor knowing nothing about that medicine or the aircraft engineers casting nothing more than a cursory glance at a plane before granting permission to fly. When heeding the doctor or while boarding the plane we take these and other basic premises for granted. Luhmann (1988) calls this *confidence*, facilitated through systems.

There are, of course, important differences between the two cases above. The interaction with a specific individual doctor may be underpinned by certain assumptions regarding the abstract system of the medical profession, but it also involves interaction dynamics and a relational proximity through which we develop further understandings of *this* professional's competence, but also of her motives and the compatibility of these with our own goals and concerns (Brown, 2008, p. 351). This interaction between a professional and patient can be seen as taking place at an 'access point' into the abstract system – 'the meeting ground of facework and faceless commitments' (Giddens, 1990, p. 83), where these facework commitments exist as more relational and interactive (rather than more abstract or symbolic) bases of trust (p. 80). Ideally, the competence of the medical expert is embodied in the caring professional.

While our experiences at access points are rooted in knowledge of abstract systems and a host of related assumptions regarding the medical profession, healthcare system and local organizational dynamics – with these forming the basis of an interpersonal (dis-)trust – so do our experiences at access points come to shape our generalized views of the abstract system (Giddens, 1990; Brown and Calnan, 2012). Broader, more or less positive, views of professional abstract systems are described by Luhmann (1979) as 'system-trust', which by way of its non-specific, non-interpersonal dynamics is qualitatively different to interpersonal trust. Both Luhmann (1988) and Giddens (1990) argue that everyday life in late modernity is characterized by an increased reliance upon such systems, implicitly involving the work of faceless expertise such as our example involving aircraft engineers. Whereas interpersonal trust is built on views of specific professionals' competence and care in light of system-trust, experiences of reliance on professionals which are wholly devoid of interaction with these professionals are purely based on 'function' (Jalava, 2006, p. 25): 'Such system trust is automatically built up through continual, affirmative experience … it needs constant feedback' (Luhmann, 1979, p. 50).

Trust, power and maintaining a monopoly of knowledge: challenges to self-regulation

A shift from confidence to trust

In seeking to assure continual affirmative experiences with professionals, regulation of professional work would seem vital for system-trust in professions. Luhmann's description of system-trust requiring ongoing positive feedback suggests that a profession's status and esteem within a society are somewhat more precarious than the coercive and monopolistic depictions of some classic texts. If a profession's status is significantly dependent upon system-trust then, according to some of Luhmann's (1988) arguments, it may only be as good as the last medicine prescription written by one of its members or the last plane granted permission to fly.

System-trust may be especially prone to lapses in a highly mediatized environment where the public's likelihood of hearing about failings is made more likely by the willingness of news media to report negative stories and the experiential immediacy of more distant dysfunctions through mediated knowledge flows (Butler and Drakeford, 2005; Warner, 2015). Failings, such as harm from medical treatment, deaths of neglected children or plane crashes, can certainly dent views of a wider profession (Warner, 2015), but Luhmann (1988, p. 104) goes on to qualify that system-trust may be protected, despite dysfunctions, through compelling performances of individual professionals when engaging with clients at access points. Positive first-hand experiences with healthcare professionals may incline patients to explain away failings as one-off aberrations (Brown and Calnan, 2012; Solbjør et al., 2012). Even amidst more regular failings, we may continue to enact trust on the basis that *our* doctor or *our* preferred airline (even though we never meet their engineers) possesses special qualities (Luhmann, 1988), regardless of problems elsewhere (Brown, 2009).

Where views of a profession as a whole are importantly shaped by ongoing encounters at access points, coupled to more enduring symbolic significance (Luhmann, 1988), then the more or less successful way expertise is embodied through a professional's presentation-of-self is fundamental to trusting (as will be considered in a later section). The concreteness of the experiential knowledge derived from direct encounters with professionals, compared with more remote media accounts, explains the relative importance of the former for trust (Brown, 2009). In the case of medical professionals in England, system-trust in professionals remained steadfastly high despite a spate of highly publicized professional failings during the mid to late 1990s, where a family doctor killed many of his patients (Harold Shipman) and where surgeons operating on infants were found to have been undertaking overly risky operations, with mortality rates unusually high as a consequence (Bristol Royal Infirmary). These were merely the two most high-profile incidents amongst many others, yet survey research suggested the percentage of the British public reporting trust in doctors remained very high at close to 90 per cent, even rising the year after Shipman's conviction for multiple murders (MORI, 2004).

While such survey research may be criticized for its reliability in measuring *trust* (this survey, for example, focused on professionals' 'veracity'), qualitative research in England involving cervical cancer patients receiving treatment in a local area where related services had suffered a number of high-profile problems also found high levels of trust in medical professionals, despite concerns about the healthcare system (Brown, 2009; see also Kuhlmann, 2006). Similarly, in Norway, Solbjør and colleagues (2012) found that patients who developed breast cancer which had not been picked up within (sometimes recent) screening often continued to trust, emphasizing the quality of care they had received, the success of the overall screening programme and explaining away their situation as an exception. Taken together, these quantitative and qualitative findings appear to counter broader discussions about a decline of trust in scientific and professional expertise (c.f. Furedi, 1997).

One way of working through this tension is to distinguish between professionals and healthcare systems, with the former being trusted more than the faceless latter. Another approach would be to return to Luhmann's conceptual distinction between confidence and trust. We noted earlier that confidence relates to taken-for-granted assumptions about an outcome, one where doubt is not experienced. Luhmann (1988) contrasts this with trust, which involves an awareness of alternative outcomes, doubt and the possibility for regret. Arguably, the professional failings reported above, alongside a more general awareness of the limitations of expertise and fallibility of experts in late modernity, have shifted patients from a position of relative confidence to one of trust, but this is qualitatively different from saying doctors are trusted less than they were (Brown, 2008). This important distinction is implicit elsewhere in the trust literature, for example in denoting a shift along a spectrum from a more blind non-reflexive trust towards more conditional-critical trust (Poortinga and Pidgeon, 2003; Calnan and Rowe, 2008), as we explore below.

The politicization of 'lost trust'

If trust in some professions has remained high while becoming more critical, it nevertheless entails a change in power dynamics around these professions and professionals' work (Dent, 2006). At the micro-level, shifts towards more critical forms of trust render different power dynamics in professional–client encounters – whereby the professional is more likely to be questioned, confronted with client perspectives and expert knowledge gathered by the client, and to be required to include the clients' concerns within any decision-making or advice-giving (Dent, 2006; Buetow *et al.*, 2009). While it is important not to exaggerate such changes and to acknowledge the extent to which more critical-conditional professional–client interactions may be dependent on the cultural capital and educational background of the client, the general direction of changes does indicate a reducing (albeit still strong) power-asymmetry and knowledge monopoly (Brown et al. 2015).

At the more meso-organizational level, that of professional regulation, the impact of changes in trust has arguably been more profound (Moran, 2003; Power, 2004; Dixon-Woods *et al.*, 2011). For while we suggested above that trust in British medical professionals had changed but not necessarily declined, the political machinations around the failings in professional practice provided a very different emphasis. Alaszewski (2002) argues that although dysfunctions in care such as those that took place at Bristol Royal Infirmary in England were not new, the failings nevertheless attracted significant media attention and were successfully politicized and 'used by the incoming [1997] Labour Government as evidence of the failure of public services and justification of its programme of modernization' (Alaszewski, 2002, p. 375).

At this broader level of analysis, the position and esteem of a profession has to be analysed in relation to both its public (client-base) and the state which enacts and maintains the legal framework by which, as we saw in the preceding section, the profession's monopoly of practice is maintained (Moran, 2003; Dent, 2006). A historical perspective on professions notes periods of relatively stable settlements involving these three groups, as well as other moments when these triangular 'compacts' break down – resulting in regulatory change (Ham and Alberti, 2002; Moran, 2003). In describing the position of the medical profession before the latter years of the twentieth century, Waring and colleagues follow Salter in denoting:

> a triangular regulatory 'bargain' that, in its ideal type, provided benefits to civil society through offering some assurance as to the standards of healthcare, benefits to the state in the form of enhanced legitimacy from civil society, and benefits to the profession in the form of trust and the privilege of self-regulation. Its practical effect was that the medical profession was allowed to monitor the conduct and performance of members, for the most part free of external scrutiny.
>
> *(Waring et al., 2010, p. 542)*

Regardless of what the British public really thought, the successful characterization of the medical profession as having lost public trust (MORI, 2004) was used by successive governments to rework this 'bargain', chiefly through a reduced autonomy of the profession – undermining self-regulation, significantly reforming the GMC, requiring revalidation and imposing increasing levels of external governance (Dixon-Woods *et al.*, 2011). Far from mere passive acceptance, elite representatives of the profession were very much involved in such restructuring, echoing and thus legitimizing notions of lost trust.

Trust, checking and control: transaction costs and inter-professional knowledge exchange

Shifts towards new forms of regulation and trust

Where professional organizations fail to successfully regulate the work of their members, to the extent that their publics become harmed, then prima facie there is a case for further intervention by the state. Or, where a professional group has come to depend on the state for much of its employment, then the state may increase its oversight of such professional work to ensure effective use of taxpayers' money. These were some of the underlying arguments behind a wave of reforms enacted in Britain over the past twenty years, especially between 1997 and 2002, which has been characterized by Moran (2003) as a period of unusually speedy and expansive regulatory reform. In contrast to the very gradual change whereby, for example, teaching had grown increasingly independent of state interference during the first half of the twentieth century, the last decade of the millennium was characterized by a paradigm shift towards a new format of regulatory politics in Britain, with manifold changes across many professions (Moran, 2003).

Le Grand (2010, p. 56) argues that the political organization of education systems or healthcare services is based around certain underlying perceptions and assumptions regarding the respective professionals involved: 'that is, the extent to which they are "knaves," motivated primarily by self-interest, or "knights," motivated by altruism and the desire to provide a public service'. As professionals have been increasingly construed as prone to mishaps and failures to act in the public or client interest, so have they also been depicted as knavish – in keeping with the narrow rational-choice models which dominate much recent policy-making logic (Taylor-Gooby, 2006). In turn, these views have underpinned various new forms of regulation which have emerged in place of the traditional compacts which had their roots in the informal 'club government' approach to regulation of the nineteenth century (Moran, 2003).

It is not new to perceive professionals as self-interested – Aneurin Bevan, a founding father of the British National Health Service (NHS) in the 1940s, famously referred to having to 'stuff [doctors'] mouths with gold' (Thomas-Symonds, 2010, p. 161) to ensure their cooperation – but the recent intensification of this more instrumental manner of overseeing professions has led to profound changes in their regulation and, accordingly, in the nature of professional work. Common emerging features of this new regulation, in Britain and elsewhere, are the result of 'complex bargains', usually involving the acceptance or imposition of some form of external oversight, with certain levels of autonomy retained in return for requiring professionals to work with more encoded forms of knowledge and guidelines of practice (Moran, 2003, p. 81). Moran draws out further common features of the legal and medical professions' experiences in terms of a much tighter and interwoven relationship between (self-)regulatory organizations and the state (p. 85).

In considering the effects of this more formal, external and imposed regulation, the medical profession in Britain again represents a prototypical case where doctors' work has been redefined in many ways by the expansion of governance and audit (Flynn, 2002; Harrison and Smith, 2003; Brown, 2011). Clinical governance, a variant of NPM, has combined a proliferation of guidelines and targets with the increased recording and 'checking' of professionals' compliance. 'Softer' forms of governance have also been described (Sheaff and Pilgrim, 2006) that impact on knowledge-work in medicine and other professions. Here, we concentrate on a number of implications of these forms of professional oversight for trust.

The impact of new forms of governance on trust and professional work

The impact of external governance and NPM reforms can be usefully conceptualized from the perspective of transaction cost economics, whereby transactions of goods, services and knowledge can be managed through *markets* incentivized via price, *bureaucratic stipulations* incentivized by hierarchy, or *trust* incentivized through social norms (Adler, 2001). These three bases of transactions are ideal-types and various combinations of these approaches will be interwoven across any organizational–professional context. Professional work has always been structured around

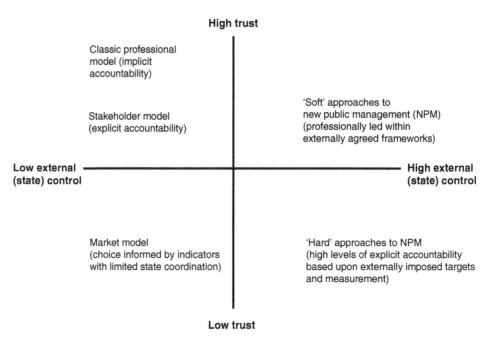

Figure 9.1 'Balancing' trust and state bureaucratic control within various governance models
Source: adapted from Rowe and Calnan (2006, p. 381).

hierarchy and financial contracts to some degree, but the move away from more informal forms of self-regulation within various configurations of NPM certainly represents a diminished role for trust (see Figure 9.1).

The shift towards a reliance upon guidelines, audit and checking not only implies a reduced trust in professionals but has been further criticized as positively undermining trust within the organizations in which professionals operate. Davies and Mannion (1999, p. 6) emphasize that while other ways of managing organizational transactions exist, the effective functioning of bureaucratic or market-oriented *alternatives* to trust are nevertheless 'underpinned' by 'softer information and informal relationships' grounded in trust. The way in which new forms of auditing professional work may undermine traditional normative-fiduciary structures and related informal commitments is therefore a concern. Where forms of audit are implemented by those outside the profession, who are perceived as not understanding the nuances and intricacies of professional work, then various forms of instrumental and subversive actions may result, from gaming to fabrication of recorded data to selective appropriation of guidelines (Bevan and Hood, 2006; Brown, 2011; Spyridonidis and Calnan, 2011).

Such deleterious effects of new forms of external regulation, through a neglect of trust, would be problematic for any organizational or working context but may be especially dysfunctional for much professional work which is innately 'knowledge intensive' (Adler, 2001, p. 216). Trust has been argued to drive efficiencies and quality outcomes in its enabling of informal knowledge exchange, refinement of practices and other key features of organizational learning (Davies and Mannion, 1999; Sheaff and Pilgrim, 2006). Forms of hierarchy and market are not inherently undermining of trust, but the variants of quasi-markets and related forms of regulatory bureaucracy which have emerged within many northern European welfare states and educational systems have resulted in forms of audit-checking which are often described as creating organizational dynamics which distract from the first-order goals of effective professional work (Rothstein, 2006) and usher in "tyrannous" tendencies (Strathern, 2000; Bevan and Hood, 2006), thus undermining quality and efficiency.

Facework and abstract systems: embodying trustworthy practice at access points

Regulatory (mis)trust impacting upon clients' (mis)trust

The preceding section noted that a perceived need to recast formats of professional regulation, based on doubts around the competence and motives of professionals, has ushered in new forms of governance which have been critiqued for impeding quality professional work but moreover for fostering 'knavish' motives rather than overcoming these: 'a system that does not trust people begets people that cannot be trusted' (Davies and Lampel, 1998 – quoted in Davies and Mannion, 1999, p. 15). Professionals acting in a more purposive-rational manner are less likely to win the trust of their colleagues, and hence new regulatory systems founded on the premise of limited trust undermine the functioning of this valuable organizational lubricant.

Stimulating more instrumental tendencies within professional work may be problematic for building trust with clients. Earlier in this chapter we briefly addressed the importance of facework for generating interpersonal trust in a particular professional, as well as for galvanizing system-trust in the broader profession. It is possible to identify a number of ways in which new forms of governance may hinder professionals' trust-building facework, though of course the nature of this facework will vary greatly across different professions and cultural settings.

Effective presentation-of-self within client encounters may be especially crucial for professionals working within health and social care contexts, not least due to the way their emotional labour, embodied interactions and hands-on care-work may provide a rather intense form of experiential knowledge, as drawn upon by the client when inferring the clinical competencies and/or caring qualities of the professional (Brown, 2008). Where the demands placed upon professionals to account for their work create a substantial bureaucratic burden, this may detract from the time which professionals have to engage in facework and trust-building activities (Brown and Calnan, 2012). Trust may still be generated 'swiftly' by skilled communicators within certain contexts, especially when certain positive starting assumptions already exist about the professional, though more time may be necessary if trust is to move beyond more calculative and superficial forms towards those based upon mutual knowledge and commitment (Dibben and Lean, 2003, p. 243). These latter deeper forms of trust relations may be very important in facilitating the knowledge exchange and cooperation between client and professional which generate quality outcomes and perpetuate trust over the longer term.

Professional–client interactions impeded by governance

There are further ways in which less-trusting governance systems may impact on professional–client trust. In our research into trust within mental health services, we found that the various professionals involved (psychiatrists, nurses, social workers) experienced high levels of uncertainty in their day-to-day work – not least regarding the diagnostic processes, notions of good care and the management of risk – which were far from straightforward in contexts of psychosis care (Brown and Calnan, 2012). Tensions emerging between the uncertainty which was so characteristic of professionals' work, on the one hand, and the bureaucratic demands for calculability and control within governance arrangements, on the other, led to many professionals describing heightened experiences of pressure and work-stress (Brown and Calnan, 2012). Stress appeared to vary in relation to level of seniority (senior psychiatrists had greater decision latitude which insulated them from stress) as well as the extent of trust demonstrated by middle managers. Where more junior professionals experienced pressurized work within more low-trust contexts, high levels of absences due to illness (primarily work-stress) were reported. Such effects could, in turn, be seen to affect the quality of care, consistency and time that professional teams were able to provide for clients.

Amidst such pressurized work environments, professionals' defensive practice may also change the very nature of their work, with a wariness of blame coming to warp the ends and means of professional practice (Power, 2003; Bevan and Hood, 2006; Brown and Calnan, 2012). In various contexts, clients may come to see governance frameworks, not least those pertaining to risk, as driving professionals' agendas ahead of their own expressed interests (Power, 2004; Rothstein, 2006). This compromising of motives which precludes putting clients first – as inferred from access-point encounters – may lead to negative views of these professionals and, correspondingly, of the profession more broadly (Brown and Calnan, 2012).

Alongside the influence of new forms of regulation and governance, there are also broader societal changes which can be seen as creating challenging dynamics for the maintenance of trust within professional–client interactions. We have already noted how demands for calculability and control from professionals, which have been described as intensifying through cultural developments within modernity, may place professionals working with uncertainty under pressure. These demands may be especially difficult to negotiate as their emergence coincides with a growing awareness of the uncertainty present within abstract systems of knowledge and the fallibility of the professionals who apply this knowledge (Giddens, 1990).

Amidst these shifting features of late modernity, professionals' presentation or veiling of uncertainty within the encounter may come to bear decisively upon trust dynamics:

> There is no skill so carefully honed and no form of expert knowledge so comprehensive that elements of hazard or luck do not come into play. Experts ordinarily presume that lay individuals will feel more reassured if they are not able to observe how frequently these elements enter into expert performance.
>
> *(Giddens, 1990, p. 86)*

Yet the masking of back-stage uncertainty by front-stage presentation has its limitations. Referring to the actions of family doctors, Fugelli (2001, p. 577) warns that where 'patients experience too large a difference between "front stage medicine" and "back stage medicine", trust is lost'.

Trust in (re-)emerging professions

Challenges to mainstream professions amidst a more critical public sphere

In earlier sections we suggested that historic shifts in regulatory structure can be seen as enabling a more homogeneously trusted profession, while concurrently distancing these professionals from *non-professionals* in the eyes of their publics (Burney, 2007). Establishing the trust of a public is thus one vital source of power for a profession; but so is discrediting outsiders. Much of the politics in the mid-nineteenth-century consolidation of medical professions across various national contexts involved scathing critiques of quackery, which professionals defined themselves against (Burney, 2007). Indeed, organizations such as the Association Against Quackery (Vereniging Tegen de Kwakzalverij) in the Netherlands remain outspoken critics of various complementary and alternative medicine (CAM) techniques within contemporary national public spheres. Undermining trust and hope in CAM is an important feature of this critical discourse (VtdK, 2010, p. 1).

This particular organization also lobbies the Dutch Ministry of Public Health and insurance providers regarding what should and should not be included within basic healthcare insurance coverage for Dutch citizens. The challenging of various 'alternative' treatments is seemingly effective, for example in recent laws in the Netherlands prohibiting claims for effectiveness on packaging of homeopathic treatments (Rijksoverheid, 2012, Art.73, para.2) and the recent limiting of tax dispensations to mainstream 'protected professions', excluding most CAM practitioners (Rijksoverheid, 2013). These and other recent policy developments elsewhere ward against narratives regarding the inexorable rise of CAM in recent years.

Yet anti-quackery claims become harder to substantiate within late-modern public spheres, where the multiplicity of scientific theories is commonly recognized, where an emphasis on evidence-based medicine is drawing attention to many interventions commonly used in 'mainstream' medicine which are evidence-deficient or where contrasting evidence of (non-)effectiveness exists (e.g. Kirsch *et al.*, 2008), and where a few CAM practices are becoming more professionalized and appealing to evidence-based reasoning (Broom and Tovey, 2008; Gale, 2014). This has led some researchers to suggest a shift away from (bio-)medical hegemony-monopoly towards a reversion to medical pluralism (Cant and Sharma, 2004), even if this cannot be seen as a straightforward unidirectional process.

Micro-dynamics in professional–client interactions: new professions winning trust through facework

Amidst these broader macro-level conditions, which render neat distinctions between system-trust in professions and system-distrust in certain outsiders harder to maintain, there exists an array of conditions at the micro-level which further assist the (re-)emergence of some former outsiders towards gradual professionalization. As addressed in the preceding section, the increasing employment of professionals within health, welfare and other state-run institutions and the later influence of various management and efficiency drives have compromised these mainstream professionals' interactions and, correspondingly, their relationships with their clients.

Mechanic (2001) argues that despite doctors' concerns to the contrary, average time spent with a patient in primary care consultations increased rather than decreased between the mid 1960s and the mid 1990s. However, this measure of 'objective' time does not take into account the increasingly negotiated rather than deferential nature of these encounters, so the subjective 'cadence' of these interactions may indeed be less satisfactory for patients and professionals alike. In contrast to the stipulated nine-minute consultations which English patients may expect with their family doctors (Mechanic, 2001), clients of CAM practitioners refer to the extent and cadence of time as one of many features which underlie their usage of these services (Siahpush, 2000). Gale summarizes Siahpush's (2000) review of reasons for the growing popularity of CAM as including 'dissatisfaction with the health outcomes of orthodox medicine; dissatisfaction with the medical encounter/doctor–patient relationship; preference for the way alternative therapists treated their patients, including being caring, individualized attention, ample time and information' (Gale, 2014, p. 807), as well as noting a preference for natural solutions, and the role of some CAM approaches in assisting sense-making amidst illness and death after the decline of organized religion. Although not mentioned explicitly in this list, processes pertaining to trust are very much implicit. As Siahpush (2000, p. 167) states, CAM practitioners are able to be far more patient-oriented in the way they may 'pay close to attention to trivial symptoms, spend a lot of time with patients and therefore gain their trust and patronization'.

The quality of interpersonal trust building may, very gradually, be furnishing an emerging system-trust which accompanies – drawing upon while helping facilitate – a creeping professionalization in some CAM fields in Britain. Broom and Tovey's research into patients' use of CAM in the often staunchly biomedical context of oncology care describes patients' preferences for the depth and holism of various CAM encounters which

> were valued, primarily, for their subjectified (rather than abstracted) and individualized (rather than depersonalized) approach to cancer care; an approach which was seen to allow for, and promote, agency, self-determinism and ultimately hope.
>
> *(2008, p. 43)*

The extent to which CAM is integrated within British oncology care varies a lot across different institutional and professional settings (Broom and Tovey, 2008), again emphasising the micro and structural dynamics of syncretism-pluralism across professional domains. Gale (2014) similarly points to some broader variations in CAM use which are highly relevant to studies of trust in (new) professions more broadly. In the United States, the increased propensity towards CAM usage amongst African-Americans who have been victims of discrimination, and/or the influence of social network 'membership' (Gale, 2014, p. 808), are two examples which underline the salience of a more nuanced and textured attentiveness to different publics and contrasting attitudes towards different professions.

Effects of wider social membership and/or marginalization may be important therefore in noting varying levels of trust in some professions and distrust in others. Distrust amongst certain marginalized groups towards hegemonic professions – which clients are compelled to use despite misgivings in doing so – helps us understand the darker side of professional monopolies, the difficulties faced in professional work and, in extreme situations, the violence and hostility experienced by some professionals more than others (Elston and Gabe, 2008; Newburn, 2014). These nuances underline the limitations of accounts of homogeneous national system-trust in professions, with Hohl and colleagues' (2013) research into variations in views of the police profession being one useful example.

Conclusion

Nuanced variations in system-trust towards professionals represent a challenge to neat analyses of professions' status and the structure of professional–client relations. They also pose a challenge to professionals themselves – in the requirement to gauge a client's attitudes and expectations and respond appropriately. Some clients will expect a more egalitarian, negotiated approach where back-stage issues of evidence and uncertainty are openly worked through when informing clients' choices. Others will neither expect nor appreciate such interactions, preferring more traditional, professional-driven encounters. The ability of the professional to accurately 'read' the client and deliver the appropriate level of (in-)formality, complexity and choice may be increasingly important.

Meanwhile, clients may be more attuned to the varying quality of professionals, with alternative sources of expert information and/or 'visible markers' such as league tables being used to negotiate trust amidst a heightened awareness of uncertainty (Greener, 2003; Kuhlmann, 2006). Assessments of the presentation-of-self nevertheless remain vital to the development of (dis-) trust in specific professionals. To the extent that clients adopt this newer more critical-conditional approach, trust in professionals necessitates more active and continual maintenance than in the past (Giddens 1990). Such trust dynamics epitomize a rather different regulatory environment which in some senses may more effectively ensure the quality of individual professional work than earlier forms of a less conditional, more enduring and blanket trust (Brown and Calnan, 2011).

As far as they are able to capture what matters, visible markers of performance applied within new governance frameworks may be useful in generating conditional trust (Kuhlmann, 2006). However, we have noted various perverse tendencies which warp the meaning of these markers and professional practices as a result. Where governance frameworks and markers are developed by professionals themselves, then their enhanced sensitivity to the subtleties of professional work and, correspondingly, their legitimacy amongst professionals, may render them highly effective in facilitating both trust and professional work which merits this trust (Kuhlmann, 2006; Brown and Calnan, 2011). But these processes may only function effectively in the absence of the more instrumental 'checking' which otherwise undermines the socio-normative fabric through which trust functions in "civilizing" practice (Brown and Calnan, 2011).

As professional work is increasingly performed within 'audit societies', the civilizing influence of trust upon professionals may be increasingly inhibited. Ironically, obstructions to effective trust relations are partly motivated (or at least justified) by ostensible crises of trust. By exploring shifting trust dynamics in the archetypal profession of medicine (Elston, 2009), especially within a national context where trust has been especially problematized and NPM 'solutions' fervently pursued, our analysis has sought to provide insights with much broader cross-professional relevance.

Amidst organizational contexts seen as becoming more faceless and bureaucratically and technologically mediated, the value of individual professional *faces* may be less obvious. Yet we must remember that 'to ask why societies incorporate their knowledge in professions is thus not only to ask why societies have specialized lifetime experts, but to ask why they place expertise in people rather than things or rules' (Abbott, 1988, p. 323). Professionals were initially trusted to deal with complexity and, while trusting these professionals has itself become more complex, both these forms of complexity are most satisfactorily resolved by interacting individuals.

References

Abbott, A. (1988) *The System of Professions: An Essay on the Division of Expert Labour.* Chicago, IL: University of Chicago Press.

Adler, P. (2001) 'Market, hierarchy and trust: The knowledge economy and the future of capitalism'. *Organization Science*, 12(2), pp. 215–234.

Alaszewski, A. (2002) 'The impact of the Bristol Royal Infirmary disaster and inquiry on public services in the UK'. *Journal of Interprofessional Care*, 16(4), pp. 371–378.

Barbalet, J. (2009) 'A characterisation of trust and its consequences'. *Theory and Society*, 38(4), pp. 367–382.

Bevan, H. and Hood, C. (2006) 'What's measured is what matters: Targets and gaming in the English public health care system'. *Public Administration*, 84(3), pp. 517–538.

Broom, A. and Tovey, P. (2008) *Therapeutic Pluralism: Exploring Experiences of Cancer Patients and Professionals.* London: Routledge.

Brown, P. (2008) 'Trusting in the new NHS: Instrumental versus communicative action'. *Sociology of Health & Illness,* 30(3), pp. 349–363.

Brown, P. (2009) 'The phenomenology of trust: A Schutzian analysis of the social construction of knowledge by gynae-oncology patients'. *Health, Risk and Society*, 11(5), pp. 391–407.

Brown, P. (2011) 'The concept of lifeworld as a tool in analysing health-care work: Exploring profession-als' resistance to governance through subjectivity, norms and experiential knowledge'. *Social Theory and Health*, 9(2), pp. 147–165.

Brown, P. and Calnan, M. (2011) 'The civilising processes of trust: Developing quality mechanisms which are local, professional-led and thus legitimate'. *Social Policy &Administration*, 45(1), pp. 19–34.

Brown, P. and Calnan, M. (2012) *Trusting on the Edge: Managing Uncertainty and Vulnerability in the Context of Severe Mental Health Problems*. Bristol, UK: Policy Press.

Brown, P., Elston, ME. and Gabe, J. (2015) From patient deference towards negotiated and precarious infor-mality: An Eliasian analysis of English general practitioners' understandings of changing patient relations. Social Science & Medicine 146:164–172.

Buetow, S., Jutel, A. and Hoare, K. (2009) 'Shrinking social space in the doctor–modern patient relation-ship: A review of forces for, and implications of, homologisation'. *Patient Education and Counselling*, 74(1), pp. 97–103.

Burney, I. (2007) 'The politics of particularism: Medicalization and medical reform in 19th century Britain'. In R. Bivins and J. Pickstone (eds) *Medicine, Madness and Social History: Essays in Honour of Roy Porter*, pp. 46–57. Basingstoke, UK: Palgrave.

Butler, I. and Drakeford, M. (2005) *Scandal, Social Policy and Social Welfare*. Bristol, UK: Polity Press.

Calnan, M. and Rowe, R. (2008) *Trust Matters in Healthcare*. Basingstoke, UK: Palgrave.

Cant, S. and Sharma, U. (2004) *A New Medical Pluralism: Complementary Medicine, Doctors and the State*. London: Taylor & Francis.

Davies, H. and Lampel, J. (1998) 'Trust in performance indicators'. *BMJ Quality and Safety*, 7, pp. 159–162.

Davies, H. and Mannion, R. (1999) 'Clinical governance: Striking a balance between checking and trusting'. Centre for Health Economics – discussion paper 165, online at: www.york.ac.uk/media/che/documents/papers/discussionpapers/CHE%20Discussion%20Paper%20165.pdf (last accessed 25 January 2016).

Dent, M. (2006) 'Patient choice and medicine in health care: Responsibilisation, governance and proto-professionalisation'. *Public Management Review*, 8(3), pp. 449–462.

Dibben, M. and Lean, M. (2003) 'Achieving compliance in chronic illness management: Illustrations of trust relationships between physicians and nutrition clinic patients'. *Health, Risk and Society*, 5(3), pp. 241–248.

Dixon-Woods, M., Yeung, K. and Bosk, C. (2011) 'Why is UK medicine no longer a self-regulating profes-sion? The role of scandals involving "bad apple" doctors'. *Social Science & Medicine*, 73(10), pp. 1452–1459.

Elston, M. A. (2009) 'Remaking a trustworthy medical profession in twenty-first century Britain?'. In J. Gabe and M. Calnan (eds) *The New Sociology of the Health Service*, pp. 17–36. London: Routledge.

Flynn, R. (2002) 'Clinical governance and governmentality'. *Health, Risk and Society*, 4(2), pp. 155–170.

Freidson, E. (1970) *Profession of Medicine: A Study of the Sociology of Applied Knowledge*. Chicago, IL: University of Chicago Press

Fugelli, P. (2001) 'Trust in General Practice'. *British Journal of General Practice*, 51, pp. 575–579.

Furedi, F. (1997) *Culture of Fear: Risk Taking and the Morality of Low Expectation*. London: Cassell.

Gabe, J. and Elston, M.A. (2008) '"We don't have to take this": Zero tolerance of violence against healthcare workers in a time of insecurity'. *Social Policy & Administration*, 42(6), pp. 691–709.

Gale, N. (2014) 'The sociology of traditional, complementary and alternative medicine'. *Sociology Compass*, 8(6), pp. 805–822.

Giddens, A. (1990) *The Consequences of Modernity*. Cambridge: Polity Press.

Greener, I. (2003) 'Patient choice in the NHS: the view from economic sociology'. *Social Theory and Health*, 1(1), pp. 72–89.

Hall, M., Dugan, M., Zheng, B. and Mishra, A. (2001) 'Trust in physicians and medical institutions: What is it, can it be measured, and does it matter?'. *Millbank Quarterly*, 79(4), pp. 613–639.

Ham, C. and Alberti, K. (2002) 'The medical profession, the public and the government'. *British Medical Journal*, 324, pp. 838–841.

Harrison, S. and Smith, C. (2003) 'Neo-bureaucracy and public management: The case of medicine in the National Health Service'. *Competition and Change*, 7(4), pp. 243–254.

Hohl, K., Stanko, B. and Newburn, T. (2013) 'The effect of the 2011 London disorder on public opinion of police and attitudes towards crime, disorder, and sentencing'. *Policing*, 7(1), pp. 12–20.

Jalava, J. (2006) *Trust as a Decision: The Problems and Functions of Trust in Luhmannian Systems Theory*. PhD thesis, University of Helsinki.

Kirsch, I., Deacon, B., Huedo-Medina, T., Scoboria, A., Moore, T. and Johnson, B. (2008) 'Initial severity and antidepressant benefits: A meta-analysis of data submitted to the Food and Drug Administration'. *PLOS Medicine*, 5(2), e45.

Kuhlmann, E. (2006) 'Traces of doubt and sources of trust: Health professions in an uncertain society'. *Current Sociology*, 54(4), pp. 607–620.

Le Grand, J. (2010) 'Knights and knaves return: Public service motivation and the delivery of public services'. *International Public Management Journal*, 13(1), pp. 56–71.

Luhmann, N. (1979) *Trust and Power*. Chichester, UK: Wiley.

Luhmann, N. (1988) 'Familiarity, confidence, trust: Problems and alternatives'. In D. Gambetta (ed.) *Trust: Making and Breaking Cooperative Relations*, pp. 94–108. Oxford: Basil Blackwell.

Mechanic, D. (2001) 'How should hamsters run? Some observations about sufficient patient time in primary care'. *British Medical Journal,* 323, pp. 266–268.

Möllering, G. (2005) 'The trust/control duality: An integrative perspective on positive expectations and others'. *International Sociology*, 20(3), pp. 283–305.

Moran, M. (2003) *The British Regulatory State: High Modernism and Hyper-Innovation*. Oxford: Oxford University Press.

MORI (2004) *In Search of Lost Trust*. London: MORI.

Newburn, T. (2014) 'Civil unrest in Ferguson was fuelled by the Black community's already poor relationship with a highly militarized police force'. *LSE American Politics and Policy* (29 Aug 2014) Blog Entry. http://eprints.lse.ac.uk/59363/ (last accessed 25 January 2016).

Parsons, T. (1975) 'The sick role and the role of the physician reconsidered'. *Millbank Quarterly*, 53(3), pp. 257–278.

Poortinga, W. and Pidgeon, N. (2003) 'Exploring the dimensionality of trust in risk regulation'. *Risk Analysis*, 23(5), pp. 961–973.

Power, M. (2003) 'Evaluating the audit explosion'. *Law and Policy* 25, pp. 185–202.

Power, M. (2004) *The Risk Management of Everything: Rethinking the Politics of Uncertainty*. London: DEMOS.

Rijksoverheid (2012) *Geneesmiddelenwet*. [Medicines Act]. The Hague: Dutch Government.

Rijksoverheid (2013) *Wet op de Omzetbelasting* [Sales Tax] 1968. The Hague: Dutch Government. Artikel 11, g, 1; Policy revision made on 14 May 2013.

Rothstein, H. (2006) 'The institutional origins of risk: A new agenda for risk research'. *Health, Risk and Society*, 8(3), pp. 215–221.

Rowe, R. and Calnan, M. (2006) 'Trust relations in health care: Developing a theoretical framework for the "new" NHS'. *Journal of Health Organization and Management,* 20(5), pp. 376–396.

Sheaff, R. and Pilgrim, D. (2006) 'Can learning organisations survive in the new NHS?'. *Organisational Science*, 1, p. 27.

Siahpush, M. (2000) 'A critical review of the sociology of alternative medicine: Research on users, practitioners and the orthodoxy'. *Health*, 4(2), pp. 159–178.

Solbjør, M., Skolbekken, J. A., Saetnan, A., Hagen, A. and Forsmo, S. (2012) 'Mammography screening and trust: The case of interval breast cancer'. *Social Science & Medicine,* 75(10), pp. 1746–1752.

Spyridonidis, D. and Calnan, M. (2011) 'Are new forms of professionalism emerging in medicine? The case of the implementation of NICE guidelines'. *Health Sociology Review,* 20, pp. 394–409.

Strathern, M. (2000) 'The tyranny of transparency'. *British Educational Research Journal,* 26(3), pp. 309–321.

Taylor-Gooby, P. (2006) 'The rational actor reform paradigm: Delivering the goods but destroying public trust?'. *International Journal of Social Quality*, 6(2), pp. 121–141.

Thomas-Symonds, N. (2010) *Attlee: A Life in Politics*. London: I.B. Tauris.

VtdK – Vereniging Tegen de Kwakzalverij (2010) 'Handelaren in valse hoop'. www.kwakzalverij.nl/756/Handelaren_in_valse_hoop (last accessed 25 January 2016).

Waring, J., Dixon-Woods, M. and Yeung, K. (2010) 'Modernising medical regulation: Where are we now?'. *Journal of Health Organization and Management*, 24(6), pp. 540–555.

Warner, J. (2015) *The Emotional Politics of Social Work and Child Protection*. Bristol, UK: Policy Press.

10

Professionalism and knowledge

Teresa Carvalho and Rui Santiago

Introduction

Sociological theories of the professions have highlighted the key role of knowledge, especially if it is connected to abstract and formal rules of science. Knowledge has been interpreted as a basic condition to perform highly specialized work, since its application assures the rationalization of tasks and solutions to solve complex problems. Training in scientific knowledge and its legitimacy through formal credentials by higher education institutions have been the main route used by professional groups to promote professionalization based on a strategy of social closure (Johnson, 1972; Freidson, 1994, 2001; Larson, 2013). Within the knowledge society, the social prominence of knowledge is even more evident, with work activities and the division of work becoming more complex and increasingly based on a more qualified workforce. In this context, new and more diversified professional groups emerge, the number of professionals increases, and, at the same time, it is expected that professions will acquire more status and prestige in societies.

The term knowledge society has been used with different meanings, although most are interrelated. It expresses the most relevant changes within the so-called post-modern and post-industrial society. Bell (1973) was, along with others such as Drucker (1993), one of the prominent authors who referred to post-modern society as knowledge society. Drucker (1959, p. 114) was also the first author to coin the terms 'knowledge work' and 'knowledge workers' to refer to highly qualified work and people, assuming that these would have a key role in the development of societies.

In assuming knowledge as an important means of wealth production, the knowledge society is also increasingly seen as a knowledge economy. Olssen and Peters (2005) argue that traditional industrial capitalism as a solution to enhance economic development is giving way to a new knowledge-based capitalism. According to these authors, the knowledge economy can be interpreted as a meta-idea legitimating and serving national interests in the face of the globalization of the competitive arena.

Other sociological perspectives present a different view. The way knowledge has become incomparably more spread through contemporary societies, and how it becomes publicly available, allows the existence of increased reflexivity mediated by expert systems (Giddens, 1990). People think and act under the influence of information produced by experts, meaning that daily interactions are based on information produced by specialists that social actors reinterpret in their actions (Giddens, 1990).

Taking these different perspectives, one can say that the terms knowledge society/knowledge economy are used as metaphors to express not only the increasing production and flow of knowledge in globalized economies but also the way knowledge cultures spread and are now embedded in society (Knorr-Cetina, 1997, 2000).

This emphasis on knowledge presents some challenges to professionals and professionalism. First, expert knowledge is increasingly contested by different social actors (Jensen et al., 2012). Second, with the democratization of higher education, new professional groups have institutionalized codified knowledge as central devices of their professional project and formal rules of science may become less distinctive to support a professional project. Third, the association of knowledge production and dissemination with markets and new public management (NPM) devices and external pressures to make organizations and professionals more accountable and manageable challenges professional autonomy. The development of rational and formal knowledge to sustain professional practices legitimates the discretionary decision-making in situations of uncertainty but, at the same time, it is this type of knowledge that allows the standardization of professional practice, which is said to constrain professional autonomy.

This chapter intends to discuss the way knowledge has been interpreted in theories in the sociology of professions and, within this framework, how nurses' professionalization can provide pertinent elements to improve reflection on the relationship between knowledge and professionalism. The analysis of the nurses' case may allow us to increase our knowledge of how a certain variety of alternatives, flowing from the interplay between different types of knowledge, can support the construction of a given professional epistemology serving a strategy of social closure. The chapter draws on empirical studies of nurses in Portugal and investigates how professional knowledge can be interpreted and what role tacit and practical knowledge and scientific knowledge may have in the professional project.

Knowledge and professional development

In the first studies of the sociology of professions, researchers identified the following four main attributes that fundamentally defined a group as a profession: (i) a body of formal and abstract knowledge, obtained through higher education training, formally attested to by a diploma, (ii) an orientation to perform service to others, (iii) self-control over the work, and (iv) high incomes and social status (Wilensky, 1964; Parsons, 1972). The acquisition of academic knowledge was the most relevant of these four basic attributes. It was perceived as serving not only societal development but also, through its application, the progress of professional practices working toward the resolution of complex social and human problems.

Advancing the application of specialized science and technology toward an increased rationalization and intellectualization of the social division of work (Brint, 1994; Freidson, 2001; Larson, 2013) has contributed substantially to the recognition of abstract and formal knowledge as a basic element of professions. Moreover, this recognition has allowed professional groups to claim an exclusive access to the professional market, even if one has to add to it the role of other institutions – such as professional associations and the state – in defining and legitimating the credentials system (Freidson, 1986).

The professions' control over labour markets was translated into social, cultural and economic power and privileges to the professions (Larson, 2013), and higher education was important in legitimating this process. At least until the 1970s, higher education institutions not only had a monopoly on abstract and formal knowledge production, but also a monopoly on training, which is the basis for the institutionalization of the cognitive support of professions – the standardization and codification of professional knowledge (Larson, 2013). From the end of World War II until the 1970s, the traditional professions enjoyed a golden age (Gorman & Sandefur, 2011).

Critical insights into the functionalism version of the sociology of professions

From the 1970s onwards, professions faced many changes, and new perspectives emerged in the sociology of professions (Freidson, 1970, 1986; Johnson, 1982; Brint, 1994, 2006; Larson, 2013), questioning the previous idealistic vision of professions and professional groups. However, the relevance attributed to the acquisition of formal, abstract and specialized knowledge has been maintained. For instance, through interpreting the sociological literature, Larson (2013) argues that, implicitly or explicitly, most of this literature takes on the idea that 'the advance of science and cognitive rationality and the related rationalisation and growing differentiation in the division of labour [are the] most significant "modern" dimensions' (p. xvi) of professions.

In his first critical insights on professions, Freidson (1970) maintained that the possession of formal and abstract knowledge by professionals protects their autonomy, exercises social dominance, and secures self-interest. To Freidson, the main source of professional power is the professional monopoly over knowledge, since it controls tasks and thus allows technical autonomy. In turn, this autonomy enables both professional self-regulation and control over important information and resources in the organizational context. In this sense, Freidson (1970) identified control over the acquisition of resources and interpersonal relationships with the client as sources of professional power.

Freidson later moved away from his criticism of two decades before (Brint, 2006) and engaged in a strong defence of professionalism, which he defined fundamentally as the occupational control of work (Freidson, 2001). In some aspects, this defence recovered one of the main elements identified by functionalists to define a professional – the normative orientation to the service of others. It seems that Freidson returned to the substantive functionalist logic underpinning professionalism through reconnecting it to the ethical value and moral code of 'doing the right thing' (Ward, 2012, p. 66). When outlining the fifth element of his ideal type of professionalism, Freidson asserts: 'an ideology serving some transcendent value and asserting greater devotion to doing good work than to economic reward' (2001, p. 180).

In a wider sense, professionalism as a third logic can be interpreted as a theoretical response to the challenges that the sociology of professions started to face in the 1970s and 1980s, which include, among other things, the increased influence of neo-liberalism, the market and NPM in knowledge production, dissemination and use. Some of these challenges are linked to the increasing domination by large organizations and the imposition of external controls. Within this context, professionalism refers to an ideological principle for organizing society, since it is based on a set of axiomatic assumptions and principles that distinguishes it from market and bureaucracy logic. The major distinction here is the social need of recognizing the monopoly of professionals 'over the *practice* of a defined body of intellectualized knowledge and skill, a discipline' (Freidson, 2001, p. 198).

This emphasis led Freidson (2001) to try to clarify the meaning of bodies of knowledge for professionalism through discussing the status and scope of the epistemological authority of professional knowledge. Freidson made a distinction between three forms of knowledge: (i) the descriptive forms, covering both science and scholarship and to which technical authority corresponded; (ii) the prescriptive forms, which were linked to social norms attached to secular and sacred forms of knowledge (as in, for instance, law, religion and ethics) and claims for moral authority; and, finally, (iii) the artistic forms, 'which deal with aesthetic norms and claim normative aesthetic authority' (Freidson, 2001, p. 158).

Elements such as a specific body of knowledge, self-control over work, and an ideal of 'service to others' formed the basis of the functionalist concept of professions; the control over the market and the technical content of the work also became important research subjects in the 1970s. Johnson (1972) and Larson (2013) rather emphasized, respectively, the professions' relations with the political and economic elite and the state and also their relations with the market and social classes.

Knowledge, social distance and social closure

The analysis of the professions by Johnson (1972) is based on a reflection over the social division of labour. Furthermore, developments in professionals' social power and domination over consumers relativized the idea of service to others portrayed by the early sociological theorizations. For Johnson (1972), the emergence of specialized occupational knowledge induces relations of socio-economic dependence and, simultaneously, relations of social distance between professionals. This social distance creates a structure of uncertainty, or indeterminacy, in the relationship between production and consumption, which results in a potential exploitation of customers by professionals. The degree of uncertainty emerges from expert knowledge and from a certain mystification produced by professionals to increase their control and autonomy over professional activities.

That uncertainty, however, may be reduced, with consequences for the professions and for consumers, a reduction which varies depending on the social context and power relations generated. To Johnson (1972), professionalism can be seen as a particular type of occupational control. It occurs when an occupation controls its work activities, but this control is only effective if the activities correspond to the fulfilment of the global functions of capital, meaning the functions of control, survival, and reproduction of labour relations.

Larson (2013) also believes that professions are an element of delimitation of the labour market. The main factor that characterizes a profession is its ability to promote its monopoly in the market for professional services, which results in controlling access to the profession (control of the education system) and market protection (licensing system). As others have proposed before, Larson's analysis focuses both on knowledge and power. Taking the medical profession as an illustrative case, Larson considers that 'the negotiation of cognitive exclusiveness was inseparable from the production and progress of (medical) knowledge' (Larson, 2013, p. 24), thus sustaining the process of 'production of professional producers' (Larson, 2013, p. 34) by higher education institutions.

Starting from a different perspective – namely, the organization and the conflicts between professional groups for the control of the jurisdictional boundaries of work – Abbott (1988) reinforces the importance of academic or scientific knowledge. According to Abbott (1988, p. 40), professional judgements in the sphere of work disputes are concentrated in the jurisdictional claims for what he named the 'three acts of professional practice'. These are (i) diagnosis (to classify a problem), (ii) inference (to reason about a problem), and (iii) treatment (to take action over the problem). Inference, the middle game of the process, also became an important issue in the determination of the professional work exclusions (or not) for other groups, particularly 'when the connection between diagnosis and treatment is obscure' (Abbott, 1988, p. 49). However, Abbott emphasized that, in most professions, the professional power over diagnosis, inference and treatment depends on linkages to a system of formal and abstract knowledge and expert skills based on academic knowledge.

More recent approaches claim that control over jurisdictional boundaries must be analysed at a global level. Faulconbridge and Muzio (2012, p. 137) call for a transnational sociology of professions since regulations, norms and cultures are being institutionalized through 'transnational professional projects tied to imperatives of neoliberal capitalism'. Taking this assumption, Seabrooke (2014, p. 50) argues that it is in the international realm that 'professionals are being professionalized to organize across jurisdictions and where professionals are mobilized to generate demand for their skills and knowledge'. In these processes professionals are more important than their associations. Using epistemic arbitrage, professionals exploit differences in professional knowledge and position some particular forms as the most appropriate to deal with some problems.

The concept of epistemic arbitrage emphasizes professional knowledge that comes from different sources of training and learning. Even if there is a relevant tradition in the analysis of knowledge related with working practices, it has only recently been incorporated into the sociology of professions.

Professional work and professional knowledge

Donald Schön (1983) reflects on knowledge related to working practices, maintaining that there are relevant differences between scientific and practical knowledge. Schön assumes professionals are reflective practitioners, meaning that they develop a learning process within the workplace in which they analyse their working experiences to learn from them. Schön (1983) and Argyris and Schön (1974) maintain that a gap is always present in professional work due to the existing discrepancy between theory and practice and between university curricula and training and professional action in the field.

This gap also generates tacit knowledge (Polanyi, 1967), based on spontaneous identifications and judgements, arising at some stages in the development of working processes. Tacit knowledge can be incorporated into professional abilities and norms and, potentially, can also be shared and socialized among professionals through formal and informal interactions. Authors such as Schön (1983) and Argyris and Schön (1974, 1995) claim the legitimacy of a new epistemology of professional knowledge constructed through action by a reflective practitioner.

More recently, and on the same lines, reflections emerge in the sociology of professions defending the existence of tensions between academic knowledge and its application in professional practice, namely, in complex tasks. The complexity of working situations and practices creates margins of indeterminacy, uncertainty and ambiguity (Freidson, 2001; Evetts, 2002), allowing discretionary or prudential judgements (Champy, 2011), which also become an important base for securing professional autonomy and a source of learning and production of professional knowledge and, in this sense, can also be assumed as incorporating professionalism and processes of professionalization.

As the knowledge society/economy and neo-liberal and NPM tendencies emerged, authors' attention moved, on one hand, to the increasing formalization and rationalization of professional knowledge, mainly underpinned by a market-based technical rationality logic, and, on the other hand, to its use and (re-)creation within working sets. The increasing need for professionals to be accountable to their organizations and to society, along with an increasing rationalization of contemporary societies, led to a tendency to rationalize and codify professional knowledge, with evidenced-based medicine (EBM) representing one of the most popular examples.

Discussion over the implications of EBM for professionals is mainly related to how the ownership of formal and rational knowledge can still be interpreted as the main source of professionals' autonomy. Some argue that EBM has the potential to limit physicians' discretion and even put their authority in question (Timmermans & Kolker, 2004). Other authors, such as Kuhlmann (2006, pp. 200–201), suggest that expert knowledge 'can also be used as a barrier against external regulation', and consequently, both formalized and tacit knowledge can be strategically used by professionals to ensure power.

Evidenced-based medicine has not been as successful as expected (Knaapen, 2013). In the face of uncertain situations and in doubt about the way knowledge can be applied in practice, it is often ignored by professionals. The incapacity for EBM to be fully applied by professionals increases interest in the importance of non-knowledge or tacit knowledge in professional practices. For instance, Knaapen (2013) contends that the failure of EBM has occurred because it focuses only on the knowledge we have and misses the knowledge we lack.

Examining the co-existence of these dual tendencies, authors are increasingly emphasizing the importance of workplace learning over formal knowledge and formal processes of learning for professional knowledge, practice and identities (Jensen, 2014; Jensen & Lahn, 2005; Smeby, 2006; Klette & Smeby, 2012). The construction of professional identities can also be interpreted as the result of a continuous process of learning. Socialization processes within higher education in a formal learning context are followed by learning in the working context, where decisions have to be taken in an uncertain, unstable and conflicting environment (Champy, 2009).

Within this context, the sociology of professions makes use of diverse concepts drawn from different disciplinary areas. For instance, Smeby and Vågan (2008) explore how the theory–practice gap is perceived by newly qualified nurses and physicians. The authors refer to different disciplinary backgrounds to define each of the three categories composing their model used to classify knowledge acquired by new professionals during their professional education: (i) the codified knowledge, which includes general knowledge, specific knowledge, planning and organizational knowledge and insight into rules and regulations, (ii) the practical knowledge related to practical skills, ability to work under pressure, ability to work independently, and (iii) the relational knowledge, comprising co-operation skills, oral communicative skills, tolerance, empathy and ethical deliberation.

Another relevant example of the way reflections on professional practical knowledge promote a conceptual drift is in the adoption of concepts such as 'epistemic object' and 'epistemic cultures' (Knorr-Cetina, 1999, p. 1) to improve the understanding of professional learning. For instance, Lahn (2011) argues that these concepts are essential to understanding professional learning, and Smeby (2006) defends the suggestion that epistemic objectivity brings into discussion the emotional base of professional work and, in this sense, is also an essential element in promoting professional identity.

Similarly, the concept of 'epistemic communities' has been adopted to express the way expert occupational groups use, share, create, and reproduce work-related knowledge (Gorman & Sandefur, 2011); the term 'informal communities of practice' (Adler *et al.*, 2008) is used to express how professionals who do not have an occupation's body of formal knowledge can share and update work-related knowledge within informal groups. In this sense, communities of practice are then social networks, developed within organizations, in which professionals work and interact, and that can contribute to contesting the legitimacy of scientific knowledge to assure distinct professional conditions. Similar to post-Fordism in industry (Ward, 2012), the pressures over professional work for short-term results and flexibility generate tacit and unknown knowledge. The practical tools to solve specific problems that these teams develop are often conceived outside the scope of the available formal and codified knowledge.

To sum up, knowledge has always been a fundamental element in the analysis of professions. However, if early studies focused mainly on the importance of formal and abstract knowledge associated with academic knowledge for professionalism and professionalization processes, recent perspectives try also to incorporate other forms of knowledge, which include both the tacit and the unknown knowledge, mostly associated with the learning process professionals develop outside academia. The next section illustrates the relationship between formal and non-formal knowledge in professionalism using a Portuguese nurses' study as an illustrative case.

The relevance of knowledge in the professionalization of nursing

After the creation of the National Health Service (NHS), and especially with the inclusion of Portugal in the European Union, in 1986, there was successful improvement in the professionalization of nursing. In 1988, nursing courses were integrated within the polytechnic subsystem of higher education, and in the 1990s the legal career statute was approved (Decree Law number 480/88), as was the creation of a professional association (Ordem dos Enfermeiros – Nursing Council) and the document that regulates the professional activities of nurses (Regulation on the Professional Exercise of Nursing, REPE). These documents established the centrality of caring notions in nursing labour practices, which were framed by a welfare state ideology and configured a professional identity based on care (Carvalho, 2014).

In this sense, Portuguese nurses have developed a relatively successful professionalization process seeking to achieve social closure. This makes it an interesting case to analyse the nurses' relation to the different types of knowledge necessary for professional development and upholding professional values. Do nurses assume that the epistemic ground of their profession embodies the interrelation between abstract and formal knowledge and tacit knowledge? How do they interpret the contribution of these two types of knowledge to their professionalism?

As in other national contexts, nurses in Portugal have sought constantly to improve their professional status. Along this route, they have emulated doctors' processes and, in this sense, have focused on defending and promoting the indispensability of academic knowledge as a means of support and, in particular, on the possibility of translating practical experience into knowledge with a scientific basis. After several attempts and political fights, framed by a specific political environment related to the integration of Portugal with the European Union and a revision of the national law for education, nurses were able to establish a traditional process of social closure.

The locus of formal and abstract knowledge in the nurses' professional project

The main support of the conceptual insights proposed in this section draw on the findings of two qualitative-interpretative studies based on 103 interviews conducted with nurses in Portugal in 2005 and 2012 (Carvalho, 2009, 2012, 2014). Data analysis from these interviews revealed that nurses recognize the centrality of the acquisition of academic knowledge in the development of their professional project. The relevance of having higher education credentials to practise nursing is particularly emphasized in relation to professionals' autonomy in the organizational context.

Empirical studies developed in other national contexts had already demonstrated this phenomenon. In an ethnographic study carried out in an English hospital, Allen (2000) concluded that nurses used knowledge and theoretical training in the organizational field as a support for the demarcation of their activities in relation to other professional groups (particularly doctors, managers and assistants).

In the Portuguese case study, nurses' discourses also revealed the importance they gave to scientific knowledge in defining their jurisdictional boundaries, particularly in relation to the medical profession. They stressed the importance of the accreditation of knowledge (Carapinheiro,

1998), based on a formal academic high-level degree, as a way to promote their professions' autonomy. Besides, nurses recognize that having this degree is a fundamental element in legitimately removing nursing from a subservient position in the field of medicine and turning it into a profession with recognized jurisdiction in the social health division of labour. The perception that training in higher education provides the necessary tools to advance professionalism and see autonomy recognized is a widely shared idea.

Assuring a greater recognition of boundaries and formal knowledge obtained through the institutional certification of expertise, based on academic training and a diploma, was seen as the main condition to promote social recognition of the profession and also to improve working conditions. In fact, nurses are aware that the opportunity to promote social closure based on a higher education diploma resulted especially in improvements in their level of income, even if in more recent years, due to economic and political changes framed by an NPM context, these achievements have been seriously questioned.

Nurses' valorization of academic or scientific knowledge is also expressed in the way they proclaim the need to promote and develop autonomous research in the field of nursing. This is an essential requisite to improve scientific knowledge learned at the highest levels of formal training in order to legitimate professional practices on a basis of rigour and rationality. In this sense, it seems that nurses are also valuing the need to develop independent scientific knowledge as a way to maintain their autonomy in a context of increasing rationalization and codification of work.

Because they face complex situations, specialized knowledge is the main way to support nurses in resolving these situations. Proclaiming the need to develop research and produce knowledge, nurses intend to reduce routines and strengthen their professional power and autonomy over what Abbott (1988) identifies as the relationship between diagnosis, inference and treatment. Moreover, again according to Abbott, increasing the degree of inference between diagnosis and treatment contributes to solidifying and improving professional jurisdiction over the nursing sphere of working processes (Brint, 1994). At the same time, the construction of a body of knowledge specific to nursing serves to support intervention in practice and in affirming the profession, and also to allow the existence of 'epistemic authority' (Cash, 1997, p. 137) in relation to society.

The attempt to create and legitimate a specific body of knowledge, based in the appeal to specific language and in the use of specific scientific methods, can also be interpreted as an attempt to enlarge the nursing epistemological scope in order to protect and increase nurses' technical authority (Freidson, 1986, 2001). Eventually, this power can be used as a way to mediate negotiations occurring in organizational practices (Strauss, 1988) and, particularly, in care practices. It seems that nurses 'do not need knowledge just as a basis for carrying out their tasks; they also have to a greater extent to defend their professional practice scientifically to other professional groups', as Smeby (2006, p. 6) states for other professionals.

Nevertheless, the centrality of formal and rational knowledge also emerges in the nurses' prospects as an instrument to internally stratify the profession through the valorization of the sub-disciplinary professional knowledge-based hierarchies. Nurses assert that career-advancement decisions are based on the acquisition of more specialized knowledge. The main argument is that the academic or scientific knowledge should be the main criterion for reaching top leadership positions. In a bureaucratic logic, academic and scientific knowledge is established as a legitimate basis for the technical authority attributed to the position.

In this sense, specialized knowledge enables the internal hierarchy in the nursing profession and simultaneously represents the possibility of expanding the professional roles and sustaining nurses' professional identity and credibility. Specialized knowledge allows vertical stratification and legitimizes the power relations within the profession. Valuing sub-disciplinary nursing fields thus appears clearly as a result of a professional ideology: the differentiation of higher technical skills would benefit at the horizontal level across the field and the profession. At the vertical level, stratification eases the legitimization of some professionals within the group. This trend seems to be ambiguous in the nurses' discourses.

Tensions and paradoxes in formal and practical knowledge in nursing

The criteria of logical consistency and rationality underlying scientific knowledge are usually presented as opposed to the traditional characteristics (spontaneous, emotional, and irrational) which frame care professions (Davies, 1995; Traynor, 1994, 1999). The mismatch between scientific knowledge and professional practice seem to cause a dilemma for Portuguese nurses, who find it difficult to deal with. Although nurses grant, indeed, a certain primacy to scientific knowledge and its application as an ideological orientation in the professionalization process, some nuances were observed in the nurses' positions, which express some paradoxes.

The professionalization of nursing is based on care assumed as the specific task in the health division of labour. But this is not enough, by itself, to promote professional development. Care has been used strategically by nurses in more recent years to claim the relevance of their work in the health division of labour within an NPM context. However, with NPM and austerity-driven political initiatives implemented in healthcare in Portugal, nurses have experienced a degradation of their working conditions and have also been losing power and status within institutions. In this context, nurses are developing a hybrid professionalism which incorporates valorization and revalorization of care, scientific knowledge and managerial values (Carvalho, 2012, 2014). These trends suggest that different and even conflicting institutional logics persist in nurses' professionalism.

Scientific knowledge is valued as a professionalization strategy but, at the same time, it is also a threat to care as the fundamental identity element in the profession. Borrowing Freidson's (2001) reasoning, nurses seem to have some difficulty combining descriptive with prescriptive forms of knowledge, or, as Smeby and Vågen (2008) argue, combining codified knowledge with relational knowledge.

The same dichotomy seems to be present in theoretical reflections. Some authors argue that the centrality of care as the essence of the profession is one of the myths of nursing and therefore is insufficient to form the basis of the establishment of a professional jurisdiction (Dingwall & Allen, 2001), while others consider that the problem is instead the attempt to sustain the process of professionalization in scientific knowledge. The particular characteristics of this type of knowledge, because it is too rational and objective and linked to the male domain, leave no room for an overall understanding of the concept of care, not capturing the essentially feminine nature of the profession (Davies, 1995).

Aligned with this perspective, Portuguese nurses expressed some criticism with regard to higher education training, maintaining that the emphasis on scientific knowledge promotes a devaluation of care, even if, as Smeby (2006) pointed out, care is a knowledge object due to its relevant importance in creating and sustaining professional identity.

The emphasis on care does not necessarily mean that Portuguese nurses are defending an alternative professionalization process that ignores scientific knowledge, as is indeed advocated by some researchers (Davies, 1995). In the nurses' view, the gap between scientific knowledge and the valorization of the relationship with the patient results mainly from a failure of the interconnection between professional schools and research on nursing or between formal education and professional practice (Smeby & Vågan, 2008). This is not just an issue in the nursing field but is also familiar to the wider professional landscape, as Argyris and Schön (1974) and Schön (1983) have tried to demonstrate. This mismatch has been, more recently, assumed by others to be highly relevant for autonomy in professional practices (Evetts, 2002; Champy, 2011).

Nurses recognize the importance of scientific knowledge in the affirmation of the authority and autonomy of the profession, due to its role in legitimating the professional practice in relation to other professional groups, but they also highlight the risks of more technologically oriented care that moves away from traditional personal or emotional care work (Carvalho, 2012, 2014). However, as a large profession trying to distance itself from a semi-profession label, Portuguese nurses complain that there is a lack of common identity and professional jurisdiction, which they see as an obstacle to professional progress (Carvalho, 2012, 2014).

Although different identity concepts were identified in nurses' discourses, three emerged as dominant (Carvalho, 2009, 2012, 2014). First, there is a discrepancy between the theory and the practice of nursing, which induces the perception that some nurses are more technologically oriented while others put greater emphasis on personal relations. The results mirror the discrepancy between a professional identity built on theoretical higher education training and an identity developed in practice (this is sometimes assumed to be a generational gap).

Second, the different cultures and dominant *modi operandi* of each health institution influence principles and practices. Third, different pathways and nursing models structured during the development of the profession in different historical moments are also pointed to as a reason for the different conceptions of the profession.

Concerning issues related to the diversity of nursing references, Hewison and Stanton (2002) stress that professional ideologies of nursing never had a logical or linear progression since Florence Nightingale's proposals. The authors also argue that there has always been a lack of agreement on the theories and models of the nature and roles of nursing. Some theories have emerged from clinical practice based on the analysis of professional and work processes; others emphasize the need to develop a priori theoretical frameworks as guides to practice.

The successive professional ideologies that have emerged since the 1960s need to be considered as a strategy to establish a professional project, strengthening the attempt to establish nursing as a profession, rather than as theoretical constructs serving as a reliable source for practice. Both the perception that nurses identify a certain lack of common references in the profession and the diversity of the professional positions also reflect the diversity of theoretical approaches and paradigms that have been observed since the second half of the twentieth century (Hewison & Stanton, 2002). Taking these factors into consideration, one can argue that Portuguese nurses do not see the profession as a homogeneous corpus but as a result of distinct epistemic cultures and also of different communities of practice.

Some nurses suggest that experiential learning and reflection over practice are important to build the expertise of nursing. The professional ideology no longer results only from scientific and technical knowledge, identified with the biomedical model as expressed through conventional or formal training, but from the field of practice. In fact, nurses emphasize in their discourses the relevance given to practical knowledge.

The importance of the practical dimension of the profession is especially highlighted when nurses refer to: (i) collective discussion over the profession's problems and practices, based on reflections of their daily activities; (ii) a closer articulation between theoretical and practical training; (iii) the adoption of an inductive attitude with respect to the notion of nursing; and (iv) the assumption of practice as a central element in the socialization of new professionals.

Learning through practice, or rather, reflecting on professional practice (Argyris & Schön, 1974; Schön, 1983) is also an important element in the construction and development of the Portuguese nurses' professional project to achieve social closure (Larson, 2013) and professionalism

(Freidson, 2001). There is indubitably the co-existence of or, at least, attempts to articulate scientific and reflective knowledge as an overall background toward the institutionalization of a nursing professional project. Care is acknowledged as a structural element of professional identity. However, distinct positions arise concerning the relevance scientific knowledge should assume. To a great extent, scientific knowledge on its own is not as capable of promoting nurses' professional status per se but only when it is interrelated with practical knowledge.

Thus, scientific knowledge is an almost inevitable structural element in sustaining the nurses' project of professionalization. In line with the importance given to it by classical literature of the sociology of the professions, Portuguese nurses also consider scientific knowledge as indispensable, since it helps to create a unique area for nursing in the social health division of labour. In particular, it strategically distinguishes nurses from other professional groups, especially physicians. Scientific knowledge also enables a hierarchical organization of nurses in sub-disciplinary specializations, which supports an expansion of roles and the construction of a professional identity, giving more credibility to academic nursing as a profession and legitimizing professional autonomy in a context of increasing rationalization and codification of work.

It is also undeniable that scientific knowledge is seen as more technical than human, removing professionals from care and close relationships with patients, thus contributing to a possible emptying of meaning and downgrading of the significance of the profession, until professional identity retreats completely. In this context, nurses add to scientific knowledge practical knowledge, which seems also to take a prominent place in their claims for professionalism. The impossibility of translating the emotional and subjective characteristics of care into the formal codes of scientific knowledge and imposing its presence as a condition to maintaining professional identity leads nurses to value, to an equal degree, the tacit and implicit knowledge flowing from professional practice and even from different epistemic communities of practice.

The attempts to articulate both scientific and practical knowledge in the Portuguese nurses' professional project are actually expressed in a new mechanism of social closure introduced by the Nursing Council. To be able to practise nursing in Portugal, one needs a higher education diploma and to be a member of the professional association. To be recognized as a member, the association requires that the candidate experience a period of ward practice in a certified clinical centre having the necessary conditions to develop nursing practices. Thus, we should pay greater attention to the role of tacit and implicit knowledge in professionalism and professionalization processes within the knowledge society.

Conclusion

The acquisition of formal and abstract knowledge, especially by higher education institutions, has been identified as an important condition of considering an occupational group a profession. While classic theories of the sociology of professions almost exclusively focused on scientific knowledge, more recent work brings into perspective the importance of the way this knowledge is used in the professional practice to overcome uncertain situations and to legitimize autonomy.

The analysis of the Portuguese case of the nursing profession demonstrates the relevance of both practical/tacit and formal/scientific knowledge in nurses' professional identity. Following the canons of the classic professions, nurses' professional project mainly relies on the jurisdiction of a body of formal or scientific knowledge, while traditional values of nursing are rooted in care, which is a more ambiguous field of knowledge. Data analysis reveals that nurses' experiences of practices, and the knowledge that results from these practices, are essential for constructing a collective identity and defining jurisdictional boundaries. Hence, the major source of identity is the concept of care, which is difficult to measure, thereby furthering the persistence of hidden and tacit knowledge.

Even if tacit knowledge is part and parcel of their professional identity, nurses tend to interpret this type of knowledge as being in tension with the scientific knowledge that foregrounds their professional project. The hegemony of scientific knowledge is rooted in its strategic relevance for building an autonomous field of practice, but nurses also value tacit and practical knowledge as the cornerstone in their constitution of a community of practices, and they perceive it as complementary to scientific knowledge. Consequently, the epistemic legitimacy to develop nurses' professional work not only derives from higher education credentials but also from reflections on shared experiences in care work. These findings challenge classic assumptions in the sociology of professions.

Enlarging nurses' epistemological scope to include tacit or practical knowledge can be interpreted as a way to protect and increase nurses' technical authority and professional jurisdiction. In this sense, the Portuguese Nursing Council gives the same weight to formal and practical knowledge, assuming both as mechanisms of social closure. In doing so, the Nursing Council is also trying to reconcile the professional project with professional identity.

The role of practical and formal knowledge in the construction of professional projects within the knowledge society is a relevant issue that needs further reflection in the sociology of professions. More attention should be given to the inductive processes of knowledge production based on professional reflexions over practices and to the way this production may be used in professional projects.

References

Abbott, A. (1988) *The System of Professions: An Essay on the Division of Expert Labor*. Chicago, IL: University of Chicago Press.

Adler, P. S., Kwon, S. W., & Heckscher, C. (2008) 'Perspective-professional work: The emergence of collaborative community'. *Organization Science*, 19(2), pp. 359–376.

Allen, D. (2000) 'Negotiating the role of expert carers on an adult hospital ward'. *Sociology of Health & Illness*, 22(2), pp. 149–171.

Argyris, C., & Schön, D. (1974) *Theory in Practice: Increasing Professional Effectiveness*. San Francisco, CA: Jossey-Bass.

——(1995) *Organizational Learning: A Theory of Action Perspective*. Boston, MA: Addison-Wesley.

Bell, D. (1973) *The Coming of Post-Industrial Society: A Venture in Social Forecasting*. New York: Basic Books.

Brint, S. (1994) *In an Age of Experts: The Changing Role of Professionals in Politics and Public Life*. Princeton, NJ: Princeton University Press.

——(2006) 'Saving the soul of professionalism: Freidson's institutional ethics and the defense of professional autonomy'. *Savoir, Tavail et Société. Knowledge, Work & Society*, 4(2), pp. 101–129.

Carapinheiro, G. (1998) *Saberes e Poderes no Hospital: Uma Sociologia dos Poderes Hospitalares*. Porto: Afrontamento.

Carvalho, T. (2009) *Nova Gestão Pública e Reformas da Saúde: O profissionalismo numa encruzilhada*. Lisbon: Edições Sílabo.

——(2012) 'Managerialism and professional strategies: A case from nurses in Portugal'. *Journal of Health Organization and Management*, 26(4), pp. 524–541.

——(2014) 'Changing connections between professionalism and managerialism: A case study of nursing in Portugal'. *Professions and Organization*, 1(2), pp. 1–15.

Cash, K. (1997) 'Social epistemology, gender and nursing theory'. *International Journal of Nursing Studies*, 34(2), pp. 137–143.

Champy, F. (2009) *La sociologie des professions*. Paris: Presses universitaires de France.

Champy, F. (2011) *Nouvelle théorie sociologique des professions*. Paris: Presses Universitaires de France.

Davies, C. (1995) *Gender and the Professional Predicament in Nursing*. Buckingham, UK: Open University Press.

Dingwall, R., & Allen, D. (2001) 'The implications of healthcare reforms for the profession of nursing'. *Nursing Inquiry*, 8(2), pp. 64–74.

Drucker, P. (1959) *Landmarks of Tomorrow*. New York: Harper.

——(1993) *Post-Capitalist Society*. New York: Basic Books.

Evetts, J. (2002) 'New directions in state and international professional occupations: Discretionary decision-making and acquired regulation'. *Work, Employment and Society*, 16(2), pp. 341–353.

Faulconbridge, J. R., & Muzio, D. (2012) 'Professions in a globalizing world: Towards a transnational sociology of the professions'. *International Sociology*, 27(1), pp. 136–152.

Freidson, E. (1970) *Professional Dominance: The Social Structure of Medical Care*. New York: Atherton Press.

——(1986) *Professional Powers*. Chicago, IL: University of Chicago Press.

——(1994) *Professionalism Reborn*. Cambridge: Polity Press.

——(2001) *Professionalism: The Third Logic*. Cambridge: Polity Press.

Giddens, A. (1990) *The Consequences of Modernity*. Cambridge: Polity Press.

Gorman, E. H., & Sandefur, R. L. (2011) '"Golden Age," quiescence, and revival: How the sociology of professions became the study of knowledge-based work'. *Work and Occupations*, 38(3), pp. 275–302.

Hewison, A., & Stanton, A. (2002) 'From conflict to collaboration? Contrasts and convergence in the development of nursing and management theory (1)'. *Journal of Nursing Management*, 10(6), pp. 349–355.

Jensen, K. (2014) 'Signing communities dealing with non-knowledge: Some cases from nursing'. *Professions and Professionalism*, 14(2), pp. 1–13.

Jensen, K., & Lahn, L. (2005) 'The binding role of knowledge: An analysis of nursing students' knowledge ties'. *Journal of Education and Work*, 18(3), pp. 305–320.

Jensen, K., Lahn, L. C., & Nerland, M. (2012) *Professional Learning in the Knowledge Society* (Vol. 6). London: Springer Science & Business Media.

Johnson, T. (1972) *Professions and Power*. London: Macmillan.

——(1982) 'The state and the profession: Peculiarities of the British'. In A. Giddens and G. Mackenzie (eds), *Social Class and the Division of Labour*, pp. 45–67. Cambridge: Cambridge University Press.

Klette, K., & Smeby, J. (2012) 'Professional training and knowledge sources'. In K. Jensen, L. Lahn and M. Nerland (eds), *Professional Learning in the Knowledge Society*, pp. 143–162. Rotterdam: Sense Publishers.

Knaapen, L. (2013) 'Being evidence-based in the absence of evidence: The management of non-evidence in guideline development'. *Social Studies of Science*, 43(5), pp. 681–706.

Knorr-Cetina, K. (1997) 'Sociality with objects: Social relations in postsocial knowledge societies'. *Theory, Culture & Society*, 14(4), pp. 1–30.

Knorr-Cetina, K. (1999) *Epistemic Cultures: How Sciences Make Knowledge*. Cambridge, MA: Harvard University Press.

Knorr-Cetina, K. (2000) 'Postsocial relations: Theorizing sociality in a postcolonial environment'. In G. Ritzer and B. Smart (eds), *Handbook of Social Theory*, pp. 520–537. London: Sage.

Kuhlmann, E. (2006) *Modernising Health Care: Reinventing Professions, the State and the Public*. Bristol, UK: Policy Press.

Lahn, L. (2011) 'Professional learning as epistemic trajectories'. In S. Ludvigsen, A. Lund, I. Rasmussen and R. Säljö (eds), *Learning Across Sites: New Tools, Infrastructures and Practices*, pp. 53–68. New York: Routledge.

Larson, Magali Sarfatti. (2013) *The Rise of Professionalism: Monopolies of Competence and Sheltered Markets*. New Brunswick and London: Transaction Publishers.

Olssen, M., & Peters, M. (2005) 'Neoliberalism, higher education and the knowledge economy: from the free market to knowledge capitalism'. *Journal of Education Policy*, 20(3), pp. 313–345.

Parsons, T. (1968) *Professions. International Encyclopaedia of the Social Sciences* (Vol. 12). New York: Macmillan Company and The Free Press.

Parsons, T. (1972) 'Culture and social system revisited'. *Social Science Quarterly*, 53(2), pp. 253–266.

Polanyi, M. (1967) *The Tacit Dimension*. New York: Doubleday.

Schön, D. (1983) *The Reflective Practitioner: How Professionals Think in Action*. London: Temple Smith.

Seabrooke, L. (2014) 'Epistemic arbitrage: Transnational professional knowledge in action'. *Journal of Professions and Organization*, 1(1), pp. 49–64.

Smeby, J. (2006) *Epistemic Cultures Among Beginning Professionals*. Working paper no 8, Center for the Study of Professions, Oslo University College.

Smeby, J.-C., & Vågan, A. (2008) 'Recontextualising professional knowledge: Newly qualified nurses and physicians'. *Journal of Education and Work*, 21(2), pp. 159–173.

Strauss, A. (1988) *Negotiations: Varieties, Contexts, Processes, and Social Order*. San Francisco, CA: Jossey-Bass.

Timmermans, S., & Kolker, E. S. (2004) 'Evidence-based medicine and the reconfiguration of medical knowledge'. *Journal of Health and Social Behavior*, 45, pp. 177–193.

Traynor, M. (1994) 'The views and values of community nurses and their managers: Research in progress-one person's pain, another person's vision'. *Journal of Advanced Nursing*, 20(1), pp. 101–109.

Traynor, M. (1999) *Managerialism and Nursing: Beyond Oppression and Profession*. Hove, UK: Psychology Press.

Ward, S. C. (2012) *Neoliberalism and the Global Restructuring of Knowledge and Education*. New York/London: Routledge.

Wilensky, H. L. (1964) 'The professionalization of everyone?'. *American Journal of Sociology*, 70, pp. 137–158.

Part III

Professions, management and leadership

Introduction

Jean-Louis Denis

The relation between professions and organizations has been a long-standing research interest in the sociology of professions and in organizational studies. The integration of professions in organizations is not a new phenomenon for non-dominant professions such as teachers and social workers. Elite professions like lawyers and medical doctors are becoming more and more involved in the organizational game (Adler *et al.*, 2008). Driven by various assumptions regarding the compatibility of these two worlds (Evetts, 2003; Noordegraaf, 2011), researchers have explored the ability of professions to protect themselves from organizational demands, to negotiate a viable modus operandi in a context of increasing organizational pressures or to see opportunities in the growing integration of professions within organizations.

Chapters in this section relate to various manifestations of such a closer connection between professions and organizations. Using some sensitizing concepts such as agency, structuration or leaderism, these authors propose an innovative reading of the co-evolution of organizations and professions in contemporary societies. Hinings provides a critical assessment of the work done on 'organizations that are primarily owned, staffed, and run by professionals, the professional service firm'. He proposes looking more closely at the transformation of professional status and work as a by-product of organizational evolution. But professions and their context of practice are not all the same, which indicates the need for more comparative work across professional groups, organizations and jurisdictions. Only through comparative research can specificities and commonalities between professional organizations and other types of organizations be properly understood.

Professionals are mutants – they take various roles in organizations and experience various identity tensions and transitions. Not only does their work context change, but also competing demands and changing expectations deeply affect them. Responses to these challenges will vary, partly due to the relative resilience of professionals. Based on an extensive review of published research of managerial-professional roles, mostly from the healthcare sector, Kirkpatrick explores the vertical and horizontal dynamics of hybridization. Professions differentiate from within through a process of restratification and across professions and organizational context. One of the key insights from this chapter is the importance of looking at hybrid roles as a manifestation of a mosaic of organizational and professional projects where co-optation and protective strategies co-exist. Although there are signs of growing hybridization, there is still a lack of accomplished research on the influence of hybrid roles on organizational adaptation and performance.

In the third chapter, Leicht contributes a socio-historical analysis of the professionalization of management, mainly based on research conducted in the US context. Although management does not align well with the ideal type of professional, the access of such professionals to university training and the development of professional associations have provided new credentials to practising managers. With fine empirical details, the chapter traces the evolving context in the twentieth century that provides a basis for the professional aspirations of managers. The professionalization of managers has implications for other professions. The more managers aspire to professional legitimacy, the more their position as agents of corporate interests may erode the professional aspirations of other groups. Such a process opens up a new perspective on control and competition among professional groups.

In the fourth chapter, Reed looks at policies and discourses related to leadership capacities, based on empirical research on public sector reforms in the UK. He explores the various factors that provide ideological legitimacy and political momentum to this call for more leadership as a way to engage professionals (and public servants and managers) in an agenda defined by policy elites. Leadership is relabelled here as an ideology. Leaderism reveals an attempt by reformers to co-opt professionals in neo-liberal reforms. Active participation of professionals in leadership roles may culminate in the erosion of their autonomy and status. In the end they become participants in changes that are not well aligned with their own values and interests.

The fifth chapter, by Denis, van Gestel and Lepage, explores the role of professionals in organizational change. Professionals have often been depicted as victims of change. The authors suggest the need for a more nuanced picture. Their analysis explores the agent capacity of professionals within organizational changes. They argue that the predominant structural approach used to mobilize professionals in change initiatives is too limited. More attention needs to be paid to the dynamics of co-evolution between professionals and organizations. Subtle processes of institutional reflexivity are involved in shaping the relationship between professionals and change. Such processes culminate in various roles enacted by professionals in organizational change, and these roles are broader than the one of leader of change.

Taken together, the chapters in this section reveal a complex and heterogeneous picture of the overlapping of professions and organizations in contemporary societies. One common trend in this research is that organizations and professions are mutually constitutive and transformative. Forces of change in these two worlds may suppress or enhance the status and influence of professionals.

References

Adler, P.S., Kwon, S.W., & Heckscher, C. (2008) 'Perspective-professional work: The emergence of collaborative community'. *Organization Science*, 19(2), pp. 359–76.

Evetts, J. (2003) 'The sociological analysis of professionalism: occupational change in the modern world'. *International Sociology*, 18(2), pp. 395–415.

Noordegraaf, M. (2011) 'Risky business: How professionals and professional fields (must) deal with organizational issues'. *Organization Studies*, 32(10), pp. 1349–71.

11

Restructuring professional organizations

C. R. (Bob) Hinings

The study of professionals in organizations and the organization of professionals has a long and distinguished history (Hinings, 2004). Initially the emphasis was on the potential for conflict for professionals working in bureaucratic organizations, reflecting the interest in the 1960s in the development of bureaucracy (Hall, 1968). This was followed by an emphasis on the jurisdictions and power of professions and their impact on organizational and societal labour markets (Freidson, 1986). In the 1980s and 90s, a further stream emerged (which had its origins in the 1960s and 1970s (Scott, 1965)) that emphasized the changing nature of professionals, acknowledging a variety of professional and organizational locations (Greenwood et al., 1990). Abbott (1988) had developed the idea of continuous competition and jurisdictional disputes between professional groups at the level of the professional system. Thus, professions and organizations, professionals in organizations, and professional organizations have been an ongoing set of issues for both organization and management theory and the sociology of organizations and professions for more than 50 years.

The last 25 years or so have seen a revival of interest in the professional organization, per se. In particular there has been a concentration on organizations that are primarily owned, staffed, and run by professionals, the professional service firm (PSF). There has been an argument that this is a distinctive form of organizational design (Brock et al., 1999; Greenwood & Empson, 2003; Empson et al., 2015). This chapter is both a review of the models and an explanation of the distinctive form of design characteristics of professional firms, centring on the professional partnership. It also addresses the ways in which these are changing, and looks at new ideas for the analysis of restructuring, including the impact of new forms on the status and work of professionals. It aims to synthesize the common threads running through the literature on restructuring.

Models of the professional firm that will be discussed include work on the differences between professional and bureaucratic/corporate forms of organization and the extent to which they are both present in PSFs; the notion of the archetype form of professional firm and how this is nested within neo-institutional theories of organization form and change. An important aspect of this is differences between professions, something that has been addressed quite recently (Malhotra & Morris, 2009; von Nordenflycht, 2010). There is a developing literature on both professional and national differences. In many respects, the systematic examination of difference is a recent development and requires a more thorough incorporation into work on PSF restructuring.

These issues lead to the central question of the restructuring of professional organizations. How can the observable changes in the organizational design of many professional firms be explained? Both institutional theory and contingency theory can provide answers to this question and, in particular, the ways in which institutional and contingent aspects of restructuring interact. In terms of institutional theory, this means examining the ideas of archetypes and archetype change which have been central to discussions of the restructuring of professional organizations. The archetype approach has to be balanced with the impact of historical contingent factors such as increasing size and specialization, and the increasing use of information technology. Also considered are the processes by which change in professional firms occurs, including the impact of broader economic factors and labour-market dynamics on changes in professional work.

There are a further set of issues that are important in answering the question of why change is occurring. The globalization of professional service firms is happening; there are changes in the nature of ownership as jurisdictions allow these firms to move away from the professional partnership. The chapter considers how these issues can be theorized within the context of professional organization restructuring from both an institutional and contingency perspective. Also to be noted is how, as professional firms grow and diversify, they are portfolios of expertise-based practices that may require differing designs.

As well as providing a summary of what we know about the restructuring of professional organizations, the chapter ends by identifying the gaps that exist in our knowledge and proposes an agenda for further research on restructuring.

Professional organizational design and restructuring: a review of the models

The origins of a concern with the supposed uniqueness of professional organizations come from a concern with the nature of a profession. There were early attempts to define the structural and value characteristics of a profession. Thus, structural aspects such as a certification system, a professional association and a code of ethics were emphasized, together with the idea of a professional culture that was built on vocation, self-regulation and autonomy, peer reference and a public service ethos. As Brock *et al.* (1999, p. 4) put it, 'the common thread is a set of professional values, beliefs and aspirations woven into the very fabric of professional firms and organizations'.

Early work by Scott (1965) suggested two models of professional structuring. One, the autonomous professional organization, was what has essentially come to be called the professional organization or the professional service firm as it is where professionals design and manage the organization. Examples are law firms, medical clinics and architectural practices. Authority rests with professionals and autonomy and collegiality are emphasized. Administrative staff are subordinate to professionals. The heteronomous professional organization is one where professionals perform the core service but are subordinate to a managerial system. Examples are universities, health systems and social work. The extent of professional autonomy is less in these organizations.

This model was taken further and systematized by Mintzberg (1979) with his idea of the professional bureaucracy. Professionals are at the operating core of the organization but within a wider bureaucratic framework. In this model, while professionals strive for autonomy and collegial control in their work, they are subject to authority systems and control instituted by either non-professionals or other professionals. Of course, Mintzberg is dealing with an ideal type: in reality, there are variations between professions. In healthcare, physicians retain high degrees of autonomy over their work and much authority. In engineering, engineers are often under the control of non-professional managers.

For three decades through the 1960s, 70s and 80s, the primary approach to understanding professional organizations was by contrasting it with bureaucratic organizations, drawing on the work of Scott (1965). This concern arose from theorizing bureaucracy as the dominant form of organization which posed a threat to professional ways of organizing. As a result, much work centred on the response of professionals to working in bureaucratic settings. Such was the centrality of theories of bureaucracy that settings where professionals worked in independent practice were ignored; there was no model for understanding such organizations. As Hinings (2004, p. 406) put it, 'the neglect of professional service firms is particularly striking in the light of the fact that the independent professional organizational setting was considered to be very important as the preferred, archetypal work environment for an autonomous professional practitioner'.

Beginning in the late 1980s and accelerating in the 90s (Greenwood et al., 1990; Brock et al., 1999), there was a rediscovery of the professionally based, private practice organization, the professional service firm or the archetype professional organization. There has been a transformation of the professional–bureaucratic distinction into professionalism and managerialism. A considerable stream of work has been generated that encompasses accounting, law, management consulting, engineering consulting and architecture, and much of this work has derived from the ideas of Greenwood et al. (1990) and Cooper et al. (1996).

Greenwood et al. (1990) started from the neglect of autonomous professional organizations by organization theorists. They argued that these organizations, exemplified by the professional service firm, had distinctive characteristics, which they labelled the P^2 archetype. This framing is within institutional theory and as such connects meaning, structures and systems. Archetypes are located in organizational fields (Greenwood et al., 2002; Pinnington & Morris, 2003), in this case, that of professional services. The concept of archetypes captures the idea of the relationship between institutional logics and organizations. 'An archetype is thus a set of structures and systems that consistently embodies a single interpretive scheme' (Greenwood & Hinings, 1993, p. 1055). Archetypes are comprised of structures, systems, practices and activities bound together by an institutional logic. This concept adds the very important dimension of interpretive schemes or institutional logics (Greenwood & Hinings, 1993); in doing that it also emphasizes the important dimension of professional logics and the professional field.

Indeed, historical formulations have emphasized the professional partnership archetype (Abbott, 1988; Greenwood et al., 1990; Greenwood & Empson, 2003), highlighting the differences from corporations in organizational structure, systems, power and politics because of the logic of professionalism (Pinnington & Morris, 2003). Logics have both symbolic and material elements; the symbolic aspects refer to meaning and beliefs, the material to structures and practices, and the two are intertwined and constitutive of one another. Indeed, Thornton et al. (2012) delineate two separate institutional orders at the level of society (amongst the six in total), the profession and the corporation with their own specific logics, legitimacy, norms, control systems, etc. In the context of PSFs, Cooper et al. (1996) identify the symbolic aspect of the professional logic as encompassing beliefs in peer control (collegiality), representative democracy, authority resting with the professional, and, consequentially, minimum hierarchy. Materially, this means that there is low differentiation, low integration, few formal rules and procedures and few levels (Malhotra et al., 2006). This P^2 archetype is located in an institutional field which legitimates this particular way of organizing through the regulatory bodies responsible for professions (Greenwood et al., 2002).

However, a major development in the study of professional organizations has been the idea that an alternative archetype for PSFs has become important, what Cooper *et al.* (1996) called the managed professional business (MPB). It represents the rise of a managerial/corporate logic in the professional sphere (Malhotra *et al.*, 2006). This logic emphasizes effectiveness, efficiency, productivity, the separation of professional and managerial roles, and growth. Materially, there are formal managerial structures and systems, hierarchies, explicit targets and the devolution of decision-making to executive teams which may include non-professionals. Thus, the logic of professionalism is de-emphasized. Greenwood *et al.* (2002) and Greenwood and Suddaby (2006) show how this alternative archetype became legitimated within the accounting institutional field. The MPB is akin to Scott's (1965) heteronomous professional organization or Mintzberg's (1979) professional bureaucracy.

So, these two models, the P^2 and the MPB, represent the tension between professional autonomy and bureaucratic control. However, more recent work has suggested that the tension is overdrawn; that there is 'a creative adaptation of leadership roles and identities in the newly globalized firm in which traditional professional values and technical expertise (are) integrated with managerial and business skills' (Greenwood *et al.*, 2006, p. 10). Studies carried out by Fenton and Pettigrew (2006) and Empson and Chapman (2006) both show adaptation in PSFs. Indeed, in terms of some of the contemporary themes of institutional theory, this suggests that logics do not necessarily compete but may be complementary, separated or combined in some way, producing a hybrid organization (Thornton *et al.*, 2012; Battilana & Lee, 2014).

Much of this literature has begged the question of what constitutes a professional organization in order not to get bogged down in the kinds of debates that dogged the discussion of professions for so many years (Abbott, 1988). But a definition is needed. Empson *et al.* (2015) suggest that there are four defining characteristics. These characteristics allow for heterogeneity among PSFs and for the fact that there are hybrid professional organizations.

1. The primary activity is the application of specialist knowledge to clients' problems through the creation of customized solutions.
2. The key assets of PSFs are the specialist knowledge of the professional members, together with their in-depth knowledge of clients.
3. Governance is exercised through extensive individual autonomy as the core producers own or control key assets. As a result, managerial authority is contingent.
4. There is a special identity where the core producers recognize each other as professionals and are recognized as such by clients and competitors.

(Empson et al.*, 2015)*

These characteristics differ from those of Mintzberg's (1979) definition of a professional bureaucracy because of his concern with structuring and Empson *et al.*'s (2015) with a more comprehensive notion of organizational governance and design. Mintzberg emphasized classic bureaucratic dimensions rather than assets, identity and governance.

Pressures and processes of restructuring

The basic theme, then, of the past 25 years of study of professional organizations is that of the encroachment of corporatism or managerialism on professionalism, seen as two logics competing for dominance (Malhotra *et al.*, 2006). And this is a more modern form of the debate that goes back to the 1950s and 70s about the relationship between professional values and practices and bureaucratic forms of organization. Historically, this has been formulated as an 'internal' issue, arising from the evolution and dominance of large-scale, bureaucratic organizations. But a number of 'external' reasons for the pressures to restructure from professional to corporate organizational models have been articulated.

Greenwood and Hinings (1996), in examining radical, archetype change, suggested that there are two generic pressures for change, market and institutional, each of which covers a number of elements. There is a sense in which market pressures are derived from a contingency theory approach while institutional pressures are from institutional theory.

Pressures to restructure: markets

Greenwood *et al.* (2002) outlined four aspects of market context: overall growth in business services; changes in the number and demands of clients; degree of competition; and globalization. These elements can be found also in the work of Greenwood and Empson (2003), Malhotra *et al.* (2006), Hinings (2004) and Empson *et al.* (2015).

There has been considerable growth in the demand for professional services in accounting, law, management consulting, engineering consulting, etc. This is a reflection of the modern economy moving from a manufacturing to a service base. As an adjunct to a concern with professional organizations, per se, there has been an increasing interest in the idea of the knowledge organization because of the centrality of knowledge to the modern, post-industrial economy. Sharma (1997, p. 758), in examining knowledge, states 'without PSFs, business as we know it, would come to a grinding halt'. In particular, there has been a shift in the demand for more complex advisory and consulting services.

The increasing demand for professional services also reflects changes in the number and demands of clients. Because clients are themselves increasingly knowledge-based and have a greater understanding of the services offered by PSFs, more is demanded by those clients (Malhotra *et al.*, 2006). There are two aspects to this: one is the idea of 'one-stop shopping' for professional services, with the expectation that the professional organization will provide a wide array of services (Cooper *et al.*, 2007). This has led to a large number of mergers and acquisitions with PSFs cutting across jurisdictional lines, accounting firms acquiring law firms, for example. The second is the client distinguishing between standardized, commodified services such as audit and services tailored to their specific needs (Malhotra *et al.*, 2006). This produces price pressures on commodified services.

Increased demand for professional services has led to new entrants and heightened degrees of competition. A prime example is the move of IBM from a producer of computer hardware to a global business advisory firm. Indeed, IBM Global Services is the largest IT consulting firm (Greenwood *et al.*, 2006).

Finally, there is the issue of globalization which is related, at least in part, to client changes. Rose and Hinings (1999, p. 43) argue that 'Global Business Advisory Firms have become global in order to maintain their relationships with clients who themselves have been progressing along the path from multinational to international, to transnational enterprise...'. Morgan and Quack (2006) point to a process of legal globalization. Sako (2009) also examines how decisions are made about which services to retain within the firm and which to outsource or offshore in a global context. She has noted the influence of professional expertise and identity on organizational design and industry structure in law firms on the decision about which service to supply. Greenwood *et al.* (2006) point out that the very largest PSFs (e.g. PricewaterhouseCoopers, Ernst and Young) are some of the world's most geographically complex with offices in nearly 150 countries and with the scale to match.

What are the consequences of these market changes for the restructuring of professional organizations? Here we draw on the insights of contingency theory. One 'simple' result of growth in services and globalization is an increase in the scale of PSFs in both sheer numbers and in services offered. And we know that increased scale is strongly related to more bureaucratic control (Donaldson, 2001). But underlying this 'simple' relationship is a more complex reality. In response to the demand for more services delivered in a global context, PSFs become more differentiated, which raises issues of integration (Rose & Hinings, 1999). Accounting, law, engineering, and management consulting firms provide a wider range of services, in more offices and more countries. Providing that wider range of services also means employing a wider range of professionals. So, there is more differentiation along functional and geographic lines.

In order to deliver a one-stop service there is a greater need for integration; there is a demand, internally, for the development of coordination mechanisms across the firm. Integration is required at a level that goes beyond previous experience (Greenwood *et al.*, 2010; Boussebaa & Morgan, 2015). New integrative roles and activities are required. In particular, there is the appearance of stronger international headquarters, business unit structures and client management teams. These organizational developments are akin to what Nohria and Ghoshal (1997) call a differentiated network structure which has a high level of complexity. What has been happening in contemporary professional organizations is the current working out of the long-standing professional–bureaucratic tensions. This contemporary outworking is emphasizing the creative integration of professional values and technical skills with managerial and business skills in the globalized PSF (Greenwood *et al.*, 2006).

Pressures to restructure: institutional

The second pressure for radical change in PSFs is that of institutional change (Greenwood & Hinings, 1996). Professions are highly institutionalized, being subject to forms of external regulation by the state and having their own internal controls through educational and certification processes controlled by professional associations (Abbott, 1988). But this institutional, regulatory context has been changing, some suggest quite radically. Leicht and Lyman (2006) argue that the emergence of neo-liberal ideologies challenges historical professional values; in other words, there is a clash of institutional logics. Indeed, the deregulation of professional markets and changes in government policy towards professional has been emphasized as part of the general literature on change in PSFs (Greenwood *et al.* 2006; Empson *et al.*, 2015). Deregulation is based on a logic that favours consumers over producers; the centrality of markets; and competition as producing efficiencies (Leicht & Lyman, 2006). Indeed, Leicht and Lyman (2006, p. 40) say, 'market logics have become institutionalized among significant actors and stakeholders in the provision of business services'.

The impact of deregulation and the logic of corporatism works both directly and indirectly on professional organization restructuring. Directly, it opens up the possibility to provide a wider range of services; the organization can become more functionally complex. Professional service firms have increased their range of services as they are allowed to move outside their particular jurisdiction. So, accounting firms and law firms merge; information technology firms move into management consulting, and so on (Quack & Schuessler, 2015). As a result, they become more differentiated. Indirectly, deregulation reinforces the trends in markets by opening up competition and, thus, has the same organizational effects as those outlined previously.

Because of deregulation, ownership of professional organizations has changed, with outside ownership and new, innovative business structures being introduced (Empson & Chapman, 2006; Greenwood & Empson, 2003). Accounting firms are providing legal services and there is a resurgent debate about multidisciplinary practices (Greenwood & Suddaby, 2006). There is a renewed focus on shifting from service to process and business model innovation, producing entirely new service delivery models.

Restructuring processes

An important part of Greenwood and Hinings' (1996) theorizing is that the impact of market and institutional pressures is not uniform across organizations. Restructuring may, or may not, take place. Indeed, there is considerable evidence to show that the attempt to restructure a professional organization to a more managerially based organization has been fraught with difficulties because of issues of legitimacy of the new model through its supposed clash with the logic of professionalism. It draws our attention to the underlying change in meaning or logics that is involved in any move from a P^2 to an MPB form of organization.

Hinings *et al.* (1991, p. 390), in their study of an attempt to restructure to a more managerial organization, say, 'the nature of the organizational change challenged the concept of partnership and ran counter to professional values'. A particular organizational element, changing the distribution of authority to a more centralized, corporate structure, was more than a 'technical' innovation: it was seen by partners in the firm as striking at the heart of what it meant to operate as a professional: collegiality, peer evaluation, autonomy, and informality of management. Similarly, Pinnington and Morris (2002) suggested that, in architectural practices, while there were elements of a managerial form of organization, the core elements of the traditional form of professional organization were not transformed. Thus, there was protection of the central elements of the professional logic.

Gardner *et al.* (2008) show that anything that challenges the professional logic is a radical innovation and therefore subject to considerable difficulty in successful restructuring. For Gardner *et al.* (2008, p. 1117), the 'structural adjustment' of 'the creation of new subunits through which new domains can be pursued' is a radical innovation. It is part of the attempt of PSFs to become more corporate. Innovation in service delivery involves moving away from the familiar and thus requires justification to those who are committed to the status quo. Establishing legitimacy for innovation involves multiple actors, such as individual professionals, partners and clients. However, the roles of these actors in establishing legitimacy varies according to the nature of the innovation. Incremental innovation can be legitimized through purely internal actors; radical innovation requires external legitimation of clients, regulators, professional associations. Greenwood *et al.* (2002) emphasize the role of theorization in legitimating new organizational forms.

In their study of law firms, Malhotra and Hinings (2015) show that organizational transformations occur through a process of continuity and change rather than disruptive upheaval. And, because of the particular organizational dynamics of commitment, logic clashes, power and internal competition, organizations respond in different ways. Because of this it is possible for continuity to overwhelm change, or for continuity and change to operate in a synthesizing manner, or for continuity and change to unfold in polarizing ways.

One specific area of innovation and restructuring is that of knowledge management. There have been attempts to codify knowledge for purposes of changing the business model to one of corporatism, where knowledge becomes a general resource of the organization. However, these restructurings run into the problems of the professional logic together with the fact that professional knowledge resides in individual practitioners. The professional emphasis on both individuality and collegiality means that schemes for organizational systems of knowledge codification are likely to be resisted. Empson (2001) shows that individual professionals fear 'exploitation' and 'contamination' when asked to share knowledge. Morris (2001) argues that, when faced with a knowledge-codification project, professionals may actually cooperate, but this is because they understand the real limits to the codification of their knowledge. 'Professionals perceive that their true value to their clients (and their source of power within their PSF) derives from their unique combination of experiences and intuition. They recognize that this knowledge is not susceptible to codification' (Empson, 2001, p. 814). Thus, the attempted restructuring often remains suspended between the two logics and their associated structures.

Professional organizations other than PSFs have been dealt with in the literature on new public management (NPM) (McNulty & Ferlie, 2002). These scholars point out that there are many tensions and paradoxes between corporate logics, as exemplified in NPM, and professional logics, especially between different principles of organizing and the attempted shift of boundaries between professions. All of these studies illustrate considerable resistance to organizational restructuring based on corporate logics and illustrate similar issues as those in the PSF literature. McNulty and Ferlie (2002, p. 362) conclude from their study of business process reengineering in healthcare, 'there were some pockets of organization change, but no organizational transformation. Change was patchy, difficult, and took much longer than originally expected.'

In summary, there are considerable, intertwined, market and institutional pressures for professional organizations to restructure, away from a purely professional mode of organizing to a more corporate/managerial one. However, the fact that such restructuring represents a move away from one archetype to another suggests that the processes will not be straightforward. Professional organizations represent a highly embedded way of organizing and professional logics are quite resistant to some changes, especially those that emphasize more centralized authority and decreased participation/collegiality (Malhotra et al., 2006).

This work represents an interesting evolution of our understanding of restructuring in PSFs. The original formulation, deriving from the historical professional–bureaucratic conflict literature suggests a degree of mutual exclusion between the P^2 and MPB archetypes. But two developments have taken place. One suggests that there is as much continuity as change in professional restructuring, including hybrid outcomes that contain elements of both archetypes. The other, which fits well with change theories, is that change from one archetype to another is hard and the outcomes of attempting to move to more managerial forms are fraught with difficulty. A major reason for this is that professionals protect their autonomy and their status in organizational change, and, from the evidence that we have so far, do that quite successfully.

Conclusions: the future agenda

It is 25 years since Greenwood et al. (1990) re-energized the study of professional organizations through the concept of the 'P^2' archetype. The aim was to draw attention to a forgotten, important organization, the professional service firm, by specifying the 'distinctive characteristics' of professional partnerships. But, as this chapter has outlined, there has been considerable concern with the restructuring of professional organizations in response to interlinked market and institutional change. Because of all the pressures and changes that have been occurring, the question is raised of the continued distinctiveness of professional organizations.

The introduction of new organizational forms and business models (Gardner et al., 2008; Barrett & Hinings, 2015) introduces a series of questions about governance, organizational form, processes of organizational change and new practices. There is a question of whether there is still a distinctive archetype for the professional organization. This raises a number of questions for research on PSFs, examining them at three levels of analysis, the professional organization, the inter-professional, and the comparative.

All of the work cited here has been done at either the professional or inter-professional level. The professional level is where organizations of one professional jurisdiction are examined, e.g. law firms or accounting firms or engineering consulting firms. Work has centred on whether they are P^2 or MPB, or some variant of those. In addition, there has been considerable work on the processes of change from one archetype to another. Malhotra *et al.* (2006, p. 197) suggest that 'future work should more closely link changes in firms' structures … with micro-level analyses of changes to professional work' as there has been little focus on these issues. A particularly important area, because of the nature of partnership, is that of leadership (Denis *et al.*, 2010; Empson & Langley, 2015). In addition, an issue for this level of analysis is that most studies have been of larger professional organizations. There is real room for analysis of differences between organizations within a particular professional jurisdiction.

At the inter-professional level, most work has been at the level of conceptualization (Malhotra *et al.*, 2006; von Nordenflycht, 2010), attempting to define the basis of differences across professional jurisdictions. More systematic analysis is needed of inter-professional similarities and differences in order to establish what archetypes actually exist and whether there are similar pressures for change in different jurisdictions. For example, Greenwood *et al.* (2006, p. 3) show that, even when looking at the largest firms in six professional sectors, they range in size from 1,000 personnel (in architecture) to 190,000 (in management consulting). The largest law firm has 6,700 employees; the largest accounting firm, 130,000. Similarly, there are major differences in the number of countries in which they operate (6–160) and the number of offices that they have (18–771). Contingency theory tells us that such variations produce differences in organization structures and systems and for the processes of organizational restructuring. There are, of course, many other differences, for example in professional values, between professional organizations in different jurisdictions that have implications for organizational form and change. More work is needed to examine such differences.

At both the professional and inter-professional level, there is an important connection with contemporary institutional theory and the idea of institutional complexity (Greenwood *et al.*, 2011). Their concern is with organizational responses when they face incompatible prescriptions from multiple institutional logics. This is the potential situation when professional organizations face both professional and corporate logics. Institutional theory has begun to theorize these situations through ideas of how organizations manage conflicting logics, suggesting that logics do not necessarily compete but may be complementary, separated or combined in some way (Thornton *et al.*, 2012). These ideas have led to discussion of hybrid organizations that manage a variety of logics through structures, systems and practices that have elements of more than one logic (Battilana & Lee, 2014). Locating the discussion of professional organization restructuring in institutional complexity and hybrid organizations would open up a fruitful area of research.

Other work that has examined a range of professional organizations has been concerned primarily with demonstrating consistencies across those organizations rather than difference (Dougherty, 2004; Anand *et al.*, 2007). These studies deal with service innovation and are very focused on the role of knowledge in developing new ideas and services. They argue that in professional organizations, knowledge is practice based and service innovation has to come from capturing that knowledge to create value for clients and by redesigning work, for instance into teams. Knowledge rests primarily with the individual professional and derives from the set of practices pursued by those individuals. There are some important issues to be followed up from this research. One is to look for difference as well as similarity (this is a problem with much of contemporary organization theory with the loss of a truly comparative perspective (King *et al.*, 2009)). Another is for research on professional organizations to systematically deal with the role of knowledge in organizing. And a third is to take the idea of innovation seriously (Barrett & Hinings, 2015).

A truly comparative level of analysis would deal with a number of important issues. One is to come to grips with the idea of knowledge-based organizations. All definitions of professional organizations have knowledge as a central element. But there are organizations that are knowledge based that are not professional according to the definitions of Empson *et al.* (2015) and von Nordenflycht (2010). The taken-for-granted argument is that professional organizations are different from non-professional organizations. But in the modern economy, there is a convergence as many organizations (e.g. those in the high-tech sector) become more like professional organizations, and the latter become more like corporations, per se. The research question becomes: is there a distinctive professional archetype, because of professionalism, or are they, in fact, becoming similar to other types of organizations? Given the importance of professional organizations to business and government, are they truly distinctive? And what are the consequences of that distinctiveness?

Another issue in comparative analysis is related to the internationalization and globalization of professional organizations. Greenwood *et al.* (2006, p. 3) show the international nature of these organizations; but some are more heavily international than others. Some are more international than non-professional organizations. How do internationalization processes compare? For example, Malhotra and Hinings (2010) argue that the internationalization processes of the mass-production organization, the disaggregated production organization, and the project-based organization/professional organization differ. Each type of organization responds differently to the focus of entry, the degree of presence and the physical presence requirements in a foreign market. As a result, there are different approaches to organizing and operating in a foreign market. This is merely indicative of questions raised by the internationalization of professional organizations, especially when compared with non-professional organizations.

Similarly, Boussebaa and Morgan (2015) identify network, project, federal and transnational organizations as different forms of the internationalization of professional service firms. What research there is highlights change towards the transnational model from a federal model, but there is little evidence about implementation and the processes of change. Given the importance of internationalization in professional organizations, more systematic work is required. We need to know more about how, for example, law firms have achieved internationalization and with what organizational form and change processes. We need to compare those forms and processes across professional jurisdictions, and, following Malhotra and Hinings (2010) and Boussebaa and Morgan (2015), we need to examine similarities and differences between professional and non-professional organizations.

There is no shortage of research topics to take the study of professional organization restructuring forward. Perhaps the most important issue is to ensure that the study of these extremely important organizations does not become overly centred on professionals per se, but becomes more connected with the current theorizing and issues in organization theory. Essentially, the revival of interest in professional organizations and their restructuring has led to them becoming an object of interest in their own right (witness the new *Journal of Professions and Organization*). As a result, their difference from non-professional organizations has become taken for granted without being tested. Yet this is an empirical question. As organization theory more generally has become concerned with knowledge-based organization, network organizations and hybrid organizations, there are clear connections with professional organizations. Studying professional organizations and their restructuring in the context of these other kinds of organizations will provide a firmer base for establishing whether and in what way professional organizations are a unique type of organization (Kirkpatrick & Noordegraaf, 2015).

References

Abbott, A. (1988) *The System of Professions*. Chicago, IL: University of Chicago Press.

Anand, N., Gardner, H. K. and Morris, T. (2007) 'Knowledge-based innovation: Emergence and embedding of new practice areas in management consulting firms'. *Academy of Management Journal*, 50(2), pp. 406–428.

Barrett, M. and Hinings, C. R. (2015) 'Service innovation in professional service firms: A review and future research directions'. In L. Empson, D. Muzio, J. Broschak and R. Hinings (eds), *The Oxford Handbook of Professional Services Firms*. Oxford: Oxford University Press, pp. 238–254.

Battilana, J. and Lee, M. (2014) 'Advancing research on hybrid organizing: Insights from the study of social enterprises'. *Annals of the Academy of Management*, 8(1), pp. 397–441.

Boussebaa, M. and Morgan, G. (2015) 'Internationalization of professional service firms: Drivers, forms and outcomes'. In L. Empson, D. Muzio, J. Broschak and R. Hinings (eds), *The Oxford Handbook of Professional Services Firms*. Oxford: Oxford University Press, pp. 71–92.

Brock, D., Powell, M. and Hinings, C. R. (eds) (1999) *Restructuring the Professional Organization*. London: Routledge.

Cooper, D. J., Hinings C. R., Greenwood, R. and Brown, J. (1996) 'Sedimentation and transformation in organizational change: The case of Canadian law firms'. *Organization Studies*, 17, pp. 623–647.

Cooper, D. J., Greenwood, R. and Hinings, C. R. (2007) 'Knowledge management in global accounting firms'. In M. Granlund (ed.), *Total Quality in Academic Accounting*. Turku, Finland: Turku School of Economics.

Denis, J.-L., Langley, A., and Sergi, V. (2010) 'Leadership in the plural'. *Academy of Management Annals*, 6, pp. 211–283.

Donaldson, L. (2001) *The Contingency Theory of Organizations*. London: Sage.

Dougherty, D. (2004) 'Organizing practices in services: Capturing practice-based knowledge for innovation'. *Strategic Organization*, 2(1), pp. 35–64.

Empson, L. (2001) 'Fear of exploitation and fear of contamination: Impediments to knowledge transfer in mergers between professional service firms'. *Human Relations*, 54, pp. 839–863.

Empson, L. and Chapman, C. (2006) 'Partnership versus corporation: Implications of alternative forms of governance in professional service firms'. *Research in the Sociology of Organizations*, 24, pp. 139–170.

Empson, L. and Langley, A. (2015) 'Leadership and professionals: Multiple manifestations of influence in professional service firms'. In L. Empson, D. Muzio, J. Broschak and R. Hinings (eds), *The Oxford Handbook of Professional Services Firms*. Oxford: Oxford University Press, pp. 163–188.

Empson, L., Muzio, D., Broschak, J. P. and Hinings, C. R. (2015) 'Researching professional service firms: An introduction and overview'. In L. Empson, D. Muzio, J. Broschak and R. Hinings (eds), *The Oxford Handbook of Professional Service Firms*. Oxford: Oxford University Press, pp. 1–22.

Fenton, E. and Pettigrew, A. (2006) 'Leading change in the new professional service firm: Characterizing strategic leadership in a global context'. *Research in the Sociology of Organizations*, 24, pp. 101–138.

Freidson, E. (1986) *Professional Powers*. Chicago, IL: University of Chicago Press.

Gardner, H., Anand, N. and Morris, T. (2008) 'Chartering new territory: Diversification, legitimacy and practice area creation in professional service firms'. *Journal of Organizational Behavior*, 29(8), pp. 1101–1121.

Greenwood, R. and Empson, L. (2003) 'The professional partnership: Relic or exemplary form of governance?'. *Organization Studies*, 24(6), pp. 909–933.

Greenwood, R. and Hinings, C. R. (1993) 'Understanding strategic change: The contribution of archetypes'. *Academy of Management Journal*, 36, pp. 1052–1081.

Greenwood, R. and Hinings, C. R. (1996) 'Understanding radical organizational change: Bringing together the old and new institutionalism'. *Academy of Management Review*, 21, pp. 1022–1055.

Greenwood, R. and Suddaby, R. (2006) 'Institutional entrepreneurship in mature fields: The Big Five accounting firms'. *Academy of Management Journal*, 49, pp. 27–48.

Greenwood, R., Hinings, C. R. and Brown, J. L. (1990) 'The P2-Form of strategic management: Corporate practices in the professional partnership'. *Academy of Management Journal*, 33, pp. 725–755.

Greenwood, R., Suddaby, R. and Hinings, C. R. (2002) 'Theorizing change: The role of professional associations in the transformation of organizational fields'. *Academy of Management Journal*, 45, pp. 58–80.

Greenwood, R., Suddaby, R. and McDugald, M. (2006) 'Introduction'. *Research in the Sociology of Organizations*, 24, pp. 1–16.

Greenwood, R., Morris, T., Fairclough, S. and Boussebaa, M. (2010) 'The organizational design of transnational professional service firms'. *Organizational Dynamics*, 39, pp. 173–183.

Greenwood, R., Raynard, M., Kodeih, F., Micelotta, E. R. and Lounsbury, M. (2011) 'Institutional complexity and organizational responses'. *The Academy of Management Annals*, 5 (1), pp. 317–371.

Hall, R. H. (1968) 'Professionalization and bureaucratization'. *American Sociological Review*, 33, pp. 92–104.

Hinings, C. R. (2004) 'The changing nature of professional organizations'. In S. Ackroyd, R. Batt, P. Thompson and P. Tolbert (eds). *Oxford Handbook of Work and Organizations*. Oxford: Oxford University Press, pp. 404–424.

Hinings, C. R., Brown, J. and Greenwood, R. (1991) 'Change in an autonomous professional organization'. *Journal of Management Studies*, 28, pp. 375–393.

King, B., Felin, T. and Whetten, D. (2009) 'Comparative organizational analysis: An introduction'. *Research in the Sociology of Organizations*, 26, pp. 3–20.

Kirkpatrick, I. and Noordegraaf, M. (2015) 'Organizations and occupations'. In L. Empson, D. Muzio, J. Broschak and R. Hinings (eds), *The Oxford Handbook of Professional Services Firms*, Oxford: Oxford University Press, pp. 92–112.

Leicht, K. and Lyman, E. (2006) 'Markets, institutions, and the crisis of professional practice'. *Research in the Sociology of Organizations*, 24, pp. 17–44.

McNulty, T. and Ferlie, E. (2002) *Reengineering Healthcare: The Complexities of Organizational Transformation*. Oxford: Oxford University Press.

Malhotra, N. and Hinings, C. R. (2010) 'An organizational model for understanding internationalization processes'. *Journal of International Business Studies*, 41, pp. 330–349.

Malhotra, N. and Hinings, C. R. (2015) 'Unpacking continuity and change as a process of organizational transformation'. *Long Range Planning*, 48, pp. 1–22.

Malhotra, N. and Morris, T. (2009) 'Heterogeneity in professional service firms'. *Journal of Management Studies*, 46, pp. 895–922.

Malhotra, N., Morris, T. and Hinings, C. R. (2006) 'Variation in organizational form among professional service firms'. *Research in the Sociology of Organizations*, 24, pp. 171–202.

Mintzberg, H. (1979) *The Structuring of Organizations*. Englewood Cliffs, NJ: Prentice Hall.

Morgan, G. and Quack, S. (2006) 'The internationalization of professional service firms: Global convergence, national path-dependency or cross-border hybridization'. *Research in the Sociology of Organizations*, 24, pp. 403–431.

Morris, T. (2001) 'Asserting property rights: Knowledge codification in the professional service firm'. *Human Relations*, 54(1), pp. 54–71.

Nohria, N. and Ghoshal, S. (1997) *The Differentiated Network Organization: Organizing Multinational Corporations for Value Creation*. San Francisco, CA: Jossey-Bass.

von Nordenflycht, A. (2010) 'What is a professional service firm? Towards a theory and taxonomy of knowledge-intensive firms'. *Academy of Management Review*, 35(1), pp. 155–174.

Pinnington, A. and Morris, T. (2002) 'Transforming the architect: Ownership form and archetype change'. *Organization Studies*, 23(2), pp. 189–210.

Pinnington, A. and Morris, T. (2003) 'Archetype change in professional organizations: Survey evidence from large law firms'. *British Journal of Management*, 14, pp. 85–99.

Quack, S. and Schuessler, E. (2015) 'Dynamics of regulation of professional service firms: National and transnational developments'. In L. Empson, D. Muzio, J. Broschak and R. Hinings (eds), *The Oxford Handbook of Professional Service Firms*. Oxford: Oxford University Press, pp. 48–70.

Rose, T. and Hinings, C. R. (1999) 'Global clients' demands driving change in global business advisory firms'. In D. Brock, M. Powell and C. R. Hinings (eds), *Restructuring the Professional Organization*. London: Routledge, pp. 41–67.

Sako, M. (2009) 'Globalization of knowledge-intensive professional services'. *Communications of the ACM*, 52(7), pp. 31–33.

Scott, W. R. (1965) 'Reactions to supervision in a heteronomous professional organization'. *Administrative Science Quarterly*, 10, pp. 65–81.

Sharma, A. (1997) 'Professional as agent: Knowledge asymmetry in agency exchange'. *Academy of Management Review*, 22, pp. 758–798.

Thornton, P., Ocasio, W. and Lounsbury, M. (2012) *The Institutional Logics Perspective*. Oxford: Oxford University Press.

12

Hybrid managers and professional leadership

Ian Kirkpatrick

Introduction

The changing relationship between professionalism and management is a topic that continues to generate debate and controversy. This is especially so with regard to how management roles and imperatives have emerged within the professions themselves. Such roles can be found across all kinds of professional services, for example, clinical directors in health, heads of department in academia, care managers in social work or managing partners in accounting and law firms (Kitchener *et al.*, 2000; Gleeson & Knights, 2006; Deem *et al.*, 2007; Empson *et al.*, 2013a; McGivern *et al.*, 2015). Increasingly this has attracted attention, not just from academics but also from policy makers and professional associations, concerned with the implications for training, education and the quality of service delivery.

Turning to the academic literature, it is now commonplace to refer to the development of these formal professional–manager roles as hybrids (Noordegraaf, 2007). The term 'hybrid' is imported from biology to refer to a 'state of being composed through a mixture of disparate parts' (Battilana & Lee, 2014, p. 400). In this regard, a 'hybrid' is not something that is entirely new and nor is it transitory, but it involves a recombination of existing elements, often in tension. The term hybrid may be applied to different levels of analysis, including whole organisational fields, single organisations or individual roles. However, only the latter concern us in this chapter, especially where hybrid roles involve a 'recombination and blurring of distinct professional and organisational modes of working' (Waring, 2014, p. 689).

Over the past twenty years, a vast literature has accumulated around this topic, focusing on the nature and impact of these hybrid professional–manager roles in a wide variety of organisational settings. Yet, while the volume of research has grown, the boundary conditions that define these roles as a discrete phenomenon remain vague. As we shall see, there also continues to be some ambiguity concerning the reasons for the development of hybrid roles and how (and why) they vary between different institutional settings. These problems are accentuated by the fragmented nature of research on this topic, much of it channelled through separate disciplines (for example, education, health policy, accounting). This means that while we have deep insights into the experience of hybrid roles in particular settings (notably in health), there has been little attempt to generalise across all professions.

In this chapter my aim is to begin to address some of these concerns by providing a roadmap to better understanding the nature and origins of hybrid professional–manager roles. To do so, my starting point will be the classic work of Freidson (1985, 1994), which represents the first serious treatment of this topic. The chapter will then propose a framework for understanding variations in the formal nature of hybrid roles within and between organisations. Lastly, I will turn to wider debates in the literature about the forces driving the creation of these roles and research focusing on how they are enacted and experienced by professionals.

Before we begin it is important to note certain caveats. As hinted already, the primary focus of this chapter will be on professionals who take on formal management roles in organisations and not on other forms of 'hybridisation'. This means that I will necessarily give less attention to debates concerning the hybridisation of professionals more generally or to the emergence of hybrid organisations or fields (Reay & Hinings, 2009). The focus on management and leadership also means that in this chapter we will be less concerned with 'hybrids' that combine professional and commercial priorities (Byrkjeflot & Jespersen, 2015). Lastly, while reference will be made to examples of hybrids across a range of professions, given the confines of space, my review of the research on the enactment of hybrid roles will be constrained mainly to the health sector as an illustrative case.

Restratification and the emergence of professional managers

Although the emergence of hybrid professional–manager roles is sometimes depicted as a recent phenomenon, we should not forget that debates on this topic are long standing. There is a considerable body of literature, for example, dating back to the 1960s, which deals at length with the changing relationship between professions and bureaucracy, both in public services and so-called autonomous professional organisations (today referred to as professional services firms (PSFs)) (Empson et al., 2013a). This literature identified classic features of 'professional bureaucracy', noting how these organisational forms were dominated by an operating core of semi-autonomous experts, specialised through education and training with strong cosmopolitan orientations (Mintzberg, 1993).

These professional organisational forms had (and still have) particular implications for 'management' and control (Bleiklie et al., 2015). On the one hand, they are formally hierarchical, often with clear lines of command, for example, between professors, associated professors and lecturers, or between partners, managers and trainee accountants. This hierarchy also represents a career system, characterised in PSFs as an 'up or out tournament' (Empson et al., 2013a). However, on the other hand, in many ways, these organisations did not (and arguably still do not) conform to the normal principles of hierarchy based on authority of position. Instead, one finds a hierarchy based on expert status, expertise seniority and authority that is ambiguous: essentially a form of 'clan control' (Ouchi, 1980). As such, the emphasis is on maintaining relations that are 'largely informal, sustaining a live and let live relationship amongst colleagues and preventing open conflict between elite and ordinary practitioners' (Freidson, 1994, p. 140). More recently, Courpasson (2000) has termed this form 'soft bureaucracy'.

This arrangement has obvious implications for systems of supervision and peer review which tended to be light touch and non-judgemental in flavour. Useful for understanding this is Ackroyd et al.'s (1989) notion of 'custodial administration'. This depicts relationships that are focused primarily on maintaining the status quo, buffering practice from external interference, where senior professionals (serving as managers) have an 'exaggerated respect for practitioner autonomy' (Ackroyd et al., 1989, p. 612). In this context, where senior professionals are viewed as first amongst equals, the emphasis is primarily on supporting the independent, self-regulating practice of junior colleagues who are assumed to be responsible, competent practitioners. As a result, the practice of rank-and-file professionals, including some forms of malpractice, may remain 'invisible' to higher levels (Kitchener *et al.*, 2000).

Although still present today, these forms of 'clan control' have always been subject to challenge, a theme picked up first by the American sociologist, Eliot Freidson (1985, 1994). Specifically, Freidson argued that all established professions were undergoing a process of res-tratification. This meant that, in response to pressures for tighter financial and management control, professions such as medicine, accounting and engineering are likely to reorganise themselves along functional lines in order to minimise the impact of external threats. As a result, in addition to the 'rank and file' of practising professionals, one now sees the emergence of stronger 'knowledge elites' and 'administrative elites'. The former comprises those professionals involved in research and education, helping to create new standards and regulations. By contrast, the 'administrative elite' refers to those professionals who actively take on formal management roles, with responsibility for the coordination and direction of rank-and-file practitioners.

These administrative elites exemplify the professional–management hybrids which are the main focus of this chapter. On the one hand, they are no different from professional administrators who (as we noted earlier) traditionally sought to protect or buffer professional practice from outside interference. Indeed, Freidson implies that the emergence of administrative elites can be viewed as a defensive strategy, a way in which professional communities might adapt to or absorb external imperatives to change in ways that are consistent with their own interests and priorities.

However, it is clear from Freidson's account that this new class of professional managers also implies a shift in the nature of intra-professional relations. He suggests, for example, that senior doctors now play a more active role in 'setting standards, reviewing performance, and exercising supervision and control' (Freidson, 1985, p. 26). While, in the past, medical administrators were largely part time and advisory, the current trend is for doctors to exercise 'formal administrative authority … analogous to "line" and "staff" authority in industry' (Freidson, 1985, p. 26).

Freidson further suggests that members of the administrative elite will adopt different orien-tations to their rank-and-file colleagues, being more attuned to the priorities of managers, iden-tifying 'as much, if not more, with the type of professional organisation they represent as with the practicing profession' (Freidson, 1994, p. 142). Where groups such as doctors are concerned, this could imply quite a radical shift in orientation. Indeed, he concludes that doctors in administra-tive roles will become focused on the 'rationalisation of practice' and on goals of '"macro care" of populations' as well as on the '"micro care" of individuals' (Freidson, 1985, p. 30). Increasingly, they may see themselves as not simply representatives or ambassadors of a particular profession, but as 'accountable for the aggregate performance of the organisation' (Freidson, 1994, p. 142).

Hence, Freidson's restratification thesis represents an important point of departure for current debates about hybrid professional–management roles. It also introduced a degree of ambiguity which still persists today. While administrative elites might seek to buffer practice and defend professional interests (similar to custodial administration), by taking on more formal manage-ment roles (and identities) they also potentially challenge the status quo. In this way, restratifica-tion represents a source of both continuity *and* radical change.

The nature and extent of hybrid professional–manager roles

Although a useful starting point, Freidson's account of the development of hybrid professional–manager roles is limited in many key respects. In particular, it says little about how 'administrative elites' may themselves be internally stratified along vertical lines within organi-sations that employ or host professionals. Nor does it say much about how this phenomenon differs between professions which, historically, have had different relationships with organisations. In what follows we explore both of these dimensions separately.

Vertical stratification

Useful for thinking about how hybrid roles may vary between different levels of an organisational (or professional) hierarchy is Causor and Exworthy's (1999, pp. 84–85) taxonomy differentiating between *three* broad categories of hybrid professional–manager: quasi-managerial practitioners, managing professionals (conventional hybrid), and general (full-time) managers.

Their first category of *practising (or rank-and-file) professionals* relates simply to those professionals involved in day-to-day service delivery. Within this group, a further distinction needs to be made between so-called 'pure practitioners' and 'quasi-managerial practitioners', who might take on various management roles, such as the supervision or mentoring of junior colleagues or non-professionals. The latter group (as I discuss below) are in effect performing various 'management' tasks that may not be formally recognised in their job descriptions or rewarded.

A second category relates to those professionals who take on formal responsibilities for management of day-to-day work of junior professionals as part of their formal role or job description. This group relates to the middle tier of hybrid – professional–managers frequently described in the literature, although even here further distinctions need to be made depending on the proportion of time spent on management. Hence Causor and Exworthy (1999) distinguish between part time 'practising managing professionals' and (full time) 'non-practising managing professionals'.

Lastly is a category of more senior 'general managers' at the strategic apex of organisations who have responsibility for overall performance. This relates to roles such as directors, chief executive officers and senior partners. Here, too, further distinctions are needed between 'professionally grounded general managers' and 'non-professional general managers' (or pure play managers). As we shall see below, in some contexts, these more senior positions are dominated entirely by professionals, while in others it is becoming more common for non-professional, specialist managers to be employed. Veronesi *et al.* (2012) note, for example, that in the UK National Health Service (NHS) clinically qualified doctors and nurses make up only 26 per cent of board members of NHS acute hospital trusts, the remainder having private sector or civil service backgrounds. In law firms, there has also recently been a rise in the proportion of (non-lawyer) management professionals relative to managing partners (Empson *et al.*, 2013b).

Hence it is necessary to differentiate between hybrid professional–manager roles which may be performed at different levels of a professional or organisational hierarchy. If anything, the need for such distinctions becomes more apparent as a larger number of so-called practising professionals are drawn into 'quasi-management' tasks. Often such activities are not recognised as 'management' but nevertheless represent a significant hidden cost for those involved. In the NHS, for example, a recent study found that around one in three clinical staff had some kind of 'managerial' role, even though the official figures put ('pure play') specialist managers at only 3 per cent of the workforce (Buchanan *et al.*, 2013).

These problems of definition are further compounded by the growing push to strengthen leadership in professions, especially in English-speaking countries (O'Reilly & Reed, 2011). In some respects, this can be interpreted as just a discursive shift or relabelling exercise. According to Martin and Learmonth (2012, p. 287), leadership offers a 'potentially attractive self-narrative for professionals', far more so than the term 'management'. However, the focus on leadership also has wider implications, highlighting the need for a larger constituency of professionals to become actively involved with the work of coordination, control and the pursuit of new innovations in service provision. This idea is given a further boost by the notion of leadership as 'collective' or 'distributed' within teams of professionals engaged in change initiatives (Fitzgerald *et al.*, 2013). Either way, the notion of leadership implies a more inclusive understanding of hybrid professional–manager roles, blurring the boundary between those who take on formal roles with the job title of 'manager' and those who find themselves involved as de facto quasi-managers (or leaders).

Horizontal: different professional and organisational contexts

The task of clearly delineating what we mean by 'hybrid professional–manager' roles is further complicated by differences in the organisational context in which they develop. Earlier we noted how forms of 'clan control' (Ouchi, 1980) might be found in *all* forms of professional organisation. However, historically these tendencies were more pronounced in some organisations than in others. On the one hand are professions such as law and (in the USA) medicine that have existed independently of organisations and (even today) retain strong occupational cultures that emphasise the importance of autonomy, fee for service and self-regulating community (Adler *et al.*, 2008). By contrast, are professions that are almost entirely dependent on organisations which underwrite access to clients, employment prospects and other resources. Classic examples of the latter are what Johnson (1972) describes as 'state-mediated' professions such as teachers, social workers and nurses, but also other groups such as engineers or management consultants in the private sector. In these contexts, what Causor and Exworthy (1999) term 'organisational assets' have always been important.

The significance of this distinction is that it raises questions about the nature and extent of change implied by the development of hybrid professional–management roles. On the one hand, these roles might be viewed as a radical break from the past, as implied in Freidson's account. This is true in contexts such as medicine, law and academia, where (as noted above) professionals enjoyed greater independence from organisations with stronger 'cosmopolitan' orientations. In these professions there also existed multiple (or parallel) hierarchies, with separate chains of command for professionals and administrators. These structures have historically served to maintain a strong sense of separation between professional and managerial domains in terms of values and skills. As such, the move towards hybrid professional–manager roles alongside the merging if these hierarchies really does imply a significant break in the way professionals have traditionally worked and (possibly also) in the career trajectories of those who take on these roles.

This same degree of change may not, however, apply to those organisations where professionals have historically operated in a more formally bureaucratic environment. Kirkpatrick *et al.* (2005), for example, differentiate between 'pure' and 'managed' professional service organisations, including schools, social services, nursing and housing departments. The latter are characterised by tighter controls and unitary hierarchies in which professional career advancement and seniority has always been associated with taking on administrative responsibilities. Here the shift towards management may to some extent only represent a formalisation or re-labelling of past practices.

Making these distinctions is not to suggest that more hierarchically organised professionals have experienced *no* change at all. As Causor and Exworthy (1999, p. 85) argue, pressures to strengthen management have 'had the effect of promoting a greater degree of internal stratification within both older and newer professional groups, and hence of enhancing the significance of the possession of managerial assets for members of professional groups in general'. As such, the point is not to downplay change. Rather it is to emphasise important sources of continuity in the development of 'administrative elites' and recognise that this process may be highly path dependent across different organisations and sectors of the economy. While in some contexts organisational (and management) demands have always been intrinsic to professional formation, in others, it is a relatively new and contested phenomenon.

Drivers of hybridisation

In this section we turn to more substantive areas of debate about hybrid professional–manager roles, starting with the question of *why* they have emerged. Here, much of what has been written falls into the same dualism which characterises the literature on professions more generally (Gleeson & Knights, 2006). On one hand is the argument that professions have been forced reluctantly to adopt these roles, while on the other is the idea that they represent 'strategic operators' actively pushing for change.

The first perspective (professions as 'victims') has already been discussed. As we saw, Freidson's restratification thesis links the emergence of hybrid roles to a variety of exogenous pressures. In public services, there have been wide-ranging moves to reform management since the early 1980s, accentuated by declining trust in the ability of professions to regulate themselves in the public interest (Saks, 2013). To remedy this, requiring professionals to become managers – turning poachers into gamekeepers – represented an obvious course (Kirkpatrick *et al.*, 2005). A very similar account of change can be found in the literature on PSFs (Empson *et al.*, 2013a). Emphasised here are pressures linked to increased competition, deregulation and technological changes that have steadily undermined the effectiveness (and legitimacy) of established models of professional partnership (Alvesson & Thompson, 2005).

Hence, in much of the literature, hybrid roles form part of a wider control strategy, a means of subtly encouraging professionals to internalise financial disciplines, consumer values and organisational priorities. As Exworthy and Halford (1999) suggest, control *of* professionals is increasingly being supplemented with control *by* professionals.

However, against this view is the argument that professionals themselves have not been entirely passive in supporting the move towards more 'managed' forms of organisation. Exworthy and Halford (1999), for example, argue that for hybrid professionals, 'management assets' (forms of generic knowledge and credentials associated with the management) are becoming more valued than traditional 'cultural assets' 'acquired through education and characterized by personal expertise in a given body of practice' (p. 133). In this respect, pull as well as push factors may lie behind the development of hybrid professional–management roles, as elite groups seek to colonise management to strengthen their own position as an aspiring 'professional–managerial class' (Hanlon, 1998).

A slightly different spin on this account of sectional interests in driving change is the link between hybrid professional–manager roles and upward 'collective mobility projects' (Kurunmäki, 2004; Kirkpatrick *et al.*, 2009, 2011). Kirkpatrick *et al.* (2011), for example, draw on the notion of a competing 'system of professions' to argue that, within public hospital settings, the jurisdiction of management has come to represent a 'contested terrain'. Focusing on the Danish hospital sector, they note how pressures to strengthen management from 1984 onwards initiated a power struggle between doctors and nurses, the latter keen to dominate management roles as a strategy for overcoming their subordinate position and 'blocked mobility'. A very similar explanation is given for why doctors in different European health systems have sought to actively engage with and develop financial expertise. According to Kurunmäki (2004, p. 328), in the Finnish case, strong engagement is partly explained by a lack of 'overt inter-professional competition between accountants and medical professionals'.

This argument that professions (or elite groups within) may be significant agents of change has been taken even further in recent work by Adler *et al.* (2008). A starting point here is that established models of professional 'community' are being challenged by competing principles of hierarchy and markets. This, however, is not necessarily leading to the destruction of professional community, but rather to its evolution into 'collaborative community' which is more responsive to contemporary demands, including those of citizens and users of professional services. Importantly, this notion of collaborative community builds in elements of hierarchy, standardisation and competition, but merges them with professional organisational principles. The results are new organisational forms which stress the need for teamwork, the balancing of individual and collective interests. This shift is also strongly associated with the 'emergence of professional–managerial roles' and a greater sense of inter-dependency and shared accountability (Adler *et al.*, 2008, p. 367).

Hence there is some debate in the literature concerning the precise mix of forces that are driving the formation of hybrid professional–manager roles. On the one hand, these can be viewed as a top-down imposition on professionals, part of a strategy aimed at subtle control and governability. On the other, it is clear that professions themselves are not passive agents in this process, but have actively supported management either because of sectional interests (of administrative elites) pushing this change or because it is perceived to be in the community interest more generally (Noordegraaf, 2007).

Research on the nature and practice of hybrids

In this section we now turn to the voluminous research that has been conducted on hybrid professional–managers *in situ*. At the risk of oversimplifying this body of work in what follows, I identify two main strands. First are studies that focus mainly on the question of the changing identity and orientation of professional–management hybrids. Second are studies that give more attention to the practices of hybrids and their impact on organisational decision-making. Often these two strands are combined in individual studies, although in most cases, primary emphasis is placed on one or the other strand. As noted earlier, to illustrate this we will draw primarily on research that has been conducted on hybrids in the health sector.

Roles and identities

There is now an impressive body of research focusing on the development of hybrid roles such as 'clinical directors' or nurse managers, across many different countries. This work highlights wide variations in how these roles are constructed both within and between national health systems, although most studies note generic features such as the importance of boundary spanning, quality assurance, communication and conflict mediation as being central to the work of these hybrid managers.

Another common theme running through this research is the challenges associated with these hybrid roles, effectively balancing two 'worlds'. Early research on clinical directors for the UK, for example, noted that 'in addition to being able to "hunt with the service providers", the clinical director must also "run with the unit managers"' (Packwood *et al.*, 1992). Ferlie *et al.* (1996) also describe how clinical directors were constantly struggling to combine clinical credibility with management expertise. Doctors in these roles frequently report hostility from colleagues (being perceived as a 'management nark' or 'turning to the dark side') (Hoque *et al.*, 2004) or feeling uncomfortable about supervising their peers (Montgomery, 1992). Indeed, few would disagree with Ferlie *et al.*'s (1996, p. 186) observation that being a hybrid professional–manager can be

181

a 'difficult and arduous task'. Similar conclusions have been reached about nurse manager roles, linking these to rising levels of stress and work intensification (Bolton, 2005; Hales *et al.*, 2012).

Given these challenges, one might expect the response of professionals to these roles to be wholly negative. Focusing on nurse line managers in the UK, Bolton (2005, p. 6) reports that a majority were 'keen to dissociate themselves from the title of manager' and felt 'uncomfortable' with new priorities of cost control and 'customer' care. Similar findings emerge from surveys of medical managers (Degeling *et al.*, 2006), which continue to note polarisation in values between general and clinical managers, especially with regard to financial matters.

Other research, however, presents a more nuanced picture of changing identities and commitments amongst hybrid managers. A notable feature of early work on medical managers, for example, is that while many professionals felt uncomfortable with these roles, others saw them in a more positive light (Fitzgerald and Ferlie, 2000). Hence, Montgomery (1992, p. 236) noted amongst some physician managers in a US sample 'a weakening commitment to the medical profession, replaced by a strengthened commitment to the organizational and corporate aspects of medicine'. Similar conclusions are drawn by Hoff (1999), who distinguished between two emergent identities: 'organization-compatible' and 'profession-compatible'.

Although framed differently, very similar conclusions about the lack of homogeneity in the population of hybrid managers have been replicated in many subsequent studies. Hence, Fitzgerald and Ferlie (2000, p. 729), looking at the UK, note how some clinical directors actively sought these positions, demonstrating a 'crusading zeal for change' by addressing 'thorny' issues such as differential levels of performance amongst colleagues. Forbes *et al.* (2004, p. 167) identify two groups: 'reluctants' and what they term 'investors' or doctors who have 'actively pursued a management opportunity as an alternative to clinical medicine'. Consistent with this picture, Doolin (2002) refers to 'enterprising clinicians' versus 'resisting clinicians', while Martinussen and Magnussen (2011) distinguish between adopting management values and remaining alienated from management values. Most recently McGivern *et al.* (2015) distinguish between 'incidental hybrids', oriented towards representing and protecting institutionalised professionalism, and 'willing hybrids', who have more developed, stronger professional–management identities. Different identities, they suggest, have implications for role enactment, ranging from: influencing the maintenance of professional standards, representing/protecting through to challenging, regulating and auditing professionalism. Similar findings emerge from studies of clinical management in European contexts, including Spain (Cascón-Pereira & Hallier, 2012) and the Netherlands (Noordegraaf, 2007).

Taking a slightly different approach, others have focused more on the tactics adopted by *individual* hybrid professionals to cope with tensions in their role. Hence Llewellyn (2001) uses the metaphor of a 'two-way window' to explore how hybrid professionals (clinical directors) juggle and combine sets of ideas from both clinical practice and management in different ways according to the situation. This theme of how individual actors manage boundaries is also picked up by Iedema *et al.* (2004) focusing on clinical managers in Australia. In this study, the authors focus on how professions actively mediate three incommensurate discourses: the 'profession-specific' discourse of clinical medicine, the 'resource-efficiency' discourse of management, and a third 'inter-personalizing discourse' which seeks to smooth over possible contradictions. In this study and others (Doolin, 2002; Cascón-Pereira & Hallier, 2012), the focus is very much on the micro-level coping practices and tacit skills of hybrid professionals who take on these roles.

Practices

The second (sometimes overlapping) strand of research mentioned earlier has focused more on the behaviour and practices of hybrid professional–manager roles. Here again, a number of themes can be discerned. The first builds on the debate already reviewed above about how hybrids might be viewed as agents of top-down control, co-opted to manage those areas of practice that are 'hard to reach' (Martin & Learmonth, 2012). A useful illustration of this approach can be found in the work of Sheaff *et al.* (2003) focusing on the role of UK general practitioner (GP) leaders who translate management imperatives (around clinical governance) to their rank-and-file colleagues. Drawing on notions of 'soft leadership', the authors identify various tactics used by clinical leads to influence change. Hence, 'institutional legitimation' involves attempts to justify greater engagement with performance targets by framing this in the wider professional (or patient) interest. A different strategy is 'liberal legitimation' or 'soft coercion', which consists of representing external threats to the organisation's survival – typically threats posed by competitors – as necessitating and legitimating managerial decisions' (Sheaff *et al.*, 2003, p. 413).

Often left ambiguous in much of this research is the question of whether this process of mediation (by hybrids) serves mainly to defend the status quo or to subtly reinforce management control. The former can be viewed as a kind of 'reverse colonisation' of management by the professions (Waring & Currie, 2009). Hence, in the Sheaff *et al.* (2003) study, while clinical leaders ensure broad compliance with management rules, at the same time, they filter out some of the most threatening aspects of these rules, allowing practising professionals 'tacitly to construct their own clinical governance policy'(Sheaff *et al.*, 2003, 419). Similar conclusions are drawn by McDonald (2012) focusing on GPs as 'chaser elites' who reconcile professional and managerial forms of regulation. However, at the same time, these practices can just as easily be interpreted as a form of intrusive control, especially when viewed through the lens of governmentality. From this perspective, hybrid managers (whether they know it or not) are helping to reconstruct professional identities and priorities, making them 'both the prisoner and the warden in the contemporary panopticon of clinical leadership' (Waring, 2014, p. 695).

A quite different strand of work on the practices of hybrid professional–managers looks at their role as knowledge brokers (Burgess & Currie, 2013; Currie *et al.*, 2015). Drawing on earlier accounts of hybrids as key boundary spanners this approach highlights the way that professionals such as doctors and nurses in middle management positions contribute to the formulation and implementation of strategy. Specifically, this is through their role as a 'knowledge broker' defined as 'an actor who uses his/her in-between vantage position to support innovation through connecting, recombining and transferring to new contexts otherwise disconnected pools of ideas' (Burgess & Currie, 2013, p. 135). Focusing on nurse managers in the English NHS, Burgess & Currie (2013) describe how these professionals contribute to emergent strategies relating to care quality improvement by brokering knowledge flows, upwards and downwards, and also laterally, traversing both organisational and occupational boundaries. They note, however, that the effectiveness and legitimacy of these knowledge brokers may depend on their standing both within professions (such as nursing) and within multi-professional hierarchies (Currie *et al.*, 2015).

Lastly is a growing literature focusing on change leadership both within single organisations and in the wider context of inter-professional networks (Currie *et al.*, 2011). As noted earlier, much of this research is not exclusively focused on hybrid managers but on a wider constituency of professionals who may contribute towards leading change. Some studies do, however, focus on the characteristics and leadership styles of professionals involved in management roles and their relative effectiveness (Hardacre *et al.*, 2010). Exploring the impact of change leadership across ten health cases, Fitzgerald *et al.* (2013), for instance, note that hybrid professional–managers play a critical role in helping to facilitate communication laterally and across boundaries and that such work required considerable 'navigation skills and knowledge' (Fitzgerald *et al.*, 2013, p. 236).

Conclusion

In this chapter, as well as summarising some of the literature on the emergence of hybrid professional–managers, I have tried to present a roadmap to help navigate this expanding field. Given the constraints of space, it has only been possible to review studies focusing on the health context, although many of the same themes are reproduced elsewhere. Examples of this include professional–managers in further education (Gleeson & Knights, 2006), higher education (Deem, 2007) and accounting (Empson *et al.*, 2013a). Taken together, this research has greatly advanced our understanding of how professionals react to hybrid roles and the implications for practice. Yet, at the same time, it is clear that much of the literature on this topic remains locked into essentially the same dualisms that characterised the original contribution of Freidson (Gleeson & Knights, 2006). The question of whether these roles serve mainly to buffer professional practice or to fundamentally challenge it in the longer term remains open. In addition to this are more specific concerns about the nature and impact of these roles which, I suggest, highlight *three* possible areas for future research.

First is a need for more comparative research to better understand the nature and development of hybrid roles, between different kinds of professions and across national contexts. A key issue here is the difference (if any) between public and private sectors. Prima facie, we might expect hybrid professional–managers in, say, law or accounting firms to behave in similar ways to their public-sector counterparts. But what difference does it make if these managers are also owners or partners of firms? On the one hand, a greater commercial focus of hybrid professional–managers may make them even more focused on controlling their rank-and-file colleagues (Byrkjeflot & Jespersen, 2015). Yet, against this is the possibility that commercial priorities (associated with ownership) will conflict with those of 'managing' colleagues, especially if the latter is viewed as a costly (administrative) overhead interfering with the real work of generating fee income (Ackroyd & Muzio, 2007).

Related to this is the need for more comparative work across different national contexts. Limited examples of this research in the health context point to potentially significant differences in the way hybrid management roles are constructed and how professionals respond to them (Kurunmäki, 2004; Kirkpatrick *et al.*, 2009). This work, however, remains in its infancy, as do understandings of how management challenges have impacted on PSFs in the private sector across different national contexts (Faulconbridge & Muzio, 2012).

A second area for future work might be to explore why professionals, often in the same organisation, respond so differently to hybrid management roles. Of course, this topic has been addressed in some of the literature. McGivern *et al.* (2015), for example, link variable motivations to the early experiences and socialisation of professions, including positive role models or mentors. Cascón-Pereira and Hallier (2012) explain different attitudes and behaviours in terms of the emotional experiences that their relations with clinicians or senior managers elicit in them. However, while these contributions are helpful, further work is clearly needed to understand why professionals (in health and elsewhere) enact management roles so differently. Possible lines of enquiry include looking at the impact of leadership training and more general organisational conditions that support professional leadership, in particular the role played by general (or pure play) managers in providing support and encouragement.

A third area for future work concerns the wider impact of hybrid professional roles. Some studies have already begun to address this concern, for example in relation to knowledge brokering and strategy formation (Burgess & Currie, 2013) or in terms of service outcomes (Fitzgerald *et al.*, 2013) and staff morale (Hales *et al.*, 2012). In the health sector, useful work has also been done to explore how professional involvement in strategic (board-level) decision-making impacts on service quality (Veronesi *et al.*, 2012). But while these studies offer clues, our understanding of the wider effects of deeper professional involvement in leadership and management remains patchy.

Pursuing these lines of inquiry will not be without certain challenges. More emphasis will need to be given to mixed methods, perhaps combining the standard approach of in-depth case studies with the use of surveys and routine data sources across whole populations. New theoretical directions may also be useful here, including a stronger engagement with mainstream institutional theory. The potential of this approach is highlighted in a number of recent studies, drawing explicitly on the idea of institutional complexity and the way hybrid professionals (such as accounting partners) make sense of and enact competing logics in their day-to-day work (Blomgren & Waks, 2015). In all these ways it may be possible to enrich future research on this topic, to better understand the way hybrid roles *have* developed so far and how they might evolve in future.

References

Ackroyd, S. and Muzio, D. (2007) 'The reconstructed professional firm: explaining change in English legal practices'. *Organization Studies*, 28(5), pp. 729–47.

Ackroyd, S., Hughes, J. and Soothill, K. (1989) 'Public sector services and their management'. *Journal of Management Studies*, 26(6), pp. 603–19.

Adler, P., Kwon, S. and Hecksher, C. (2008) 'Professional work: the emergence of collaborative community'. *Organization Science*, 19(2), pp. 359–76.

Alvesson, M. and Thompson, P. (2005) 'Post-bureaucracy?'. In Ackroyd, S., Batt, R., Thompson, P. and Tolbert, P. S. (eds) *The Oxford Handbook of Work and Organisation*. Oxford: Oxford University Press, pp. 485–507.

Battilana, J. and Lee, M. (2014) 'Advancing research on hybrid organizing: Insights from the study of social enterprises'. *The Academy of Management Annals*, 8(1), pp. 397–441.

Bleiklie, I., Enders, J. and Lepori, B. (2015) 'Organisations as penetrated hierarchies: environmental pressures and control in professional organisations'. *Organization Studies*, 36(7), pp. 873–96.

Blomgren, M. and Waks, C. (2015) 'Coping with contradictions: hybrid professionals managing institutional complexity', *Journal of Professions and Organization*, 2(1), pp. 78–102.

Bolton, S. (2005) '"Making up" managers: The case of NHS nurses'. *Work, Employment and Society*, 19(1), pp. 5–24.

Buchanan, D. A., Parry, E., Gascoigne, C. and Moore, C. (2013) 'Are healthcare middle managers jobs extreme jobs?'. *Journal of Health Organization and Management*, 27(5), pp. 646–64.

Burgess, N. and Currie, G. (2013) 'The knowledge brokering role of the hybrid middle level manager: The case of healthcare'. *British Journal of Management*, 24, pp. S132–S142.

Byrkjeflot, H. and Kragh Jespersen, P. (2015) 'Three conceptualizations of hybrid management in hospitals'. *International Journal of Public Sector Management*, 27(5), pp. 441–58.

Cascón-Pereira, R. and Hallier, J. (2012) 'Getting that certain feeling: The role of emotions in the meaning, construction and enactment of doctor managers' identities'. *British Journal of Management*, 23(1), pp. 130–44.

Causor, G. and Exworthy, M. (1999) 'Professionals and managers across the public sector'. In Exworthy, M. and Halford, S. (eds) *Professionals and the New Managerialism in the Public Sector*. Buckingham, UK: Open University Press.

Courpasson, D. (2000) 'Managerial strategies of domination, power in soft bureaucracies'. *Organization Studies*, 21(1), pp. 141–161.

Currie, G., Grubnic, S. and Hodges, R. (2011) 'Leadership in public services networks: Antecedents, process and outcome'. *Public Administration*, 89(2), pp. 242–64.

Currie, G., Burgess, N. and Hayton, J. (2015) 'HR practices and knowledge brokering by hybrid middle managers in hospital settings: The influence of professional hierarchy'. *Human Resource Management*, 51(3), pp. 793–812.

Deem, R., Hillyard, S. and Reed, M. (2007) *Knowledge, Higher Education, and the New Managerialism: The Changing Management of UK Universities*. Oxford: Oxford University Press.

Degeling, P., Zhang, K., Coyle, B., Xu, L. Z., Meng, Q.Y., Qu, J. B., and Hill, M. (2006) 'Clinicians and the governance of hospitals: A cross-cultural perspective on relations between profession and management'. *Social Science & Medicine*, 63(3), pp. 757–75.

Doolin, B. (2002) 'Enterprise discourse, professional identity and the organizational control of hospital clinicians'. *Organization Studies*, 23(3), pp. 369–90.

Empson, L., Muzio, D., Broschak, J. and Hinings, B. (2013a) *Oxford Handbook of Professional Service Firms.* Oxford: Oxford University Press.

Empson, L., Cleaver, I. and Allen, J. (2013b) 'Managing partners and management professionals: institutional work dyads in professional partnerships'. *Journal of Management Studies*, 50(5), pp. 808–44.

Exworthy, M. and Halford, S. (1999) 'Professionals and managers in a changing public sector: Conflict, compromise and collaboration?'. In Exworthy, M. and Halford, S. (eds) *Professionals and the New Managerialism in the Public Sector.* Buckingham, UK: Open University Press, pp. 1–17.

Faulconbridge, J. and Muzio, D. (2012) 'Professions in a globalizing world: Towards a transnational sociology of the professions'. *International Sociology,* 27(1), pp. 136–52.

Ferlie, E., Ashburner, L., Fitzgerald, L. and Pettigrew, A. (1996) *The New Public Management in Action.* Oxford: Macmillan.

Fitzgerald, L. and Ferlie, E. (2000) 'Professionals: back to the future?'. *Human Relations*, 53(5), pp. 713–39.

Fitzgerald, L., Ferlie, E., McGivern, J. and Buchanan, D. (2013) 'Distributed leadership patterns and service improvement: Evidence and argument from English healthcare'. *The Leadership Quarterly*, 24(1), pp. 227–39.

Forbes, T., Hallier, J. and Kelly, L. (2004) 'Doctors as managers: investors and reluctants in a dual role'. *Health Services Management Research*, 17(3), pp. 167–76.

Freidson, E. (1985) 'The reorganization of the medical profession'. *Medical Care Review*, 42, pp. 11–35.

Freidson, E. (1994) *Professionalism Re-born: Theory, Prophesy and Policy*, Cambridge: Polity Press.

Gleeson, D. and Knights, D. (2006) 'Challenging dualism: Public professionalism in troubled times'. *Sociology*, 40(2), pp. 277–95.

Hales, C., Doherty, C. and Gatenby, M. (2012) *Continuity and Tension in the Definition, Perception and Enactment of First Line Management Role in Healthcare.* London: NIHR.

Hanlon, G. (1998) 'Professionalism as enterprise: Service class politics and the redefinition of professionalism'. *Sociology*, 32, 1, pp. 43–63.

Hardacre, J., Cragg, R., Flanagan, H., Spurgeon, P. and Shapiro, J. (2010) 'Exploring links between NHS leadership and improvement'. *International Journal of Leadership in Public Services,* 6, pp. 26–38.

Hoff, T. J. (1999) 'The social organization of physician-managers in a changing HMO'. *Work and Occupations,* 26(3), pp. 324–51.

Hoque, K., Davis, S. and Humphreys, M. (2004) 'Freedom to do what you are told: Senior management team autonomy in an acute NHS Trust'. *Public Administration*, 82(2), pp. 355–75.

Iedema, R., Degeling, R., Braithwaite, J. and White, L. (2004) 'It's an interesting conversation I'm hearing: The doctor as manager'. *Organization Studies*, 25(1), pp. 15–33.

Johnson, T. (1972) *Professions and Power.* London: Macmillan.

Kirkpatrick, I., Ackroyd, S. and Walker, R. (2005) *The New Managerialism and Public Service Professions.* London: Palgrave.

Kirkpatrick, I., Kragh-Jespersen, P., Dent, M. and Neogy, I. (2009) 'Medicine and management in a comparative perspective: The cases of England and Denmark'. *Sociology of Health and Illness*, 31(5), pp. 642–58.

Kirkpatrick, I., Dent, M. and Kragh-Jespersen, P. (2011) 'The contested terrain of hospital management: Professional projects and healthcare reforms in Denmark'. *Current Sociology*, 59(4), pp. 489–506.

Kitchener, M., Kirkpatrick, I. and Whipp, R. (2000) 'Supervising professional work under new public management: evidence from an "invisible trade"'. *British Journal of Management*, 11(3), pp. 213–26.

Kurunmäki, L. (2004) 'A hybrid profession: The acquisition of management accounting expertise by medical professionals'. *Accounting Organizations and Society*, 29(3), pp. 327–47.

Llewellyn, S. (2001) 'Two way mirrors: Clinicians as medical managers'. *Organization Studies*, 22(4), pp. 593–624.

McDonald, R. (2012) 'Re-stratification revisited: The changing landscape of primary medical care in England and California'. *Current Sociology*, 60(4), pp. 441–55.

McGivern, G., Currie, G., Ferlie, E., Fitzgerald, L. and Waring, J. (2015) 'Hybrid manager-professionals' identity work: The maintenance and hybridization of medical professionalism in managerial contexts'. *Public Administration*, 93(2), pp. 412–32.

Martin, G. P. and Learmonth, M. (2012) 'A critical account of the rise and spread of "leadership": The case of UK healthcare'. *Social Science & Medicine*, 74(3), pp. 281–88.

Martinussen, P. A. and Magnussen, J. (2011) 'Resisting market-inspired reform in healthcare: The role of professional subcultures in medicine'. *Social Science & Medicine*, 73(2), pp. 193–200.

Mintzberg, H. (1993) *Structure in Fives: Designing Effective Organisations*. London: Prentice Hall.

Montgomery, K. (1992) 'Professional dominance and the threat of corporatization'. *Current Research on Occupations and Professions*, 7, pp. 221–40.

Noordegraaf, M. (2007) 'From "pure" to "hybrid" professionalism: Present-day professionalism in ambiguous public domains'. *Administration & Society*, 39(6), pp. 761–85.

O'Reilly, D. and Reed, M. (2011) 'The grit in the oyster: Professionalism, managerialism and leaderism as discourses of UK public services modernization'. *Organization Studies*, 32(8), pp. 1079–101.

Ouchi, W. G. (1980) 'Markets, bureaucracies and clans'. *Administrative Science Quarterly*, 25, pp. 129–41.

Packwood, T., Keen, J. and Buxton, M. (1992) 'Process and structure: Resource management and the development of sub-unit organisational structure'. *Health Services Management Research*, 5(1), pp. 66–76.

Reay, T. and Hinings, C. R. (2009) 'Managing the rivalry of competing institutional logics'. *Organization Studies*, 30(6), pp. 629–52.

Saks, M. (2013) 'Regulating the English healthcare professions: Zoos, circuses or safari parks?'. *Journal of Professions and Organization*, 1(1), pp. 84–98.

Sheaff, R., Rogers, A., Pickard, S., Marshall, M., Campbell, S., Sibbald, B., Halliwell, S. and Roland, M. (2003) 'A subtle governance: Soft medical leadership in English primary care'. *Sociology of Health and Illness*, 25(5), pp. 408–28.

Veronesi, G., Kirkpatrick, I. and Vallascas, F. (2012) 'Clinicians on the board: What difference does it make?'. *Social Science & Medicine*, 77, pp. 147–55.

Waring, J. (2014) 'Re-stratification, hybridity and professional elites'. *Sociology Compass*, 8/5, pp. 688–704.

Waring, J. and Currie, G. (2009) 'Managing expert knowledge: Organizational challenges and managerial futures for the UK medical profession'. *Organization Studies*, 30(7), pp. 755–78.

13

The professionalization of management

Kevin T. Leicht

Introduction

There has been a widespread and continual debate about whether or not business management is making a bid for professional status, on a par with law, medicine, the college professoriate, and other well-established professional groups (see Clegg & Palmer, 1996; Skaggs & Leicht, 2005; Locke & Spender, 2011). Professional work and professionalism is at once a cultural label, a label for work viewed as socially and culturally important, and a career aspiration for many looking for stability in labor markets that lack it (see Leicht, 2016). In most treatments by researchers and the public, *professional work* encompasses those whose work (a) is defined by the application of theoretical and scientific knowledge to tasks tied to core societal values (health, justice, financial status, etc.), (b) commands considerable autonomy and freedom from oversight, except by peers in the same profession, and (c) claims to have exclusive or nearly exclusive control over a task domain linked to the application of the knowledge imparted to professionals as part of their training (Leicht & Fennell, 2001, pp. 25–30).

The questions surrounding the professionalization of management are occurring in a context where there is widespread upheaval over the status of professional work. This upheaval is well represented in the current literature (see Evetts, 2006, 2011, 2013; Suddaby *et al.*, 2007; Suddaby & Viale, 2011). The professions represent the quintessential triumph of Durkheimian occupational communities over and above the mass-society-based anonymity of impersonal markets and the grinding rigidity of bureaucracies. Over the past 30 years, there has been a serious and very thoughtful attempt to evaluate the overall state of professional work, the role that professional work plays in a globalized post-industrial society, and its likely future. Many scholars now focus on autonomy and control over task domains as the major markers of professionalism (cf. Abbott, 1988). And many scholars look with some skepticism on the claims to exclusivity that would-be professions make, in particular focusing on the economic and social benefits to professionals that result from social closure (see Larsen, 1977; Collins, 1990; for management, see Khurama, 2007; Locke & Spender, 2011).

This chapter briefly examines business management as a professional project in light of this widespread reassessment of professional work. The argument in this chapter is that managerial history and contemporary management behavior point to a drive toward professional status and that recent developments in the financialization of the economies of the developed world has only increased the professional claims of the managerial class (see Skaggs & Leicht, 2005; Leicht & Lyman, 2006).

Professional autonomy and professional projects

A *professional project* is a set of activities that attempt to define and defend an occupation's task domain from competing occupational groups and the actions of immediate workplace stakeholders (see Abbott, 1988). A *profession* (for our purposes) is an occupational group whose knowledge base is linked to theories and complex intellectual ideas and whose status and prestige is based on the relationship between occupational tasks and key societal values (see Leicht & Fennell, 2001, 2008). The profession defines the occupational group whose incumbents are deemed worthy of societal rewards for performing important and complex tasks. Professional projects describe how professional incumbents (and their professional associations) defend the profession's task domain from encroachment by would-be competitors.

According to Freidson (1986) and Abbott (1988), most professional projects attempt to (1) enhance the autonomy and freedom of action for occupational members under a set of well-defined professional prerogatives (Freidson, 1986); and, (2) defend a specific task domain from encroachment by competing occupational groups and stakeholders (Abbott, 1988). Managerial occupations have been and continue to be deeply involved in professional projects that defend task domains against interference by competing stakeholders (stockholders, employees, governments, etc.) while attempting to increase their freedom of action. Ironically, some of these activities harm the professional projects of long-standing professions and would-be professional groups alike.

My argument here is that historical and contemporary management practice is oriented toward increasing practitioner autonomy in response to environmental shocks and the scrutiny of external stakeholders (see also Skaggs & Leicht, 2005). The shifts from sole proprietor to scientific management, human relations management, and human resources management occurred at the same time as the Carnegie, Ford, and Rockefeller Foundations sought to place management education front and center in attempts to professionalize management (see Khurama, 2007). This produced big changes in how managers were trained and created a semi-closed, credential-driven labor market for managers. But the growing dominance of economics and the economic crisis of the late 1970s led to the questioning of all forms of professional expertise. It is at this point that managers reinterpreted their professional role as 'interpreters of markets'. While this reinvention has been rocked by crises associated with financial scandals and the 2008 global recession, this is where the management professional project stands now as of 2014. The conclusion discusses a few of the implications of this new professional claim by managerial elites. But the roots of this professional project started much earlier.

Sole proprietorships and entrepreneurialism, 1860–1910

Around the mid nineteenth century, sole proprietorships were the dominant form of firm ownership in the United States. Corporate organizational forms existed but their use was limited to public works ventures (Hurst, 1970). Most businesses were owned and managed by the same person, who supplied much, if not all, of the investment capital (Berle & Means, 1932).

The dominant form of employee organization was the inside contract (see Stone, 1974). Entrepreneurs would contract with individual craft workers to perform different operations associated with the production process. The craft worker would then hire assistants to actually perform the operations outlined in the contract. In sharp contrast to the entrepreneur, who was invested heavily in a single firm where ownership and management were lodged in the same individual, craft workers possessed vital human capital skills that were portable (see Marglin, 1974; Stone, 1974; Montgomery, 1979; Form, 1987).

Toward the end of the century, the capital demands of rapid industrialization required larger investments than individual entrepreneurs could manage. As a result, the corporate form was beginning to emerge as the preferred arrangement in for-profit enterprises (Berle & Means, 1932). The corporate form of capital structure divided property rights, separating the suppliers of capital from those who acted on their behalf. This split produced the professional domain that came to be occupied by managers (Berle & Means, 1932; Abbott, 1988; Fligstein, 1990).

On the shop floor, entrepreneurs possessed little or no knowledge of how jobs were performed. The skills required to perform necessary tasks were largely controlled by craft guilds or learned through apprenticeship from other craft workers (Wren, 1994). Due to the almost proprietary nature of craft knowledge, employees possessed a great deal of freedom and mobility (Stone, 1974). Craft workers were independent entrepreneurial contractors.

From entrepreneurialism to scientific management, 1910–1940

As firms grew and investors were less involved in the day-to-day operations of specific firms, managers became a vital intermediary representing the interests of owners in the production process. Managers wanted to defend their task domain while investors sought to tie compensation schemes for managers to returns on their investments so that the interests of managers and investors would coincide (see Edwards, 1979). Both groups lacked a mechanism for increasing control and productivity in organizations. Scientific management was one such mechanism.

Frederick Taylor, the father of scientific management, believed production inefficiencies were due to variations in work methods. Taylor (1903, 1911) felt that these inefficiencies could be reduced by studying the work process itself. Systematic study would yield insights into the most efficient production methods. Managers would record these procedures for the purposes of training their present and future employees. With all of the workers following standardized procedures based on the conservation of time and motion, worker productivity would increase.

Although the rapid growth of Taylor's ideas can be attributed to the productivity concerns of investors, another reason for the quick acceptance of this method was that scientific management reduced managers' reliance on skilled employees and increased their professional autonomy. Scientific management broke the knowledge monopoly of skilled contractors. This allowed managers to make greater productivity, hours, and wage demands which served to stabilize the production process (see Braverman, 1974; Edwards, 1979; Gordon *et al.*, 1982).

From scientific management to human relations, 1930s–late 1960s

Beginning around 1910 and continuing throughout the 1930s, scientific management became a major guide to managerial thought and practice in the United States (Wren, 1994). The Great Depression of the 1930s would alter the relationship between managers and workers in fundamental ways.

In the early 1930s, the unemployment rate in the USA rose to approximately 25 percent. Congress expressed concern for the plight of workers by passing the Norris-La Guardia Act in 1932. This Act strictly limited the use of injunctions against unions and outlawed the use of 'yellow-dog' contracts (contracts stating that the worker could not join a labor union as a condition for employment). In exchange, management enjoyed widespread protections from strikes and boycotts. The loopholes in the Act and the economic climate of the Depression meant that they could merely dismiss striking workers and replace them with others at a lower wage (Cihon & Castagnera, 1988).

Meanwhile, investors continued to reduce their risk by pursuing the corporate organizational form. The corporate organizational form also increased employee dependence on large corporations. In 1909, there was one small manufacturing firm for every 250 people in the United States; by 1929, there was only one for every 900 people. The increase in the ratio of people to firms was (partially) the result of the growth in the corporate form (from the speech of Senator Wagner, Congressional Record 1935) as well as immigration and the movement of labor from farms to the cities (see Bogue, 1959). And in 1937, when the Supreme Court upheld the constitutionality of the National Labor Relations Act (NLRA, also known as the Wagner Act), it signified the first time that both the judicial and legislative branches were in agreement regarding employees' increased dependence on large corporations.

The liabilities of scientific management in a new institutional environment

With the Supreme Court's 1937 decision to uphold the constitutionality of the NLRA, the employment relationship changed dramatically, affecting the professional autonomy of managers. Unionization and collective bargaining became options available to workers. Government restrictions on managers' ability to bargain and terminate employees had the effect of increasing the degree of uncertainty associated with investment in a firm, as volatility in earnings was now more likely. Both developments represented substantial intrusions on managerial autonomy. The human relations approach was one managerial response to this shifting landscape.

Enter human relations management

Although it is often identified with the Hawthorne studies in 1929, the human relations approach would not find its way into the management mainstream until the mid 1940s (Sherman & Bohlander, 1992; Wren, 1994). Unlike scientific management's focus on production efficiency, the human relations approach focused on aspects of human behavior as these affected the firm. One area of attention focused on managers' ability to be sensitive to the needs and feelings of their employees and to recognize the individual differences among them. This approach also emphasized the need for increased worker participation and employee-centered supervision (Sherman & Bohlander, 1992; Wren, 1994).

The human relations approach was radically different from its predecessor that stressed the use of time–motion studies to achieve uniformity and maximum efficiency. This extreme shift in emphasis was an attempt on the part of managers to regain professional autonomy and control over their work environment. Given the prevailing legal environment of the late 1930s, the use of scientific management would only exacerbate existing tensions between managers and employees. It would increase the uncertainty of continued, stable profits and heighten investor scrutiny of managerial decision-making. What managers needed, given labor's increased power in organizational matters, was a method that would appease workers in order to prevent them from exercising their newly created rights.

This attempt at appeasement was embodied in the human relations approach to management. By focusing on such areas as the needs and feelings of workers, managers could hopefully avoid any costly confrontations (Bendix, 1956; Braverman, 1974) and stabilize firm output (Gillespie,

1991). This would have the effect of reducing labors' power, decreasing investors' scrutiny of managerial actions, and restoring managerial autonomy.

From human relations to human resource management, late 1960s–2000

From the passage of the NLRA to the late 1950s, unionization in the United States increased rapidly. In 1935, 13.2 percent of the non-agricultural work force was unionized; by 1960, this figure had grown to over 30 percent (Hamermesh & Rees, 1988). After 1960, these percentages began falling (Freeman & Medoff, 1984; Hamermesh & Rees, 1988). Researchers have provided numerous explanations for this decline, from continued government intervention and the institutionalization of union efforts to successful 'union-busting' on behalf of corporations (Cihon & Castagnera, 1988; Hamermesh & Rees, 1988). As union membership began decreasing after 1960, the bargaining power of employees started to decline as well.

The development of internal labor markets

The internal labor market (ILM) consists of well-defined job ladders, with movement up these ladders dependent upon the acquisition of firm-specific skills (see Pfeffer & Cohen, 1984). The development of ILMs was the result of complex institutional and environmental interactions between government intervention in manpower activities, industrial unions, and growing personnel departments (Baron et al., 1986). Industrial unions were ambivalent about some aspects of ILMs – many of the provisions that increased management's control over the work process protected workers from layoffs and arbitrary treatment (see Gordon et al., 1982; Baron et al., 1986).

ILMs altered the relationship between firms and employees in a dramatic fashion. An employee would join the organization at a particular point of entry and move up the organization by way of a highly defined job ladder. As workers progressed through the organization, they acquired skills that tended to be highly firm-specific (Pfeffer & Cohen, 1984). Workers were tied to their current organization because movement to new organizations would result in decreased wages because the skills accrued at the old firm would not be transferable to the new one (cf. Lincoln & Kalleberg, 1982; Burawoy, 1985). The development of ILMs during the 1960s caused the welfare of many employees to become highly dependent on the success of their current workplace. But ILMs do not keep investors from moving their financial capital to other locations and ILMs give managers a stable labor pool to draw from.

The rise of portfolio investment strategies

Concurrent with the growth of ILMs, other technical developments were unfolding that would dramatically affect investors' exposure to firm-specific uncertainties. Post-depression regulations made the stock market much more efficient in terms of access to information, reducing the risk associated with stock ownership. The expansion in the number of stocks traded and the number of companies available for purchase further reduced the firm-specific dependence of investors by increasing capital mobility.

An important event in decreasing the dependence of investors came in 1952, when Harry Markowitz published his work on portfolio selection. Markowitz (1952) hypothesized that by focusing on the standard deviations of stocks, as well as the covariance between them and the market, investors could diversify away nearly all the firm-specific risk inherent in any one stock, exposing themselves only to the risk of the overall market. With portfolio investment tools, investors could now exercise control over a number of firms without being exposed to the risk of any one.

Shifts in the backgrounds of top corporate executives

By the 1970s, managerial autonomy was increasing as workers became immersed in firm-specific ILMs and investors were shedding firm-specific uncertainties by diversifying their portfolios. These changes were accompanied by a shift in the backgrounds of top executives. Prior to the 1970s, the ranks of top management were filled with individuals whose training and corporate background involved marketing, sales, and engineering. Beginning in the 1970s, a growing number of top executives with finance backgrounds were being selected for key positions in organizations (Fligstein, 1990). As this cadre of managers grew, portfolio investment theory began to emerge as the organizing mechanism for large firms (see Fligstein, 1990).

This change in organizing principles and backgrounds of top executives produced a major split within the managerial ranks. Human relations management was built from a different set of principles that were not isomorphic with the new financial tools of top management. The human relations paradigm was designed to pacify employees in response to newly created union power. But decreasing union ranks and ILMs were making this pacification unnecessary. These occurrences, along with the conflict in ideology between top executives and mid-level personnel managers, led to the rise of human resource management. But the environmental change that greatly increased the role and prestige of financial management was the economic crises of the 1970s and 1980s and the prevailing rise of neoliberal market ideologies in their wake.

Enter the human resource management paradigm

Human resource management reflects the underlying tenets of portfolio theory as practiced by top managers. The decision by top managers to diversify was based on the notion that the whole was more important than the individual parts of the organization. Top managers would add and discard firms based on their financial contribution to the overall corporation, while the welfare of the individual firms under the corporate umbrella was of secondary importance. Human resource management viewed employees in a similar fashion. Workers were no longer seen as important in and of themselves (as in the human relations approach). Rather, the employees were viewed in the context of their contribution to the specific firm, with decisions to add or discard employees reflecting this heuristic (Sherman & Bohlander, 1992; Wren, 1994).

Though this is a far cry from the previous perspective where worker satisfaction was of paramount concern, this shift from human relations to human resource management was a reaction to environmental changes affecting the professional autonomy of managers. Managers, whose future was increasingly tied to the performance of the individual firms they managed (see Donaldson, 1963), sought to reduce their dependence on specific employees and make the employment relationship more predictable (Monsen & Downs, 1965). They further sought to align their managerial paradigm with the dominant paradigm of portfolio investment theory as articulated by the new cadre of top managers. The increase in the use of ILMs and the decrease in the strength of unions made this possible. Most of the changes involved in the shift from human relations to human resource management were invisible to non-supervisory employees on a day-to-day basis. What did change slowly was the implied contract between managers and employees regarding their place within the larger corporation (Rubin, 1999).

When viewed in historical context, the paradigmatic shift from human relations to human resource management was an attempt by firm-level managers to enhance their professional autonomy. As top managers in conglomerate corporations continued to manage using the 'corporation-as-portfolio' model, the productivity of the workforce at the firm level became of paramount importance to firm-level managers. If the productivity of a particular firm within the conglomerate began to decline, the inclination on the part of top-level managers would be either divestiture or liquidation. In order to remain in the conglomerate, firm-level managers needed a continually productive workforce; this constraint affected the autonomy of firm-level managers. Human resource management supplied the analytical tool necessary for firm-level managers to obviate much of this impact and regain their autonomy.

Parallel developments: the Keynesian crisis and the rising salience of markets and ideologies

In the last 30 years, the rise of neoliberal political and economic ideologies has threatened the expert claims of professional groups and the logic of professional organization as an alternative to and protector of client and public welfare. The 1970s and early 1980s brought inherent crises to prevailing post-war economic arrangements and a questioning of the role of professional expertise in wide areas of social and economic life. This historic change was triggered by the crisis of Keynesian economics in the mid 1970s and the implications this crisis presented for a post-industrial future dominated by technical and administrative expertise (see Bell, 1976; Leicht & Lyman, 2006; Leicht & Fennell, 2008). This change is reflected in the Western European context by the rise of new public management ideas in professional civil service bureaucracies (Bourgeault et al., 2009; Leicht et al., 2009; Kuhlmann et al., 2009).

The contemporary situation of management and the professions can be contrasted with the early- to mid-1960s predictions regarding the spread of professional expertise and reliance on liberal-technocratic professionals in the new post-industrial developed world (see, for example, Bell, 1976; Frank et al., 1995; Frank, 1997). In this world of the future, professions and knowledge-based work roles develop in response to the demands of post-industrial capitalism. The process of filling these jobs and the larger societal adjustments that come with the demand for highly educated workers (educational expansion, credentialing, longer stretches of time in school, and mass higher education) create a professional elite that applies their specialized knowledge to a broad range of problems. Managers, and especially the professionalized manager envisioned by the Carnegie Commission and the post-war Eisenhower, Kennedy, and Johnson administrations, were an integral part of a post-war economy actively managed for the public good.

This view of a post-industrial world where knowledge experts would manage the economy in the name of full employment, low inflation, and general prosperity was challenged by two developments: (1) the crisis in Keynesian economics that resulted from the stagflation and economic stagnation of the 1970s; and (2) the subsequent inability of skill-based models to explain rising income and earnings inequality among professionals and between professionals and non-professional groups. These developments led to a broad-based questioning of the relationship between technological expertise and general social welfare while also leading to serious questioning of the ability and desirability of attempting to manage the economy (cf. Stein, 1995).

The new neoliberal consensus (see Reich, 2012; Stiglitz, 2013) takes free markets and moves them from their place as part of the technical environment of organizations to an all-encompassing role in the institutional environment of organizations. The traditionally defined professions have always walked a tightrope between the institutional logic of professional practice centered on professional–client relationships, autonomy, collegiality, and professional ethics on the one hand, and a technical environment stressing market efficiency, technological change, and organizational innovation on the other (see Malhotra *et al.*, 2006; Leicht & Lyman, 2006; Cummings, 2011). Management was no exception to this trend.

The present challenge of neoliberalism as an economic and political ideology has profound implications for the professions as coherent occupational entities. Many of these challenges are clarified if we take the colloquialisms of the new neoliberal consensus and contrast those with traditional conceptions of professional practice and the concept of expert labor (see Leicht & Fennell, 2008):

1. *Consumers know best.* Any attempt to interfere with, regulate, or affect consumer choice costs consumers money. This means that any interference with service provision (such as licensing procedures, legally defined monopolies over task domains, competency tests, and other devices for restricting professional service provision) extracts costs that are rarely if ever justified. Consumers of services will eventually reward competent, scrupulous providers and punish incompetent, unscrupulous ones. All that is necessary is to let the market do its work with the dollars of the consuming public voting for best practices.
2. *Markets will determine what is right.* The market becomes the locus of human perfection (see Giddens, 1994). No expert can make, guide or direct choices in the ways that markets will. No authority can make the wise choices that markets can make. Let markets do their job and stay out of it.
3. *No credentialing or licensing.* These are simply attempts to collect monopoly rents. Consumers will naturally be led to choices that are best for them, and credentialing and licensing are just an attempt to extract windfall profits at the expense of consumers.
4. *No codes of ethics.* Markets will naturally reward those who behave in the best interests of those who purchase professional services. Information about ethical and unethical practices can be sorted out in the wash and those practitioners who do what clients want them to do and who act in their best interests will win out in the end.
5. *Competition will lower fees and salaries.* Service delivery from a variety of professional groups, in a variety of settings, with a wide range of organizational arrangements will keep fees and salaries low and service delivery of the best quality.

In European contexts, the 1970s and 1980s and the accompanying economic recessions and deindustrialization led to a widespread questioning of the salience of European models of capitalism (cf. Esping-Anderson, 1989; Ironside & Seifert, 2003; Rifkin, 2004; Fourcade, 2006; Bourgeault *et al.*, 2009; Leicht *et al.*, 2009). Because professional practice (and especially the delivery of health care and education) have much more extensive ties to the public sector in most European countries, the main response to this general crisis in confidence (for professional groups) was the rise of new public management (NPM). While NPM is a label applied to a diverse set of reforms, ideas, and ideologies (cf. Savoie, 1995; Manning, 2001), the general thrust of NPM initiatives is to subject the provision of public service by professionals to market forces through disaggregation, competition, and incentivization (see Dunleavy *et al.*, 2005; Leicht *et al.*, 2009):

Disaggregation – splitting up large public sector bureaucracies into much smaller units, flattening organizational hierarchies and constructing management information systems that facilitate non-bureaucratic forms of control;

Competition – to separate purchasers and providers so that more activities can be subjected to competitive bidding and provision through multiple providers, both public and private. These competitive pressures are designed to replace hierarchical decision-making as the arbiter of appropriate action in the name of efficiency;

Incentivization – a general movement away from rewarding service providers in terms of diffuse public service or professional norms and toward specific performance incentives that are pecuniary and directly measurable. This impact has been especially serious for professional groups (see Kirkpatrick *et al.*, 2011; Dunleavy *et al.*, 2005).

The specific manifestations of NPM vary from place to place and affect a wide array of professional groups. Attempts to implement NPM concepts in the UK National Health Service (NHS) in particular have been controversial (see Ironside & Seifert, 2003). As with attempts to bring market incentives to professional practice in the USA (see Scott *et al.*, 2000), there are very few examples of successful implementation of NPM concepts in European professional health services (see especially Bottery, 1996; Thompson & Reschenthaler, 1996; Kaboolian, 1998; Lynn, 1998; Christensen & Laegreid, 1999; Scott *et al.*, 2000; Dulneavey *et al.*, 2005). The criticisms of NPM in these contexts revolve around the disarticulation between public service and revenue maximization, and the inability to 'get prices right' in the provision of services and intermediate goods that are government-supported natural monopolies.

The crisis of Keynesian economics discussed earlier, and the economic reasoning that followed, was an expression of skepticism about the role that professional expertise plays and the championing of a new market-based, spontaneous order as a source of revived prosperity and growth for economies, communities, and individuals (cf. Stein, 1995). Politically (especially in the United States) libertarian neoliberals were able to unite with the cultural right in a conservative alliance that defeated both left and right corporatism (Antonio, 2000).

Management as a professional project in a globalized, neoliberal world

The post-1970s growth and spread of neoliberal ideology has placed contemporary management practice in an ironic position. On one side, managers have played a central role in attacking the professional prerogatives of other professions and would-be professional groups (see Khurana, 2007). On the other side, managers have not been spared the axe as globalized financialization and deregulation created a 'market for corporate control' that ties managers' well-being to short-term investment returns.

In spite of the direct attacks on the job security of some segments of management, the spread of a globalized, neoliberal institutional environment represents a definitive step in the direction of permanently professionalizing management. The rapid development of business consulting and fee-for-service compensation that is the hallmark of the subcontracting process represents the definitive step in the direction of further professionalization for management (see also Leicht & Lyman, 2006). Indeed, one can see this development placing professionalized managers on a par with physicians and lawyers in their ability to establish and maintain independent, fee-for-service practice delivery to corporate clients. In this sense, management may be headed in the same direction as auditing services in accounting.

Undoubtedly, one continuing avenue of contestation will focus on attempts by professional groups to engage in social closure through controls on recruitment and task domains (Abbott, 1988, 1991; Khurana, 2007). This is a long-standing theme in scholarship on the professions, and the rewards accruing to managers are no exception to this rule. In the current climate, market claims represent the legitimation of rewards already received regardless of their relationship to actual competition. This is most obvious in the case of CEO compensation in the USA and UK. This is far from a new mechanism for the continual existence of professional work (Hughes, 1958; Larsen, 1977). The fact that a decentralized, market-based environment exists doesn't seem to limit the rewards accruing to the successful, but it changes the narrative account used to define and describe success.

The most likely avenues now for the professionalization of management are associated with interpreting markets, making or creating markets, and providing financial services. Managers service the needs of corporations and investors seeking to maximize unearned income in political environments where unearned income receives special favors. Not only do the earnings of these financial service occupations derive from the new dominance of profits, dividends, and other capital rents but the compensation systems provide these would-be professionals with direct benefits from the unearned income they generate for others (see, for example, Leicht & Lyman, 2006).

Unfortunately for others' claims over task domains, training, and earnings from a job, the new management occupations generate short-term profits for their clients by marketizing and disarticulating others' work, outsourcing and downsizing back-office activities, and otherwise attacking protected sources of earned income. The current political and economic climate directly rewards them for doing so (Khurana, 2007). In this ironic sense, business schools now teach their students how to undermine the workplace claims of the middle classes, the very group the rest of the developed world's universities train (Leicht & Fitzgerald, 2014). The managerial prerogatives asserted under the neoliberal dynamic reward professionalized managers for attacking others' claims to a stake in the economic system and this dynamic shows no signs of changing soon.

References

Abbott, A. D. (1988) *The System of Professions: An Essay on the Division of Expert Labor*. Chicago, IL: University of Chicago Press.

Abbott, A. D. (1991) 'The future of professions: Occupation and expertise in the age of organization'. *Research in the Sociology of Organizations*, 8, pp. 17–42.

Antonio, R. (2000) 'After post-modernism: reactionary tribalism'. *American Journal of Sociology*, 106, pp. 40–87.

Baron, J. N., Dobbin, F. R. and Jennings, P. D. (1986) 'War and peace: The evolution of modern personnel administration in US industry'. *American Journal of Sociology*, 92, pp. 350–83.

Bell, D. (1976) *The Coming of Post-Industrial Society*. New York: Basic Books.

Bendix, R. (1956) *Work and Authority in Industry: Ideologies of Management in the Course of Industrialization*. New York: Harper & Row.

Berle, A. A. Jr. and Means, G. C. (1932) *The Modern Corporation and Private Property*. New York: Macmillan.

Bogue, D. J. (1959) *The Population of the United States*. Glencoe, IL: Free Press.

Bottery, M. (1996) 'The challenge to professionals from new public management: Implications for the teaching profession'. *Oxford Review of Education*, 22, pp. 179–97.

Bourgeault, I. L., Benoit, C. and Hirschkorn, K. (2009) 'Introduction: Comparative perspectives on professional groups: current issues and critical debates'. *Current Sociology*, 57, pp. 475–85.

Braverman, H. (1974) *Labor and Monopoly Capital*. New York: Monthly Review Press.

Burawoy, M. (1985) *The Politics of Production: Factory Regimes Under Capitalism and Socialism*. London: Verso Press.

Christensen, T. and Laegreid, P. (1999) 'New public management: Design, resistance, or transformation? A study of how modern reforms are received in a civil service system'. *Public Productivity and Management Review*, 23, pp. 169–93.

Cihon, P. J. and Castagnera, J. O. (1988) *Labor and Employment Law*. Boston, MA: PWS-Kent.

Clegg, S. and Palmer G. (1996) *The Politics of Management Knowledge*. Thousand Oaks, CA: Sage.

Collins, R. (1990) 'Changing conceptions in the sociology of the professions', in R. Torstendahl and M. Burrage (eds), *The Formation of Professions: Knowledge, State and Strategy*, pp. 11–23. London: Sage.

Cummings, S. L. (ed.) (2011) *The Paradox of Professionalism: Lawyers and the Possibility of Justice*. Cambridge, UK: Cambridge University Press.

Donaldson, G. (1963) 'Financial goals: management vs stockholders'. *Harvard Business Review*, May–June, pp. 116–29.

Dunleavy, P., Margetts, H., Bastow, S. and Tinkler, J. (2005) 'New public management is dead – long live digital-era governance'. *Journal of Public Administration Research and Theory*, 16, pp. 467–94.

Edwards, R. (1979) *Contested Terrain*. New York: Basic Books.

Esping-Anderson, G. (1989) *Three Worlds of Welfare Capitalism*. Oxford, UK: Polity.

Evetts, J. (2006) 'Introduction: Trust and professionalism: Challenges and occupational changes'. *Current Sociology*, 54, pp. 515–31.

Evetts, J. (2011) 'A new professionalism? Challenges and opportunities'. *Current Sociology*, 59, pp. 406–22.

Evetts, J. (2013) 'Professionalism: Value and ideology'. *Current Sociology*, 61, pp. 778–96.

Fligstein, N. (1990) *The Transformation of Corporate Control*. Cambridge, MA: Harvard University Press.

Form, W. (1987) 'On the degradation of skills'. *Annual Review of Sociology*, 13, pp. 29–47.

Fourcade, M. (2006) 'The construction of a global profession: The transnationalization of economics'. *American Journal of Sociology*, 112, pp. 145–94.

Frank, D. J. (1997) 'Science, nature, and the globalization of the environment, 1870–1990'. *Social Forces*, 76, pp. 409–35.

Frank, D. J., Meyer, J. W. and Miyahara, D. (1995) 'The individualist polity and the prevalence of professionalized psychology: A cross-national study'. *American Sociological Review*, 60, pp. 360–77.

Freeman, R. A. and Medoff, J. L. (1984) *What Do Unions Do?* New York: Basic Books.

Freidson, E. (1986) *Professional Powers: A Study of the Institutionalization of Formal Knowledge*. Chicago, IL: University of Chicago Press.

Giddens, A. (1994) *Beyond Left and Right: The Future of Radical Politics*. Stanford, CA: Stanford University Press.

Gillespie, R. (1991) *Manufacturing Knowledge: A History of the Hawthorne Experiments*. Cambridge, UK: Cambridge University Press.

Gordon, D. M., Edwards, R. and Reich, M. (1982) *Segmented Work, Divided Workers: The Historical Transformation of Work in the United States*. Cambridge, UK: Cambridge University Press.

Hamermesh, D. S. and Rees, A. (1988) *The Economics of Work and Pay*, 4th edn. New York: Harper & Row.

Hughes, E. C. (1958) *Twenty Thousand Nurses Tell Their Story: A Report on Studies of Nursing Functions Sponsored by the American Nurses Association*. Philadelphia, PA: Lippincott.

Hurst, J. W. (1970) *The Legitimacy of the Business Corporation in the Law of the United States, 1780–1970*. Charlottesville, VA: Virginia University Press.

Ironside, M. and Seifert, R. (2003) *Facing Up to Thatcherism*. Oxford, UK: Oxford University Press.

Kaboolian, L. (1998) 'The new public management: Challenging the boundaries of the management vs. administration debate'. *Public Administration Review*, 58, pp. 189–93.

Khurana, R. (2007) *From Higher Aims to Hired Hands: The Social Transformation of American Business Schools*. Princeton, NJ: Princeton University Press.

Kirkpatrick, I., Dent, M. and Kragh Jespersen, P. (2011) 'The contested terrain of hospital management: Professional projects and healthcare reforms in Denmark'. *Current Sociology*, 59, pp. 489–506.

Kuhlmann, E., Allsop, J. and Saks, M. (2009) 'Professional governance and public control: A comparison of healthcare in the United Kingdom and Germany'. *Current Sociology*, 57, pp. 511–29.

Larsen, M. S. (1977) *The Rise of Professionalism*. Berkeley, CA: University of California Press.

Leicht, K. T. (2016) 'Market fundamentalism, cultural fragmentation, post-modern skepticism, and the future of professional work'. *Journal of Professions and Organization*, 3, pp. 103–17.

Leicht, K. T. and Fennell, M. L. (2001) *Professional Work*. Oxford: Blackwell.

Leicht, K. T. and Fennell, M. L. (2008) 'Institutionalism and the professions', in R. Greenwood, C. Oliver, R. Suddaby and K. Sahlin-Andersson (eds), *Handbook of Organizational Institutionalism*, pp. 375–92. Thousand Oaks, CA: Sage.

Leicht, K. T. and Fitzgerald, S. T. (2014) *Middle-Class Meltdown: Causes, Consequences and Remedies*. New York: Routledge.

Leicht, K. T. and Lyman, E. C. W. (2006) 'Markets, institutions, and the crisis of professional practice'. *Research in the Sociology of Organizations*, 24, pp. 17–44.

Leicht, K. T., Walter, T., Sainsaulieu, I. and Davies, S. (2009) 'New public management and new professionalism across nations and contexts'. *Current Sociology*, 57, pp. 581–606.

Lincoln, J. R. and Kalleberg, A. L. (1982) *Culture, Control and Commitment*. Cambridge, UK: Cambridge University Press.

Locke, R. T. and Spender, J. C. (2011) *Confronting Managerialism: How the Business Elite and their Schools Threw our Lives Out of Balance*. New York: Zed Books.

Lynn, L. E. (1998) 'The new public management: How to transform a theme into a legacy'. *Public Administration Review*, 58, pp. 231–37.

Malhotra, N. T. M., Morris, T. and Hinings, C. R. (2006) 'Variation in organizational form among professional service organizations'. *Research in the Sociology of Organizations*, 24, pp. 171–202.

Manning, N. (2001) 'The legacy of new public management in developing countries'. *International Review of Administrative Sciences*, 67, pp. 217–312.

Marglin, S. (1974) 'What do bosses do? The origins and functions of hierarchy in capitalist production'. *Review of Radical Political Economics*, 6, pp. 33–60.

Markowitz, H. M. (1952) 'Portfolio selection'. *Journal of Finance*, 7, pp. 77–91.

Monsen, R. and Downs, A. (1965) 'A theory of large managerial firms'. *Journal of Political Economy*, 73, pp. 221–36.

Montgomery, D. (1979) *Worker's Control in America*. Cambridge, UK: Cambridge University Press.

Pfeffer, J. and Cohen, Y. (1984) 'Determinants of internal labor markets in organizations'. *Administrative Science Quarterly*, 29, pp. 550–72.

Reich, R. (2012) *Beyond Outrage: What's Gone Wrong with Our Economy and Democracy and How to Fix It*. New York: Vintage Books.

Rifkin, J. (2004) *The European Dream*. New York: Penguin.

Rubin, B. A. (1999) *Shifts in the Social Contract: Understanding Change in American Society*. New York: Sage.

Savoie, D. (1995) 'What's wrong with the new public management?'. *Canadian Public Administration,* 38, pp. 112–21.

Scott, W. R., Ruef, M., Mendel, P. J. and Caronna, C. A. (2000) *Institutional Change and Healthcare Organizations*. Chicago, IL: University of Chicago Press.

Sherman, A. W. Jr. and Bohlander, G. W. (1992) *Managing Human Resources*. Cincinnati, OH: Southwestern Publishing.

Skaggs, B. C. and Leicht, K. T. (2005) 'Management paradigm change in the United States: A professional autonomy perspective'. *Research in the Sociology of Work*, 15, pp. 125–52.

Stein, J. (1995) *Monetarist, Keynesian, and New Classical Economics*. Cambridge, UK: Cambridge University Press.

Stiglitz, J. (2013) *The Price of Inequality: How Today's Divided Society Endangers Our Future*. New York: W. W. Norton.

Stone, K. (1974) 'The origins of job structures in the steel industry'. *Review of Radical Political Economics*, 6, pp. 61–97.

Suddaby, R. and Viale, T. (2011) 'Professionals and field-level change: Institutional work and the professional project'. *Current Sociology*, 59, pp. 423–42.

Suddaby, R., Cooper, D. J. and Greenwood, R. (2007) 'Transnational regulation of professional services: governance dynamics of field-level organizational change'. *Accounting, Organizations and Society*, 32, pp. 333–62.

Taylor, F. W. (1903) *Shop Management*. New York: Harper & Row.

Taylor, F. W. (1911) *The Principles of Scientific Management*. New York: Harper & Row.

Thompson, F. and Reschenthaler, G. B. (1996) 'The information revolution and the new public management'. *Journal of Public Administration Research and Theory*, 6, pp. 125–44.

Wren, D. A. (1994) *The Evolution of Management Thought*, 4th edn. New York: Wiley.

14

Leadership and 'leaderism'

The discourse of professional leadership and the practice of management control in public services

Michael I. Reed

Introduction

From the early 1990s onwards, policy-making elites across a range of national governments have initiated a complex package of programmes, technologies and practices aimed at developing 'leadership capacity' within public services (O'Reilly & Reed, 2011; Reed & Wallace, 2015). These programmes, technologies and practices have been framed within a generic rhetoric or discourse – what Fairclough (2010) calls an 'imaginary' – of 'public service modernisation' that focuses upon a debilitating paucity of 'leadership capacity' as constituting the major obstacle to reforms that will make public services more flexible, efficient, consumer-led and organizationally adaptable.

This emergent 'imaginary' of 'leaderism' has played a crucial role in legitimating a range of institutional and organizational changes that have impacted on public service professionals in complex, and often contradictory, ways (Noordegraaf & Steijn, 2013). Nevertheless, the 'general direction of travel' in which these reforms have driven public service professionals is relatively clear in that they have generated a configuration of interconnected structural, cultural and technical innovations that have progressively subjected professional workers to a much more intrusive, demanding and constraining 'regime of control' over the last two decades or so (Ackroyd, 2013). While some professional groups may have become relatively adept at 'creating new spaces of agency within the expanding market of public services' (Newman, 2013, p. 47), most have found themselves adapting to a new control regime that selectively recombines elements of marketization, surveillance and sanctioning. Again, there may be room for 'localized mediation and variation' in the organizational technologies through which policy reforms are implemented within specific sectors and locales – where various forms of 'network governance' seem to be playing an increasingly important role Newman (2013). However, most public service professionals now find themselves operating within institutionalized environments in which the imaginary of 'leaderism' has progressively challenged the once dominant occupational ideology of 'professionalism' and its associated occupational practices of 'expert judgement' and 'regulated autonomy'.

This chapter will trace the process whereby the discourse of 'leaderism' and its escalating impact on the organization and management of the work of public service professionals has developed over the last two decades or so. It will set out the key analytical features of 'leaderism', contrasting them with both 'professionalism' and 'managerialism', while drawing on the results of a large-scale empirical study of public service leadership development initiatives in the health and education sectors within England undertaken between 2006 and 2009 (Economic and Social Research Council, grant number RES-000-23-1136 'Developing Organization Leaders as Change Agents in the Public Services'; Reed & Wallace, 2015). Finally, it will draw out the wider implications of the preceding analysis for the much more 'hybridized' forms of network governance and professional management that have emerged in the course of the last 20 years.

The grit in the oyster

In 2004, the then UK Secretary of State at the Department of Education and Skills (DfES), the Right Honourable Charles Clarke MP, stated that 'the grit in the oyster is leadership. We need leadership at all levels' (National College for Schools Leadership (NSCL), 2004, p. 2). He wasn't alone in his assertion that 'leadership', however construed, was the critical mechanism that would transform public services from bureaucratic dystopias into entrepreneurial dynamos. Over a decade, successive reports for the Organisation of Economic Co-operation and Development (OECD, 2001, 2010) identified shortfalls in leadership capacity and development as constituting the major obstacles to achieving much-needed reform of public institutions and organizations. Substantial enhancement of leadership capacity throughout the public services, generated through massively improved leadership development provision, was seen as the key to achieving the 'quantum leap' in performance that the former were required to attain within the much more openly competitive and resource-constrained environments in which they were embedded.

Over the last decade or so, many OECD governments have been more than prepared to make major investments in the provision of leadership development programmes for their public services in which private sector management consultancies, often working in tandem with universities and other public providers, 'have proven to be potent sources of ideas about public service leadership and its development' (Wallace et al., 2011, p. 2). Irrespective of, potentially significant, differences in history, culture, context and content, public services leadership development programmes have been dominated by a generic paradigm of what 'leadership is' and how it might be most appropriately developed that draw their inspiration from the ideas and techniques associated with 'transformational leadership' within the private sector. This 'visionary' conception of leadership, as originally promulgated by high-profile 'guru academics' such as Bennis and Nanus (1985) and Bass (1990), became much more influential, particularly in the UK, during the 1990s, when successive New Labour governments led by Tony Blair 'promoted a discourse of public service leadership as a means of fostering the kind of system-wide transformation it envisaged, as well as promoting organisational success' (Newman, 2005, p. 196).

However, this government-promoted discourse of 'radical public service transformation through entrepreneurially empowered public leadership' didn't emerge out of thin air. Indeed, it grew out of a discourse and practice of 'new public management' (NPM) that had become increasingly influential from the mid 1980s onwards in creative and innovative ways to form a rather different kind of 'discursive imaginary' shaping contemporary political debate about public sector reform from that envisaged under NPM (Hood, 1991; Du Gay, 2005; Fairclough, 2010; O'Reilly & Reed, 2011; Ward, 2014). NPM articulated a theory and practice of public service organization and management that promised to transform public service delivery through the diffusion of competitive market mechanisms – or, at the very least, a simulacrum of market competition – and the widespread structural and cultural changes which the latter demanded in relation to performance evaluation and monitoring. By the mid 1990s, what had begun as a relatively prosaic and technocratic series of reforms focused on organizational design and managerial control had become infused with a potpourri of ideas and techniques drawn from neo-liberal ideology which legitimated system-wide changes in the philosophy and practice of public service management.

As Fairclough (2010) maintains, if they are eventually to gather sufficient ideological legitimacy and political momentum to offer a coherent and sustainable vision of the 'paradigm shift' which public service organization and management must undergo, discursive imaginaries such as NPM have to be 'theoretically adequate' and 'practically adequate' – that is, they must carry sufficient intellectual conviction and operational credibility if they are to stand any chance of being translated into organizational reality. He also points out that there are likely to be contradictions and tensions within any discursive imaginary between the demands of 'theoretical adequacy' and the constraints of 'practical adequacy' insofar as the latter inevitably compromise the integrity of the former and dilute its ideological purity. In the case of NPM, this can be most clearly seen in its failure to design and implement a control regime that effectively emasculates, rather than periodically contains, public service professionalism – both as an occupational ideology and as an organizational reality. Thus, a number of researchers and commentators (Newman, 2001; Dent & Whitehead, 2002; Farrell & Morris, 2003; Flynn, 2004; Pollitt & Bouckaert, 2011; Ward, 2014) have identified the series of ideological oscillations and organizational compromises that NPM underwent during the 1990s and 2000s as it struggled to come to terms with the institutional resilience of professional power and authority within public services.

Of course, public service professionalism and professionals were forced into making a mirror-image series of adaptations to and compromises with the control regimes that waves of NPM-inspired reforms imposed on the public sector during the 1990s and 2000s – ranging from various forms of audit and performance review to the larger-scale institutional and cultural transitions entailed in business process re-engineering and network governance (McLaughlin et al., 2002; McNulty & Ferlie, 2004; Miller, 2005; Newman, 2005, 2013; Clarke et al., 2007; Pollitt, 2007; Martin et al., 2009; Power, 2014). Yet, professional power and authority, though battered and bruised by more than a decade of ideological, structural and organizational transitions within public services, which undoubtedly strengthened managerial control and weakened professional autonomy, refused to 'lie down and die'. This was so even in the face of the growing political power and influence of neo-liberalism within elite circles and the pervasive ways in which it began to seep into every institutional nook and cranny of public service provision, organization and management during the 2000s.

The neo-liberal turn

The significance of neo-liberalism for reconfiguring and revivifying NPM as a discursive imaginary that would legitimate 'second-' and 'third-'wave public sector reforms, particularly in 'Anglo-American' political economies and welfare systems such as the USA, UK, Australia and New Zealand during the 2000s, cannot be underestimated (Jessop, 2007, 2014; Peck, 2010; Harvey, 2011; Crouch, 2013; Dardot & Laval, 2013; Mirowski, 2013; Gamble, 2009, 2014; Davies, 2014). Neither should we underestimate the practical/operational significance of neo-liberalism to the extent that it instigated 'an open-ended and contradictory process of politically assisted market rule … that has always been about the capture and re-use of the state in the interests of a pro-corporate, free-trading market order' (Peck, 2010, pp. xii–9). By elevating 'market-based principles and techniques of evaluation to the level of state-endorsed norms' (Davies, 2014, p. 6), neo-liberalism advances, through the political, economic and cultural power of its dominant elites occupying command positions within financial, political and administrative institutions, a strategic vision of how public services and their professional workers should be transformed. As Ward has recently suggested:

> NPM can be seen as the central mechanism through which neo-liberalism reconfigured not only the larger political economy of nation states but also the ordinary, day-to-day institutions where people receive services and work.... NPM sought to fold or redirect the professionals who work in public organizations under the wing of managerial authority by creating mechanisms that required a shifting of accountability from the internal ethical and disciplinary protocols of the public professionals themselves to either public sector managers or outside auditors who were said to represent the interests of various institutional 'stakeholders', taxpayers or the public in general.
>
> *(2014, p. 50)*

Ward (2014, pp. 52–58) also argues that 'under the direction of neo-liberal politicians and ministry and agency heads, NPM introduced a number of wide-ranging changes in the way public organizations around the world operated'. He identifies six key changes lying at the core of NPM as it became more widely infected by neo-liberal discourse and doctrine: first, the legitimation and operationalization of private-sector practices directed to forcing costs down and progressively reducing public expenditure; second, widespread marketization to root out the pathologies of corporatist bureaucracy; third, the introduction of a customer service culture in which consumer choice becomes a practical reality; fourth, a continuous drive towards organizational devolution as exemplified in devolved budgets, outsourcing and contracting; fifth, selective 'unbundling' and privatization of services and functions in order to achieve a much reduced 'operational core' drawing on agency staff to supplement the core professional employees remaining; and finally, the continuing casualization of professional and support labour through work disaggregation, segmentation and specialization, reversing much of the team-based and networked forms of working that had been previously in vogue.

Overall, Ward (2014, p. 56) concludes that this interrelated package of neo-liberal-driven NPM reforms was strategically focused on disempowering public professionals by directly challenging and undermining their 'claim over the exclusive control over the domain of expertise and specialized knowledge'. Also, professional autonomy became even further diluted and compromised through the process of corporatizing and casualizing professional work in public service organizations and the consequent power shift towards the auditing system and market-based competition which it necessarily entailed.

While Ward's analysis provides a powerful interpretation of the generic impact of neo-liberal-driven NPM reforms and their particular implications for public service professionalism and professions, he is not without his critics. For some of the latter (Fergusson, 2000; Pollitt, 2007; Goldfinch & Wallis, 2010), analyses such as that proffered by Ward engage in a form of 'discursive determinism' in which the rhetoric of NPM is taken at face value to the extent that it confuses 'talk' with 'action' and presupposes a political and organizational convergence around a monolithic view of 'managerialism' that is belied by real-world practice. Instead of a comprehensive paradigm shift towards a managerially dominated world in which professionals are 'on tap' rather than 'on top', these critics see a much messier pattern of change in which there is a much more complex and diverse process of interactions between ideas, interest and actors (Goldfinch & Wallis, 2010, p. 1103) in which a 'post-NPM world' is emerging that is much less fixed and constraining than analysts such as Ward suggest. Nevertheless, this group of critics indicate that the 'post-NPM world' is one in which public service professionals will still struggle to protect their power base and preserve their cultural authority due to further reductions in public expenditure and other structural pressures that reinforce their marginalization under the full force of neo-liberal-style NPM.

Other critics (Currie, 1997; McNulty & Ferlie, 2004; Thomas & Davies, 2005; Noordegraaf & Steijn, 2013) contend that over-deterministic analyses of the internal coherence and external impact of neo-liberal-style NPM substantially underestimate the capacity for 'professional resistance' – not simply to stop or at least slow down the torrent of change released by the latter but also to offer alternative conceptions of public service professionalism better suited to the 'new times' in which we now live (Clarke *et al.*, 2007). As Newman (2013) has recently argued, the new forms of 'network governance' emerging in a post-NPM world seem to offer public service professionals the political and organizational space to reinvent themselves as 'partnership leaders' within new configurations of health and social care grounded in civil society and relatively free from the top-down bureaucratic controls symptomatic of neo-liberal-style NPM. However, she also notes that these network forms of governance will blur and sometimes challenge the institutionalized boundaries between established 'jurisdictional domains' (Abbott, 1988; Macdonald, 2006) and the external occupational labour market shelters that they supported (Freidson, 1973, 2001). The former are also likely to call for more hybridized forms of work organization, occupational control and institutional governance in which the nature and role of 'leadership' and its relationship with 'professionalism' becomes even more critical to the future development of public services.

Leaderism

As we have already seen, the turn towards a neo-liberal-driven agenda and programme of NPM reforms within 'Anglo-American' welfare systems from the mid 1990s onwards generated a parallel discourse about the nature and role of 'leadership' within public services. The latter also opened up further debate about the nature and role of 'professionalism' within public services as they began to develop much more complex patterns of institutional governance and organizational design in which 'hierarchy, markets and networks' vied for attention as providing the core principles underpinning political decision-making and work co-ordination (Thompson, 2003; Du Gay, 2005; Moran, 2007).

As a discourse of public service reform, leaderism emerges in the 1990s as a response to the inherent theoretical limitations and practical failures of NPM. In particular, it offers public service professionals a much more positive position and role in the brave new world of network governance than that assigned to them by NPM as the latter's turn towards neo-liberal doctrine and practice reinforces its endemic authoritarian and polarizing tendencies (O'Reilly & Reed, 2011; Teelken *et al.*, 2012; Reed & Wallace, 2015). Insofar as neo-liberal NPM pushes towards a 'low trust' corporate culture and structure in which increasingly refined control regimes have to be designed and implemented to ensure that the sectional interests of professionals are kept in check, then it promotes a selective segmentation and intensification of expert work that further damages professional collegiality and authority (Ward, 2014). Leaderism promises to counteract these divisive and fragmenting tendencies in that it pushes back against the re-bureaucratization of service provision – now around market competition and performance management – by advocating a much more 'high trust', inclusive and self-governing form of public service organization in which professionals are to play a strategic role in co-ordinating and supporting co-produced services.

Neo-liberal NPM may have been the ideological and organizational incubator of leaderism during a period of 'hyper-innovation' in public service policy and practice, when successive central governments 'have strengthened central control but also strengthened sources of opposition to central control'(Moran, 2007, p. 192). Nevertheless, leaderism – once it has gathered sufficient ideological momentum and political support from 'advocacy coalitions or networks' of political, economic and professional elites who are increasingly dissatisfied with neo-liberal NPM's capacity to deliver the substantive reforms that it promises (Goldfinch & Wallace, 2010) – begins to undermine the intellectual coherence and policy standing of its progenitor. This is particularly the case in relation to the latter's perceived failure to offer any lasting solution to the 'leadership question' in public service organization and delivery and to the role that professionals are to play in shaping and co-ordinating the much more complex and hybridized pattern of public service provision that neo-liberal NPM, however unintentionally, has bequeathed.

Leaderism emerges in the 1990s, initially as a response to the perceived rigidity of NPM thinking and practice. Subsequently, it gathers force as an elite-driven discourse that interprets and legitimates narratives of public service reform in which signifiers such as 'modernization', 'co-production', 'consumerism', 'competition' and 'self-governance' come to play an increasingly strategic role (Newman, 2005, 2013; Clarke, 2005; Clarke *et al.*, 2007). Over time, this increasing emphasis on the critical role of 'leadership', within a profoundly changed configuration of contextual conditions wrought by neo-liberal NPM, generates a reorientation of accountability mechanisms and processes within the new pattern of public governance taking shape in 'Anglo-American' welfare systems. In particular, public service professionals are increasingly identified, in a wide range of governmental reports and policy documents (O'Reilly & Reed, 2011; Reed & Wallace, 2015), as having a central role to play in shifting the accountability focus away from top-down, technocratic and bureaucratic management and towards bottom-up, consumer and market-driven imperatives. Thus, it's the newly empowered professionals, rather than the increasingly remote and isolated bureaucratic technocrats, who have the key leadership role to play in taking public service reform forward into a new post-NPM phase in which the 'citizen-consumer' (Clarke *et al.*, 2007) becomes the critical provider and arbiter of 'user choice' and 'competitive collaboration'.

By no means does this shift in accountability from 'management' to 'leadership' entail a dismantling of the auditing and surveillance regimes that neo-liberal NPM has imposed on public service professionals; nor does it facilitate anything like a return to the levels of professional work autonomy and collegiate self-governance enjoyed under 'bureau-professionalism' (Newman, 1998; Ward, 2014). But it does suggest a growing ideological accommodation between managerialism and professionalism in which the technocratic 'theory of leadership' implicit within the former is firmly rejected and the exclusive 'theory of expertise' carried by the latter is modified to form a discursive hybrid within which 'transformational leadership' and 'network governance' can be selectively recombined in line with the dictates of 'democratic or militant consumerism' (O'Reilly & Reed, 2011).

Initially mobilized as an elite-driven discourse of public service reform to correct the authoritarian tendencies and technocratic excesses of neo-liberal NPM, leaderism has developed into a narrative of 'post-NPM reform' within which recalcitrant elite and middle-ranking professionals can be co-opted into a modernizing project. The latter is seen as generating a much more complex world of dispersed public service networks focused on satisfying escalating consumer demands in a competitive market environment in which the central state removes itself to a synoptic, overseeing role rather than the highly proactive and interventionist role characteristic of neo-corporatist welfare-state systems (Reed & Wallace 2015). Within this modernizing project, leaderism allocates a crucial role to public service professionals; they become the facilitators of and mediators between dispersed public service networks that provide the vital co-ordinating mechanisms ensuring 'joined-up' service provision and governance within a competitive environment in which private sector corporate providers, mutual/non-profit making organizations and various forms of partnership agencies vie for service contracts. Thus, a hybridized world of public service organization and delivery seems to call for a hybridized form of public service professionalism in which core principles of exclusive expert power, authority and control have to be substantially modified to accommodate a much broader spectrum of 'stakeholder interests and values' which are significantly more demanding in relation to 'access', 'voice' and 'choice'.

Polyarchic governance and professional leadership

Previous discussion has suggested that leaderism, as a discourse of public service reform, has exerted a significant impact on reform policy and practice within 'Anglo-American' welfare systems since the mid 1990s. As the latter struggle to come to terms with a world of rising consumer demand and expectations, savage cuts in public expenditure, and a neo-liberal governing ideology and practice deeply suspicious of, not to say openly hostile towards, the concept of collective public service provision in any shape or form, then the search for policy initiatives and programmes which speak to this cacophony of voices becomes ever-more urgent and politic.

Leaderism has the protean qualities and 'brilliant ambiguity' that are well suited to this complex public service world of hybridized organizational forms and networked governance regimes within which ruling financial, political, administrative and professional elites still retain strategic power and control (Reed, 2012a, 2012b; Reed & Wallace, 2015). Yet, the latter still have to construct and sustain viable governance mechanisms through which they can draw in a much wider and increasingly vociferous range of 'stakeholder interests and values', while retaining the political and organizational capacity to ensure that their long-term material interests and ideological predilections are protected.

Some commentators have identified the return of early twentieth-century-style plutocratic elite rule under the ideological hegemony and political dominance of neo-liberal theory and practice in 'Anglo-American' welfare systems over the last 30 years or so. Plutocracy is a system of political rule by an economically powerful and socially exclusionary elite unrestrained by any consideration of resistance from middle and lower order groups locked into a hierarchically stratified power structure exhibiting relatively high levels of institutional cohesiveness, stability and continuity (Pahl & Winkler, 1974; Rothkopf, 2008; Mount, 2012; Ward, 2014).

Others have argued for a more complex model of contemporary elite rule in which a hybrid regime of strategic oligarchic control at the centre and delegated pluralistic stakeholder operational control at the periphery begins to emerge in the form of 'polyarchic governance' within the more complex and unstable conditions prevailing in contemporary political economies and welfare systems (Dahl, 1971; Courpasson & Clegg, 2012). Courpasson and Clegg (2012, pp. 68–74) define polyarchic rule as a hybrid form of governance that synthesizes selected aspects of oligarchic domination and pluralistic interest group participation:

> polyarchic bureaucracy is a model of resistance and competition between resisters for elite inclusion, whose performance as 'resistance bearers' establishes their claims for elite inclusion. It therefore dilutes bureaucracy by selecting non-oligarchs among those individuals as potential and *competing* candidates for elite inclusion. As a result, authority still resides in the bureaucratic control of the organization's upper echelons, but access to these positions is open to those whose performativity in creative 'projects of resistance' is tangible, according to criteria determined by the managerial oligarchy, including leadership of dissenting coalitions.
>
> *(Courpasson & Clegg, 2012, pp. 72–73 emphasis in original)*

Within polyarchic modes of governance, a central oligarchy unobtrusively retains strategic control over middle- and lower-level elites by opening up the hierarchically containable horizontal exercise of delegated leadership and influence. This is achieved through two, linked, institutional innovations: first, through a controlled decentralization of governing routines within 'rules of the game' that proscribe any open and direct challenge to the authority of 'the centre' to set and control the political–strategic agenda; second, through the promotion of multiple channels of participation and contestation that allow a range of stakeholder interest groups and their local leaders to pursue their interests in ways that do not threaten the domination of the central oligarchy. In this way, polyarchy establishes a hybrid governance regime through which ruling elites can achieve a modus vivendi between sustaining the structural mechanisms required to retain oligarchical power and facilitating a form of 'controlled stakeholder engagement' that gives the impression of grass-roots participation. As Monbiot (2014) notes, it has now become routine practice for both private and public sector corporations to develop polyarchic forms of governance in order 'to stakeholderise every conflict ... they embrace their critics, involving them in a dialogue that is open in the same way that a lobster pot is open, breaking down critical distance and identity until no one knows who they are any more'.

Selznick (1949) anticipates many of the key features of polyarchic governance in his classic study of the complex ways in which formal and informal mechanisms of 'co-optation' were deployed by policy and administrative elites within the Tennessee Valley Authority (TVA) to neuter the agency's more radical founding policies and programmes (Reed, 2009). However, more recent research on the worsening position of 'knowledge professionals' under the pressures exerted by neo-liberal NPM (Ackroyd, 2013; Ward, 2014) suggests that these mechanisms of co-optation have become even more well developed and now constitute the main levers of 'soft power' that are increasingly combined with more conventional 'hard power' systems of surveillance and control required to sustain polyarchic modes of governance in public services.

Indeed, the more hybridized institutional forms that polyarchy generates assigns a pivotal role to 'leadership' at all levels of the, now streamlined and flattened, hierarchical authority structures through which elite rule is reproduced and legitimated. 'Leadership' becomes the key process through which the much more internally complex, dynamic and unstable forms of network governing that polyarchy instantiates are contained and controlled in ways that enable public service organizations to survive within institutional environments characterized by much higher levels of economic insecurity and political uncertainty (Newman, 2005, 2013). Effective political leadership and management, within and across national, sectoral and local levels of public service organization and delivery, looms large within institutional environments in which competing, and often conflicting, 'institutional logics' based on markets, hierarchies and networks have to be brought into some sort of viable organizational alignment. Once open contestation, opposition and resistance to established policy orthodoxy becomes acceptable to the 'powers that be' – as long as it does not seem to threaten their structural domination and strategic control – in ways that would have been inconceivable under the 'club regulation' of public services which emerged in the late Victorian era and dominated for much of the next century (Moran, 2007). Conversely, under polyarchic governance, effective political leadership and management, at all levels, is at a premium to the extent that it provides the key co-ordinating and control mechanism through which some semblance of continuity and cohesion emerges out of bewildering organizational complexity.

Increasingly, it is public service professionals who are being offered, trained and developed for these overarching leadership roles because they are seen as occupying the key co-ordinating nodes within the governance regimes which are taking shape in contemporary public service networks, and only they have the required expertise and skill to make the latter work under conditions of extreme economic constraint and political instability (O'Reilly & Reed, 2011). Our research (Wallace *et al.*, 2011; Reed & Wallace 2015) indicates that this is increasingly the current institutional context and organizational situation within which growing numbers of UK public service professionals find themselves – that is, being required to take on leadership roles and relationships within hybridized, polyarchic governance regimes which involve a considerable degree of political risk and insecurity for them and their organizations. In a major Economic and Social Research Council (ESRC)-funded, qualitative study – involving a critical discourse analysis of 128 policy documents and 218 semi-structured interviews with 163 informants (55 informants were interviewed twice) from within UK central government, national leadership development bodies, service organizations, senior managers and professional leaders in the English health and education service sectors – we attempted to trace the development and impact of 'leaderism' under a succession of New Labour governments between the mid 1990s and early 2000s.

What we discovered was a highly complex pattern of polyarchic governance emerging in these two sectors where senior health and educational professionals were incrementally being drawn into a political process where they were expected, by policy elites, to 'make the hybrid happen' due to their technical expertise, organizational centrality and cultural status. Whatever the decline in occupational power and operational autonomy that 'rank-and-file' public service professionals were suffering under a neo-liberal NPM regime that imposed more intensive and intrusive controls on their organizational lives, these very same public service professionals were expected to 'hold the system together' and to convince service users, or 'customers', that all was well with the integrity and quality of the service they were receiving. While UK central government policy elites orchestrated a 'twin-track approach' to public service reform – that is, an approach focused simultaneously on service marketization and re-regulation – they also directed much of their attention and effort to the resourcing, design and management of the national leadership development bodies (NLDBs) through which this new vision of 'leaderism' was to be inculcated and legitimated. In turn, this demanded that much of the pre-existing organizational architecture of local government-based control and management of education and health services be dismantled and replaced with a panoply of devolved budgets, local initiatives and delegated accountability overseen by a neo-liberal state elite exercising 'remote control' through various quasi-independent agencies. It was the senior public service professionals in schools, hospitals, general medical practices and universities who were now expected to provide the cultural and organizational leadership through which this increasingly fragmented and fissured hybrid governance system could achieve at least some degree of operational integration and strategic coherence.

At the core of this discourse of leaderism – which a substantial majority of our interview informants 'bought into', admittedly with varying degrees of sector-specific and occupation-specific variation and mediation – lay an eliding of sectional interests with supposedly universally shared collective interests which both 'leaders' and 'followers' were required to harness and pursue. By glossing over and subsuming seemingly intractable conflicts of interests and values between different groups within an overarching discourse of 'mediated consensus' that homogenizes and neutralizes the structural sources of such conflicts, leaderism provides an ideological mechanism through which neo-liberal elites can reproduce their power and control within polyarchic governance systems.

Our research revealed the various, sometimes subtle sometimes not-so-subtle, mechanisms and modes through which this overarching 'discursive imaginary' of leaderism – as the key process facilitating public service modernization – was constructed, promoted and legitimated.

First, leaderism is promulgated through a wide range of, usually, central government-generated policy and training and development documents (48 central government, health and education documents; 7 documents addressed to NLDBs; 56 NLDB documents and 17 sectoral professional association and other 'stakeholder documents') analysed in our research. The latter revealed a consistent pattern of central government departments and devolved agencies advocating and orchestrating a much closer partnership, indeed 'advocacy coalition', between policy elites and professional leaders to drive through a programme of change in schools, universities, hospitals, general medical practices and primary care trusts that would transform them from professional bureaucracies into entrepreneurial networks. It also revealed the ideological significance of leaderism as providing a crucial discursive mechanism whereby sectional interests and conflicts, within and between political, administrative and professional groups, are dissolved in favour of a greater collective good defined and communicated by superordinate elites who are presumed to embody the latter. Thus, 'transformational public service reform' requires strong, customer-focused and performance-driven leadership from senior professionals within and across different sectors and levels of public service delivery in order to ensure that it becomes more than a paper exercise and metamorphoses into an operational reality (UK Treasury, 2000; Office of Public Services Reform, 2002; Strategy Unit, 2006, 2008).

Second, in order to mobilize the 'right kind of leaders' who will take the public service reform agenda forward in ways that central government departments approve of, they establish 'national leadership development bodies' for schools, universities, colleges, hospitals and other health-care agencies that are tasked with identifying, training and developing the new professional leadership cadres who will deliver modernized services keenly attuned to the demands of globalized market competition and the organizational flexibility it requires. These NLDBs, at least in their initial set-up phase, are allowed some degree of intellectual and organizational space to be creative and innovative in terms of the design and delivery of the training and development packages they offer to the new cohorts of incoming public service professionals – usually recruited from public service professionals already performing management roles within their respective sectors. However, this space is, in most cases, relatively quickly closed down and colonized by standardized forms of training and development focused on delivering neo-liberal-driven reform initiatives and programmes.

Third, our programme of qualitative, in-depth interviewing undertaken with over 200 public service professionals in health and education (in some cases involving 'before' and 'after' interviews with those who had been on training and development courses offered by their NLDBs), as well as a small group of policy elites located within the central government apparatus involved in orchestrating and delivering this change agenda, demonstrated that the majority of them had been acculturated into a broad acceptance of the values and norms prioritized by leaderism (Reed & Wallace, 2015). Again, while there is some degree of sector-specific mediation and variation evident in our informants' interview responses, these can still be accommodated within a generic narrative of public service reform in which they see themselves as playing the key strategic role of 'change agents' carrying through a long-term process of cultural and organizational transformation in which competitive markets, tight performance management, entrepreneurial flexibility and network-mediated delivery are the dominant values and realities. While they retain a strong allegiance to their core professional service values and claim to have played a mediating role by implementing required changes in a sympathetic way within their particular occupational domains and organizational jurisdictions, they are also politically astute concerning the overall direction and trajectory of public service change and the much 'harder' accountability regimes that will delimit the room for manoeuvre in delivering the latter.

Conclusions

Leaderism is a highly versatile and dynamic discursive imaginary which allows public service professionals to see themselves as change agents within an overarching process of public sector reform in which the policy priorities embodied in neo-liberal ideology and the values embedded in delegated professional autonomy can be creatively recombined within a hybridized form of polyarchic governance. As a reform discourse within public services, leaderism has the capacity to span intra-professional and extra-professional boundaries at a time when managerialism seems to be waning as a primary source of occupational identity and organizational status (Carroll & Levy, 2008; Ford & Harding, 2007).

Yet, we should not underestimate how pervasive neo-liberal NPM has become within contemporary public services organizations and the much-changed institutional contexts in which they are located. Leaderism may have been grafted on to the former as an innovative discursive imaginary which softens and mediates the harshness, if not brutality, of the free-market populism that neo-liberal NPM has brought in its wake. Political and administrative elites located within the central government machinery of 'Anglo-American welfare systems' have co-opted public service professional elites into an ideology of institutional leadership and organizational change in which they play the key role of facilitating and protecting a process of rolling cultural transformations where market competition, enhanced private sector provision, semi-independent service delivery networks, intrusive performance management regimes and consumer choice move from the periphery to the core of public service ethos and order. Also, there is increasing evidence to suggest (Buchanan et al., 2007; Bolden et al., 2008; Ferlie et al., 2013) that further hybridization of governance structures and organizational forms has occurred where the ideological remit of neo-liberal NPM and leaderism runs strongest and seems to have pushed and pulled public service professionals into a closer accommodation with market-based reforms.

Of course, there is considerable system-level and sector-level variation in the extent to which public service professionals have been forced into 'making the hybrid happen'. Recent research on 'Continental European', as opposed to 'Anglo-American' welfare systems (Noordegraaf & Steijn, 2013), indicates that the former provide public service professionals with the ideological resources and discursive imaginaries to resist the worst excesses of neo-liberal NPM and leaderism. Organizational professionals located in certain European public services systems operate within an institutional context in which corporatist-style 'bureau professionalism' has been significantly more ideologically robust and organizationally resilient in the face of the neo-liberal NPM onslaught. Consequently, they have been better placed to maintain sector-level regimes and local-level practices in which professional autonomy, often working in collaboration with community groups and other interested stakeholders, can be sustained as a core ingredient of public service provision and organization.

It is also true to say that the hybrid system of managed markets and professional leadership that has emerged within polyarchic governance regimes has its own internal tensions and external pressures. Neo-liberal NPM continues to push, relentlessly, in the direction of marketized public services coupled with performance management systems that deracinate professional work autonomy and threaten to reduce 'professionals' to the status of 'technicians' or 'bureaucrats', as predicted by Freidson (2001). On the other hand, leaderism strives to preserve whatever vestiges of professional occupational control and work discretion remain as necessary prerequisites for the continuance of (at least the façade of) organizational self-governance and co-produced services. By emphasizing the vital importance of 'practice-based leadership' of a distributed or collaborative kind, selective mediations and interpretations of leaderism can be made more appealing to established public service professions and professionals prepared to take on hybrid 'professional/leader' roles and the space they can open up for creative innovation.

In this way, the underlying stability of polyarchic governance regimes within public services now dominated by neo-liberal NPM, never that secure at the best of times, depends on maintaining a complex and delicate balancing act between 'strategic control' from the centre and 'delegated control' at the periphery. While strategic control from the centre keeps sector- and local-level innovation within acceptable bounds, delegated control at the periphery sustains the semblance of professional leadership required to convince voters, clients and customers that their needs and demands remain a vital part of the equation determining how, when and where their public services are provided and organized.

This delicate but crucial balancing act between strategic and delegated control under polyarchic governance is likely to come under increasing strain as the, seemingly ineluctable, pressures for further substantial, not to say savage, reductions in public expenditure intensify (for example, see UK Chancellor's Autumn Statement presented to the House of Commons on 3 November 2014). Public sector professionals will be at the 'organizational sharp-end' of these intensifying pressures for more public spending cuts under an expenditure regime of 'permanent austerity' (Ackroyd, 2013). The ideological attractiveness and the discursive versatility of leaderism may begin to wane somewhat under these conditions as the space for creative innovations in occupational collaboration and organizational innovation begins to narrow once more.

Much will depend on the willingness and capacity of professional groups throughout the public services to adapt selected elements of their core occupational structures and practices to the 'logic of consumerism' that neo-liberal NPM has imposed with some considerable political force and organizational acumen in recent years. However, this process of selective adaptation will need to ensure that whatever hybrid discursive imaginary emerges out of it – such as the 'citizen-consumer' and the concept of 'civic professionalism' which accompanies it (Clarke *et al.*, 2007) – it will need to be robust enough to sustain the structural and cultural preconditions of professionalism as constituting the 'third logic' of occupational ordering within public service organizations in the twenty-first century. There is little doubt that the more apocalyptic predictions about the deprofessionalization and proletarianization of expert work in the twenty-first century considerably underestimate the structural power and cultural capital that professionalism continues to enjoy (Reed, 2007). Nevertheless, it is also the case that public service professionals, certainly within Anglo-American welfare systems, have faced, and will continue to face, major challenges to their authority and control which will further constrain their organizational autonomy and weaken their occupational identity.

Acknowledgements

The research reported in this chapter was funded by the Economic and Social Research Council (ESRC), Award No: R-000-23-1136 'Developing Organization Leaders as Change Agents in the Public Services'. The views expressed in this chapter are those of the author and do not represent the views of the ESRC.

References

Abbott, A. (1988) *The System of the Professions*, London: University of Chicago Press.

Ackroyd, S. (2013) 'Professions, professionals and the "new" government policies: A reflection of the last 30 years', in M. Noordegraaf and B. Steijn (eds), *Professionals under Pressure: The Reconfiguration of Professional Work in Changing Public Services*, Amsterdam: Amsterdam University Press, pp. 21–39.

Bass, B. (1990) 'From transactional to transformational leadership: Learning to share the vision'. *Organizational Dynamics*, 18, pp. 19–31.

Bennis, W. and Nanus, B. (1985) *Leaders: The Strategies for Taking Charge*, New York: Harper & Row.

Bolden, R., Petrov, G. and Gosling, J. (2008) *Developing Collective Leadership in Higher Education*, Final Report, London: Leadership Foundation for Higher Education.

Buchanan, D., Addicott, R., Fitzgerald, L., Ferlie, E. and Baeza, J. (2007) 'Nobody in charge: Distributed agency in health care'. *Human Relations*, 60(7), pp. 1065–90.

Carroll, B. and Levy, L. (2008) 'Defaulting to management: Leadership defined by what it is not'. *Organization*, 15(1), pp. 75–96.

Clarke, J. (2005) 'Performing for the public: Doubt, desire and the evaluation of public services', in P. Du Gay (ed.), *The Values of Bureaucracy*, Oxford: Oxford University Press, pp. 211–32.

Clarke, J., Newman, J., Smith, N., Vidler, E. and Westmarland, L. (2007) *Creating Citizen Consumers: Changing Publics and Changing Public Services*, London: Sage.

Courpasson, D. and Clegg, S. (2012) 'The polyarchic bureaucracy: Cooperative resistance in the workplace and the construction of a new political structure of organizations', in D. Courpasson, D. Golsorkhi and J. Sallaz (eds), *Rethinking Power in Organizations, Institutions and Markets*, Research in the Sociology of Organizations, Vol. 34, Bingley, UK: Emerald Publishing, pp. 55–80.

Crouch, C. (2013) *Making Capitalism Fit for Society*, Cambridge: Polity Press.

Currie, G. (1997) 'Contested terrain: the incomplete closure of managerialism in the health service'. *Health Service Management*, 23(4), pp. 123–32.

Dahl, R. (1971) *Polyarchy; Participation and Opposition*, New Haven, CT: Yale University Press.

Dardot, P. and Laval, C. (2013) *The New Way of the World: On Neoliberal Society*, London: Verso.

Davies, W. (2014) *The Limits of Neoliberalism: Authority, Sovereignty and the Logic of Competition*, London: Sage.

Dent, M. and Whitehead, S. (eds) (2002) *Managing Professional Identities: Knowledge, Performatives and the 'New' Professional*, London: Routledge.

Du Gay, P. (ed.) (2005) *The Values of Bureaucracy*, Oxford: Oxford University Press.

Fairclough, N. (2010) *Critical Discourse Analysis: The Critical Study of Language*, 2nd edn, London: Longman.

Farrell, C. and Morris, J. (2003) 'The neo-bureaucratic state: Professionals, managers and professional managers in schools, general practices and social work'. *Organization*, 10, pp. 129–56.

Fergusson, R. (2000) 'Modernizing managerialism in education', in J. Clarke, S. Gewirtz and E. McLaughlin (eds), *New Managerialism, New Welfare?*, London: Sage, pp. 202–21.

Ferlie, E., Fitzgerald, L., McGivern, G., Dopson, S. and Bennett, C. (2013) *Making Wicked Problems Governable? The Case of Managed Networks in Healthcare*, Oxford: Oxford University Press.

Flynn, N. (2004) 'Soft bureaucracy, governmentality and clinical governance: Theoretical approaches to emergent policy', in A. Gray and S. Harrison (eds), *Governing Medicine: Theory and Practice*, Maidenhead, UK: Open University Press, pp. 1–26.

Ford, J. and Harding, N. (2007) 'Move over management: we are all leaders now'. *Management Learning*, 38(5), pp. 475–98.

Freidson, E. (1973) *Professions and Their Prospects*, New York: Sage.

Freidson, E. (2001) *Professionalism: The Third Logic*, Cambridge: Polity Press.

Gamble, A. (2009) *The Spectre at the Feast: Capitalist Crisis and the Politics of Recession*, Basingstoke, UK: Palgrave Macmillan.

Gamble, A. (2014) *Crisis without End? The Unravelling of Western Prosperity*, Basingstoke, UK: Palgrave Macmillan.

Goldfinch, S. and Wallis, J. (2010) 'Two myths of convergence in public management reform'. *Public Administration* 88 (4), pp. 1099–115.

Harvey, D. (2011) *The Enigma of Capitalism and the Crises of Capitalism*, London: Profile Books.

Hood, C. (1991) 'A public management for all seasons'. *Public Administration*, 69 (1), pp. 3–20.

Jessop, B. (2007) *State Power: A Strategic-Relational Approach*, Cambridge: Polity Press.

Jessop, B. (2014) 'The free economy and the sovereign state'. *Renewal*, 22(3/4), pp. 81–90.

Macdonald, K. (2006) 'Professional work', in M. Korczynski, R. Hodson and P. Edwards (eds), *Social Theory at Work*, Oxford: Oxford University Press, pp. 356–87.

McLaughlin, K., Osborne, S. and Ferlie, E. (eds) (2002) *New Public Management: Current Trends and Future Prospects*, London: Routledge.

McNulty, T. and Ferlie, E. (2004) 'Process transformation: Limitations to radical organizational change within public service organizations'. *Organization Studies*, 25, pp. 1389–412.

Martin, G., Currie, G., and Finn, R. (2009) 'Leadership, service reform, and public-service networks: The case of cancer-genetics pilots in the English NHS'. *Journal of Public Administration Research and Theory*, 19, pp. 769–94.

Miller, D. (2005) 'What is best value? Bureaucracy, virtualism and local governance', in P. Du Gay (ed.), *The Values of Bureaucracy*, Oxford: Oxford University Press, pp. 233–54.

Mirowski, P. (2013) *Never Let a Serious Crisis Go to Waste: How Neoliberalism Survived the Financial Meltdown*, London: Verso.

Monbiot, G. (2014) 'How have these corporations colonized our public life?'. *The Guardian*, 8 April.

Moran, M. (2007) *The British Regulatory State: High Modernism and Hyper-Innovation*, Oxford: Oxford University Press.

Mount, F. (2012) *The New Few or a Very British Oligarchy*, London: Simon & Schuster.

National College for Schools Leadership (2004) *Annual Report and Accounts Performance Review 2003–2004*. Nottingham, UK: National College for Schools Leadership.

Newman, J. (1998) 'Managerialism and social welfare', in G. Hughes and G. Lewis (eds), *Unsettling Welfare: The Reconstruction of Social Policy*, London: Routledge, pp. 333–74.

Newman, J. (2001) *Modernizing Governance: New Labour, Policy and Society*, London: Sage.

Newman, J. (2005) 'Bending bureaucracy: Leadership and multi-level governance', in P. Du Gay (ed.), *The Values of Bureaucracy*, Oxford: Oxford University Press, pp. 191–210.

Newman, J. (2013) 'Professionals, power and the reform of public services', in M. Noordegraaf and B. Steijn (eds), *Professionals under Pressure: The Reconfiguration of Professional Work in Changing Public Services*, Amsterdam: Amsterdam University Press, pp. 41–53.

Noordegraaf, M. and Steijn, B. (eds) (2013) *Professionals under Pressure: The Reconfiguration of Professionals Work in Changing Public Services*, Amsterdam: Amsterdam University Press.

OECD (2001) *Public Service Leadership for the 21st Century*, Paris: Organisation for Economic Co-operation and Development.

OECD (2010) *Making Reform Happen: Lessons from OECD Countries*, Paris: Organisation for Economic Co-operation and Development.

Office of Public Services Reform (2002) *Reforming Our Public Services: Principles into Practice*, London: Office of Public Services Reform.

O'Reilly, D. and Reed, M. (2011) 'The grit in the oyster: Professionalism, managerialism and leaderism as discourses of public services modernization'. *Organization Studies*, 32(8), pp. 1079–101.

Pahl, R. and Winkler, J. (1974) 'The economic elite: Theory and practice', in P. Stanworth and A. Giddens (eds), *Elites and Power in British Society*, Cambridge: Cambridge University Press, pp. 102–22.

Peck, J. (2010) *Construction of Neoliberal Reason*, Oxford: Oxford University Press.

Pollitt, C. (2007) 'New Labour's re-disorganization: Hyper-modernism and the costs of reform – A cautionary tale'. *Public Management Review*, 9(4), pp. 529–43.

Pollitt, C. and Bouckaert, G. (2011) *Public Management Reform: A Comparative Analysis*, 3rd edn, Oxford: Oxford University Press.

Power, M. (2014) 'Risk, social theories, and organizations', in P. Adler, P. Du Gay, G. Morgan and M. Reed (eds), *The Oxford Handbook of Sociology, Social Theory, and Organization Studies: Contemporary Currents*, Oxford: Oxford University Press, pp. 370–92.

Reed, M. (2007) 'Engineers of human souls, faceless technocrats or merchants of morality? Changing professional forms and identities in the face of the neo-liberal challenge', in A. Pinnington, R. Macklin and T. Campbell (eds), *Human Resource Management: Ethics and Employment*, Oxford: Oxford University Press, pp. 171–89.

Reed, M. (2009) 'Bureaucratic theory and intellectual renewal in contemporary organization studies', in P. Adler (ed.), *The Oxford Handbook of Sociology and Organization Studies: Classical Foundations*, Oxford: Oxford University Press, pp. 559–84.

Reed, M. (2012a) 'Masters of the universe: Power and elites in organization studies'. *Organization Studies*, 33(1), pp. 203–22.

Reed, M. (2012b) 'Theorizing power/domination and studying organizational elites: A critical realist perspective', in D. Courpasson, D. Golsorkhi and G. Sallaz (eds), *Rethinking Power in Organizations, Institutions and Markets, Volume 34, Research in the Sociology or Organizations*, Bingley, UK: Emerald Publishing, pp. 21–54.

Reed, M. and Wallace, M. (2015) 'Elite discourses and institutional innovation: Making the hybrid happen in English public services'. *Research in the Sociology of Organizations*, 43, Bingley, UK: Emerald Publishing, pp. 269–302.

Rothkopf, D. (2008) *Superclass: The Global Power Elite and the World they are Making,* London: Little, Brown.

Selznick, R. (1949) *The TVA and the Grass Roots*, Berkeley, CA: University of California Press.

Strategy Unit (2006) *The UK Government's Approach to Public Service Reform – a Discussion Paper*, London: Cabinet Office.

Strategy Unit (2008) *Realizing Britain's Potential: Future Strategic Challenges for Britain*. London: Cabinet Office.

Teelken, C., Ferlie, E. and Dent, M. (eds) (2012) *Leadership in the Public Sector: Promises and Pitfalls*, London: Routledge.

Thomas, R. and Davies, A. (2005) 'Theorizing the micro-politics of resistance: New public management and managerial identities in the UK public services'. *Organization Studies*, 26, pp. 683–706.

Thompson, G. (2003) *Between Hierarchies and Markets: The Logic and Limits of Network Forms of Organization*, Oxford: Oxford University Press.

UK Treasury (2000) *Public Services Productivity: Meeting the Challenge*. A joint report by the Public Services Productivity Panel. London: HM Treasury.

Wallace, M., O'Reilly, D., Morris, J. and Deem, R. (2011) 'Public service leaders as change agents – For whom?', *Public Management Review*, 31, 963–96.

Ward, S. (2014) *Neoliberalism and the Global Restructuring of Knowledge and Education*, London: Routledge.

15

Professional agency, leadership and organizational change

Jean-Louis Denis, Nicolette van Gestel and Annick Lepage

Introduction

Over the past two decades, the diversification and fragmentation of professional roles has progressively developed (Currie, Lockett, and Suhomlinova, 2009; Noordegraaf, 2011a; Adler and Kwon, 2013). More professions with more sub-specialties have created a complex web of experts in various sectors of activities (Evetts, 2003). This web relates to organizations that increasingly operate in flexible (international) networks or chains and often outsource work to third parties. The growing fragmentation of organizations is in turn affecting the changing nature of professional work, with greater diversification among professionals and professional interests (Scott, 1982; Cooper *et al.*, 1996; Noordegraaf, 2011a). In parallel, a growing convergence and proliferation of control structures has been witnessed, as 'professional practice in many sectors is increasingly driven by pressure for revenue generation and accountability to the state and to avoid legal prosecution' (Leicht and Fennell, 1997, p. 219). The traditional view of professional practice as self-regulating and based on 'peer group control' is supplemented with bureaucratic measures for professional production that push toward a greater embodiment of professions within organized settings and the development of strategies to better control risks (Courpasson, 2000; Noordegraaf, 2011a, 2011b; Adler and Kwon, 2013).

Against this background, two contrasting notions have emerged as to how professionals are connected to organizational change. One notion is that organizational change is imposed on professionals (Ackroyd and Muzio, 2007; Adler and Kwon, 2013) with detrimental consequences for their status and autonomy (Evetts, 2011; Hupe and Van der Krogt, 2013). Professionals increasingly must report their decisions to complex systems of accountability for the purpose of remuneration and must spend a growing share of their time on administrative work rather than on supporting their clients (Evetts, 2011). Negative impacts of organizational change on professional status and work are recognized within a broad diversity of research on corporatization (Waring and Bishop, 2013), proletarianization (Reed, 2007), or deskilling of professionals (Currie, Finn, and Martin, 2009) and are associated with a group of sociological theories labelled as 'mutation theories' (Adler and Kwon, 2013).

An alternative, more positive, approach is based on the premise that professionals act as co-creators of organizations and organizational transformations (Suddaby and Viale, 2011). From this perspective, it is argued that professionals are able to influence their work environment, especially when they collaborate (Adler and Kwon, 2013), despite increasing pressures for accountability and transparency and despite multiple regulatory requirements that are often difficult to reconcile (Noordegraaf, 2011a; Hupe and Buffat, 2014). According to this more optimistic notion about the relationship between professionals and organizational change, professionals are viewed as 'agents who possess and develop their own strengths' (Noordegraaf et al., 2014, p. 2) rather than as victims who lack the capability to influence the organizational context according to professional needs and values.

Given these contrasting notions, this chapter aims to clarify and discuss the assumptions and conditions related to the roles and involvement of professionals in organizational change, in line with professional aims and values. We focus on the capability of professionals to develop and deliver their services in a context of various demands and challenges, which may even lead to new roles such as organizational leaders of change.

The chapter is structured as follows. First, we briefly discuss the changing context of professionals in organizations that influence their agency and consequently their role in shaping organizational change. Second, we present a number of concepts from the literature – 'organized professionalism' (Noordegraaf, 2011a), 'governmentality' (Miller and Rose, 2008), and 'pluralistic organizations' (Denis et al., 2007) – that we find useful in examining the link between professional agency and organizational change. Finally, we discuss the implications of these concepts for research and practice.

The context of changing relationships between professionals and organizations

The organization of professional occupations has evolved greatly over the past few decades (Scott, 1982; Muzio et al., 2013). Organizational boundaries have weakened as professional services have been deregulated, global competition has increased within and between professions, and work contexts have changed (Noordegraaf, 2011a; Adler and Kwon, 2013). Some of the changes have involved professionals moving away from solo practices to small organizations or group practices to join the ranks of larger professional organizations (Adler et al., 2008; Evetts, 2011). Overall, professional organizations have gone through a process of inter-archetype transformation because institutional values and ideologies have evolved over the years toward increased reciprocal influence between these two worlds (Cooper et al., 1996; Suddaby and Greenwood, 2001).

The new public management (NPM) appears to be important to the understanding of this context for public professionals and organizations (Currie et al., 2009; Evetts, 2011). Inspired by practices from the private sector, NPM reformists are trying to measure and optimize professional work (Adler and Kwon, 2013). Traditional accountability models such as 'peer group control' are no longer perceived as sufficient to guarantee the performance of professional organizations (Scott, 1982; Adler and Kwon, 2013), and new techniques and guidelines for cost control and production are being implemented to improve the performance of professional work. These organizational changes inspired by NPM may have consequences for professional agency in terms of lower autonomy and a decrease in work motivation (Evetts, 2003).

Along with global and regulatory pressures, accessibility of information and the proliferation of communication channels available to clients have transformed the environment of professionals and their organizations (Ackroyd and Muzio, 2007; Faulconbridge and Muzio, 2008; Currie and White, 2012; see also the chapter by Tonkens in this volume). Clients now have more opportunities to become informed actors, and they expect professionals to reduce the uncertainty related to their needs and requests (Dingwall, 2008; Adler and Kwon, 2013). The diversification and complexity of customer needs regarding professional work has consequences for organizations and professions, with the client increasingly being seen as able to perform a more regulating role (Ackroyd and Muzio, 2007; Cooper et al., 1996; Faulconbridge and Muzio, 2008) rather than being a passive actor (Hupe and Buffat, 2014).

Given these contextual changes, both organizations and professionals are more and more being invited to play active roles in adapting to contextual pressures (Muzio et al., 2013). They are challenged to become actively engaged in an 'assimilation process' in order to maintain, develop, and implement new practices. Without professional engagement in developing such practices, organizational changes in routines, values, and norms cannot be institutionalized (Suddaby and Greenwood, 2001). In the next section, we present some vital concepts from the literature to understand the various ways that professional agency can be related to organizational change.

Professionals as leaders of organizational change: three concepts

Three recently developed central concepts are used in this chapter to understand the role of professionals in organizational changes: 'organized professionalism', 'governmentality', and 'pluralistic organizations'. We selected these concepts to move beyond mutation theory (Adler et al., 2008) in order to explore and understand how transitions in professional organizations and professions may represent opportunities for professional agency. Each of the three concepts has received considerable attention in the literature without their having been related to one another in an explicit way. In this section, we compare and contrast the assumptions, opportunities, and consequences of the three concepts to provide valuable insights into the nature and conditions of professional agency in organizations.

Organized professionalism

The notion of 'organized professionalism' has been proposed to define and understand the emergence of a new synthesis between professions and organizations in contemporary societies. This convergence of organizational logic and professional logic is considered in itself a process of change, as underlined by Noordegraaf (2011b, p. 469): 'Traditionally, professionals are *not* "made" to act as organizational members. They are made into "professional" workers who treat cases and clients as effectively and responsibly as possible.' This new convergence is based on evolving contingencies, task complexity, interdependence, and responsibilities (Noordegraaf, 2011a, 2011b). The notion of organized professionalism does not address a new phenomenon, but one could argue that the interest in this concept is symptomatic of increased pressure to renew and, in some cases, to intensify the relationships between organizations and professions. Given the purpose of our chapter, we reconstruct a representation of professional agency within this idea of organized professionalism.

Underlying the concept of organized professionalism is the assumption that both sides of the relationship (professions and organizations) respond to societal demands for changes in the nature of their relations, roles, and positions. Noordegraaf (2011a) invites us to go beyond promulgating dualisms (e.g. occupational versus organizational control, professionals versus managers) to better understand how both professions and organizations mutually adapt to evolving contingencies. He identifies this gap in the contemporary literature on professionals and organizations:

> Although they highlight the potential interweaving of organizational and professional domains, they generally portray organizational and professional behaviour as intrinsically

conflicting. They do not really clarify whether and how organizations and professionals can work together in the face of contextual change.

(Noordegraaf, 2011a, p. 1350)

The concept of organized professionalism has been useful in identifying the elements that favour the involvement of professionals in organizational change, for example, changing work preferences, a need to adapt professional work to the delivery of services in inter-professional teams, and regulatory measures to better regulate the quality and safety of professional services. Implementing the organized professionalism agenda is even presented as a necessary condition to ensure the joint legitimacy of professions and organizations. In our view, professional agency materializes within this context as a result of the growing interdependence of organizational performance and professional virtuosity (Waring and Currie, 2009; Muzio et al., 2013).

According to Noordegraaf (2011b), these changes are also partly shaped and promoted by the work of professional associations and institutions of higher education, which have progressively incorporated new standards in professional practices, a process documented empirically by Kitchener and Mertz (2012) in the case of American dentistry. These professional associations often get involved in change processes and act as leaders of change from outside the organizations, for example by advocating for new standards of practice. According to Noordegraaf, organizations, professionals, and managers are jointly (more or less) defining connective organizational standards that put professional practices in a broader context. Professional practices thus become more collective and organized in this process.

In the conclusion of his article on organized professionalism, Noordegraaf (2011a) suggests that such convergence between professions and organizations will not materialize automatically. Despite the ambition to transcend the conflictual dynamic assumed by mutation theories, politics and power relations will remain in the realm of so-called 'organized professionalism' and may limit the penetration of organizational principles in the professional world. Consequently, we argue that to better understand the role of professionals in organizational change, we need to identify the conditions under which managers and professionals perceive their collaboration for change as an effective strategy to respond to new societal demands. In other words, we need to understand how demands for a renewal of the relationship between professions and organizations are translated into transformative capacities and to identify what role professional agency plays in this process.

Engaging professionals in organizational change

Managerial elites cannot by themselves reconstruct expert organizations and transcend the dichotomies between professionals and managers and between occupational and organizational control (Noordegraaf, 2011a). The involvement, collaboration, and leadership of professionals are essential in this process. As we noted, the growing role of professional associations (Noordegraaf, 2011b; Kitchener and Mertz, 2012) in generating and prescribing standards for practice improvement (Timmermans and Epstein, 2010; Brunsson, Rashe, and Seidle, 2012) generates a set of changes that are professionally induced. Again, we are not describing a new phenomenon here. Professional associations have long been involved in the governance of professions in the United States, Canada, and Europe. However, we refer here to an intensification of their role in promoting innovations in practice. For example, quality and safety of care have been emphasized in the work performed by professional associations in many jurisdictions. We believe that changes in professional practice can only be activated and implemented through the development of an organizational context that is receptive to them, as has been suggested in recent works on clinical governance in the healthcare sector (Bohmer, 2011).

According to Noordegraaf, within the context of 'organized professionalism' the involvement of professionals as protagonists of change is structured around three dimensions of professional work: (i) their involvement in the improvement of practices through the use of evidence in order to better manage risks of all sorts (Noordegraaf, 2011a; Adler and Kwon, 2013); (ii) their participation in teams and in the development of an extended multi-professionalism as a resource for the adaptation of services to evolving expectations and needs of clients (Evetts, 2003; Falconbridge and Muzio, 2008; Noordegraaf, 2011a); and (iii) the development of competencies that reflect a more salient organizational ethos and imperatives within professionals' mindsets (Muzio *et al.*, 2011; Noordegraaf, 2011a; Waring and Bishop, 2013). In all these spheres, strict bureaucratic and external control is not considered a viable solution to societal demands for greater accountability and more effective professional services (Flynn, 2004; Adler *et al.*, 2008). For example, the translation of practice guidelines in healthcare into effective practices is mediated by a complex social process of learning and adaptation in which professional leaders play a key role (Ferlie *et al.*, 2005; Noordegraaf, 2011a).

Engagement of professionals in teams is favoured by organizational contexts where more distributed forms of leadership are valued (Denis *et al.*, 2012). More collaborative forms of work require broad and coercive regulations (external governance) but also relate to intense work by and with professionals within organizations to create the conditions for collaboration (Ferlie *et al.*, 2005; Currie and White, 2012). Adler and colleagues (2008) have documented the various dimensions and processes involved in such a collaborative shift in organizing professional work. Overall, there is a growing consensus around the need to organize professional practices on a more collective basis to support learning, effectiveness, and innovation (Orlikowski, 2002). The motivation behind such involvement of professionals in change processes is driven by the preservation of value-rationality as a fundamental principle of professional action (Adler *et al.*, 2008).

According to our assessment of the concept of organized professionalism, professionals will thus play an essential leadership role in renewing work arrangements and adapting their work to complexity and interdependence. It is through their leadership and agency that transformations of organizational processes are based on expert advice, and that learning and collaboration are maintained and expanded under changing circumstances (Noordegraaf, 2011a). While the concept of 'organized professionalism' thus opens up a valuable approach to understanding the roles of professionals in organizational change, we believe that more attention should be given to the tensions and ambiguities associated with the process of convergence between organizational goals and professional practices. In the next sections we elaborate on the potential conflicts and uncertainties in professional roles related to organizational change, building on the concepts of 'governmentality' and 'pluralistic organizations'.

Governmentality

Critical thoughts on the role of professionals in leading change have recently been articulated in the works of the Anglo-governmentalists, with their growing interest in empirical application of Foucault's works to the study of broad societal transformations and their consequences for day-to-day practices (Rose *et al.*, 2006; Martin *et al.*, 2013). For example, in a study of criminal justice, Rose (2000) suggests that regulations and control in contemporary society cannot be understood properly without attention to the problem of agency:

> And mobility and contestability is further enhanced by the fact that contemporary strategies for the government of conduct, far from seeking to crush and eliminate the capacities for action of those persons and forces they act upon, on the contrary seek to foster and shape

such capacities so that they are enacted in ways that are broadly consistent with particular objectives such as order, civility, health or enterprise.

(p. 323)

Agency is an inextricable component of the contemporary governmentality project. The creation of space to activate new forms of control in organizations requires the active participation of agents with their potential for resistance to and reframing of forms of control (Ferlie *et al.*, 2012; Martin *et al.*, 2013). Pressures to develop and impose new forms of control are considered instances of organizational change in professional settings.

Our objective in this chapter is not to provide a systematic analysis of the tensions or complementarities between disciplinary power and governmentality, as proposed by Martin and colleagues, but to use the recent studies to explore the question of professional agency in organizational change. Anglo-governmentalists have found in the works of Foucault a conceptual apparatus to examine processes of change, such as the use and spread of more diffuse control or regulatory practices (Miller and Rose, 2008). Somewhat distinct from the 'organized professionalism' approach, their interest lies in how change is produced and reproduced through less visible or tangible processes. The concept of 'governmentality' raises the question of how to think about professional agency in a context that focuses on imposing control through monitoring and transparencies and on the embodiment of control through complex internalization processes (subjectification). Such control may end up in self-discipline and a less conscious participation of professionals in transformations.

According to the governmentality approach, the emergence of new control systems in professional settings is intimately related to the constitution of new knowledge such as data and information on risks, quality, and safety. New regulatory regimes take shape through systematic use of this knowledge that makes the activities of professionals more visible for scrutiny. Recent studies in healthcare, for example, have suggested that these regimes cannot develop and proliferate without the active participation of informed agents such as professionals (Ferlie *et al.*, 2012; Martin *et al.*, 2013; Ferlie and McGivern, 2014). Professional agency and the ambition to impose control on professional work thus co-exist somewhat. The process of subjectification that is central to the concept of governmentality cannot take form without the involvement of professionals in creating the conditions for their own subjectification.

Recognizing the role of professional agency in the governmentality concept leaves open the question of the distributed nature of their capacities to shape new regimes of control. A long-standing hypothesis of the sociology of professions suggests that only a specific segment of professions, a new professional elite, will actively participate in the governmentality project. The proliferation of standards (Muzio and Kirkpatrick, 2011; Noordegraaf, 2011a), standard setters (Cooper *et al.*, 1996; Ackroyd and Muzio, 2007; Currie *et al.*, 2009; Adler and Kwon, 2013), and decision-support tools (Frey *et al.*, 2013) in various professional practices is certainly symptomatic of a growing investment by a professional elite in generating new systems and devices. These changes simultaneously contribute to rethinking and reframing professional autonomy (Evetts, 2003) and to potentially improving professional practice (Adler and Kwon, 2013), but they leave aside the question of the participation of the majority of professionals in these transformations in day-to-day working life.

From a different angle, professionals can participate in the shaping and leadership of change based on their own values, experiences, and views. They not only become involved as a professional elite to generate the tools that are used in the new context of 'organized professionalism' but from a governmentality perspective, professionals within organizations (the operators as opposed to the regulators) can also deploy resistance or reinterpret imposed control or regulatory regimes (Rose *et al.*, 2006; Adler *et al.*, 2008; Currie *et al.*, 2009; Waring and Currie, 2009). They are active agents in the contextualization of these new forms of control (DiMaggio, 1991; Waring and Bishop, 2013), as exemplified by the notion of organizational closure (Faulconbridge and Muzio, 2008; see also Muzio *et al.*, 2011; Noordegraaf *et al.*, 2014) where professionals recreate work arrangements in organizations that in the end protect their core values and aspirations.

While the governmentality approach is coherent with the idea of professional agency (Evetts, 2003), the use of agency capacity in the context of organizational change is thus more problematic here at first sight than in the works on 'organized professionalism'. From a governmentality perspective, professionals can be affirmative in their response to growing institutional reflexivity and can intervene in the co-evolution of power and knowledge, as exemplified by the generation of tools and systems to regulate practices. Professionals are not necessarily subjugated by these 'new systems', and their reactions cannot be limited to the internalization of norms with its consequences in terms of self-discipline.

However, one must keep in mind that the governmentality project also represents risks for the professional project. The imposition of new standards on practice may culminate in a kind of subjugated agency where participation in meeting more demanding standards can lead to an intense competition among professionals that may undermine collegiality as a legitimate collective form of control (Teelken, 2015). As Evetts (2003) suggests, the dynamic of performance and competition may culminate in a restratification of professions where emerging professional elites are involved in the creation and recreation of norms for higher performance. Such potential perverse effects on professions and professionalism of their active engagement with new standards has not been explicitly discussed by Adler and colleagues (2008) when they propose collaborative work as the essence of the new professional ethos.

These potential perverse effects are at first sight difficult to reconcile with the study of Faulconbridge and Muzio (2008) on lawyers in organizations. They, as we noted above, suggest that professionals are able to achieve a kind of organizational closure as an act of mediation between broad social forces, their day-to-day practices, and their professional norms. Faulconbridge and Muzio (2008) suggest that, similar to professional roles in organized professionalism, professionals lead changes in these firms by participating in a process of adaptation of professional aspirations to organizational or corporate goals. For professionals, leading organizational change will thus imply their capacity to shape this process of institutional reflexivity to achieve an acceptable equilibrium between professional and organizational projects.

While the principle of organizational closure offers a plausible solution to the dilemma of renewing the relations between professions and organizations without putting professional aims and ethos too much at risk, recent analysis of professions and professionalism indicates that much effort is needed to achieve such a level of protection (Falconbridge and Muzio, 2008; Adler and Kwon, 2013).

Our discussion of professionals and organizational change from a governmentality perspective suggests that professionals can take an active role in translating new forms of control and standards for their work context in line with what they value. In doing so, they may build on practices of professionals to translate change into workable options for their development in, for example, a study on major transformations in the forest industry in Canada, as discussed by Zietsma and Lawrence (2010). These authors identify a set of practices that support the ability of actors to create a protected space within the field where innovation and experimentation with new models become possible. By analogy, professionals may invent and deploy practices in such experimental settings to create effective mediations between new external forms of control and self-regulation.

We now turn to another vital concept, that of pluralistic organizations, to understand the opportunities and limits of professional agency in a context of organizational change to improve our understanding of the plural context in which professionals operate.

Strategic change in pluralistic organizations

One way to characterize organizational context as a setting for the role of professionals in leading change is found in the notion of pluralistic organizations (Denis *et al.*, 2007). The term refers to organizations with multiple goals and commitments and where authority is conferred upwards (Cooper *et al.*, 1996). Empirical studies of strategic change in pluralistic organizations (Denis *et al.*, 2007; Currie *et al.*, 2009; Martin *et al.*, 2009) have documented the various roles of professionals in change processes. For example, a representation of professional agency in bringing about changes in pluralistic contexts is captured through a study on collective and distributed leadership (Denis *et al.*, 2012). In their study of knowledge brokering among professionals within the National Health System (NHS), Currie and White (2012) show that professionals perform a kind of rhetorical work that impacts on organizational or field-level changes. The valuation of new frames like 'integration of care' helps some professional groups to gain agency in front of predominant professional groups and at the same time shapes a reformative template. While there is asymmetry among professional groups in their ability to lead change processes within organizations, the capacity of some groups to mobilize new reformative templates or ideas in their day-to-day work appears critical in developing leadership roles in change (Cloutier *et al.*, 2015).

In fact, the notion of profession has been intimately linked to the one of change. In a paper on professions as institutions, Scott (2008) insists that professional projects can only be achieved and sustained by the constant exercise of agency. Professionalism is a contested and unstable construct that needs to be constantly reaffirmed and transformed through professional agency. According to Scott (2008), the roles of professionals in the production of changes can be classified in three categories: creators, carriers, and clinical professionals. Creators invent transformative ideas that change professions, their practices, and consequently organizations. Examples of creators are found in the invention of new models of intervention like the advanced chronic disease management model in healthcare special education policies (see, e.g. Ontario Ministry of Education 2006), or community health nursing (De Blok and Pool, 2013). Carriers are the disseminators who propagate new ideas in a given field and, consequently, play a transformative role. Clinical professionals bring about changes through the application of knowledge to specific cases and through incremental adjustments in practices. In all these roles, professionals are agents of change who mobilize their power and resources to achieve their projects.

In pluralistic contexts, distributed capacities (expertise, influence, legitimacy) mean that professionals are in a position to shape change. However, professional agency not only impacts professional projects but also reverberates to reflect the broader organizational and institutional processes (Suddaby and Viale, 2011). In contrast to the concept of organized professionalism, the literature on distributed leadership and pluralistic organizations does not emphasize that professional and organizational projects converge due to a set of contingencies. In this literature, leadership is defined as 'the dispersion of leadership roles across organizations, and even beyond their boundaries, as a variety of people relay leadership responsibilities over time to achieve important outcomes' (Denis *et al.*, 2012, p. 241). It is recognized here that contradictions and resistance permeate the processes of organizational change (Denis *et al.*, 2002; Currie *et al.*, 2009; Martin *et al.*, 2009), and the idea of professions as an endogenous force of change is considered in more problematic terms. Even change is problematized as an emergent phenomenon with uncertain boundaries. Professionals shape change through their day-to-day practices, but these changes are not necessarily aligned with corporate or organizational goals.

The idea of professional leadership as an adequate representation of professionals' agency in organizational change is challenged by an empirical study by Reed and colleagues (see Chapter 14 by Reed in this Companion). They found that the call for professional leadership to implement large-scale restructuring in public services in England revealed intense pressures by reformers to transform sectors and activities, with negative impact on the status and autonomy of professionals and civil servants. They consider this situation as an illustration of 'leaderism', where a call for a voluntary engagement in reforms masks the imposition of policies by a central authority that impacts negatively on the public sector. Leadership is equivalent here to a discourse used to enrol professionals in change and transformations potentially in conflict with their values and interests. Leadership discourses thus may permeate change processes and influence how professionals connect with changes in their day-to-day work. To understand the roles of professionals in organizational changes, we therefore need to analyse how broad reformative templates and structural determinants (for example, neo-liberal reforms) shape and influence the micro-practices of professionals involved in formal and informal leadership roles, and inversely as well. The framing of professional agency in organizations within a highly distributed context with severe pressures for change needs to be explored in more detail.

A review on plural forms of leadership (Denis *et al.*, 2012) argues that a key challenge for contemporary organizations is to channel the latent leadership capacity that is embodied in the knowledge of professional workers. The involvement of various actors in leadership roles may be performed within the context of a variety of ideological positions and objectives, as studies on leaderism suggest. Works on collective and distributive leadership also suggest that professional agency is a key asset in structuring a group of leaders who can support (or not!) organizational change. To maintain a kind of collective agency in leading change is, however, a challenge, and demonstrates the fragility of leadership roles and positions in pluralist organizations (Denis *et al.*, 2002). When professionals get involved in leading change, they necessarily share their leadership roles with other powerful actors and broader organizational interests (Suddaby and Viale, 2011). Such sharing of positions and the negotiation of goals and objectives may be a source of increased differentiation among professionals, where those who carry on the 'organizational agenda' for change can gain access to powerful positions within their field.

Discussion

For many years, the theorizing of professions as linked to organizations has been dominated by a focus on the controversial relationship between the two worlds. The relationship between professionals and organizations has been portrayed extensively as dichotomous and intrinsically conflicting (Waring and Currie, 2009). Organizations are perceived as investing in structural approaches and managerial instruments to discipline professionals rather than in strategies to rely on and develop professional commitment (Adler and Kwon, 2013). Recently, we have begun to observe more optimistic views on the relationship between professions and organizations, suggesting the idea of co-evolving strategies of professionals and organizations in response to endogenous and exogenous demands (e.g. changes in client–professional relationships, new government regulations, and global pressures for competition). Work by Adler and Kwon (2013) on professional communities as a form of social organization that develops within formal organizational structures suggests that tensions can be transcended. Similarly, works by Noordegraaf (2011a, 2011b, 2014) see in the intensification of reciprocal relations between organizations and professions a new synthesis that also transcends tensions and contradictions. Based on our discussion of three vital concepts in understanding professional agency and leadership – organized professionalism, governmentality, and strategic change in pluralistic organizations – we argue that both propositions (pessimistic or optimistic) are probably too simplistic to convey a realistic picture of professions and organizational change. Although we believe that there is room for professional agency in positively influencing organizational change, we have argued all along in this chapter that such positive accommodations imply a demanding process of investments and change on the part of both organizations and professions.

Opportunities and challenges to professional agency related to organizations and change cannot be captured by a focus on either controversy or harmony. Based on the three concepts of professional agency on which we focus, we suggest that there are many (and competing) meanings of professionals as leaders of change. We argue for an understanding of professional agency as involving opportunities for leadership in terms of co-evolving strategies with organizations, as well as resistance to developments that are perceived as suppressing or denying professionals' specific qualities and contributions. Commitment and resistance are considered intrinsic properties of how professional agency develops within the context of changes. We believe that the way in which professionals develop their agency and collaborate with organizations is always a political process contingent on the interests and values of the participants and their ability to advance them while being conscious of their dependence upon organized settings in their quest for professional virtuosity and legitimacy.

Our reading of the literature indicates that it would be wise to move away from a unitary view of professionalism and professions in their relation to organizational change. Gaining distance from a unitary view should not be made at the expense of a more realistic and less normative approach to the role of professionals as leaders of organizational change. The idea of professionals as leaders of change can, in fact, be misleading when the real issue is how professionals exert agency to reformulate the professional project in the context of change and how this reformulation is associated (or not) with more active or explicit leadership roles in driving change. We need also to take into account that professionals shape change through their activities and practices. For example, the concept of organized professionalism is implicitly attached to the idea that professional and organizational transformations are co-constitutive and can co-evolve in response to endogenous and exogenous changes. Organizational adaptation becomes impossible without professional agency. However, the view that is promoted of professional agency where a variety of contingencies create an inevitable convergence and harmonization between professions and organizations is probably too deterministic.

Studies of governmentality identify how professionals, through various mechanisms of subjectification, become agents of change. The propensity of professionals to lead change is (at least partly) nurtured by their involvement in a process of institutional reflexivity. The exposure of professionals to new regimes of governance shapes the expression of their agency and creates new leadership opportunities. The consequences for the professional ethos of involvement in such leadership roles is an open empirical question. As noted before, studies based on the concept of leaderism are sceptical of the capacity of professional leadership to promote productive relationships between organizations and professions. Studies on pluralistic organizations have revealed how professionals in such contexts participate actively in a non-linear process of change marked by contradictions, tensions, and collaboration among a wide range of actors. The ability to secure a position as a leader of change in such a context is challenging even for powerful professionals. Moreover, the consequences of professional agency as expressed in leadership roles are problematic and may in the end undermine professionals' ability to exert influence.

In sum, we suggest that there is much more variation in leadership roles of professionals than is implied in either a focus on problematic aspects of the relationship between professionals and organizations or a positive view in regard to opportunities for agreement and co-creation. Based on the literature review in this chapter, we emphasize that the notion of professionals as leaders of change is multifaceted. Leadership cannot be associated only with attempts to generate proportional organizational and professional benefits. There are other ways for professionals to demonstrate agency that do not align with how their organizations seek to adapt to changing environments. One can argue that passivity or resistance, in particular for more powerful professions, is also a demonstration of their agency in a context of change. Professionals may resist specific changes to protect their values and aspirations, which is in itself a demonstration of their agency and leadership. Such resistance may not necessarily imply the continuation of traditional systems and practices.

The literature review also demonstrates that different outcomes may occur following the intensification of organizing in professional practices (Ferlie *et al.*, 2005; Falconbridge and Muzio, 2008). Professionals may find ways to accommodate these new pressures for accountability, higher reliability, and greater responsiveness to clients' needs, or they may see in change challenges to professional projects and aspirations. Thus, in all cases, professionals develop strategies to influence and deal with the evolving context of their practice (Noordegraaf, 2011a; Adler and Kwon, 2013; Muzio *et al.*, 2013). We suggest that more attention should be paid in future research to how professional agency plays out in actual organizational change processes – a promising avenue to better understand how organizational and professional transformations are intimately linked.

Conclusion

This chapter reveals that many changes in the context of professional practice and the embodiment of professionals in organized work settings have an impact on professionals and their work; however, professionals' roles in organizational change can only be elucidated by studying the evolution of their capacity for agency in these situations. It has often been suggested that professionals in leadership roles should go beyond taking a traditional attitude of protecting autonomy and improving material positions and move beyond their usual tasks of delivering professional services (Evetts, 2003). In line with these studies, we suggest a more dynamic and practice-based approach to understanding how professionals get involved in organizational transformations (Denis and Van Gestel, 2015).

One consequence of a dynamic and practice-based approach is to better understand how professionals become closely involved in processes of decision-making on organizational change (Suddaby and Viale, 2011; Muzio *et al.*, 2013). Such involvement, as we have seen, can take various forms. It also implies the possibility that professionals may develop generative mechanisms to reframe their work and autonomy (Reed, 2009). Examples of such generative mechanisms can be found in the collaborative organizational community as one of the main foundations of contemporary professional work (Adler *et al.*, 2008) and in a more explicit recognition of the distributed aspects of leadership in professional or expert organizations and their consequences for the expression of leadership in change processes (Denis *et al.*, 2012).

References

Ackroyd, S., and Muzio, D. (2007) 'The reconstructed professional firm: Explaining change in English legal practices'. *Organization Studies*, 28(5), pp. 729–47.

Adler, P. S., and Kwon, S.-W. (2013) 'The mutation of professionalism as a contested diffusion process: Clinical guidelines as carriers of institutional change in medicine'. *Journal of Management Studies*, 50(5), pp. 930–62.

Adler, P. S., Kwon, S.-W., and Heckscher, C. (2008) 'Perspective-professional work: The emergence of collaborative community'. *Organization Science*, 19(2), pp. 359–76.

Bohmer, R. M. (2011) 'The four habits of high-value health care organizations'. *New England Journal of Medicine*, 365(22), pp. 2045–47.

Brunsson, N., Rasche, A., and Seidl, D. (2012) 'The dynamics of standardization: Three perspectives on standards in organization studies'. *Organization Studies*, 33(5–6), pp. 613–32.

Cloutier, C., Denis, J.-L., Langley, A., and Lamothe, L. (2015) 'Agency at the managerial interface: Public sector reform as institutional work'. *Journal of Public Administration Research and Theory*, online *doi: 10.1093/jopart/muv009*.

Cooper, D. J., Hinings, B., Greenwood, R., and Brown, J. L. (1996) 'Sedimentation and transformation in organizational change: the case of Canadian law firms'. *Organization Studies*, 17(4), pp. 623–47.

Courpasson, D. (2000) 'Managerial strategies of domination: power in soft bureaucracies'. *Organization Studies*, 21(1), pp. 141–61.

Currie, G., and White, L. (2012) 'Inter-professional barriers and knowledge brokering in an organizational context: The case of healthcare'. *Organization Studies*, 33(10), pp. 1333–61.

Currie, G., Finn, R., and Martin, G. (2009) 'Professional competition and modernizing the clinical workforce in the NHS'. *Work, Employment and Society*, 23(2), pp. 267–84.

Currie, G., Lockett, A., and Suhomlinova, O. (2009) 'The institutionalization of distributed leadership: A "Catch-22" in English public services'. *Human Relations*, 62(11), pp. 1735–61.

De Blok, J., and Pool, A. (2013) *Community nursing: Humanity above bureaucracy.* (Dutch title: Buurtzorg, menselijkheid boven bureaucratie.) The Hague: Boom Uitgevers.

Denis, J.-L., and Van Gestel, N. (2015) 'Leadership and innovation in healthcare governance'. In E. Kuhlmann, R. H., Blank, I. L. Bourgeault, and C. Wendt (eds), *The Palgrave international handbook of healthcare policy and governance* (pp. 425–41). Palgrave Macmillan.

Denis, J.-L., Lamothe, L., and Langley, A. (2002) 'The dynamics of collective leadership and strategic change in pluralistic organizations'. *Academy of Management Journal*, 44(4), pp. 809–37.

Denis, J.-L., Langley, A., and Rouleau, L. (2007) 'Strategizing in pluralistic contexts: Rethinking theoretical frames'. *Human Relations*, 60(1), pp. 179–215.

Denis, J.-L., Langley, A., and Sergi, V. (2012) 'Leadership in the plural'. *Academy of Management Annals*, 6(1), pp. 211–83.

DiMaggio, P. J. (1991) 'Constructing an organizational field as a professional project: US art museums, 1920–1940'. In P. J. DiMaggio and W. W. Powell (eds), *The new institutionalism in organizational analysis* (Vol. 17). Chicago, IL: University of Chicago Press.

Dingwall, R. (2008) *Essays on professions.* Aldershot, UK: Ashgate.

Evetts, J. (2003) 'The sociological analysis of professionalism: Occupational change in the modern world'. *International Sociology*, 18(2), pp. 395–415.

Evetts, J. (2011) 'A new professionalism? Challenges and opportunities'. *Current Sociology*, 59(4), pp. 406–22.

Faulconbridge, J., and Muzio, D. (2008) 'Organizational professionalism in globalizing law firms'. *Work, Employment and Society*, 22(1), pp. 7–25.

Ferlie, E., and McGivern, G. (2014) 'Bringing Anglo-governmentality into public management scholarship: The case of evidence-based medicine in UK health care'. *Journal of Public Administration Research and Theory*, 24(1), pp. 59–83.

Ferlie, E., Fitzgerald, L., Wood, M., and Hawkins, C. (2005) 'The nonspread of innovations: The mediating role of professionals'. *Academy of Management Journal*, 48(1), pp. 117–34.

Ferlie, E., McGivern, G., and FitzGerald, L. (2012) 'A new mode of organizing in health care? Governmentality and managed networks in cancer services in England'. *Social Science & Medicine*, 74(3), pp. 340–47.

Flynn, R. (2004) '"Soft-bureaucracy", governmentality and clinical governance: theoretical approaches to emergent policy'. In A. Gray and S. Harrison (eds), *Governing medicine.* Maidenhead, UK: Open University Press.

Frey, B. S., Homberg, F., and Osterloh, M. (2013) 'Organizational control systems and pay-for-performance in the public service'. *Organization Studies*, 34(7), pp. 949–72.

Hupe, P., and Buffat, A. (2014) 'A public service gap: Capturing contexts in a comparative approach of street-level bureaucracy'. *Public Management Review*, 16(4), pp. 548–69.

Hupe, P., and Van der Krogt, T. (2013) 'Professionals dealing with pressures'. In M. Noordegraaf and B. Steijn (eds), *Professionals under pressure* (pp. 55–72). Amsterdam: Amsterdam University Press.

Kitchener, M., and Mertz, E. (2012) 'Professional projects and institutional change in healthcare: The case of American dentistry'. *Social Science & Medicine*, 74(3), pp. 372–80.

Leicht, K. T., and Fennell, M. L. (1997) 'The changing organizational context of professional work'. *Annual Review of Sociology*, 23, pp. 215–31.

Martin, G. P., Currie, G., and Finn, R. (2009) 'Reconfiguring or reproducing intra-professional boundaries? Specialist expertise, generalist knowledge and the "modernization" of the medical workforce'. *Social Science & Medicine*, 68(7), pp. 1191–98.

Martin, G. P., Leslie, M., Minion, J., Willars, J., and Dixon-Woods, M. (2013) 'Between surveillance and subjectification: Professionals and the governance of quality and patient safety in English hospitals'. *Social Science and Medicine*, 99, pp. 80–88.

Miller, P., and Rose, N. (2008) *Governing the present: Administering economic, social and personal life*. London, UK: Polity Press.

Muzio, D., and Kirkpatrick, I. (2011) 'Introduction: Professions and organizations: A conceptual framework'. *Current Sociology*, 59(4), pp. 389–405.

Muzio, D., Kirkpatrick, I., and Kipping, M. (2011) 'Professions, organizations and the state: Applying the sociology of the professions to the case of management consultancy'. *Current Sociology*, 59(6), pp. 805–24.

Muzio, D., Brock, D. M., and Suddaby, R. (2013) 'Professions and institutional change: Towards an institutionalist sociology of the professions'. *Journal of Management Studies*, 50(5), pp. 699–721.

Noordegraaf, M. (2011a) 'Risky business: How professionals and professional fields (must) deal with organizational issues'. *Organization Studies*, 32(10), pp. 1349–71.

Noordegraaf, M. (2011b) 'Remaking professionals? How associations and professional education connect professionalism and organizations'. *Current Sociology*, 59(4), pp. 465–88.

Noordegraaf, M., Van Loon, N., Heerma, M. and Weggemans, M. (2014) 'Professional capability: Towards a positive approach to professionals in the public sector'. *Paper for the Netherlands Institute of Government (NIG) conference*, Delft University of Technology, 27–28 November 2014.

Ontario Ministry of Education. 2006 *Education for All: The Report of the Expert Panel on Literacy and Numeracy*. www.edu.gov.on.ca/eng/document/reports/speced/panel/speced.pdf.

Orlikowski, W. J. (2002) 'Knowing in practice: Enacting a collective capability in distributed organizing'. *Organization Science*, 13(3), pp. 249–73.

Reed, M. (2007) 'Engineers of human souls, faceless technocrats or merchants of morality? Changing professional forms and identities in the face of the neo-liberal challenge'. In A. Pinnington, R. Macklin, and T. Campbell (eds), *Human resource management: Ethics and employment* (pp. 171–89). Oxford: Oxford University Press.

Reed, M. (2009) 'Critical realism: Philosophy, method, or philosophy in search of a method'. In D. A. Buchanan and A. Bryman (eds), *The Sage handbook of organizational research methods* (pp. 430–48). London: Sage.

Rose, N. (2000) 'Government and control'. *British Journal of Criminology*, 40(2), pp. 321–39.

Rose, N., O'Malley, P., and Valverde, M. (2006). 'Governmentality'. *Annual Review of Law and Social Science*, 2, pp. 83–104.

Scott, W. R. (1982) 'Managing professional work: Three models of control for health organizations'. *Health Services Research*, 17, pp. 213–40.

Scott, W. R. (2008) 'Lords of the dance: Professionals as institutional agents'. *Organization Studies*, 29(2), pp. 219–38.

Suddaby, R., and Greenwood, R. (2001) 'The colonization of knowledge: Commodification as a dynamic of change in professional service firms'. *Human Relations*, 54(7), pp. 933–53.

Suddaby, R., and Viale, T. (2011) 'Professionals and field-level change: Institutional work and the professional project'. *Current Sociology*, 59(4), pp. 423–42.

Teelken, C. (2015) 'Hybridity, coping mechanisms and academic performance management: Comparing three countries'. *Public Administration*, 93 (2), pp. 307–23.

Timmermans, S., and Epstein, S. (2010) 'A world of standards but not a standard world: Toward a sociology of standards and standardization'. *Annual Review of Sociology*, 36, pp. 69–89.

Waring, J., and Bishop, S. (2013) 'McDonaldization or commercial re-stratification: Corporatization and the multimodal organisation of English doctors'. *Social Science & Medicine*, 82, pp. 147–55.

Waring, J., and Currie, G. (2009) 'Managing expert knowledge: Organizational challenges and managerial futures for the UK medical profession'. *Organization Studies*, 30, pp. 755–78.

Zietsma, C., and Lawrence, T. B. (2010) 'Institutional work in the transformation of an organizational field: The interplay of boundary work and practice work'. *Administrative Science Quarterly*, 55(2), pp. 189–221.

Part IV
Global professionalism and the emerging economies

Introduction

Ivy Lynn Bourgeault

Introduction

By the very nature of the esoteric body of knowledge that is captured and marketed by modern professions, they transcend national boundaries. In this section, we touch upon some of the unique variations of the globalized professions of accounting and finance with that of healthcare – which bookends this section. In between, we examine three case studies of the unique context of local professionalism in the emerging economies of post-colonial South Africa and India and the shift from communist to post-communist Russia. Together these papers begin to address some of the key gaps in our knowledge left by typical analyses of the professions focused on Anglo-American societies.

We begin, first, with Colin Haslam's contribution entitled, 'Accountancy, finance and banking: The global reach of the professions'. The argument Haslam develops in this chapter is that the institutions governing the accountancy and allied finance professionals actively contribute to the ongoing development of the financialized global banking business model. The accounting profession and its associated institutions are prima facie guided by a conceptual framework which places the 'investor' at the centre of resource stewardship and corporate governance. This governing framework serves two interrelated objectives: first, the need to report to investors about resource stewardship and, second, the need to contribute to the efficient functioning of capital markets for investors. That is, accounting and finance professionals are an active ingredient driving financial innovation and adaptation within the financialized banking business model. Indeed, accounting and finance professionals are not only called upon to develop new financial products but are handsomely rewarded if this contributes to generating higher profits. But accounting and finance professionals need to ensure that resources are stewarded in a 'prudential' manner and they need to focus on preserving financial stability in the 'public interest'. The recent banking crisis and increasingly lengthy charge sheet of poor conduct and excessive risk taking calls into question the legitimacy of accounting and financial specialists in relation to safeguarding society. Indeed, Haslam describes how there has been a need for a public relations effort to restore trust in the accounting and finance profession after the financial crisis. He concludes that the accounting and finance profession needs to redefine its purpose and objectives and play its role in limiting the moral hazard arising from a financialized banking business model. This would require a substantial reorientation in the conceptual framework that governs the behaviour and priorities of the accounting and finance professional in our banks.

In the following chapter, 'Professions and professionalism in emerging economies: The case of South Africa', Debby Bonnin and Shaun Ruggunan describe how the key transformations witnessed in the South African professions reflect a post-apartheid project of racial and, to a lesser extent, gendered transformation. The primary purpose of their chapter is to consider how this transformation project is affecting South African professionals. The chapter examines recent developments in professions in South Africa, highlighting four key developments. First, they detail the strategies developed by the state, professional bodies and educational/training institutions to effect racial transformation in the composition of traditional professions. Second, they outline key developments in the state regulation of some of the traditional professions. Third, they detail how state-led projects of the professionalization of the public service were aimed at racial and gender transformation as well as raising standards of service delivery. Fourth, the emergence of the professionalization of new groups (for example, security guards) is described as a strategy for credentialing and organizing better working conditions. The theme of transformation, access and the removal of barriers underlie all of these developments.

In 'India International (Inc): Global work and the (re-)organization of professionalism in emerging economies', Swethaa Ballakrishnen details how professionalism is being reorganized in the face of the dramatic increase in the globally focused nature of professional work. She focuses in particular on the new kinds of transnational workflows and value chains, where professionals are being organized, valued and oriented in ways that did not exist even a few decades ago. Since much of this emergence is unprecedented, new forms of work and new types of workers have found themselves introduced into novel professional spaces that contest existing prestige, professional identity and internal stratification. And while these phenomena have affected institutions worldwide, their effect has been particularly strong in emerging countries like India that newly support the supply end of these operations. In her chapter, Ballakrishnen traces the organization and emergence of three different, but related, high-status professional spaces in India: law, management consulting and information technology, chosen for their comparative advantage in terms of neo-liberal influences on style and scope of their changes. Across these cases, she pays particular attention to the ways in which gender negotiations have played out for these different professions. The situation for high-status professionals, she argues, has been largely ignored by the vast gender and work literature in India, which has been restricted to the circumstances of women in low-skilled labour. This gap offers her a chance to look more closely at variations in this neo-liberal organizational emergence.

We then travel to the Russian Federation with Elena Iarskaia-Smirnova and Roman Abramov's carefully laid-out argument in 'Professions and professionalization in Russia'. They argue that in order to understand the situation of the professions, one must recognize the more central role of the one party-state and the historical changes that occurred before, during and after the period of state socialism. They begin by noting how classic sociological approaches to the study of professions were conducted from a perspective typical for the Anglo-American context while in Continental Europe and other contexts, occupational groups may not be the main actors in these processes. Professionalization here thus may be promoted 'from above' by the state, which plays the main role in the development of the professions. But in the case of socialist Russia, one must take into account how the single-party bureaucratic and at times autocratic state provided the professions with additional ideological frames and functions. Their chapter focuses on the pre-socialist, state-socialist and post-socialist periods of the history of professions and professionalization in Russia. Their case analysis reveals how the professions have responded to a number of dramatic shifts in the economy and in doing so shaped how they fit

into changing societal structures. The Soviet state created a new map of the professional structure, eliminating or 'reforging' the old and promoting the new occupational groups. The analysis
of the role of women in particular in the development and evolution of professions demonstrates
how the (re)forming of the gendered identity of occupations was linked to the reinforcement of
the state's authority. Overall, these authors argue that professions have either been a focal part of
changes or quite an aside, but usually the professions have been resilient even under such serious
and rapid transformations in Russian history.

We conclude this section with the chapter on 'Professions and the migration of expert labour'
that I undertake with colleagues Sirpa Wrede, Cecilia Benoit and Elena Neiterman. We argue
that, whereas internationally mobile professionals find many more opportunities than in the past,
the migration of professionals across countries is not in itself a new phenomenon. The bulk of
this literature has, however, been somewhat atheoretical – or at least not touched by professions
theory, and neither has professions theory been extended to address these trends. We provide an
overview of the literature on the migration of health professionals, arguing that they constitute a
particularly interesting case that transcends the continuum between purely transnational labour
markets and persistent nationally rooted professional occupations. To capture the situatedness of
professional mobilities, we distinguish between *migration* and *integration*, proposing a pluralistic
conceptual framework that begins to tease apart the inputs into the migration and integration of
expert labour through the particularities of migrating health professionals. This analytic framework separates micro, meso and macro influences, with an emphasis on the often neglected
meso-analytic level, which highlights the important contributions to these trends that the professions literature can play.

Together the chapters in this section encourage us to challenge some hard-and-fast assumptions we have about the ties professions have to national contexts, but at the same time how those
national contexts can differ dramatically from those which have dominated the professions and
professionalism literatures heretofore.

16

Accountancy, finance and banking

The global reach of the professions

Colin Haslam

Introduction

The argument developed in this chapter is that the institutions governing the finance and accountancy profession and their members actively contribute to the ongoing development of the financialized global banking business model. Accounting and finance professionals are an active ingredient driving financial innovation and adaptation within the financialized banking business model. Professional finance and accounting executives are employed in a range of internal positions within the global banking business model, for example in regulators' offices, ratings agencies, brokerages, underwriting, valuation, trading (buy and sell side) and asset and liability governance committees. These accountancy and finance professionals also have an important collective stewardship role which is centred on securing the financial interests of shareholders. This stewardship function and purpose is reinforced and amplified by professional institutions that operate within a conceptual framework geared towards preserving the interests of investors. Thus the general process of setting regulatory standards, financial disclosure practices and the ongoing training and accreditation of accounting and finance specialists is directed towards securing the financial interests of a bank's shareholders.

The global banking business model has also become increasingly complex (see Blundell-Wignall *et al.*, 2013), but, fundamentally, banks are financial intermediaries that convert liabilities (household deposits) into different types of assets (loans). Banks make their money from margin spreads between interest paid on deposits and interest received on assets (loans made) in addition to obtaining service-related commission fees. The recent financial crisis revealed the extent to which a financially interconnected and networked universal banking business model was not only fragile but that disruption to its functioning compromised global financial market stability, triggering the need for state intervention and emergency funding. This once relatively simple national banking business model has evolved and adapted over time to become increasingly universal and financialized. That is, senior accounting and finance personnel are incentivized to develop more exotic financial products, which generate returns for a bank's shareholders but also inflate risk within the financial system. This financialized evolution of the global banking business model is predominantly driven by accounting and finance professionals. The knowledge of these professionals is employed to promote and record the outcome of financial innovation which is focused on leveraging returns on capital for bank shareholders. It is a business model that requires a constant feed of innovative financial products and services that instrumentally seek to extract returns for shareholders, but this is often at the expense of promoting financial stability and the public interest. The pressure to earn higher returns has encouraged banks to employ the knowledge of accounting and finance experts to displace operations outside of regulatory control and, in the extreme, this has even involved rigging or manipulating financial product markets. A *Guardian* article (12 November 2014) 'Banks pay out £166bn over six years: a history of banking misdeeds and fines' revealed that the global banking industry has racked up more than £166bn in fines for selling on toxic assets, inappropriate selling and marketing of mortgage-backed securities, fixing the London interbank interest rate (Libor) and rigging foreign exchange markets.[1]

Accounting and finance professionals are thus not only called upon to develop new financial products but are handsomely rewarded if this contributes to generating higher profits on shareholder funds. For example, in the run-up to the last financial crisis, banks employed a process of asset securitization, that is, selling on packaged-up household mortgage loans to raise additional funds to further expand bank lending. Buyers of these packaged-up loans were not fully aware of the potential default risk embedded within these complex structured loan packages. When household mortgage charge-off rates started to increase, it was not clear how much of these packaged-up and securitized mortgages were at risk, and so their values quickly collapsed (Heilpern *et al.*, 2009). Altunbas and colleagues observe that:

> The huge accumulation of risk that subsequently materialized during the recent crisis raises significant doubts as to whether banks face the right incentives to manage risk effectively on behalf of depositors and investors. Indeed structural developments in the banking industry have probably helped distort incentives towards more risk-taking.
>
> *(Altunbas* et al.*, 2011, p. 10)*

Thus the combination of innovation coupled with financial incentives modified the stewardship of resources towards the manipulation of financial arrangements within the banking system to generate leverage, that is, inflated profits for a bank's shareholders, but at the risk of financial system instability. Within this evolving banking business model, accounting finance professionals and their representative institutions promote and legitimize the development of new products, like securitized assets and other complex collateralized products.

The banking business model is facilitated by an underlying conceptual framework that governs the objectives and responsibilities of professional accountants and financial specialists. The accounting professional bodies and accounting standards-setting agencies such as International Accounting Standards Board (IASB) define their general objectives, which are set out in the accounting conceptual framework.

> In a broad sense a conceptual framework can be seen as an attempt to define the nature and purpose of accounting. A conceptual framework must consider the theoretical and conceptual issues surrounding financial reporting and form a coherent and consistent foundation that will underpin the development of accounting standards.
>
> *(ACCA website)[2]*

This governing conceptual framework serves two interrelated objectives: first, the need to report to investors about resource stewardship and, second, to contribute to the efficient functioning of capital markets for investors. It has been argued that after the financial crisis, a different professional project is required, one that serves the 'public interest' where resource stewardship is focused on promoting 'financial stability' rather than capital market efficiency (Maystadt, 2013). Schwarz *et al.* (2014) observe that, with regard to the banking system, accounting has the power to modify financial stability:

> Financial institutions have to meet capital requirements in order to cover any potential losses arising from their activity. Accounting rules influence the amount of capital that is available.... With the aim of preserving financial stability, central banks should analyse the risks stemming from certain accounting rules and contribute directly to the discussions on accounting standards, particularly during the course of the standard-setting process.
>
> *(Schwarz* et al., *2014, p. 5)*

The institutions that govern the professions of accounting and finance have, for some time, encouraged us to think differently about the stereotype of accountants and finance professionals as simply 'bean counters'. This image is being challenged by the professional bodies and replaced by an alternative that describes accounting and finance professionals as providing a sophisticated function which can contribute towards ethical responsibility and safeguarding the economy. In a survey report commissioned by the UK professional accountancy body, the Association of Chartered Certified Accountants (ACCA), Helen Brand notes that:

> Improvement must begin with a greater self-awareness since the accountancy profession's views of itself do not always match up to those of the wider public. Old fashioned stereotypes of accountants as bean counters must give way to a more accurate representation of the functions they fulfil today – which range from financial reporting through to strategic business advice and planning. Accountants can help to ensure that businesses behave in an ethically responsible way and that the rules and regulation of the land, which have been designed to safeguard the future of the economy, are adhered to.[3]

This public relations effort is designed to restore trust in the accounting and finance profession after the financial crisis. In 2013, Philippe Maystadt's report on the role of accounting and its professional bodies implicates the accounting profession in the recent financial crisis. This report argues that accounting and finance professionals need to ensure that resources are stewarded in a 'prudential' manner and that professional accountants and financial managers need to focus on preserving financial stability in the 'public interest'. Maystadt's argument is that the process of accounting and its representation in financial information is more than a mere 'language convention' but a means through which behaviour can be modified. Maystadt reports that:

> Policy choices in the field of accounting involve public interest stakes that should be considered more thoroughly. Recent examples include the links with prudential requirements for banks or insurance companies, the rules applicable to the shadow banking system, the impact on long-term investment or access to financing for SMEs (Small and Medium Enterprise). Accounting standards are more than a mere language convention. By influencing the behaviour of actors in financial markets, they can have an impact on the stability of those markets.
>
> *(Maystadt, 2013, p. 5)*

The argument developed in the next section of this chapter is that accounting and finance professionals operate within a banking business model that is financially leveraged. This financial leverage is required so that shareholders can generate a relatively high return on their equity funds invested in a bank. In order to sustain high financial returns for a bank's shareholders, accounting and finance professionals are constantly working to develop innovative financial products and services. In this respect, accounting and finance professionals and their representative professional institutions are therefore key stakeholders involved in the development of the banking business model in terms of its regulation, development of new products and governance. In a following section we turn to consider the role of institutions that represent the collective interests of professional accountants. These international institutions are guardians of a conceptual framework for corporate financial management and resource stewardship. The conceptual framework sets out the purpose and objectives of accounting, and these are reinforced through professional development, technical exams and regulatory supervision. The key purpose set out in the conceptual framework is that accounting and finance professionals are in the service of investors so as to facilitate capital market efficiency. It follows that the key objectives of the accounting and finance professional are to ensure that resource stewardship and governance arrangements within banks align with the needs of investors. The accounting profession has continued to modify the conceptual framework that moderates this behaviour but it still remains firmly entrenched with meeting the needs of investors.

In a final section to this chapter, it is argued that accounting and finance specialists and their professional institutions could play a different role, for example safeguarding and encouraging structural reform to reduce the instability inherent within the international banking business model. This would require a substantial adjustment in both the purpose and objectives of the conceptual framework that governs the accounting and finance profession, as well as changes in the agenda for professional training and development and regulatory interventions. This reorientation is a serious challenge to accounting and finance professionals and their representative institutions. For example, safeguarding in the banking business model could include the need for regulatory interventions to protect households and non-financial firms that place their savings and pension funds into banks and are exposed to significant financial risk if banks do fail. This could also include stress-testing financial innovations in the interest of financial market stability and the public interest.

Accounting for the financialized banking business model

Andreas Nölke (2012) observes that 'financialization characterizes a situation where capitalism is affected by a dominance of the financial sector (financial elites, income, institutions and motivations) relative to the productive sector. This dominance may be detected in various observations, such as neo-liberal economic policy, the ascendancy of shareholder value'.[4] Andersson et al. (2014) and Haslam et al. (2012) observe that core financial services in the United States account for roughly 6 per cent of GDP, and across a range of advanced economies, the average is between 6 and 8 per cent of GDP (Greenwood and Scharfstein, 2012, p. 1). Yet the IMF 2014 Financial Stability Report reveals that total outstanding bank assets are 160 per cent of global GDP.[5] Thus banking, as an activity, accounts for a relatively small share of global GDP but a significant share of global financial assets (loans outstanding), which are effectively financed by the savings and pensions of households and invested assets of non-financial firms.

The average bank operates with very thin income margins, that is, the difference between income received from assets (loan interest and commission fees) and payments made to depositors in the form of interest paid. Thus liquidity risk forces banks to innovate so as to manipulate their working capital on a daily basis to try and balance the short-run behaviour of depositors (liabilities) with the need for banks to issue relatively long-term loans (assets). The average bank

Table 16.1 Income to assets ratio: top 1,000 global banks

	Income (return) to total assets ratio %
2008	1.9
2009	2.4
2010	2.7
2011	2.6
2012	2.5

Source: www.capgemini.com/resource-fileaccess/resource/pdf/trends_in_the_global_banking_industry_2013.pdf.
Data extracted from chart on page 4.

Table 16.2 Banking leverage and return on equity

	Return on total assets (ROA)%	Shareholder equity to total assets %	Return on equity (ROE) %[a]
2008	1.9	0.1	19
2009	2.4	0.1	24
2010	2.7	0.1	27
2011	2.6	0.1	26
2012	2.5	0.1	25

Source: the author.
a. ROE = [ROA / (equity / assets)]; ROE = [2 / 0.10]; ROE = 20%.

generates a very slim 2–2.5 per cent profit margin on their total assets/loans (see Table 16.1) after paying their employee costs. A further significant challenge to the banking business model is asset price risk and the possibility that a reduction in the value of assets (loans outstanding), even of relatively modest proportions, could force a bank into insolvency. For example, in the recent financial crisis, many US banks were forced to the brink of insolvency when just 3 per cent of US households defaulted on their mortgages and these needed to be charged off against bank profits and shareholder equity (see Heilpern *et al.*, 2009; Haslam *et al.*, 2012).

In Table 16.2 we assume that an average bank is required to hold 10 per cent of total assets as shareholder equity (the so-called regulatory capital funds provided by shareholders). This requirement to put in equity equivalent to just 10 per cent of total assets facilitates a process of financial leverage. That is, a modest return on assets of just 2 per cent can be converted into a 20 per cent return on equity because the equity to assets ratio is just 10 per cent:

As Stefan Ingves, Chairman of the Basle Committee on Banking Supervision (the standard-setter for the prudential regulation of banks), observes, banks operate with very high leverage.

> Leverage in banking is far higher than in other industry sectors. For example, the average leverage ratio across 10 of the world's largest listed non-financial companies is on the order of 50%. That is, on average these companies fund their assets around 50:50 with debt and equity. In banking, a more common ratio is 95:5.
>
> *(Ingves, 2014, p. 1)*

We can contrast banking with an average business that would finance its total assets with roughly 50 per cent debt and 50 per cent equity funds. Banks might be funding 95 per cent of their assets with debt and 5 per cent with shareholder equity. The incentive to reduce the amount of shareholder funds relative to total assets is a powerful one because the lower the equity to total assets ratio, the higher the return on equity (ROE). In the banking business model, shareholder equity doubles as the banks' regulatory capital, that is, the financial buffer that absorbs any losses on assets such as on a defaulting loan which needs to be written off because it will not be repaid.

> Unlike normal companies, banks are in the business of issuing loans to individuals and businesses – which means that if those individuals and businesses default on their loans, the bank loses money.
>
> Think about what happens in accounting terms if an asset – loans in this case – goes down: something on the liabilities & shareholders' equity side of the balance sheet must go down to match it.
>
> In the best case scenario, this will be the bank's shareholders' equity: it acts as a buffer to cover losses on assets.[6]

A bank's shareholder equity (or regulatory capital) is set by external banking regulations (Basle III[7]) using an accounting formula that identifies a bank's 'risk adjusted assets'. That is, the equity buffer required by a bank is set by the share of assets (loans) that are deemed to be at risk. The more assets a bank holds on a balance sheet graded at no risk (what the Standard and Poor's credit rating agency terms AAA), the less shareholder equity (regulatory capital) is required. Thus, banks will try to maximize the share of total assets that are AAA 'risk free' so as to reduce equity funding (regulatory capital). In the run-up to the last financial crisis, banks employed a process of 'asset securitization' to bundle up assets (mortgages and loans) and sell these on. The purchasers of these sold-on loans would often be investment banks which would themselves issue bonds (securities) to raise funds to purchase these sold-on bank assets (mortgages and loans). This financial innovation was known as asset 'securitization' and served to increase the share of bank assets (loans) rated as AAA and hence deemed to be of little risk. Securitization had the impact of reducing a bank's risky assets and thus also the need for regulatory capital (shareholder funds). As early as 1999, the Basle Committee noted the increasing sophistication of banking financial products and how the largest banks were finding ways to avoid the limitation which fixed capital requirements (the need for shareholder funds) placed on their risk-taking relative to their capital (see Basle Committee, 1999).

In a speech in 2013, Andrew Haldane (a member of the Financial Policy Committee in the Bank of England) presented Charts 16.1 and 16.2. These reveal the extent to which, in the run-up to the financial crisis, risky assets held in total banks' assets fell from 70 to just over 30 per cent of total assets. Chart 16.2 then reveals that because the share of risky assets in total assets is reduced, the need for regulatory capital (shareholder funds) also reduced. For this group of banks, at the time of the financial crisis, the value of assets (loans outstanding) was 30 times larger than regulatory capital, that is, shareholders were putting up just 3 per cent of total assets as a buffer against asset write-downs (bad loans).[8]

Asset securitization is a financial innovation designed to reduce a bank's risk-weighted-assets and need for the shareholder to provide funding. These arrangements came undone in the run-up to the financial crisis because securitized assets, thought to be to safe collateral because they were deemed to be AAA rated, contained a significant amount of risk. David Rule, Executive Director, Prudential Policy at the Bank of England, observed that 'securities financing markets may be important but the financial crisis demonstrated that they can also be fragile. Securities thought to be "safe" collateral, such as AAA-rated mortgage-backed securities and peripheral European sovereign bonds, became "risky" collateral' (see Rule, 2014, p. 5).

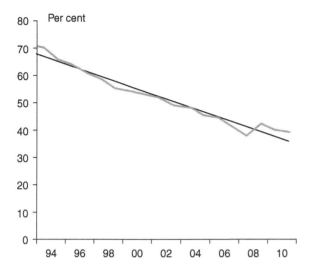

Chart 16.1 Average risk weights

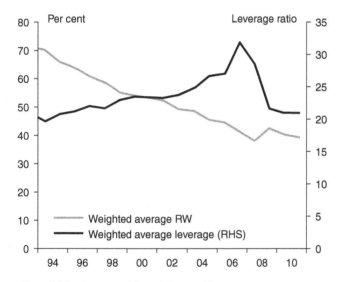

Chart 16.2 Average risk weights and leverages

The regulatory response to the banking crisis has been to tighten up the process by which risky assets are assessed so as to force banks to increase the amount of regulatory capital held on their balance sheets and which is available to absorb asset write-downs. Lysandrou and Nesvetailova (2014) observe, in relation to tightening bank regulation, that 'it takes me about two hours to assemble a team of finance geeks and lawyers to devise a product or a transaction that would bypass any new rule or regulation coming our way'.[9] Banks, for example, are deepening 'shadow banking' networks, that is, setting up new financial intermediaries that are not subject to regulatory oversight.[10] The IMF Global Financial Stability Report observes that so-called shadow banks operating outside government-regulated banking systems are providing more credit because many traditional banks now lack adequate credit capacity to support economic recovery. This expansion of so-called shadow banking is 'shifting risks that borrowers won't repay their loans to shadow banks',[11] further obscuring financial risk and heightening the potential for another financial crisis. Driving this underlying process of financial innovation are the accounting and finance specialists that understand how to set up special purpose vehicles (SPVs), arbitrage differences in regulatory environments and move transactions on and off balance sheets to generate financial leverage. Again Lysandrou and Nesvetailova remind us that:

> Today, behind the facade of any major banking conglomerate, there is a plethora of entities, transactions and quasi-legal cells. Many of them are 'orphaned' from the visible part of the bank by complex legal and financial operations and often embedded in offshore financial havens, yet they have become integral to the functioning of our banks.[12]

According to the Financial Stability Board (2013), this growth in shadow banking 'represents on average about 24% of total financial assets, about half of banking system assets and 117% of GDP. These patterns have been relatively stable since the crisis' (Financial Stability Board, 2013, p. 2). The financialized banking business model is fuelled by financial innovation, which, as Minsky points out, can become increasingly speculative in nature because risk within the financial system cannot easily be contained (Minsky, 1992). The fundamental driver of this risk-taking is the pursuit of financial leverage by banks, because this increases the return to shareholders but leaves households and other depositors with their money in a business model that can rapidly become financially unstable. The recent financial crisis revealed that banks could not contain or hedge their risk because this was displaced onto the state and taxpaying households (Andersson *et al.*, 2014).

The conduct and behaviour of finance and accounting professionals and their contribution to a fragile and ethically damaged banking business model continues to unfold as we hear about inappropriate lending practices, tax-avoidance schemes, mis-selling of insurance products and interest rate swaps and Libor rate fixing (the average interbank interest rate). Sam Fleming in a *Financial Times* article observes that: 'The big European banks could face another $50bn of fines and litigation costs after setting aside or paying out more than $80bn since 2009, according to Morgan Stanley. Banks have been hit by hefty fines in relation to rigging of the Libor interest rate benchmark and other violations. They are also awaiting the outcome of a big multinational probe into alleged foreign exchange market rigging'.[13] These fines alone represent a significant charge against European banks' regulatory capital and threaten, yet again, to undermine its financial viability.

We finally turn to consider how the institutions that represent the accounting and finance profession are implicated in the process of financializing the banking business model.

Accounting for the professional bodies: governance and stewardship

Sikka *et al.* argue that

> Ever since its professionalisation, accountancy bodies have sought to portray accounting as an independent, objective and neutral constructor of the state of corporate affairs. A common institutional response to scandals has been to reconstruct confidence in accounting by tweaking the regulatory and disciplinary apparatuses, without necessarily scrutinising the conceptual, social and theoretical basis of accounting.
>
> *(2007, see also Sikka and Willmott, 1995)*

In this section we review and question the broad objectives set out in the accounting conceptual framework that governs the purpose of financial reporting, standards setting and the stewardship of resources. Scrutinizing the conceptual framework provides useful insight into the way in which the professional training and development of accounting and finance specialists is geared towards representing the interests of a narrow group of stakeholders: the investors. This conceptual framework also facilitates a broader set of values that have become culturally embedded in the finance and accounting professions in terms of setting priorities and justification of behaviour surrounding the stewardship of resources.

Within professional accounting and financial resource management there has been an ongoing debate about the general purpose of the accountants' conceptual framework for informing a narrow or broader group of stakeholders about the stewardship of a firm's resources. Zeff (1999) considers the evolution of the conceptual framework governing financial disclosure in the United States and observes that, in 1966, the American Accounting Association (AAA) published a pioneering monograph entitled 'A Statement of Basic Accounting Theory (ASOBAT)'. According to Zeff, ASOBAT introduced the notion of 'decision usefulness' of financial statements as 'the process of identifying, measuring, and communicating economic information to permit informed judgments and decisions by users of the information' (AAA, 1966, p. 1). The primary users of disclosed information are the 'investors' or, more specifically, shareholders who use reported earnings figures to make valuation estimates and assess financial risk.

The American Institute of Certified Professional Accountants Committee Report: 'Objectives of Financial Statements (the Trueblood Report)' (AICPA, 1973) reinforced the need for the accounting and finance professions to generate information about the stewardship of resources useful for investors. Significantly, the Trueblood Report discussed the possibility of multiple values to describe performance and resource stewardship to a range of user groups, proposing also that social goals are no less important than economic goals. This theme about the role and purpose of resource stewardship and its responsibilities to investors or to a broader group of stakeholders is highlighted again in the International Integrated Reporting Council report (IIRC, 2013). The International Accounting Standards Board (IASB, 2013) is also currently engaged in clarifying the purpose of the accounting conceptual framework. Regardless of this ongoing debate, the conceptual framework is still firmly focused on providing information about resource stewardship that is decision-useful to 'investors' as primary stakeholders and providers of risk capital.

> The primary users of general purpose financial reporting are present and potential investors, lenders and other creditors, who use that information to make decisions about buying, selling or holding equity or debt instruments and providing or settling loans or other forms of credit.
>
> ...
>
> The primary users need information about the resources of the entity not only to assess an entity's prospects for future net cash inflows but also how effectively and efficiently management has discharged their responsibilities to use the entity's existing resources (i.e., stewardship).
>
> *www.iasplus.com/en-gb/standards/other/framework*

Thus the conceptual framework that governs the purpose and objectives and work of professional accountants establishes a bias towards active interventions that support the process of resource stewardship that aligns with the interests of shareholders. A substantial amount of academic research has been commissioned by the professional bodies to evaluate the contribution of 'accounting and finance' to aligning managerial and investor interests in terms of reducing risk to investors and their cost of capital. The ICAEW 'Reporting Business Risks: Meeting Expectations' Report calls for better information from accounting and finance professional about risks, observing that:

> Improved information on risk also allows investors to make better-informed decisions as to how they will choose to influence the actions of firms' managers and where they will put their money. It should therefore result in both more effective stewardship of individual firms and a more efficient allocation of resources. In addition, external reporting of risks should encourage firms to improve their management of risks.
>
> *(ICAEW, 2011, p. 2)*

There has been growing demand in recent decades for businesses to report more and better information about the risks they face. The demand for better reporting about stewardship and governance, especially for banks, intensified after the global financial crisis of 2007, reflecting a view that banks previously failed to provide adequate information about their risks. A further comprehensive review of the academic evidence on financial reporting, resource stewardship and capital market efficiency has also been carried out by the Institute of Chartered Accountants in England and Wales (ICAEW, 2014). This research report reveals the extent to which the international convergence of accounting practices and stewardship of resources contributed towards improving capital market efficiency for investors. This comprehensive survey of the academic research summarizes the results as 'mixed and inconclusive' and says that: 'It is not possible, however, to draw indisputable conclusions on the overall effects of mandatory International Financial Reporting Standard (IFRS) adoption based on the available research. Different researchers arrive at different conclusions' (ICAEW, 2014, p. 6).

The difficulty with the 'capital market efficiency' project in accounting and finance is that there are contradictory forces at play because the object of 'governance' has been to align the interests of managers (as stewards of resources) with those of their investors demanding lower risks and a higher return on capital. This alignment of managerial and investor interests is captured in the theory of shareholder value (i.e. the theory of how financial metrics such as return on capital employed (ROCE), Economic Value Added (EVA™) and earnings per share (EPS) are incorporated into executive remuneration packages to align managerial and shareholder interest). Senior corporate personnel, including finance and accounting specialists, are rewarded with substantial bonuses and stock options if their firms hit specified financial targets which are assumed to correlate with a firm's stock market value. This link between financial performance and executive pay often promotes additional risk-taking as a means to boost short-run performance at the expense of stability and the financial viability of the firm as a going concern. A UK House of Lords Banking Supervision and Regulation Economic Affairs Committee observed that:

> irresponsible compensation packages 'incentivised bankers to' book short-term profits based on excessively risky behaviour which increased systemic risk in the financial system and weakened the medium and long-term prospects and profitability of the bank
>
> *www.publications.parliament.uk/pa/ld200809/*
> *ldselect/ldeconaf/101/10110.htm: para 194*

Critics of this drive for shareholder value suggest that it generates contradictory outcomes more broadly in terms of economic prosperity. Martin Wolf observed in the *Financial Times* that: 'Unfortunately, we have made a mess of this. That mess has a name: it is "shareholder value maximisation". Operating companies in line with this belief not only leads to misbehaviour but may also militate against their true social aim, which is to generate greater prosperity' (Wolf, 2014). Maximizing shareholder interest and its impact on the banking business model in the UK was the subject of a Banking Supervision and Regulation Economic Affairs Committee, which observed that:

> In most sectors of the economy, corporate governance is primarily concerned with protecting shareholder rights, and maximising shareholder value. If a non-financial firm collapses its shareholders and bondholders lose money, employees' jobs are lost and customers need to find another supplier. But there are few external effects. Bank failures on the other hand tend to have far-reaching external effects. The special nature of banks makes their corporate governance more complex.
>
> *www.publications.parliament.uk/pa/ld200809/*
> *ldselect/ldeconaf/101/10110.htm*

Mitigating the social risk generated by dysfunctional governance of the global banking business model is made more difficult by the fact that banks are now generally protected by state-sponsored deposit insurance funds, are still too large to fail or operate with a tacit government guarantee of a bailout. This all adds fuel to the fire of moral hazard because banks can pursue financial innovation and risk-taking and, in the event of failure, society and governments (the public and taxpayers) pick up the bill. In the next section, we argue for a significant reorientation in the nature of the accounting conceptual framework, one that redefines the role and contribution of the accounting and finance professional. This also needs to include the professional institutions that represent finance and accounting specialists. Institutional reform and a reorientation of values are required to transform their role as custodians that are safeguarding a broader set of stakeholder interests. In the following section we introduce a business-models approach to structuring a conceptual framework governing the behaviour and priorities of finance and accounting professionals.

Banking as a business model: stakeholders and corporate governance

We can account for a firm's business model as the outcome of interactions with a complex network of stakeholders, where these relations serve to broadly define the nature of a firm's business model (Haslam *et al.*, 2012). Haslam and colleagues argue that these stakeholder relations are being constantly manipulated by firms, within their business model, to generate financial return. Jacobides (2009) observes that 'many "BM (Business Model) innovations" are either changes *within* IA [Industry Architecture]; or changes *of* IA' (emphasis in original). The drivers of these changes to a firm's business model result from interactions with a range of stakeholders, both primary and secondary, and include customers, employees, suppliers, advisers, credit ratings agencies, industry and valuation analysts, consultants, regulatory and professional institutions, to name a few. Primary and secondary stakeholder relations not only help to broadly define the nature of a firm's business model in terms of its governance but also influence a firm's general value proposition in terms of its liquidity solvency and sustainability. Bukh and Nielsen (2010) argue that the value of the 'business model' is that it offers up a new management technology that can inform disclosure to investors.

> Thus, we perceive the business model as a management technology that helps management communicate and share its understanding of the business logic to external stakeholders, in our case primarily analysts and investors.
>
> *(Bukh and Nielsen, 2010, p. 11)*

The accounting and financial institutions are moving closer towards employing a business-models approach to disclosure of information about the stewardship of financial resources. For example, a 'business-models' approach to disclosure informs the International Financial Reporting Standard 9 (IFRS9) (Accounting for Financial Instruments), that is, that judgements can be made about valuation (historic cost or market value) of financial assets depending upon a firm's business model. IFRS9 reinforces the need for finance and accountancy professionals to investigate the nature of counterparty arrangements involved in financial transactions and how these might impact on risk. The ICAEW has published a report on 'Business Models in Accounting: The Theory of the Firm and Financial Reporting' (2010), and a recent European Financial Reporting Advisory Group (EFRAG) research report: 'The Role of the Business Model in Financial Statements' considers how a business-models reporting framework could modify the fundamental qualitative characteristics of the conceptual framework, namely: relevance and faithful representation, comparability, timeliness and comprehension (EFRAG, 2013). The IIRC also challenges the accounting profession to report to a broader group of stakeholders (IIRC, 2013, p. 4). However, these research reports do not have a clear position on what constitutes a firm's business model. In this chapter, we suggest that a firm's business model can be described as the outcome of material stakeholder relations that broadly describe the key activity characteristics of firms in their business model. Marshall and Lennard (2014) have a more developed notion of how the nature of a firm's business model, combined with a prudent approach to resource stewardship, might inform the accounting conceptual framework. That is:

> By setting out an alternative rationale, based on the idea of a business model and prudence, we attempt to demonstrate their significance and hence reinforce our view that the Conceptual Framework should specifically acknowledge or refer to them.
>
> *(p. 1)*

Marshall and Lennard construct two business model typologies within which resource stewardship and prudent governance can be framed, referring to the first type as 'value added' businesses and the second as 'price change' businesses. These labels correspond to the fact that the first type of business adds value by its own activities, whilst the second makes its profits through its skill in forecasting price changes (Marshall and Lennard, 2014, p. 3). In contrast, Haslam *et al.* (2015) argue that a business-models approach to financial reporting and resource stewardship could be presented as a management technology to reveal information about the firm's broad stakeholder relations (Haslam *et al.*, 2015). This might include information about how stakeholder relationships are enhancing or degrading a reporting entity's value proposition, instrumentally in terms of liquidity and solvency and normatively in terms of the quality and trust embedded in these relationships. Accounting and finance professionals need to be charged with reporting about how resource stewardship in relation to a variety of key stakeholders is sustaining the business from a holistic point of view. This alternative perspective on the nature of business models provides a useful framing device because it increases our understanding about how stakeholder relations are being managed both instrumentally and normatively. Within a business-models framework of analysis, stewardship is broader than just delivering for 'investors' but includes securing trust and compliance across a broader stakeholder network to reduce moral hazard. A business model–stakeholder agency approach to resource stewardship would provide the grounding for a new conceptual framework for accounting and finance professionals (Haslam *et al.*, 2015). This would demand a significant reorientation by the governing institutions, which currently define their primary role as representing investors and the efficient functioning of capital markets rather than safeguarding and stability in the public interest.

Discussion and conclusions

The argument developed in this chapter is that the institutions governing the accountancy and allied finance professionals have contributed and are actively contributing to the development of a financialized global banking business model. The accounting profession and its associated institutions are prima facie guided by a conceptual framework which places the investor at the centre of resource stewardship and corporate governance. The recent banking crisis and increasingly lengthy charge sheet of poor conduct and excessive risk-taking calls into question the legitimacy of accounting and financial specialists in relation to safeguarding society. This risk-taking is amplified by shareholder value performance metrics wired into remuneration packages that encourage accounting and finance executives to financialize the banking business model.

The banking business model operates with profit margins on assets (loans), generally around 2 per cent. This thin operating margin on assets can be converted into a relatively high return on equity only if shareholder funds are a small fraction of total assets, say less than 10 per cent. Because shareholder funds are such a small proportion of total assets, this generates financial leverage for shareholders, as a 2 per cent margin on assets can be converted into a 20 per cent return on equity. In banking, shareholder equity doubles as regulatory capital which *should* absorb any losses arising from risky assets (lending by banks) that need to be written off. This regulatory capital itself depends upon a calculation based on the share of a bank's assets that is deemed to be 'risky'. Banks can manipulate assets classified as 'risky' through financial product innovations such as securitization and exotic forms of collateralization. Accountancy and finance professionals are key actors here because they provide regulatory, technical and valuation/reporting services and thereby have influence over the stewardship of resources. The drive to maximize shareholder return on equity, within the banking business model, exposes other stakeholders, including households, non-financial firms and governments, to considerable risk because risk is no longer hedged in a financialized banking business model. The lesson we draw from the banking crisis is that technical fixes designed to contain risk will not be adequate because the banking business model is by its nature highly leveraged and geared towards the financial interests of shareholders. There is still a high probability that future financial disturbance in the banking system will not be contained but displaced into society. We already know that banks are migrating operations into 'shadow-banking' arrangements to avoid regulations that will increase their regulatory capital.

The accounting and finance profession needs to redefine its purpose and objectives and play its role in limiting the moral hazard arising from a financialized banking business model. This would require a substantial reorientation in the conceptual framework that governs the behaviour and priorities of the accounting and finance profession in our banks (see Haslam *et al.*, 2015). The conceptual framework governing this behaviour could be reprogrammed towards stakeholder governance where material stakeholder relationships are defined by the type of business model within which a firm is located. In the case of the banking business model, arrangements between banks and their stakeholders will still be instrumentally managed to 'make money' but this will need to be tempered with a normative requirement to safeguard trust across a broad(er) group of stakeholders if we are to limit moral hazard to society.

Notes

1 Banks have been fined for a series of attempts to manipulate and rig financial markets so as to extract financial advantage to banks against society: www.theguardian.com/business/2014/nov/12/banks-fined-200bn-six-years-history-banking-penalties-libor-forex.

2 The conceptual framework is an overarching description of the purpose and function of financial reporting and outlines the way in which resource stewardship should align with shareholder interests: www.accaglobal.com/uk/en/student/exam-support-resources/fundamentals-exams-study-resources/f7/technical-articles/conceptual-framework-need.html.

3 For a more lengthy report about the need for professional accounting and finance bodies to regain trust, see www.accaglobal.com/uk/en/discover/news/2012/09/public-value.html.

4 Andreas Nölke observes that recent measures for financial market regulation did not affect financialization in any substantial way. Policies regarding increased transparency for rating agencies, the registration of hedge fund managers and increased capital requirements for banks do not really reduce the degree of financialization: www.academic-foresights.com/Financialization.html.

5 This IMF report provides technical data about banks' assets to GDP: https://www.imf.org/external/pubs/ft/gfsr/2014/02/index.htm. It also points out that executive pay and risk are related and that there needs to be an appropriate alignment of bank executives' compensation with risk (including the risk exposure of bank creditors), deferment of some compensation, and providing for clawbacks.

6 This article provides a good review of bank regulatory capital and why we need it: https://samples-breakingintowallstreet-com.s3.amazonaws.com/60-BIWS-Bank-Regulatory-Capital.pdf.

7 Basle III regulations are about improving the banking sector's ability to absorb shocks arising from financial and economic stress, whatever the source, and improving risk management and governance to strengthen banks' transparency and disclosures: www.bis.org/bcbs/basel3.htm.

8 Andrew Haldane's presentation reveals that in the pre-crisis boom, bank leverage rose steadily to reach historically unprecedented levels. This signalled high and rising bank risk: www.bankofengland.co.uk/publications/Documents/speeches/2013/speech657.pdf.

9 Nesvetailova argues that current academic studies of shadow banking illustrate that secrecy, lack of transparency, complexity and opacity have become essential ingredients of today's financial innovation: www.opendemocracy.net/ourkingdom/anastasia-nesvetailova/shadow-banking-or-why-black-holes-are-important-in-global-financia.

10 See www.financialstabilityboard.org/wp-content/uploads/r_131114.pdf.

11 The IMF notes that shadow banking increases investor risk because it is outside of the regulated sphere of normal banking: www.ibtimes.com/shadow-banks-could-compromise-global-financial-stability-imf-says-1701089.

12 Relying on long, complex and opaque structures of credit creation, many visible banks are able to enlarge their de facto size, often creating undetected leverage and thus adding to the problem of 'too big to fail': www.taxjustice.net/2014/02/28/quite-anywhere-shadow-banking-offshore-system/.

13 The fines paid by banks could have a significant impact on their financial viability: www.ft.com/cms/s/0/c9b75846-084c-11e4-9afc-00144feab7de.html#axzz3RKyl2uBe.

References

Altunbas, Y., Manganelli, S. and Marques-Ibanez, D. (2011) *Bank Risk During the Financial Crisis: Do Business Models Matter?* European Central Bank, Working Paper No 1394. www.ecb.europa.eu/pub/pdf/scpwps/ecbwp1394.pdf (last accessed 27 January 2016).

American Accounting Association (AAA) (1966) *A Statement of Basic Accounting Theory.* Evanston, IL: AAA.

American Institute of Certified Public Accountants (AICPA) (1973) *Objectives of Financial Statements* (Trueblood Report): New York. http://3197d6d14b5f19f2f440-5e13d29c4c016cf96cbbfd197c579b45.r81.cf1.rackcdn.com/collection/papers/1970/1973_1001_TruebloodObjectives.pdf (last accessed 27 January 2016).

Andersson, T., Lee, E., Theodosopoulos, G., Yin, Y. P. and Haslam, C. (2014) 'Accounting for the financialized UK and US national business model'. *Critical Perspectives on Accounting*, 25(1), pp. 78–91.

Basle Committee (1999) *Capital Requirements and Bank Behaviour: The Impact of the Basle Accord*, Working Paper No.1. www.bis.org/publ/bcbs_wp1.pdf (last accessed 27 January 2016).

Blundell-Wignall, A., Atkinson, P. and Roulet, C. (2013) 'Bank business models and the Basel system: Complexity and interconnectedness'. *OECD Journal: Financial Market Trends*, 2. www.oecd.org/finance/Bank-Business-Models-Basel-2013.pdf (last accessed 27 January 2016).

Bukh, P. N. and Nielsen, C. (2010) 'Understanding the health care business model: The financial analyst's point of view'. *Journal of Health Care Finance*, 37, pp. 8–25.

EFRAG (2013) *The Role of the Business Model in Financial Statements*. Available online: www.efrag.org/files/PAAinE%20-%20Business%20Model/140415_Business_Model_Research_Paper.pdf.

Financial Stability Board (2013) *Global Shadow Banking Monitoring Report*, Bank for International Settlements, Switzerland. www.financialstabilityboard.org/wp-content/uploads/r_131114.pdf (last accessed 27 January 2016).

Greenwood, R. and Scharfstein, D. (2012) *The Growth of Modern Finance*, Harvard Business School and National Bureau of Economic Research (NBER). www.people.hbs.edu/dscharfstein/growth_of_modern_finance.pdf (last accessed 27 January 2016).

Haslam, C., Andersson, T., Tsitsianis, N. and Yin, Y. P. (2012) *Redefining Business Models*, London: Routledge.

Haslam, C., Andersson, T., Tsitsianis, N. and Geadle, P. (2015) 'Accounting for business models: increasing the visibility of stakeholders'. *Journal of Business Models*, 3(1), pp. 62–80 http://journals.aau.dk/index.php/JOBM/article/view/1066/811 (last accessed 27 January 2016).

Heilpern, E., Haslam, C. and Andersson, T. (2009) 'When it comes to the crunch: What are the drivers of the US banking crisis?'. *Accounting Forum*, 33(2), pp. 99–113.

IASB (2013) *A Review of the Conceptual Framework for Financial Reporting*, Discussion paper DP/2013/1. www.ifrs.org/Current-Projects/IASB-Projects/Conceptual-Framework/Discussion-Paper-July-2013/Documents/Discussion-Paper-Conceptual-Framework-July-2013.pdf (last accessed 27 January 2016).

ICAEW (2010) *Business Models in Accounting: The Theory of the Firm and Financial Reporting*. Information for Better Markets Initiative. London: ICAEW. Available online: www.icaew.com/~/media/Files/Technical/Financial-reporting/Information%20for%20better%20markets/BMIA%20published%20report.pdf.

ICAEW (2011) *Reporting Business Risks: Meeting Expectations*. Information for Better Markets Initiative. London: ICAEW. Available online: www.icaew.com/~/media/corporate/files/technical/financial%20reporting/information%20for%20better%20markets/ifbm/rbr%20final.ashx (last accessed 13 February 2016).

ICAEW (2014) *The Effects of Mandatory IFRS Adoption in the EU*. www.icaew.com/en/technical/financial-reporting/information-for-better-markets/ifbm-reports/the-effects-of-mandatory-ifrs-adoption-in-the-eu (last accessed 27 January 2016).

IFRS (2014) *IFRS 9 Financial Instruments*. www.ifrs.org/current-projects/iasb-projects/financial-instruments-a-replacement-of-ias-39-financial-instruments-recognitio/documents/ifrs-9-project-summary-july-2014.pdf (last accessed 27 January 2016).

IIRC (2013) *Consultation draft of the International Framework*. London: IIRC. www.theiirc.org/consultation-draft2013/ (last accessed 27 January 2016).

Ingves, S. (2014) 'Banking on leverage'. Keynote address to the *10th Asia-Pacific High-Level Meeting on Banking Supervision* jointly organised by the Basle Committee on Banking Supervision. www.bis.org/speeches/sp140226.pdf (last accessed 27 January 2016).

Jacobides, M. (2009) 'Business models in context: Some biased reflections'. *AoM Meetings*, Chicago, IL. www.businessmodelcommunity.com/fs/Root/8v2h8-AoM2009BusinessModelsymposimMGJ.pdf (last accessed 27 January 2016).

Lysandrou, P. and Nesvetailova, A. (2014) 'The role of shadow banking entities in the financial crisis: A disaggregated view'. *Review of International Political Economy*, 22(2), pp. 257–279.

Marshall, R. and Lennard, A. (2014) 'The reporting of income and expense and the choice of measurement bases', *Accounting Standards Advisory Forum*, June. www.ifrs.org/Meetings/MeetingDocs/ASAF/2014/May/06%20Conceptual%20Framework.pdf (last accessed 27 January 2016).

Maystadt, P. (2013) 'Should IFRS Standards be more European?'. http://ec.europa.eu/finance/accounting/docs/governance/reform/131112_report_en.pdf (last accessed 27 January 2016).

Minsky, H. P. (1992) *The Financial Instability Hypothesis*. Working Paper No. 74, The Jerome Levy Economics Institute of Bard College. www.levyinstitute.org/pubs/wp74.pdf (last accessed 27 January 2016).

Nölke, A. (2012) 'Financialization'. *Academic Foresights*, 4. Available online: www.academic-foresights.com/Financialization.pdf.

Rule, D. (2014) 'Regulatory reform, its possible market consequences and the case of securities financing'. *Federal Reserve Bank of Chicago Annual International Banking Conference*. www.bankofengland.co.uk/publications/Documents/speeches/2014/speech774.pdf (last accessed 27 January 2016).

Schwarz, C., Karakitsos, P., Merriman, N. and Studener, W. (2014) *Why Accounting Matters: A Central Bank Perspective*. Occasional Paper Series, 153. www.ecb.europa.eu/pub/pdf/scpops/ecbop153.pdf (last accessed 27 January 2016).

Sikka, P. and Willmott, H. (1995) 'The power of "independence": Defending and extending the jurisdiction of accounting in the UK'. *Accounting, Organizations and Society*, 20(6), pp. 547–581.

Sikka, P, Haslam, C., Kyriacou, O. and Agrizzi, D. (2007) 'Professionalizing claims and the state of UK professional accounting education: some evidence'. *Accounting Education: An International Journal*, 16(1), pp. 3–21.

Wolf, M. (2014) 'Opportunist shareholders must embrace commitment'. *Financial Times*, 26 August. www.ft.com/cms/s/0/6aa87b9a-2d05-11e4-911b-00144feabdc0.html#axzz3RRrxhtS0 (last accessed 27 January 2016).

Zeff, S.A. (1999) 'The evolution of the conceptual framework for business enterprises in the United States'. *Accounting Historians Journal*, 26, pp. 89–131.

17

Professions and professionalism in emerging economies

The case of South Africa

Debby Bonnin and Shaun Ruggunan

Introduction

South African sociology has not paid much attention to the sociology of professions in any formal way (Bonnin and Ruggunan 2013). While there has been a strong focus on the sociology of work and economic sociology, this has focused primarily on the labour movement and its strategies of organising and servicing blue-collar workers as well as the labour process and the conditions of production (Buhlungu 2009). Whilst middle-class professions have historically been 'studied' by South African sociologists (see Marks 1994; Nzimande 1991; Walker 2005), these analyses, with the exception of Gilbert's work (1998) on community pharmacists, have not been framed within the established theoretical contexts of the sociology of professions. Instead, South African sociologists have been preoccupied with racial inequalities in accessing professional labour markets (Marks 1994; Walker 2005). Given South Africa's racialised history and current context, this focus is appreciated. However, since the advent of a post-Apartheid South Africa in 1994, professions and their milieus are assuming an increasingly important space in the South African social and political landscape. This chapter identifies four shifts in post-Apartheid South Africa that motivate a need to engage, theoretically, empirically and practically in a sociology of professions. Two simultaneous processes occurred that spurred these four shifts: the dismantling of Apartheid and the increased opening-up of the economy to globalising (post-Fordist) processes.

South Africa held its first democratic election in 1994. The post-Apartheid government moved swiftly to dismantle legislated racism. They paid particular attention to the labour market and, within a few years, had passed a number of pieces of legislation – the key acts designed to remove discrimination and promote equity in the labour market were the Labour Relations Act, the Employment Equity Act and the Skills Development Act. Following these pieces of legislation were various other processes – transformation charters aimed at specific industries or professions, attempts to deracialise ownership of the economy through black economic empowerment, legislation aimed at specific professions, etc. – all aimed at deracialising the economy, the labour market and ultimately professions and occupations within that labour market.

The second process that marked the post-1994 period was the integration of the South African economy into the global economy. The Apartheid economy had been built on import-substitution policies. This insulation was reinforced when economic sanctions were implemented by the international community. In the post-1994 period, the South African government ensured the South African economy became globally integrated through the lowering of import tariffs and the lifting of capital controls. They also attempted to change the basis on which the South African economy's accumulation strategy rested – to shift it from a commodity-based to an export-orientated economy.

In this chapter we argue that these two processes contributed to the four shifts. First, there are the strategies developed by the state, professional bodies and educational/training institutions to effect racial transformation in the composition of traditional professions. Second, distinguished from these broad measures are specific interventions in the regulation of some professions, with a key theme of access and equity. Third, there is a state-led project of the professionalisation of public services, with the twin goals of racial and gender transformation and as a strategy to raise standards of service delivery. Fourth, discourses have emerged of the professionalisation of new groups (for example, security guards) as a strategy for credentialing and organising better working conditions for employees. The theme of transformation, access and the removal of barriers underlie all of these developments.

Racial transformation in the composition of the traditional professions

Historically, the Apartheid state's professional project operated as a form of social closure based primarily on race, that is, to the exclusion of black South Africans (by black we mean African, Indian and Coloured)[1] and, to a lesser extent, gender and its intersections. White middle-class South Africans enjoyed superior and privileged access to professional education, training and labour markets. This shaped the 'profile' of the South African professions in very stark and particular ways.

South Africa provides one of the most explicit examples of forced or legislated social closure into professions based on race classification and identity that is in keeping with structural accounts of professional social closure (Murphy 1986). As will be demonstrated, these legacies still shape the post-Apartheid professional labour market despite efforts at transformation. On the other hand, post-structural accounts have suggested that there are subtler ways of achieving professional social closure and thus controlling entry into a profession, mobility within a profession and the ways in which different groups experience a profession. These forms of post-structural controls revolve around identities. In Western democracies, it is often about the ways in which racial and ethnic minorities, women and gay men experience entry and mobility within professions. For example, Rumens and Kerfoot (2009) describe the disciplinary power of professions on gay men's sexuality and its consequences for mobility within professions. Bolton and Muzio's (2008) work on gender segmentation in the law profession is another example. Examples from the global South that are published in English are fewer, but notable examples show the ways in which caste produces professional identities in India (Sidhu 2011) and the ways in which gender stratifies professions in Mexico (Ruiz 2012).

In Apartheid South Africa, universities served as an initial form of racialised social closure into professions. Tertiary institutions were segregated on the basis of race and ethnic group. Of the twenty-one universities, nine were for Africans (further segregated according to ethnic groups), two catered for Coloureds and Indians (one each), with the remaining fifteen for white South Africans (but divided between English-language and Afrikaans-language universities).

Those allocated to black South Africans often did not offer the tertiary qualifications that would enable a professional qualification. For example, no 'black' universities were allowed to offer the Certificate in the Theory of Accounting (CTA), a qualification required by all those who wished to become chartered accountants (Hammond *et al.* 2012: 337), and only 'whites-only' technikons (technical colleges) offered qualifications in textile design, ensuring that no black textile designers were able to qualify (Bonnin 2013). The only black university that offered an engineering degree accredited by the Engineering Council of South Africa was the University of Durban-Westville (a university for Indians) (Engineering Council of South Africa 2014).

The Apartheid state did not want to play a direct role in the day-to-day or primary welfare of African people and thus allowed black South Africans access to certain types of professions that would allow 'blacks to look after blacks'. It was uncomfortable with the idea of 'white hands' on 'black bodies' or 'black hands' on 'white bodies' in the fields of medicine and nursing, for example, hence they allowed black South Africans entry into these professions albeit in a controlled and segregated manner (Marks 1994). Black nurses were also not allowed to rise beyond certain ranks so as to avoid a situation where black nurses gave instructions to white nurses (Marks 1994). This ceiling on rank was also present in the other professions open to black South Africans. Other professions where blacks were allowed access included social work, teaching, and law. Professions outside the idea of 'social welfare' were not viewed as requiring black South African participation since they were not directly related to social welfare issues. This was in keeping with the ideas of separate development.

In 1957, there were 3,000 black nurses on the nursing register, in 2013, there were 129,000 nurses on the register, over 80 per cent of whom were classified as black South Africans (SANC). This is representative of South Africa's larger racial demographics. Nurses are divided almost evenly between auxiliary and professional nurses, though less equitably between the public and private sectors, with most nurses (60 per cent) situated in the public sector (Wildschutt and Mqolozana 2008).

For social workers, the same racialised thinking applied in terms of the training and education of black social workers. The logic of Apartheid dictated that, given that South African welfare services were racially divided, it 'made sense' for black social workers to be trained separately since they would only service black communities (Mazibuko *et al.* 1992). Separate professional bodies, divided along racial and ideological lines, also existed for social workers as recently as 2006 (Sewpaul 2012). In 2006, there were 11,100 registered social workers in South Africa, of whom 50 per cent were black South Africans (Lund 2010). These numbers have not gone up significantly since then due to the limited intake of social workers by universities (less than a thousand a year of which less than 50 per cent graduate) [personal communication, Dr Rubeena Partab, Social Worker, 5 March 2015]. The National Association of Social Workers in South Africa no longer keeps race-based figures on social workers, so census data has to be relied on (Lund 2010).

Black South Africans could study law at any approved black university. Theoretically, they could then practise law anywhere in South Africa. The reality, however, was that black lawyers were forced to practise in black townships and 'homelands' only. In order to practise in an urban area – a synonym for 'white area' – black lawyers had to seek official permission from the state. The state would assess the case and issue a permit. These permits were rarely issued (Midgley and Godfrey 2007). Unsurprisingly, law as a profession became dominated by white South Africans and, as Midgley and Godfrey (2007) demonstrate, white male South Africans. The types of law that were practised also took on a racial element. Black lawyers primarily specialised in criminal and sometimes human rights cases. Establishing a lucrative practice was difficult given that the entire judiciary and legal personnel outside the black homelands were white.

However, blacks had to attend the university allocated to their ethnic group, which restricted the possible number of black graduates into those professions. For example, for much of the twentieth century, the University of Natal Medical School was the only institution which admitted black doctors (see Noble 2013). In 1976, Medunsa, a medical university, opened. Situated in the far north of the country, its role was to train African doctors, dentists and allied health professionals (Hayes and Lee 1995). In some cases, blacks could apply for ministerial permission to study at white institutions, but in order for the application to be successful the applicant had to argue that the course they wished to study was not available at their designated ethnic institution. Even then, there were restrictions; for example, black medical students at the University of Cape Town were not allowed to work with white cadavers.

Acquiring (and blocking access to) the requisite formal education was the first tool in creating social closure in the Apartheid professional labour market. The second tool was the professional bodies themselves. Gatekeeping into all professions was controlled through state policy – a key piece of legislation was the 'job colour bar', which reserved skilled occupations for whites and was controlled through Clause 77 of the 1956 Amendment to the Industrial Conciliation Act. This legislation formalised what had previously been the norm of reserving skilled jobs for whites. But professional bodies both supported and rubber-stamped the state's racialised system of access into professions.

Black professionals, with the exception of those involved in health or welfare, were seen as 'non-essential' to the needs of the South African labour market and found it difficult to find employment within 'white' South Africa. Besides lawyers having to seek permission to set up a practice in 'white areas', Hammond *et al.* (2009: 710) make the point that professionals were 'specifically targeted for deportation to the Homelands'. Furthermore, employers (often linked to international firms) actively participated in keeping the professions white through the utilisation of forms of closure that excluded blacks. Black professionals who were fortunate enough to graduate with an appropriate qualification and to find articles or a clerkship were then faced with individual prejudices that resulted in them being refused job experience once employed (see Hammond *et al.* 2009, 2012). Recounting their experiences, black clerks talked about sitting in the offices doing photocopying while their white counterparts were assigned to audit teams (Hammond *et al.* 2012).

The racialised legacies of these policies continue to resonate in contemporary South Africa, specifically in the engineering, accountancy and medical professions. For example, in 2000, there were only 220 black chartered accountants in South Africa (Hammond *et al.* 2012: 335); by 2010, this number had increased to 1,738 (Solidarity, 2012: 6). The work of Hammond *et al.* (2009) demonstrates that, while many accounting practices introduced 'new South African programmes' in order to increase the number of qualified black accountants, the cultures of professional closure mitigated against the success of these projects.

In order to bring about racial transformation the state has developed a number of policies – the main components are around employment equity, black economic empowerment (BEE) and sector transformations. The Employment Equity Amendment Act (2014) (first passed in 1996) requires companies employing more than fifty employees to put in place measures to increase the representation of designated groups (i.e. black, women and disabled people) as well as submit an annual report to the Department of Labour indicating progress. In their 2013/14 Annual Report, the Employment Equity Commission reports that over the last three years an increasing number of employers have not only complied by submitting reports but have submitted accurately completed reports. BEE legislation (the Broad-based Black Economic Empowerment Act was passed in 2003) and policies require companies to submit various information indicating employment demographics, ownership and shareholding structures, supplier demographics, etc. in order to receive a BEE rating. Their BEE rating will provide an indication of the extent to which companies have 'transformed' and enable them to qualify for contracts, etc.

While the state has some influence (through legislation, for example) in regulating and promoting racial transformation, given that many of these professionals work in the private sector, the roles of employers, professional bodies, education and training bodies and organised labour are pivotal in this process. Professional bodies and training institutions have implemented a number of joint programmes to bring about transformation. For example, the South African Institute of Chartered Accountants (SAICA) has developed a Chartered Accountancy Profession Charter (see Perumal *et al.* 2012) to identify measures that need to be implemented to bring about racial and gendered transformation in the profession. The SAICA has also established the Thuthuku Programme, which manages a bursary and education fund for the training of black accountants. The project has two components: supporting maths education at school level through focusing on scholars with aptitude and providing bursaries and support at tertiary level for the education and training of black students who wish to enter the accountancy profession.

Whilst state legislation (employment equity and black economic empowerment legislation) can and has acted as a catalyst to increase quantitative racial diversity by forced compliance (through employment equity legislation, for example), very little is known about the qualitative experiences of black South Africans attempting to cross or who have crossed the 'colour bar' into the traditional (i.e. law, accountancy, engineering and medical) professions. Quantitative measures indicate progress, albeit slow, in the racial transformation of the labour markets for these four professions. A recent study (2012) by the Solidarity Trade Union (a more politically conservative trade union grouping) provides us with the following figures. In 1999, approximately 350 African attorneys were admitted, by 2008, the number had increased to approximately 430 annually. The total number of African charted accountants increased from 301 in 2002 to 1,738 in 2010. When looking at professional engineers, the number of black engineers increased from approximately 20 registering in 1994 to 50 registering in 2008. Examining the number of medical practitioners registered, one notes that there were just over 5,000 African medical practitioners registered in 2007 and this had increased to just over 7,000 in 2010. Interestingly, Solidarity makes a great show of these numbers, showing how the number of black chartered accountants has increased by 477 per cent and the number of attorneys by 37 per cent, thus making a case for the significant advancement of blacks in the professions (Solidarity 2012). However, we would suggest that such conclusions are incongruous given that the starting base of Africans in almost all the professions is so low that such percentage increases are in fact not as significant as the figures might suggest.

Looking more closely at the legal profession, one finds that racialised patterns remain today despite the legislated deracialisation of the profession. As Midgley and Godfrey (2007) state, most law firms are white-owned and offer internships or 'articles' to white law graduates. He further contends that, despite the racial democratisation of training and education in the professions, black law graduates are faced with more barriers in seeking employment than white graduates. Professional bodies have been asked to intervene in this regard. For example, in 2011, of all first-year law students, 78 per cent were black, 22 per cent white, 54 per cent were women and 46 per cent men. In the same year, of the 3,751 LLB graduates, 68 per cent were black, 32 per cent white, 59 per cent women and 41 per cent men (Nel 2013). At the level of advocates who fell under the umbrella of the General Council of the Bar (as at April 2012), 1,367 were white men, 366 white women, 295 African men, 89 African women, 47 Coloured men, 37 Coloured women, 114 Indian men and 69 Indian women. There seems to be greater equity at the rank of attorney. Of the 20,077 practising attorneys in 2011, 36 per cent were black and 64 per cent were white. Women constituted 34 per cent and men 66 per cent (Nel 2013).

What is needed is a more nuanced understanding of why the total numbers of black professionals in these fields is so low. Here the sociology of professions can contribute to understanding how social closure or gatekeeping (racial and gendered) in these professions occurs. A study by Hammond *et al.* (2009, 2012) gives some indication of the way in which the lived experience of professional closure has discouraged black articled clerks from qualifying as chartered accountants. Drawing on the theoretical framework postulated by Murray, Hammond *et al.* (2009: 706) identified the informal colour bar as manifested through language and cultural competencies as key components of professional closure. Furthermore, they demonstrate that the class inequalities created under Apartheid persisted in post-Apartheid society 'making it increasingly difficult to discern whether racial barriers or class barriers limited opportunities for blacks in public accounting' (Hammond *et al.* 2009: 717). A later study by Perumal *et al.* (2012) indicated differences of opinion between managers and trainees on the effectiveness of transformation measures. But such studies are a rarity; a lot more are needed in order for us to understand the challenges facing the deracialisation of the professions.

Furthermore, very little is known about the career mobility of black professionals once they are credentialed into these professions. The work of Hammond *et al.* (2009, 2012) does give some insight when they inform us that most black accountants, once qualified, left the 'Big Accounting Firm' in which they had served their articles, given the hostile atmosphere they had encountered there. Such experiences and the limited research in this area is a further challenge to the sociology of professions in South Africa.

New developments in the state regulation of professions

One of the concerns in the professions literature is the control of work by professionals themselves as well as their ability to self-regulate the profession (Adams 2015). A recent review (Bourgeault *et al.* 2009: 479) indicates that 'issues of work organisation, organisational change / restructuring and relations with the state / regulation were the most frequently cited macro issues examined'. The professions in South Africa have not escaped these concerns.

The most obvious example has been the state's focus on equity and the demands for professions to address this through affirmative action or a particular focus on training and access to resources for black and female professionals, as discussed above. There have been a number of debates within various professional bodies in recent years. The medical profession has been increasingly unhappy about the introduction of a year of community service prior to recently graduated doctors being able to register – this is in addition to two years' internship once they have completed their university degree (Erasmus 2012). In many cases, the community service is being used to respond to the shortage of doctors in small towns and rural areas, but the medical profession claims there seems to be little benefit in terms of the training of the doctors.

A more recent controversy in the medical profession relates to the recent signing into law of Sections 36 to 40 of the National Health Act, which state that all health professionals who wish to open a private practice will need to apply to the Department of Health for a 'certificate of need', which will give them permission to work in their chosen location ('Docs to be told where to work', *The Times*, 23 May 2014). The acquisition of such a certificate will be compulsory from April 2016. The purpose of the legislation is to ensure that health professionals are not over-concentrated in affluent urban locations, thus speaking to the need for access to health care. While the Act was passed ten years ago, this section was not originally promulgated (in 2005, doctors had marched to Parliament in protest), until the President did so unexpectedly. This generated substantial criticisms from health professional organisations, including the biggest doctors' organisation, the South African Medical Association. However, acting on the advice of the state law advisor, the Department of Health has asked the President to withdraw the promulgation of this section (Kahn 2015). Nevertheless, it appears the reprieve is only temporary, with the Department of Health saying it needs more time to craft the regulations (Kahn 2015).

There have also been recent interventions by the state in the regulation of the law profession ('Controversial Bill ends legal fraternity's self-regulation', *Mail & Guardian*, 13 November 2013). In 2013, the Legal Practice Bill was passed by parliament and promulgated by the President in November 2014. Amongst a number of controversial aspects, the Bill will abolish the current law societies (divided between attorneys and advocates[2]) and replace them with a 'legal practice council', many critics argue that this will 'erode the independence of the legal profession as it brings an end to the long tradition of self-regulation by the legal fraternity' ('Controversial Bill ends legal fraternity's self-regulation', *Mail & Guardian*, 13 November 2013). Initially, the Bill sought to remove the distinction between the professions of advocates and attorneys, and only after urgent pleas by professional bodies were these professional distinctions retained. Nevertheless, attorneys would dominate the new Council and many in the legal profession are concerned that a Council dominated by attorneys (with the Chair and Vice-Chair nominated by government) would be making regulations for advocates. Others, like well-known human rights advocate George Bizos 'were opposed to a situation where the executive would be granted far-reaching powers to control important aspects of the functioning of the profession' ('Controversial Bill ends legal fraternity's self-regulation', *Mail & Guardian*, 13 November 2013). For the government, the Legal Practice Bill was part of ensuring transformation in the legal profession and allowing government to ensure that citizens have a voice in the policies and practices of a profession that affects their daily life (Brand South Africa 2014). The Legal Practices Council came into effect on 1 February 2015, which brought into effect the transitional body, the National Forum on the Legal Profession, in preparation for the formation of the Legal Practice Council.

These developments point to an interventionist state that is wanting to have a say in the way professions regulate themselves, particularly with regard to access to professions by those who have been previously excluded, as well as to ensure that professions serve the public good.

State-led project of professionalisation

The Apartheid state implemented a racialised public service professionalisation project, which culminated in a white Afrikaner-dominated public service. The interventions, primarily affirmative action but also educational bursaries and preferential employment, shifted working-class white South Africans into middle-class professions within the state bureaucracy. To address this history, the post-Apartheid state project of professionalisation is targeted simultaneously at racial and gender transformation and the professionalisation of the public service. This is implemented through legislative reforms that target affirmative action favouring blacks and women and remove legislated barriers to employment. But it is also a class-based project in its attempt to grow a professional African middle class.

State intervention in the public sector

Apartheid policy ensured a white, and primarily Afrikaner, male-dominated public sector. It was a primary source of employment for the white population and was used as a mechanism to empower (economically and politically) Afrikaans-speaking whites. For much of the twentieth century, only white males and single white women were allowed to be employed in the public service. It was only in 1961 that the Public Services Joint Advisory Board recommended that married women could retain their jobs, and only in 1977 (in the wake of the Soweto crisis) that the South African Cabinet approved a policy that allowed 'non-whites' to be employed by the public service – with the proviso that this was only done on an ad hoc basis to meet the needs of the moment (see Swanepoel *et al.* 2005: 173). The idea that blacks could not be placed in a position of authority over whites prevailed. As with other areas of professional service work, separate departments were created to allow blacks to serve blacks. Nevertheless, there were large wage differentials between occupations at the same level in these racially separate departments.

By the time of the political transition in 1994, this legacy of race and gender discrimination remained. A 1999 study by Muthien (cited in Swanepoel *et al.* 2005) showed that even though women were able to compete freely against men for posts, a glass ceiling remained. A gender breakdown of the public service showed that women were at a much lower skill level than men and mostly located in the nurturing positions associated with the female gender. Black employees were primarily located in their 'own' departments within homelands and black townships, while the public service in urban locations was still dominated by whites. In an effort to address this, the Transitional Executive Council froze all vacancies and promotions and then advertised 11,000 posts in a major affirmative action drive (Swanepoel *et al.* 2005).

A slew of legislation aimed at transforming the public service and removing the effects of decades of legislated occupational closure based on race and gender was introduced in the post-1994 period. This included legislation that was specifically aimed at public services; for example the White Paper on Transformation in the Public Service (1995), the Public Service Law Amendment Act (1997), the White Paper on Human Resource Management in the Public Sector (1997), the White Paper on Public Service Training and Education (1997), as well as the more general employment equity legislation discussed above. The purpose of these state interventions was not only to remove the barriers to access and discriminatory measures that had ensured blacks, women and the disabled were not able to access these occupations in the same way as whites and men could (for example in the 1997 Public Service Law Amendment Act) but also to actively change the employment profiles of the public service. This was done through the implementation of a rigorous affirmative-action policy. The 1995 White Paper set targets for all government departments; these stated that there should be at least 50 per cent black representation at management level by 1999. Additionally, 30 per cent of all new appointments to middle and senior management were to be female. According to Thompson and Woolard (2002: 2), these goals were seen as minimum national targets. A more comprehensive affirmative-action policy was outlined in the 1998 White Paper on Affirmative Action in the Public Service, the Public Service Regulations stipulated that each department needed to include in their annual report precise information regarding their progress for the preceding year. Guiding all this legislation was the South African Constitution (Act No 108 of 1996) that stated that 'public administration must be broadly representative of the South African people, with employment management and personnel practices based on ability, objectives, fairness and the need to redress the imbalances of the past to achieve broad representation' (South Africa 2014: 29).

The question that arises is how successful were these measures. A study by Thompson and Woolard (2002) shows that by 2001, there had been a large increase in the total number of managers in the public service as well as an increase in the absolute number of Africans employed. While all race groups experienced an absolute increase in the total number of managers in the public service during this period, Africans show the greatest increase. By 2001, 63 per cent of managers were black. However, when one examines senior management specifically the picture is slightly different. In 1994, senior management (i.e. Director to Director-General level) was 94 per cent white and 95 per cent male (South Africa 2014). By 2001, whites still occupied a significant number of senior management posts, 45.5 per cent, which, as Thompson and Woolard (2002) observe, is out of proportion with their 12.3 per cent representation in the total population but still a significant shift from the position in 1994. Thus, as they observe, the proportion of whites in these senior management positions had been slowly decreasing since 1994.

By the end of the following decade, according to the Presidency's Twenty Year Review (South Africa 2014), the transformation of the public service had made further significant progress. A total of 1.3 million people were employed between national and provincial government. Of these, 57 per cent were female and 43 per cent male; 91 per cent were black (80 per cent African) and 9 per cent white (South Africa 2014: 29). The situation at senior management level had now changed significantly, even within the past decade: by 2011, 87 per cent of senior management were black. However, the position of women was still less than representative, and women were still to be found in the lower levels of the public services. While women made up 57 per cent of public service employees, only 38 per cent of senior managers are female (South Africa 2014: 30).

State attempts to professionalise the public sector

There is also a recognition by the state that the public sector has to become professionalised, and public service workers at managerial levels need to adopt and engage in 'professional' milieus and certification as a strategy to improve service delivery (see South Africa 2014: 31–38). The Twenty Year Review by the Presidency (South Africa 2014: 20) refers to the National Development Plan (NDP) in its admission that there is, what it terms 'an unevenness in capacity that leads to uneven performance in the public service'.

The term 'professional culture' is a key theme running through the NDP developed by the National Planning Commission in 2011 and subsequently adopted by the state (in particular, see Chapters 9, 10, 13 and 14). It contends that there is a need to build a more professional culture amongst educators, health workers and public sector workers. Whilst professionalism and professional culture is not explicitly defined in the NDP (professional status, skill, certification and competence seem to be at the heart of its discussion on professionalism), these are related to improving the accountability and service delivery of the state. Thus the NDP correlates effective public service delivery with inculcating a new professionalism (through training) and professional culture amongst public service workers. On the 8 March 2013, Public Service and Administration Minister, Lindiwe Sisulu, taking her cue from the NDP, stated that the state has a vision for a professional public service that does not include cadre deployment (*Daily News*, 8 March 2013). A Human Sciences Research Council study (*Daily News*, 8 March 2013) shows that only 0.4 per cent of managers employed by the public services have the requisite professional qualifications to effectively practise their jobs. This supports research findings in the Department of Health identifying a lack of professional managerial qualifications in the health sector as a major contributor to lack of public health. A consequence was that 100 hospital chief executives were replaced by candidates with 'professional' qualifications. In addition, the Department of Health has recently put in place minimum competency requirements for hospital managers (South Africa 2014: 32).

Another area that has recently fallen under the spotlight has been the competencies and qualifications of municipal managers and municipal chief financial officers (CFOs). Following concerns about the competencies of municipal managers and CFOs, the legislation governing their appointment and conditions of service was amended in 2007; after a period of grace in which they could ensure their qualifications would be in order (see 'Gordhan throws municipal staff a lifeline', *Sunday Independent*, 6 April 2014), those who have not complied now face dismissal. The daily newspaper *The Sowetan* ('Municipal managers to lose jobs', 10 March 2015) reports that the Minister for Co-operative Governance and Traditional Affairs Pravin Gordhan has indicated that action will be taken and at least thirty-six under-qualified municipal managers face dismissal. There are strong correlations between dysfunctional local municipalities and under-qualified municipal managers and CFOs. In this respect, the professional project is about producing a capable state through professionalisation (Bonnin and Ruggunan 2013).

The sociology of professions has drawn empirically from the development of professions in the global North to make theoretical points about the state and its role in the development of professions globally. While there is some recognition of differences between the USA, Europe and the UK, there is a tendency to theorise this particular role as normative. The limited but growing literature that examines the way in which race, caste and gender influences professional closure in post-colonial settings (see Hammond *et al.* 2009: 706), suggests that the role played by the modernising enlightenment state or the welfare state is just one trajectory amongst others. While this is an area that requires more research to understand the way in which the colonial and post-colonial state intervened in the development of professions in the South, the literature needs to acknowledge the specificity of the theoretical arguments around the role of the state.

Emergence of new groups of professionals/occupations

A fourth trend in the South African professions landscape is that the discourse of professionalism extends beyond what have traditionally been seen as expert or high-skill occupations. New occupational groups have emerged that are attempting to professionalise through strategies of credentialing, organising through new 'professional bodies' as opposed to union-based organising.

The professionalisation of new groups (those groups that sit outside the classical and traditional professions) in South Africa is occurring at three levels. The first is the professionalisation of blue-collar low-skilled/low-status occupations such as security guards; the second level targets occupations that require some tertiary education such as a diploma or undergraduate degree, such as media professionals, public relations professionals and air traffic controllers; the third level consists of occupations that require postgraduate or professional postgraduate qualifications, such as MBAs or other management-type qualifications. Common to all three levels is the belief that professionalisation will protect the status (symbolic or material) of these occupations.

Professionalisation of low-skilled occupations

South Africa has one of the largest private security industries in the world, but traditional attempts by unions to service security guards have not substantively increased their symbolic or material conditions of work. The formation of the professional body's register of 'qualified' security guards may be viewed as an alternative to unions in its attempt to organise security guards with regard to certification, industry-standard wages and codes of conduct. However, as work by Sefalafala and Webster (2013) has demonstrated, professionalisation of low-skilled/low-status occupations is often a top-down approach servicing the needs of employing bodies rather than workers themselves. The industry gets guards with some level of training who have complied with security checks and are credentialed by the professional body, and the guards themselves have the status of working for a 'better' company at industry-set wages. In this sense, professionalisation serves as a strategy of discipline and control.

In some cases, professionalisation processes represent attempts by both the state and/or existing professional bodies to incorporate and regulate occupations that lie outside of their control. An example of this are attempts to regulate and accredit professional healers and traditional surgeons (involved in traditional circumcisions) by the state. While the Traditional Health Practitioners Act was signed into law in 2008 and the Interim Traditional Health Practitioner Council of South Africa was inaugurated in 2013, the current struggle is more about internal regulation for human resource management purposes than recognition by the wider community. While these trends are not unique to South Africa (see, for example, the work on homeopaths by Saks (2003)), it is suggested that, in the context of a society that excluded and marginalised many of these occupations on the basis of the race of the practitioners and/or ideas of cultural superiority, these developments could add a different nuance to the existing literature.

Professionalisation of higher-skilled occupations

For occupations that require higher skill levels but don't necessarily enjoy high status, such as public relations or media occupations, attempts to professionalise are targeted at increasing social capital (networking) and symbolic capital (prestige) of these occupations. This is achieved by attempts to control who can gain access to practise these occupations.

High-skill and high-status professions such as those in the management field are also under transition in South Africa. For example, generic management as a discipline, profession and practice is giving away to more specialised forms of professional management, such as supply-chain management, human resources development management, marketing management and financial management. Each of these sub-fields of management is trying to establish itself as a unique profession and epistemic centre of its own. Business schools in South Africa are observing a decline in students registered for general management studies and an increase in students wanting to pursue more specialised forms of management, as these specialist forms of management potentially enjoy more symbolic and economic capital. In this sense, South Africa is following similar trends to Western countries.

We would suggest that this strategy is about both increasing status and cornering access to a labour market for both management professionals and security workers. These strategies acquire urgency given that so many are denied access to decent work, employment and protection in the labour market.

Conclusion

In this chapter we identified and discussed four shifts in the professional milieu in South Africa. We argued that the theme of transformation, access and the removal of barriers underlies all of these developments. From these discussions, three trends have emerged. The first is that race structures professions in very material ways. For South Africans, race determines access to professional labour markets and it determines where people are positioned within these markets. This does not discount post-structural accounts of race as one of many identities used to negotiate or deny entry into labour markets, but in the South African context, race has been reified in very material ways. Despite the efforts towards transformation, this continues to be the case in the post-Apartheid era.

Second, we observe an active project of racial and, to a lesser extent, gendered transformation which is led by an interventionist state. This is a state-led attempt to control and address historic forms of social closure based primarily on race but also around gender. The success of this project is variable, with the public sector experiencing rapid and deep racial transformation whilst the private sector has experienced a much slower transformation of professions. These interventions go beyond labour market legislation and we see the state intervening in the regulation of some of the traditional professions. The South African case is different from most other projects of achieving equity in workplaces and professions in that the emphasis is not on the representativeness of minorities in these professions but the representativeness of the majority of the country's demographic groups in these professions.

Whilst the legislated social closure of the South African case could be viewed as exceptional, it nevertheless resonates with Witz's (1992) arguments that the state is an agent of professional closure. She contends that professional projects can be projects of professional closure led by a mostly patriarchal capitalist state. Whilst her work examines the gendered nature of how these projects are articulated, it does support our argument that the Apartheid state very much engaged in a racialised and, to a lesser extent, patriarchal professional closure project. The post-Apartheid state continues to engage in a professional project; however, its agency is devoted to democratising this in terms of both race and gender.

Third, whilst we can quantitatively measure how 'transformed' certain professions have become through labour market statistics, South African sociologists know little about black or female professionals' qualitative experiences of professional trajectories and entry into these professions. What is needed is a more nuanced understanding of why the total numbers of black professionals in these fields is so low. We know because of the disproportinate numbers of black and female professionals that social closure has found new forms in post-Apartheid South Africa, but we do not know how this becomes operational and how it might intersect with class. This remains an important task for the sociology of professions in South Africa.

Furthermore, this discussion shows that there needs to be a wider exploration of the role played by the post-colonial state in the professions. The story of professions and the modernising enlightenment state or the welfare state is but one amongst others.

Notes

1 In Apartheid South Africa, all South Africans were classified by the 1950 Population Registration Act according to their 'race'. Those of African descent were known as Africans; those who originated from the Indian sub-continent were called Indians; those of mixed-race were known as Coloured; and, those of European descent, white. Collectively, Africans, Indians and Coloureds were called black – this was a political term used in opposition to Apartheid terminology which over the years changed the various terms.
2 White South Africans are over-represented amongst 'advocates'.

References

Adams, T. (2015) 'Sociology of professions: International divergences and research directions', *Work Employment and Society*, 2(1), pp. 154–165.

Bolton, S. and Muzio, D. (2008) 'Can't live with 'em; can't live without 'em: Gendered segmentation in the legal profession', *Sociology*, 41 (1), pp. 47–64.

Bonnin, D. (2013) 'Race and gender in the making and remaking of the labour market for South African textile designers'. Paper presented to the *British Sociological Association Work, Employment and Society Conference*, University of Warwick, 3–5 September.

Bonnin, D. and Ruggunan, S. (2013) 'Editorial: Towards a South African sociology of professions', *South African Review of Sociology*, 44(2), pp. 1–6.

Bourgeault, I., Benoit, C. and Hirschkorn, K. (2009) 'Introduction: Comparative perspectives on professional groups. Current issues and critical debates', *Current Sociology*, 57(4), pp. 475–485.

Brand South Africa (2014) 'New body to regulate SA's legal practitioners', 29 September 2014. www.southafrica.info/about/salpc290914.htm#.VQXNg-G1f0w (last accessed 15 March 2015).

Buhlungu, S. (2009) 'South Africa: The decline of labour studies and the democratic transition', *Work and Occupations*, 36(2), pp. 145–161.

Engineering Council of South Africa (2014) *University Degrees Accredited as Meeting the Educational Requirement for Registration as a Professional Engineer.* Document E-20-PE, 5 November 2014. www.ecsa. co.za/education/EducationDocs/List_of_AccrUniv_E-20_PE.pdf (last accessed 16 April 2015).

Erasmus, N. (2012) 'Slaves of the state: Medical internship and community service in South Africa', *The South African Medical Journal*, 102(8), pp. 655–658.

Gilbert, L. (1998) 'Community pharmacy in South Africa: A changing profession in a society in transition', *Health & Place*, 4, pp. 273–285.

Hammond, T. Clayton, B. and Arnold, P. (2009) 'South Africa's transition from apartheid: The role of professional closure in the experiences of black chartered accountants', *Accounting, Organisations and Society*, 34, pp. 705–721.

Hammond, T., Clayton, B. and Arnold, P. (2012) 'An "unofficial" history of race relations in the South African accounting industry, 1968–2000: Perspectives of South Africa's first black chartered accountants', *Critical Perspectives on Accounting*, 23, pp. 332–350.

Hayes, M. and Lee, A. (1995) 'MEDUNSA and the training of black doctors for South Africa', *Academic Medicine*, 70(2), pp. 115–121.

Kahn, T. (2015) 'Plans to regulate where doctors work put on ice', The South African Optometric Association website www.saoa.co.za/index.php/contacts-us/directors/2-latest/291-plans-to-regulate-where-doctors-work-put-on-ice (last accessed 27 January 2016).

Lund, F. (2010) 'Hierarchies of care work in South Africa: Nurses, social workers and home-based care workers', *International Labour Review*, 149(4), pp. 495–509.

Marks, S. (1994) *Divided Sisterhood: Race, Class and Gender in the South African Nursing Profession.* Johannesburg: Wits University Press.

Mazibuko, F., McKendrick, B. and Patel, L. (1992) 'Social work in South Africa: Coping with apartheid and change'. In M. C. Hokenstad, S. K. Khinduka and J. Midgely (eds) *Profiles in International Social Work.* Washington: NASW Press, pp. 129–142.

Midgley, R. and Godfrey, S. (2007) *Scarce and Critical Skills: Law Professionals.* Report for Labour and Enterprise Policy Research Group, University of Cape Town.

Murphy, R. (1986) 'Weberian closure theory: A contribution to the ongoing assessment', *The British Journal of Sociology*, 37(1), pp. 21–41.

Nel, A. (2013) 'Too many whites are still advocates, attorneys', CensorBugbear. www.censorbugbear.org/africa/south-africa/too-many-whites-are-still-advocates-attorneys (last accessed 27 January 2016).

Noble, V. (2013) *A School of Struggle: Durban's Medical School and the Education of Black Doctors.* Pietermaritzburg: UKZN Press.

Nzimande, B. (1991) *The Corporate Guerrillas: Class Formation and the African Corporate Petty Bourgeoisie in Post-1973 South Africa.* PhD thesis, University of Natal.

Perumal, R., Perumal, S. and Mkhize, M. (2012) 'Transforming the accountancy profession through broad-based black economic empowerment', *Alternation Special Edition*, 5, pp. 122–139.

Ruiz, M. (2012) 'Time demands and gender roles: The case of the big four company in Mexico', *Gender Work and Organisation*, 19(5), pp. 532–554.

Rumens, N. and Kerfoot, D. (2009) 'Gay men at work: (Re)constructing the self as professional', *Human Relations*, 62(5), pp. 763–786.

Saks, M. (2003) *Orthodox and Alternative Medicine: Politics, Professionalisation and Health Care.* London: Sage.

Sefalafala, T. and Webster, E. (2013) 'Working as a security guard: The limits of professionalization in a low status occupation', *South African Review of Sociology*, 44(2), pp. 76–97.

Sewpaul, V. (2012) 'How social work in South Africa entered a new era'. *The Guardian*, 5 July 2012. http://gu.com/p/38np9/sbl (last accessed 28 February 2015).

Sidhu, J. (2011) *The Interplay between Caste and the Accounting Profession in India.* Australia: University of Ballarat.

Solidarity (2012) *South African Transformation Monitor.* Pretoria: Solidarity Research Institute.

South Africa (2014) *Twenty Year Review: South Africa 1994–2014,* Pretoria, The Presidency. www.20yearsoffreedom.org.za/20YearReview.pdf (last accessed 14 March 2015).

Swanepoel, B., van der Westhuizen, E., Erasmus, B. Schenk, H. and Wessels, J. (2005) *South African Human Resource Management for the Public Sector.* Cape Town: Juta.

Thompson, K. and Woolard, I. (2002) *Achieving Employment Equity in the Public Service: A Study of Changes Between 1995–2001.* University of Cape Town, Development Policy Unit, Working Paper 02/61.

Walker, L. (2005) 'The colour white: Racial and gendered closure in the South African medical profession', *Ethnic and Racial Studies*, 28(2), pp. 348–375.

Wildschutt, A. and Mqolozana, T. (2008) *Shortage of Nurses in South Africa: Relative or Absolute?* Report for South African Department of Labour, Pretoria.

Witz, A. (1992) *Professions and Patriarchy*. London: Routledge.

18

India (International) Inc.

Global work and the (re-)organization of professionalism in emerging economies

Swethaa Ballakrishnen

Introduction

The increasing prominence of new kinds of knowledge work around the world has reoriented the ways in which we think about professionalism and organizational change (Evetts, 2003). Especially with new kinds of transnational workflows and value chains, professionals are being organized, valued and oriented in ways that did not exist even a few decades ago. Since much of this emergence is unprecedented, new forms of work and new types of workers have found themselves introduced into novel professional spaces that contest existing prestige, professional identity and internal stratification. And while these phenomena have affected institutions worldwide, their effect has been particular in emerging countries like India that newly support the supply end of these operations.

Naturally, the extent of this transformation has been widespread and many sectors have encountered new types of professionalization (and, in turn, professionals) over the last few decades that contrast with, extend and/or alter pre-existing boundaries. In this chapter, I trace the organization and emergence of three different, but related, high-status professional spaces in India that have responded to this demand for new types of global work, law, management consulting and information technology (IT). I choose to focus on these three fields because their comparative introspection offers a unique lens to evaluate emergence in global contexts. Particularly, while each of these sectors has undergone transformation as a result of globalization, their neoliberal extensions have varied in both style and scope. Further, as one way of understanding internal stratification, I pay especial attention to the ways in which gender negotiations have played out in these different kinds of professional spaces. The vast gender and work literature in India has been restricted to women in low-skilled labor – using this lens of gender to dissect the different kinds of high-status professional emergence offers us a chance to look more closely at variations in this neoliberal organizational emergence.

To unpack these variations, I organize this chapter as follows. First, I outline the ways in which new types of professional emergence and reorganization have occurred in these three sectors. Second, I highlight the organizational differences in the three cases and analyze the impact it has had on internal gender stratification. Finally, I use these comparative genesis findings to illustrate the ways in which globalization of work has introduced new professional spaces for the contestation of prestige and power. I argue that professional spaces that are built on institutionally settled organizational forms (for example, consultants in a Mumbai office of a global consulting firm) are likely to be different from professional emergence that is devoid of a Western prototype (for example, domestic law firms that do international work). Similarly, I highlight that there tend to be differences in the ways in which older professions with set institutional scripts (e.g. law) vary from other kinds of professional spaces that have emerged as a response to entirely neoliberal demands in the marketplace (e.g. information technology).

By engaging in this comparative exercise, I expect these accounts to inform us significantly about professional boundary creation, contestation and institutional adaptation in the emerging world.

Global professions go to India

In his seminal work on the sociology of professions, Macdonald (1995) lays out how the professions are ripe ground for investigating the sociological heartlands of culture, monopoly, closure and stratification. While Macdonald's 'professional project' was fundamentally interested in Western economies and hierarchy, over the last three decades, sociologists have returned to his theoretical premise in attempts to understand more global patterns of occupational and organizational change (Cooper and Robson, 2006; Faulconbridge and Muzio, 2012).

The impetus for this is obvious, with the expansion of international business over the last three decades, new kinds of organizational forms, processes and phenomena have emerged as necessary solutions to sustain and supplement different models of global production. And as a response to the demand for efficient and territory-agnostic services, we have seen a rise in complex 'transnational' (Bartlett and Goshal, 1999) or 'globally integrated' (Palmisano, 2006) organizations across the world that purport to blur the boundaries between the local and the global (Prahlad and Doz, 1999).

For emerging economies like India, the novelty of this organizational emergence has been doubly pertinent. First, research focusing on the subcontinent's new identity as a service provider has been quick to highlight the ways in which these new businesses and organizations have influenced both economic and political context (Evans, 1995; Dossani, 2008). Second, these new kinds of global organizations and workspaces have offered a chance for Indian professional workforces to be employed in unprecedented ways, in terms of both structure and culture. Research on Indian elite professional workforces reveals that these new global organizations have been pivotal in creating new cultures of professionalism (Khadria, 2001; Mirchandani, 2004; DiMello and Sahay, 2007) and are seen as avenues to claim new forms of legitimate and social capital (Mirchandani, 2004; Radhakrishnan, 2011; Nadeem, 2011; Ballakrishnen, 2012). Thus, together, these organizations have influenced the creation and sustenance of new professional spaces and, with them, new kinds of professionals.

At the same time, given India's market liberalization, there has been a natural variance in the structural conditions that set up these different professions. By the end of the twentieth century, the professional landscape for law in India had begun to dramatically change following a range of financial reforms in 1991 that opened the markets to foreign investment,[1] but not all markets were exposed to foreign intervention and attention in the same way. In turn, this staggered liberalization set in place different emergence trajectories for these spaces and professionals alike.

The 1991 reforms conceived brand new professional spaces that had never before existed like IT and management consulting. But even in sites where there was no complete overhaul, the reforms introduced novelty and organizational change to existing professional spaces. In professions like law, for instance, the reforms spearheaded new actors and clients that demanded

Table 18.1 Field and firm emergence for major Indian professions

Field	Post-1991	Global organization	New organization
Consulting	*	*	*
IT	*	*	*
Accounting		*	*
Banking		*	*
Law			*

a professional emergence that could cater to new kinds of transactional work which had not existed before, such as international mergers and acquisitions and global public offerings.

The sectors also vary in the ways in which they relate to their global counterparts. While organization in consulting and IT has followed a traditional multinational corporation (MNC) model with control and ownership often with a global organization, organization in law has been less in touch with Western organizational scripts. No doubt globalization changed the kinds of work that came under the purview of lawyers. But as new organizational entrants to a settled professional system, a strong domestic political movement resisted the entry of global lawyers and practice firms. Law remained internally regulated and outside the professional purview of international firms – adding yet another layer of specificity to this emergence story.

Thus, while globalization of markets has produced neoliberal sectors like IT that are intrinsically dependent on international value chains and organizations, sectors like law continue to be deeply nationally regulated, leaving foreign firms as distant frameworks of inspiration. It is through this prism of novelty and emergence that I seek to review these new professional workspaces in India. Especially from the perspective of how these professional spaces have organized professionals, it is clear that these different factors have been integral in their respective emergence histories. In particular, I argue that three core structural factors are central to this emergence, especially in terms of determining environments for professionals in these firms: (a) field and practice novelty, (b) global exposure and (c) barriers to entry for professionals (see Table 18.1). Together, I argue that these factors have come together to produce distinct strains of globalization – *mainstream, fringe* and *responsive*, and it is to the exploration of these differential histories that I turn in this chapter.

India's information technology sector: mainstream globalization

Even for the non-nuanced observer, the explosion of the IT sector has been the capstone of globalization in the local professional landscape. One of the fastest growing industries in the country, IT contributes to 8.1 percent of India's GDP, a significant growth from 1.2 percent in 1998, when it was first introduced as part of the country's national priority mandate by the Vajpayee government (NASSCOM, 2014). But it is not just national significance that makes this industry prime for the study of global influences in professionalization – at 38 percent of all exports, IT also accounts for the single largest share of India's total service exports. And with a presence in over 52 countries, 500 global client destinations and over 1,000 cross-border acquisitions and captive organizations, the IT sector has been a prime site of mainstream professional globalization.

I highlight these over the wealth of other statistics that the National Association of Software and Services Companies (NASSCOM) declares every year on the industry to illustrate three main dimensions of this sector's professional workforce. First, more than any other sector, IT has been the most prominent in revolutionizing 'work' in local contexts. For instance, over half the knowledge professionals working in this sector are graduates with professional degrees in engineering or, to a smaller extent, medicine, accounting, law (NASSCOM, 2014). While professions like law, accounting and consulting have been influenced by global forces to varying degrees (as I will elaborate later in this chapter), none of them have been to the same extent as in the IT industry, just in terms of scope.

Second, as the country's highest-impact sector employing over 3 million professionals, IT is also India's largest private sector employer – a drastic change from the pre-liberalization sectors that were predominantly publicly owned. Particularly, scholarship on the emergence of the IT industry (Evans, 1995; Singh, 2000; Chanda, 2002; Dossani, 2008) has marked the relevance of this move from public to private as an important factor in creating professional ideology at the level of the workers. Satish Deshpande, for example, emphasizes how the shifting of the developmental state has meant a shift in the emergence of the middle class – with differentiated elites becoming the predominant producer of ideologies that the middle class consumed (Deshpande, 2003). Thus, the sector has been all-important in ushering in a new set of global ideologies in public imagination that has included bureaucratic norms and non-partisan management.

Third, the newness of the IT sector not only influenced the move in ownership from public to private, it also introduced a new set of global actors – clients, investors, management, organizations, etc. – who were part of the framework of this professionalization. As a neoliberal industry with no preexisting frameworks in the domestic context, these professional spaces have been inherently embedded in their global identities. Nowhere else has the proliferation of global firms and industry infiltrated local conscience and economy to the same extent (Singh, 2000).

Together, the scope and nature of the sector's proliferation has meant that global scripts have influenced more organizations and workers in this sector than any other – resulting in a more mainstream transformation of what 'global' means to workers, organizations and even more common cultural parlance. It would not be a stretch to say that local professionalization as a function of global influence is more likely to be thought of in terms of this sector than any other.

But this impact on globalization and private ownership did not mean changes at the macro level alone. And a prominent brand of recent scholarship has focused on not just the institutional proliferation of these sectors but also the intermittent connection between these macro influences and micro identities (Nicholson *et al.*, 2000; Van den Broek, 2004; Taylor and Bain, 2005; D'Mello, 2005; Chakravartty, 2006; Radhakrishnan, 2011; Nadeem, 2011; Aaftaab, 2012).

For young graduates, especially, global IT firms and career paths have become prominent destinations to invest their aspirational capital. The impact of globalization on emerging country elites, particularly in terms of understanding the systemic reproduction of internal hierarchies, has been well documented (for example, across different international adaptive contexts, see Dezalay and Garth 2002, 2010). In contrast, the case of IT work in India has been pertinent; as a movement not restricted to just the elites, it has meant a reorientation of India's newly mobile middle class (Singh, 2009; Nadeem, 2011). Recent research on global attitudes (Milanovik, 2013) shows that the main 'winners of globalization' have been the middle classes of emerging market economies. And as a fiscally profitable sector not riddled with traditional bureaucratic practices, India's IT sector has become the core destination for middle-class college aspirants keen on collecting these rewards.

Management consulting in India: globalization at the fringes

While human resource consultants and company managers existed prior to liberalization reforms in 1991, it was only following liberalization that global management consulting firms brought their practices to India. And to the extent that we limit our analysis to novelty alone, the emergence of this professional field was not all that different from IT. But, unlike IT, which took the service industry by storm and reshaped the public consciousness of 'international work', the professionalization of India's management consultants happened at a considerably different scale. For instance, despite having been introduced to the Indian market at around the same time, consulting is, at best, a USD 1.5 billion market (Source Global Research, 2013) as compared to the estimated USD 150 billion market that is the IT industry (NASSCOM, 2015). Similarly, while IT employs 3 million workers, most management consulting firms have between 50 and 400 client-facing consultants – thereby working in an entirely different framework of operation and infiltration.

But despite these differences, both sectors professionalized under the serious influence of globalization, albeit through different mechanisms. Similar to the IT sector, management consulting firms are privately owned and managed with predominantly bureaucratic scripts focusing on industry best practices and attention to global comparisons. But the trigger for these formations is slightly different – while IT companies were organizing their professional spaces in response to global clients, practices and ideology (see, for example, Radhakrishnan, 2011, Nadeem, 2011 and Aaftaab, 2012), consulting firms have had easier access to these global scripts as Indian offices of foreign firms. Although these firms often find resistance to organizational standardization in these local contexts, they predominantly operate in standard MNC fashion, following structural cues from their original global blueprints. Similarly, while IT professionals are situated in new organizations set up to respond to foreign clients, workflows and practices, management consulting firms are new institutions set up *by* multinational entities interested in exploring Indian markets. Finally, these sectors attract and retain a very different type of professional worker. The scale of IT operations in India allowed for a range of professionals to be recruited – thereby widening the opportunity window for more and more Indians to partake in the mobility project. In contrast, the smaller management consulting sector maintained a much more restrictive recruitment process that limited itself to elite graduates from the country's top business and engineering schools.

They are, however, important sites for understanding the ways in which professional identities and margins have been shaped by globalization in the emerging-country context. Particularly, even though they affect only a small proportion of the population, these elite professional sectors are crucial in their role as shaping India's new professional elite class. Nowhere is this more obvious than in the comparison of median salaries between professionals in these two sectors. While the median starting salary for a systems engineer in Mumbai, India, is INR 546,302 a year (about USD 9,000/yr), starting consultant salaries are about four times that amount at INR 20,00,000 (about USD 32,552/yr) *and* they include a performance-based variable bonus of up to INR 600,000 (about USD 9,766). By offering entry-level salaries that were unthinkable at senior levels even a few decades ago, these new firms and global cultures offer to a new (even if very small) generation of young Indians a chance at speed mobility that is not feasible in the much larger IT sector. Thus, subject to very high entry barriers, these outposts of global professional service firms advance incrementally higher rewards to a much more limited pool of talented, upwardly mobile Indian graduates.

India's corporate law firms: responsive globalization

Unlike service professions like IT and management consulting that were direct products of the 1991 federal liberalization reforms that internationalized Indian markets, corporate law firms in India have emerged in another slight variation. While it was indeed new markets and clients that set up the demand for these firms, unlike IT and management consulting, this avenue for professional work emerged *within* an already pre-existing professional framework. Further, unlike most other sectors, nationalist regulation continues to restrict the entry of foreign firms into the Indian professional market for legal services. Thus, while most of IT and management consulting has emerged in a way scripted by organizational connections to Western firms and markets, the Indian sector for legal services offers a new contrast to the globalization process by being the only elite professional sector to remain entirely closed to foreign investment and global firm moderation.

I focus on the emergence of corporate law firms and professionals within them for the purposes of this comparative exercise because it offers prime context for extending the preceding two examples of global professionalism and reorganization. Although a small part of the larger Indian legal profession, these firms are crucial examples of neoliberal professional reorganization and a formidable 'corporate elite' (Papa and Wilkins, 2011) within the larger, more traditional legal profession – a set-up that affords insight into the ways in which global influences are moderated in established sectors. But the Indian corporate law firm case is also interesting for the range of other ways in which it varies from other forms of global impact in the reorganization of work. Two factors are of particular relevance for this emergence: first, the phased opening of domestic industries to foreign direct investment following India's market liberalization in 1991 and, second, a closed market for legal services that prohibited direct entry of foreign law firms into the Indian landscape.

As I have argued elsewhere (Ballakrishnen, 2013), first, new kinds of transactional work (e.g. mergers and acquisition) came under the professional purview of Indian lawyers as the opening of the domestic market in general brought to India new kinds of international and cross-border transactions work that required domestic legal advice and representation.[2] Second, unlike the traditional organization of litigation practice, which consisted mainly of lawyers connected by kinship or similar background working in small offices (Dezalay and Garth, 2010), this transactional work did not have pre-existing organizations ready to receive it. As a consequence, firms that did corporate work were new organizations that evolved to meet this new transactional sophistication. Third, for the first time, a lot of this transactional work, especially in the most prestigious of these firms, included a strong international component, where either the work or the clients were non-domestic. Finally, since a combination of regulatory factors limited the entry of international law firms into the Indian legal market, the emergence of these new 'global' firms, unlike its counterparts in other Asian countries (e.g. Liu, 2008), was without direct structural support or intervention.

All of this also meant that following 1991, there was a sudden influx of new kinds of corporate transactional work that was being demanded by Indian and global clients alike. India's rapid industrial growth had changed the kind of work that lawyers were beginning to be transactionally involved in, and booming domestic markets meant existing clients of many firms were now beginning to retain lawyers for new kinds of business negotiations involving project finance, general corporate expansion, secured debt and banking. Much of this work required not just lawyers who could represent clients in courts but solicitors who would give legal advice on corporate transactional law and practice. It was to respond to this need that new kinds of bureaucratically organized enterprises – present-day corporate law firms loosely modeled on the Western law firm – emerged in the Indian landscape in the early 1990s.

Professionals within this sector add a new kind of nuance to the workings of globalization in India. First, unlike IT and consulting, their emergence was not couched in field-novelty since the legal profession in India was not in itself new. Second, unlike the large firms in IT and consulting, these organizations were not managed and operated by multinational entities. As local firms responding to global markets without actual blueprints of how global organizations worked, these firms were especially impressive sites of understanding professional emergence in more diluted global environs. They show us the power of firms responding to cultural norms and institutional standards without actual relationships to their parent scripts. It is this variety of globalization that is *responsive* to external triggers without actually being attached to it that sets these firms apart structurally from their peers.

Women in professional work

The micro-level prominence of these sectors' professional emergence has not been missed by the wealth of research over the last three decades. While the first wave of research on these sectors focused on the relevance of globalization as a harbinger of new jobs, this has since been replaced by research that pays particular attention to the interplay between local characteristics and their resultant intersections with global agendas (Arun and Arun, 2002; Kelkar *et al.*, 2002). In particular, a global agenda and influences have been critical in reshaping the construction of the 'modern' Indian woman, especially as regards impacts on motherhood, family, consumption and nation (Fernandes, 2000; Donner, 2008; Radhakrishnan, 2011). Even so, there remain stark differences in the ways gender plays out in these different sectors. First, I set out the ways in which gender plays out in predominant accounts of high-status work in India. Then, to help unpack the different frameworks that shape emergence across these various sectors, I tease out the ways in which gender plays out in each of these sectors. Feminization of these firms is a useful way to understand emergence because it gives us insight into how these environments are experienced by actors within them. It also gives us tangible ways of understanding the impact of these various strands of globalization as they apply to professional emergence.

Gender and high-status work in India

Not unlike evidence from other parts of the world, in the Indian context, studies on women and work outside of agriculture remain primarily concerned with the informal sector and low-wage employment (e.g. Swaminathan, 2012; Paul, 2009; Raju and Bagchi, 1993). With the advent of liberalization, there has been some indication of an increase in the different types of work available to women, but this too has been confined largely to routine, segregated and task-intensive labor (Mukherjee, 2004) within sectors like IT (e.g. Jhabvala and Sinha, 2002), outsourcing (Patel, 2010), foreign export (Jeyaranjan and Swaminathan, 1999) and telemarketing (Gothoskar, 2000). To the extent that there is research on professional workforces, it confirms an essentialist prejudice to feminization in select family-friendly sub-fields like obstetrics and gynecology for women doctors (Sood and Chadda, 2010), 'customer-relations'-friendly human resource positions for women managers (Gupta *et al.*, 1998) or communication-related manager posts for female engineers (Patel and Parmentier, 2005). In addition, research on women within high-prestige professional tracks shows that they are subject to persistent gender role expectations and penalties for deviance. For instance, Patel and Parmentier (2005) show that female engineers in India from elite engineering schools (IITs) continue to be on the periphery of employing organizations with large socio-economic disparities when compared to their male peers. Work on women in academia and science more generally (Gupta and Sharma, 2002) shows that there is a strong patriarchal bias to female participation and promotion within elite organizations. Other research on highly educated women shows that while women match and sometimes surpass men at entry levels within prestigious organizations, they advance at rates that are much less significant than their male peers who started with them (Kumar, 2001). Similarly, research on women in the Indian managerial workforce testifies to strong entry constraints (Jain, 1975), fewer opportunities for within-organization training and education (Buddhapriya, 1999), a resistance to women in positions of power (Nath, 2000; Naqvi, 2011) and an overall male bias (Gulhati, 1990), even among managers who think of their organizations as meritocratic (Gupta *et al.*, 1998).

Thus, in the Indian case more generally, workforce feminization has followed this expected trend of being either essentialism-driven or low-prestige work. For instance, in the Indian example of legal reorganization and firm formation, the process-outsourcing example is less persuasive as a true site of innovative gendering of work because these firms are relatively low prestige compared to large law firms and corporate practice. Much like other examples of feminization, this concentration of women in lower-prestige work is not uncommon (England, 1992). The case of large concentrations of women in Indian legal process outsourcing units (LPOs) is still noteworthy, but it is not as unique because it is circumscribed by the lower prestige of these jobs. And in the few cases where highly educated women have managed to break entry barriers into prestigious workforces, their advancement and value has varied significantly from that of their male peers.

Women in IT: traditional advantages

Gender ratios in India's IT sector – about 31 percent – do not trail behind global estimates of the female workforce in similar fields. However, this blanket representation is not indicative of the barriers to advancement and sustainability that women face on entry.

Marissa D'Mello's (2005) exhaustive account of the literature from over a decade ago continues to offer a good paradigm to view the way gender works in Indian mainstream globalization. In her account, D'Mello argues that a range of social and cultural limitations came in the way of women entering and advancing in the workforce, including inherent socialization, gendered workplace expectations and mobility handicaps. And from accounts since then, these barriers to entry continue to persist to some extent – evidenced by the fact that women continue to be represented at lower levels of power and often in female-type jobs (see e.g. Jhabvala and Sinha, 2002).

Although this mainstream globalization has not been a magic wand with powers to completely eradicate existing cultural notions of patrifocal power, it *has* brought about changes in terms of redefining the role of the transnational global worker. For instance, Radhakrishnan's (2011) recent work on globalization and identity formation in India's 'silicon valley' reveals that these new professional workspaces do indeed help reorient the construction of dominant ideology and give women a chance to reinvent their access to professional work. Seen as 'good work' that supports families while being morally upright, this global IT work has offered India's new middle-class woman an opportunity to champion a new identity at work without losing leverage of an important prior identity tied to her morality. At the same time, Radhakrishnan warns that this trumping of gender is not without other structural disadvantages, and not all women can stake a claim to these advantages – the very ability of transnational Indians to prioritize family and work differently, she argues, is a reiteration of a strain of class-based stratification.

Women in management consulting: restricted advantages

Unlike the IT sector, whose growth and prominence is well documented, research on elite service professionals is much more scarce. As still nascent industry that is yet to infiltrate the local market to its full potential, most of the data about the sector is restricted to industry-level observations. From my own fieldwork on high-status professionals in Mumbai, India, which included a consultant sample (Ballakrishnen, 2015), I find that women in management consulting practices raise standard issues that scholars studying gender in elite workforces have long identified as the persistent problem of sustaining egalitarian workplaces: gender-typed essentialism (Pierce, 1996), sustainability of female careers (see Kay and Gorman, 2008 for a review), lack of adequate mentorship (Epstein, 1981; Blake-Beard, 2001), male-friendly partner composition (Chambliss and Uggen, 2000; Gorman, 2005) and overall gender-based stratification (Epstein, 2000). While consultants enter at about the same rates as professionals in the IT workforce (30 percent in top firms), attrition is high, especially among women. Many women move to less-prestigious 'back-office' roles that don't involve time-intensive client handling, and few manage to get promoted to senior levels of partnership, especially when also faced with dual responsibilities of marriage and motherhood.

Further, in contrast to Radhakrishnan's findings that women found global IT work as a fair compromise between morality and work opportunity, women in international consulting firms saw the failure of gender representation at senior levels as a function of being supplanted in the Indian context. Even though consulting firms had more committed gender programs, mentoring networks and other scheduled structural incentives for women to do well, many professionals thought these measures didn't 'stick' *because* they were housed in an Indian socio-cultural environment where expectations and externalities – by way of families, peers and clients – stood in the way of realizing the more egalitarian outcomes that were possible in less patriarchal environments. Take, for example, this male consultant's explanation for why women were poorly represented in senior positions within elite consulting firms even though the firm was committed to being inclusive:

> They have a chance of choosing flexible work hours, they can certainly pick projects that are closer to where they want to be, but even with all that, women leave.... There is no difference between men and women – in fact, the only time it makes a difference, is in promotion. But that is because the amount of time you need to invest is more and so, then, it matters. But it doesn't matter to the firm – if you do as much work as a man, you'll get your promotion – but it probably matters to family and neighbors who will not want a woman to spend so much time at work outside the house.

This assumption that the firm is doing everything it can to help women integrate better into professional life but that it is the women who are not taking advantage of it speaks directly to the variance in background assumptions and expectations that inhabit these different workspaces. By seeing the organization as agentic ('*in fact, the push is to encourage women to stay*'), the firm was absolved in this professional's mind and any gender disadvantage was solely on the slate of the woman professional and the endogeneity of her environment.

Women in elite law firms: Unusual advantages

In drastic contrast to both these cases – and in contrast to its own larger field – the case of women in India's elite corporate law firms poses a puzzle. In the country's most prestigious and largest corporate law firms, women are one half the population, not just at entry but at more senior levels of partnership.

This is peculiar for a range of reasons. Existing and recent research (Schultz and Shaw, 2003; Michelson, 2013) all point to a consistent and increasing global feminization of the legal workforce. But while these accounts have suggested the lagging of certain Asian countries in this trend (Kay and Gorman, 2008), it is not until recent comparative research (Michelson, 2013) on the demography of the legal workforce internationally that we have had any grasp of how vast the disparity is, particularly in the Indian context. Not only has India – like its other Asian counterparts – had a lower rate of feminization of the profession, this research suggests that it has the *lowest* rate of feminization. Women in most Western countries represent 30 percent (USA) to 50 percent (Finland) of the workforce, and while representation in other Asian countries is lower (about 10–20 percent), the percentage of women in the Indian professional landscape has remained flat at about 5 percent (Michelson, 2013).[3]

Further, even though the legal profession remains predominantly male and hierarchical at the country level, recent accounts of feminization and success for women lawyers within certain types of legal firms poses a second important puzzle. From these accounts, women do well within two types of firms. They do well in LPOs where research (Ballakrishnen, 2012) shows that they not only join in comparable numbers to men but also have moderate to high success in being hired and promoted to managerial and training positions. And second, there is evidence (Ganz, 2012) that they do well in two large 'international' law firms[4] where they not only enter at the same rate as their male peers, but also get promoted and rewarded on 'track' with these peers (India Business Law Journal, 2012). In other words, in the country's largest and most prestigious firms, men and women are equally represented not just at entry level but also at partnership.

Thus, at both of these levels of entry and success, the particular and limited case of Indian women working in large, global-style corporate law firms offers an interesting contrast to traditional accounts. First, the Indian legal profession is a notable exception to this otherwise consistent trend of feminization within the profession globally. Second, in spite of this context of a highly gendered professional workforce (or, as one can argue, because of it), certain firms in India seem to be delivering highly egalitarian advantages to their women lawyers, not just at the level of entry but at the levels of advancement and success. This is a rhetoric that is salient not only in the general context of what we know from the women and professions literature but particularly in the context of India, where women are so poorly represented in other positions of power. Together, this sets up a unique context for understanding the negotiation of gendered hierarchies in these spaces.

Discussion

The variance in these three professional cases gives us a quick snapshot of the imperialist possibilities of the Western professional model. Not only do structural and environmental differences cause firms to emerge differently, they also afford their inhabitants very different experiences of globalization. In particular, three kinds of structural conditions predominantly impact this variance in gender outcomes across these sites. The first is the novelty of the field and practice area. As new firms doing new work, all of these firms have the potential to renegotiate pre-existing frameworks of identity and propriety (Ridgeway, 2009). But the advantage of the Indian corporate law firm case is that, in addition to being a new sub-field, regulatory restrictions also require that it be subject to domestic ownership and management.

Together, this primes a second structural condition that is relevant in predicting this variance – global exposure. Indian corporate law firms as local firms responding to global clients without access to global emergence scripts seem naturally capable of affording gender egalitarian workspaces. Unlike consulting firms and IT firms that 'do' globalization in a standard MNC manner, elite corporate law firms as elite domestic firms *responding* to a foreign market of clients and competition are structurally different in the ways they absorb and replicate international cues and standards for emergence. They are owned and managed domestically, but have an important audience – foreign clients – and this places on them an onus to respond to

Table 18.2 Structural characteristics of Indian professional emergence

	Field + practice novelty			Global exposure		Barriers to entry		Globalization type
	Novel field	Novel organization	Novel work	Global clients	Global ownership	Supply	Scope	
IT	*	*	*	*	*	Varied	Broad	Mainstream
Management consulting	*	*	*		*	Elite		Fringe
Corporate law		*	*	*		Elite		Responsive

standards of international meritocracy. While large corporate law firms did work for domestic clients, a large part of their work was to service international clients. As the sole providers of legal services, this monopoly on the service market meant not just that they were emerging in a market where they had to negotiate their legitimacy but also that they were emerging in a market where their interaction was rife with sophisticated actors who did not prime gender in interactions in the same ways that peers in other firms who were facing more traditional clients were likely to face.

A third structural condition that remains relevant in the construction of this gender-friendly emergence are the barriers to entry to these professional workspaces. Corporate law firms are also significantly aided in creating egalitarian environments by the ways in which their supply pool is recruited and socialized in their schools. As a small part of the larger legal profession, these firms attract and retain the best students from the most prestigious law schools. But in this, too, there is the added advantage of novelty – prestigious law schools in India, the National Law Schools, are new institutions that emerged alongside these corporate law firms post-liberalization. Hiring from a gender-egalitarian graduating pool differentiated this elite supply significantly from the consulting firms that recruited from established elite schools that were more traditional and deeply gendered. In the case of IT firms, the vastness of the field also means that barriers to entry are relatively lower and more variant. While here, too, the firms are new and the work is new, the hiring pool is riddled with strong gendered biases.

Together, the ways in which gender plays out in these different professional spaces give us one slice of the relevant structural characteristics set up by different strands of globalization (see Table 18.2). In the IT sector, the more diffuse and *mainstream* version of globalization reaches more people and assumes a more general format of what is assumed to be 'international' or 'global'. In turn, this vast proliferation and its assorted allied assumptions allow gender hierarchies to be renegotiated in the name of being 'global' and 'moral' (Radhakrishnan, 2011). But the broad scope of the field results in a much less concentrated pool of professional women, especially at the more senior levels. Consulting firms are advantaged by field and practice novelty, but because their clients are mostly local, women feel distinctly gender primed in interactions. Thus, while institutionally similar to IT in terms of being a product of neoliberalism, consulting firms, unlike their mainstream peers, are sites of *fringe* globalization. Not only do these sectors operate on different scales, these firms are also much less a part of mainstream professional consciousness as fewer people realistically aspire to enter and succeed in these firms. Indian corporate law firms, as new firms doing new work but within regulatory restrictions that inhibit access for foreign corporate firms, emerge in an interesting vacuum that bodes well for their professional inhabitants. On the one hand, they are new sites doing new work without steeply gendered expectations of the ideal worker (Acker, 1990). At the same time, regulatory circumscriptions mean that these firms are emerging under the *expectations* of globalization rather than the rewards of it – setting them up to be competition-fearing organizations with strong hurdles of legitimacy to overcome. As new firms with no global associations to lend them weight, their competition in the international market depends on the marketing of their modernity. This *responsive* globalization is possibly born out of an organizational commitment to be competitive in international markets and the over-compliance to gender neutrality is one way in which they appease these assumed concerns (Ballakrishnen, 2015).

Conclusion

I have used these comparative genesis findings to illustrate the ways in which globalization of work has introduced new professional spaces for the contestation of prestige and power. I argue that professional spaces that are built on institutionally settled organizational forms are likely to be different from professional emergence that is devoid of a Western prototype. Similarly, I highlight that there tend to be differences in the ways in which older professions with set institutional scripts vary from other kinds of professional spaces that have emerged as a response to entirely neoliberal demands in the marketplace. In turn, each of these comparisons yields different outcomes when viewed through the lens of gender representation and parity. While each of them relies on globalization and global impetus at varying degrees, the ways in which they translate to internal accounts of stratification are distinct. Together, these findings give us one way to begin to dissect the ways in which reorganization and adaptation of professional frameworks happen in an emerging-country context.

Notes

1 In 1991, the government shifted to a more open economic policy that included, predominantly, a greater involvement of the private sector and the first move towards codified foreign direct investment. With particular regard to the impact this liberalization has had on the legal profession and law firms, see the recent work of Krishnan, who argues that 'liberalization has enhanced the powers of these lawyers already at the higher end of the pyramid' (2013, p. 4).

2 As Papa and Wilkins (2011) explain, 'Before 1991–1992, conventional corporate legal activities such as project, finance, investment law, intellectual property protection and environment regulation, were almost unknown in India and there was practically no market demand for junior or senior lawyers for any assignment coming from outside the country (ICRIER 1999).'

3 Even the less conservative estimates by the Bar Council of India stagnate this number at about 10%, Bar Council of India. 2010. Statement of total number of advocates enrolled with the State Bar Councils as on 01/02/2010. Available at http://120.138.244.28/advocates/num-advocates.php.

4 I refer to these large law firms as 'international' not because they are global law firms in India. Note that India's legal market is closed, leaving international business in the hands of domestic law firms that have had to restructure themselves and respond to this global transactional workload.

References

Aaftaab, Nadeed Gina (2012) *Branding a Global Identity: Labor Anxieties, Conspicuous Consumption and Middle Class Culture in Hyderabad, India.* PhD dissertation, University of Minnesota.

Acker, Joan (1990) 'Hierarchies, jobs, bodies: A theory of gendered organizations'. *Gender and Society* 4(2), pp. 139–158.

Arun, Shoba, and Arun, Thankom (2002) 'ICTs, gender and development: Women in software production in Kerala'. *Journal of International Development* 14(1), pp. 39–50.

Ballakrishnen, Swethaa (2012) '"I love my American job": Professional prestige in the Indian outsourcing industry and global consequences of an expanding legal profession'. *International Journal of the Legal Profession* 19(2–3), pp. 379–404.

Ballakrishnen, Swethaa (2013) *Women in India's 'Global' Law Firms, Comparative Gender Frames and the Advantages of New Organizations*. Globalization Lawyers and Emerging Economies (GLEE) Working Paper Series, Harvard Law School Program on the Legal Profession.

Ballakrishnen, Swethaa (2015) *'Same Same' But Different: Accidental Feminism and Unintended Parity in India's Professional Firms*. PhD dissertation, Stanford University.

Bartlett, Christopher A., and Ghoshal, Sumantra (1999) *Managing Across Borders: The Transnational Solution*, Vol. 2. Boston, MA: Harvard Business School Press.

Blake-Beard, Stacy D. (2001) 'Taking a hard look at formal mentoring programs: A consideration of potential challenges facing women'. *Journal of Management Development* 20(4), pp. 331–345.

Buddhapriya, Sanghamitra (1999) *Women in Management*. New Delhi: APH Publishing.

Chakravartty, Paula (2006) 'White-collar nationalisms'. *Social Semiotics* 16(1), pp. 39–55.

Chambliss, Elizabeth, and Uggen, Christopher (2000) 'Men and women of elite law firms: Reevaluating Kanter's legacy'. *Law & Social Inquiry* 25(1), pp. 41–68.

Chanda, Rupa (2002) *Globalization of Services: India's Opportunities and Constraints*. New York: Oxford University Press.

Cooper, David J., and Robson, Keith (2006) 'Accounting, professions and regulation: Locating the sites of professionalization'. *Accounting, Organizations and Society* 31(4), pp. 415–444.

D'Mello, Marisa (2005) '"Thinking local, acting global": Issues of identity and related tensions in global software organizations in India'. *The Electronic Journal of Information Systems in Developing Countries* 22. Available online at www.ejisdc.org/ojs2/index.php/ejisdc/article/view/164 (last accessed 27 January 2016).

D'Mello, Marisa, and Sahay, Sundeep (2007) '"I am kind of a nomad where I have to go places and places"… Understanding mobility, place and identity in global software work from India.' *Information and Organization* 17(3), pp. 162–192.

Deshpande, Satish (2003) 'The centrality of the middle class'. In Satish Deshpande, *Contemporary India: A Sociological View*, pp. 125–150. India: Penguin Books.

Dezalay, Yves, and Garth, Bryant G. (eds) (2002) *Global Prescriptions: The Production, Exportation, and Importation of a New Legal Orthodoxy*. Michigan, MI: University of Michigan Press.

Dezalay, Yves, and Garth, Bryant G. (2010) *Asian Legal Revivals: Lawyers in the Shadow of Empire*. Chicago, IL: University of Chicago Press.

Donner, Henrike (2008) *Domestic Goddesses: Maternity, Globalization and Middle-Class Identity in Contemporary India*. Aldershot, UK: Ashgate.

Dossani, Rafiq (2008) *India Arriving: How This Economic Powerhouse Is Redefining Global Business*. New York: AMACOM Division of American Management Association.

England, Paula (1992) 'From status attainment to segregation and devaluation'. *Contemporary Sociology* 21(5), pp. 643–647.

Epstein, Cynthia Fuchs (1981) *The Woman Lawyer*. Chicago, IL: University of Chicago Press.

Epstein, Cynthia Fuchs (2000) 'Women in the legal profession at the turn of the twenty-first century: Assessing glass ceilings and open doors'. *University of Kansas Law Review* 49, p. 733.

Evans, Peter B. (1995) *Embedded Autonomy: States and Industrial Transformation*, Vol. 25. Princeton, NJ: Princeton University Press.

Evetts, Julia (2003) 'The sociological analysis of professionalism: Occupational change in the modern world'. *International Sociology* 18(2), pp. 395–415.

Faulconbridge, James R., and Muzio, Daniel (2012) 'Professions in a globalizing world: Towards a transnational sociology of the professions'. *International Sociology* 27(1), pp. 136–152.

Fernandes, Leela (2000) '"Nationalizing the global": Media images, cultural politics and the middle class in India'. *Media, Culture & Society* 22(5), pp. 611–628.

Ganz, Kian (2012) 'Amarchand promotes 13 partners, 70% women, in boon to corporate, comp, lit'. Available online at www.legallyindia.com/201205052795/Law-firms/amarchand-promotes-13-partners-70-women-in-boon-to-corporate-comp-lit (last accessed 12 February 2016).

Gorman, E. H. (2005) 'Gender stereotypes, same-gender preferences, and organizational variation in the hiring of women: Evidence from law firms'. *American Sociological Review* 70(4), pp. 702–728.

Gothoskar, S. (2000) 'Teleworking and gender'. *Economic and Political Weekly* 35(26), pp. 2293–2298.

Gulhati, Kaval (1990) 'Attitudes toward women managers: Comparison of attitudes of male and female managers in India'. *Economic and Political Weekly* 25(7/8), pp. M41–M48.

Gupta, A., Koshal, M., and Koshal, R. J. (1998) 'Women managers in India: Challenges and opportunities'. *Equal Opportunities International* 17(8), pp. 4–18.

Gupta, Namrata, and Sharma, Arun K. (2002) 'Women academic scientists in India'. *Social Studies of Science* 32(5–6), pp. 901–915.

India Business Law Journal (2012) India Business Law Directory, available online at www.indilaw.com/pdfs/Directory%20of%20Indian%20Law%20Firms.pdf (last accessed 12 February 2016).

Jain, D. (ed.) (1975) *Indian Women*. New Delhi: Ministry of Information and Broadcasting.

Jeyaranjan, J., and Swaminathan, P. (1999) 'Resilience of gender inequities, women and employment in Chennai'. *Economic and Political Weekly* 34 (16/17), pp. 17–24.

Jhabvala, R., and Sinha, S. (2002) 'Liberalization and woman worker'. *Economic and Political Weekly* 37(21), pp. 2037–2044.

Kay, Fiona, and Gorman, Elizabeth (2008) 'Women in the legal profession'. *Annual Review of Law and Social Science* 4, pp. 299–332.

Kelkar, G., Shrestha, G., and Veena, N. (2002) 'IT industry and women's agency: Explorations in Bangalore and Delhi, India.' *Gender, Technology and Development* 6 pp. 63–84.

Khadria, B. (2001) 'Shifting paradigms of globalization: The twenty-first century transition towards generics in skilled migration from India'. *International Migration* 39(5), pp. 45–71.

Krishnan, Jayanth K. (2013) 'Peel-off lawyers: Legal professionals in India's corporate law firm sector'. *Socio-Legal Review* 9(1), pp. 1–59.

Kumar, N. (2001) 'Gender and stratification in science: An empirical study in the Indian setting'. *Indian Journal of Gender Studies* 8(1), pp. 51–67.

Liu, S. (2008) 'Globalization as boundary-blurring: International and local law firms in China's corporate law market'. *Law and Society Review* 42(4), pp. 771–804.

Macdonald, K. M. (1995) *The Sociology of the Professions*. California: Sage.

Michelson, Ethan (2013) 'Women in the legal profession, 1970–2010: A study of the global supply of lawyers'. *Indiana Journal of Global Legal Studies* 20, p. 1071.

Milanovic, B. (2013) 'Global income inequality in numbers, in history and now'. *Global Policy* 4(2), pp. 198–208.

Mirchandani, K. (2004) 'Practices of global capital, gaps, cracks and ironies in transnational call centres in India'. *Global Networks* 4(4), pp. 355–373.

Mukherjee, M. (2004) 'Women and work in the shadow of globalisation'. *Indian Journal of Gender Studies* 11(3), pp. 275–290.

Nadeem, S. (2011) *Dead Ringers: How Outsourcing Is Changing the Way Indians Understand Themselves*. Princeton, NJ: Princeton University Press.

Naqvi, F. (2011) 'Perspectives of Indian women managers in the public sector'. *Indian Journal of Gender Studies* 18(3), pp. 279–309.

NASSCOM (2014) *Indian IT-BPM Industry: Collaborating For Growth*. NASSCOM Report, available at www.nasscom.in/indian-itbpm-industry-collaborating-growth.

NASSCOM (2015) *India IT-BPM Overview*, available at www.nasscom.in/indian-itbpo-industry.

Nath, D. (2000) 'Gently shattering the glass ceiling: Experiences of Indian women managers'. *Women in Management Review* 15(1), pp. 44–52.

Nicholson, B., Sundeep, S., and Krishna, S. (2000) 'Work practices and local improvisations with global software teams: a case study of a UK subsidiary in India.' *Proceedings of the IFIP Working Group 9.4 Conference on Information Flows, Local Improvisations and Work Practices*.

Palmisano, Samuel J. (2006) 'The globally integrated enterprise'. *Foreign Affairs* 85(3), p. 127.

Papa, M., and Wilkins, D. B. (2011) 'Globalization, lawyers and India: Toward a theoretical synthesis of globalization studies and the sociology of the legal profession'. *International Journal of the Legal Profession* 18(3), pp. 175–209.

Patel, R. (2010) *Working the Night Shift: Women in India's Call Center Industry*. Stanford, CA: Stanford University Press.

Patel, R., and Parmentier, M. J. C. (2005) 'The persistence of traditional gender roles in the information technology sector: A study of female engineers in India'. *Information Technologies and International Development* 2(3), pp. 29–46.

Paul, T. (2009) *Women Empowerment through Work Participation*. Delhi: New Century Publications.

Pierce, Jennifer L. (1996) *Gender Trials: Emotional Lives in Contemporary Law Firms*. Berkeley, CA: University of California Press.

Prahalad, Coimbatore Krishna, and Doz, Yves L. (1999) *The Multinational Mission: Balancing Local Demands and Global Vision*. New York: Simon & Schuster.

Radhakrishnan, S. (2011) *Appropriately Indian: Gender and Culture in a New Transnational Class*. Durham, NC: Duke University Press.

Raju, S., and Bagchi, D. (1993) *Women and Work in South Asia: Regional Patterns and Perspectives.* London: Routledge.

Ridgeway, Cecilia L. (2009) 'Framed before we know it: How gender shapes social relations'. *Gender & Society* 23(2), pp. 145–160.

Schultz, Ulrike, and Shaw, Gisela (eds) (2003) *Women in the World's Legal Professions.* London: Bloomsbury.

Singh, A. (2009) *Globalization of Services and the Making of a New Global Labor Force in India's Silicon Valley.* PhD dissertation, University of California, Santa Barbara.

Singh, Y. (2000) *Culture Change in India.* Jaipur: Rawat Publications.

Sood, M., and Chadda, R. K. (2010) 'Women in medicine: A perspective'. *Indian Journal of Gender Studies* 17(2), pp. 277–285.

Source Global Research (2013) *The India Consulting Market*, available at www.sourceglobalresearch.com/our-reports.

Swaminathan, P. (ed.) (2012) *Women and Work*. New Delhi: Orient Blackswan.

Taylor, P., and Bain, P. (2005) '"India calling to the far away towns": The call centre labour process and globalization'. *Work, Employment and Society* 19(2), pp. 261–282.

Van Den Broek, D. (2004) 'Globalising call centre capital, gender, culture and work identity'. *Labour and Industry* 14(3), pp. 59–75.

19

Professions and professionalization in Russia

Elena Iarskaia-Smirnova and Roman Abramov

Introduction

Classic sociological approaches to the study of professions were conducted from a perspective typical of the Anglo-American context, while in Continental Europe and other contexts, occupational groups may not be the main actors in these processes. Professionalization here thus may be promoted 'from above' by the state, which plays the main role in the development of the professions (Siegrist 1990). But states also differ. In the case of socialist Russia, one must take into account the role of the ruling Communist Party. In fact, it was the single-party bureaucratic and at times autocratic state that provided the professions with additional ideological frames and functions.

In order to study the professions in Russia, where the party-state has had a much more central role in the organization of social life than have governments in capitalist or mixed economies (Jones 1991), one needs to consider the historical changes that occurred before, during and after the period of state socialism (Krause 1991, p. 5). This chapter will focus on the pre-socialist and state-socialist periods of the history of professions and professionalization in Russia.

We begin with a brief glance into the history of the modernization reforms of the eighteenth century to see the origins of the strong role of the state in the institutionalization of the professions. Then we consider the important changes that occurred in the late nineteenth century, in the course of liberal reforms, which affected a transformation of social structure, opened the way for new occupations and expanded opportunities for professionalization.

Then we describe the dynamic and complex remapping of professional structure within the society after the socialist revolution. After that, we turn to a discussion on how the new understanding of professions was formed and revised throughout recent Soviet history and conclude by outlining the main trends of professionalization processes in pre-socialist and socialist Russia as well as a short outline of what changes have occurred in the post-Soviet state.

Professions and professionalization before socialism

The training of technical experts was established by the state at the beginning of eighteenth century in the fields of military engineering, medicine and mining, as well as for ministerial officials

(Raeff 1966). The engineering, legal and medical professions were given priority as army-related occupations, which has developed their authority in close relation with the autocratic policies in Russia since those times.

In addition to the dominant role of the state in Russia, professional autonomy was also limited by the strong estates (*soslovie*) order formed there by the eighteenth century. This structure offered social groups a legal form of collective organization (Freeze 1992, pp. 47–48). Belonging to an estate was inherited by birth. While many professional occupations had been developing in tsarist Russia, they lacked official definition and group identity other than through these estates (Frame 2005, p. 1028; Pomeranz 1999).

The devastating outcomes of the Crimean War (1854–56) showed the insufficient industrial and technological development and lack of trained personnel in military and civilian occupations in Russia. These conditions threatened to undermine the empire's position among the European powers (Ringlee 2010). The liberal 'Great Reforms' implemented from the late 1850s abolished serfdom, enabling increased physical, social, and intellectual mobility (Balzer 1996, p. 56). While the estates were not abolished, they were subject to democratization and professionalization. The reforms targeted public enlightenment, expanded educational opportunities, and modernized and professionalized both military and civilian educational institutions (Ringlee 2010), and in the late nineteenth century opportunities for women to study at university were opened up.

The women's movement had fought for more opportunities for training in new and existing professions. In late Imperial Russia, women increased their participation in such high white-collar occupations as teachers, especially in Moscow and other large cities, and were gradually occupying medical practice, starting at less prestigious levels, since 'medicine was becoming an acceptable occupation for female graduates; a number of leading feminists were doctors' (Edmondson 2004, p. 231).

The process of professionalization in late Imperial Russia was reflected in the language. In a famous edition of the Russian dictionary of those times (Dahl 1865) we cannot find the word *professiia* [profession], but there is a word 'professor' interpreted as a mentor and a teacher of the university. However, the term *professiia* was used in a sense of an occupation in relation to the actual work of educated people.

Although Russia was a country with a predominantly agrarian economy, by the late nineteenth century, the Great Reforms and the development of capitalism had led to the expansion of the social group of so-called *raznotchintsy* (literally, 'men of various ranks'), most of whom were professionals (engineers, doctors, lawyers, teachers, university professors). The local councils (*zemstvo*) required trained employees – statisticians, clerks, architects, postal employees, etc., and leading professions such as engineers, doctors, teachers, lawyers, university professors and state bureaucrats only then began to emerge and consolidate as separate entities (Balzer 1996). The professional ideal grew among them 'based on expertise and selection by merit' (Bailes 1996, p. 40) in contrast with the hereditary principles of *soslovie* and the ideals of profit and market competition of Russian entrepreneurs (Freeze 1992, p. 41). The entrepreneurial middle class in late Imperial Russia was rather weak. Between 1850 and 1914, professional occupations grew here faster than did such groups as the merchants, industrialists and bankers (Bailes 1996, p. 41).

While, for some professional occupations, economic issues of low status, low pay, unemployment and altruism were important vehicles of self-organizing for professionalization (Balzer 1996), in most cases, it was the state that spurred professional organization. The Russian Technical Society was established in 1866, and soon thereafter Chemical, Physical, Mining, Medical and other societies appeared as well. They organized conferences, published research works, edited professional journals. As the state established modern professional occupations and intervened in their development, the professionals were faced with the dilemma to 'free themselves from the tutelage of the state, while still using the state for their own ends' (Bailes 1996, p. 45).

The important role of the state prevented professional occupations from being fully autonomous or self-regulating, but their frustration with the state provided a basis for cohesion. Many educated professionals were deeply disappointed with the tsarist regime and developed a rich and sincere critical culture of Russian intelligentsia (Nahirny 1982). Both the government and professionals began to take an official interest in acute welfare issues (Edmondson 2004, p. 231). Spreading their views through journals, conferences, and professional associations, as well as through the educational system and the broader media, professionals formed circles, trying to influence government decisions and carry out direct social change in such areas as education, health, defense and the economic development (Bailes 1996, p. 42).

Political dissent increased after liberal reforms. Many liberal policies were abandoned by the new tsar, Alexander III, who reduced the authority of *zemstva* and reinforced the role of the secret police. At the same time, he developed economic policies and, by the beginning of the twentieth century, Russia was undergoing modernization of industry and transportation; but political modernization was stuck. Before the revolutions of 1905 and 1917, Russia faced a huge complex of political, socio-economic and cultural contradictions (Hutchinson 1999; McKean and Thatcher 2005). The rights of the workers were in devastating condition, and the well-being and health of the population deteriorated. A politically active minority of radical and liberal intelligentsia spurred the revolutionary waking of the masses.

This was again reflected in changes in terminology. After the bourgeois revolution in 1905, the mention of *professiia* also occurs in relation to the industrial labor occupations, especially in publications concerned with criticisms of the poor situation of workers, for instance of women typists in typography (Svavitskii and Sher 1909, p. 42), or in relation to the activities of *professional'nyi soyuz* [trade unions].

In sum, although agriculture was the main occupation in pre-revolutionary Russia, many modern professions began to emerge. They were developed under conditions of rigid state control and the embeddedness of professional work in the administrative system, on the one hand, and the advent of self-organizing communities demanding greater political, civil and social rights, on the other (Ryavec 2003). This complex map was swept aside by the socialist revolution in 1917, which launched further radical changes in the social structure of Russian society and effected deep transformation of the professional identities and ways of life of various occupational groups.

Rethinking professions and professionalization during the first decades of state socialism

The processes of economic and social modernization began immediately after the Bolshevik Revolution in 1917, which required the establishment of new or modifications to existing institutions of industrial management, health care, education, the police, legal system, and technology. In the framework of 'central planning', an extensive party-state administration tried to comprehensively regulate all economic activities (Mrowczynski 2012) and the welfare of the citizens. New hierarchies started to grow.

In the initial post-revolutionary period, labor legislation was reformed in order to displace capitalist elements of labor relations and to change occupational structure. The proletariat was proclaimed as a hegemon of socialist revolution. In the words of Sarah Ashwin (2000) The main role of women was as levers through which the regime could gain increased control over society (p. 3), and their liberation was to 'free' human resources to 'serve the communist cause' (p. 5).

From the late 1920s to the end of the 1940s, health care for industrial workers became a priority. Doctors were under pressure by the state, which was interested in maximizing the use of human resources. Behind the scenes, they were instructed to reduce the sick-list as much as possible. As M. Field argues (1972, cited in Krause 1991, p. 13), the medical profession in the USSR turned from a relatively small and prestigious professional group into a mass occupation with the elite of academicians and famous doctors, on the one hand, and poorly paid ordinary practitioners, on the other, with the growing proportion of women among them.

The Central Research Institute of Labor, established by the direct order of Lenin in 1921 and directed by Alexei Gastev, studied various legal, medical, social, and psychological aspects of work. The word *professiia* was widely used at this time to denote any occupation. Thus, the traditional distinction between professions and occupations was not as clearly delineated in USSR/Russia as in Anglo-Saxon contexts.

Soviet sociologist and economist Stanislav Strumilin and his colleagues elaborated the first Soviet classification of occupations to be used in the first census of 1920 (Klassifikatsiia 1921; Strumilin 1921; see also Abramov 2014). The 1921 annual edition of statistics contains data arranged by 29 groups of professions, including agricultural, forest, miners, textile workers, builders, workers of communication, transport, nutrition, hygiene, art, education, finance, medicine, pharmacy, Soviet *sluzhashchie* [educated employees], and *chernorabochie* [laborers] (TsSU 1922). The census instructions defined a 'profession' as 'an occupation to which a surveyed person is adjusted most of all according to a special training or to a previous job, even though this profession is not his main occupation' (TsSU 1920, p. 18). These instructions reflected the precarious situation of many educated professionals and other populations facing unemployment, famine, persecution, and displacement in the first years after the revolution and civil war. As the instruction said, it might be the case that a given person had not engaged in his profession for a long time, examples being factory workers, peasants or craftsmen, doctors, etc. Overall, 'profession nowadays is only a secondary occupation', the census instruction said (TsSU 1920, pp. 18–19).

Soviet attempts to rationalize industrial production were associated with methods of scientific management, and issues of professionalization were crucial in this regard. But the model of the managerial generalist adopted from American business could not be fully applied in a non-market context. In the 1920s, 'many managers opposed professionalization as a threat to their careers and their positions while ideologues opposed it on the ground that it threatened to cut off channels of social mobility' (Beissinger 1988, p. 189). The official doctrine declared that the Soviet Union was a 'workers' state'. The legacy of this ideology prevented professionalization until very late periods of socialist history. Nevertheless, over time, the levels of education increased and managerial functions became more sophisticated and specialized. In the mid 1930s, only 14 percent of Soviet enterprise directors had a higher education, by 1965, this share had increased to one third, and as late as 1970 that figure had risen to 42 percent (Beissinger 1988, p. 210). The status of all white-collar occupations, especially professions that connect with administrative and managerial labor also increased.

A new system of privileges constituted new Soviet classes despite the regime's rhetoric of universality and equality. The political and administrative ruling class consisted of the regional and national political and economic elite: leaders of the Party organizations at different levels, and heads of industrial plants and ministerial departments. This professional bureaucracy, called the 'new class' by Djilas (1983), developed its own lifestyle and subculture. A special closed education and training system was established for them, with high career opportunities for the graduates and strictly secured entrance for outsiders. Until the collapse of the Soviet Union, they held the political and administrative authority in the country.

The social and occupational structure of socialist society was changing in the course of military-industrial modernization, and the functional specialization led to the development of modern Soviet professions (Jones and Grupp 1987, p. 5). The range and scope of these professions was quite similar to many other industrial countries of the time. The main emphasis was on the rise of engineering professions and, of course, an intelligentsia loyal to the regime, doctors and lawyers, writers, artists, and teachers – the 'workers of ideological front'. Some professions did not emerge at all while others were prohibited for decades. Some scientific fields (e.g. sociology and psychology) were suppressed after being labeled as ideologically incorrect, and in many cases, the leading professionals in these disciplines were terrorized and executed (Graham 2004). For example, as official state policy did not recognize the existence of social problems, a need for social work could not be explicitly articulated, and this profession did not exist in Soviet Russia until the end of state socialism. Its functions were implemented by other occupations, namely by the welfare officers whose work was directed by strict ideological instructions to distinguish between 'ours' and 'alien elements'.

Professional organizations

Professional associations were allowed but groups would be closely monitored. Any possible sign that group interests deviated from those of the proletarian dictatorship could be interpreted as anti-Soviet activity. Public groups of engineers, agronomists, physicians, and teachers were subject to official sanctions from the Soviet security apparatus (Finkel 2007, pp. 67–68). Fine arts groups were under strict pressure as well.

The state encouraged the development of forms of self-government, for instance, youth organizations, scientific-technical societies or trade unions. These not only nurtured collective activities and provided people with symbolic resources and informal relations but also assisted the Party and the state in ruling the country and managing the particular industries. The scientific-technical societies supported by the state since 1921 were an important form of collectivity of the professionals. They promoted popularization of science and technology, supported creative initiatives, encouraged the enthusiasts of labor. Later, in 1954, they were relegated under the jurisdiction of the *professional'nye soyuzy* [trade unions]. Trade unions united all workers, peasants, and employees of all occupational groups (intelligentsia) as well as students of vocational and higher educational institutions. They were defined as schools of communism, were led by the Party and contributed to the building of socialism. In addition to the trade unions, a number of professional associations were (re)established, but they were subordinate to the trade unions and the state.

In the first half of the 1930s, a system of *tvorcheskie soiuzy* [creative unions] was established in the USSR (unions of composers, artists, architects, theater people), as the guilds providing internal ideological control over the activities of their members. A creative union was a hybrid organization (Wilensky 1964). It combined professional and bureaucratic functions and was neither a trade union nor a professional association. Wilensky considered this mix of professions and bureaucracy as a barrier to professionalization. In the case of Soviet liberal arts, these creative unions executed strict control over their members under the guidance of the Party and security apparatus. At the same time, the unions gave their members a huge advantage in conducting professional activities: guaranteed fees, provided social benefits, gave orders for novels, paintings, songs, etc. In fact, the possibilities for official work in the field of liberal arts without membership of a professional creative union were rather limited (Tomoff 2006). The unions were communities with a strong monopoly power over the jurisdiction of their activities and a high level of social closure. As such, the creative unions existed before the collapse of the USSR.

The political context of professionalization

The word *professionalizatsiia* [professionalization] in the 1920s–30s had to do with the division of labor and development of a certain vocation. This meant that people should master their skills and learn new knowledge, move to the next qualification, learn more and promote themselves further. However, specialization of knowledge and labor was perceived as a possible risk to the ideals of social homogeneity. Thus at some points professionalization was considered as a threat to equality that might alienate a person and his/her work from the masses and restore class differences.

The New Economic Policy (NEP) and industrial modernization in 1921–28 required technical specialists, but Soviet industry lacked its own engineers. In the first stage of economic modernization, the Soviet government encouraged import of technology and knowledge, creating a concession with foreign capital and inviting foreign engineers on a temporary basis. The word *spetsy* (from the 'spetsialist' –specialist, a professional expert) denoted professionals with pre-revolutionary and foreign backgrounds, who often were treated with suspicion and replaced at the first opportunity by experts who had non-bourgeois social origins and had received their training under the state socialism (Fitzpatrick 1998).

Some *spetsy*, for instance the tsarists engineers, were among the Russian professional groups 'that adapted relatively successfully to Soviet power' (Balzer 1996, p. 55). But in many other cases, the displacement of the 'old professionals' took the form of political repression. Many scientists and engineers had also been working in secret labs in prisons named *sharashka* since the late 1920s, during Stalin's political purges when numbers of professionals were arrested (and many were also murdered). A famous Soviet writer and dissident, Alexander Solzhenitsyn, based one of his novels on autobiographical experiences of working in such *sharashka* in 1947–50.

The attacks on the 'old professionalism' served Stalin's plan of nurturing a new communist elite (Fitzpatrick 1979) as well as a new professionalism (Graham 1993). This intolerance towards 'old' professionals as 'the remains of bourgeoisie' was legitimized in terms of class inequality. According to the Marxist logics (Marx 2007[1867]), *intelligentsia* was serving the needs of capitalist production and helping capital to exploit manual labor. Besides, after the socialist revolution, radical criticism of educated professionals was not required any more as it could have undermined the Soviet power. However, the state acknowledged the usefulness of intellectual forces. Thus, instead of posing as the conscience of the nation, *intelligentsia* became 'the collective noun used in referring to all those performing mental labor in the service' of Soviet country (Finkel 2007, p. 227).

By the eve of World War II in 1941, the professional communities had lost their autonomy; many old pre-revolutionary professionals were replaced by the new Soviet specialists whose socialization took place in the Soviet educational institutions. Both old and new specialists became state servants, providing control over the population, ideological support to the regime and technical rearmament of industry and the army.

The devastation of the war, shortage of consumer goods and food, and political terror that continued in the post-war period, made life after the war very difficult for all Soviet people. The voluntary compliance of citizens became increasingly important to the functioning of Soviet society (Ashwin 2000, p. 14). Women should continue to study and work and be successful in professional life, but at the same time they were called upon to produce more children 'to hold the family together, to comfort her shell shocked husband and to support his aspirations' (Dunham 1990, p. 214). While the achievements of women in the public sphere were growing indeed, the post-war Soviet literature 'presented the public success of a woman as problematic if it served to undermine the masculinity of the man with whom she was involved' (Ashwin 2000, p. 15). According to the census, by 1959, the majority of the population was still employed in physical (manual) labor, while women had already taken over men in the fields of intellectual labor (TsSU 1961, pp. 24–25).

After Stalin's death, the mass repressions ended. The so-called political 'thaw' in the years of Khrushchev meant 'a gradual pull-back of the Party, and especially of its ideologies, from most of the everyday functioning of the medical, legal, academic, and engineering professions' (Krause 1991, p. 9). An increase of medical personnel became an important goal of health-care policy. The overall number of doctors doubled between 1940 and 1950, and Soviet society was flooded with young doctors (Burton 2007), with a growing proportion of women among them. Nevertheless, the medical profession lagged far behind in medical technology in comparison with the West (Krause 1991, p. 14). Although the number of graduated physicians rapidly grew, their wages still remained low.

The post-war economic recovery made it possible to significantly raise the quality of life of the population in the 1960s. Under the economic growth in Khrushchev's era, urbanization and general modernization of life continued (Clements 1991, p. 273). Some possibilities were opened up for the democratization of public life, literature and art. These major changes affected the nature of professions. During that period, a new generation of Soviet *intelligentsia* appeared called 'the sixties' generation, with its subculture, ethos and political preferences (Alekseeva and Goldberg 1990).

A new scientific and technical intelligentsia

In the post-war period, intellectual occupations, which require mass higher education, grew rapidly. The intelligentsia, defined in the census as 'workers of intellectual labor', was as big as 20 percent of the population in 1959, with 54 percent of this group being women (TsSU 1961, pp. 24–25). The profession of engineering was developing faster than any other because it was associated with technological development being the highest priority of the Soviet state, which was investing in technical training and salaried jobs of engineers in the military and space research, as well as in energy, communication, and other civilian branches (Krause 1991). An increase in the funding of engineering and science affected not only science academics but also the professoriate (Krause 1991, p. 21). A group of Soviet *scientific and technical intelligentsia* appeared to become the structural center of professionalized occupations in the USSR.

These people graduated from polytechnics and universities in engineering and natural sciences and went to work in the expanding sector of science as well as in the research and development division of industry. Often they were the first generation in their families who managed to get a higher education and to secure a 'white-collar job'. Professional autonomy in different subgroups of the scientific and technical intelligentsia was different and depended on the arrangements within the particular industry (Josephson 1997). They worked in applied research institutes, higher education, engineering offices and laboratories at the factories, at the Academy of Sciences of the USSR, and in organizations and industries in the secret factories and 'closed towns' which implemented strategic military orders. A number of such secret towns, plants and research had been built by the beginning of the World War II within the Soviet military–industrial complex for creating and producing weapons, space and missile technology (Rowland 1996; Brown 2013).

These technological areas were in a paradoxical situation: on the one hand, they were under the heavy supervision of the secret services. On the other hand, technical experts received more resources for creativity than in civil science or civil engineering, their work was relatively better paid, and censorship concerned them less than ordinary Soviet citizens (Klumbyte and Sharafutdinova 2014). Dmitry Sakharov and some other well-known political dissidents and civil society activists belonged to the elite of the scientific and technical intelligentsia. In addition to the secret towns, a number of *naukograds* (scientific towns) were built in the same period. These were devoted to basic research and a lot of researchers were concentrated in those areas.

The emphasis on technological modernization also concerned the development of the medical profession. During the Khrushchev era, the quality of training for doctors and improvements in medical technology began to be a new emphasis in state policy (Krause 1991, p. 14). A large increase in the number of medical personnel was accompanied by a shift in the organization and scope of Soviet health care (Burton 2007). This reform was in accord with the international trend towards the specialization of the medical profession and the hierarchization of specialists over generalists (Burton 2007). Compared to an ideal image of the Russian doctor from the writings of Chekhov and Bulgakov, the professionalism of the Soviet physicians during the 1950s and 60s also included subordination to the unified national public health system and an emphasis on possession of current scientific knowledge and technology.

Inspired by the liberalization policy of Khrushchev during the political 'thaw' and by the achievements of Soviet science in the 1960s, the scientific and technical intelligentsia developed a work ethic based on selflessness, honesty, responsibility, and dedication to work. They also held a contempt for bureaucratic hierarchy and the demonstration of a broad erudition that goes beyond the narrow professional knowledge.

Professional autonomy of school teachers was rather low; in their work they followed the national curriculum and a standard textbook. But during the period of 'thaw', along with the reform of education in 1961–66, a movement of 'educational innovators' emerged oriented towards the upbringing of a 'creative person'. The government's attitude toward this movement was contradictory: it encouraged some 'innovative teachers', while the others experienced bureaucratic pressure from local authorities. These innovations did not affect the work environment of Soviet teachers and did not promote their professional status and position of power in society (Kerr 1995).

At the end of the 1960s, against the backdrop of political frosts and the beginning of the Brezhnev 'stagnation' period, the mood of the scientific and technical intelligentsia changed: apathy and indifference became more prominent and the commitment to work in films and literature was replaced by focus on family values.

Professions and social structure: an emphasis on social equality

A canon of official Marxism-Leninism during the 1950–80s prescribed social scientists to follow a simple model of social structure, as declared by Stalin in the 1930s. Workers and collective farmers had been appointed the main classes of socialist society, the former being a 'hegemon of Revolution', and the *intelligentsia* formed a 'thin layer', which supposedly recruited its members from workers and peasants. Soviet ideology in the Khrushchev period emphasized the goal of social equality and the homogeneity of the socialist society (Podmarkov 1973).

In spite of this focus on social equality, labor conditions, wages, benefits and the prestige of working occupations varied greatly in different industries. The better trained and qualified 'blue collars' were working in the enterprises of the military-industrial complex, whereas agricultural engineering, food industry and a number of other areas lacked skilled workers. In general, in the 1970–80s, the prestige of working occupations began to fall.

Equality between the sexes in the professions was ambivalent in nature. Although the number of women with higher education exceeded that of men, female specialists in medicine and science, for instance, were rarely promoted to the top positions. The proportion of women at all levels of management was low even in such professions where women constituted an overwhelming majority of workers (Boutenko and Razlogov 1997, p. 65). This situation was legitimized in public discourse on traditional gender roles, which in the late 1960s and 1970s became even stronger than in the post-war period. Female characters in the cinema of the 1970s were shown as struggling with family/work imbalance, and a 'strong' professional woman would be shown as being unhappy in her personal life (Bulgakova 1993, pp. 172–173).

Professions and professionalization in late socialism

The processes of urbanization during the Khrushchev 'thaw' period (1955–64) were accompanied by the formation of the Soviet model of consumer society (Chernyshova 2013). The service sector (trade, repair, beauty industry) was actively expanding in the cities and, therefore, such occupations as shop assistants, hairdressers, masters of home-appliance repair, tailors and fashion designers became widespread. They were presented as important occupations. Nevertheless, the prestige of the work in these areas was not high. Needless to say, the vast majority of human resources in this area were women. The low social status and level of remuneration were often compensated by shadow part-work for private orders.

Soviet sociologists in the 1970s singled out the following social features of a profession: special training, level of qualification, societal recognition (Podmarkov 1973, p. 103). During the 1970–80s, under the rule of Leonid Brezhnev, the Soviet economy was failing and many professionals experienced hard times. The economic slowdown resulted in a deficit of goods and services and led to the emergence of widespread shadow occupations, which filled the gaps in the provision of goods and services throughout the country (Eaton 2004). *Fartsovshchiki* (black-marketeers) and *spekulyanty* (profiteers), private shadow tailors, dentists, builders, real estate brokers and others were the underground pioneers of market economy, and their experience was later in demand in the early stages of legalization of capitalism in Russia.

By the end of the Soviet era, the scientific and technical intelligentsia had become a large socio-professional group, losing its former autonomy and working enthusiasm of the 1960s. The reasons for this were stagnation of innovative industries, fewer opportunities for upward social mobility, and a relative decrease in the level of wages. A rapid increase in the numbers of students and graduates of higher engineering education led to a drop in the quality of education. Similarly, school teaching began to lose its prestige, along with a fall in wages and further loss of autonomy. By the end of the 1980s, the bulk of the teaching corps was women, as men found this work undervalued (Kerr 1995).

By the mid 1980s, women comprised 50 percent of the engineers and 80 percent of the physicians in the USSR. They also constituted 83 percent of all employees in retailing, 82 percent in health care and other social services, and 75 percent in education. Most of these women were employed in low-paid, low-status jobs, and female professionals generally worked at the lowest positions (Clements 1991, p. 274).

Some professional initiatives, such as the movement of educators–innovators and creative workshops, were encouraged. In the arts and social sciences, alternative intellectual movements appeared (Kind-Kovacs and Labov 2012). These processes demonstrated that, for some professions, certain niches were opened, enabling autonomy and creative pursuits.

Field (1991) noted the hybrid character of the medical profession under socialism, which he refers to as a 'combination of political powerlessness and clinical (professional) powerfulness' (p. 58). Although professionals were subordinated by the state, it is hard to underestimate the innovative and proactive work of many doctors in protecting the health of their populations. Some medical professionals succeeded in manipulating the rigid bureaucratic system, in particular through the informal charging of fees (Riska and Novelskaite 2011, p. 83).

By the end of the Soviet period, control over professional groups was still strict, while at the same time, the role of informalities also was growing. Work-related networks endured and provided support based on shared work-based identity (Knudsen 2014). Professional life was arranged through various informal practices, relations, negotiations, and mutual dependence (Ledeneva 1998). Informal relations were not just a characteristic of relations between managers and workers (Romanov 1995), they governed all aspects of the life of the Soviet enterprise and helped maintain production (Ashwin 2000, p. 143).

In spite of adjusting to and manipulating the existing system through the wide range of informal practices, by the end of *perestroika* all occupational groups were rather critical towards the circumstances of their work.

A glance into post-Soviet professionalism: challenges and changes, 1990s–2010s

In the 1990s, a radical transformation occurred in Russia causing crucial changes in the labor market for all occupational groups. A rapid marginalization of many professionals took place. Doctors, school teachers and engineers working for the public sector suffered chronic delay in wage payments and their salaries were extremely low. These so-called 'new poor' joined the ranks of the precariat labor force, and became craftsmen, laborers, taxi drivers, 'shuttle traders', as well as commercial agents, real estate brokers, various kinds of managers and business consultants. Many of them were employed on a temporary informal basis.

The situation improved somewhat during the first decade of the twenty-first century with economic growth, but the status of professionals employed in the public sector still lags behind the status of professionals working in the private sector, due to social reforms in recent years aimed at improving efficiency and cost reduction. The result is a revision of contract principles between the professional communities and the state: instead of long-term relationships of governmental support to expert professional activities, there are now commercialized contracts based on limited duration and job insecurity.

The destruction of the socialist economy and erosion of the Soviet professionalism opened up new opportunities for such occupations that met the needs of the new market realities and were compatible with profound social change. A number of strategies of professionalization proved to be effective under such circumstances. First, in the course of market reforms, new business occupations appeared and a layer of small entrepreneurs started to grow. Many of these new occupations tried to acquire some institutional attributes by licensing education programs and establishing associations, while others remain non-professionalized, and still others were only short-term responses to the period of economic and social turbulence.

Second, intellectual professions which were widely suppressed by or limited to serving the ideological needs of the Party and the government during Soviet times have been transformed or (re)established, with many opportunities to develop. The legal profession has been enlarged and has proliferated; new communities of attorneys, notaries, judges were established, and some of them receive high public recognition for the clearly pronounced civic position (for instance the Bar Association in Moscow and other large cities).

Political and civil liberalization has led to the emergence of professional organizations engaged in human rights work and journalism. The Union of Journalists indeed became an organization advocating freedom of expression and journalists' rights in times of political and military crises. At the same time, work commissioned by media owners was another side of the new journalist autonomy in post-socialist Russia.

The state reforms in various fields have opened new channels for the emergence of new occupations and changes in the types of professionalism in existing ones. For example, the armed forces began to gain privates and NCOs under contract. So-called *kontraktniki* in the 'tax police' also significantly changed the functions and ways of organizing of the tax authorities, and a new governmental department has been established dealing with emergency situations as a special-forces rescue service with its own identity and structure. Social work has re-emerged as a fully-fledged profession and relevant education in this area was established as early as 1991.

Economic growth and a new 'consumer revolution' has changed the socio-economic landscape in Russia since the beginning of 2000. In addition, the internet has become a big industry, including media and entertainment, thus not only contributing to the emergence of new occupations and professions but also transforming models of professionalism, including freelance and online employment. In the following period of increased quality of life, there was a need for new occupations and specializations, whose activity is connected with servicing new consumer habits. Beauty, spa, feng shui specialists, counselors, sports instructors and many others often take the form of informal employment and precarious labor, but they are widespread and form a new model of professionalism.

At the present stage of Russian welfare policy, the government has made the development of occupational standards in the social service domain a priority. In the situation of a lack of strong professional public organizations, trade unions, or associations of customers, it is rather difficult to formulate occupational standards from the 'bottom up'. The first versions of these standards were elaborated with major participation of the representatives of higher education. The government has actively reformed education, science, social services and health care. This has significantly affected the autonomy, nature of work and the status of such 'traditional' professions as teachers, doctors, and academic workers. Managerialism and focus on 'effectiveness' constitute the ideology of social reform and education.

In contemporary Russia, the boundaries of occupations are becoming more fluid, the strategies of professionalization more flexible and resources for constructing professional identity more diverse. The classic elements of professionalism (state regulation, academic community and professional identity) in many occupational fields, are complemented by market logic (advertising, market conditions and user satisfaction), and culture used as 'social capital' (Iarskaia-Smirnova and Romanov 2008). Furthermore, the success or failure of professional services and their legitimacy depends on various conditions, in particular: successful advertising, market conditions, and demand from, and satisfaction of, the target group.

The post-Soviet situation is characterized by the significant transformation of the role of the state, the social support ideology, and the models and tools of social policy. The creation of an expert community from above leads to increasing the level of professionals' engagement by the authorities. To determine the content of professional standards from below is difficult due to the lack of strong professional community organizations and trade unions. A new model of professionalism is based on reduction of the state's contribution in the welfare state and the creation of conditions for monopolization and cross-sector collaboration, as well as on pursuing microeconomic efficiency and decentralization of the welfare state. These processes are leading to the proliferation of occupational fields and diversification of institutional conditions for the development and transformation of professional ethos and discourses. In addition, the consequences of such processes may include the building of new hierarchies within the professions as well as the segmentation and/or consolidation of occupations, and deprofessionalization, managerialization and proletarianization in key areas of the welfare state, such as health care, education, social work and various forms of care work, as well as governmental and municipal management.

Conclusion

The Russian case reveals how the professions have responded to a number of dramatic shifts in the economy and in doing so shaped how they fit into changing societal structures. As our overview has shown, they have either been a focal part of changes or quite an aside, but usually the professions have been resilient, even under such serious and rapid transformations in Russian history.

The professional occupations developed throughout Russia's history of reforms and revolutions, wars and political purges, economic and societal modernization. As sociologists have noted, regulation is one of the key variables in the research of occupational groups (Mrowczynski 2012). Regulation may be conducted by the state or by corporate governance. The 'third logic' is self-regulation provided by the professionals themselves. This is typical for the situation of a profession in the 'free market', where it can control and maintain its specific status by controlling the entrance of newcomers and the socialization of admitted specialists during their work (Freidson 2001). While in the West occupational groups advocated for greater state involvement in the battle against the laissez-faire ideology of free markets (Abbott 1988), in late imperial Russia, society lacked the strong enterpreneurial ideal that could have limited the role of the state. Although dependent on the state, the professions strived to achieve some autonomy and opportunities for self-regulation.

In capitalist countries, professionals in hierarchic organizations became subject to managerial authority, and the trends of deprofessionalization and 'proletarianization' of educated labor occurred (Larson 1977). Within the institutional context of state socialism, similar consequences were caused by the state's penetration into the lives of the professions. The party-state encompassed all spheres of regulation, including the granting of a certain level of collective autonomy to some occupations (Mrowczynski 2012).

The Soviet state created a new map of the professional structure, eliminating or 'reforging' the old and promoting the new occupational groups. The analysis of the role of women in the development of professions demonstrates how the (re)forming of the gendered identity of occupations was linked to the reinforcement of the state's authority. While in comparison to earlier eras, female participation in employment increased greatly in the late Soviet period, a widespread gender stereotyping still legitimized unequal arrangements of work and affected the educational and vocational choices of girls and women. The strengthening discourse on traditional gender roles justified the inequality in the workplace.

The official propaganda glorified labor valor and qualification of workers, doctors and teachers, in some cases, challenging, repressing and eliminating whole groups of professionals. The status boundaries between professionals and ordinary people were appreciable. The specialized knowledge, skills, jargon and mutual support built the ground for cohesion. Social relations of mutual aid and favors were particularly significant under socialism. The internal values, norms and definitions embedded informally into the everyday practice of work and relations with co-workers and clients engendered the rules of conduct and boundaries of collective identity. All these sides constituted the internal and external, corporate and public, frames of the gendered professional project, both for individual occupations and for the society as a whole.

Throughout history, the collective identity of the professions was often formed in close association with the state apparatus. This essential legacy of Russian imperial culture when the state was still the main source of status and identity, has remained under socialism, and it partly retains its force in post-Soviet Russia (Becker 2011). The state attempted to streamline the ever-changing ways of division of labor into different sectors and industries. These attempts did not always result in the concerted development of a valid classification of occupations. Nor did it define a single standard list, which in addition was not keeping up with the pace of change in the real life of professions and organizations. Besides, the division of responsibilities between different public agencies in an attempt to standardize the world of professions caused a mismatch of action and results. These discrepancies still remain in certain aspects, although in the early 2000s, the documents were subject to substantial revision. In the late 1990s and throughout the 2000s–2010s in Russia, the map of professions was changing very fast. New stages of professionalization have been initiated in different occupational fields, both from below, through the activity of business and trade unions, and from above, through a series of government regulations.

Acknowledgment

This chapter consists of findings that emerged from a project carried out with the support of the Basic Research Programme of the National Research University, Higher School of Economics, Moscow, in 2015.

References

Abbott, A. D. (1988) *The System of Professions: Essay on the Division of Expert Labor.* Chicago, IL: University of Chicago Press.

Abramov, R. (2014) *The History of Sociological Research on Occupations and Professions in the USSR 1960–80s: Ideological Frameworks and Analytical Resources.* Higher School of Economics Research Paper No. WP BRP 40/SOC/2014. http://papers.ssrn.com/sol3/papers.cfm?abstract_id=2430178 (last accessed 27 January 2016).

Alekseeva, L., and Goldberg, P. (1990) *The Thaw Generation: Coming of Age in the Post-Stalin Era.* Pittsburgh, PA: University of Pittsburgh Press.

Ashwin, S. (2000) 'Introduction: Gender, state and society in soviet and post-soviet Russia'. In Sarah Ashwin (ed.), *Gender, State and Society in Soviet and Post-Soviet Russia.* London and New York: Routledge, pp. 1–29.

Bailes, K. E. (1996) 'Reflections on Russian professions'. In H. D. Balzer (ed.), *Russia's Missing Middle Class: The Professions in Russian History.* Armonk, NY: M.E. Sharpe, pp. 39–54.

Balzer, H. D. (1996) 'The engineering profession in tsarist Russia'. In H. D. Balzer (ed.), *Russia's Missing Middle Class: The Professions in Russian History.* Armonk, NY: M.E. Sharpe, pp. 55–88.

Becker, E. M. (2011) *Medicine, Law, and the State in Imperial Russia.* Budapest: CEU Press.

Beissinger, M. R. (1988) *Scientific Management, Socialist Discipline, and Soviet Power.* Cambridge, MA: Harvard University Press.

Boutenko, I. A., and Razlogov, K. E. (1997) *Recent Social Trends in Russia 1960–1995.* Montreal: McGill-Queen's University Press.

Brown, K. (2013) *Plutopia: Nuclear Families, Atomic Cities, and the Great Soviet and American Plutonium Disasters.* Oxford: Oxford University Press.

Bulgakova, O. (1993) 'The hydra of the Soviet cinema: The metamorphoses of the Soviet film heroine'. In L. Attwood (ed.), *Red Women on the Silver Screen.* London: Pandora Press, pp. 149–174.

Burton, Ch. (2007) 'Zdravookhranenie v period pozdnego stalinisma i dukh poslevoennogo gosudarstva blagodenstviia, 1945–1953 gody' [Public health in the period of late Stalinism and the ghost of the postwar welfare state, 1945–53]. *Zhurnal issledovaniia sotsial'noi politiki* [*Journal of Social Policy Studies*], 5(4), pp. 541–558.

Chernyshova, N. (2013) *Soviet Consumer Culture in the Brezhnev Era.* London: Routledge.

Clements, B. E. (1991) 'Later developments: Trends in Soviet women's history, 1930 to the Present'. In B. E. Clements, B. A. Engel, and Ch. Worobec (eds), *Russia's Women: Accommodation, Resistance, Transformation.* Berkeley, CA: University of California Press, pp. 267–277.

Dahl, V. (1865) *Tolkovyi slovar' zhivago velikoruskago iazyka* [*The Explanatory Dictionary of the Living Great Russian Language*]. *Part 2.* Moscow: Tipografia Lazarevskago instituta vostochnykh iazykov, pp. 629–1351.

Djilas, M. (1983) *The New Class: An Analysis of the Communist System.* San Diego, CA: Harcourt Brace Jovanovich.

Dunham, V. S. (1990) *In Stalin's Time: Middleclass Values in Soviet Fiction* (updated edition). Durham, NC: Duke University Press.

Eaton, K. (2004) *Daily Life in the Soviet Union.* Westport, CT: Greenwood Press.

Edmondson, L. (2004) 'Feminism and equality in an authoritarian state: The politics of women's liberation in late imperial Russia'. In Sylvia Paletschek and Bianka Pietrow-Ennker (eds), *Women's Emancipation Movements in the Nineteenth Century: A European Perspective.* Stanford, CA: Stanford University Press.

Field, M. (1972) 'The taming of a profession: Early phases of Soviet socialized medicine'. *Bulletin of the New York Academy of Medicine,* 48(1), pp. 83–92.

Field, M. (1991) 'The hybrid profession: Soviet medicine'. In A. Jones (ed.), *Professions and the State: Expertise and Autonomy in the Soviet Union and Eastern Europe.* Philadelphia, PA: Temple University Press, pp. 43–62.

Finkel, S. (2007) *On the Ideological Front: The Russian Intelligentsia and the making of the Soviet Public Sphere.* New Haven, CT: Yale University Press.

Fitzpatrick, S. (1979) 'Stalin and the making of a new elite, 1928–1939'. *Slavic Review.* Vol. 38, pp. 377–402.

Fitzpatrick, S. (1998) 'Intelligentsia and power: Client-patron relations in Stalin's Russia'. In M. Hildermeier, *Stalinismus vor dem zweiten Weltkrieg.* Neue Wege der Forschung. Munich: Oldenbourg Wissenschaftsverlag, pp. 35–54.

Frame, M. (2005) 'Commercial theatre and professionalization in late imperial Russia'. *The Historical Journal,* 48(4), pp. 1025–1053.

Freeze, G. L. (1992) 'Between estate and profession: The clergy in imperial Russia'. In M. L. Bush (ed.), *Social Orders and Social Classes in Europe since 1500: Studies in Social Stratification.* London and New York: Longman, pp. 47–65.

Freidson, E. (2001) *Professionalism, the Third Logic: On the Practice of Knowledge.* Chicago, IL: The University of Chicago Press.

Graham, L. (1993) *The Ghost of the Executed Engineer: Technology and the Fall of the Soviet Union.* Cambridge, MA: Harvard University Press.

Graham, L. (2004) *Science in Russia and the Soviet Union: A Short History.* Cambridge Studies in the History of Science. Cambridge: Cambridge University Press.

Hutchinson, J. F. (1999) *Late Imperial Russia: 1890–1917.* Toronto: Addison-Wesley Longman Limited.

Iarskaia-Smirnova, E., and Romanov, P. (2008) 'Culture matters: Integration of folk medicine in health care in Russia'. In E. Kuhlmann and M. Saks (eds), *Rethinking Professional Governance: International Directions in Health Care.* Bristol: The Policy Press, pp. 141–154.

Jones, A. (ed.) (1991) *Professions and the State: Expertise and Autonomy in the Soviet Union and Eastern Europe.* Philadelphia, PA: Temple University Press.

Jones, E., and Grupp, F. W. (1987) *Modernization, Value Change and Fertility in the Soviet Union.* Cambridge and New York: Cambridge University Press

Josephson, P. R. (1997) *New Atlantis Revisited: Akademgorodok, the Siberian City of Science.* Princeton, NJ: Princeton University Press.

Kerr, St. T. (1995) Teachers' continuing education and Russian school reform'. Paper prepared for presentation at the *Conference of the American Association for the Advancement of Slavic Studies,* October 28, 1995, Washington, DC: University of Washington, available at http://faculty.washington.edu/stkerr/concrut.htm (last accessed 27 January 2016).

Kind-Kovacs, F., and Labov, J. (eds) (2012) *Samizdat, Tamizdat, and Beyond: Transnational Media During and After Socialism.* New York: Berghahn Books

Klassifikatsiia (1921) *Klassifikatsiia zanyatii, proizvodstv i otraslei truda dlia razrabotki Vserossiiskoi demografichesko-professional'noi perepisi 1920 g.* [*Classification of occupation, industries and branches of labor for elaboration of All-Russian demographic-professional census of 1920*]. Moscow: Tsentral'noe Statisticheskoe Upravlenie.

Klumbyte, N., and Sharafutdinova, G. (eds) (2014) *Soviet Society in the Era of Late Socialism, 1964–1985.* Plymouth, MA: Lexington Books.

Knudsen, I. H. (2014) 'Moonlighting strangers met on the way: The nexus of informality and blue-collar sociality in Russia'. In J. Morris and A. Polese (eds), *The Informal Post-Socialist Economy: Embedded Practices and Livelihoods.* London and New York: Routledge.

Krause, E. A. (1991) 'Professions and the state in Eastern Europe and the Soviet Union: theoretical issues'. In A. Jones (ed.), *Professions and the State: Expertise and Autonomy in the Soviet Union and Eastern Europe.* Philadelphia, PA: Temple University Press, pp. 3–41.

Larson, M. (1977) *The Rise of Professionalism: A Sociological Analysis*. Berkeley, CA: University of California Press.

Ledeneva, A. (1998) *Russia's Economy of Favours: Blat, Networking and Informal Exchange*. Cambridge, UK: Cambridge University Press.

McKean, R. B., and Thatcher, I. D. (2005) *Late Imperial Russia: Problems and Prospects*. Manchester, UK: Manchester University Press.

Marx, K. (2007[1867]) *Capital: A Critique of Political Economy*. Vol. I, Part I The Process of Capitalist Production. New York: Cosimo.

Mrowczynski, R. (2012) 'Self-regulation of legal professions in state-socialism: Poland and Russia compared'. In *Rechtsgeschichte – Legal History Rg* 20 170–188, available at http://rg.rg.mpg.de/en/article_id/802 (last accessed 27 January 2016).

Nahirny, V. C. (1982) *The Russian Intelligentsia: From Torment to Silence*. New Brunswick, NJ: Transaction Publishers.

Podmarkov, V. G. (1973) *Vvedenie v promyshlennuyu sotsiologiyu. Sotsial'nye problemy promyshlennogo proizvodstva* [*Introduction into the industrial sociology. Social problems of industrial production*]. Moscow: Mysl'.

Pomeranz, W. (1999) '"Profession or estate"? The case of the Russian pre-revolutionary'. *Advokatura*, SEER, 77(1).

Raeff, M. (1966) *Origins of the Russian Intelligentsia: The Eighteenth-Century Nobility*. New York: Harcourt, Brace and World.

Ringlee, A. J. (2010) *The Instruction of Youth in Late Imperial Russia: Vospitanie in the Cadet School and Classical Gymnasium, 1863–1894*. A thesis submitted to the faculty of the University of North Carolina at Chapel Hill in partial fulfilment of the degree of Master of Arts in the Department of History Chapel Hill 2010, available at https://cdr.lib.unc.edu/indexablecontent/uuid:2b680298-d907-4425-a210-3c1a1fdaa745 (last accessed 27 January 2016).

Riska, E., and Novelskaite, A. (2011) 'Professionalism and medical work in a post-soviet society: Between four logics'. *Anthropology of East Europe Review*, 29(1), pp. 82–93.

Romanov, P. (1995) 'Middle management in industrial production in the transition to the market'. In S. Clarke (ed.), *Management and Industry in Russia: Formal and Informal Relations in the Period of Transition*. Aldershot: Edward Elgar, pp. 182–211.

Rowland, R. H. (1996) 'Russia's secret cities'. *Post-Soviet Geography and Economics*, 37(7), pp. 426–462.

Ryavec, K. W. (2003) *Russian Bureaucracy: Power and Pathology*. Oxford: Rowman & Littlefield.

Siegrist, H. (1990) 'Professionalization as a process: Patterns, progression and discontinuity'. In M. Burrage and R. Torstendahl (eds), *Professions in Theory and History: Rethinking the Study of the Professions*. London, Newbury Park, New Delhi, pp. 177–202.

Strumilin, S. G. (1921) 'K voprosu o klassifikatsii truda' [On the question of labour classification], *Organizatsiia truda* [*Organization of labor*], 1, pp. 2–6.

Svavitskii, A., and Sher V. (1909) *Otcherk polozheniia rabotchikh petchatnogo dela v Moskve: po dannym ankety, proizvedennoi Obshchestvom rabotchikh graficheskikh iskusstv v 1907 godu*. St. Petersburg: Imperatorskoe russkoe tekhnicheskoe obshchestvo.

Tomoff, K. (2006) *Creative Union: The Professional Organization of Soviet Composers, 1939–1953*. Ithaca, NY: Cornell University Press.

TsSU (1920) *Vseobshchaia perepis' 1920 goda. Demografichesko-professional'naia i sel'sko-khozyaistvennaia, s uchetom promyshlennykh predpriiatii* [*General Census. Demographic-professional and agricultural, industrial enterprises taken into account*]. Moscow: Tsentra'noe statisticheskoe upravlenie.

TsSU (1922) *Statisticheskii ezhegodnik-1921* [*Statistial Annual Edition*], Trudy Tsentral'nogo Statisticheskogo upravleniia [Works of the Central Administration of the Statistics], VIII (3). http://istmat.info/files/uploads/29739/statezh_1921_trud.pdf (last accessed 27 January 2016).

TsSU (1961) *Narodnoe khozyaistvo SSSR v 1960 godu. Statisticheskii ezhegodnik* [*The economy of the USSR in 1960. An annual statistical edition*]. Moscow: Tsentral'noe statisticheskoe upravlenie pri Sovete Ministrov SSSR.

Wilensky, H. L. (1964) 'The professionalization of everyone?'. *American Journal of Sociology*, 70, pp. 137–158.

20

Professions and the migration of expert labour

Towards an intersectional analysis of transnational mobility patterns and integration pathways of health professionals

Ivy Lynn Bourgeault, Sirpa Wrede, Cecilia Benoit and Elena Neiterman

Introduction

Whereas internationally mobile professionals find many more opportunities than in the past, the migration of professionals across countries is not in itself a new phenomenon. Indeed, the esoteric nature of professional knowledge is such that it can transcend national boundaries, at least theoretically. What is new is the number of countries participating in the transnational migratory movements of professionals, the rapid increase in the pace of the movement of professionals internationally, the impermanency of their migration decisions, and the growing politicization of migration (Castles and Miller, 2003). These new dynamics are transforming not only the lives of the internationally mobile professionals but the overall composition of the professional workforce and its social organization. In this chapter we use the concept 'mobilities' in parallel to migration to denote how the numerous new patterns of spatial mobility of professionals are transforming the social organization of professions, in ways that disrupt the very idea of professions as nationally bounded social phenomena. Indeed, we argue that a better understanding of professional mobilities has implications for all future theorizing about professions in the era of transnational globalization.

Transnational mobilities of professionals occur in new types of social networks and economic contexts that shape the mobility patterns and integration pathways of professionals. These complex mobilities can be seen as a reflection of economic globalization and the related increasing competition for international talent that has brought about new transnational flows and mechanisms (Yeates, 2009). This increased pace of professional migration raises important equity concerns, including the emigration of highly trained professionals ('brain drain') from so-called 'source' countries of the less-resourced south to destination countries in the more-resourced global north (cf. Kapur and McHale, 2005).

Internationally mobile professionals, whose strategic actions can maximize their economic circumstances and earning potential within a globalizing market, may possess significant mobility capital, defined as capacities and competencies, in relation to the surrounding physical, social and political affordances for movement (Kaufmann *et al.*, 2004). Differential capacities and potentials for mobility are identified in the literature with the concept of 'motility', referring to 'the manner in which an individual or group appropriates the field of possibilities relative to movement and uses them' (Kaufmann and Montulet, 2008, p. 45). While professional expertise per se constitutes an attractive resource in the context of global competition for expert labour, professions differ when it comes to motility (i.e. the ease with which their expertise travels). For example, many areas of engineering, commercial and corporate law, economics, consulting and accounting have been directly influenced by the rise of an international arena of professional business, giving rise to a transnational labour market linked to such new types of service work; these are the types of *transnational professionals* to which Sassen (1988, 1998, 2007) refers in her analyses. By way of contrast, many human service professions, such as health care, teaching or social work, continue to be shaped by a low degree of mobility due to the ties that bind them to specific national settings and to the strict rules regarding skills assessment requirements (cf. Bourgeault *et al.*, 2010; Wrede, 2010).

Professional mobilities are also highly gendered, classed and 'racialized' in ways that condition both who can be mobile and how and what kind of consequences particular mobility patterns have in origin and destination countries. While traditionally migration was analysed as 'male' movement, today women often outnumber men in transglobal movement (Camilin *et al.*, 2014; Ryan, 2002), although some countries continue to restrict women's migration due to patriarchal ideologies (Kingma, 2006). The literature now speaks of a feminization of migration, referring to how more women are migrating, not only in the professions, though the caring professions are most notable. Women's migration has given rise to *global care chains*, a term first coined by Hochschild (2000) to denote how migrant care workers fill the care deficits left by women's increased labour force participation in destination countries but at the same time women's emigration creates care deficits in their countries of origin.

This chapter considers transnational professional migration and integration from an intersectional perspective recognizing the interconnectedness of professional identities and associated hierarchical structures relating to, for example, gender, ethnicity, race and class at different levels of society (cf. Anthias, 2012). We undertake this examination through the case of the health-care professions, with a specific focus on medicine and nursing. The health-care professions constitute a particularly interesting case that transcends the continuum between purely transnational labour markets and persistently nationally rooted professional occupations.

Health-care delivery in the global north represents a labour-intensive growth industry. Despite welfare state austerity, the demand for more health-care workers is constantly growing due to demographic and epidemiological trends of population ageing and the rising prevalence of multiple chronic conditions. The demand for health labour is compounded by the ageing of the local health workforces. Not surprisingly, recruiters of health professionals from high-income countries scout for new labour pools globally; in the OECD 11 per cent of employed nurses and 18 per cent of employed doctors were foreign-born (OECD, 2007, p. 162). The sheer magnitude of the flows of internationally mobile health professionals has sparked significant policies to address the ethics of international recruitment practices globally (e.g. World Health Report, 2006, 2010).

To capture the situatedness of professional mobilities, we need also to distinguish *mobility/ migration* – the decision to leave a country for another – and the *settlement/integration* of the mobile professionals into a particular local professional labour market. Moreover, integration is more complex than the attainment of licensure to practice; it also concerns broader social and cultural integration. The drivers of professional migration briefly noted above may be similar across types of professions – but the integration processes and possibilities for internationally mobile professionals are very much tied to the integration pathways that are available in local contexts, particularly for the highly regulated health professions. Such complexity calls for analytical approaches that not only are sensitive to context but serve to tease apart the complex drivers of migration from the forces influencing the integration of migrating health professionals.

In this chapter, we review the literature examining the migration and integration of health professionals to help elucidate the distinction between globalized migration and localized integration. We then draw upon theoretical inspirations from the overlapping sociology literatures on migration, the professions and globalization, with an aim of outlining a pluralistic conceptual framework for the intersectional analysis of professional mobilities that recognizes that migration and integration have their interlinked but separate, complex dynamics. This analytic framework separates micro, meso and macro influences. The meso level, we argue, is particularly important to more fully understand local professional integration processes whereby transnationally mobile professionals are integrated into a local labour market that is controlled nationally or subnationally. An emphasis on the integration pathways that are constituted through interactions and mechanisms that operate at meso level also highlights the important contributions to these trends that literature on the professions can play and that has heretofore been neglected.

Health professional migration: an overview of micro, meso and macro influences

Health professional migration is a multi-layered phenomenon with a complex history. Historically, an internationally mobile workforce generally moved along established pathways between countries that often had their roots in colonial ties (see e.g. Choy, 2003). This was particularly notable of the Commonwealth countries and exemplified through the historically relatively straightforward migration of doctors and nurses among the UK, Australia, Canada and South Africa. From a colonial perspective, the Filipino government was the first to tap into the expanding health labour demand brought about by neoliberal globalization in the 1980s (Choy, 2003). The dynamics of health professional migration thus reflect the deep social-economic and political divisions that have come to be identified as the North–South divide that underpins the global inequalities between affluent countries and countries that lack resources. In the 1990s and 2000s, governments in the global south as well as private firms, often located in the global north, followed suit. In the present context, numerous source countries already cater for nearly all countries of the global north. While the numbers of mobile health professionals recruited to different countries varies, it is obvious that workforce planning in the global north has become a transnational practice that is structured by the uneven social development in different parts of the world.

In order to analyse the multi-layered nature of health professional migration, it is helpful to tease apart the various levels of analysis prevalent in its literature. We begin with the more *micro* or individually focused level of analysis which emphasizes the motivational factors affecting individual migration decisions, including how the migration and integration processes are experienced personally. The next most frequent focus in the literature is at the *macro* or political economic level which addresses, among other issues, the impact of globalization on labour markets for professional services, the impact of health professional migration on source and destination countries, and how these processes are shaped by intersecting inequalities. In general, there has been a neglect of the *meso* or institutional factors, including the roles played by intermediaries such as employers, professional certifying and regulatory bodies, professional associations and trade unions in destination countries (Bach, 2003). It is important to note that the teasing apart of these factors is for heuristic purposes only, because there is, as we will argue further below, significant interaction of the different levels.

Micro/individual level of analysis

The mainstream literature on health professional migration is dominated by a more or less implicit rational-choice perspective that focuses on the health professionals who migrate, analysing the social, political but largely economic reasoning underpinning their decisions to migrate. This labour-market-oriented research often emphasizes how certain 'push' and 'pull' factors operate at a micro or individual level, although some of the push and pull factors are often a direct result of macro, structural forces. *Pull* factors include the individual perceptions or experiences of better and more comfortable living and working conditions, and higher wages and opportunities for advancement (Aiken *et al.*, 2004). Overall, the literature identifies poor wages, economic instability, poorly funded health-care systems, the burdens and risks of AIDS and safety concerns as factors that *push* health professionals to leave less-resourced countries (Aiken *et al.*, 2004; Robinson and Carey, 2000).

Although this model is often cited in the migration literature, it tends towards a taxonomy, listing and describing factors, with little attention to the dominance of some factors over others, the root causes of some of these individual factors at a broader level and the interrelationship between push and pull factors. Kingma (2006) notes, for instance, that 'pull factors' do not solely account for mass exodus of health-care professionals from less-resourced areas of the world. Walton-Roberts (2015) similarly critiques this approach for focusing almost exclusively on labour-market conditions and failing to appreciate the role played by the broader political economy and local health professional educational systems, which we discuss more fully below. This perspective can also be critiqued for neglecting colonial relations, gender and other social divisions in its analysis of the migration dynamic (Hagopian *et al.*, 2005). We add to these critiques that analyses focusing on push and pull factors may result in a narrow understanding of the reasoning that goes into decisions to migrate. If people are primarily approached as labour-market agents, ignoring both their private concerns and other than economic work-related aspirations, including those of professional character.

Researchers have also been interested in the integration experiences of health-care workers in their countries of destination. Despite significant differences in the countries of origins of migrating professionals, they experience remarkably similar processes of struggling to become integrated. Research shows that newly immigrated professionals often feel alienated from other members of their profession when integrated (Neiterman *et al.*, 2015) and report discrimination in their new workplaces. Indeed, the majority of these studies deal with the racism and discrimination that health-care workers face in the country of destination (Alexis and Vydelingum, 2004; Collinds, 2004; Hagey *et al.*, 2001; Larsen, 2007). Qualitative studies often explore how immigrant health workers are discriminated against according to race and denied career opportunities (Allan *et al.*, 2004; Dicicco-Bloom, 2004; Turrittin *et al.*, 2002). The instances of discrimination and racism at the workplace are especially prevalent in the nursing literature (Allan *et al.*, 2004; Dicicco-Bloom, 2004; Hagey *et al.*, 2001; Kingma, 2006), but it is also evident of women physicians (Giri, 1998), suggesting the importance of accounting for gender as an important dynamic in racism and discrimination.

While experiences of racism and discrimination of health workers have been documented by researchers, less is known about the process of *integrating* into a new country's local labour and culture of practice. Indeed, much of the literature on health labour migration at the micro level lacks knowledge of the psychosocial experiences of health-care immigrants and how they negotiate the labyrinth of policies and procedures to practise their profession. A great deal of what we know comes from the studies undertaken by Shuval and her colleagues (Bernstein and Shuval, 1998; Shuval, 1995, 1998, 2000) of the massive emigration of physicians from the Soviet Union to Israel when it had an open, non-selective migration policy. Not surprisingly, these studies found that Soviet physicians who migrated to Israel and who were working in their profession had significantly higher well-being scores than those not working as physicians. Yet many of those physicians who were working in their chosen profession were dissatisfied with their allocation to less prestigious practice settings, with the lack of recognition of their professional backgrounds, and with the questioning of their authority by patients. The salience of professional identity is critical among immigrants who see their occupational status as core to their self-identity (Bernstein and Shuval, 1998). How this was experienced differentially by male and female physicians and those of different minority backgrounds was noted.

Building on this analysis, Neiterman et al. (2015) compared the situation of physicians migrating and integrating in Canada and Sweden utilizing the theoretical literature on *othering* and *belonging*. They argued that the construction of professional identity among migrating physicians necessitates constant comparison between 'us' – immigrant physicians, and 'them' – local doctors. In this process, one's ethnicity and professional status are intertwined with the experience of being seen as 'other'. Adjusting to the local culture of practice, migrating health professionals undergo a process of professional resocialization, learning the new professional landscape simultaneously with learning the cultural norms of the host country (see also Neiterman and Bourgeault, 2015a).

In brief, the micro literature focuses on both the migration and integration processes, and in recent years the traditional focus on push-pull factors has expanded to include, alongside political and economic reasons, also personal motives for migration. Increasingly, intersectional approaches that account for social divisions and cultural processes have started to appear.

Macro/political-economic level of analysis

While micro-level studies have expanded in scope, they still often remain under-contextualized. Macro-level analyses augment the micro dimension in a way that links the migration of health-care workers to broader economic forces. These analyses often take an ethical standpoint; authors opposing the migration of health professionals highlight the losses to the less-resourced countries of their highly qualified health-care personnel (Ahmad et al., 2003; Buchan, 2004; Jeans, 2006; Labonté et al., 2006), while the proponents of such movement highlight the economic benefits that remittances of migrant health-care workers return to their countries of origin (cf. Guarnizo, 2003). Similarly, the cost–benefit analysis of the use of the imported health-care workforce in the countries of destination has demonstrated how the recruitment of health-care workers from abroad helps more resourced countries to save millions on the training of health-care personnel (Labonté et al., 2006). These and other ethical concerns are raised in a context where recruitment is emerging as a growing, increasingly transnational industry (e.g. Pittman et al., 2010), and where there is a huge discrepancy between countries with high burdens of disease and disability and wealthier and comparatively well-resourced countries (Eckenwiler, 2014).

Because of the ethical dilemmas of recruiting health personnel from less-resourced nations, the British National Health Service (NHS) produced a Code of Practice for NHS employers involved in the international recruitment of health-care professionals (NHS, 2001) prohibited direct recruitment of nurses from Africa. It did not, however, initially cover private sector employers, but because the NHS recruits from private employers, its own Code was circumvented. African nurses continued to emigrate to the UK (Aiken et al., 2004). Later Commonwealth countries in 2004 developed a similar Code of Practice, but it too was limited by coverage and lacked an enforcement mechanism. These limitations hold true to a certain extent for the WHO Code recently signed by all countries in 2010, even though it covers the widest possible range of employers in both the public and private sectors, and includes NGOs, professional associations and regional health authorities (Bourgeault *et al.*, forthcoming). Notwithstanding the ethical issues arising from active recruitment, another ethical dilemma associated with the international migration of health professionals is in their effective integration when they choose to migrate so as not to let their skills go to waste (Bourgeault, 2007). This issue has only been addressed in the most recent WHO Code. These codes have, however, failed to stem the tide of migrating health workers largely because they are voluntary, have no financial implications, and because they are difficult to apply to the rapidly growing involvement of private-sector recruitment agencies (Labonté *et al.*, 2006; Tankwanchi *et al.*, 2014).

The resulting flows of human and economic capital from lower- to higher-resourced countries can be linked to the historically colonial nature of the relationship between nations. In the past, old colonial ties gave rise to migration pathways between Australia, Canada and the UK, similarly to the migration in the Nordic region, where low cultural distance facilitated health professional mobility (Bourgeault and Wrede, 2011). Drawing on post-colonial theory, McNeil-Walsh (2004) seeks to explain the migration and easy integration of South African nurses to the UK. She describes how Britain, as a colonial power, shaped the structure of South African society, including its health-care delivery and education system. South Africans therefore had an immigration advantage with policies that recognized their British-like credentials and immigration policies which favoured those who hailed from the former colonies to move to Britain without restriction. Any thorough analysis of current migration trends cannot, according to McNeil-Walsh (2004), ignore this historical context. The historical context in which migration of health-care workers was established from the colonies also cannot be reduced to simple economic explanations. For instance, scholars have found the culture of migration to be firmly rooted in Nigerian and Ghanaian physicians' visions of their medical future – to move to the West upon completion of their education (Hagopian *et al.*, 2005).

Other literature stresses the importance of looking beyond the particular policy contexts of the nation state, or its pre-existing colonial ties, to understand the broader impact of trade agreements, such as the European Union (EU), the World Trade Organization (WTO), the North American Free Trade Agreement (NAFTA) and the General Agreement on Tariffs and Trade (GATT) on the flow of health labour (Bach, 2003; Orzak, 1998). These trade agreements urge national governments to reduce or eliminate requirements and regulatory devices that impede or block the movement of goods and services. So where national boundaries historically separated licensing, regulatory and credentialing systems, the facilitation of enhanced international trade in services may weaken the autonomy and authority of nationally based professional regulatory systems (Orzack, 1998).

The EU, for example, has been keen to promote the free movement of labour as well as encourage migration into certain regions and sectors. The EU has established an inclusive model of mutual recognition of qualifications in which a number of regulated health professionals, including physicians and nurses, are free to work in any other member states. Similarly, NAFTA has made it easier for some Canadian nurses to find work in the USA (Aiken *et al.*, 2004), but there has not been a similar migration of nurses from Mexico to the United States, due largely to issues of educational equivalence (Squires, 2011). This speaks to the importance of the meso regulatory level, discussed more fully below.

The overarching GATT also facilitates increased labour migration because of its efforts towards aligning the competency and recognition requirements for health professionals between countries. This has had important impacts on the education systems in source countries, shifting their orientation from local health-care needs to global health workforce markets. Indeed, there are over-arching trends towards the internationalization of health professional education which is typically focused on standards in well-resourced countries of the north. Choy's (2003) analysis of the nursing export labour policy of the Philippines reveals how its educational system under US neo-colonialism became structured toward US health-care market demands, with most nursing schools following US-based curricula and utilizing US-based textbooks. Walton-Roberts (2015) describes this in the case of nursing training in India, and specifically on how the increasingly private and indeed corporate health-care training systems evolving in India are more and more aligned with the production of professionals dominated by US-based curricula and orientated to globally integrated health labour markets. She argues for a global political economy approach in order to better understand the impact of the rise of international health human resource systems and circuits and how practices originating outside of the state, involving interaction and integration across and between places and scales, are comprising, altering and constraining 'national' processes (p. 375).

In sum, macro-level analyses help to elucidate the broader contextual factors influencing migration, why health professionals move from where and to where, and also in terms of highlighting dynamics related to gender, 'race' and ethnicity. Attention to the meso level of analysis would, however, help to contextualize the agency of migrating health professionals by elucidating some of the structural constraints on their actions when they attempt to and become integrated into local labour markets.

Meso/institutional level of analysis

As noted above, meso-level analyses are less frequent in the health professional migration literature. It is not accidental that the notable exceptions focus more on professional integration processes than the migration decision. Diallo (2004) elucidates the distinction between the migration decisions and actions of health professionals and the contextual factors and forces influencing their integration into the local professional market. In Figure 20.1, Diallo (2004) teases apart the process and outcomes of migration from integration and also captures both the primary and return migration trajectory that may be evidenced for some migrating health professionals. In addition, the figure helps us to visualize how skills can be lost to source countries (i.e. 'brain drain') but also to destination countries (i.e. the 'brain waste' issue noted above) when migrating health professionals work in sectors other than health.

One of the earliest scholars to undertake a more meso-level analysis of the integration of health professionals is Shuval and colleagues (1995; Bernstein and Shuval, 1998) in the examination of

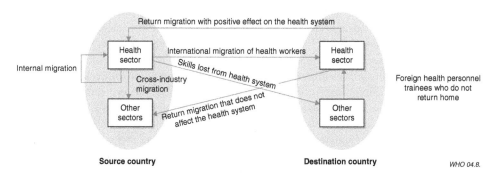

Figure 20.1   Migration and integration dynamics in source and destination countries

301

the experiences of Russian émigré physicians in Israel discussed above. The context in Israel for these integration efforts was marked by an already oversaturated medical market exemplified by under- and unemployment. The migration of over 12,000 Jewish physicians from the Soviet Union between 1989 and 1994 essentially doubled the supply of physicians in Israel. Although there has never been overt opposition to the entry of immigrants by the established medical profession in Israel, Shuval (1995) describes three key strategies undertaken in response to this flooding of the medical labour market: (1) the Israeli medical profession applied stringent quality control with regard to the licensure of migrating physicians, including the same qualifying examinations as those administered to Israeli medical graduates, but strictly limited to general practice in the primary care system; (2) senior Israeli physicians exerted full control of the employment options for Russian émigrés in the local health-care system; and (3) Israeli physicians promulgated widespread negative stereotypes regarding the professional skills of immigrant physicians. These three strategies together served to exclude a sizeable proportion of the émigré physicians from practising as physicians in Israel.

Groutsis' (2003) examination of the integration paths of overseas doctors in Australia focuses similarly on the meso level. She juxtaposes the role of the state, as the major driver of policy shifts enabling the migration of overseas-qualified health-care professionals, with the role of the local medical profession, a group that has exercised its professional power to operate above and beyond the state's interest in controlling health professional supply conditions. Groutsis' (2003) analysis reveals how the medical profession's strict control of the registration of migrating physicians, and therefore their labour market access, through its licensure examination was met with a more activist approach by the state. This was afforded through policy 'work arounds', such as the *Areas of Need* programme, which enabled the direct recruitment of overseas-trained doctors with a restricted licence to work in remote locales for a period of up to ten years.

Similarly, studies of professional integration in Nordic countries have problematized other features of professional integration. As noted above, the member countries of the EU are obligated to mutually recognize the professional qualifications of professionals from other member countries. EU rulings do, however, recognize the need for language controls which thus become the key focus for defining the conditions of entry for mobile EU nationals (see European Commission, 2013). A Norwegian study focusing on the experiences of health professionals found that even when they were working in their profession, they often encountered exclusion related to a dynamic in which 'Norwegianness', defined as locale-specific cultural knowledge, has emerged as an important informal criterion of competence (Dahle and Seeberg, 2013). Other Nordic research has uncovered similar ethnic hierarchies in organizations that do not recognize the institutional racism involved in work organization that privileges locale-specific cultural knowledge (Laurén and Wrede, 2008); deteriorated terms of employment within welfare services, as well as institutional racism negatively impacting the families of the mobile professionals (Isaksen, 2010); and the rise of 'migrancy' as an exclusionary boundary within the medical profession that assigns immigrant doctors to low-prestige positions within the profession (Salmonsson, 2014).

Thus, one of the key problematics at the meso level is how migrating health professionals integrate and the multiple meanings this has both for their integration context and for their social position in the destination country. Integration involves admittance into often highly regulated fields of practice controlled by local professional organizations, as well as assimilation into the culture of the health-care system and local health professional practice. For example, in the case of the Russian émigré physicians in Israel who were able to secure a licence, they expressed dissatisfaction with the questioning of their authority by Israeli patients (Bernstein and Shuval, 1998), showing that complex ethnic boundaries may result from the integration of foreign personnel, requiring attention from the perspective of discrimination.

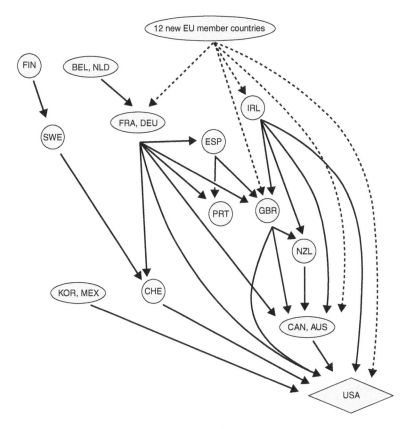

Figure 20.2 Chain migration across OECD countries

Source: OECD (2007), International Migration Outlook 2007, OECD Publishing, Paris, http://dx.doi.org/10.1787/migr_outlook-2007-en.

The gendered dynamics of health professional migration in the era of transnational mobilities

More recent analyses of health professional migration depict an even more complex picture than the terms 'source' and 'destination' country entail, emerging in the current era of transnational health professional mobilities. Some countries can be both source and destination, to varying degrees. For example, while Canada has both historically and more recently relied on migrating health professionals to help solve shortages in particular areas and sectors, there have been, from time to time, laments about its own health-care 'brain drain' to the United States. Similarly, while Ireland still provides a great deal of nursing labour to neighbouring countries, especially, it has recruits from other labour markets, most notably the Philippines (Yeates, 2004). Beyond this dynamic, there is an increasing trend of 'chain' migration and 'transition' countries, particularly through the Middle East (of which we know very little), which reflects a decreasing permanence of professional migration. Figure 20.2 represents this type of chain migration using the OECD countries as an example.

Some of the reasons behind particular chains of migration may reflect post-colonial ties between specific localities, as noted above. Other drivers result from the global political economy of the increasingly prevalent bilateral and multilateral agreements, both those that explicitly address health professional migration as well as those agreements for which health professional migration is incidental (e.g. trade agreements).

Scholarly research framed by approaches rooted in globalization and feminist political economy have increasingly studied such mobilities as gendered (Walton-Roberts, 2015). The literature on the migration of nurses has particularly considered how gender is implicated in the migration decisions of health-care workers through gender discrimination, inequality, traditional societal attitudes towards female migration and gender-based networks (e.g. Adhikari, 2013; Byron, 1998; Ryan, 2008). Ryan's (2008) work on Irish nurses who migrated to Britain in the post-war period reveals, for instance, that most of them were encouraged to migrate by female relatives, especially sisters, aunts and cousins. Adhikari (2013) illustrates how female nurses in Nepal are encouraged to migrate by their families as their migration is seen as collective family investment. Although the same could be said about male migration, female migration is a relatively new phenomenon because it overcomes previous (and in some places continued) restrictions on women's mobility which are rooted in patriarchal relations. Moreover, being a son who migrates versus being a daughter has very different social implications, not the least of which are social issues of purity and economic issues of family remittances. It is also important to note that the gendered meanings of family ties change over time. Transnational mobilities may serve to disrupt traditional gender roles and relations within the family at a relatively rapid pace, as shown by George's (2005) examination of the migration of nurses from Kerala, India, to the United States.

As noted above, the concept of 'global care chains' has also been applied in the case of more highly skilled health professional work. Yeates (2004), for example, argues that the concept enriches our understanding of the complex relationship between international migration and care-giving, which helps to contextualize the migration of nurses. The burden of the global care chain can have multiplicative negative effects on the lives of these women in terms of increased workload and social isolation (Bourgeault, 2015; Eckenwiler, 2014).

When examining the process of professional integration, gender is similarly important to consider. Some researchers have found, for example, that women physicians seem to adjust to a new system better than men (Remennick and Ottenstein-Eisen, 1998), but others have noted greater psychological distress among female health professionals who migrate (Factourovich *et al.* 1996). Given that they tend to shoulder greater family responsibilities, many female migrating health professionals have been found to delay the process of accreditation, retraining and occupational integration in favour of supporting their male spouse (Bernstein and Shuval, 1998; Neiterman and Bourgeault, 2015b).

In a comparison of the experiences of discrimination among nurses and doctors coming to Canada from abroad, Neiterman and Bourgeault (2015b) found that there is an interplay of ethnic, gender and professional inequalities in the instances of discrimination and racism to which these migrating health professionals are exposed in their workplace (cf. Hankivsky *et al.*, 2010). Migrating nurses tend to be exposed to more instances of discrimination and racism than physicians. The status of the medical profession can serve as a shield of protection from the experiences of racism and discrimination. That is, the relatively high status of the profession of medicine and the lower status of nursing, a profession considered inherently 'feminine', suggests that the role of gender and professional status intersect in the experiences of discrimination.

In sum, the emergence of globalized health labour markets entails that mobility pathways become more diverse, but these mobilities continue to be structured by gender that intersects with other local and global forms of inequality, such as ethnicity, 'race' and class. These sociocultural hierarchies further intersect with conceptions of professionalism and skill that are always situated and socially constructed along gender lines (Wrede, 2010).

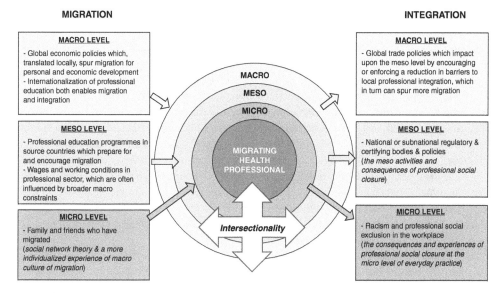

MIGRATION

INTEGRATION

Figure 20.3 A pluralistic conceptual framework of professional migration and integration

Source: reprinted from *Bulletin of the World Health Organization*, 82/8, Kassoum Diallo', 'Data on the Migration of Health-Care Workers: Sources, Uses and Challenges', p.602, copyright 2004.

Building a pluralistic framework for the intersectional analysis of mobility patterns and integration pathways of health professionals

We have made the case for the importance of a multi-layered analysis that includes micro, meso and macro levels, with attention to the intersections of gender, ethnicity, class, etc. as cross-cutting features. In this section we will use this structure to develop a conceptual framework that marries theoretical approaches to migration and professions with theoretical insights from studies of globalization and transnationalism. Instead of lamenting 'the absence of a single, coherent, interdisciplinary theory that is able to explain the full complexity of the migration processes' (de Haas, 2010), we argue for the need to be more pluralist in seeking different and ideally complementary theories to explain the different layers of the factors and forces influencing professional migration in a way that links these analyses.

We propose a pluralistic conceptual framework of theories, not an overarching theory in and of itself. Figure 20.3 begins to tease apart the various layers of analysis and their impact on migration and integration separately (though there are some for which there is overlapping influence) and maps some of the different theories next to the factors and forces they emphasize; we highlight in the text below a few of these theoretical perspectives, particularly those which draw upon professions theory. An intersectionality lens, described above as including critical social divisions such as gender, ethnicity, class, etc., cuts across all levels of analysis as well as the migration and integration processes. This is important because the, identification of interlinkages is necessary in order to grasp the complexities of mobility patterns and integration pathways.

Micro-level theoretical inputs

We acknowledged above that health professionals from different countries and in different professions have access to differential capacities and potentials for mobility. It is important to note how more conventional understandings of migration tend to ignore such differences and instead assign ample room for individual migrants as strategic actors. This kind of research on expert labour tends to draw from classical migration theory that builds on neoclassical economic theory and economic spatial analyses. For example, such approaches assume that migration decisions are powerfully influenced by how individuals assess supply and income differentials (without acknowledging how these differentials arise). Early migration studies sought to demonstrate how such assessments lead to an equilibrium of workers moving to a context of low supply and higher incomes (e.g. Harris and Todaro, 1970). Other early theories of migration developed spatial approaches, focusing, for example, on an interplay between distance and opportunities for migrants (Stouffer, 1940) or on ways that migrants move within established 'streams' where there is a pre-existing flow of workers and information (Lee, 1966).

Analyses that assume the autonomy of professional migrants as strategic actors shaping their transnational careers have an intuitive appeal and may indeed be undertaken, but in and of itself this is an insufficient and inadequate framework for analysing mobility patterns and integration pathways. There is agency involved, but there are also structural determinants which ultimately affect the weight of push and pull factors. This perspective does not, as Hazarika (2015) describes, 'take into consideration factors such as human capital characteristics, segmentation of destination country labour markets as well as immigration policies that are important determinants in the migration process' (p. 22).

Social and cultural dimensions are also explored in migrant network theories (Massey *et al.*, 1993), which are described as 'sets of interpersonal ties that connect migrants, former migrants, and non-migrants in origin and destination areas through bonds of kinship, friendship, and shared community origin' (p. 448). Massey *et al.* (1993) further argue that migrating can become self-perpetuating once a critical mass of migrants establishes a de facto social structure enabling migration. Connell (2008) writes about how such a culture of migration is endemic to the Pacific Islands such that the retention of health workers seems impossible.

With respect to the integration side of the framework, we could draw more fully on professional socialization theory to examine how the integration experiences of mobile health professionals involve a process of professional *re*socialization (Neiterman and Bourgeault, 2015a). These reworked concepts are helpful in denoting how migrating health professionals must learn a new local professional culture in their new country, layering over their original professional socialization in their home country.

Meso-level theoretical inputs

Meso-level theoretical inputs are at the local labour market level reflecting both economic supply and demand factors that affect social-closure activities of professional groups. Here we can build upon Shuval (1995) and colleagues' (Bernstein and Shuval, 1998) application of a professional closure model by broadening this to include a more dual or parallel systems focus from the work of Abbott (1988). Shuval explored the intra-professional tensions in the Israeli medical profession when confronted with the massive emigration of physicians from the Soviet Union by drawing upon a professional closure model (Parkin, 1979). Briefly, this approach delineates how *exclusion* based on credentials serves to limit and control the supply of entrants to professional practice, depending on the key market factors of need, supply and distribution. Using this approach, Shuval describes how Israeli physicians maintained control over international medical graduates in a highly saturated medical market.

To expand, social-closure theorists within the sociology of professions describe the relations *between* professions when boundaries of professional jurisdiction are negotiated within a single-system perspective (Abbott, 1988); they also analyse the dynamics *within* professions, such as the inclusion or exclusion of particular subgroups. Indeed, Witz (1992) utilized the concepts of inclusion and exclusion to describe the historical treatment of women in medicine in Britain. Analyses of the dynamics of inclusionary and exclusionary social closure strategies have tended to focus more narrowly on the dynamics within a nationally bound profession. Indeed, these internal dynamics within nationally bound health systems (and their consequences) are increasingly under scrutiny/surveillance and/or problematized by a range of stakeholders external to national systems.

What might be useful would be an expansion of Abbott's (implicitly nationally focused) system to include dual or *parallel systems of professions* in 'source', 'destination' and transit countries influencing the migration pathways of health professionals. Visually, these could be represented by the two circles in Figure 20.1 as the 'source system' and the 'destination system', acknowledging the important distinctions made in that figure. Inclusion and exclusion could still be utilized as the main tools of social closure. Migration (in, out and return) of the parallel systems could be considered as *external system disturbances* (drawing upon Abbott's terminology) influencing jurisdiction within nationally bound professions. But there are also a number of other external system disturbances reflecting more macro-level inputs (codes of practice, trade agreements, etc.), which would enable a natural tie from meso- to macro-level analyses. This conceptualization would also enable the recognition of highly segregated/regulated internal systems – which could help to address what is sometimes a 'brain waste' phenomenon in destination countries. It would also help to recognize the inequalities between 'source' and 'destination' countries – which addresses the more typically discussed 'brain drain' issues.

While a professional closure model may be useful in helping to explain the dynamics within a profession, it sometimes does not fully attend to the broader political and economic factors, including relations between various professional organizations and government agencies, which are critical to examine in the case of the integration of health professionals trained abroad. It can, however, incorporate a gender and intersectionality lens, as discussed above. Witz's (1992) discernment of different types of gendered social closure strategies, for example, represents an as yet untapped resource in gendered analyses of health professional migration. That is, just as Witz (1992) encouraged us to gender the actors of professional projects, we argue here that we need to gender migrating health professionals. Gender matters in decisions to migrate and in the opportunities that male and female migrating health professionals have in integrating into local labour markets.

Macro-level theoretical inputs

Attention to the global political economy in research on the migration of health professionals draws from the rise of critical theorizing about globalization with roots in, among others, Wallerstein's (1974) World System's Theory. Wallerstein's perspective is an important example of the historical-structural theoretical approach that describes how goods and capital flow from the powerful 'core' to the 'periphery' in search of raw materials, labour and new consumer markets. In the current context, critical approaches within a post-colonial global sociology seek to develop a sociology of connections that takes seriously the histories of interconnection that have shaped the current global inequalities (Bhambra, 2014). As implemented in the study of professional mobilities, Wallerstein's theory of a world organized as centres and peripheries and Bhambra's sociology of connections would allow us to understand professional mobility from peripheral locales in less-resourced countries to central locales in more-resourced countries and through them to marginal positions in their professional order as constitutive of the histories of the professions (see Bhambra, 2014, p. 155). This means recognizing that modern professions emerged in a colonial world, and that contemporary patterns of mobility make use of such historical connections as well as global ideas (Wrede, 2010).

Currently, the debates are formed around the practices of transnational communication and the impact of migration on the home and hosting countries' economies and cultures (Levitt, 2001; Orum, 2005). While transnational studies incorporate many aspects of inquiry to better capture the dynamic of the relationship between migrants, host countries, and the countries of origin, scholars continue to engage in methodological and theoretical debates about what constitutes 'transnationalism', as well as how it should be studied and measured (Levitt and Jaworsky, 2007). Although definitions rendered by researchers of the transcultural movement vary, the vast majority of scholars appear to agree that research on migrants should contextualize the agency of migrants in the structural and institutional dynamics of both countries. This new approach is reflected in many works looking into the experiences of immigrants in their countries of destination. Scholars often link migrants' personal experiences to the structural forces in their home countries and the modes of communication that shape their experiences as newcomers in their countries of destination (Behnke *et al.*, 2008; Calavita, 2006; Waldinger *et al.*, 2007)

The sociology literature has addressed the issue of professional migration as one of the key features in economic globalization. Sassen (1988, 1998, 2007), for example, describes the tensions between *transnational* economies and national *migration* policies. The author notes that 'There is a causal relationship between immigrant receiving countries, foreign investment, and political-military and cultural involvement, on the one hand, and immigrant flows, on the other' (Sassen, 2007). Transnational economic policies, such as the World Bank's Structural Adjustment Policies, have been critical in encouraging the large-scale out-migration of workers she terms an *offshore proletariat*. On the opposite end of the spectrum of the division of labour, she also describes the portable rights of a *new transnational professional class*, acquired through free-trade agreements, the International Monetary Fund and other such supranational institutions which can supersede national migration policies. These are indeed important insights but they may be less relevant to highly regulated local markets of certain professional domains, such as in health care. That is, national or subnational regulatory policies may still limit the integration of migrating professionals despite the system of health professions. Such regulations may serve as a mechanism for gatekeeping that may result in the emergence of a migrant division of labour within health professions where the transnationally mobile health professionals only have access to specific positions, not to equal inclusion (see Yeates, 2009; Wrede, 2010). This not only speaks to the continued importance of meso-level analysis, it also highlights how it is important to tease apart factors and forces influencing migration and those influencing integration. These are two overlapping yet distinct processes with different inputs and outputs.

In terms of the gender dimensions of translocal economic connections, Sassen's (2002) analysis of the current transnational migration of women for largely female-typed activities identifies centres and peripheries as dynamic configurations, that is, as global cities and as sets of survival circuits emerging as a response to growing impoverishment of governments and whole economies in the global south. Even though Sassen's ideas have often been applied to lower-skill workers, analyses that recognize the intersected inequalities ordering professional mobilities benefit from recognizing these connections as survival circuits that are often complex, involving multiple locations and sets of actors constituting increasingly global chains of traders and 'workers'. Indeed, it is evident that health-care systems in the global north can build new economies of health care on the availability of supposedly rather valueless economic actors – low-wage and poor health professionals, the majority of whom are women.

Conclusion

In this chapter, we have categorized the literature on health professional migration according to different levels of analysis to inform the creation of a pluralistic theoretical framework that draws upon migration, globalization and professions theory. Our aim has been to build a basis for capturing the complexity of contemporary mobility patterns and integration pathways that are structured by intersecting global and local inequalities. A framework enabling interconnected theories recognizes the complexity of the migration and integration processes in a way that encourages us to look in new places for new connections and mechanisms that are disrupting and transforming migration and integration processes. It explicitly acknowledges that although health professionals are rational agents, their agency is structured by the different degrees of mobility they have access to and integration pathways. It also encourages us to undertake research in ways that do not ignore these new connections, thus avoiding the situation where our scholarship has less and less relevance to what is happening on the ground. It is meant to be a framework within which to situate one's analysis and to acknowledge that there are other relevant levels that should not be ignored but that may not necessarily be the focus of one's analysis. The next challenge is to develop a sound methodology to capture the impact of these complex migration and integration processes. Another possible direction is to develop typologies to help to analyse the uneven distribution of mobility capital among professionals from different countries and different professions.

References

Abbott, A. D. (1988) *The System of Professions: An Essay on the Division of Expert Labor*. Chicago, IL: University of Chicago Press.

Adhikari, R. (2013) 'Empowered wives and frustrated husbands: Nursing, gender and migrant Nepali in the UK'. *International Migration* 51(6), pp. 168–179.

Ahmad, A., Amuah, E., Mehta, N., Nkala, B. and Singh, J. A. (2003) 'The ethics of nurse poaching from the developing world'. *Nursing Ethics* 10(6), pp. 667–670.

Aiken, L. H., Buchan, J., Sochalski, J., Nichols, B. and Powell, M. (2004) 'Trends in international nurse migration'. *Health Affairs* 23(3), pp. 69–77.

Alexis, O. and Vydelingum, V. (2004) 'The lived experience of overseas black and minority ethnic nurses in the NHS in the South of England'. *Diversity in Health and Social Care* 1(1), pp. 13–20.

Allan, H. T., Larsen, J. A., Bryan, K. and Smith, P. (2004) 'The social reproduction of institutional racism: Internationally recruited nurses' experiences of the British health services'. *Diversity in Health and Social Care* 1(2), pp. 117–125.

Anthias, Floya (2012) 'Transnational mobilities, migration research and intersectionality'. *Nordic Journal of Migration Research* 2(2), pp. 102–110.

Bach, S. (2003) *International Migration of Health Workers: Labour and Social Issues*. Paper prepared for the Sectoral Activities Department, International Labour Office, July.

Behnke, A., Taylor, B. A. and Parra-Cardona, J. R. (2008) '"I hardly understand English, but": Mexican-origin fathers describe their commitment as fathers despite the challenges of immigration'. *Journal of Comparative Family Studies* 39, pp. 187–205.

Bernstein, J. and Shuval, J. T. (1998) 'The occupational integration of former Soviet physicians in Israel'. *Social Science & Medicine* 47(6), pp. 809–819.

Bhambra, Gurminder K. (2014) *Connected Sociologies*. London: Bloomsbury Academic.

Bourgeault, I. L. (2007) 'Brain drain, brain gain and brain waste: Programs aimed at integrating and retaining the best and the brightest in health care'. *Canadian Issues / Thémes Canadiens*, pp. 96–99.

Bourgeault, I. L. (2015) 'The double isolation of immigrants undertaking older adult care work'. In C. Stacey and M. Duffy (eds) *Caring on the Clock*. New Brunswick, NJ: Rutgers University Press, pp. 117–125.

Bourgeault, I. L. and Wrede, S. (2011) 'Caring across borders: Contrasting the contexts of nurse migration in Canada and Finland'. In C. Benoit and H. Hallgrimsdottir (eds) *Valuing Care Work: Comparative Perspectives*. Toronto: University of Toronto Press, pp. 65–86.

Bourgeault, I. L., Neiterman, E., LeBrun, J., Viers, K. and Winkup, J. (2010) *Brain Gain, Drain and Waste: The Experiences of IEHPs in Canada*. Available for download: www.healthworkermigration.com (last accessed 28 January 2016).

Bourgeault, I. L., Labonté, R., Packer, C., Runnels, V. and Tomblin Murphy, G. (forthcoming) 'Knowledge and potential impact of the WHO Global Code of Practice on the international recruitment of health personnel: Does it matter for source and destination country stakeholders?'. *Human Resources for Health*.

Buchan, J. (2004) 'International rescue? The dynamics and policy implications of the international recruitment of nurses to the UK'. *Journal of Health Services Research and Policy* 9(1), pp. 10–16.

Byron, M. (1998) 'Migration, work, and gender: The case of post-war labour migration from the Caribbean to Britain'. In M. Chamberlain (ed.) *Caribbean Migration: Globalised Identities*. London: Routledge, pp. 226–242.

Calavita, K. (2006) 'Gender, migration, and law: Crossing borders and bridging disciplines'. *International Migration Review* 40(1), pp. 104–132.

Camlin, C. S., Snow, R. C., and Hosegood, V. (2014). 'Gendered patterns of migration in rural South Africa'. *Population, Space and Place* 20(6), pp. 528–551.

Castles, S. and Miller, M. J. (2003) *The Age of Migration* (3rd edn). New York & London: The Guilford Press.

Choy, C. (2003) *Empire of Care: Nursing and Migration in Filipino American History*. Durham, NC: Duke University Press.

Collinds, E. M. (2004) *Career Mobility among Immigrant Registered Nurses in Canada: Experiences of Caribbean Women*. Toronto: University of Toronto Press.

Connell, J. (2008) 'Niue: embracing a culture of migration'. *Journal of Ethnic and Migration Studies* 34(6), pp. 1021–1040.

Dahle, Rannveig and Seeberg, Marie Louise (2013) '"Does she speak Norwegian?" Ethnic dimensions of hierarchy in Norwegian health care workplaces'. *Nordic Journal of Migration Research* 3(2), pp. 82–90.

Diallo, K. (2004) 'Data on the migration of health-care workers: Sources, uses and challenges', *Bulletin of the World Health Organization* 82(8), pp. 601–607. www.who.int/bulletin/volumes/82/8/en/601.pdf (last accessed 28 January 2016).

Dicicco-Bloom, B. (2004) 'The racial and gendered experiences of immigrant nurses from Kerala, India'. *Journal of Transcultural Nursing* 15(1), pp. 26–33.

Eckenwiler, L. (2014) 'Care worker migration, global health equity, and ethical place-making'. *Women's Studies International Forum* 47, pp. 213–222.

European Commission (2013) *Modernisation of the Professional Qualifications Directive: Frequently Asked Questions*. Memo Brussels, 9 October 2013. http://europa.eu/rapid/press-release_MEMO-13-867_en.htm (last accessed 1 July 2015).

Factourovich, A., Ritsner, M., Maoz, B., Levin, K., Mirsky, J., Ginath, Y., Segal, A. and Natan, E. B. (1996) 'Psychological adjustment among Soviet immigrant physicians: Distress and self-assessments of its sources'. *Israel Journal of Psychiatry and Related Sciences* 33(1), pp. 32–39.

George, S. (2005) *When Women Come First: Gender and Class in Transnational Migration*. Berkeley, CA: University of California Press.

Giri, N. M. (1998) 'South Asian women physicians' working experiences in Canada'. *Canadian Woman Studies* 18(1), pp. 61–64.

Groutsis, D. (2003) 'The state, immigration policy and labour market practices: The case of overseas-trained doctors'. *The Journal of Industrial Relations* 45(1), pp. 67–86.

Guarnizo, L. E. (2003) 'The economics of transnational living'. *International Migration Review* 37(3), pp. 666–699.

de Haas, H. (2010) 'Migration and development: A theoretical review'. *International Migration Review* 44(1), pp. 227–264.

Hagey, R., Choudhry, U., Guruge, S., Turrittin, J., Collins, E. and Lee, R. (2001) 'Immigrant Nurses' Experiences of Racism'. *Journal of Nursing Scholarship* 33(4), pp. 389–394.

Hagopian, A., Ofosu, A., Fatusi, A., Biritwum, R., Essel, A., Hart, L. G. and Watts, C. (2005) 'The flight of physicians from West Africa: Views of African physicians and implications for policy'. *Social Science & Medicine* 61(8), pp. 1750–1760.

Hankivsky, O., Reid, C., Cormier, R., Varcoe, C., Clark, N., Benoit, C. and Brotman, S. (2010) 'Exploring the promises of intersectionality for advancing women's health research'. *International Journal for Equity in Health* 9(5), pp. 1–15.

Harris, J. R. and Todaro, M. P. (1970) 'Migration, unemployment and development: A two-sector analysis'. *The American Economic Review* 60(1), pp. 126–142.

Hazarika, I. (2015) *Flight of International Medical Graduates: A Cross-Country Comparative Study Examining Key Events in the Trajectory*. PhD thesis, University of Melbourne.

Hochschild, A. R. (2000) 'Global care chains and emotional surplus value'. In W. Hutton and A. Giddens (eds) *On The Edge: Living with Global Capitalism*. London: Jonathan Cape.

Isaksen, L. W. (2010) 'Transnational care: The social dimensions of international nurse recruitment'. In L. W. Isaksen (ed.) *Global Care Work: Gender and Migration in Nordic Societies*. Lund: Nordic Academic Press, pp. 137–157.

Jeans, M. E. (2006) 'In-country challenges to addressing the effects of emerging global nurse migration on health care delivery'. *Policy, Politics, & Nursing Practice* 7(3), pp. 58S–61S.

Kapur, D. and McHale, J. (2005) *Give Us Your Best and Brightest: The Global Hunt for Talent and Its Impact on the Developing World*. Washington, DC: Center for Global Development.

Kaufmann, V. and Montulet, B. (2008) 'Between social and spatial mobilities: The issue of social fluidity'. In W. Canzler, V. Kaufmann and S. Kesselring (eds) *Tracing Mobilities: Towards a Cosmopolitan Perspective*. Farnham and Burlington, VT: Ashgate, pp. 37–56.

Kaufmann, V., Bergman, M. and Joye, D. (2004) 'Motility: Mobility as capital'. *International Journal of Urban and Regional Research* 28(4), pp. 745–756.

Kingma, M. (2006). *Nurses on the Move: Migration and the Global Health Care Economy*. Ithaca, NY and London: ILR Press.

Labonté, R., Packer, C. and Klassen, N. (2006) 'Managing health professional migration from sub-Saharan Africa to Canada: A stakeholder inquiry into policy options'. *Human Resources for Health*, 4(22). Available online: www.human-resources-health.com/content/4/1/22 (last accessed 28 January 2016).

Larsen, J. A. (2007) 'Embodiment of discrimination and overseas nurses' career progression'. *Journal of Clinical Nursing* 16(12), pp. 2187–2195.

Laurén, J. and Wrede, S. (2008) 'Immigrants in care work: ethnic hierarchies and work distribution'. *Finnish Journal of Ethnicity and Migration* 3(3), pp. 20–31.

Lee, E. S. (1966) 'A theory of migration'. *Demography* 3(1), pp. 47–57.

Levitt, P. (2001) 'Transnational migration: Taking stock and future directions'. *Global Networks* 1(3), pp. 195–216.

Levitt, P. and Jaworsky, B. N. (2007) 'Transnational migration studies: Past developments and future trends'. *Annual Review of Sociology* 33, pp. 129–156.

McNeil-Walsh, C. (2004) 'Widening the discourse: A case for the use of post-colonial theory in the analysis of South African nurse migration to Britain'. *Feminist Review* 77, pp. 120–124.

Massey, D. S., Arango, J., Hugo, G., Kouaouci, A., Pellegrino, A. and Taylor, J. E. (1993) 'Theories of international migration: A review and appraisal'. *Population and Development Review* 19(3), pp. 431–466.

Neiterman, E. and Bourgeault, I. L. (2011) 'Conceptualizing professional diaspora: international medical graduates in Canada'. *Journal of International Migration and Integration* 12(3), pp. 39–57.

Neiterman, E. and Bourgeault, I. L. (2015a) 'Professional integration as a process of professional resocialization: Internationally educated health professionals in Canada'. *Social Science & Medicine* 131, pp. 74–81.

Neiterman, E. and Bourgeault, I. L. (2015b) 'The shield of professional status: Comparing discriminatory experiences of IENs and IMGs in Canada'. *Health* 19(6), pp. 615–634.

Neiterman, E., Salmonsson, L. and Bourgeault, I. L. (2015) 'Navigating through otherness and belonging: A comparative case study of international medical graduates professional integration in Canada and Sweden'. *Ephemera: Theory and Politics in Organization* 15(4), pp. 773–795.

NHS (Department of Health, UK) (2001) *Code of Practice for NHS Employers Involved in the International Recruitment of Healthcare Professionals*. http://webarchive.nationalarchives.gov.uk/+/www.dh.gov.uk/en/Publicationsandstatistics/Publications/PublicationsPolicyAndGuidance/DH_4006781 (last accessed 28 January 2016).

OECD (2007) 'Immigrant health workers in OECD countries in the broader context of highly skilled migration'. *International Migration Outlook*. www.oecd.org/els/mig/41515701.pdf (last accessed 28 January 2016).

Orum, A. M. (2005) 'Circles of influence and chains of command: The social processes whereby ethnic communities influence host societies'. *Social Forces* 84(2), pp. 921–939.

Orzack, L. (1998) 'Professions and world trade diplomacy: National systems and international authority'. In V. Olgiati, L. Orzack and M. Saks (eds) *Professions, Identity, and Order in Comparative Perspective.* Onati: Institute for International Study of the Sociology of Law.

Parkin, F. (1979) *Marxism and Class Theory: A Bourgeois Critique.* New York: Columbia University Press.

Pittman, P. M., Folsom, A. J. and Bass, E. (2010) 'US-based recruitment of foreign-educated nurses: Implications of an emerging industry'. *American Journal of Nursing* 110(6), pp. 38–48.

Remennick, L. I. and Ottenstein-Eisen, N. (1998) 'Reaction of new Soviet immigrants to primary health services in Canada'. *International Journal of Health Services* 28(3), pp. 555–574.

Robinson, V. and Carey, M. (2000). 'Skilled international migration: Indian doctors in the UK'. *International Migration* 38(10), pp. 89–108.

Ryan, J. (2002) 'Chinese women as transnational migrants: Gender and class in global migration narratives'. *International Migration* 40(2), pp. 93–116.

Ryan, L. (2008) '"I had a sister in England": Family-led migration, social networks and nurses'. *Journal of Ethnic and Migration Studies* 34(3), pp. 453–470.

Salmonsson, L. (2014) *The 'Other' Doctor: Boundary Work within the Swedish Medical Profession.* Unpublished PhD dissertation, Uppsala University.

Sassen, S. (1988) *The Mobility of Capital and Labor: A Study in International Investment and Labor Flow.* Cambridge: Cambridge University Press.

Sassen, S. (1998) *Globalization and Its Discontents: Essays on the New Mobility of People and Money.* New York: The New Press.

Sassen, S. (2002) *Global Networks, Linked Cities.* Hove, UK: Psychology Press.

Sassen, S. (2007) *A Sociology of Globalization.* New York: W.W. Norton.

Shuval, J. (1995) 'Elitism and professional control in a saturated market: Immigrant physicians in Israel'. *Sociology of Health and Illness* 17(4), pp. 330–365.

Shuval, J. (1998) 'Credentialling immigrant physicians in Israel'. *Health & Place* 4(4), pp. 375–381.

Shuval, J. (2000) 'The reconstruction of professional identity among immigrant physicians in three societies'. *Journal of Immigrant Health* 2(4), pp. 191–102.

Squires, A. (2011) 'The North American Free Trade Agreement (NAFTA) and Mexican nursing'. *Health Policy and Planning* 26, pp. 124–132.

Stouffer, S. A. (1940) 'Intervening opportunities: A theory relating mobility and distance'. *American Sociological Review* 5(6), pp. 845–867.

Tankwanchi, A., Vermund, S. H. and Perkins, D. D. (2014) 'Has the WHO global code of practice on the international recruitment of health personnel been effective?'. *The Lancet Global Health* 2(7), pp. e390–e391.

Turrittin, J., Hagey, R., Guruge, S., Collins, E. and Mitchell, M. (2002) 'The experiences of professional nurses who have migrated to Canada: Cosmopolitan citizenship or democratic racism?'. *International Journal of Nursing Studies* 39, pp. 655–667.

Waldinger, R., Lim, N. and Cort, D. (2007) 'Bad jobs, good jobs, no jobs? The employment experience of the Mexican American second generation'. *Journal of Ethnic and Migration Studies* 33(1), pp. 1–35.

Wallerstein, I. (1974) *The Modern World System I, Capitalist Agriculture and the Origins of the European World Economy in the Sixteenth Century.* New York: Academic Press.

Walton-Roberts, M. (2015) 'International migration of health professionals and the marketization and privatization of health education in India: From push-pull to global political economy'. *Social Science & Medicine* 124, pp. 374–382.

WHO (2006) *Working Together for Health.* World Health Report. Geneva: World Health Organization.

WHO (2010) *Global Code of Practice on the International Recruitment of Health Personnel.* Geneva: World Health Organization.

Witz, A. (1992) *Professions and Patriarchy.* London: Routledge.

Wrede, Sirpa (2010) 'Nursing: Globalization of a female-gendered profession'. In E. Kuhlmann and E. Annandale (eds) *The Palgrave Handbook of Gender and Healthcare.* Basingstoke: Palgrave Macmillan, pp. 437–453.

Yeates, N. (2004) 'Broadening the scope of global care chain analysis: Nurse migration in the Irish context', *Feminist Review,* 77, pp. 79–95.

Yeates, Nicola (2009) *Globalizing Care Economies and Migrant Workers: Explorations in Global Care Chains.* Basingstoke, UK: Palgrave Macmillan.

Part V
Sectoral analysis
Case studies

Introduction

Mike Dent

Elsewhere in this Companion we have chapters on specific professions, including accountancy (Haslam, Chapter 16) and law (Ballakrishnen, Chapter 18), but these are discussed in connection with the specific themes of globalisation in Part IV. In this final part of the Companion, we take the opportunity to examine specific professions, or groups of cognate professions, in terms of how they are responding to current challenges.

We start with the professions of the academy, the professors and their colleagues. Muzzin and Martimianakis examine the academic profession historically and globally, providing us with a richly detailed account of their contemporary and variegated condition internationally. Next, we have Mausethagen and Smeby's comparative analysis of the teaching profession and the impact of the rationalisation processes contained within current educational policy. From education we move to health, with Nancarrow and Borthwick's consideration of inter-professional working within health care. They consider two case studies, the first looks at the boundary role issues surrounding foot surgery, as between surgeons and podiatrists, while the second tells of more flexible working and sharing of responsibilities for tasks across professions in the case of the rural allied health generalist in remote rural parts of Australia. In the next chapter, on social work, the emphasis of Webb's account is less on the practice of social work and more on the role and importance of theory in the ongoing pursuit of professional identity. Finally, we consider a putative profession, namely journalism, that is currently having to consider its future in light of the possibilities provided by the internet and digitalisation. Here Schnell considers the different Anglo-American and continental European journalistic traditions and the impact of the new technologies and changing media consumption patterns for the profession. She makes a good case for the survival of the fourth estate of news media journalists in the face of the ubiquitous blogs, tweets and Facebook observations and commentaries provided by amateurs and others.

What we see with all of these professional groups, in their different guises, is that they are having to adapt and change in the face of new political, social and technological realities, globally and nationally. The resulting situation for these professionals is now far more fluid and challenging than ever before.

21
The professoriate and professionalism in the academy

Linda Muzzin and Maria Athina (Tina) Martimianakis

Introduction

This chapter explores three different literatures that contribute to a portrait of contemporary professors as professionals: comparative studies of faculty, research theorizing inequity in academia, and recent writing about the professoriate in the context of the 'knowledge economy'. All three types of scholarship tend not to relate the professoriate and other academic professions to writing about other professions or work in general and so we must read 'between the lines' to get some sense of the professional cultures or identities inside post-secondary institutions.

To anchor arguments about the professoriate and academic professionalism within the sociology of professions, we begin with Freidson's thesis (2001) that professions are a 'third logic', distinct from the state or the market, as experts controlling to various extents not only the conditions of their work but the very production of knowledge, an observation he derived from his ethnographies of physicians and, to a lesser extent, the American academy (Freidson, 1970). He later modified this to argue that an elite faction of a profession could retain its autonomy when pressures from the state seemed to have limited its power (Freidson, 1984). Despite the embedding of professors in the state in European countries, writers seem to agree that the professoriate displays aspects of a third logic even if they have not adopted this term. They have differed in their accounts of what this logic actually is, variously relating it to medieval 'guild power' (Krause, 1996); the power of dons recruited from the ruling class and their freedom to shape the academy (Annan, 1999); the power of the disciplines linked to the system of departments that either recruit or are referred applicants based on the departmental discipline (Abbott, 2000; Musselin, 2010); the recognition by the courts of a right called 'academic freedom'; and to the institution of tenure, or unique granting of job security for life to professors (Chait, 2002; Musselin, 2010).

But by the end of the 1990s, writers agreed that this key aspect of professionalism was on the wane. There were different arguments about exactly how professional autonomy had declined – whether it was a slow erosion from powers held in medieval times; a decline from a high point in the twentieth century; or that autonomy had only been achieved in particular places but not in others and would eventually disappear worldwide. A parallel equity literature argued that the academy is deeply segmented with only a small elite having autonomy, much as Freidson had argued for the medical profession (1984). The first three of these arguments will be examined in the first section, citing three authors making the various arguments, and the last in a separate section on equity. In contrast to the generally pessimistic tone of comparative studies and much of the equity literature, the emergent field known as knowledge production dealt with in the last section of this chapter is mixed about the status of faculty in an era of globalization, with its images of privatization, marketization, commodification, financialization and neoliberalism. Some authors continue the 'decline' and 'equity' themes of earlier studies, worrying about the decentring of the professor, fragmented faculty identities and exploitation of an underclass. Others are quite hopeful and even expansive about the robustness of professorial creativity and the production of knowledge, even if professors are just one kind of 'knowledge worker' among many. And most promising is a critique by so-called 'third world' scholars of the first world's academic obsession with globalization.

Traditional and comparative studies

Professional autonomy in the form of academic freedom and tenure are central concepts in traditional discussions about the power of the professoriate and the university as a societal institution. In the German system, *Lehr* and *Lernfreiheit* (freedom of teaching and learning) are principles assumed to be originally present. Academic freedom and tenure are defined in the 1940 statement by the American Association of University Professors (AAUP), which described the granting of individual professors the right to freedom of research and the publication of results, in the classroom discussing their subject, and from institutional censorship 'when they speak as citizens'. The document also stated that 'after the expiration of a probationary period, teachers or investigators should have permanent or continuous tenure, and their service should be terminated only for adequate cause, except in the case of retirement for age, or under extraordinary circumstances because of financial exigencies' (AAUP, 1940). Academic freedom and the granting of tenure were assumed to be in synchrony with each other,[1] with judgements dependent on a 'company of equals' for the admission and recognition of any one individual (Freidson and Rhea, 1963).

The early sociology of professions literature leans heavily in the direction of Anglo-America. This is why Krause's (1996) assessment of what he terms the 'guild power' of medicine, law, engineering and academia in the USA, Britain, France, Italy and Germany is so useful. Guild power was the historical power obtained by guilds of craftsmen in Europe between 1100 and 1500. In applying this concept to professions, Krause defines it as that power of association that historically challenged the feudal system and permitted creation of a *universitas* in the medieval Latin (1996, p. 3) controlling entrance, education and dues. Guild power also includes control of the workplace and the market, as well as the profession's relation to the state, which resonates with Freidson's description of a 'third logic'. Each chapter in Krause's book outlines the particularities of the professions in the five countries and then compares them, revealing wide national variations in the prestige and power of the academic profession, from a high in Germany and Italy (1996, p. 262) to a low in Britain. He argues that scholars' guilds have held on to their autonomy longer than the other professions 'under local and national protection and subsidy' (1996, p. 6) in all five countries, coping with attacks on guild powers by early capitalism, the church and central bureaucratic states (as in France). Globalization happened early to the professoriate with its Latin *lingua franca*, and this advantage persists to this day with English as the global language of the sciences.

Like Abbott (2000), Krause traces the robustness of the US professoriate in particular to the founding of disciplinary societies about a century ago and the recruitment of entrants via the unique departmental structure of the US university. These links to disciplinary control are also made by Musselin for France and Germany (2010). In the USA, she describes those with tenure functioning as 'almost autonomous employees with a set of prescribed freedoms and responsibilities' (2010, p. 68), which include teaching for the majority (the locals) and research for a minority of elites (the cosmopolitans). But Krause rejects both Abbott's faith in the invincibility of the disciplinary system as well as neo-Marxist accounts of the irretrievable proletarianization of academia over time, emphasizing that a profession does not die – only its guild power waxes and wanes (1996, p. 283). Consistent with the two other comparative studies examined here, he concludes that in specific countries, some academic guild powers have been limited. For example, during the Thatcher era in Britain, tenure was abolished, and with massification of higher education, control over the workplace and the market has been at least partially lost (1996, p. 22). US guild power waxed from 1935 to 1965, but has waned since then, facing administrative apparatuses and globalization. Wherever these losses have occurred in recent times, Krause argues, state rationalization has been the cause.

At about the same time that Krause's historical comparisons appeared, Slaughter and Leslie (1997) cast doubt on the robustness of the autonomy of the professoriate vis-à-vis the neoliberal state in Australia, Canada, the UK and USA over the period from 1980 to 1995, identifying and tracing a deepening corporatization and commercialization of the university, which they termed academic capitalism. They traced a 'money trail' which showed greater investment in research at the expense of teaching in US universities over the period. In *Academic Capitalism* and subsequent writing, they documented the key effect on individual faculty members as eroding their autonomy through spending their time chasing research grants and publications rather than devoting time to teaching or the public good. While university administrators were identified as leading academic capitalism, Slaughter and colleagues argued that faculty on the ground either actively pursued corporate research funding and patents or participated unhappily in such entrepreneurial activities without being able to effectively resist them. Perhaps their most persuasive observation that faculty autonomy has declined is their argument about the 'unbundling' of faculty activity and replacement of tenured faculty with contingent faculty and vocationally oriented middle management performing many research, teaching and student-service activities that were formerly the responsibility of faculty in the countries studied. Veblen (1918[1957]) had been the first to argue that the importation of entrepreneurial professions into the American university would challenge autonomy over faculty work and the curriculum. He critiqued the corporate pandering of university presidents (sarcastically labelled 'captains of erudition') to the corporate elite. Slaughter and colleagues' contemporary research is dominated by observations about the American professoriate, supplemented by Australian research and analysis of the situation in the UK and Canada, which they see as exhibiting the same changes in faculty work due to processes of globalization. Unlike Krause, they do not contrast how faculty careers play out in the various states but instead point to their similarities. Is the American experience generalizable? Academic capitalism resulting from an erosion of state funding had been described by many previous authors in different countries, including Etzkowicz and Leydesdorff (1996), who used the metaphor of the 'triple helix' to identify the three logics of the market, state and academy; Welch (2002) in Australia; and Newson and Buchbinder (1986) in Canada, who made an early argument that boards of post-secondary institutions were heavily peopled by corporate leaders. These authors have continued to publish evidence of the effects of entrepreneurial activity on the faculty of their respective countries, lending credence to the argument that academic capitalism has transformed professorial and institutional autonomy in relation to the market over the past several decades. Or is this just sour grapes about the (imagined) loss of a golden age (Scott, 2007)? We will return to this argument below.

Because they focus on countries with historically well-developed post-secondary sectors, the two Anglo-American and European studies reviewed to this point do not reveal very well a global view of the situation of faculty. Altbach's (1996, 2003) comparison of academics in 14 countries appearing at the same time as those of Krause and Slaughter and colleagues partially addressed this problem. (None of the three cites the others.) Based on his original study of academic freedom and a subsequent book called *The Decline of the Guru*, Altbach highlights the organizational differences among faculty in Asia, North and South America, Europe and Africa, theorizing a centre–periphery model within which universities in developing countries are closely modelled on those of their colonizers. He relates this pattern to either the imposition of the colonizing nation's university system within the captured nation continued in the postcolonial era or the adoption of the colonizer's system rather than developing a new system. This is consistent with the observations that we will make in the next section about the deeply segmented nature of the academy and the exclusion of indigenous knowledges worldwide.[2] At his time of writing, Altbach pointed out that even though over half of the 'world's 80 million postsecondary students' are in developing or middle-income countries, 'very little is known about the professionals who are responsible for teaching and learning in those universities' and what little is known 'is not positive' (2003, p. 1). Perhaps reflecting the hold of colonizing nations, he argues that, overall, the faculty in most countries of the world do not share the colonizers' tradition of academic freedom (2003, p. 15). Nor have most professors attained the northern standard of a doctorate. As such, Altbach terms them 'a profession on the periphery' (2003, p. 3) which looks for leadership to the faculty of the north. Although there are some elite universities among the countries he studied, they maintain the language of the northern colonizers; for example, English and French are entrenched in Africa, not African languages. English is typically the language of instruction and research publication in northern journals. Like Slaughter and colleagues, Altbach relates leadership in research in the north to 'close relationships with multinational corporations' (2003, p. 4) and an 'international labor market for scholars and scientists' (2003, p. 7) that flows from south to north, as do international students, corroborated by the international survey undertaken by Welch (1997). This is the proverbial 'brain drain' that continues to impoverish the 'third world' in what is called the 'knowledge economy'.

In the intervening years to our time of writing, much progress has been made in documenting conditions of faculty outside the Anglo-American world, and there is a dreary consistency about their conclusions. Altbach argues that academic freedom for professors was never present in most of the world; Slaughter and colleagues agree with many previous and subsequent authors that the notion of what may at one time have been a university working for the public good in the centre has lost its way. And even Krause, who sees some guild power maintained in European states, admitted at his time of writing that professorial proletarianization is waxing in the global economy.

Research theorizing inequity and knowledge production in academia

While comparative studies reached for a 'grand narrative' of the professoriate, there emerged a parallel literature of in-depth investigations of inequity within the professoriate.[3] This separate sociological literature began to document processes of exclusion for women professors from the academy (especially in science) as well as locating and publishing their achievements in the UK, New Zealand, Canada and the USA (e.g. Acker, 1994). The sociology of professions literature had documented gendered exclusionary practices in professions as early as the 1980s (Witz, 1992). But the feminist movement burst onto the scene of Anglo-American universities in the latter part of the twentieth century, bringing with it critical feminist scholars who argued that women also brought a different epistemology to male-dominated fields (e.g. Haraway, 1988). This was theorized as 'standpoint theory' by Dorothy E. Smith in Canada, focusing on the social sciences (1987) and by Sandra Harding in the USA, focusing on the sciences (1986). Eventually,

Harding generalized her argument to the dominance of neocolonial science over local knowledges all over the world in the production of a Eurocentric academy (1998). The academy also became a site for activism for gay and lesbian rights (e.g. Lorde, 1984), as well as for queer theorists who focus on knowledge production and queering the academy (e.g. Butler, 1999).

Preceding and paralleling this first-world feminist and sexuality literature, there had been emancipatory calls that pointed to the Eurocentric academy as the source of oppression of racially minoritized and Indigenous populations and the knowledge production within them as laced with colonial visions of the 'Other' (Said, 1978). But these early feminist, anti-colonial and other emancipatory efforts have been largely superseded by more recent postcolonial and poststructural arguments that either acknowledge their essentialism as 'strategic' or reject the essentialism inherent in characterizing all women as oppressed or all colonized groups as having the same experience (e.g. Loomba, 1998). Alternatively, they emphasize the intersectionality of race, gender, sexuality and ability as axes of oppression; or write from specific locations about the history of specific regions, such as New Zealand (e.g. L. Smith, 1999).

Historically, gender, race, class and sexuality movements linked their social projects to mere access to education and employment in the academy. But case studies of professors identified a 'chilly climate' once such groups were within the academy, challenging notions that merely increasing numbers of the so-called marginalized groups eliminates discrimination (Hall and Sandler, 1982; Wagner et al., 2008). Further, the voices of feminist, anti-racist and queer scholars contesting Eurocentric knowledge production in their writings continue to build and expose the mechanisms by which the fields of science, medicine and engineering have come to dominate other fields. The valuation of research activities over teaching activities is also evident across fields, with marginalized groups differentially involved in these activities. The Kogan and Teicher collection (2007), which includes China and India, explores this theme, and a critical scholar reading between the lines can see that marginalization in the academy cuts across multiple intersecting axes of inequities of race, gender, class and sexual orientation, based on notions of perceived 'relevance' or the socio-economic importance of one's activities and knowledge. Perhaps the fastest growing research on the professoriate focuses on the inequities visited on 'just in time' or contingent faculty. The explosive growth of contingent faculty in some jurisdictions, replacing tenured and tenure stream faculty, signals a progressive loss of autonomy by faculty and their challenges in negotiating the conditions of their work with administrative apparatuses. This is illustrated in the Welch survey (1997) as well as a more recent comparative study conducted by Stromquist and colleagues (2007).

The Stromquist study links the equity and comparative literatures, citing both Altbach's *Decline of the Guru* as well as the unbundling of faculty work in advanced capitalism in countries beyond Anglo-America. From this composite review of the tertiary sectors in Mexico, Brazil, Peru, Denmark, Russia and South Africa, a portrait of increasing diversification of higher education emerges that is structurally linked to economic determinants (funding arrangements between the state and higher education institutions and employment arrangements between institutions and their faculty). While they note an overall pattern of segmentation across the education sectors, it is clear that situations for faculty differ across countries. Notable is the distinction they make between publicly funded and privately funded universities. Stromquist and colleagues argue that institutions that have been able to hold on to public sector status, such as in Denmark, have to a large extent been able to 'protect … academic personnel', while 'the not for profit sector is moving towards an unstable professoriate, poorly paid, hired mostly on a per-hour basis, and for whom sharing in academic governance is a distant dream' (2007, p. 114). While the private sector in higher education has always been present in some countries, Stromquist and colleagues note the dramatic shift from full-time to contingent faculty in Mexico, Brazil and

Peru and the poorly paid professoriate of Russia, who must resort to additional part-time work to make a living (2007, p. 114).

There is also a 'feminization trend in private institutions' in Russia (Stromquist *et al.*, 2007, p. 130), where 58 per cent of faculty working in private tertiary institutions are women holding multiple positions to make ends meet. Indeed, gender and other differences, first identified as an equity issue in the UK, the USA, Australia and Canada (e.g. Abbas and McLean, 2001; Muzzin, 2008) is present globally. For example, Welch's (1997) data show that women tend to be stuck mainly in their country of birth, in what he terms the 'indigenous' sector of the professoriate, suggesting that 'the opportunity to travel and study abroad actively discriminates against women academics' (1997, p. 329). That is, they are anchored to their respective teaching and administrative posts, not able to experience the pleasures of Mannheim's 'free floating intellectual' (1936).[4] In one of many examples, Mazawi (2005) describes how the Saudi Arabian professoriate has very few avenues to influence government policy, and male Saudi professors are in the most profitable disciplines and hold the most prestigious ranks. As a result, 'women do not control the production of knowledge and are more involved in teaching than research' (2005, p. 242). It is significant that the equity literature does not bend to the idea that inequity is a permanent and incontestable aspect of the academy that negates professorial autonomy. Certainly the goal of feminist, anti-racist and queer theorists has been to identify inequity so as to change it. Literature that identifies these inequities writ large in the 'global marketplace' visualizes an alternative future. For example, Welch (2002), in an extended discussion on 'going global' in Australia, contrasts Jane Knight's (1995) concept of 'internationalization' with sinister aspects of 'globalization'. Internationalization focuses on the 'common good' embodied in organizations 'such as the United Nations and its charter' (Welch, 2002, p. 434). Welch also refers to growing resistance to 'the economic model of globalization [that] threatens to overwhelm prospects for more creative and more democratic pedagogies in higher education' (2002, p. 464), concluding that higher education is 'Janus faced' with 'one side facing towards twentieth century ideals of cooperation and … peace and social justice, while the other side faces toward increasing integration of universities … into the world of deregulated global business' (2002, p. 469).

The 'decentred professor' in the global knowledge economy?

In this section, we turn to an international literature that has emerged in the past decade that speculates about the effects on the professoriate of the 'networked society', new public management, academic capitalism and globalization along with fledgling investigations of the construction of professorial identities.

In comparison to visions of academia in decline, a more postmodern (and thus uncertain and sometimes hopeful) approach is offered in a recent book by Peters, Marginson and Murphy on the 'creative economy' (2009). Peters (2009), in a chapter in that book, points out that however one theorizes it, there is agreement that we have moved from one set of relations to a new one in which mass communication is made possible because digital goods defy the laws of scarcity. How does this affect the professoriate? Arguably, in material terms, the 'space' of higher learning is no longer contained within the walls of the university. This is not a new concept in the academy, where 'distance learning' is normalized. But Welch (1998), for one, contends that the cumulative postmodern disruption of 'conventional assumptions regarding knowledge' itself (including questioning the role of theory in knowledge production and the primacy of the disciplines as organizing structures of the academy), has destabilized the notion that only professors have expertise. There has been a continuing controversy about the idea that the hegemony of knowledge created by theory-driven experimental scientists and carried out within universities, or 'Mode 1 knowledge', is being superseded by 'Mode 2 knowledge', which is 'socially distributed, application oriented, transdisciplinary and subject to multiple accountabilities' (Nowotny *et al.*, 2003, Martimianakis and Muzzin, 2015). Welch sees this displacement as a process of deprofessionalization in traditional sociological terms, or as a decentring of professorial identities in postmodern terminology (1998, p. 5). As information is available to billions of people in real time, never before have so many people in so many strata had the capacity to contribute to knowledge-making without formally being 'in' the university. Those involved now can learn from academics and non-academics worldwide, without having to leave their homes.

Marginson (2009), like Peters, doesn't jump to the conclusion that these are negative developments. At the level of volition of the individual professor, he teases out selective philosophies of 'freedom' that have been considered to characterize the professor's everyday work, pointing out that it is still possible to do work conceived by someone else and that '[n]ew ideas may emerge under conditions of necessity' (2009, p. 92). Drawing on the idea that the ability to do good does not necessarily privilege the agent, Marginson points to professors who may choose poorly paid employment to be able to 'make a difference' as an 'independent entity', with the will and 'power to act' (2009, pp. 98–99). He sees a 'deep complementarity' between professorial 'individual agency and the social setting' (2009, p. 100) and theorizes that in research, 'the project of self-construction is never finished' (2009, p. 101). At the level of the university, leading scholars are present, and research training (at the nexus of teaching and research) is virtually monopolized along with advanced credentialing, even though more research may take place in KFOs (knowledge-forming organizations) outside the university. Marginson points to research achievement as the core of university status – a magnet that draws students and scholars alike. New public management (NPM) has resulted in what he terms 'organizational convergence' across KFOs towards innovation discourse, a point explored at length by Martimianakis (2011; Martimianakis and Muzzin, 2015) in her research on faculty identity in medicine and engineering, where the boundaries between industry and the university have been particularly permeable and faculty can become their own entrepreneurs. However, Marginson insists that boundaries between these institutions are 'robust in the face of efforts to break them down' (2009, p. 106).

The vast majority of the literature published recently on the academy does not take such an accommodating view of the professorial transition into a knowledge economy. One disturbing observation is that equity literature produced by academics outside disciplinary spaces, originally associated with resistance to disciplinarity from the margins, can be circled back through mainstream global educational policy. This stripping of critical content is possible because international organizations such as the OECD, the World Bank and UNESCO advocate for strategies of innovation that call for the wide adoption of interdisciplinary research as a way to make knowledge production relevant without attending to the ontological differences and historical politics of that research (Martimianakis, 2011). Thus, applied forms of knowledge-making, at the core of neoliberal innovation-discourse, can reconfigure even academics working for equity, as professors are encouraged to extend their work in industry and community contexts to 'engender creativity'. Faculty become not professionals but service providers (Martimianakis and Muzzin, 2015). Performance indicators are normalized and discourses of 'accountability', 'transparency', 'productivity' and 'relevance' appear in university mission statements. Broadbent and Laughlin (1997) have theorized this as an 'accounting logic', generally questioned by a range of professionals who do not see such discourses as relevant to their work as professionals but who acquiesce as managed professionals. With receding state involvement in the financing of massified public education, tertiary institutions around the world are described as actively pursuing a vicious cycle of pursuing funds while overproducing graduates who join the professorial precariat. Buildings, departments and entire faculties (even seats in lecture halls) are renamed to commemorate endowments, and faculty resistance to this market takeover of academic space seems to have little effect. There is worldwide competition for students, standardization of curricula and 'poaching' of highly skilled labour.

The global shrinking of tenure-track positions and expansion of more contingent and flexible employment arrangements lead Bousquet to lament that the 'disappearance of the professoriate' (2008, p. 71) will not be caused by technological replacement but through a restructuring of labour (though we would argue the two are linked). Levin and Shaker (2011), studying the self-representations of full-time non-tenure track faculty, describe this growing segment of the professoriate as having 'dualistic identities' which mirror their hybrid work arrangements – partly 'profession' and partly 'job'. Although Scott (2007) feels they 'still manage their own time and operate as relatively free-standing professionals' (2007, p. 208), Levin and Shaker argue that their lack of job security and capacity to influence decision-making means restricted self-determination and low self-esteem. To succeed, they must be agile workers, life-long learners, participating in continual self- and organizational improvement. Knowledge workers are also not necessarily PhD trained nor in professorial positions. New roles within the academy, including the faculty developer, the consultant, and the community or industry partner, are increasingly common in university classrooms and research laboratories.

This NPM (Broadbent and Laughlin, 1997; Dent and Whitehead, 2002) in theory is all about reproduction, standardization and homogenization; it has no regard for intellectual freedom; and there has been unprecedented government interference in university affairs. Still, Marginson (2009) argues that professors and other academic professionals have been able to create 'bounded niches' for themselves, sometimes by not being tied to one master. Kolsaker (2008), examining the English situation, concludes that faculty can tolerate and even sustain managerialism, just as Nixon (1997) had observed earlier, describing university teachers in the UK as focused on their core professional responsibilities to their students, learning as a public good, and collegiality.

Perhaps the most important development in the literature on globalization and the professoriate is an occasionally perceptible shifting of the gaze away from the centre to admit a writer from the 'third world' who critiques how it is viewed through Anglo-American professorial eyes. Said's (1978) *Orientalism* was an early example, but Samir Amin's critique of American, European and Chinese constructions of globalization in *Maldevelopment* (2011) stands out as another voice from what Altbach terms 'the periphery'. Subotzky (1999), also working in the so-called periphery, offers a model of the contemporary university based on a higher education–community partnership model that is an alternative to the 'entrepreneurial university'. Using South Africa as a case study, Subotzky outlines the social benefits of expanding knowledge-making into the community as well as the intrinsic benefits to the professoriate in having the capacity to make a difference socially in ways that are consistent with the 'intrinsic' mission of the university.

Appadurai (2000) has made a general critique of the way the academy 'has found in globalization an object around which to conduct its special internal quarrels' where multiple case studies and comparisons have 'an increasingly parochial quality' (2000, p. 2). Instead, he urges academics to stop navel-gazing and use their 'academic imagination' to study 'globalization from below', especially the activities of cash-strapped NGOs working for social justice worldwide ('grassroots globalization'). As he puts it, 'it is also the faculty through which collective patterns of dissent and new designs for collective life emerge' (2000, p. 6). Notably, he critiques an outmoded form of 'research' that sees geographic spaces as stable, when populations are mobile; that aims to be value-free and run all findings through a traditional assessment apparatus for replicability (2000, p. 11); that aims for a respectable 'shelf life' (2000, p. 12); and that uses an alienating vocabulary of 'fora such as the World Bank, the UN system, the WTO, NAFTA, and GATT' (2000, p. 17). He asks, '[c]an we find ways to legitimately engage scholarship by public intellectuals here [in the USA] and overseas whose work is not primarily conditioned by professional criteria of dissemination?' (2000, p. 14). His answer is that this would involve stepping back from 'abstractions that constitute our own professional practice to seriously consider the problems of the global everyday' (2000, p. 18).

Conclusion

The three bodies of literature reviewed here on the professoriate and other knowledge workers in the academy span comparative, critical equity and postmodern theoretical perspectives. Comparative views that emerged in the 1990s from the first world are by their nature mainstream and oriented to global narratives. The equity literature, a view from or of marginalized groups, is by its nature emancipatory, and oriented towards social justice, whether it appears in the first or third worlds. And the newest literature, a situated view rather than from 'nowhere' (Haraway, 1988), is local, self-reflexive, situated and open-ended, dwelling as it does in everyday professional practice.

Several futures are suggested by our review. There is enough evidence to conclude that Freidson's 'third logic' has survived in the form of elite professors. This group can be seen as retaining its academic freedom to produce knowledge (albeit on the backs of Welch's 'indigenous' professors). In fact, Marginson's excursus on creativity seems to fit the elite professor who jetsets around the world doing research while, as part of a gendered, racialized process, lesser faculty take care of students and other business (salvaging their professionalism through devotion to their students and the public good rather than basking in the glamour of being a research star or a talk-show intellectual). This, of course, depends on their embodying the kind of professionalism that supports a system of inequality – not the ideal outcome.

An alternative conclusion could be that the great experiment of the internet, Google and Wikileaks, promises a true emancipation of knowledge historically produced in the siloes of dons' jurisdictions, disciplines or colonial enclaves that is as significant as the industrial revolution. Although warnings of 'inconvenient truths' echo in our minds about professorial autonomy and the internet, we could choose to believe that creativity, as described in this chapter, for example, by Marginson, Kolsaker, Nixon and others, will survive under conditions of limited free will.

Finally, as processes of internationalization unfold, we could imagine a third development – that all of the resistance to accounting logic and segmented hierarchies of academic professionals documented here would continue to make headway led by visionary third-world scholars. There is evidence that we are on that road: there are now voices urging us to rethink what we count as research and knowledge, and we do have inspiring proposals from indigenous scholars on the table. For example, Linda Tuhiwai Smith (1999) calls for a decolonizing of academic research; Shiva (2008) asks for a reworking of disciplines to include multiple knowledges; and while Amin (2011) calls for a delinking of the south from the north, Subotzky (1999) and many others present visions of the university as emancipatory rather than colonizing; and Appadurai (2000) suggests that a good first step in the direction of these proposals would be for elite academics to just 'reverse [their] gaze' from problems of the academy to the plight of the impoverished world.

Notes

1 Recent court cases in North America have conflated the concept of institutional autonomy of universities and individual professorial freedom, with rulings tending to favour institutional powers rather than the individual (Gillin, 2002; O'Neil, 2005). The power of professional (rather than academic) administrators where universities have autonomy from the state is relevant here, as is the decline of individual professorial freedoms and security (Kogan and Teichler, 2007).
2 'Indigenous' here refers to a wider demographic than Aboriginal, to which the word commonly refers.

3 For example, Foucauldian analysis moves beyond 'grand narratives' to examine how professors construct their identities via the uptake of dominant discourses such as neoliberalism (Martimianakis, 2011; Davies and Bansel, 2010). Circulating discourses operate as taken for granted 'truths' that govern spaces and the people within them (termed governmentality), making certain activities and institutions more visible than others and bringing objects and subjects into being.

4 Mannheim argued that the professoriate was able to escape the relativity of its position, viewing 'the peculiarity of our own mode of life' (1936, p. 47). Such 'free-floating intellectuals' are said to have declined in Ango-American democracies, although Scott (2007) claims these 'celebrities' are alive and well and serve to brand the professoriate.

References

AAUP (1940) 'Our programs: Protecting academic freedom', www.aaup.org/our-work/protecting-academic-freedom (accessed 4 February 2016).

Abbas, A. and M. McLean (2001) 'Becoming sociologists: Professional identity for part-time teachers of university sociology', *British Journal of Education* 22(3), pp. 339–352.

Abbott, A. (2000) 'The disciplines and the future', in S. Brint (ed.) *The Future of the City of Intellect*, California: Stanford University Press, pp. 205–230.

Acker, S. (1994) 'Contradictions in terms: Women academics in British universities', in *Gendered Education*, Maidenhead: Open University Press, pp. 134–150.

Altbach, P. (ed.) (1996) *The International Academic Profession: Portraits of Fourteen Countries*, Princeton, NJ: Carnegie Foundation for the Advancement of Teaching.

Altbach, P. (ed.) (2003) *The Decline of the Guru: The Academic Profession in Developing and Middle Income Countries*, New York: Palgrave Macmillan.

Amin, S. (2011) *Maldevelopment: Anatomy of a Global Failure*, Cape Town: Fahamu Press.

Annan, N. (1999) *The Dons: Mentors, Eccentrics and Geniuses*, Chicago, IL: University of Chicago Press.

Appadurai, A. (2000) 'Grassroots globalization and the research imagination', *Public Culture* 12(1), pp. 1–19.

Bousquet, M. (2008) *How the University Works: Higher Education and the Low-Wage Nation*, New York: New York University Press.

Broadbent, J. and R. Laughlin (1997) 'Accounting logic and controlling professionals: the case of the public sector', in J. Broadbent, M. Dietrich and J. Roberts (eds) *The End of the Professions? The Restructuring of Professional Work*, London: Routledge, pp. 34–49.

Butler, J. (1999) 'Preface', in *Gender Trouble: Feminism and the Subversion of Identity*, New York: Routledge, pp. vii–xxvi.

Chait, R. (ed.) (2002) *The Questions of Tenure*, Cambridge, MA: Harvard University Press.

Davies, B. and P. Bansel (2010) 'Governmentality and academic work: Shaping the hearts and minds of academic workers', *Journal of Curriculum Theorizing* 26(3), pp. 5–20.

Dent, M. and S. Whitehead (eds) (2002) *Managing Professional Identities: Knowledge, Performativity and the 'New' Professional*, London: Routledge.

Etzkowitz, H. and L. Leydesdorff (1996) *Universities in the Global Knowledge Economy: A Triple Helix of Academic-Industry-Government Relations*, London: Cassell.

Freidson, E. (1970) *Profession of Medicine*, New York: Harper & Row.

Freidson, E. (1984) 'The changing nature of professional control', *Annual Review of Sociology* 10, pp. 1–20.

Freidson, E. (2001) *Professionalism: The Third Logic: On the Practice of Knowledge*, Chicago, IL: University of Chicago Press.

Freidson, E. and B. Rhea (1963) 'Processes of control in a company of equals', *Social Problems* 11, pp. 119–131.

Gillin, C. (2002) 'The bog-like ground on which we tread: Arbitrating academic freedom in Canada', *Canadian Review of Sociology and Anthropology* 39(3), pp. 301–322.

Hall, R. and B. Sandler (1982) *The Classroom Climate: A Chilly One for Women?* Washington DC: Association of American Colleges. Retrieved from http://files.eric.ed.gov/fulltext/ED215628.pdf, October 5, 2014.

Haraway, D. (1988) 'Situated knowledges: The science question in feminism and the privilege of partial perspective', *Feminist Studies* 14(3), pp. 575–599.

Harding, S. (1986) *The Science Question in Feminism*, Ithaca, NY: Cornell University Press.

Harding, S. (1998) *Is Science Multicultural? Postcolonialisms, Feminisms and Epistemologies*, Bloomington, IN: Indiana University Press.

Knight, J. (1995) 'A national study on internationalization at Canadian universities', in H. DeWit (ed.) *Strategies for Internationalization of Higher Education: A Comparative Study of Australia, Canada and the USA*, Amsterdam: International Association for International Education and OECD, pp. 99–120.

Kogan, M. and U. Teichler (eds) (2007) *Key Challenges to the Academic Profession*, Paris: UNESCO Forum on Higher Education Research and Knowledge. International Centre for Higher Education Research. (INCHER Kassel).

Kolsaker, A. (2008) 'Academic professionalism in the managerialist era: A study of English universities', *Studies in Higher Education* 33, pp. 513–525.

Krause, E. (1996) *Death of the Guilds: Professions, States, and the Advance of Capitalism, 1930 to the Present*, New Haven, CT: Yale University Press.

Levin, J. and G. Shaker (2011) 'The hybrid and the dualistic identity of full-time non-tenure-track faculty', *American Behavioural Scientist* 55(11), pp. 1461–1484.

Loomba, A. (1998) *Colonialism/Postcolonialism*, London and New York: Routledge.

Lorde, A. (1984) 'The master's tools will never dismantle the master's house', in *Sister Outsider: Essays and Speeches*, Freedom, CA: The Crossing Press, pp. 110–113.

Mannheim, K. (1936) *Ideology and Utopia: An Introduction to the Sociology of Knowledge*, International Library of Psychology, Philosophy and Scientific Method, reprinted by New York: Harcourt, Brace, Jovanovich.

Marginson, S. (2009) 'Intellectual freedoms and creativity', in M. Peters, S. Marginson and P. Murphy (eds) *Creativity and the Global Knowledge Economy*, New York: Peter Lang, pp. 91–123.

Martimianakis, M. A. (2011) *Discourse, Governance and Subjectivity: Knowledge-Making in Engineering and in Medicine*, Doctoral Dissertation. Department of Theory and Policy Studies, OISE, University of Toronto.

Martimianakis, M. A. and L. Muzzin (2015) 'Discourses of interdisciplinarity and the shifting topography of academic work: generational perspectives on facilitating and resisting neoliberalism', *Studies in Higher Education*, 40(8), pp. 1454–1470.

Mazawi, A. E. (2005) 'The academic profession in a rentier state: the professoriate in Saudi Arabia', *Minerva* 43, pp. 221–244.

Musselin, C. (2010) *The Market for Academics*, New York: Routledge.

Muzzin, L. (2008) 'How fares equity in an era of academic capitalism?' in A. Chan and D. Fisher (eds) *The Exchange University: The Corporatization of Academic Culture*, Vancouver BC: UBC Press, pp. 105–124.

Newson, J. and H. Buchbinder (1986) *The University Means Business*, Toronto: Garamond.

Nixon, J. (1997) 'Regenerating professionalism with the academic workforce', in J. Broadbent, M. Dietrich and J. Roberts (eds) *The End of Professions? The Restructuring of Professional Work*, London: Routledge, pp. 86–103.

Nowotny, H., P. Scott and M. Gibbons (2003) 'Mode 2 revisited: The new production of knowledge', *Minerva* 41(3), pp. 179–194.

O'Neil, R. (2005) 'Academic freedom past, present and future beyond September 11', in P. Altbach, R. Berdahl and P. Gumport (eds) *American Higher Education in the Twenty-First Century: Social, Political and Economic Changes* (2nd edn), Baltimore, MD: Johns Hopkins University Press, pp. 91–113.

Peters, M. (2009) 'Introduction: Knowledge goods, the primacy of ideas and the economics of abundance', in M. Peters, S. Marginson and P. Murphy (eds) *Creativity and the Global Knowledge Economy*, New York: Peter Lang, pp. 1–22.

Peters, M., S. Marginson and P. Murphy (eds) (2009) *Creativity and the Global Knowledge Economy*, New York: Peter Lang.

Said, E. (1978) *Orientalism*, New York: Vintage Books, Random House.

Scott, P. (2007) 'From professor to "knowledge worker": Profiles of the academic profession', *Minerva* 45, pp. 205–215.

Shiva, V. (2008) 'Democratizing biology: Reinventing biology from a feminist, ecological and third world perspective', in Alison Jagger (ed.) *Just Methods*, Boulder, CO: Paradigm Publishers, pp. 433–445.

Slaughter, S. and L. Leslie (1997) *Academic Capitalism: Politics, Policies and the Entrepreneurial University*, Baltimore, MD: Johns Hopkins University Press.

Smith, D. E. (1987) *The Everyday World As Problematic*, Toronto: University of Toronto Press.

Smith, L. T. (1999) *Decolonizing Methodologies*, London: Zed Books.

Stromquist, N., M. Gil-Anton, C. Colatrella, R. Mabokela, S. Obakeng and E. Balbachevsky (2007) 'The contemporary professoriate: Towards a diversified or segmented profession', *Higher Education Quarterly* 61(2), pp. 114–135.

Subotzky, G. (1999) 'Alternatives to the entrepreneurial university: New modes of knowledge production in community service programs', *Higher Education* 38, pp. 401–440.

Veblen, T. ([1918]1957) *The Higher Learning in America*, New York: Hill & Wang.

Wagner, A., S. Acker, and K. Mayuzumi (eds) (2008) *Whose University Is It Anyways? Power and Privilege on Gendered Terrain*, Toronto: Sumach Press.

Welch, A. (1997) 'The peripatetic professor: The internationalization of the academic profession', *Higher Education* 34, pp. 323–345.

Welch, A. (1998) 'The end of certainty? The academic profession and the challenge of change', *Comparative Education Review* 42(1), pp. 1–14.

Welch, A. (2002) 'Going global? Internationalizing Australian universities in a time of global crises', *Comparative Education Review* 46(1), pp. 433–471.

Witz, A. (1992) *Professions and Patriarchy*, London: Macmillan Press.

22

Contemporary education policy and teacher professionalism

Sølvi Mausethagen and Jens-Christian Smeby

Introduction

In this chapter, we address changes in teacher professionalism following contemporary education policy developments. During the past couple of decades, the teaching profession has been subject to changes in expectations and in the governance of their work. A number of countries have introduced a relatively new set of public management approaches in education that emphasize the combined power of performance measurement, quality indicators, goal setting, incentives, accountability, and marketization to mobilize teachers' work effort and raise student achievement (Fuller, 2008). These initiatives are typically framed within a broader discourse of raising overall student achievement and reducing social inequality (Heilig, 2011). On the one hand, these initiatives aim to enhance teaching quality and to ensure a basic standard for all students; on the other hand, they push for standardization and micromanagement, which can undermine professional autonomy and professionalism. In addition, the issue of evidence-based practice is related to these developments through debates over what characterizes teachers' knowledge base and how teacher education should be organized to prepare 'high-quality' teachers (Darling-Hammond and Lieberman, 2012). Thus, investigating trends in teacher education is important for identifying and discussing new policy expectations towards teacher professionalism.

Traditional notions of professional knowledge, autonomy, and responsibility have been redefined in many ways by more recent policy developments emphasizing evidence-based practice and responsibility for outcomes. Yet the profession itself often highlights conceptualizations of professionalism that emphasize individual autonomy and experience-based knowledge, making teacher professionalism a somewhat contested idea. This development has also influenced teacher education. On the one hand, more solid, research-based teacher education is emphasized; on the other hand, teacher education programmes have become more differentiated and practice oriented (Smeby, 2015). Dichotomies such as professionalization from above and from within have been developed to describe such changes (Evetts, 2003). At the same time, somewhat conflicting ideas of professionalism can coexist and create dilemmas for teachers in their work. Furthermore, professionalization strategies are more complex than the simple dichotomy 'from above and from within' would suggest. Therefore, a need exists for more insight into how far new governing modes 'travel' into classrooms so as to address how the teaching profession deals with such contradictory professional expectations. The ways in which tensions are made prominent and resolutions subsequently attempted are understudied. In this chapter, we explore empirical studies that address changes in teacher work and teacher education, suggesting that this body of research can supply important insight into the dynamics of contemporary educational policy expectations towards teacher professionalism.

We begin by outlining the broader policy developments so as to provide a background for interpreting the expectations placed on teachers and teacher education. Following a discussion of (changes in) teacher professionalism, we review studies published from the year 2000 onwards, focusing on how research studies on changes in teacher professionalism have developed over time so as to highlight the many continuities in teachers' work rather than primarily focusing on dichotomies. We argue that new policy expectations can be experienced as dilemmas rather than as fundamental shifts in work and professionalism. Finally, we suggest the need for reconceptualizing teacher professionalism so as to understand changes in teacher work and teacher education, as well as how the phenomena are addressed in existing and future studies.

International policy developments

The shifting education policy climate of the past few decades provides a starting point for identifying the broader political context in the discussion on teacher professionalism. Two incidents are especially prominent. First, policy developments in the United States and England in the 1980s played an important role in formulating an agenda for restructuring education. Second, the Organisation for Economic Co-operation and Development (OECD) became increasingly involved in the field of education, particularly from the 1990s onwards.

Developments in the United States and England during the 1980s marked seminal moments for restructuring education. The report *A Nation at Risk*, published in the United States in 1983, was the most prominent. Its aim was to restructure the education system. The report conveyed a message of a fundamental national crisis, one that could endanger the American economy and, ultimately, its national security; that is, the United States was in danger of not maintaining its position internationally unless standards in education systems were raised. A series of reforms followed, of which the most important and comprehensive was the *No Child Left Behind* Act of 2001 (NCLB). This act was based on four basic principles: increased accountability, increased flexibility and local control, expanded options for parents, and the prioritization of teaching methods that have been proven to work (Fuller, 2008). A similar development occurred almost in parallel in England. The 1988 *Education Reform Act* emphasized national regulations on educational performance targets, inspections, regular testing of students, and the publication of these results (Priestley and Biesta, 2013). Within teacher education, the United States and England have also undertaken programme reforms in the direction of accountability, evidence-based teaching, and standards (Darling-Hammond and Lieberman, 2012).

International organizations such as the OECD play an increasingly important role in initiating the legitimization of new reform initiatives in national policy development (Martens *et al.*, 2007). Since the early 1990s, the OECD has published widely on educational indicators. These indicators have been further developed through *Education at a Glance*, a compendium of education statistics that has been published regularly since 1992, and the Programme for International Student Assessment (PISA), an international assessment of the skills and knowledge of fifteen-year-olds that has been performed every three years since 2000. The OECD also publishes country background reports and thematic reviews as well as reports on issues related to teacher education, for example, the 2005 report titled *Teachers Matter: Attracting, Developing and Retaining Effective Teachers*. Together, such activities present domestic policymakers with a quite different access to educational data than had been previously available, data that have increasingly become a prominent focus for different stakeholders within the field of education. Educational policies and practices, however, are adapted from the traditions and culture as part of the national and local context in which they are embedded (Ozga and Jones, 2006). As such, the specific national backdrop is of importance in understanding how policy developments towards a greater emphasis on educational accountability play out, for example, in terms of trust in the profession.

The timing of the increase in test-based accountability coincides with the OECD's initiatives, and accountability has increasingly become the dominant policy of action in the quest for improving educational 'quality' and efficiency in the United States and most European countries, as well as several Asian countries (Fuller, 2008). This policy development must be viewed in terms of a broader background in which education is regarded as a crucial part of economic prosperity in knowledge societies. This background is important when discussing the changes in expectations that have occurred in the teaching profession as well as how these changes have been largely enacted through the introduction of new governing modes and performance-based managerialism from the 1980s onwards (Clarke and Newman, 1997). However, before we explore what characterizes teacher professionalism based on recent empirical studies from the field, we will present various concepts that have been developed to describe how the new policies have affected and challenged teacher professionalism.

Teacher professionalism

Sociologists have returned to the concept of professionalism in efforts to understand challenges related to knowledge-intensive work and expectations towards accountability and professionals' use of evidence in their work (Smeby, 2015). The term 'professionalism' is broadly used to describe competent individuals who perform tasks adequately and appropriately. Typically, this term is used to describe certain qualities related to the ways in which practices are performed (Molander and Terum, 2008). 'Being a professional' and 'being professional' are connected but not always the same (Hargreaves and Fullan, 2012). Moreover, professionalism can be construed with different meanings (Ozga and Lawn, 1981) and used to challenge or to defend the status quo (Hall, 2004). Teacher professionalism is often described as situational and contradictory over time and among actors (Ozga and Lawn, 1981; Mausethagen and Granlund, 2012) and is typically related to the political 'struggle' to define what teachers' work should be and how it should be specified in the curriculum (Hall, 2004).

Distinguishing between professionalism as constructed from above and professionalism from within (Evetts, 2003) can be an advantageous perspective for illuminating developments where actors assign different meanings to the concept of professionalism and where different views are expressed regarding what will enhance or impair the professionalization of teachers (Mausethagen and Granlund, 2012). Professionalization from within can be outlined through the concept of occupational professionalism put forward by Evetts (2003). This discourse builds on normative value systems that, first and foremost, are constructed within professional groups. To the teaching profession, an interpretation of professionalism as a value system would typically emphasize trust in teachers' workplace relationships, use of discretion, and use of expert judgement in the best interests of the students. Moreover, trust is given to professionals based on the competence they have gained through the education system and the internal control that goes on within the professional community. Consequently, externally imposed rules would be minimized and discretion maximized. By contrast, organizational professionalism is conceptualized as new governing modes that increasingly use control and increased standardization of work procedures (Evetts, 2003). This can be described as professionalization from above, in that the enhancement of professionalism is related to developments such as the introduction of accountability policies, the implementation of standards, and evidence-based practice. At the rather extreme end of this line of thought, teachers are mainly seen as victims of bureaucratization and accountability, thereby becoming deprofessionalized. According to Evetts (2003), these policy developments can reduce the use of discretion and prevent the application of so-called service ethics. Both discretion and service ethics have been regarded as highly important in teaching, for instance, as stated in Dan Lortie's (1975) seminal work titled *Schoolteacher: A Sociological Study*. However, it can be argued that discretion and service ethics represent more stable aspects of teaching that are not so easily altered by policy initiatives.

Research on changes in teacher professionalism under new policy expectations increased from the year 2000 onwards, and this increase must be related to the reconstructions of teachers' work that have taken place during the same time period. Many studies have described the changes in teachers' work in terms of a 'performativity discourse' (Jeffrey, 2002) or a 'managerial-ist professionalism' (Sachs, 2001; Furlong, 2005) in an attempt to capture the idea of effective and accountable teachers who carry out tasks of high quality, as described by external standards. The opposites of these forms are presented as a 'humanistic discourse' (Jeffrey, 2002) and an 'individual-ized professionalism' (Furlong, 2005). The use of such dichotomies is prominent in studies from England in particular, but it is also evident in studies from several other countries. Helgøy and Homme (2007) distinguish between 'old professionalism' and 'new professionalism' in a study on Swedish and Norwegian teachers, with old professionalism referring to professional practice as relying on formal education, occupational monopoly, and licensing and with new professional-ism emphasizing individual responsibility in the meaning of teachers' ability to perform and act strategically and to be accountable. Similarly, Simons and Kelchtermans (2008) make use of the terms 'profession-oriented' and 'market-oriented' forms of professionalism to reflect a shift in teacher education policies in the Netherlands.

Sachs (2001) introduces the terms 'entrepreneurial identity' and 'managerial professionalism' and contrasts this with a so-called 'activist identity' and 'democratic professionalism'. Democratic professionalism is used to describe collaborative, cooperative action between teachers and other stakeholders, whereas managerial professionalism is concerned with how teachers to a greater extent are placed in a line of authority in terms of being accountable for reaching measurable outcomes (see also Day, 2002). Locke *et al.* (2005) use the terms 'professional-contextualist pro-fessionalism' and 'technocratic-reductionist professionalism' to describe a shift in the conceptu-alizations of teacher professionalism accompanying new educational reforms. The former term connotes the integrity and reflectiveness of practitioners, enabling the development of diverse human capabilities, intrinsic motivation, and commitment, whereas the latter term is described as involving skilled technicians, competence development, the production and attainment of spe-cific learning outcomes, extrinsic motivation, and contractual compliance. Similarly, a 'technicist model of professionalism' (Tummons, 2014) is used to describe the introduction of standards in teacher education and the failure of these standards to recognize the professional knowledge and competence of teachers.

The models proposed by Evetts and the various dichotomies presented above portray differ-ent contrasting images of teachers – that is, teachers are portrayed as acting altruistically or out of self-interest, as being competent reflective practitioners or restricted technicians, and as prac-tising old or new professionalism. These dichotomies are mainly analytical distinctions and not always based on empirical work. However, in the daily work of teachers, these dichotomies are more likely to coexist and create tensions and dilemmas that have to be negotiated and resolved. In the rest of the chapter, we concentrate on the growing number of empirical studies exploring the consequences of the new policies on central dimensions of teacher professionalism. First, we present studies focusing on responsibility, accountability, and autonomy. Thereafter, we turn to studies that mainly address teachers' knowledge base and educational programmes. Finally, we explore whether there is a need for reconceptualizing teacher professionalism.

Responsibility, accountability, and autonomy

Issues of responsibility, accountability, and autonomy are closely related. Several studies on changes in teacher professionalism focus on how the redefinitions of teacher responsibility, introduced through educational reforms in the past two decades in particular, have more or less dramatically changed teachers' work, with the reduction in teachers' classroom autonomy often being highlighted. This reduction in teachers' autonomy may also have to do with more emphasis on evidence-based practice and the use of prescribed curriculum material. Broadly, these aspects are related to the introduction of managerial accountability (Sinclair, 1995), referring to the focus on the monitoring of inputs and outputs, leadership practices, and the participation of all actors in improving educational outcomes. However, defining managerial accountability as educational accountability would imply a rather narrow definition of what can be described as professional accountability (Conway and Murphy, 2013). Teachers have always practised based on their professional knowledge and moral, relational forms of responsibility. This situation raises the following important questions: To what extent do accountability policies and practices challenge the professional forms for accountability based on professional knowledge and moral and relational concerns? To what extent does managerial accountability travel into classrooms? How do teachers negotiate what can be experienced as challenging their professional accountability? Concerning the organizational aspect of the profession, managerial accountability is mainly found to be challenging the forms of professional accountability and the status and legitimacy of the teaching profession and steering teachers' work in the direction of more standardization and less classroom autonomy.

Positive and negative developments

An examination of the performative aspect of teaching across a range of empirical studies in which teachers report on how they experience accountability reveals various developments. On the positive side, studies are concerned with how accountability demands can give clear signals about what is important in the curriculum, make expectations of what should be taught more explicit, be corrective to existing practices and beliefs, provide evidence of instructional practices that make a difference for students, function as effective diagnostic tools, and lead to more collaboration among teachers in schools, which in turn develops their work (e.g. Locke *et al.*, 2005; Wilkins, 2011; Little, 2012). On the negative side, studies report on 'teaching to the test', the narrowing of the curriculum, the reduced attention given to certain subjects, the use of more traditional teaching methods, the adoption of a more teacher-centred approach to teaching, the decreased emphasis on the development of caring relationships with students, the increase in the tracking and labelling of students, and the development of hierarchical and competitive relationships involving teachers within a school (e.g. Day, 2002; Jeffrey, 2002). These findings point to how changes in professionalism seem to have a different interpretation when this issue is investigated from the perspective of teachers' everyday work.

Several of the more recent empirical studies also address issues regarding how different perceptions about professionalism and accountability coexist and how this development could have an effect on new generations of teachers entering the field and on issues of knowledge and ideals for teaching. For example, studies from the USA, England, and Norway show that the younger generation of teachers is more positive towards a stronger emphasis on performance and seems to balance issues of accountability and autonomy better, without feeling that their teaching identity is necessarily being threatened (Wilkins, 2011; Mausethagen, 2013; Stone-Johnson, 2014). Furthermore, Terhart (2013) discusses how teachers often ignore or misuse data from performance tests, proposing that this finding should be interpreted as the profession having mixed reactions rather than as expressing resistance. He argues that teacher resistance reflects 'an inconvenient truth' and that there is a need for various ways to interpret 'resistance' to new policy expectations. For example, Terhart describes how teachers who adequately use information from assessments have already developed a culture of internal evaluation and how many teachers welcome change and consider it to be necessary. Teachers' reactions to accountability are therefore, he argues, not simply a matter of adaptation or resistance, but rather of mixed experiences, reactions, and attitudes. In a similar vein, Hardy (2012) seeks to add nuance to arguments about the impact of accountability policies on teachers' practices by providing empirical evidence of the effects of such processes. For example, schools where self-esteem is an issue might be influenced differently, and teachers should not be viewed as simply passive victims because there are complex practices and processes at play when studying changes in teachers' work and professionalism. Moreover, such developments point to the complexity of managerial accountability in education. There is a call to uphold a less dichotomous perspective when discussing issues related to accountability and autonomy.

Continental European vs Anglo-American traditions

These developments should also be viewed against the backdrop of the various national contexts and described as either 'high trust' or 'low trust' contexts. However, in the past two decades in particular, there has been a shift in several national curricula from formulating broader aims and content towards outlining student competences and learning outcomes. On the one hand, new curricula are often marked by the adoption of a progressive education approach (i.e. active learning, child-centred approaches); on the other hand, they emphasize educational outcomes, performativity, and teacher centrality (Priestley and Biesta, 2013). This development can be viewed in light of differences between a continental European tradition and an Anglo-American tradition in terms of how teacher autonomy has been framed historically through the curriculum. According to Hopmann (2015), two dominant patterns of curriculum control exist – process control and product control – from which different vocabularies for how to construct the expectations of teachers' work and teachers' responsibilities are established. The former is the so-called continental or licensing system, which exercises weak external control of educational outcomes. The latter is the product-centred system of external controls. This system is used, for example, in the United States. Within this tradition, external control of products or outcomes through testing and assessments has been considered important. The curriculum is outcome based, and the basic claim for teacher expertise has been effective teaching (Hopmann, 2015). However, in the tradition of process control, an input-based curriculum has been the main instrument for state control. Different outcomes have been allowed, depending on the work of local teacher groups and the performance of procedures in accordance with the national curriculum; the outcomes themselves have not been evaluated.

A prominent example of a country with 'high trust' policies is Finland, where the state frames teachers as autonomous developers of the curriculum rather than as deliverers of the curriculum (Westbury *et al.*, 2005; Mølstad, 2015). The positioning of teachers as deliverers is more prominent in countries where prescribed learning outcomes are used (Priestley and Biesta, 2013) and teaching standards are introduced in teaching and in initial teacher education

(Goepel, 2012). In his comparison of student teachers in England, Norway, and Germany, Czerniawski (2011) finds that the English student teachers were more marks-oriented and concerned with being accountable to actors outside schools, whereas the Norwegian and German student teachers were mainly concerned with being accountable to students and parents. In Norway and Germany, however, basic education and teacher education have also undergone development in the direction of placing more emphasis on the 'competent teacher' and on the measurement of outcomes – a development largely legitimized through the medium scores obtained in international comparisons such as the PISA (Blömeke, 2006; Mausethagen and Granlund, 2012). This is also interesting in terms of how the teaching profession in Norway and Germany has historically been governed mainly through input regulations rather than the outcomes of education (Sivesind, 2008). The Anglo-American tradition of curriculum control is increasingly influencing the continental tradition. Yet it is possible that the continental tradition may still have far-reaching implications in that, for example, teacher education continues to be viewed as a highly important institution for ensuring the provision of high-quality teachers in the future, which is somewhat in contrast to developments in England and the United States (Furlong, 2005; Darling-Hammond and Lieberman, 2012).

Teaching standards

In addition to the increased emphasis on outcomes, some countries (including England, Australia, and the United States) have introduced teaching standards as an effective way to express professionalism and uphold public trust (Goepel, 2012). The tensions that arise when teaching standards are discussed are similar to those that surface in the discussion on accountability. Even though there are arguments stating that following standards and being accountable are inherent in teacher professionalism, research shows that contemporary policy developments and accompanying government tools have changed teachers' classroom autonomy and room for decision-making in terms of what and how to teach (Menter and Hulme, 2013). Because these standards have been mainly introduced by governments, they can be described as representing professionalization strategies from above, existing under the umbrella of improving performance and professionalism (Day, 2002; Evans, 2008). However, professional organizations have also taken part in this work (Mulcahy, 2011), situating it as an example of a professionalization strategy from within. Another approach to standards is advocated by Mulcahy (2011), who, despite questioning the belief in teaching standards as a way of enhancing the quality and performance of teachers, argues that standards are important for defining key aspects of work if they take the enactment of standards in the classroom as their starting point rather than the description of pre-existing realities. As such, this may also point to how the profession could be involved in defining standards instead of simply handing this responsibility over to external actors to define and control them.

These contemporary policy developments also involve the preparation of teachers and future teachers in working within the new organizational contexts and the importance of teacher competence in balancing diverse expectations and setting priorities in the future. For example, teacher educators can use teaching students' experiences with testing and standardization in preparing them for work – not least because the coming generations of teachers will most likely have been educated within the new forms of curricula and in the use of testing and evaluation data. How and to what extent teacher education programmes are preparing teaching students to handle a new context for their work are, however, relevant questions to ask.

Knowledge base and educational programmes

Teacher professionalism also involves the characteristics of the knowledge base and educational programmes. Evans (2008) uses the dichotomy of 'limited professionalism' and 'extended professionalism'. At one end of the continuum are teachers who practise and base their work primarily on experience-based knowledge and what happens daily in the classroom; at the other end are teachers who practise 'extended' professionalism, using theories underpinning pedagogy and didactics while upholding a broader view of what education means. Consequently, the further a teacher moves towards extended professionalism, the more often the teacher combines theory and practical experience in a more integrated fashion. As such, this example also points to how issues of teachers' professional knowledge are seemingly less dichotomously represented in the literature than issues of accountability.

Research-based education

Internationally, there have been calls for more research-based educational practice and for teacher education to become more research based (Darling-Hammond and Lieberman, 2012). A review of the international literature on teachers' use of research shows that to a limited extent there exists a culture that supports and values research. Moreover, researchers on teachers and teacher education are challenged particularly in relation to the context, generalizability, and validity of their research (Hemsley-Brown and Sharp, 2003). Two of the most prominent barriers to teachers' use of research are reported to be a lack of time and a lack of readily accessible sources (Williams and Coles, 2007). Studies also emphasize that teachers' concerns need to be given greater weight when research agendas are set and funding is allocated and that more collaboration between researchers and practitioners needs to be developed (Vanderlinde and van Braak, 2010). Trent (2012) finds that student teachers see a difference between how much they are involved in research in the teacher education programme and what they anticipate will be possible when they start working in schools, believing that it will be difficult to assume the identity of a 'teacher–researcher'. Trent calls for more attention to be paid to the creation of learning communities comprising students, teachers, and teacher educators. Yet teachers and educational researchers who are involved in common development projects often appear to hold different beliefs about what constitutes relevant knowledge and research (Joram, 2007), which can create barriers to the use and perceived value of research.

The call for research-based knowledge and evidence-based practice is also contested. On the one hand, the argument is that the development of a more rigorous and relevant knowledge base is a way to strengthen the status and legitimacy of the profession – as well as the performative aspects of teaching, including its effectiveness (Hargreaves, [1996] 2007). On the other hand, the argument is that evidence-based practice in teaching is unrealistic and undesirable because teaching is too complex and requires critical analysis. Such developments would also strengthen the accountability aspects in education and push for more standardization of classroom practices (Hammersley, 2013), thereby reducing teacher autonomy. A more modest approach to the question of research-based knowledge and evidence-based practice is to emphasize the importance of context in terms of generalizing findings in education research (Shavelson and Towne, 2002). Another approach is to highlight the importance of scientific knowledge as a part of teachers' knowledge base; yet how and to what extent research should be put into use must be placed in the hands of teachers to use at their discretion.

'On-the-job training'

Another important trend in teacher education is the development of alternative pathways into teaching, including pathways that provide 'on-the-job training' in countries such as England, the United States, and the Netherlands. The Teach First programme in England is an employment-based route into teaching (Townsend, 2011). After earning a disciplinary degree, mainly in maths or the natural sciences, trainees join Teach First and their university partners for six weeks of intensive training. Upon completion of this training, they teach at a school in a low-income community for two years, during which time they achieve a postgraduate certificate in education, are paid a full-time salary, and are given real responsibility in the classroom from day one. Trainees are also supported with professional development, coaching, and opportunities to network with supporters from other industry sectors. The implementation of this type of programme may be viewed as a response against academic and research-based teacher education. There is a concern that school-based preparation has become much too prominent and that trainee teachers do not spend enough time on practice-based components of preparation. There is also a claim that the development of new pathways into teaching is 'market driven' and represents efforts to reduce standards (MacBeath, 2012). Moreover, even though these schemes can draw high-quality entrants into teaching, research shows that these strategies fail because most of these teachers drop out within a few years (Hargreaves and Fullan, 2012). Research also points to the danger posed by the growing movement in the United States to focus on core instructional practices and standards in teacher education at the expense of other aspects of teaching that are fundamental in developing teachers' abilities to exercise judgement in the best interests of their students (Zeichner, 2012).

Look to Finland

Darling-Hammond and Lieberman (2012) argue that Finland in particular has developed a sophisticated teaching profession, with all teachers holding a master's degree that encompasses both strong subject matter and pedagogical preparation and that integrates research and practice. Many teachers in Finland also pursue a doctoral degree and then remain in the teaching profession. Furthermore, Westbury *et al.* (2005) describe the Finnish research-based approach to teaching as a foundation for classroom autonomy and a way to pursue an expanded understanding of teachers' work. In addition, Niemi and Nevgi (2014) show that Finnish student teachers learn critical thinking skills and independent inquiry strategies, as well as many other skills necessary in research, and that these general scientific inquiry skills are as important for the teaching profession as for their own professional development. Niemi and Nevgi conclude that for teachers to have the ability to use research and contribute to the development of professional knowledge, they need to gain experience in conducting research during their pre-service education. However, it is important to point out that many factors have contributed to Finland's educational fame, including the status of the teaching profession and the extreme competitiveness of recruitment to teacher education in Finland (Sahlberg, 2012).

The focus on an appropriate academic knowledge base and training at the master's level as a foundation for maintaining autonomy may be considered a strategy of 'extended' professionalism and professionalization from within, whereas the focus on accountability, standards, and practice-based teacher education is more in line with strategies for 'limited' professionalism and professionalization from above. Some countries, such as Finland, have strongly highlighted the importance of a research-based foundation for teacher responsibility and autonomy, whereas other countries have challenged the idea that there is a knowledge base for teaching, thereby questioning the role of universities in preparing teachers for their work. Other countries attempt to combine both approaches by extending teacher education and making it more specialized and by holding teachers more accountable for student outcomes (Mausethagen and Granlund, 2012). Such developments may also point to how the distinction between professionalism from above and from within is somewhat imprecise and that the different strategies instead exist together and might be more intertwined and multifaceted than they are often represented to be. In the next section, we therefore argue that there is a need to reconceptualize professionalism.

Reconceptualizing teacher professionalism

On the one hand, the existing literature on changes in teacher professionalism in the past two decades has emphasized a shift in teachers' work and teachers' education, as well as in the status and legitimacy of the profession. On the other hand, the existing research also points to mixed reactions towards new modes of governing and expectations towards teachers' knowledge base. Moreover, we argue that there are reasons to move beyond the use of dichotomies to describe such changes following policy developments and that the distinction between professionalization from above and from within is too simplistic to describe the complexity involved in the use of professionalization strategies in knowledge-intensive societies.

From dichotomies to dilemmas

In studies published after 2010 in particular, we find an interesting shift in terms of the conceptualizations of professionalism. Compared with previous studies addressing these phenomena, studies conceptualized changes in teachers' work and professionalism more in the direction of dilemmas or tensions rather than dichotomies. For example, with 'dilemmatic spaces', Fransson and Grannäs (2013) refer to ways of connecting the ongoing formation of identity in relation to dilemmas. In particular, they refer to dilemmas that teachers experience between official, recommended, learned, and tested curricula, as well as how such dilemmas can help to construe new perspectives. Rather than focusing on major shifts in teacher identities, researchers should direct their attention to dilemmas so as to deepen the understanding of the complexity in educational contexts. In a similar vein, Wilkins et al. (2012) introduce the concept of 'liminality'. Their research is concerned with how teacher identities are in transition when new teachers adjust to the workplace in a broader context of an increasingly performative agenda. In their discussion on the in-between situation that new teachers face in terms of possessing different ideals towards the teaching profession, Wilkins et al. argue that accountability demands do not necessarily lead to the emergence of a truly performative professional and that the character of teacher–student interactions in particular has a defining impact on teachers' motivation, thereby adding to this complexity.

In another article, Wilkins (2011) introduces the label of a 'post-performative teacher', representing a generation of teachers whose experience as students has been that of an increasingly performative schooling system in England. He finds that these younger teachers are neither compliant nor resistant to accountability policies. They are still largely motivated by affective rewards in teaching (but have clear career ambitions) and are aware of the potential conflicts between accountability demands and the desire for autonomy. Together, the studies from Wilkins (2011) and Wilkins et al. (2012) point to developments among a younger generation of teachers that serve to challenge some of the dichotomies used in the literature. Similarly, Stone-Johnson (2014) uses the concept of 'parallel professionalism'. She finds that groups of teachers in the

United States understand professionalism differently and that a new generation of teachers accommodates new demands in a more neutral fashion. Given the complexity of teacher professionalism, Stone-Johnson finds that accountability and standardization can make one feel both in more control and in less control as a teacher. Furthermore, Stillman (2011) introduces the term 'productive tensions' to describe how accountability-related pressure also leads to important professional learning and instructional improvement by creating productive tensions so that teachers challenge their existing beliefs and practices. In teacher education, new governing modes are found to create some of the same dilemmas. For example, Solbrekke and Sugrue (2014) find that Irish teacher educators attempt to find legitimate compromises between what they describe as the logic of responsibility and the logic of accountability.

Data use in education

Moreover, there has been a recent increase in studies that give more attention to how teachers use data derived from new assessment tools and what factors at school seem to foster positive learning cultures which not only focus on learning outcomes in a narrow sense but also are characterized by broader pedagogical discussions (Coburn and Turner, 2011; Little, 2012). A closer examination of the growing literature on data use reveals that studies often report on how the focus on different forms of data on student outcomes has led to increased collaboration among teachers, thereby drawing attention to the assessment, development, and justification of their own teaching practices. This development in the literature also mirrors the increase in new sources of knowledge that teachers are expected to handle, analyse, and make use of in their work. In addition, it suggests that teachers need to develop and hold additional competences – competences that could also be seen as ways of enhancing teacher professionalism and not only as ways of decreasing professionalism and professional autonomy.

Together, these developments and what can be described as 'new' conceptualizations may point to a slight shift in the research on teachers' work. More recent studies also attend to the dynamics of managerial accountability in terms of how teachers find ways to negotiate between the different aims for which they are accountable and the specific demands that are put forth, for example, through standardized testing. The emphases on teachers' sense of professionalism and how they enact it under accountability demands seem to have shifted towards a greater concern with the dilemmas that teachers face rather than being 'pro' or 'con' to a stronger performative culture in education. This shift may point to how teachers are becoming more aware of the fact that by justifying their everyday work in the classroom, teachers could also contribute to increasing the status and legitimacy of the profession.

Tensions

Whereas a great deal of existing research on teacher professionalism has been characterized by an extensive use of dichotomies that strengthen a notion of 'before' and 'now' in terms of teachers' work, several studies also highlight how different ideals towards professionalism are likely to exist together. The increase in empirical studies shows that, in the context of everyday work in the classroom in particular, implications of policy shifts are experienced as tensions rather than as dramatic shifts in teacher work. Moreover, we argue that it is perhaps time for the somewhat one-dimensional view on changes in professionalism centring on dichotomies, such as occupational and organizational professionalism and professionalization from above and from within, to be replaced by more multi-dimensional perspectives that focus on tensions and dilemmas rather than dichotomies. This also implies that a range of contextual factors exists that should be taken into account when changes in teacher professionalism – for example, different curricula traditions and views on teacher education – are investigated.

Conclusion

This chapter has examined changes in teacher professionalism in the context of contemporary education policy developments. The restructuring of teachers' work in education policy has been addressed and conceptualized in various ways by researchers. We report on a shift of focus in the literature – from studies on the dramatic change in the status and work of teachers to those on how this change is often experienced by teachers, thereby creating dilemmas in their work. These dilemmas derive both from expectations towards being accountable for outcomes and from expectations towards using different knowledge sources. We therefore argue that issues surrounding teachers' knowledge base and the different educational programmes leading into teaching should be seen in relation to that of increased external control of professional work. This implies being attentive not only to the context of the studies being conducted but also to the research designs. There is a need for more robust research in this area, for example, comparative studies, observation studies, and studies that investigate issues of teacher professionalism on different institutional levels. Thereby, the use of organizational perspectives could add valuable insights into changes in teachers' work and professionalism (e.g. Noordegraaf, 2013). The ways in which teachers are educated to work in more knowledge-intensive societies could also be more closely investigated to enhance knowledge about what characterizes teachers' work, education, and professionalism in new work contexts.

References

Blömeke, S. (2006) 'Globalization and educational reform in German teacher education'. *International Journal of Educational Research* 45 (4–5), pp. 315–324.

Clarke, J. and Newman, J. (1997) *The Managerial State: Power, Politics and Ideology in the Remaking of Social Welfare.* London: Sage.

Coburn, C. and Turner, E. O. (2011) 'Research on data use: a framework and analysis'. *Measurement: Interdisciplinary Research and Practice* 9 (4), pp. 173–206.

Conway, P. F. and Murphy, R. (2013) 'A rising tide meets a perfect storm: New accountabilities in teaching and teacher education in Ireland'. *Irish Educational Studies* 32 (1), pp. 11–36.

Czerniawski, G. (2011) 'Emerging teachers – emerging identities: Trust and accountability in the construction of newly qualified teachers in Norway, Germany, and England'. *European Journal of Teacher Education* 34 (4), pp. 431–447.

Darling-Hammond, L. and Lieberman, A. (2012) 'Teacher education around the world: What can we learn from international practice?'. In Darling-Hammond, L. and Lieberman, A. (eds), *Teacher Education around the World: Changing Policies and Practices.* Hoboken, NJ: Taylor & Francis.

Day, C. (2002) 'School reform and transitions in teacher professionalism and identity'. *International Journal of Educational Research* 37 (8), pp. 677–692.

Evans, L. (2008) 'Professionalism, professionality and the development of education professions'. *British Journal of Educational Studies* 56 (1), pp. 20–38.

Evetts, J. (2003) 'The sociological analysis of professionalism'. *International Sociology* 18 (2), pp. 395–415.

Fransson, G. and Grannäs, J. (2013) 'Dilemmatic spaces in educational contexts: Towards a conceptual framework for dilemmas in teachers work'. *Teachers and Teaching: Theory and Practice* 19 (1), pp. 4–17.

Fuller, B. (2008) 'Overview: Liberal learning in centralizing states'. In Fuller, B., Henne, M. K. and Hannum, E. (eds), *Strong States, Weak Schools: The Benefits and Dilemmas of Centralized Accountability.* Bingley, UK: Emerald.

Furlong, J. (2005) 'New Labour and teacher education: The end of an era?'. *Oxford Review of Education* 31 (1), pp. 119–134.

Goepel, J. (2012) 'Upholding public trust: An examination of teacher professionalism and the use of Teachers' Standards in England'. *Teacher Development* 16 (4), pp. 489–505.

Hall, C. (2004) 'Theorising changes in teachers' work'. *Canadian Journal of Educational Administration and Policy* 32, pp. 1–14.

Hammersley, M. (2013) *The Myth of Research-Based Policy and Practice*. Los Angeles, CA: Sage.

Hardy, I. (2012) '"Managing" managerialism: the impact of educational auditing on an academic "specialist" school'. *European Educational Research Journal* 11 (2), pp. 274–289.

Hargreaves, A. and Fullan, M. (2012) *Professional Capital: Transforming Teaching in Every School*. New York: Teachers College Press.

Hargreaves, D. H. ([1996] 2007) 'Teaching as a research-based profession: Possibilities and prospects'. In Hammersley, M. (ed.), *Educational Research and Evidence-Based Practice*. London: Sage.

Heilig, J. V. (2011) 'Understanding the interaction between high-stakes graduation tests and English learners'. *Teachers College Record* 113 (12), pp. 2633–2669.

Helgøy, I. and Homme, A. (2007) 'Towards a new professionalism in school? A comparative study of teacher autonomy in Norway and Sweden'. *European Educational Research Journal* 6 (3), pp. 232–249.

Hemsley-Brown, J. and Sharp, C. (2003) 'The use of research to improve professional practice: A systematic review of the literature'. *Oxford Review of Education* 29 (4), pp. 449–470.

Hopmann, S. (2015) 'Didaktik meets Curriculum' revisited: historical encounters, systematic experience, empirical limits. NordSTEP 1(2), pp. 14–21.

Jeffrey, B. (2002) 'Performativity and primary teacher relations'. *Journal of Education Policy* 17 (5), pp. 531–546.

Joram, E. (2007) 'Clashing epistemologies: Aspiring teachers', practicing teachers', and professors' beliefs about knowledge and research in education'. *Teaching and Teacher Education* 23 (2), pp. 123–135.

Little, J. W. (2012) 'Understanding data use practice among teachers: The contribution of micro-process studies'. *American Journal of Education* 118 (2), pp. 143–166.

Locke, T., Vulliamy, G., Webb, R. and Hill, M. (2005) 'Being a "professional" primary school teacher at the beginning of the 21st century: A comparative analysis of primary teacher professionalism in New Zealand and England'. *Journal of Education Policy* 20 (5), pp. 555–581.

Lortie, D. C. (1975) *Schoolteacher: A Sociological Study*. Chicago, IL: University of Chicago Press.

MacBeath, J. (2012) 'Teacher training, education or learning by doing in the UK'. In Darling-Hammond, L. and Lieberman, A. (eds), *Teacher Education around the World Changing Policies and Practices*. Hoboken, NJ: Taylor & Francis, pp. 66–80.

Martens, K., Rusconi, A. and Leuze, K. (2007) *New Arenas of Education Governance: The Impact of International Organizations and Markets on Educational Policy Making*. Basingstoke: Palgrave Macmillan.

Mausethagen, S. (2013) 'Accountable for what and to whom? Changing representations and new legitimation discourses among teachers under increased external control'. *Journal of Educational Change* 14 (4), pp. 423–444.

Mausethagen, S. and Granlund, L. (2012) 'Contested discourses of teacher professionalism: Current tensions between education policy and teachers' union'. *Journal of Education Policy* 27 (6), pp. 815–833.

Menter, I. and Hulme, M. (2013) 'Developing the teacher – or not?'. In Priestley, M. and Biesta, G. (eds), *Reinventing the Curriculum: New Trends in Curriculum Policy and Practice*. London: Bloomsbury Academic.

Molander, A. and Terum, L. I. (2008) 'Profesjonsstudier: en introduksjon'. In Molander, A. and Terum, L. I. (eds), *Profesjonsstudier*. Oslo: Universitetsforlaget.

Mølstad, C. E. (2015) 'State-based curriculum-making: Approaches to local curriculum work in Norway and Finland'. *Journal of Curriculum Studies* 47(4), pp. 441–461.

Mulcahy, D. (2011) 'Assembling the "accomplished" teacher: The performativity and politics of professional teaching standards'. *Educational Philosophy and Theory* 43 (suppl. 1), pp. 94–113.

Niemi, H. and Nevgi, A. (2014) 'Research studies and active learning promoting professional competences in Finnish teacher education'. *Teaching and Teacher Education* 43, pp. 131–142.

Noordegraaf, M. (2013) 'Reconfiguring professional work: Changing forms of professionalism in public services'. *Administration & Society*. doi: 10.1177/0095399713509242 (last accessed 28 January 2016).

Ozga, J. T. and Lawn, M. A. (1981) *Teachers, Professionalism and Class: A Study of Organized Teachers*. London: Falmer Press.

Ozga, J. and Jones, R. (2006) 'Travelling and embedded policy: The case of knowledge Transfer'. *Journal of Education Policy* 21 (1), pp. 1–17.

Priestley, M. and Biesta, G. (2013) 'Introduction: The new curriculum'. In Priestley, M. and Biesta, G. (eds), *Reinventing the Curriculum: New Trends in Curriculum Policy and Practice*. London: Bloomsbury Academic.

Sachs, J. (2001) 'Teacher professional identity: Competing discourses, competing outcomes'. *Journal of Education Policy* 16 (2), pp. 149–161.

Sahlberg, P. (2012) 'The most wanted: Teachers and teacher education in Finland'. In Darling-Hammond, L. and Lieberman, A. (eds), *Teacher Education around the World: Changing Policies and Practices*. Hoboken, NJ: Taylor & Francis, pp. 1–21.

Shavelson, R. J. and Towne, L. (eds) (2002) *Scientific Research in Education*. Washington, DC: National Academy Press.

Simons, M. and Kelchtermans, G. (2008) 'Teacher professionalism in Flemish policy on teacher education: A critical analysis of the Decree on Teacher Education (2006) in Flanders, Belgium'. *Teachers and Teaching: Theory and Practice* 14 (4), pp. 283–294.

Sinclair, A. (1995) 'The chameleon of accountability: Forms and discourses'. *Accounting, Organizations and Society* 20 (2/3), pp. 219–237.

Sivesind, K. (2008) *Reformulating Reform: Curriculum History Revisited*. A thesis submitted in partial fulfilment of the Requirements of the University of Oslo for the Degree of Doctor of Philosophy. Oslo: University of Oslo.

Smeby, J.-C. (2015) 'Academic drift in vocational education?'. In Smeby, J.-C. and Sutphen, M. (eds), *From Vocational to Professional Education: Educating for Social Welfare*. London: Routledge.

Solbrekke, T. D. and Sugrue, C. (2014) 'Professional accreditation of initial teacher education programmes: Teacher educators' strategies: Between "accountability" and "professional responsibility"?'. *Teaching and Teacher Education* 37, pp. 11–20.

Stillman, J. (2011) 'Teacher learning in an era of high-stakes accountability: Productive tension and critical professional practice'. *Teachers College Record* 113 (1), pp. 133–180.

Stone-Johnson, C. (2014) 'Parallel professionalism in an era of standardisation'. *Teachers and Teaching: Theory and Practice* 20 (1), pp. 74–91.

Terhart, E. (2013) 'Teacher resistance against school reform: Reflecting an inconvenient truth'. *School Leadership & Management* 33 (5), pp. 486–500.

Townsend, T. (2011) 'Searching high and searching low, searching east and searching west: Looking for trust in teacher education'. *Journal of Education for Teaching* 37 (4), pp. 483–499.

Trent, J. (2012) 'Research engagement as identity construction: Hong Kong preservice teachers' experiences of a compulsory research project'. *Teacher Development* 16 (2), pp. 145–160.

Tummons, J. (2014) 'The textual representation of professionalism: problematising professional standards for teachers in the UK lifelong learning sector'. *Research in Post-Compulsory Education* 19 (1), pp. 33–44.

Vanderlinde, R. and van Braak, J. (2010) 'The gap between educational research and practice: Views of teachers, school leaders, intermediaries and researchers'. *British Educational Research Journal* 36 (2), pp. 299–316.

Westbury, I., Hansén, S.-E., Kansanen, P. and Björkvist, O. (2005) 'Teacher education for research-based practice in expanded roles: Finland's experience'. *Scandinavian Journal of Educational Research* 49 (5), pp. 475–485.

Wilkins, C. (2011) 'Professionalism and the post-performative teacher: New teachers reflect on autonomy and accountability in the English school system'. *Professional Development in Education* 37 (3), pp. 389–409.

Wilkins, C., Busher, H., Kakos, M., Mohamed, C. and Smith, J. (2012) 'Crossing borders: New teachers co-constructing professional identity in performative times'. *Professional Development in Education* 38 (1), pp. 65–77.

Williams, D. and Coles, L. (2007) 'Teachers' approaches to finding and using research evidence: An information literacy perspective'. *Educational Research* 49 (2), pp. 185–206.

Zeichner, K. (2012) 'The turn once again toward practice-based teacher education'. *Journal of Teacher Education* 63 (5), pp. 376–382.

23

Interprofessional working for the health professions

From fried eggs to omelettes?

Susan Nancarrow and Alan Borthwick

Introduction

Interprofessional team work has become the mantra of early twenty-first-century health workforce training, development and delivery. Interprofessional team work involves professions from different disciplines training or working together to understand, and in some cases adopt, roles traditionally performed by others. The motivation for interprofessional team work stems from complex client or patient needs that require the input of a range of different professional perspectives or expertise. It is also designed to overcome problems of workforce fragmentation and specialisation that mean that no single discipline can meet complex client needs, particularly in light of demographic changes likely to increase demand for healthcare provision.

The ideal espoused by interprofessional collaboration suggests a certain interchangeability of roles, such that professional identities are supressed for the sake of harmonious team functioning. However, in contrast, there is evidence suggesting that effective team functioning depends on clearly defined and communicated roles, which is arguably more challenging when roles are interchangeable. The latter point assumes that professions and roles/tasks are intertwined. In other words, roles may be defined by professional title, and both may confer status on their practitioners, ensuring each is likely to be defended rather than seamlessly transferred from one to another (Larson 1977; Hugman 1991). Reinforcing the link between roles and title requires professions to hold on to the defining components of their roles (often the 'virtuoso' roles) while delegating the non-essential or non-defining tasks (the dirty work) (Hugman 1991; Zetka 2011).

This notion of interprofessional working, therefore, suggests that there is a professional 'core' of tasks which continues to define that profession but also a more generic periphery of tasks that can be shared across a range of professions without challenging the 'professional core' (Zetka 2011). The negotiation of the boundaries between those tasks that are shared and those that are maintained by professions is key to the sociology of interprofessional team work. Metaphorically, this could be compared to a fried egg, where the yolk represents the clearly delineated core skills maintained by the profession while the white represents the peripheral, interchangeable components. We argue that the current model of professionalism is similar to a fried egg, and this is illustrated in Case Study 1.

Yet there is evidence of a shift towards a more competency-based approach to interprofessional team work (Case Study 2), where the function of the whole team supersedes the identities of the individual professional constituents. The ultimate extrapolation of this concept is a generalist practitioner with no defining professional core, but who adopts a range of interchangeable tasks, perhaps to meet specific population needs (Stressing and Borthwick 2014). A move away from professions to a competency-based workforce could be seen to more closely represent an omelette, where the core and peripheral tasks are no longer differentiated along professional lines, but tasks are allocated on the basis of skills and risk. The result is a more homogeneous workforce, where the individual components are no longer recognisable and the team functions as a whole, rather than as a disaggregated group of individuals vying to deliver virtuoso roles (Hugman 1991).

The use of metaphor is becoming increasingly valued as a way of shaping our understanding of complex concepts (Cornelissen 2005). There are a small number of examples of metaphors used to describe attributes of professions. Professions have been described in terms of landscapes and hierarchies (Liljegren 2012). Saks use the metaphors of zoos, circuses and safari parks to describe the regulation of English healthcare professions (Saks 2013b). These metaphors have the advantage that they enable complex power relationships to be embedded (more akin to Abbott's (1988) models).

The fried egg–omelette metaphor is more functionally focused and illustrates the core–periphery separation versus the homogeneity of profession roles which could be seen to be the ultimate extrapolation of an interprofessional team. We have selected two case studies of different approaches to interprofessional team work, illustrated using the fried egg–omelette metaphor.

The first case study highlights the ongoing role boundary dispute over the contested domain of foot surgery, in which both orthopaedic and podiatric surgeons compete for space. In the absence of exclusive control, each seeks different goals – orthopaedic surgeons demand hegemony, podiatric surgeons assert legitimacy. The second is the development of a rural generalist allied health practitioner in northern Australia, which involved the explicit identification of professional roles and tasks using a tool designed specifically for that purpose (the Calderdale Framework, Smith and Duffy 2010). The roles and tasks were then amalgamated and analysed for similarities that could meet specific patient needs. In other words, they regrouped around patient needs and logic, rather than traditional professional boundaries, potentially enabling the whole to function as separate entities, but as a single discrete entity to achieve a specific goal.

The two case studies illustrate re-profiling of health-professional roles using interdisciplinary work, but from two distinct perspectives. Case Study 1 examines interprofessional role negotiation involving vertical substitution, in which the negotiated role (surgery) is traditionally owned by the medical profession. Case Study 2 looks at roles negotiated across professions with relatively equal status, and in a context of workforce shortages, or horizontal substitution (Nancarrow and Borthwick 2005).

Case Study 1: Contested titles and role boundaries in foot surgery

In his seminal work on the profession of medicine, Eliot Freidson remarked that 'legally or otherwise, the physician's right to diagnose, cut and prescribe is the centre around which the work of many other occupations swing, and the physician's authority and responsibility in that constellation of work are primary' (Freidson 1970, 1988). What this conveys is the extent to which, at the time, the medical profession enjoyed an almost exclusive social and cultural authority over healthcare practices. It is also instructive that Freidson identified three core elements as central to medical practice and authority, particularly that of surgery.

Since the Medical Act (1858) in the UK brought together the three disparate practitioner classes of physician, barber surgeon and apothecary, the practice of invasive surgery has largely been viewed as a skillset which could only be undertaken by individuals trained as medical doctors and registered as such by the General Medical Council (GMC) (Berlant 1975; Freidson 1988). Curiously, the Act itself, viewed as a concession to liberal political values, revoked earlier privileges accorded to the medical profession and permitted 'anyone to practise who wished to' (Berlant 1975). Indeed, the growth of political liberalism ensured opposition to monopolistic practices and thus restrictive licensure, in spite of the assertion by physicians that they should be exempt from considerations of free market exchange, as they provided services rather than engaging in trade. In asserting the difference between a profession and a trade, they hoped to remove themselves from the vagaries of a free market with open competition. In reality, a deal was struck in which the amalgamation of physicians, surgeons and apothecaries into a single class, registered as such, was combined with acceptance of the official doctrine of *caveat emptor* and the freedom of individuals to choose their healer (Berlant 1975). Therein lay the seeds of a modern conflict, most clearly evident in the ongoing dispute between two variants of 'surgeon': a medically trained version (orthopaedic surgeons) and a non-medically trained type (podiatric surgeons) (Borthwick 2000).

Invasive foot surgery, once the exclusive province of the medically trained orthopaedic surgeon, is today practised by suitably trained podiatrists as well (Borthwick 2000, 2001). It was not so much a change in the law which enabled this transition, but a decline in medical power and dominance in healthcare, and a shift in the health policy agenda (Kuhlmann and Saks 2008). Contemporary concerns over the sustainability of health service provision for an ageing population, coupled with a growth in chronic disease and a reduction in manpower resources, led to a series of health policy initiatives aimed at maintaining services and their quality through workforce redesign and role flexibility, necessarily demanding a break from the 'traditional' professional division of labour (Cameron and Masterson 2003; Nancarrow and Borthwick 2005). However, this has not been seamlessly achieved, and interprofessional disputes continue to flare in notable areas of practice, especially where role and task domains central to medical practice are contested. Perhaps unsurprisingly, medical opposition to podiatric surgery has been led by the speciality of orthopaedics, given the similarity in role boundaries across the two groups (Borthwick 2000).

Medicine, of course, continues to occupy a position of relative authority and leadership within the health division of labour, and challenges to its exclusive control of key tasks and roles are likely to meet firm resistance, especially when offered by professions with less power (Hugman 1991). Much has been written about the hierarchical power structures in healthcare, and the dominance of medicine throughout most of the twentieth century (Freidson 1970, 1988; Larkin 1988; Willis 1989). Equally, the gradual erosion of medical power since the 1970s has been clearly traced, following the ascendency of anti-monopolistic neoliberal governments across the Western world (Larkin 1995; Moran 2002; Willis 2006). Neoliberal concerns with fiscal restraint, free market competition and professional accountability in healthcare have led to policies threatening to professions wishing to retain exclusive control over roles and role boundaries (Evetts 2002; Kuhlmann and Saks 2008; Evetts 2011).

Moves to introduce interprofessional working, education and training have been evident across the anglophone world, and have been hailed as a solution to the problems facing modern healthcare provision, premised on the need to break down 'traditional professional boundaries' and demarcations in practice (Department of Health 2008a, 2008b). Yet a tendency to accept these policies uncritically, as 'common sense', has masked the resulting tensions between professions attempting to renegotiate revised roles and boundaries (Kitto *et al.* 2011).

Within the field of surgery, a number of strategies have been adopted as a defence against encroachment on established work jurisdictions, such as the incorporation of new technologies to aid specialisation and expertise, which in turn may also force a re-evaluation of core roles (Zetka 2003). The importance of 'core' roles, identified as those tasks 'central to … self-worth and status', is clear in as much as professions 'care most about their core task. They generally attempt to control these performances and establish protective boundaries around them' (Zetka 2003). Other tasks are viewed as less central, and still others as 'demeaning', which are thus discarded, often by delegation (Zetka 2003).

For orthopaedic surgeons, foot surgery undoubtedly constitutes a perceived 'core' role, albeit one relegated to the status of a relatively minor activity within the wider spectrum of 'core' practices, and one often delegated to junior staff in training (Macnicol 2002; Kelly *et al.* 2011). In the United Kingdom and Australia podiatric surgery has emerged over the last forty-year period, in which it gradually became established within mainstream healthcare. As foot surgery was a 'core' role within medicine, this development was always likely to provoke a reaction from the speciality of orthopaedics. At stake were three factors. At the start, the exclusive right of medically qualified individuals to undertake invasive surgery was a largely taken-for-granted assumption (Borthwick 2000). It had hardly occurred to the profession that anyone other than a medically qualified person would or could seek to undertake surgery. Next, once alternative providers of surgery had emerged and become established, the medical profession sought to impose oversight of their practices, maintaining its leadership role whilst ensuring non-medical practitioners were firmly constrained and afforded little more than technician status in terms of the practical application of standardised techniques (Borthwick 2000). Finally, as independent non-medically qualified surgical practitioners flourished, moves to impose a restriction on the use of key professional titles emerged, reflecting a bid to retain symbolic power through exclusive access to prestigious titles implying leadership, seniority and expertise (Macnicol 2002; Getty 2010).

Each of these three features follows a chronological course, reflecting the gradual decline in medical authority and the arrival of the workforce redesign agenda. Conceptually, it is a transition which is perhaps most clearly illuminated when viewed through both a Weberian and Bourdieusian lens (Saks 1983; Bourdieu 1985, 1989; Saks 2013a). With the former, disputes over territorial acquisition of tasks and roles, and claims over abstract and expert knowledge are sharply illustrated. With the latter, the importance of the symbolic power of professional title is neatly captured, as a form of symbolic capital over which the struggle for legitimacy is fought. Crucially, what this case study reveals is that the interprofessional conflict between orthopaedic and podiatric surgeons continues to smoulder in part because the monopoly of surgical practice has not yet been fully disestablished. Indeed, a re-emergent medical monopoly might be reasserted should current efforts to enlist government support in a bid to fully protect key titles succeed.

In short, pressure to adopt interprofessional working in the sphere of surgery has foundered on two counts – first, because the dominant discourse of medicine continues to undermine efforts by non-medical providers to attain full recognition and legitimacy, and second because podiatric surgeons continue both to refuse to work in multiprofessional teams overseen by orthopaedic surgeons, and to assert the right to independent practice. Together, these factors unwittingly move each toward a form of monopoly: an orthopaedic campaign to enable restrictive legislative change which would confine surgery to the medically qualified, and a podiatric assertion of rights to practise without overarching medical control. In combination, these features militate against role flexibility and appeal to professional accreditation and standards as a means to maintain established monopolies. Arguably, neither trend will meet the needs of the changing population, as both serve professional rather than patient requirements. Attempts to incorporate both may constitute a remaking of traditional boundaries and barriers, thus 'retro-fitting' professional monopolies and preventing meaningful change in the interests of those who most need it.

Foot surgery as a medical prerogative

In the UK, the Medical Act (1983) appears at face value to offer clarity in giving legal force to the protection of medical titles (UK Government 1983). In fact, it may have achieved the opposite. Ambiguity abounds in the interpretation of the provisions which protect specific titles – notably 'doctor of medicine' and 'surgeon'. Whilst the provisions also address a 'holding out' clause, which renders illegal any attempt by non-medically qualified individuals to 'wilfully or falsely' imply that they are registered medical practitioners, they neither restrict the practice of medicine or surgery, nor prevent the use of titles which appear similar but arguably avoid any wilful or false insinuation of medical status. Certain prior precedents had been set by cases arising in the first half of the twentieth century. In the case of Jutson v. Barrow [1936] 1 KB 236, the title 'manipulative surgeon' had been used by a non-medically qualified individual who had no relevant qualifications to support his claim, and he was duly convicted. In the second case, Younghusband v. Luftig [1949] 2 All ER 72, a qualified German physician who was not entered on the UK's GMC register, used the title 'MD, Berlin' or 'MD BLN'. In this instance, the accused was acquitted, as his use of title did not, in the eyes of the court, constitute 'wilfully and falsely' implying he was registered as a medical doctor with the GMC. In the latter case, Lord Goddard declared that the ambiguity generated by these cases left a 'complete fog'. At the heart of these cases was the need to demonstrate 'clear and unambiguous' intent (*mens rea*) (Ward and Akhtar 2011). Perhaps as a result of this ambiguity, the matter has not yet been tested in a court of law, and thus lacks resolution. One side might argue that the use of the title 'podiatric surgeon' or 'consultant podiatric surgeon' implies that the title-holder is deliberately seeking to mislead patients into thinking that he or she is a registered medical practitioner. Equally, it may be argued that use of the prefix 'podiatric' ensures a degree of clarity in that it actively states the title holder is a podiatrist practising surgery. However, as a former President of the Royal College of Surgeons (RCS) admitted, until competition arose in the form of podiatrists practising surgery, the RCS had assumed its Royal Charter gave it exclusive powers over who might practise surgery, but this proved not to be so (Borthwick 2000).

Transition from exclusion to delegation to dispute over title

Once it became apparent to the RCS that it was possible for non-medical healthcare professionals to undertake surgical training and to incorporate surgical skills within their scope of practice, it sought to contain the problem by insisting that the best means of providing such a service would be through multidisciplinary teams led by medically qualified surgeons. In part, the logic for this arrangement lay in access to the full range of hospital infrastructure and support, which would, it was presumed, be absent if carried out by non-medically qualified surgeons. Medical doctors still held exclusive authority over the allocation of hospital beds and had 24-hour hospital care available to them, with on-call services throughout the night. Non-medically qualified podiatrists could not hope to offer a similar range of support mechanisms independently. What they could offer, however, was a range of foot surgical operations carried out under local anaesthetics on a day-care basis, thus providing a cheaper alternative (Borthwick 2000). Attempts to impose a hierarchy of medical sovereignty, issued by the Joint Consultants Committee of the

British Medical Association as well as the RCS, did not enjoy the support of the Department of Health, which had reason to commend the timeliness and cost effectiveness of an alternative provider of care at a time when the policy agenda promoted GP (general practitioner) fund-holding and competitive tendering for service contracts. In such a political climate, podiatric surgery was able to gain a foothold in mainstream healthcare provision, and many of its practitioners attained positions of authority as independent 'consultant'-grade podiatric surgeons in the National Health Service.

Use of the terms 'podiatric surgeon' and 'consultant podiatric surgeon' by podiatrists practising foot surgery then grew in importance, as it became evident that medicine could not impose medical supervision and delegation of work on podiatric surgeons, who could operate independently. Orthopaedic surgeons focused attention thereafter on the 'misuse' of 'their' title by non-medically qualified practitioners. A public campaign ensued, waged in the press and media, designed to convince the public of the illegitimacy of podiatrists' use of the term 'podiatric surgeon'. An article in *The Times* announced that the British Orthopaedic Trainees Association had 'declared open war' on podiatric surgeons, who 'had no medical qualifications at all' (Hawkes 2004). Subsequent articles referred to the 'hijacking' of medical titles such as 'surgeon', to the 'hoodwinking' of the public by podiatric surgeons who would 'mislead' and 'deceive' the public by their use of title (Goldacre 2004; Getty 2010). Most notable was the assertion that podiatrists should adopt the title 'surgical podiatrist' to differentiate themselves from medically qualified surgeons, but that they might add 'chief', 'grand high' or 'most senior' if they so desired (Rawlins 2011). This was what Bourdieu referred to as the 'struggle for the production and imposition of the legitimate vision of the social world', and he recognised the importance of title in that equation: 'it is not the relative value of the work that determines the value of the name, but the institutionalised value of the title that can be used as a means of defending or maintaining the value of the work' (Bourdieu 1989).

Case study 2: Establishment of a rural allied health generalist

Workforce shortages in rural and remote areas of Australia are well documented. Health services outside metropolitan areas have difficulty attracting, retaining and supporting nursing, medical and allied health staff (Humphreys *et al.* 2009). At the same time, rural and remote residents have poorer health status than those in urban communities.

Interprofessional working is proposed as one solution to help meet skills shortages or increase workforce efficiency by enabling workers to adopt a suite of skills that can best meet the needs of the patient or context, rather than be explicitly bound to a defined professional repertoire.

Several strategies have been introduced to help overcome the difficulties of health service accessibility in rural communities by introducing more innovative and flexible ways of working. In particular, the shortage of practitioners has meant that the existing rural and remote workforce has had to develop a broader repertoire of more generalist skills (Quilty *et al.* 2014). In some cases, such approaches have been contentious. For example, the University of Queensland attempted to introduce training to develop a physician assistant role. This role was designed to provide a way to address rural health workforce shortages by introducing a new worker who could adopt some components of work traditionally performed by the medical profession (Saunders 2011). However, medical opposition thwarted this approach, and the training was withdrawn. Similarly, the expansion of nursing roles through nurse practitioner has met with a rocky path in Australia due to medical opposition (Appel and Malcom 2002).

Notably, these new roles represent attempts at vertical substitution, where the new professions are attempting to encroach on boundaries that are the traditional domain of the medical profession. These examples, and the podiatry–surgeon case study, illustrate interprofessional role negotiations in which the new or expanding role presented a challenge to the medical monopoly.

In contrast, this case study describes the strategic identification and negotiation of tasks which could be shared across, and delegated by, six allied health professions working in rural and remote Australia. The project described in this case study used a structured workforce tool (the Calderdale Framework) to identify and negotiate a suite of generic tasks that could be shared across a range of allied health professionals working in rural and remote areas of northern Australia.

The context for this study is important. Most existing studies of interprofessional role negotiation explore the role dynamics between practitioners working within existing co-located teams (King *et al.* 2015), hence role negotiation becomes dependent on a range of locally contextual factors such as the individual personalities, the clinical requirements and the setting in which the care is provided. The unique contribution of this project is that it explicitly sought to identify generic tasks at a macro level, beyond the context of the individual teams, with a view to developing a generalisable set of core generic activities. Second, the rural context of this study is important. Rural and remote practice creates a relatively unique set of circumstances that are known to breed innovation (Wakerman and Humphreys 2011). It is generally accepted that rural and remote health practitioners require a broader skill base than metropolitan workers, due in part to the varied client load and the inability to sustain specialities across smaller population groups (Nielson 2014; Quilty *et al.* 2014). Another necessity of rural practice is a greater reliance on team work and multidisciplinary practice. Rural practice is particularly well placed to support opportunities for interprofessional practice and skill sharing. The term rural 'generalist' is widely used to describe a practitioner who works in a rural area; however, the term is not clearly defined. Rural generalism refers broadly to the breadth of patient case-load and/or diversity of skill mix to meet these needs. Another important feature that differentiates this case study from others examining role renegotiation is that it takes place between professions with relatively equal status, and notably, in the absence of any direct medical involvement.

The Greater Northern Australia Regional Training Network (GNARTN) Rural and Remote Generalist: Allied Health Project was funded by the Australian Government to develop training models for practitioners working in rural and remote areas (Nielson 2014). The project was also designed to inform health services in the development of skill-sharing models, supported by appropriate risk management and governance structures.

Five teams across rural and remote regions of northern Australia participated in the project. Staff employed by each service were trained in the use of the Calderdale Framework (Smith and Duffy 2010). The Calderdale Framework is a facilitated process that implicitly separates tasks or competencies from professional jurisdictions. The process involves working with clinicians to break down clinical interventions into defined functions and tasks. The tasks are analysed according to the level of risk and skill associated with performing that task and the frequency with which the task is performed. Using a consensus approach, the practitioners determine which tasks are appropriate to delegate to another worker. Those tasks deemed to be appropriate for delegation are then defined in terms of specific competencies.

The participating teams were required to have two or more allied health professions working within a team-based multidisciplinary model of care. The allied health professions involved were occupational therapy, physiotherapy, speech language pathology, dietetics and nutrition, podiatry, social work, and allied health assistants.

Only data pertaining to clinical tasks were analysed. Non-clinical tasks (such as care coordination, administrative/operational, student supervision) were excluded from the data collection.

Non-clinical tasks were considered essential to all professions, therefore not considered to be negotiable across professional boundaries.

The participating professions identified 337 unique tasks. Of these, 127 were deemed as appropriate for skill sharing across allied health professionals with appropriate training and governance support. Of those tasks that were identified as appropriate for skill sharing, 40 per cent were currently only performed by a single discipline, but 60 per cent were deemed to be multidisciplinary (already performed by more than one discipline). The project also identified a large number of tasks performed by allied health professionals that could be delegated to the allied health assistant workforce, but less than one third of these potentially delegable tasks were being delegated.

The tasks were then clustered into functional or diagnostic categories rather than professional groupings. Thirteen clusters were proposed, namely: activities of daily living (ADL) and function; mobility and transfers; prevention of foot morbidity in high-risk groups; children's development; cognition and perception; communication; psycho-social; fatigue, sleep and energy conservation; pressure care, skin and wounds; diet and nutrition; neuro-musculoskeletal and pain; cardiovascular fitness and exercise tolerance; and continence assessment and basic intervention. Following validation of these groupings by other allied health professionals, these clusters were designed to form the basis of future clinical training programmes for rural and remote allied health practitioners. The aggregated task clusters were then analysed according to which of the six practitioners could contribute to the delivery of these activities. Interestingly, in more than half of the clusters, two or more professionals were considered to deliver those roles. For example, the ADL cluster incorporated the activities of ADL screening and assessment, assessment and prescribing home modifications, equipment relating to ADL and function, and functional training in the ADL. All disciplines other than podiatry were considered to contribute to this activity. Interestingly, only 20 per cent of occupational therapy tasks and 26 per cent of physiotherapy tasks were perceived to be unidisciplinary.

An example of a shared task is lymphedema management, which involved tasks that are common across physiotherapy and occupational therapy. The clusters that accounted for the greatest proportion of shared skills were activities of daily living and mobility and transfers.

Staff supported the project and processes of role negotiation between allied health practitioners. The majority of participants supported the notion of greater delegation by practitioners within the team. Feedback from participants suggested that the process, far from being threatening, enabled staff to gain a greater understanding of each other's roles.

Under the guise of person-centred care, this case study challenges several of the accepted assumptions about professionalism. Where traditional literature on the sociology of the professions focuses on the exclusionary practices of professions (Abbott 1988), this study used a structured, democratic, negotiated approach to identify a suite of tasks that could be shared by more than one profession, with strong support for this process by the six disciplines involved. Further, the tasks were regrouped around logical clinical functions rather than historic professional repertoires.

The explicit identification of a set of tasks, the attribution of a level of skill and risk to these tasks, and renegotiation of these tasks challenges the very assumptions underpinning professionalism. Professional work is distinguished from non-professional work through the interweaving of occupational content and institutional control to establish occupational closure (Noordegraaf 2007). In this case study, in the context of the rural shortages and under the guise of person-centred care, the professions codified their practice into tasks, which they then willingly redistributed on the basis of skill and risk levels.

The focus on patient-centred care in the rural context became the overriding priority of this group. In other words, the functional purpose of the team superseded the professional boundaries of the professions involved. A similar approach was identified by Carmel (2006) in an analysis of intensive care teams. In this study, despite tensions between the nursing and medical professions involved, the occupational boundaries were obscured using a strategy that Carmel labelled 'incorporation' as a way to reinforce the intensive care project. This created organisational boundaries that differentiated the intensive care team within the hospital organisation.

Similarly, the cooperation of the allied health professionals as part of the GNARTN project could be seen as the incorporation of allied health profession roles through the transprofessional negotiation of competencies for the purpose of developing the rural generalist project or role.

An extrapolation of this approach, and the ultimate in interprofessional team work, is the privileging of the function of the team over the professional roles of the individuals comprising the team. In this case, the team could be described as functioning as an *organism*, towards which the synergies of the single components align to achieve a single purpose. An example of a team functioning as an organism was illustrated by Morey and colleagues in the emergency department. In this case, they found that in times of stress, the team focused on the delivery of a function rather than on the negotiation of individual tasks (Morey *et al.* 2002).

> From these larger teams, ad hoc teams are formed to respond to emergent events such as resuscitations. In this model, teamwork is sustained by a shared set of teamwork skills rather than permanent assignments that carry over from day to day.
>
> *(p. 1555)*

This interprofessional case study is relatively unusual in many ways. In contrast to the podiatry–surgeon negotiations, the allied health professions are relatively equal in status. The professions involved are state funded, so there is no fee for service negotiation involved (i.e. less competition). Interestingly, there are no regulatory boundaries or restrictions around the reallocated tasks. The case study takes place in a rural context and it may be that the rural context is associated with lower-status tasks that are more easily delegated. This reinforces the notion that the 'core' roles, especially those occupied by more powerful professions (vertical substitution) are more likely to be contested and defended (Zetka 2011), but the lower status, more 'peripheral' tasks are more likely to be shared or shed (Hugman 1991).

The GNARTN case study suggests that the allied health practitioners have accommodated or modified part of their identity to allow the sharing of roles, or a 'negotiated order' at a local level, where things just 'get done' by by-passing the usual norms (Carmel 2006). However, in contrast to other examples of this practice, which normally take place within a single team or organisation, this negotiated order has taken place at a wider, systems level (albeit, an informal system).

Discussion

The growth of interprofessional team work reflects neoliberal values that are patient, rather than profession centred. It has progressed on the assumption that professional boundaries can be renegotiated to meet the needs of patients. The two case studies presented in this chapter illustrate this interprofessional role renegotiation from two discrete perspectives. The first reinforces the maintenance of professional boundaries and role negotiation along speciality lines. This role renegotiation takes place between professions with unequal status, under the guise of medical dominance around regulated tasks.

The second case study illustrates an almost exemplary approach to interprofessional team work, where professions of similar status use a democratic process to renegotiate their tasks around groupings based on function or need rather than historic professional boundaries.

The juxtaposition of these case studies suggests several important points around role negotiation in interprofessional team work. Interprofessional role boundaries were more easily negotiable across professions that had relatively equal status than within the traditional professional hierarchy imposed by the podiatrist–surgeon. The rural context of workforce shortages was both a driver and facilitator of interprofessional role negotiation, creating opportunities for innovation in service delivery. Similarly, the renegotiation of tasks was simplified when there were no regulatory implications.

Reflecting the omelette and fried egg metaphor, the yolk is the 'core' professional tasks while the white is the peripheral roles which can be shared across professions. In the case of the podiatrists/surgeons, both are vying for a part of the yolk, the foot surgery, when the surgery can be seen as a core component of the surgeon's activities. The surgical tasks are high risk, highly skilled and highly invasive, therefore highly regulated.

The functional focus of the allied health project enabled the sharing of competencies across professions to achieve an organisational identity (the omelette), as opposed to reinforcing discrete professional identities (the fried egg). The adoption of formalised tools, such as the Calderdale Framework used by the GNARTN project, offers scope to achieve large-scale competency-based skill as opposed to localised renegotiation of roles. It may then be possible within a single organisational setting, with an established organisational project, that the professions can move in and out of their tasks to adopt functions to achieve a common negotiated goal, then move back into their professional identities.

The analysis of the data from the Calderdale Framework in the GNARTN project showed that in the rural allied health service context, the proportion of unique 'core' tasks performed by each profession was actually relatively small. While not as homogeneous as an omelette, the overall effect of the interprofessional project was to take away the core and replace it with functions (the 13 domains), which could be seen as the omelettes. They are still currently configured around a disciplinarily base; however, the fact that they have distilled these functions away from the professions suggests the potential for a much more homogeneous approach – more akin to the omelette, where the core (yolk) and periphery (white) are blended to form a single profession (the omelette). The reconfiguration of a distinctive skillset to service a particular market is suggestive of Zetka's (2003) turf logics. The subsequent loss of professional identity associated with the omelette model illustrates the concepts of post-professionalism or Dent and Whitehead's 'culture of performativity' (2002).

Through these cases, we draw a distinction between Abbot's (1988) competition for jurisdictional spaces, illustrated through the disputes that arise over 'core' tasks (where combatants appeal to public audiences and judicial means to defend their exclusive rights to high-status tasks or titles) and the less-skilled, lower-status roles and tasks that are negotiated on the basis of competencies.

Conclusion

Professional roles within interprofessional work can be seen to be negotiated across a continuum. At one end of the spectrum, an interprofessional team can be seen to function as a single, functionally focused unit where the professional roles are subordinated to the goals of the team (omelette model). At the other end of the continuum, is the fried-egg model in which professions maintain their core (yolk) and work within a negotiated framework of sharing of peripheral roles (whites). In reality, interprofessional roles are not static, and individual professionals and teams may move between the omelette and fried-egg states.

The case studies also highlight the importance of enabling context in the negotiation of role boundaries. A scarce task or role performed in a less-regulated environment is potentially more vulnerable to encroachment, and will face fewer barriers to encroachment (Nancarrow and

Borthwick 2005). Conversely, there are likely to be more active policies to facilitate encroachment of the scarce roles in these contexts. In addition, taking the role negotiation outside the clinical context objectified the process and removed much of the politics that might have been present in a more contained and politically charged clinical setting.

References

Abbott, A. (1988) *The System of Professions: An Essay on the Division of Expert Labour.* Chicago, IL, Chicago University Press.

Appel, A. L. and P. Malcom (2002) 'The triumph and continuing struggle of nurse practitioners in New South Wales, Australia'. *Clinical Nurse Specialist* 16(4), pp. 203–210.

Berlant, J. (1975) *Profession and Monopoly: A Study of Medicine in the United States and Great Britain.* Los Angeles, University of California Press.

Borthwick, A. (2000) 'Challenging medicine: The case of podiatric surgery'. *Work, Employment and Society* 14(2), pp. 369–383.

Borthwick, A. (2001) 'Occupational imperialism at work: The case of podiatric surgery'. *British Journal of Podiatry* 4(3), pp. 70–79.

Bourdieu, P. (1985) 'The social space and the genesis of groups'. *Theory and Society* 14(6), pp. 723–744.

Bourdieu, P. (1989) 'Social space and symbolic power'. *Sociological Theory* 7(1), pp. 14–25.

Cameron, A. and A. Masterson (2003) 'Reconfiguring the clinical workforce'. In C. Davies (ed.) *The Future Health Workforce.* Basingstoke, Palgrave Macmillan, pp. 68–86.

Carmel, S. (2006) 'Boundaries obscured and boundaries reinforced: Incorporation as a strategy of occupational enhancement for intensive care'. *Sociology of Health & Illness* 28(2), pp. 154–177.

Cornelissen, J. P. (2005) 'Beyond compare: Metaphor in organization theory'. *Academy of Management Review* 30(4), pp. 751–764.

Dent, M. and S. Whitehead (2002) 'Configuring the "new" professional'. In *Managing Professional Identities. Knowledge, Performativity and the 'New' Professional.* London, Routledge, pp. 1–18.

Department of Health (2008a) *Framing the Contribution of the Allied Health Professionals.* London, Department of Health.

Department of Health (2008b) *Modernising Allied Health Professions (AHP) Careers: A Competence Based Career Framework.* London, Department of Health.

Evetts, J. (2002) 'New directions in state and international professional occupations: Discretionary decision making and acquired regulation'. *Work, Employment and Society* 16(2), pp. 341–353.

Evetts, J. (2011) 'A new professionalism? Challenges and opportunities'. *Current Sociology* 59(4), pp. 406–422.

Freidson, E. (1970) *Professional Dominance: The Social Structure of Medical Care.* New York, Atherton Press.

Freidson, E. (1988) *Profession of Medicine: A Study of the Sociology of Applied Knowledge.* London, University of Chicago Press.

Getty, J. (2010) 'Medical job titles: What's in a name?' *The Telegraph,* 13th October.

Goldacre, B. (2004) 'It's all in a title'. *The Guardian,* 16th September.

Hawkes, N. (2004) '"Consultant" treading on doctors' toes'. *The Times,* p. 15.

Hugman, R. (1991) *Power in the Caring Professions.* Basingstoke, Macmillan.

Humphreys, J., *et al.* (2009) 'Improving workforce retention: Developing an integrated logic model to maximise sustainability of small rural and remote health care services'. *Canberra: Australian Primary Health Care Research Institute.* http://files.aphcri.anu.edu.au/research/full_report_10797.pdf (last accessed 28 January 2016).

Kelly, J. C., P. J. Groarke, E. Flanagan, J. Walsh and M. M. Stephens (2011) 'Foot and ankle surgery: The Achilles heel of medical students and doctors'. *The Foot* 21, pp. 109–113.

King, O., S. Nancarrow, A. Borthwick and S. Grace (2015) 'Contested professional role boundaries in health care: a systematic review of the literature'. *Journal of Foot and Ankle Research* 8(1), pp. 1–9.

Kitto, S., J. Chesters, J. Thistlethwaite and S. Reeves (2011) *Sociology of Interprofessional Health Care Practice: Critical Reflections and Concrete Solutions.* New York, Nova Science Publishers.

Kuhlmann, E. and M. Saks (2008) *Rethinking Professional Governance: International Directions in Healthcare.* Bristol, Polity Press.

Larkin, G. (1988) 'Medical dominance in Britain: Image and historical reality'. *The Millbank Quarterly* 66(Suppl 2), pp. 117–132.

Larkin, G. (1995) 'State control and the health professions in the United Kingdom: Historical perspectives.' In T. Johnson, G. Larkin and M. Saks (eds) *Health Professions and the State in Europe*. London, Oxford University Press.

Larson, M. (1977) *The Rise of Professionalism: A Sociological Analysis*. London, University of California Press.

Liljegren, A. (2012) 'Key metaphors in the sociology of professions: occupations as hierarchies and landscapes'. *Comparative Sociology* 11(1), pp. 88–112.

Macnicol, M. (2002) 'Warning on podiatrists "posing" as surgeons'. *Hospital Doctor*, 23rd May.

Moran, M. (2002) 'Health professions in international perspective'. In J. Allsop and M. Saks (eds) *Regulating the Health Professions*. London, Sage.

Morey, J. C., *et al.* (2002) 'Error reduction and performance improvement in the emergency department through formal teamwork training: Evaluation results of the MedTeams project'. *Health Services Research* 37(6), pp. 1553–1581.

Nancarrow, S. and A. Borthwick (2005) 'Dynamic professional boundaries in the healthcare workforce'. *Sociology of Health & Illness* 27(7), pp. 897–919.

Nielson, I. (2014) *Rural and Remote Generalist: Allied Health Project*. Greater Northern Australia Regional Training Network.

Noordegraaf, M. (2007) 'From "Pure" to "Hybrid" professionalism: Present-day professionalism in ambiguous public domains'. *Administration and Society* 39(6), pp. 761–785.

Quilty, S., D. Valler and J. Attia (2014) 'Rural general physicians: Improving access and reducing costs of health care in the bush'. *Australian Health Review* 38(4), pp. 420–424.

Rawlins, R. D. (2011) 'Non-doctors' use of the title "consultant podiatric surgeon" DOES mislead patients'. *British Medical Journal online* doi: 10.1136/bmj.d4241.

Saks, M. (1983) 'Removing the blinkers? A critique of recent contributions to the sociology of professions'. *Sociological Review* 31(1), pp. 1–21.

Saks, M. (2013a) 'The limitations of the Anglo-American sociology of the professions: A critique of the current neo-Weberian orthodoxy'. *Knowledge, Work and Society* 1(1), pp. 13–31.

Saks, M. (2013b) 'Regulating the English healthcare professions: Zoos, circuses or safari parks?' *Journal of Professions and Organization*. doi: 10.1093/jpo/jot001.

Saunders, C. (2011) 'Turf war over physician assistants'. *Medical Journal of Australia* 194, pp. 256–258.

Smith, R. and J. Duffy (2010) 'Developing a competent and flexible workforce using the Calderdale Framework'. *International Journal of Therapy and Rehabilitation* 17(5), pp. 254–262.

Stressing, S. and A. Borthwick (2014) 'The impact of workforce redesign policies on role boundaries in "generalist" podiatry practice: Expert member views within the professional body'. *Journal of Foot and Ankle Research* 7(52). Online: doi:10.1186/s13047-014-0052-7.

UK Government (1983) *The Medical Act*. London, The Stationery Office.

Wakerman, J. and J. S. Humphreys (2011) 'Sustainable primary health care services in rural and remote areas: Innovation and evidence'. *Australian Journal of Rural Health* 19(3), pp. 118–124.

Ward, R. and A. Akhtar (2011) *Walker and Walker's English Legal System*. Oxford, Oxford University Press.

Willis, E. (1989) *Medical Dominance: The Division of Labour in Australian Healthcare* (2nd edn). London, George Allen & Unwin.

Willis, E. (2006) 'Introduction: Taking stock of medical dominance'. *Health Sociology Review* 15(5), pp. 421–431.

Zetka, J. R. (2003) *Surgeons and the Scope*. London, Cornell University Press.

Zetka, J. R. (2011) 'Establishing specialty jurisdictions in medicine: The case of American obstetrics and gynaecology'. *Sociology of Health & Illness* 33(6), pp. 837–852.

24

Professional identity and social work

Stephen A. Webb

Introduction

Issues of professional identity in social work have been vexed by conceptual ambiguity, lack of consensus about core attributes and problems in identifying what counts in the constitution of identity. Studies have tended to focus on the following matters: social workers' professional identity formation; the framing of key tensions around social workers' professional identity; issues which convey the narrative represented by social workers in talking about their role, values and work; and the context in which professional identity is formed in preparation for front-line practice. This muddled terrain is further complicated by the fact that several competing theoretical perspectives have been deployed to help make sense of matters of professional identity. At a practical level, the extent to which front-line workers have to fulfil a narrow set of socially coded values, regulated by a professional body, as part of identity maintenance has been a troublesome and much debated matter for social work. As will be shown in this chapter, it is fair to say that issues of professional identity in social work are contestable. A mix of competing rationalities and values are involved in attempts to locate the specificities of front-line practice, social work education and policy which make up professional identity for social work.

Professional identity – or how a social worker thinks of herself or himself as a social worker – is often defined as a practitioner's professional self-concept based on attributes, beliefs, values, motives and experiences (Ibarra, 1999; Schein, 1978). Despite a growing interest in matters of professional identity in social work, researchers know relatively little about how identities are formed among practitioners who carry out complex, challenging and often ambiguous public sector functions (Baxter, 2011). The aim of this chapter is to examine the concept of professional identity as it relates to social work. This will facilitate greater theoretical clarity and map possible alternatives, such as the institutional logics perspective, to afford a better understanding of the field of social work. The chapter focuses on the significance of professional socialisation, workplace culture, boundary maintenance, jurisdiction disputes and inter-professional tensions with health, education and the police. The chapter highlights the importance of beliefs as well as attachment and sense of belonging for the study of professional identity (Rothausen *et al.*, 2015). Professional identification is often associated with increased personal accomplishment. The importance of identity formation as mainly social and relational in nature is attenuated.

Here it is concerned with narratives of recognition, trust, gossip and organisational rituals within hierarchal settings.

From these different perspectives, it is apparent that the notion of professional identity is a complex one, and a cursory examination of the literature reveals that there is a great deal of contestability and range of views about the significance of identity in social work and professional development. Moreover, as will be seen, professional identity is not a stable entity; it is an ongoing process of interpretation and customisation which is shaped by contextual workplace factors. In this respect, identity formation is viewed as more interactive and more problematic than the relatively straightforward adoption of the role or category of 'professional social worker'. Given the historical and increasing importance of professionals in all types of organisations (Wallace, 1995), and given the centrality of identity in how practitioners make sense of and 'enact' their workplace environments (see Weick, 1995), addressing issues of professional identity construction and 'being professional' is timely. In the section which follows, attention is drawn to the contestable nature of professional identity and the way this impacts on its various characterisations in social work.

Professional identity: background to a contestable concept

The literature on professional identity has consistently revealed its contestable and changing nature. This is in part due to the rapid changes that occur in organisational, workplace and professional life and the wider links to economic and political change. Professional identity does not come ready-made but is continually fashioned in the movements along ways of organisational and professional life. We need to consider the constant re-localisation, re-embodiment and re-distribution of social worker as practitioner to get a grasp on the dynamics of professional identity. As Dent and Whitehead explain:

> Being professional becomes more than a means by which the individual navigates the increasingly choppy waters of organizational life. Being professional suggests a context of meaning and values, whereby the lawyer, judge, lecturer, human resource manager, banker and so on is experientially located through the particular narratives and discourses which accrue with and around that identity position.
>
> *(2002, p. 5)*

The fact that individuals occupy multiple subject positions and shift, manoeuvre and negotiate within and across these adds to the complexity of thinking about professional identity. This leads Dent and Whitehead to conclude that 'Identity is neither stable, nor a final achievement' (2002, p. 11).

The literature on identity and identification in organisational settings (Ashforth *et al.*, 2008) suggests two core phenomena are at work in identity formation and maintenance: belonging and attachment. This formulation is reflected in the institutional logics conception of identity discussed below (Thornton and Ocasio, 2008; Thornton *et al.*, 2012). Ashforth and Mael's (1989) classic study summarises the precursors and consequences of professional identity as consisting of three main factors: distinctiveness, prestige and the salience of out-groups. Distinctiveness refers to a profession's values and practices in relation to other comparable groups (teachers, nurses or occupational therapists); prestige, the hallmark of professional identity, is the second factor with an emphasis on status, reputation and credentials. The final antecedent factor, which again highlights the significance of relational factors, is identified as salience of the out-group, whereby awareness of the out-group, those who do not belong, reinforces an awareness of one's in-group (1989, p. 21).

As Payne notes:

> The identity of the profession of social work has often seemed unclear and contested, and social workers in the UK have felt their identity to be bound up in specific roles provided for in legislation, rather than in broader conceptions of their potential role.
>
> *(2006, p. 138)*

Nevertheless, there are plenty of examples of an increased uptake and recognition of the significance of professional identity for social work in statements from associations, groups and researchers across the international stage (Wiles, 2013; Levy *et al.*, 2014). In 2011, the European network group TiSSA (The international 'Social Work and Society' Academy*)* invited scholars and practitioners from different countries to share their experiences and a vision of professional identity which will impact on current social policies and promote participative welfare initiatives. The group claimed 'professional identity is continuously developed in the triangle of education, organisation and individual practice' (www.socmag.net/?p=494). The American Board of Examiners in Clinical Social Work (2002) position statement *Professional Development and Practice Competencies in Clinical Social Work* calls for practitioners to demonstrate 'evidence of the full integration of a professional identity and responsible professional role' (https://www.abecsw.org/images/Competen.PDF). A feature of the Australian Association of Social Workers' mission is the 'promotion of professional identity'. A South African report (2008) commissioned by the Department of Labour talked about factors which 'caused for social workers in South Africa over the past decade what many authors have referred to as a crisis of professional identity and confidence' (Lombard, 2005, p. 2). Woochan Shim and colleagues (2009) carried out an extensive empirical study of professional identity, job satisfaction, and retention of licensed social workers in South Korea. They showed that professional identity was significantly associated with enhanced job satisfaction. While research has internationally focused on matters of professional identity, few government policies have paid specific attention to its significance in delineating the parameters of social work practice.

A rare exception is Scotland's *Changing Lives: Report of the 21st Century Social Work Review* (2006), which made explicit references to the significance of professional identity in maintaining a central role for social work. The Report was described as the basis for 'the biggest overhaul of social work in Scotland for 40 years'. As William Roe, Chair of the 21st Century Social Work Review put it:

> The review group was asked to take a fundamental look at all aspects of social work and make recommendations on how services should be developed to meet the future needs of Scotland's people.
>
> *(2006, p. 2)*

The Report reflects the problems that beset social work and focused particularly on issues of professional identity. The report states:

> There is an urgent need for social work to clarify its professional identity in order to establish clear roles for individual social workers.
>
> *(2006, para. 8.4, p. 39)*

The Report goes further in identifying the core values and moral commitment in the make-up of social work's professional identity. The skills social workers possess are underpinned by this shared set of values.

> The professional identity of social work need not be inextricably linked to specific organisational structures. Rather, professional identity should be based more on core values and principles in order to distinguish the nature of the social worker's contribution from that of individuals working within other agencies and to protect against the threat of boundary erosion as the result of development in other professions. Issues of recruitment and retention to social work are inextricably linked to the issue of professional identity.
>
> *(2006, para. 8.5, p. 39)*

The danger of boundary erosion is recognised here but, as we shall see below, the research literature tends to maintain that professional identity is intimately locked into aspects of organisational culture. The Scottish review dramatically concluded:

> the 'crisis' in social work is mainly a matter of professional identity that impacts on recruitment, retention and the understanding of the profession's basic aims.
>
> *(2006, p. 8)*

The crisis in social work *is* regarded a crisis of professional identity. Whether issues of professional identity actually constitute a crisis for social work, or whether we are simply dealing with a matter of concern remains debatable. Evoking the language of crisis often occurs when a state of affairs does not comfortably fit with pre-existing categories or arrangements. Talk about crisis can either unsettle or stabilise professional boundaries, but it does have the effect of making the discursivity of social work more visible to public and politicians.

Professional socialisation, workplace relations and identity regulation

Being labelled 'unprofessional' is equivalent to striking the fear of God into many social work practitioners. Indeed, to be accused of being 'unprofessional' is used as a powerful shaming device. Social workers who transgress risk bringing their credibility, reputation and professionalism into question. In educational settings, social work students can be failed on fieldwork placements for 'being unprofessional'. 'Professional misconduct' is an offence likely to be investigated by the Health and Care Professions Council in England and Wales. Indeed, Grant and Kinman (2012) reported that social workers regarded it as 'unprofessional' to admit that traumatic cases affected them emotionally and that not mixing your personal life with work is considered as 'being professional'.

The significance of professional socialisation has consistently been acknowledged as a crucial factor in the formation of identity (Loseke and Cahill, 1986; Freund *et al.*, 2014). It is worth noting that a major criticism is that it regards professionals as subject to a deterministic process of moulding and as essentially passive recipients. Goldenberg and Iwasiw describe professionalisation as:

> a complex and interactive process by which the content of the professional role (skills, knowledge, behaviour) is learned and the values, attitudes, and goals integral to the profession and sense of occupational identity which are characteristic of a member of that profession are internalized.
>
> *(1993, p. 4)*

The principles of identity formation articulated in social work have recently been used to examine the process through which social workers acquire their professional identities.

Socialisation – with its complex networks of social interaction, role models and mentors, experiential learning, and explicit and tacit knowledge acquisition – influences each learner, causing them to gradually think, act, and feel like a social worker. Some research has discussed how role models provide professional identities that one can 'try on' to see if they fit (Ibarra, 1999). Helpful distinctions have emerged between *socialisation for work*, which corresponds primarily with experiences of qualifying professional education, and *socialisation by work*, which focuses on experiences *in situ* (Cohen-Scale, 2003). Normative protocols, rules and standards are learnt on a formal level (for example, work-based professional development training) and in informal contexts in contact with peer group, experienced role models and service users. This is a dynamic process whereby practitioners anticipate and pre-empt the actions of other social workers. The transformation process of newly qualified social workers to professionals is essentially an acculturation process during which the values, norms and performative rituals of the social work profession are gradually internalised (Hodgson, 2005; Grant *et al.*, 2016).

Identity work is pivotal in understanding how practitioners embed themselves into organisational life. It is through workplace cultures of socialisation that professional identities are partly developed in relation to discourses of recognition (practitioner competence and professional values), with newly qualified social workers displaying what they consider to be desirable professional identities of confidence, capability and suitability. Indeed, for some practitioners, 'being professional' and being oppositional are necessarily antithetical. This means that professional identity formation can act negatively and may not necessarily be a good thing when the possibility of organisational coercion comes into the frame. Workplace organisations exert influence on individual practitioners in part through identity and identification but also through the regulation of professional conduct. Professional identity exhibits a logic which inscribes 'autonomous' professional practice within a network of accountability and professional conduct which is governed at a distance. In social work, professionalism is autonomous to the extent to which the conditions of autonomy have already been inscribed in particular forms of conduct embodied in the notion of 'professional competence' and regulation (Fournier, 1999).

Professional conduct is deemed extremely important in social work, with accusations of being unprofessional having the effect of hardening an already risk-averse culture. As Fournier (2001) points out, the quest for professionalism reveals significant disciplinary tendencies. Professionalism can be understood as a disciplinary technique, one largely exercised through the label 'professional'. In the same way that no one wishes to be deemed incompetent, thus privileging the idea that given competencies are essential for a successful career, so no one wishes to be labelled unprofessional. Fournier argues that practitioners:

> will work harder and be more conscientious in the interests of the company if they believe themselves to be acting professionally, rather than as subordinates.
>
> *(2001, p. 118)*

Thus, as Dent and Whitehead remark: 'being professional' appears to act in the interests of all concerned and so doing becomes a universal mantra (2002, p. 3). As Goffman noted, 'being a professional' means adopting the 'rhetoric of training which marks off the professional from the layperson'. He says that 'the licensed practitioner is someone who is reconstituted by his learning experience and is now set apart from other men [sic]' (1959, p. 49). This means engaging in impression management and forming a visible identity in dress, attitude, vocabulary and empathy. For Goffman, speech, expressive behaviour, and demeanour embody intentions. In *Asylums*,

Goffman (1961) discussed how organisations instil tacit acceptance and conformity through inducements. In his work on face-saving, he emphasised how professionals are expected to use talk, with ritual care, to present an image of self-control and dignity. Anecdotally, it's often remarked how social workers struggle to detach the 'personal' from the 'professional' and how it's difficult not to take their work home with them. Reflecting on this mix of cognitive and affective work, De Montigny goes as far as to claim that 'Being a social worker is not just a job. It's a way of life' (1995, p. 57).

As Barbour and Lammers contend, the institutionalisation of a professional identity can be conceptualised as 'the emergence, establishment, and sedimentation of what it means to hold a particular position or engage in a particular activity in the context of the larger, generic notion of profession' (2015, p. 38). On-the-job learning activities are crucial in this respect. Emphasising the processual nature of power, Alvesson and Willmott comment on the phenomenon of identity regulation as a restrictive feature of organisational control (Alvesson, 2001; Alvesson and Willmott, 2002). They demonstrate how employees are enjoined to develop self-images, narrative repertoires and work orientations that are deemed congruent with narrow managerially defined objectives. The iteration of self-identity and identity work regulation is likely to be keenly felt for middle and service managers in social work as they are squeezed between different constituencies. Alvesson and Willmott's focus on identity extends and deepens themes developed within other analyses of normative institutional control. They develop empirical material to support and illustrate:

> how managerial intervention operates, more or less intentionally and in/effectively, to influence employees' self-constructions in terms of coherence, distinctiveness and commitment.
>
> *(2002, p. 619)*

They argue that organisational control is achieved through the self-positioning of employees within managerially driven discourses about work through which they may become more or less identified and committed. This leaves the distinct possibility that identity regulation is performed as much through micro practices, and is reflexively negotiated by practitioners, as it is through top-down processes.

I recall a recent visit to a local authority social services department in Scotland and a vivid manifestation of corporate regulation as it is increasingly assimilated into the physical workspaces of front-line social workers. I was told how practitioners were allowed to decorate their workspace but the colours used had to be explicitly the same as the corporate colours of the local authority organisation. Should their colour scheme not match the corporate colours, it would be removed. What was most surprising about this corporate socialisation was the manner in which it was accepted and indeed in some cases seen as a positive. It was imagined that colour-coded corporate uniformity contributed to a neat, tidy and ordered workplace environment, one that gave off an air of professionalism and one where the distractions of non-corporate colours were absent.

According to Schultz *et al.* (2000), however, it is not enough to insist on employee behaviour conforming to whatever management deems a desirable narrative or vision. The behaviour that supports a corporate reputation or brand needs to be more deeply rooted; it needs to be thoroughly embedded in the organisation's identity. Our corporate colour-coded social workers must feel the message they are sending with their behaviour, not just go through the motion of conformity. Indeed, studies of identity resistance have, according to Thomas (2008), contributed to an appreciation of the role of agency in resistance, extending the focus and definition of resistance to include more routinised, informal, and often inconspicuous forms in everyday professional practice. Kärreman and Alvesson (2009) imaginatively take this further in developing the concept of 'counter-resistance'. They maintain that professionals do in fact resist the pressures that public sector employers place upon them, but they internalise this resistance. Rather than jeopardise their position in the organisation by openly expressing their resistance, they develop an internal discourse which embodies their conflicting perceptions. Whilst employers may perceive that the professional is conforming to the organisational demands of micro-management practices, the suppression of this resistance can ultimately give way to sudden and unexpected ruptures of discontent.

It has been shown how professional identity is a vehicle for understanding the interaction between work organisations and identity (Alvesson *et al.*, 2008; Vough, 2012) and its consequences for the service users and organisations served by professionals (Korica and Molloy, 2010). Since professionals are organisationally situated, a better understanding of their identities needs to take differences in workplace culture, credentials and professional status into account. In social work, the differences between practitioners working in children and family teams and those working with disabled service users may be significant. Smith (2003), for example, considers the poor relation of residential child care to the rest of social work. He regards the former as marginalised in a professional training curriculum which fails to reflect the essential task of group care and is preoccupied with overriding child protection concerns of safety and regulation. Smith claims that:

> Any more discrete professional identity for residential child care will also need a pedagogy that supports the professional task. It should certainly draw on the academic disciplines of psychology and sociology which underpin social work training but would be usefully widened to include insights from education, philosophy and anthropology.
>
> *(2003, pp. 247–248)*

In emphasising the relation between reputational status as it is bound to various types of professional qualification (vocational versus formal learning) and workplace conditions, Smith goes on to say that this:

> marginalization is structurally reinforced in poorer conditions of service and through the proposed institutionalization of qualification structures of inferior status and dubious efficacy.
>
> *(p. 249)*

It is important to recognise that gender divisions and gender bias play a significant role in this context. Throughout the 1980s and 1990s, certification, registration and licensure for social workers – but not social care assistants – marched rapidly throughout the developed Western world. The social workers were often women who struggled to gain formal professional recognition and comparable pay conditions until the establishment of bodies like the General Social Care Council in the UK and the Council on Social Work Education (CSWE) in the USA. Men have been noticeably absent on the front line of services, but are more prominent in managerial roles. According to General Social Care Council (GSCC) figures, over 75 per cent of qualified social workers in England are female (*The Guardian*, 25 July 2014). In a UK study that looked at students' motivations to train as social workers, Furness (2007) found that, from 2002 to 2005, 83 per cent of total registrations for all pathways in social work were women. The idea that men's gendered identity is vulnerable and easily undermined when they do 'women's work' might be a significant factor in this respect. Practitioners' gender will play a significant role in the formation of professional identity. Given the care ethics of social work and its welfare role, it's likely that women social workers understand their gender and professional identities as compatible.

It's also important to mention here that there is a powerful 'practice wing' in social work often sourced by techniques invented in the field itself and readily accepted – aside from some conflicts with psychiatrists and clinical psychologists – outside of it. This accounts for significant internal tension within social work. Many qualifying programmes in social work are obsessive about so-called 'practice learning curricula' and heavily resourcing 'placement visits'. Clinical practice fieldwork predominates the US social work education curriculum. The introduction of structural and systemic family therapy techniques in the 1990s are good examples of this sort of skills-based practice orientation. External competitive pressures were evident with the shaping of this internal boundary making. There was a prevailing view, for example, that counselling psychology tended to produce practitioners who were better trained for direct work with clients. The production of 'professionally competent practitioners' who would engage with evaluative direct work such as risk assessment and behaviour modification techniques to protect the public was also crucial in this respect. In front-line practice, professionals and service users alike are more likely to be concerned with whether a social worker has the current skills and competencies needed to meet the service-user needs than with the social worker's academic knowledge base. In the UK, pressures of the increasingly dominant practice wing drove the BASW (British Association of Social Workers) in directions often unpalatable to academics dedicated to general theory and foundational concept building in social work.

That the dominance of this practice agenda may have pushed the academic and practice wings apart and in doing so weakened social work's intellectual jurisdiction by inhibiting theoretical originality and methodological innovation has not been properly researched. Neither have there been any studies on the way the hardening of the practice wing resulted in a professional bunker mentality within the academy and undermined social work's academic status and reputation with other traditional social science disciplines such as sociology and psychology. Nevertheless, there is no escaping the fact that academic credentials, especially with national research evaluation exercises, which are being carried out across a range of countries, proves a crucial resource for applied social work and keeps it closely tied to academic social work.

Institutional logics perspective and the interplay of structure and agency

This section discusses a contemporary approach to conceiving of professional identity for social work. It is suggested that we need a much richer understanding of how social workers locate themselves in micro relations and interpret their institutional context. Powell and Colyvas (2008) emphasise that these micro-institutional relations are fairly mundane, aimed at interpretation, alignment, and muddling through. With increasing refinement in conceptualising the relation between workplace and identity, the institutional logics perspective makes a rich and lively contribution to thinking about professional identity.

As Barbour and Lammers note:

> The concept of institutional logics is distinctively suited to the study of professional identity, because it provides resources for understanding the interplay of institutional and organizational structures *and* the communicative enactment and individual negotiation of professional identity and identification.

(2015, p. 14)

For this perspective, professional identity is thus embedded in a mix of different modes of institutional reasoning. The notion of a logic or rationality captures the existence of ideas of what it is to be a 'professional' that are independent from but related to, enacted in, and shaped by the day-to-day actions of practitioner professionals in particular workplace organisations.

The core assumption of the institutional logics approach is that:

> the interests, identities, values, and assumptions of individuals and organizations are embedded within prevailing institutional logics.
>
> *(Thornton and Ocasio, 2008, p. 100)*

These authors also observed that institutional logics provide a conceptual link between 'individual agency and cognition and socially constructed practices and rule structures' (p. 101). This perspective provides a useful trajectory of connecting professional identity to workplace cultures and public institutions. In developing ideas of Friedland and Alford (1991) and Thornton (2004), Thornton, Ocasio and Lounsbury show sources of identity to be the 'building blocks [that] specify the organizing principles that shape individual and organizational preferences' (2012, p. 54; Friedland, 2012) in workplace cultures. Identity, it is argued, conveys behavioural repertoires for individuals, including knowledge of the following:

> who they are, their logics of action, how they act, their vocabularies of motive, and what language is salient.
>
> *(Thornton et al., 2012, p. 54)*

Often these institutional logics can be in conflict or contradictory. Thus Blomgren and Waks (2015) report on the way that various rationalities incorporating a democratic logic, a professional logic, a managerial logic, and a market logic collide as micro processes of institutional complexity. This leaves open the distinct possibility of role conflict for professional social workers and particularly team leaders. Similarly, Sachs's (2001) study on teachers demonstrated how different institutional rationalities were at odds with each other in shaping professional identities. Two logics of democratic and managerial professionalism were identified. Democratic professionalism emerged from the teaching profession itself, while managerial professionalism was reinforced by employing authorities through their policies on professional development with their emphasis on accountability, performance and effectiveness.

Hybrid types of professional identity emerge from these institutional logics. The two identities characterised were the entrepreneurial-careerist and the activist identity. These identities were not fixed; at various times and in various contexts, teachers moved between or ambivalently conflated these two professional identities, creating role conflict. Studies of professional identity could usefully focus on contested, violated or changing aspects of professions to bring the salient factors into sharp relief. Indeed, Barley and Tolbert (1997) suggest researchers explicitly focus on:

> forces initially exogenous to the system under study that create disturbances – e.g., changes in technology, new regulations or laws, major economic shifts, etc.
>
> *(1997, pp. 103–104)*

The existence of contested institutional logics means that practitioners are more likely to accentuate beliefs about the constituting features of professional identity and various boundary roles. Thornton (2004) observed that professional identities are characterised by group affiliations as well as roles that are defined in part by other roles, so, for example, social workers' identities are sustained in part by the enactment of out-group roles by the police, care assistants, foster carers, administrators, teachers and occupational therapists, as well as by service users and carers.

Customisation of identity in workplace settings

One of the most influential and highly cited studies which adopts and sophisticates the institutional logics perspective is Pratt *et al.* (2006) 'Constructing professional identity: The role of work and identity learning cycles in the customization of identity among medical residents', which develops a process approach through which professional identity is constructed and negotiated. Here the importance of sense-making as doing, acting and interacting is emphasised. Thus the crux of any definition of professional identity must emphasise its relational properties. For Weick *et al.* (2005), conceptions of identity and institutional logics are relational, fashioned not only through projections of self and others' perceptions, but also through scripted interactions in relation to what others are 'supposed to do' in any given situation.

Our recent study of newly qualified social workers in Scotland elicited a similar pattern of identity splitting in accounts given of the first few months of employment in local authority social services (Grant *et al.*, 2016). The uncertainties surrounding the transition to work and the lack of a comfort zone which easily accommodates task functions meant that newly qualified social workers often resorted to scripts and accounts they'd previously procured in their qualifying training. It is likely that after several months in practice, newly qualified social workers will have moved from an *identity-patching* to an *identity-enriching* process. In the transmission of competences adapted to the job market, social validation and peer groups plays an important role in forming and maintaining professional identities. In the analysis of processes of identity customisation, Pratt *et al.* found that social validation took one of two forms:

> The first form was largely initiated by senior physicians and peers and involved validating how well a particular resident was performing as a resident. The second form of validation appeared to be initiated by the residents and involved identifying specific role models. Unlike identity customization processes, the validation processes were highly similar across the three groups of residents.
>
> *(2006, p. 254)*

In our study of newly qualified social workers, we similarly found they were able to assess their performance compared to their colleagues' through an active grapevine and shadowing of more experienced practitioners (Grant *et al.*, 2016). They often found this informal ready-at-hand networking and feedback on performance by colleagues more useful than formal evaluations and supervision. The informal contact of newly qualified social workers, notably through peer groups or shadowing, represents shared advantages, such as access to information, and a greater sense of professional similarity and expectations. Feedback through informal channels, gossip and stories helps form social workers' identities by shaping their behaviour and values. Much hinges on their symbolic and performative production. By learning what they, and others, are doing wrong and consequently how the work should be performed, they change how they view themselves as social workers. Although the room to manoeuvre is strictly limited, the 'states of worth' of a practitioner cannot be wholly predetermined; newly qualified social workers undertake reality tests, find stable references and codify institutional protocol; they have to interact and negotiate in order to discover their relative worth in the organisational setting (Stark, 2011).

Boundaries, partnership and multi-professional work

As Bourdieu shrewdly observed:

> What is at stake in the struggles about the meaning of the social world is power over the classificatory schemes and systems which are the basis for the representation of groups and therefore of their mobilization and demobilization.
>
> *(1984, p. 479)*

This gets at the heart of issues of professional identity and its boundary making. Boundaries, as involving both elements of social structure and process, are important to the study of professional identity because they mediate almost every aspect of organisational life. Abbott's (1988) study of professions, professional boundaries and turfs mapped fields of jurisdiction between those professions and turfs. His model helps explain inter-professional conflict. Professions pro-act and react by seizing openings and reinforcing or casting off their earlier jurisdictions:

> Professions' claims for legitimate control are judged by various 'audiences': the state, the public, co-workers in the workplace. These external judgments ratify professions' claims, thereby making them efficacious against competitors.
>
> *(Abbott, 2005, p. 246)*

Social work as conceived by Abbott is a complex turf which needs to be defended in a systems approach to professions. He deploys a 'network-constitutive approach' to examine the way social work emerges out of a set of social 'boundary groups' with different types of jurisdiction claims at stake (Abbott, 1995, p. 546). A typical example of boundary conflict and competing jurisdiction claims are tensions in child protection between the police and social work over access to national data and risk assessment of sex offenders. In the UK, multi-agency public protection arrangements (MAPPA) attempt to conflate professional roles but are often resisted by social workers because they impose a quasi criminal justice and authoritative statutory role. The police will typically informally control access to ViSOR (Violent and Sex Offender Register) – a computer system which provides a UK multi-agency information sharing tool – thus reducing the potential for sharing and storing critical information on sex offenders. The emerging integration agenda between health and social care will further test the silo effect of professional boundaries and territorial claims.

Professional territories and areas of responsibility are delineated, privileges acquired and assured, and claims on material resources enforced. Nesting occurs within professions but a danger for identity occurs when they lose their singular separation because of the overwhelming number of linkages binding them. As Hudson (2002) has observed, there are three critical areas in which these rivalries are played out between different professions:

- professional identity, jurisdiction and territory;
- relative status and power of professions;
- different patterns of discretion and accountability between professions.

Abbott focuses on the aspect of jurisdiction for social work, which is related to exclusivity and exclusion, that is, the ability to make discrete claims for expert knowledge and assure authority over a certain professional realm, agent or object. Professional success for social work depends on the ability to maintain jurisdictional control over the client-relevant expert knowledge, exercise the tactics of depredation and expand legitimate spheres of intervention. Legitimacy comes from the power over particular work tasks and functions and external recognition. Boundaries between social work, counselling and mental health professions and psychology are examples of the contested and divided nature of jurisdictional claims. Payne notes that the NICE (2004) guidance on palliative care, for example, defines four levels of psychological support, the lower levels provided by generic professionals, such as nurses and social workers, with more expert levels provided by accredited counsellors, which may include appropriately post-qualified social workers and psychologists (2006, p. 141). Specialist training plays a key role in this respect. Presently, in the UK, the British Prime Minister David Cameron is proposing dementia training for all health-care staff in an attempt to improve the quality of care (Perraudin, 2015). This will be provided to a range of health-care personnel from hospital porters to surgeons, but at the exclusion of social workers. In the process of client differentiation, dementia becomes a space of intervention, diagnosis, inference and treatment, which Abbott calls 'potentially professionalizable work' of coherent jurisdiction, previously:

> constituted under loose, commonsense understandings, such as 'getting dotty' before it became 'senile dementia', 'organic brain syndrome', and eventually 'Alzheimer's disease'.
>
> *(Abbott, 2005, p. 249)*

Contrary to Abbott's characterisation of the ubiquity of professional turf wars and of jurisdiction claims as perpetually in dispute, Payne is optimistic about the potential of multi-professional teams in providing coherence and solidity for social work identity. This, he imagines, bodes well for the integration agenda of health and social care in the UK. He contends that:

> social work's professional identity may be seen as fairly stable, emerging in patterns of relationships with other occupational groups, reducing the social need to establish and defend its institutional position. Multi-professional teams are a major site in which stable professional identities might emerge.
>
> *(2006, p. 140)*

Using the case of palliative social work, he points to the prospects of multi-professional case discussions and journal clubs where different professionals lead discussion of publications, contributing to a shared perception of the role of the different professions. The ways in which professional groups with a sense of identity can use such mechanisms to influence the shared conception of their own profession are discussed. In summarising the prospects of a more seamless inter-professional mix, Payne uses the notion of communities of practice to hail the possibility of practitioners effectively developing stable professional identities by negotiating knowledge and demonstrating practice in multi-professional teams, rather than trying to maintain professional boundaries (2006, p. 149). Based on an empirical study of general practitioners, community nurses and social workers in northern England, Hudson (2002) offers a similar optimistic account of the potential for inter-professional work and seamless integrated provision.

In empirically researching the related sub-field of health social work, Beddoe (2013) is less optimistic about the potential for inter-professional harmony. Examining the credentials of health social work in institutional settings, she shows how social work's claims for knowledge are weak, which in turn impacts on professional identity and status in multidisciplinary settings (McMichael, 2000). Focusing on issues such as hospital discharge, Beddoe reports on how integration will be dependent on organisational culture, including resource allocation and local perceptions of professional boundaries. Lymbery (2005) similarly argues that effective partnership working within health and social care will be hard to achieve, particularly in the light of significant differences in power and culture between various occupational groupings and the inherently competitive nature of professions jostling for territory in the same areas of activity. Complex power relations, inclusionary/exclusionary strategies, and inter-professional status dynamics come to the fore in this context. In the UK, much of the policy thrust has been at the level of inter-organisational working rather than at the level of inter-professional partnerships. The extent to which identities can be forged which transcend the traits of particular professions and provide the most effective basis for the delivery of integrated provision and the achievement of organisational outcomes remains unclear.

Abbott (1995) maintains that social work is perpetually at the mercy of changes in other professions. Following the logic of his argument, it's conceivable that social work will increasingly come to assume the role of a discipline which functions to make connections across boundaries of other disciplines. Connecting together services provided largely by other professions and on behalf of clients and users will become its primary function. Under this scenario and using Abbott's technical language, the function of social work increasingly takes on the form of what he calls 'advisory jurisdiction', that is, a weaker and less stable form of control based on professions already possessing independent jurisdictions of their own. With health and social care, for example, under advisory jurisdictions:

> one profession [social work] seeks a legitimate right to interpret, buffer or partially modify actions another profession [health] takes within its own full jurisdiction.
>
> *(Abbott, 1988, p. 75)*

Traditionally, this is referred to as the tension between the medical and social model often manifest in areas like mental health. Here we can envisage potential pressure of other occupations that occupy a broadly similar position to social work – e.g. nursing and occupational therapy – to claim aspects whose jurisdiction currently forms part of the social worker's role. In particular, this is likely to be the case with assessments of older people and those with a disability.

For Abbott, an advisory jurisdiction is the 'bellwether of inter-professional conflict', dual identities do not occur and hybridity leads to the professional control of one group over another (1988, p. 76). Historically, as Abbott points out:

> social workers have often conceded control to other professions, a cession that, for example, was quite explicitly made in psychiatric social work.
>
> *(1995, p. 559)*

The main conclusion is that since its main area of jurisdiction is heavily dependent on the state and government funding, 'the profession is perpetually in a precarious position' (1995, p. 560). This precarity is made even more fragile by the fact that the general public view social work as a 'helping profession' which works with the most feared and despised populations. Many of social work's clients are not so much dispossessed as politically controversial; not only criminals, the poor, and the mentally ill, but also the problem schoolchildren, the drunk drivers and the child abusers (Abbott, 1995, p. 561). In contradistinction to, say, nursing and teaching, the professional identity of social work continues to suffer in the public eye from their client associations.

Conclusion

This chapter has considered a number of important and complex issues that inform professional identity in social work. This is an area that has been under-researched and is influenced by personal beliefs and attributes, early socialisation experiences, and contextual workplace factors. The chapter has drawn attention to the value of the emerging institutional logics perspective to consider how social work organisations influence and shape cognition and action in front-line practitioners and agencies, and how they are in turn shaped by them. Perhaps the most decisive factor framing the agenda for social work around matters of professional identity in the UK is the important integration policy reform in health and social care. Care coordination and partnership arrangements, along with moves towards self-directed support and the personalisation of provision, are increasingly reframing key roles and tasks for different professionals. The prospect for what Abbott (2005) calls competing jurisdictional claims of expertise and knowledge within the system of professions makes working life increasingly uncertain for social work and thus brings matters of professional identity much more to the fore.

References

Abbott, A. (1988) *The System of Professions: An Essay on the Division of Expert Labor*, Chicago, IL: University of Chicago Press.

Abbott, A. (1995) 'Boundaries of social work or social work of boundaries?', *Social Service Review*, 69, pp. 545–562.

Abbott, A. (2005) 'Linked ecologies: States and universities as environments for professions', *Sociological Theory*, 23(3), pp. 245–274.

Alvesson, M. (2001) 'Knowledge work: Ambiguity, image and identity', *Human Relations*, 54(7), pp. 863–886.

Alvesson, M. and Willmott, H. (2002) 'Identity regulation as organizational control: Producing the appropriate individual', *Journal of Management Studies*, 39(5), pp. 619–644.

Alvesson, M., Ashcraft, K. L. and Thomas, R. (2008) 'Identity matters: Reflections on the construction of identity scholarship in organization studies', *Organization*, 15(1), pp. 5–28.

Ashforth, B. E. and Mael, F. (1989) 'Social identity theory and the organization', *The Academy of Management Review*, 14(1), pp. 20–39.

Ashforth, B. E., Harrison, S. H. and Corley, K. G. (2008) 'Identification in organizations: An examination of four fundamental questions', *Journal of Management*, 34(3), pp. 325–374.

Barbour, J. B. and Lammers, J. C. (2015) 'Measuring professional identity: A review of the literature and a multilevel confirmatory factor analysis of professional identity constructs', *Journal of Professions and Organization*, 2(1), pp. 38–60.

Barley, S. R. and Tolbert, P. (1997) 'Institutionalization and structuration: Studying the links between action and institution', *Organization Studies*, 18(1), pp. 93–117.

Baxter, J. (2011) *Public Sector Professional Identities: A Review of the Literature*, Milton Keynes, UK: Open University.

Beddoe, L. (2013) 'Health social work: Professional identity and knowledge', *Qualitative Social Work*, 12(1), pp. 24–40.

Bourdieu, P. (1984) *Distinctions: A Social Critique of the Judgment of Taste*, translated by Richard Nice, Harvard, NY: Harvard University Press.

Blomgren, M. and Waks, C. (2015) 'Coping with contradictions: Hybrid professionals managing institutional complexity', *Journal of Professions and Organization*, 2(1), pp. 78–102.

Cohen-Scale, V. (2003) 'The influence of family, social, and work socialization on the construction of the professional identity of young adults', *Journal of Career Development*, 29(4), pp. 237–249.

De Montigny, G. A. J. (1995) *Social Working: An Ethnography of Front-line Practice*, Toronto: University of Toronto Press, Scholarly Publishing.

Dent, M. and Whitehead, S. (eds) (2002) *Managing Professional Identities: Knowledge, Performativities and the 'New' Professional*, London: Routledge.

Fournier, V. (1999) 'The appeal to "professionalism" as a disciplinary mechanism', *The Sociological Review*, 47(2), pp. 280–307.

Fournier, V. (2001) 'Amateurism, quackery and professional conduct: the constitution of 'proper' aromatherapy practice'. In M. Dent and S. Whitehead (eds), *Managing Professional Identities: Knowledge, Performativities and the 'New' Professional*, London: Routledge, pp. 116–137.

Friedland, R. (2012) 'Book review: Patricia H. Thornton, William Ocasio and Michael Lounsbury 2012 The Institutional Logics Perspective: A new approach to culture, structure, and process', *Management*, 15(5), pp. 582–595.

Friedland, R. and Alford, R. R. (1991) 'Bringing society back in: Symbols, practices, and institutional contradictions'. In W. W. Powell and P. J. DiMaggio (eds), *The New Institutionalism in Organizational Analysis*, Chicago, IL: University of Chicago Press, pp. 232–263.

Freund, A., Cohen, A., Blit-Cohen, E. and Dehan, N. (2014) 'Professional socialization and professional commitment in social work students: A longitudinal study', *Academy of Management Proceedings*, 2(1) http://proceedings.aom.org/content/2014/1/10679 (last accessed 29 January 2016).

Furness, S. (2007). 'An enquiry into students' motivations to train as social workers in England', *Journal of Social Work*, 7(2), pp. 239–253.

Goffman, E. (1959) *The Presentation of Self in Everyday Life*, New York: Doubleday.

Goffman, E. (1961) *Asylums: Essays on the Social Situation of Mental Patients and Other Inmates*, Garden City, NY: Anchor Books.

Goldenberg, D. and Iwasiw, C. (1993) 'Professional socialization of nursing students as an outcome of a senior clinical preceptorship experience', *Nurse Education Today*, 13(1), pp. 3–15.

Grant, L. and Kinman, G. (2012) 'Enhancing wellbeing in social work students: Building resilience in the next generation', *Social Work Education*, 31(5), pp. 605–621.

Grant, S., Sheridan, L. and Webb, S. A. (2016) 'Newly qualified social workers' readiness for practice in Scotland', *British Journal of Social Work*, in press.

Hodgson, D. (2005) 'Putting on a professional performance: Performativity, subversion and project management', *Organization*, 12(1), pp. 51–68.

Hudson, B. (2002) 'Interprofessionality in health and social care: The Achilles heel of partnership?', *Journal of Interprofessional Care*, 16(1), pp. 7–17.

Ibarra, H. (1999) 'Provisional selves: experimenting with image and identity in professional adaptation', *Administrative Science Quarterly*, 44(1), pp. 764–791.

Kärreman, D. and Alvesson, M. (2009) 'Resisting resistance: Counter-resistance, consent and compliance in a consultancy firm', *Human Relations*, 62(8), pp. 1115–1144.

Korica, M. and Molloy, E. (2010) 'Making sense of professional identities: Stories of medical professionals and new technologies', *Human Relations*, 63(12), pp. 1879–1901.

Levy, D., Shlomo, S. B. and Itzhaky, H. (2014) 'The building blocks of professional identity among social work graduates', *Social Work Education*, 33(6), pp. 744–759.

Lombard, A. (2005) 'Impact of social services on human, social and economic development and the promotion of human rights in South Africa', *Social Work/Maatskaplike Werk*, 41(3), pp. 2–15.

Loseke, D. R. and Cahill, S. E. (1986) 'Actors in search of a character: student social workers' quest for professional identity', *Symbolic Interaction*, 9(2), pp. 245–258.

Lymbery, M. (2005) 'United we stand? Partnership working in health and social care and the role of social work in services for older people', *British Journal of Social Work*, 36 (7), pp. 1119–1134.

McMichael, M. (2000) 'Professional identity and continuing education: A study of social workers in hospital settings', *Social Work Education*, 19(2), pp. 175–183.

Payne, M. (2006) 'Identity politics in multiprofessional teams palliative care social work', *Journal of Social Work*, 6(2), pp. 137–150.

Perraudin, F. (2015) 'David Cameron announces dementia training for all NHS staff', *The Guardian*, 21 February. www.theguardian.com/society/2015/feb/21/david-cameron-dementia-training-nhs-staff.

Powell, W. W. and Colyvas, J. A. (2008) 'Microfoundations of institutional theory'. In R. Greenwood, C. Oliver, R. Suddaby and K. Sahlin (eds), *The Sage Handbook of Organizational Institutionalism*, London: Sage.

Pratt, M. G., Rockmann, K. W. and Kaufmann, J. B. (2006) 'Constructing professional identity: The role of work and identity learning cycles in the customization of identity among medical residents', *Academy of Management Journal*, 49(2), pp. 235–262.

Rothausen, T. J., Henderson, K. E., Arnold, J. K. and Malshe, A. (2015) 'Should I stay or should I go? Identity and well-being in sensemaking about retention and turnover', *Journal of Management*, published online: doi: 10.1177/0149206315569312.

Sachs, J. (2001) 'Teacher professional identity: Competing discourses, competing outcomes', *Journal of Education Policy*, 16(2), pp. 149–161.

Schein, E. H. (1978) *Career Dynamics: Matching Individual and Organizational Needs*, Reading, MA: Addison-Wesley.

Schultz, M., Hatch, M. and Larsen, M. H. (2000) *The Expressive Organization: Linking Identity, Reputation, and the Corporate Brand*, Oxford: Oxford University Press.

Scottish Executive (2006) *Changing Lives: Report of the 21st Century Social Work Review*, Edinburgh: Scottish Executive.

Shim, W. S. and Hwang, M. J. (2009) 'Professional identity, job satisfaction, and retention of licensed social workers in Korea', *Asia Pacific Journal of Social Work*, 19(1), pp. 82–95.

Smith, M. (2003) 'Towards a professional identity and knowledge base: Is residential child care still social work?', *Journal of Social Work*, 3(2), pp. 235–252.

Smith, M. (2005) 'Applying ideas from learning and teaching in higher education to develop professional identity: The case of the MSc in advanced residential child care', *Child and Youth Care Forum*, 34 (4), pp. 261–279.

Stark, D. (2011) *The Sense of Dissonance: Accounts of Worth in Economic Life*, Princeton, NJ: Princeton University Press.

Thomas, R. (2008) 'Critical management studies on identity: Mapping the terrain'. In M. Alvesson, T. Bridgman and H. Willmott (eds), *The Oxford Handbook of Critical Management Studies*, Oxford, Oxford University Press.

Thornton, P. (2004) *Markets From Culture: Institutional Logics and Organizational Decisions in Higher Education Publishing*, Stanford, CA: Stanford University Press.

Thornton, P. and Ocasio, W. (2008) 'Institutional logics'. In R. Greenwood, C. Oliver, K. Sahlin and R. Suddaby (eds), *The Sage Handbook of Organizational Institutionalism*, Thousand Oaks, CA: Sage, pp. 99–128.

Thornton, P., Ocasio, W. and Lounsbury, M. (2012) *The Institutional Logics Perspective: A New Approach to Culture, Structure and Process*, Oxford: Oxford University Press.

Vough, H. (2012) 'Not all identifications are created equal: Exploring employee accounts for workgroup, organizational, and professional identification', *Organization Science*, 23(1), pp. 778–800.

Wallace, J. (1995) 'Corporatist control and organisational commitment among professionals: The case of lawyers working in law firms', *Social Forces*, 73(3), pp. 811–840.

Weick, K. (1995) *Sensemaking in Organizations*, Thousand Oaks, CA: Sage.

Weick, K., Sutcliffe, K. and Obstfeld, D. (2005) 'Organizing and the process of sensemaking', *Organization Science*, 16(4), pp. 409–421.

Wiles, F. (2013) 'Not easily put into a box: constructing professional identity', *Social Work Education*, 32(7), pp. 854–866.

25

Journalism and its professional challenges

Christiane Schnell

1. Introduction

During recent decades, it has become particularly evident that professions do not exist in a vacuum independent of social, economic, political, or technological developments, but rather they experience fundamental structural changes due to the transformation of their contextual conditions. This is even more true of the field of journalism, whose professional status has always been fragile. As journalism has never been able to develop a stable monopoly of jurisdiction, Abbott has described it as a 'permeable occupation' (Abbott, 1988, p. 225). Legally, journalism is an 'open profession', because preventing anyone from expressing themselves in the media by demanding a licence or a particular qualification would come into conflict with the fundamental right to freedom of expression. Nevertheless, journalism has developed a professional ideology that claims objectivity and autonomy and assumes the role of a publicly legitimized gatekeeping authority in media communication (Lewis, 2012).

From today's perspective, the professionalization of journalism can be best understood in relation to the development of the mass media during the twentieth century. During that time, journalists established themselves as experts of media communication, and their professionalization was based on controlling content creation, in particular in respect to 'the news'. Journalism grew as an occupational group and functional role with the technological development and market expansion of the media system, from press to radio broadcasting to television. However, the rise of new media affects journalism much more fundamentally than earlier changes to the media system ever did.

Digital technology has changed newsroom processes and given journalists new tools. New outlets have emerged within the traditional media and in new media production, which are competing and accomplishing conventional types of publication (Witchge and Nygren, 2009, p. 41). Therefore, journalists increasingly have to be able to work in different formats and to handle many types of technology, since internet production requires new working routines and since news selection differs from the traditional outlets. Nevertheless, the principles of new media have further blurred the boundaries of journalism; the relationship between production and consumption and between professionals and amateurs has become highly contested. Moreover, the progressing commercialization of the media challenges the concept of professionalism and professional identity in this field. Journalists are becoming increasingly torn between the contradictory demands of economic profitability, taking political positions, and the imperatives of proper intellectual work. This has been particularly pronounced since the balance between financial and journalistic motives has changed towards global competition in the course of the internationalization of the media system.

This chapter discusses the dimensions of professionalism and the professionalization of journalism, beginning with a brief summary of the various historical pathways of its professionalization in the Western hemisphere (Section 2). Because of the structural openness or permeability of the occupation, journalists refer to professional values in order to legitimize their claim for autonomy and a normative role. Section 3 therefore deals with the ideal-typical traits of the professional ideology. The professionalization of journalism implies the development of an academic discipline in terms of research, building up a theoretical body, and establishing academic education. How academization, professional identity and skill development are interrelated in this process is analysed in Section 4. After dealing with the already mentioned changes resulting from the digitization and commercialization of the media in Section 5, two interpretations of the current development of journalism are discussed (Section 6). What the future perspectives of professional journalism might be is considered in the seventh and final section.

2.   Pathways of journalistic professionalization

The development of the journalistic profession in Western democratic societies has followed historically different pathways but has been influenced by the Anglo-American model. Therefore, the historically rooted institutional conditions have served as nation-bound frameworks in which distinct profiles of journalism emerged throughout the twentieth century. In the literature, three to four main historical-institutional concepts of Western journalism are described (Esser and Umbricht, 2013; Mancini, 2005; Polumbaum, 2010; Williams, 2005).

The Anglo-American model is discussed as the dominant model of professional journalism (Mancini, 2005). It is called the 'liberal' or 'social responsibility model' (Siebert *et al.*, 1956) or the 'professional model' (Tunstall, 1977) and has become a reference model for measuring and judging journalistic behaviours in other countries. Authors such as Esser and Umbricht (2013) refer here to the ideal-typical concept of news work, which is outlined in the article 'Journalism as an Anglo-American invention' (Chalaby, 1996). From today's perspective, it is obvious that the 'objectivity' that characterizes this model can first be understood in the sense of political neutrality. It emphasizes objectivity, implying that news should be recorded in a detached and neutral way (Schudson, 2001). Concerning journalistic practice, a value orientation is asserted that stresses both objectivity and a reporting style distinct from comment or interpretation (Mancini, 2005). The frame of journalism as a 'watchdog' over politics is rooted in the liberal ideology and corresponds with the commercialized structure of the Anglo-American press. Journalism claims professional autonomy but isn't distinctively concerned with the limitations of journalistic freedom resulting from market regulation and economic dependencies.

Journalism studies have stressed the contrast between Anglo-American professionalism and continental European traditions in journalism. However, the Anglo-American ideal of journalistic professionalism has been progressively imported and adapted in newsrooms throughout continental Europe. The general picture has also changed with the expansion and internationalization of media production in recent decades. In order to understand the similarities and differences of the journalistic field, the systems of media production and the social and political preconditions for professionalization in Europe are still of interest. One line of differentiation is drawn between a highly politicized literary style in south or central

Europe and a corporatist style allocated to the more northern European countries (Hallin and Mancini, 2004).

France and Italy are labelled typical representatives of the southern European pathway and are characterized by a greater emphasis on interpretation and commentary than on factual reporting. A mix of 'news and views' is typical of these journalistic traditions, implying that opinion is prioritized over reportage (Chalaby, 1996). This style is based on deep-seated literary roots that have continued to exist in a context of elite orientation and limited readership. It corresponds with newspapers' chronically weak financial situation and a greater dependency on state aid and political favouring (Mancini, 2000; Esser and Umbricht, 2013, 991f.). Strong press–party ties and a comparatively late development of journalism as an independent profession are the reason that the professional culture of 'watchdog reporting' has not been able to prosper properly in this context. The literature also indicates that the media's intricate involvement in this polarized context tends towards its misuse in political disputes.

The corporatist model is based on the principle of consensus democracies with an emphasis on compromise and power sharing. This model spans the German-speaking, Benelux, and Scandinavian countries. With some variation, the political system in these countries is characterized by a wider range of political parties and organized groups that ideally resolve their differences in partnership and come to consensual decisions through bargaining and negotiation. This socio-political framework has supported the development of strong ties between newspapers, political parties, and organized social forces, and thus also a partisan reporting style. Though press partisanship might have weakened over recent decades, this political structure and 'offshoots of the literary tradition stemming from southern countries' has featured opinionated reporting (Esser and Umbricht, 2013, p. 991; Mancini, 2005). Different from the more polarized Mediterranean system, the literary tradition is less pronounced here, and the connections to politics are explained with a consensus around welfare state democracy instead of instrumentalization. In other words, the ideal of a neutral professionalism and information-oriented journalism has prevailed in these corporatist news systems against the background of a moderate degree of external pluralism and a legacy of commentary-orientated journalism. Switzerland and Germany are typical representatives of the liberal version of corporatism, with an intermediate position between the central European model and the Anglo-American system. This could be explained by Switzerland and Germany's geographic proximity to France and Italy and the direct American influence on German media politics after the Second World War (Esser and Umbricht, 2013, p. 992).

Last but not least, the British model is also differentiated from the type of professional journalism developed in the United States. It is described as a mixed model that apparently incorporates elements from more than one historical-institutional pathway. A relatively strong segment of sensational, negative, and interpretative journalism is considered to characterize the British case. Therefore, the idea of pure journalistic professionalism is traditionally relativized and has led to a rather partisan national press (Hallin and Mancini, 2004).

This brief overview indicates how journalistic cultures have been influenced by the interplay between society, political frameworks, and the media system. The concept of professionalized journalism was born within the context of the Anglo-American system, and the professionalization of the journalistic occupation during the twentieth century was characterized by the merging of the standards of professional journalism in the varying media systems. The ideology of journalism as an independent profession was established in the Western hemisphere, in particular, between the 1960s and the 1990s (Schnell, 2007). Regarding the external and internal understanding of journalistic professionalism, the core values of this role model are still the reference points. They justify the special social status of journalists and even the current challenges of professional journalism due to the ongoing changes of media production and consumption and are evaluated related to these values.

3. Professional ideology

During the twentieth century, journalism developed as an academic-based discipline and an object of systematic self-reflection. A consensual body of knowledge and a widely shared understanding of key theories and methods emerged. Reconstructing the relation between media and society, the functional role of journalism was interpreted as a gatekeeping authority in the media system. Journalists drew upon their expert role and their responsibility for 'what the world needs to know' as an important feature of democracy.

Even though a lack of coherence is problematized and discussed in the literature, the conceptualization of journalists as representatives of the public is the main legitimization for journalists' claims of professional autonomy (Breen, 1998; Löffelholz, 2000; McNair, 2003; Deuze, 2004). As the boundaries of journalism are 'permeable' and not institutionally secured, journalists tend to refer to professional standards to distinguish themselves from other occupational groups and sustain some operational closure, thereby keeping outside forces at bay (Deuze, 2005, p. 447). Moreover, the ideology of professionalism has been identified as an instrument in the hands of journalists to neutralize the hierarchy in news-organization and media corporations (Soloski, 1990).

The paradoxical consequence of the absence of institutional boundaries in journalism has been a very distinct and narrow definition of what a 'real' journalist is and what parts of media production are considered examples of 'real' journalism. As journalism developed with the industrialization and emergence of the press as the first mass medium, the ideal of journalism refers to news work and newspaper journalism and more or less ignores the diversity of journalistic work, which often includes editorials, comments, reviews, consumer advice, and also domains outside that of 'hard news', such as entertainment, celebrity and everyday life. Most scholarly work on journalism has focused on institutional news journalism, and even the research on so-called 'alternative' journalism suggests that journalists across genres and media types invoke more or less the same ideal-typical value system when discussing and reflecting on their work (Van Zoonen, 1998; Sparks, 1992). These evaluations have shifted subtly over time yet have always served to maintain the dominant sense of what journalism is (and should be) (Deuze, 2005, p. 444; McNair, 2003).

Therefore, five discursively constructed ideal-typical traits that form the core values of the professional ideology of journalism can be identified (Deuze 2005, pp. 447ff.; Golding and Elliott 1979; Kovach and Rosenstiel, 2001): the public service ideal, objectivity, autonomy, immediacy, and ethics.

The *public service ideal* is the main legitimizing feature of journalism, implying that journalists share a sense of 'doing it for the public'. The figure of the 'watchdog' or the claim of a fourth estate stands for this self-perception. Overall, journalistic work is interpreted as important to the public – as consumers but even more as citizens – insofar as journalism's public task is conceptualized as promoting democratic deliberation (Deuze, 2005; Merritt, 1995).

Objectivity is a key element, particularly in Anglo-American professional self-perception (Mindich, 1998). Although recent approaches question whether any information is objective in the sense of value neutrality, academics and journalists revisit this value through synonymous concepts such as fairness, professional distance, detachment, and impartiality in order to define and legitimize what media practitioners do. The claim of objectivity makes professionals immune to critique, but, as Deuze (2005) reports, the critical reappraisal of objectivity also supports it as an 'ideological cornerstone of journalism' (p. 448).

Of course, the claim of professional *autonomy* plays an important role in the field of journalism. As in the established professions, autonomy is demanded in different directions and encompasses freedom of opinion, free media, and protection from censorship as well as the independence of journalistic work from market forces and newsroom hierarchies. Whereas the general claim for autonomy unifies editors, media companies, and journalists, it is supposed to defend the interests of journalists within their working environment so that they will not have to subordinate themselves to editors' expectations. Instead, this autonomy could strengthen journalists' need to be adequately supported in their work, probably through further training and education (Weaver, 1998). Because of the fragility of editorial autonomy, changing working conditions resulting from technological innovations tend to be met with doubts (Singer, 2004).

Immediacy has always played an important role in the journalistic working culture. Fast decision-making and hastiness are part of the professional habitus, corresponding with the defining principle of 'news' – the novelty of information. With regard to the technological development and the emergence of real-time publishing in the so-called 'non-stop' 24/7 digital environment, the notion of speed has become more ambivalent as it increases the conflict between prudence and fact (Deuze, 2005; Hall, 2001).

Last but not least, the development of a professional code of *ethics* has been another central element of the professionalization of journalism. Regardless of contextual differences, the commitment to truth and objectivity are key dimensions of ethical guidelines as they legitimize the claim of autonomy and societal trust and recognition (Hafez, 2002; Ryan, 2001). Historically, this process took place in the first half of the twentieth century. After the emergence of professional associations of journalists in many countries during the nineteenth century, first efforts were made to organize the journalistic field on an international level. In 1896 the 'Union Internationale des Associations de Presse' (UIAP) was founded in Budapest (Kutsch, 2008). The first formalization of a professional code of ethics was the adoption of the Code of Bordeaux by the International Federation of Journalists in 1956 (Nordenstreng and Topuz, 1989).

4.   Academization and skill development

Academization has been another important aspect of the professionalization of journalism, starting in the late nineteenth century, but mainly taking place in the second half of the twentieth century. Journalism studies have evolved principles of teaching, learning, and researching journalism, which were adopted at an international level (Deuze, 2005, p. 443). However, a persistent scepticism against academic journalism could be observed in the field until recently. To hold a university degree has been relatively common for journalists for quite some time, but often it would be from other academic areas, such as social or political science, that were meant to build up their analytical skills or to widen their intellectual horizons without directly preparing students for journalistic practice (Schnell, 2007). Journalism studies show evidence of the shift from a 'profession of talent' to a 'profession of qualification', whereas established journalists still tend to doubt that universities could prepare new entrants for the 'realities' of journalistic work (Donsbach, 2014; Kepplinger, 2011). For the former generation of journalists, which was socialized within the 'old industry model', journalism was understood as a craftwork that was learned in the environment of the newsroom (Bromley, 2013). In the continental European context, the critical stance against a presumably just-technically-prepared 'graduate journalism' originated from the traditional idea of journalists as intellectuals and independent writer personalities (Marr, 2004). However, there has, in fact, been a steady increase in the number of university courses and degrees, and journalism has become a graduate occupation during recent decades. As Frith and Meech conclude, by the end of the 1990s there had developed a peculiar disjunction between the reality of how people did become journalists and the ideology of how they should become journalists, between the empirical evidence that journalism was now a career for graduates and the editorial suggestion that it should not be.

(Frith and Meech, 2007, p. 139)

In contrast to established professions, the relation between society and journalism is in a constant process of redefinition, and the profession is in a more reactive than proactive role of defining its position in relation to society. In the UK, for example, the role of journalism has also been discussed in respect to social closeness and how journalism might keep in touch with the 'ordinary people', implying that the academic elite would not be able to communicate the right things in the right way and represent their reality (ibid.). In Germany, the idea of an intellectual avant-garde was much more accepted in the second half on the twentieth century, but the need for practical learning and socialization in the field was emphasized as well.

In terms of professionalization, academization mirrors the development of a theoretical body of journalistic knowledge and an attempt at the self-regulation of the occupational field. Therefore, priority has been given to education and socialization in a professional culture, which is conducted by the described values and principles. On the other hand, academization has not been an instrument of social closure, but rather the opposite. Against the background of changing market conditions, the growth of journalistic university programmes and degrees has contributed to enhanced competition in the journalistic labour market. As a result, academization has not stabilized the social status of journalists even though a university degree has more or less become a standard, if not a formal, requirement within the field over time. An interpretation of the academization of journalism as a successful collective upwards mobilization would be misleading. A more adequate interpretation seems to be that academic education and training have taken over parts of the reproduction of journalistic culture and offered training that is no longer provided within the general journalistic working conditions (Schnell, 2008; De Burgh, 2005).

Another important transformation that takes place within the frame of academization results from the technological development that is summarized by the term digitization. Technological innovations have always influenced journalism and led to new specializations, but new media have generated an unprecedented and widespread proliferation of new technologies, new genres, platforms, and industries. As a result of this development, technical skills have grown in importance in relation to the traditional core skills of writing and information gathering. It is claimed that journalists need to be more skilled at doing technical tasks and that more working time is being taken up in dealing with technical problems. Whether this should be interpreted as a de-skilling, a change, or an extension of professional skills is controversial. According to Örnebring (2010), re-skilling, multi-skilling, and de-skilling occur simultaneously. New training programmes have been designed to teach journalism in the new media environment, considering that a broader skill base is needed within these segments of the news-gathering process from investigation to production (Deuze, 2005). Despite the need for qualification and acquiring new skills, new media has led to a redesigning of journalism. Taking over parts of the production leads to an expanding control over more stages of production but is also time-consuming; therefore, writing and investigating tend to take a backseat (p. 67) (Örnebring, 2010).

5. Changing context conditions and new media

Parallel to the development of journalistic professionalism, the structural preconditions of media production changed fundamentally. The manifold dimensions of change are interconnected, and the consequences with regard to journalism are complex. In addition to technological advancement, the literature discusses social change in general (which also includes a transformation of the audience), changing political and legal frameworks, and, of course, structural changes of media systems as concentration processes take place at the national and international levels (Knoche, 2007). In this section, some of the direct effects on journalistic working practice are discussed, along with the profound changes in the concept of journalistic professionalism associated with the ongoing processes of computerization, digitization, multimedia production, and interactivity (Lievrouw and Livingstone, 2002; Wise, 2000).

The emergence of a new type of journalism has been discussed since the 1990s. This new type is often entitled cyber-journalism or network journalism and is adapted to the online media logic (Dahlgren, 1996). In contrast to the traditional ideal of news production, which is characterized by a more or less individualistic top-down process, editorial organization patterns of multimedia journalism are much more team-based and include participatory elements. Moreover, the technique of storytelling differs from mono-media production insofar as multimedia journalists have to organize content differently and produce story 'packages' that can be integrated in digital network technologies instead of writing single stories, probably repurposed in multiple formats (Deuze, 2005 p.451). These changes are challenging the traditional self-conception and the professional ideology of journalists and catalysing new tensions in the industry and among journalists. However, the development of new media goes far beyond concrete editorial organization. It is embedded in and interlaced with the transformation of the media economy, which is increasingly being driven by commercialism and market rationality (Dickinson, 2007; Cottle, 2003). In continental Europe, where the cultural landscape (including the media) has traditionally been assumed to be predominantly 'public territory', a shift has taken place from public cultural services to a prospering private-commercial domain within progressively internationalizing market structures. Audio-visual media, newspapers and magazines, the book trade, and music are in the hands of globally operating media companies. Overall, capital considerations and 'shareholder value' have grown in importance in media production and changed the labour market and working conditions in the journalistic field (Schnell, 2007; Hallin, 1996). Against this background and combined with the 24-hour multimedia news cycle of news media, immediacy has been evolving more and more from a key value in the journalistic culture to a contradiction of journalistic liability and diligence (Blair, 2004). Digitization has accelerated the news process and afforded a 'discourse of speed' (Hampton, 2004), which tends to overlap with other criteria of journalistic labour. Many authors criticize the fact that this development has become stronger and more encompassing over time, and journalistic work practices have needed to adapt to the pressure of immediate publication and broadcasting.

After all, the discourse of speed appears as a mechanism of economic competition insofar as the technology is used to rationalize the news process in the very narrow sense of increasing the output and reducing the costs of media production. In effect, this can be interpreted as a devaluation of the traditional principles of journalistic professionalism (i.e. news gathering according to the principles of verification, ethical clarity, and depth) and as a shift in occupational control from journalists to managers (Higgins-Dobney and Sussman, 2013; Ursell, 2003). Instead of using new technologies to support elaborate investigation, many journalists seem to carry out desk jobs and have to take over technical production (Witchge and Nygren, 2009, p. 55). Örnebring (2010, p. 64) sees a risk of a 'proletarianization' of journalism in this development in which technology becomes a tool 'that allows managers to implement organizational changes aimed at making journalistic labour more cost-effective and more easily controlled'.

Another aspect of change resulting from digitization and convergence is the conceptualization of the producer–consumer relationship (Bardoel and Deuze, 2001; Neuberger and Quandt,

2010). With the increase of interactivity, the hierarchical relationship between producers and users is blurring, which is discussed in the literature of journalism studies as a challenge of 'one of the most fundamental "truths" in journalism: the professional journalist is the one who determines what publics see, hear, and read about the world' (Deuze, 2005, p. 451; Singer, 1998; Löffelholz, 2000; Hall, 2001; Pavlik, 2001). The more or less unlimited access to information in the digital era is changing the jurisdiction of journalistic professionalism from the level of the generation of information to the level of supporting consumers to cope with the flood of information (Schnell, 2008). At the same time, journalists have to consider a rising social complexity resulting from changes in the social structure and multiculturalism (Deuze, 2005). This is identified as another problem of journalists' role perception in contemporary society by authors of journalism studies because the active awareness of social diversity contradicts the valued detachment of society that has been the traditional ideal of journalistic professionalism (Golding, 1994; MacGregor, 1997; Quandt and Schweiger, 2008).

In sum, these brief discussions of the technical, economic, and social dimensions of new media affect the core values of journalistic professionalism. As described, the public service ideal in a multimedia context is 'not the same safe value to hide behind like it used to be in days of print and broadcast mass media' (Deuze, 2005, p. 455). It is much more difficult to meet a general public interest and therefore to legitimize professional authority in a public that is characterized by individualization and an audience considered to be becoming increasingly fragmented. This seems to be even truer since new media also imply a further loss of control in respect to the reception of information in the face of surfing the internet and shrinking attention spans. As a consequence of this development, theories of journalism indicate a shift towards a notion of serving the public that is increasingly based on a bottom-up principle. Instead of pretending to be responsible for what people need to know (or not), journalism has to take over the role of the moderator of the 'conversations society has with itself' and offer filters and interpretations with regard of the overload of accessible information (Deuze, 2005; Carey, 1989 [1975]).

Additionally, the value of journalistic objectivity is being questioned insofar as it follows the common understanding of 'getting both sides of the story' (Deuze, 2005). The increasing similarities of different media cultures in new-media production, combined with news platforms that support interactivity and direct feedback from the audience, are challenging journalists more than ever before with a plurality of interpretations of reality. As a result, the core value of objectivity appears much more against the background of social complexity. Moreover, the value of autonomy, which was developed as a concept at the individual level, now has to be reflected in a more transparent and sometimes even participatory news environment. Obviously, as argued before, immediacy potentially turns from a value to a menace of journalistic professionalism, in particular if the quality and depth of news and information are not adequately valued in the context of online publishing. Last but not least, journalists might refer to ethics to defend against structural changes or commercial, audience-driven, or managerial encroachment, but they will need to rethink their ethical standards in order to be able to deal with new conditions of working and publishing.

These very general aspects of change do not sufficiently reflect the diversity of journalistic genres and practices but summarize the challenges of new media for the concept of professional journalism. The concept of journalists as a social authority and representatives of the public, which was developed within the expansion of mass media, has lost power against the background of changing technical, economic, and social preconditions (Bardoel, 1996). Compared with traditional professions, journalism is not institutionalized as a profession, but it has to react to these developments. Despite this, a rethinking of what journalism is or could be is claimed by journalism studies and also from a general perspective of the sociology of professionalism (Claussen, 2012).

6. Structural heteronomy and new identities

Regarding the interpretation of the current developments in the field of journalism, at least two general directions can be differentiated. One analysis refers to the structural changes of the media with regard to the precariousness and heteronomy with which journalists are increasingly being confronted. The other strand of argumentation focuses on new movements aiming at a redefinition of the role of journalism in contemporary society. Both interpretations assume that the ideology of professional journalism has functioned as social cement and kept the field together in the past but is beginning to crumble and generate new factions and subgroups.

The first analysis regards the ideology of professional journalism as a discourse that extenuates deprofessionalizing working conditions and an economically driven rationalization of media production. Traditionally, journalistic professionalism was embedded in working structures in which journalists and utilizers were seen as a symbiosis with regard to the autonomy of media production (Schnell, 2008). Instead of this community with a shared culture, journalistic labour is being increasingly regulated by singular and temporary commitments that are based on project work and mostly comply with pragmatic rules. The traditional figure of the publisher, as fulfilling a dual role of media entrepreneur and publicist personality, has vanished. Now journalists are being hired by managers who are often educated in business administration and think in economic categories. As a result of economic rationality and the logic of multi-media production, journalism can be seen as being partly deinstitutionalized and confronted with market regulation in terms of daily journalistic practices, labour market conditions, and also careers (Manske and Schnell, 2010). Thus, the traditional career ladder, which assumed a regulated upgrading from local to regional to national press, has also lost reliability and become 'chaotic', while competition between aspirants has grown tremendously (Frith and Meech, 2007; Tunstall, 1996).

Against the backdrop of working conditions whose social and moral foundations seem to be already undermined, the call for journalistic professionalism can be reconstructed as an ideological façade. Analyses are based on a Foucauldian interpretation, relating in particular to how work is controlled by the appeal of professionalism. The attractive and identity-giving professional ideal becomes a mechanism of control to the benefit of the employer if journalists anticipate the call for self-control as professional working behaviour despite growing heteronomy and social precariousness (Aldridge and Evetts, 2003; Fournier, 1999). In this perspective, journalistic ideology is understood as a stable concept that is adequate for the small elite of established journalists who work for the rare renowned high-standard publications. Beyond that, the 'discourse of professionalism' merely feigns the relevance, autonomy, and responsibility of professional work and animates new 'media workers' to fulfil what they are expected to. A transformation or adaption of the concept of journalism does not fall under this analytical perspective. The ideology developed in the twentieth century seems to survive as a sacrilege.

The second analytical perspective also refers to journalistic ideology but focuses more on the redefinition of the role of journalism in society. Journalistic professionalism is not only regarded as a discourse that gives individual orientation, but also as a basis for the definition of professional jurisdiction and collective boundaries (Zelizer, 2004, p. 33). Therefore, the professional core of journalism serves a collection of shared and continuously contested values that define how proper journalists should act and what they should aim towards (Ahava, 2013). In this approach, not only are external influences such as economic, socio-cultural, technological, and political developments taken into consideration, but so too are internal influences within the professional culture of journalism, which deliberately aim to shape and challenge the classical values. One of these internal drivers has, for example, been the public or civic journalism movement.

Public journalism is a reform movement that aims to build a new relationship between journalism and society, particularly by encouraging active deliberation and public discussion. The peak of the movement was between 1990 and 2003 in the United States, but some elements of the participatory practice are still being conducted in the non-American context (Haas, 2007). Even before new media featured interactivity, there were experiments with media communication to improve comprehension and to involve the audience in the journalistic process. The movement of civic or public journalism was intended to be a critique of the traditional concept of professional journalism, which is based on detachment and separation and a view of the public from above. The critique formulated by public journalism was that the traditional interpretation of professional ethics tended to fail in the aim of supporting social deliberation and democratic discourse. The debate concerning public journalism is interesting with regard to the development of the occupational field in general because it reveals that the ideology of professionalism could also work as a source of professional reflexivity and change. Of course, the movement emerged historically before, or rather, at the beginning of the era of digitization, but it exemplifies how journalism proactively responds to social changes or to a rising awareness of the complexity of the public discourse. The movement of public journalism was built by a subgroup within the journalistic field that could be seen as a 'new moral community' from within the occupational field (Schnell, 2009).

7. Conclusions

Journalism went through a process of professionalization against the background of the development of the mass media during the twentieth century. The ideology of professional journalism, stemming from the Anglo-American context, has now merged into different media systems in Western industrialized societies. On the one hand, the concept of professionalism was initially very similar to those of established professions, but on the other hand, journalism could not institutionalize as a classic profession because the paradigm of the freedom of expression counteracts professional exclusivity. Within the expansion of the media industries, journalism has nevertheless become a relatively strong occupational group and has pursued its further professionalization, in particular by building systematic knowledge and developing academic training.

Journalism has always had blurry boundaries and a weak definition of who is allowed to call him- or herself a journalist. However, there is a strong element of journalistic professionalism within the ideology of journalism that has both worked as a legitimization and provided a hierarchical structure within the field. The ideal-typical professional journalist has always worked in the domain of institutionalized news. As long as news production has been understood to be a unique genre and a core task of media communication, this ideology has quite successfully worked as a regulatory feature and allowed the concept of professional journalism to reproduce over time. The vast spectrum of social positions between the privileged and the precarious, which has always characterized the field of journalism, has not hindered but rather strengthened the concept of professional journalism because it has functioned as a culture with blurred inequalities, hierarchies, and economic dependency to a certain extent.

As a consequence of the rapid revolutionary development of digitization and the accelerated economic dynamics of market expansion, internationalization, and concentration, journalism has been fundamentally challenged. On the one hand, the true flexibility of journalistic skills and potential roles has allowed for an efficient adaption to new technologies and working structures; on the other hand, the already-existing ambivalence of the ideology of journalistic professionalism has apparently been reinforced. While professional values such as autonomy, objectivity, diligence, and the claim that journalism is a service to the public are still of relevance – indeed they seem to be becoming more important as a stronghold against a fully commercialized media industry – it also seems that the dazzling appeal of journalism is to some degree detracting from the disintegration of contemporary media production.

Compared with other occupational groups within the media sector, journalism established its functional role at the beginning of mass-media communication, when information was a much more restricted good that was difficult to reproduce and share. The importance of journalism to society was thereby historically more or less manifest, even though autonomy and public legitimization had been contested continuously throughout history. In the world of new media, journalistic control over the mediated public sphere seems to fade, and it appears as if professional journalism has to be redefined or might already be redesigned by the commercial forces that are currently governing the media industries. Journalists are trying to strengthen the demarcation against other online news sources, but the more that news is generated outside the established structures, the more they are running the risk of becoming one of many actors within the public sphere. While they still have a privileged access to many sources of information, the expectation that journalists act as representatives of the public is fundamentally affected by the transformation of the media (Witschge and Nygren, 2009, p. 55).

The historical pathway of professionalization that the classic professions have followed will obviously not be repeatable in contemporary societies. Hence, the attempt to organize the developments of the journalistic field in a system of de- and re-professionalization only makes sense in the framework of an empirical approach that focuses on a concrete section within the whole complex. Nevertheless, the journalistic field is interesting for the debate on the challenges to professionalism in general. In particular, in connection with the development of an information or knowledge society, the consequences for journalism, an occupation that operates in the centre of information production, will be significant (Hesmondhalgh, 2006). Furthermore, journalism foreshadows a general change in the knowledge–power nexus that will also have an effect on the traditional professions. Two dimensions of the new requirements of professionalization that are currently appearing within journalism are particularly important here.

First is the understanding of professional expertise as not based on a monopoly of knowledge as claimed by the traditional professions, but rather on a particular competence of filtering, selection, and interpretation of knowledge. Therefore, the functional role of journalism could be described as that of a 'navigator' or a 'compass' in the everyday flood of information that has become all too nebulous for the consumer. With regard to the concept of the knowledge society, the underlying idea is that journalism contributes to the transformation of information into knowledge, but now in a less hierarchical and more cooperative or discursive relation to the public, the collective client of journalists (Schnell, 2008).

Second, journalism traditionally derives from individual commitment to the concept of self-reliant work and from the anticipation and defence of moral maxims. This intangible bond inherent in journalistic work can be interpreted as a concealed potential for exploitation. The reliance on intrinsic motivation and symbolically loaded offers of identification tends to induce self-discipline and voluntary self-exploitation, especially in the highly commercialized fields of the media industries. As a consequence, containing such developments is becoming (and also must become) a requirement of individual and collective professionalization. Therefore, defining professional jurisdiction involves the protection of workers against unreasonable demands and more or less forced self-exploitation. Furthermore, professional values, which reflect the tension between normative requirements and the structural pressures of media production, could provide individual professionals with guidelines for selective action between competing structural, moral, and social expectations and targets. A final decision has yet to be reached whether this emerging model of journalism reflects a framework for a new type of professionalism.

References

Abbott, A. (1988) *The System of Professions: An Essay on the Division of Expert Labor*, Chicago, IL: University of Chicago Press.

Ahva, L. (2013) 'Public journalism and professional reflexivity'. *Journalism* 14(6), pp. 790–806.

Aldridge, M. and Evetts, J. (2003) 'Rethinking the concept of professionalism: The case of journalism'. *British Journal of Sociology* 54(4), pp. 547–564.

Bardoel, J. (1996) 'Beyond journalism: A profession between information society and civil society'. *European Journal of Communication* 13(11), pp. 283–302.

Bardoel, J. and Deuze, M. (2001) '"Network journalism": Converging competences of media professionals and professionalism'. *Australian Journalism Review* 23(2), pp. 91–103.

Blair, J. (2004) *Burning Down My Master's House: My Life at the New York Times*, Beverleyey Hills, CA: New Millennium Press.

Breen, M. (ed.) (1998) *Journalism: Theory and Practice*, Paddington, Australia: Macleay Press.

Bromley, M. (2013) 'The "new majority" and the academization of journalism'. *Journalism* 14(5), pp. 569–586.

Carey, J. (1989 [1975]) *Communication as Culture: Essays on Media and Society*, Boston, MA: Unwin Hyman.

Chalaby, J. K. (1996) 'Journalism as an Anglo-American invention: A comparison of the development of French and Anglo-American journalism, 1830s–1920s'. *European Journal of Communication* 11(3), pp. 303–326.

Claussen, D. S. (2012) 'If even journalism professors don't know what journalism is, then all really is lost'. *Journalism & Mass Communication Educator* 67(4), pp. 327–331.

Cottle, S. (2003) 'Media organization and production: Mapping the field'. In S. Cottle (ed.) *Media Organization and Production*, London: Sage, pp. 3–24.

Dahlgren, P. (1996) 'Media logic in cyberspace: repositioning journalism and its publics'. *Javnost/The Public* 3(3), pp. 59–72.

De Burgh, H. (2005) *Making Journalists*, London: Routledge.

Deuze, M. (2004) 'What is multimedia journalism?'. *Journalism Studies* 5(2), pp. 139–152.

Deuze, M. (2005) 'What is journalism? Professional identity and ideology of journalists reconsidered'. *Journalism* 6(4), pp. 442–464.

Dickinson, R. (2007) 'Accomplishing journalism: Towards a revived sociology of a media occupation'. *Cultural Sociology* 1(2), pp. 189–208.

Donsbach, W. (2014) 'Journalism as the new knowledge profession and consequences for journalism education'. *Journalism* 15(6), pp. 661–677.

Esser, F. and Umbricht, A. (2013) 'Competing models of journalism? Political affairs coverage in US, British German, Swiss, French and Italian newspapers'. *Journalism* 14(8), pp. 989–1007.

Frith, S. and Meech, P. (2007) 'Becoming a journalist: Journalism education and journalism culture'. *Journalism* 8(2), pp. 137–164.

Fournier, V. (1999) 'The appeal to "professionalism" as a disciplinary mechanism'. *The Sociological Review* 47(2), pp. 280–307.

Golding, P. (1994) 'Telling stories: Sociology, journalism and the informed citizen'. *European Journal of Communication* 9, pp. 461–484.

Golding, P. and Elliott, P. (1979) *Making the News*, London: Longman.

Haas, T. (2007) *The Pursuit of Public Journalism: Theory, Practice and Criticism,* New York: Routledge.

Hafez, K. (2002) 'Journalism ethics revisited: A comparison of ethics codes in Europe, North Africa, the Middle East, and Muslim Asia'. *Political Communication* 19(2), pp. 225–250.

Hall, J. (2001) *Online Journalism: A Critical Primer*, London: Pluto Press.

Hallin, D. (1996) 'Commercialism and professionalism in American news media'. In J. Curran and M. Gurevitch (eds) *Mass Media and Society*, London: Arnold, pp. 243–64.

Hallin, D.C. and Mancini, P. (2004) *Comparing Media Systems: Three Models of Media and Politics*, New York: Cambridge University Press.

Hampton, M. (2004) *Visions of the Press in Britain, 1850–1950*, Champaign, IL: University of Illinois Press.

Hesmondhalgh, D. (2006) 'Bourdieu, the media and cultural production'. *Media Culture & Society* 28(2), pp. 211–231.

Higgins-Dobney, C. L. and Sussman, G. (2013) 'The growth of TV news, the demise of the journalism profession'. *Media Culture & Society* 35(7), pp. 847–863.

Kepplinger, H. M. (2011) *Journalismus als Beruf: Theorie und Praxis öffentlicher Kommunikation*, 6th edn, Wiesbaden: VS Verlag.

Knoche, M. (2007) 'Medienkonzentration'. In B. Thomas (ed.) *Mediensysteme im internationalen Vergleich*, Konstanz: UVK Verlagsgesellschaft, pp. 122–144.

Kovach, B. and Rosenstiel, T. (2001) *The Elements of Journalism*, New York: Crown Publishers.

Kutsch, A. (2008) 'Journalismus als Profession: Überlegungen zum Beginn des journalistischen Professionalisierungsprozesses in Deutschland am Anfang des 20. Jahrhunderts'. In A. Blome and H. Böhning (eds) *Presse und Geschichte: Leistungen und Perspektiven der historischen Presseforschung*, Bremen: Edition Lumière, pp. 289–325.

Lewis, S. C. (2012) 'The tension between professional control and open participation'. *Information, Communication & Society* 15(6), pp. 836–866.

Lievrouw, L. and Livingstone, S. (eds) (2002) *Handbook of New Media: Social Shaping and Consequences of ICTs*, London: Sage.

Löffelholz, M. (ed.) (2000) *Theorien des Journalismus*, Opladen: Westdeutscher Verlag.

MacGregor, B. (1997) *Live, Direct and Biased? Making Television News in the Satellite Age*, London: Arnold.

McNair, B. (2003) *Sociology of Journalism*, London: Routledge.

Mancini, P. (2000) 'Political complexity and alternative models of journalism: The Italian Case'. In J. Curran and M. J. Park (eds) *De-Westernizing Media Studies*, London: Routledge, pp. 264–278.

Mancini, P. (2005) 'Is there a European model of journalism?'. In H. De Burgh (ed.) *Making Journalists: Diverse Models, Global Issues*, London: Routledge, pp. 77–93.

Manske, A. and Schnell, C. (2010) 'Arbeit und Beschäftigung in der Kultur- und Kreativwirtschaft'. In F. Böhle, G. Voss and G. Wachtler (eds) *Handbuch Arbeitssoziologie*, Wiesbaden: VS Verlag, pp. 699–728.

Marr, A. (2004) *My Trade: A Short History of British Journalism*, London: Macmillan.

Merritt, D. (1995) 'Public journalism: Defining a democratic art'. *Media Studies Journal* 9(3), pp. 125–132.

Mindich, D. (1998) *Just the Facts: How 'Objectivity' Came to Define American Journalism*, New York: New York University Press.

Neuberger, C. and Quandt, T. (2010) 'Internet-Journalismus: Vom traditionellen Gatekeeping zum partizipativen Journalismus?'. In W. Schweiger and K. Beck (eds) *Handbuch Online-Kommunikation*, Wiesbaden: VS Verlag, pp. 59–79.

Nordenstreng, K. and Topuz, H. (eds) (1989) *Journalist: Status, Rights and Responsibilities*, Prague: International Organization of Journalists.

Örnebring, H. (2010) 'Technology and journalism-as-labour: Historical perspectives'. *Journalism* 11(1), pp. 57–74.

Pavlik, J. (2001) *Journalism and New Media*, New York: Columbia University Press.

Polumbaum, J. (2010) 'Comparative models of journalism'. In C. H. Sterling (ed.) *Encyclopaedia of Journalism*, Los Angeles, CA: Sage, pp. 338–342.

Quandt, T. and Schweiger, W. (eds) (2008) *Journalismus online: Partizipation oder Profession?*, Wiesbaden: VS Verlag.

Ryan, M. (2001) 'Journalistic ethics, objectivity, existential journalism, standpoint epistemology, and public journalism'. *Journal of Mass Media Ethics* 16(1), pp. 3–22.

Schnell, C. (2007). *Regulierung der Kulturberufe in Deutschland: Strukturen, Akteure, Strategien*, Wiesbaden: Deutscher Universitäts-Verlag.

Schnell, C. (2008) 'Public good or free market? Cultural professions in Germany and the European copyright regulation'. *European Societies* Special Issue 1/2008, Professions in Europe, pp. 633–650.

Schnell, C. (2009) 'Solidarität trotz Individualisierung? Befunde aus dem Feld der Kulturberufe'. In R. Castel, and K. Dörre (eds) *Prekarität, Abstieg, Ausgrenzung. Die soziale Frage am Beginn des 21. Jahrhunderts*, Frankfurt am Main: Campus, pp. 334–344.

Schudson, M. (2001) 'The objectivity norm in American journalism'. *Journalism* 2(2), pp. 149–170.

Siebert, F., Peterson, T. and Schramm, W. (1956) *Four Theories of the Press*, Urbana, IL: University of Illinois Press.

Singer, J. (1998) 'Online journalists: Foundation for research into their changing roles'. *Journal of Computer-Mediated Communication* 4(1). Online: doi: 10.1111/j.1083-6101.1998.tb00088.x.

Singer, J. (2004) 'Strange bedfellows: The diffusion of convergence in four news organizations'. *Journalism Studies* 5(1), pp. 3–18.

Soloski, J. (1990) 'News reporting and professionalism: Some constraints on the reporting of the news'. *Media, Culture and Society* 11(4), pp. 207–228.

Sparks, C. (1992) 'Popular journalism: theories and practice'. In P. Dahlgren and C. Sparks (eds) *Journalism and Popular Culture*, Thousand Oaks, CA: Sage, pp. 24–44.

Tunstall, J. (1977) *The Media Are American*, New York: Columbia University Press.

Tunstall, J. (1996) *Newspaper Power*, Oxford: Clarendon Press.

Ursell, G. (2003) 'Creating value and valuing creation in contemporary UK television: or "dumbing down" the workforce'. *Journalism Studies* 4(1), pp. 31–46.

Van Zoonen, L. (1998) 'A professional, unreliable, heroic marionette (M/F): Structure, agency and subjectivity in contemporary journalisms'. *European Journal of Cultural Studies* 1(1), pp. 123–143.

Weaver, D. H. (ed.) (1998) *The Global Journalist: News People Around the World*, New Jersey: Hampton Press.

Williams, K. (2005) *European Media Studies*, London: Hodder Arnold.

Wise, R. (2000) *Multimedia: An Introduction*, London: Routledge.

Witschge, T. and Nygren, G. (2009) 'Journalism: A profession under pressure?'. *Journal of Media Business Studies* 6(1), pp. 37–59.

Zelizer, B. (2004) *Taking Journalism Seriously: News and the Academy*, London: Sage.

Index